Read This First:
Europe

PAUL HARDING

LONELY PLANET PUBLICATIONS
melbourne ◆ oakland ◆ london ◆ paris

Read This First: Europe
1st edition – June 2000

Published by
Lonely Planet Publications Pty Ltd ABN 36 005 607 983
90 Maribyrnong St, Footscray, Victoria 3011, Australia

Lonely Planet Offices
Australia Locked Bag 1, Footscray, Victoria 3011
USA 150 Linden Street, Oakland, CA 94607
UK 10a Spring Place, London NW5 3BH
France 1 rue du Dahomey, 75011, Paris

Printed by
The Bookmaker International Ltd
Printed in China

Photographs
Many of the images in this guide are available for licensing from Lonely Planet Images.
email: lpi@lonelyplanet.com.au
Web site: www.lonelyplanetimages.com

Front cover photograph
Guggenheim museum of Modern Art, Bilbao, Spain (Guy Moberly, LPI)

10 9 8 7 6 5   3 2 1

ISBN 1 86450 136 7

LEGEND

BOUNDARIES
International
Regional
Disputed

HYDROGRAPHY
Ocean, Coastline
River, Creek
Intermittent River, Creek
Lake
Salt Lake
Spring, Rapids
Waterfalls

TRANSPORT & ROUTES
Ferry Route
Flight Path
Two/Three Day Itinerary
One Week Itinerary
Two Week Itinerary
One Month Itinerary

AREA FEATURES
Park, Reserve
Other Countries
Urban Area

CAPITAL .... National Capital
Capital .... Regional Capital
City .... City
Town .... Town
Village .... Village
Airport
Archaeological Site
Beach
Border Crossing
Castle
Cave
Chalet or Hut

MAP SYMBOLS
Church or Monastery
Mountain or Hill
National Park
Pass
Point of Interest
Ski Field
Tomb
Temple

CONTENTS ▶▶

The Lonely Planet Story

The story begins with a classic travel adventure – Tony and Maureen Wheeler's 1972 journey across Europe and Asia to Australia. Useful information about the overland trail did not exist at that time, so Tony and Maureen published the first Lonely Planet guidebook to meet a growing need among the backpacker community.

Written at a kitchen table and hand-collated, trimmed and stapled, *Asia on the Cheap* became an instant local bestseller, inspiring thoughts of another book. A further 18 months in South-East Asia resulted in their second guide, *South-East Asia on a shoestring*, which they put together in a backstreet Chinese hotel in Singapore in 1975. The 'yellow bible', as it quickly became known to backpackers around the world, soon became the guide to the region. As we go to print, it has sold almost 750,000 copies, still retaining its familiar yellow cover. A 10th anniversary edition has recently been released and includes a story and photographs by Tony recalling the 1975 trip.

Today Lonely Planet publishes more than 450 titles, including travel guides, city guides, diving guides, city maps, phrasebooks, trekking guides, wildlife guides, travel atlases and travel literature. The company is the largest independent travel publisher in the world; an international company with offices in Melbourne, Oakland, London and Paris.

However, some things haven't changed. Our main aim is still to help make it possible for adventurous travellers to get out there – to explore and better understand the world. At Lonely Planet we believe that travellers can make a positive contribution to the countries they visit – if they respect their host communities and spend their money wisely. Since 1986 a percentage of the income from each book has been donated to aid projects and human rights campaigns across the world.

INTRODUCTION ▶▶

Europe is the classic big trip. Whether it's your first time or a return visit, a six month backpacking odyssey or a whirlwind two week tour, Europe evokes more familiar icons and must-see sights than any other continent on Earth.

For many first-time travellers it is the obvious destination choice. There is a huge cultural diversity squeezed into a relatively small space – you can flit from country to country, with a new language, new currency, and a new way of life, with consummate ease. Notwithstanding the usual pitfalls of travel (and the occasional overindulgence in German beer), Europe is 'easy' to travel in. Even Eastern Europe, having wrenched itself out of those Communist Soviet bloc days, is becoming more 'westernised' and travel-friendly every year. They may not always be cheap, but there are plenty of planes, trains and buses to get you around and always a warm bed at the end of the day.

Europe represents so many things. To some it is world-class museums and galleries such as the British Museum in London or the Louvre in Paris, or the soaring, elaborate churches and cathedrals you'll find all over the Continent.

Scope of Europe

The 36 countries covered in this book occupy a total area of approximately 5.7 million sq km, slightly less than three-quarters of the size of Australia or the 48 'continental' states of the USA. To make comparisons in linear terms, the distance from London to Ankara is comparable to that between Los Angeles and Chicago; that between Dublin and Athens equates to a direct line between San Francisco and St Louis; while that between Lisbon and Helsinki is comparable to the distance between San Francisco and Columbus, Ohio. With one exception, all cities dealt with in this book are closer than the distance between the Australian cities of Perth and Brisbane, or between Los Angeles and New York. The exception is the distance between Reykjavik and Ankara, which is comparable to that between Miami and Seattle.

But the density of European inhabitation is of course much greater than that of Australia, and, at an average density of about 101 people per square kilometre, is almost four times the density of the USA. The total population of approximately 575 million is more than double that of the USA, even though the landmass is only about two-thirds of the American territory.

Europeans are reasonably evenly spread over the land, with more than half of the countries close to the average population density. But the Netherlands, which supports 16 million inhabitants on only 41,863 sq km – less than the size of Estonia or Denmark, which are home to 1.5 and 5.3 million people respectively – has a density of almost four times the average. The Scandinavian countries, on the other hand, have much smaller person-land ratios than the average. Finland, about eight times the size of the Netherlands, has less than a third of the Netherlands' population. Iceland, more than double the size of the Netherlands, has a density of less than three inhabitants per square kilometre. Norway's density is about 13 people per square kilometre, while Sweden, more than 10 times the size of the Netherlands, supports a population only slightly more than half of the Netherlands.

introduction

For others it's the dazzling light and the beaches and islands of southern Europe, or the manic festivals of Spain and Italy. For still others it's the chance to hike through magnificent Alpine scenery or cycle through the patchwork hills of Tuscany.

Europe is a great mix of past and present. After visiting medieval towns and centuries-old castles, there are the pubs, bars, cafes and pulsating nightlife of cities like London, Barcelona and Copenhagen. And many of your experiences in Europe will be less tangible; along the way you'll meet many people – locals and travellers from around the world – who will enhance your journey, and perhaps even your life.

If you're about to start planning your first European trip, you probably have visions of enjoying some or all of these aspects of the Continent; of boarding a train in Berlin and hopping off in Venice, of ferrying around the Greek islands or wandering through ancient Roman ruins. These things are all possible – even in a trip of one month or less you can fit in a surprising amount without keeling over. All it takes is a little planning, a dash of spirit and a desire to have new experiences.

The important thing is to go. Now that you've made the first step, read on, cast aside all self-doubt and buy that plane ticket. Don't worry that you mightn't have a good time (you will), or that you'll get run over by a Vespa in Rome (you probably won't) or even that you can't afford it (start saving) – just go. You'll have the experience of a lifetime, a head full of happy memories and, in all probability, a lifelong passion for travel.

PLANNING

Unless you have unlimited travelling time and equally unlimited funds (and who does?), some serious pretrip planning will go a long way towards maximising your experience and minimising any problems.

Planning doesn't necessarily mean working out a daily itinerary and sticking to it like glue – flexibility is the key to enjoyable independent travel – but you'll feel better about the trip by sorting out the broad details well before you set off and by focusing on what you want to do when you actually arrive in Europe.

Some questions to ask during the planning stage are: do you want to travel alone or with others? How much time and money will you have? Would you prefer to see a broad section of the continent, or to concentrate on getting to know one country in depth? Are there certain activities – for example, trekking, skiing or cycling – that you enjoy and want to incorporate into your trip? Do you like meeting other travellers or would you rather be out on your own? Are you more interested in exploring Europe's varied landscapes and natural attractions or in immersing yourself in its museums, architecture and cultural attractions? Or are you in it for a good time, with plenty of nightlife and festivals?

Allow yourself the versatility to make changes on the road because eventually you'll find yourself doing something you never dreamed of. You might alter course and end up in a Turkish bath in Budapest when you were headed for a tapas bar in Barcelona. It's all part of the joys of independent travel.

What Kind of Trip?

ORGANISED TOURS

Travellers often dismiss the idea of an organised tour as being too restrictive or lacking in the sort of adventurous spirit they're after. But for many, particularly first-time travellers who may be worried about travelling alone, a tour has obvious advantages.

For a start, everything is done for you. Accommodation is booked, itineraries are planned, a busload of travelling companions is laid on, transport is taken care of, and a good tour guide can be very informative. But these very factors are also the drawbacks with tours. There's little flexibility and no option to change your itinerary. Having the tour coach for transport and the busload of travelling companions is great fun but it tends to isolate you from the local people and culture.

Organised tours are also more expensive than going it alone. You can expect to pay at least US$50 to US$70 a day on an average tour (for 18 to 35 year-olds), which doesn't include spending money. The cheaper end of the scale will probably mean camping.

There are dozens of companies offering tours around Europe in many different permutations, including specialist tour groups (cycling, walking etc).

Some of the main companies catering to younger travellers include:

AESU Travel – This is a US operator specialising in 18-35 European tours staying in hotels and with meals included. Tours range from eight to 37 days (US$80 to US$90 per day). Look it up at www.aesu.com.

Contiki – The biggest in the 18-35 tour market and generally recognised as the 'party' tours, Contiki is a reliable operator with a wide range of European trips. Trips start at a quick 10 day jaunt covering eight countries to the 37 day European Adventure or a 45 day camping trip. You can find Contiki on the Web at www.contiki.com.

Discover Tours – A budget European tour outfit running shorter, more specialised tours. Its Web address is www.europetour.com.

Top Deck – This UK-based company concentrates mainly on budget camping and accommodation trips along similar lines to Contiki. Its combo tours also include all meals. Tours range from 14 to 49 days and are generally slightly cheaper than the equivalent Contiki trips. Look Top Deck up at http://dialspace.dial.pipex.com.

Trafalgar Tours – A more upmarket and pricey outfit that's been around for a while. Various tours cater to all age groups. Trafalgar Tours is at www.trafalgartours.com.

GOING IT ALONE

As daunting as it may seem at first, travelling solo has many advantages. Europe is full of backpackers who are also going it alone, so the chances that you will remain alone for long are slim. Meeting people seems to become easier – or at least more of a priority – when you travel alone. It also gives you more of a chance to meet local people because you are more likely to be approached for conversation if you are alone (the flip side is that you may receive unwanted attention). The luxury of being free to go where you want and when you want shouldn't be underestimated and you will probably find you are more receptive to new experiences and more open to the cultures and people surrounding you.

Travelling solo poses no particular difficulties in Europe and you'll probably find that it strengthens your independence and character. If you're tempted by the idea of solo travel, but are unsure as to whether you have the temperament for it, give it a trial run in a brief trip at home before heading to Europe. If you find yourself craving companionship after a few days, perhaps it's time to start looking for a travel partner.

TRAVELLING WITH FRIENDS

Travelling with a friend or two eliminates the potential isolation and loneliness of solo travel. It also has practical advantages: you can split up when looking for rooms; you'll save money on accommodation, taxis and in national parks or wilderness areas where the cost of hiring guides or boats can be shared; and, you will have moral support when facing unfamiliar or tricky situations. With a small group, you can also consider options such as hiring a car for a few days in order to reach areas that are difficult to get to.

Remember that a good friend (or a good spouse) doesn't necessarily make a good travel companion. It's important to determine whether you both enjoy travelling in the same way and have similar priorities for the trip. For example, some people prefer planning things out to the last detail, while others like

FINDING SUITABLE TRAVEL PARTNERS

There are several ways to find a companion for your trip if you don't happen to know anyone who is interested and able to travel at the same time you are. Good places to start include travel magazines, university and community centre bulletin boards, and Internet travel sites – many of which have advertisements for prospective travel partners. You can also post your own ad through any of these mediums. If you do find a travel partner this way, arrange to meet before setting off and, ideally, do a short trip together closer to home to ensure you are compatible.

Joining an organised tour is another possibility (see Organised Tours earlier in this chapter): you may find someone to team up with for further travel when it finishes. Some travellers set off solo and head to a spot with the specific intention of finding a travel mate. London, in particular, is full of backpackers seeking other travellers to team up with. Here you'll find pubs, hostels and clubs frequented by travellers, or which have travellers notice boards. The free weekly *TNT Magazine* has a classifieds ads section for travel companions.

Your Route

Only the trip itself can beat the excitement of spreading out all the maps, opening the guidebooks and just imagining the possibilities. You could never hope to cover the whole continent in one trip, so some basic decisions have to be made. Do you try to cover as many countries as possible, zipping from capital to capital, or do you choose a few countries or cities and explore them in depth?

The first decision is where you intend to start and finish your journey. It's possible to fly into one city and out of another, or you could plan a loop trip. London is a major hub for flights into Europe and an excellent starting point for any trip, as are Paris, Amsterdam, Frankfurt, Athens and Vienna.

Also consider the mode of transport you intend to use while in Europe. Rail travel is probably the best single way of covering a large area, but there is also a comprehensive network of international and domestic buses. Buying or hiring a car offers you the ultimate in flexibility, but it can isolate you from other travellers and the locals. You'll probably use a combination of train, bus, ferry and foot to get around – see the Getting Around section in the While You're There chapter for more details.

The following sections outline some route options for travelling into and around Europe. When planning your route, make sure it is based on the way you want to travel and includes the sights and activities that interest you, but be realistic. There's not much point allowing only a day or two for major cities, missing many of the sights and being totally exhausted at the end of your trip.

Here are a few tips for planning a European itinerary:

City-to-city – Pick a few cities that you absolutely must visit (London, Paris, Berlin, Prague, Vienna, Venice, Florence and Barcelona are popular choices). Allow at least two or three days in each and a day to travel between them, and research at least one day trip from each city (eg Versailles from Paris, Pisa from Florence, Verona from Venice). Add a few days for impromptu side trips or just relaxing somewhere, and a few days for possible travel-related delays. See how many days that adds up to – if it's more than the length of your trip you may be forced to cut back. If not, keep planning.

The country approach – Pick two, three or four countries that you really want to visit and allow one to three weeks (or more) for the larger countries, five to 12 days for smaller ones. Consider whether they are close together or whether you'll have to make lengthy trips to cross between them. Within each country allow around three days in the capital and the remainder in lesser known towns, villages or scenic areas (eg mountains, lakes and historic regions).

Flexibility – Once you've come up with an itinerary that suits you, stuff it in your backpack and do your best to ignore it. The best way to travel independently is with the attitude that you have the flexibility to change plans on a whim. Other travellers and people you meet on the road will have a big impact on where you end up going. Be open to advice, but don't throw your own plans out the window just because some guy tells you Stuttgart is 'unmissable' (but neglects to tell you he thinks that because it has a great collection of motor museums).

Burn out – Don't try to see too much in too short a time. Europe is a big place. If you expect to see London, Lisbon, Oslo and Istanbul in one trip, you're in for a hell of a lot of travel. Travel steadily, pack in a lot of sightseeing each day if you wish, but allow time for relaxation and plan your route so that you can take in places of interest in reasonably short hops, rather than zigzagging across the continent. (Taking overnight train trips may involve exceptions to this rule.)

OVERLAND ROUTES

While most people fly directly into Europe, it's possible to approach by an overland route, either from Russia or the Middle East, or by ferry from Africa.

Overland travel requires careful research into current visa situations, travel advisories and border crossing regulations to ensure your proposed route is feasible.

Trans-Siberian Railway

Few rail journeys can conjure up mystery and romance like the Trans-Siberian Railway. Actually, there are three separate rail routes. The 'true' Trans-Siberian trip takes seven days to travel from the eastern Siberian city of Vladivostok to Moscow. Ferries will get you from Niigata in Japan to the port of Nakhodka near Vladivostok. From Moscow there are plenty of rail connections to Berlin, Helsinki, Munich, Budapest and Vienna. The Trans-Manchurian line from Beijing to Moscow crosses the China-Russia border at Manzhouli-Zabaikalsk, and the Trans-Mongolian line connects Beijing and Moscow via the Mongolian capital of Ulaan Baatar. Both these routes take six days.

Conditions on board the trains are rough, and theft is rampant. If you can afford it, travel deluxe class, which has two-bed cabins, showers and better security. Economy-class cabins will do at a pinch. Fares seem to vary enormously depending on where you buy the ticket, but a 2nd class fare is around US$490 from Vladivostok and US$282 from Beijing. In Europe, you can purchase tickets through The Russia Experience in the UK (☎ 020-8566 8846, www.travel .world.co.uk) and STA Travel (www.sta-travel-group.com), among others. In China, try China International Travel Service in Beijing (☎ 010-6515-8570) or

Monkey Business in Hong Kong (☎ 852-2723 1376, www.monkeyshrine.com). In the US, try Red Star Travel (☎ 800-215 4378, www.travel2russia.com), although it deals mainly with extended tours making numerous stops. *Trans-Siberian Handbook* (Trailblazer Publications) by Bryn Thomas is a useful and detailed guide.

From Africa

Entering Europe from Africa will require a ferry trip, although it is possible to go overland along the Middle Eastern route from Egypt through Israel, Jordan, Syria and into eastern Turkey.

From Morocco it's a short ferry ride from the main port of Tangier to Algeciras (Spain) or Gibraltar. There are also regular ferries from Ceuta in Spanish Morocco to Algeciras, and from Melilla, also in Spanish Morocco, to Almeria (Spain). There's a 38 hour car-ferry from Tangier to Sète in southern France.

From Tunisia there are weekly ferries from Tunis to the Italian ports of Genoa and Trapani (Sicily). There are more frequent ferries from Tunis to Marseille in southern France.

From Egypt, there's one boat from Alexandria to Antalya in Turkey, and one from Port Said to Lemessos in Cyprus.

From the Middle East

Turkey is the link between the Middle East and Europe. It's possible to enter Turkey overland from Syria by taking a bus from Aleppo or Damascus to Antakya. You can also cross from Iran via the border post at Bazargan to Dogubeyazit in eastern Turkey. Research these border crossings carefully and make sure you have the appropriate visas for each country.

ROUTES IN EUROPE

The combination of possible routes in Europe boggles the mind. The following loop routes are suggestions only, covering major places of interest, plus a few off-beat areas given the constraints of time and distance. They are based on a two to three month trip. If your time is limited to less than one month, you'll really have to concentrate on a smaller area or spend a lot of time on overnight trains. Following is information on general routes within Western, northern (Scandinavia), Eastern and southern Europe. For suggested itineraries within each country, see the country profiles later in this book.

Western Europe

Western Europe is probably the most popular region with first-time travellers. There's so much to see in Britain, Germany and France alone, before you start on Ireland, the smaller Benelux countries and the Alps of Austria and Switzerland. Travel here is very easy, though rail travel is expensive if you don't have a pass.

Starting from London, you'll probably want to spend some time in Britain and Ireland. There are good hop-on hop-off backpacker buses operating through England, Wales, Scotland and Ireland which provide a good alternative to public transport. At least try to visit Edinburgh, Bath or Oxford and perhaps Dublin and the west coast of Ireland. From England you can take a ferry across to the Netherlands, Belgium or France, and all can be included in your trip. You could start with a couple of days in Amsterdam, then visit Brussels and Bruges and perhaps tiny Luxembourg and the Moselle Valley. Spend a week or more touring Germany including Berlin, Munich and the Black Forest region, or perhaps Hamburg and the Rhine River valley. Don't miss Vienna and Salzburg in Austria, or the mountain panoramas of the Jungfrau (Interlaken) and Geneva in Switzerland. From there you can head down to Lyon and the south of France for some beach action. Head up to Paris and, if you have time, explore some of the Loire Valley, before returning to London.

Northern Europe (Scandinavia)

For the purposes of this section, northern Europe refers to Scandinavia and the Baltic states (Estonia, Latvia and Lithuania). This area is best visited in summer when the days are long and sunny. Extensive travel in Scandinavia will require the use of quite a few cross-sea ferries, which makes getting around all the more interesting.

A tour of northern Europe can begin in London. From England you can take a ferry to Stavanger or Bergen in Norway, to Esbjerg in Denmark or Gothenburg in Sweden. If the thought of sea travel makes you turn green, take the short ferry (or Channel Tunnel) across to Calais (France) or Ostende (Belgium), then take a train across to Hamburg and up to Copenhagen. From Denmark it's a very short hop into Sweden. If you head up the west coast via Gothenburg into Norway you can explore Oslo then take the superb railway journey to Bergen. Explore some of Norway's western fjords then head back across to Sweden and its capital, Stockholm. From there you can cross by ferry to Turku or Helsinki in Finland, have a sauna, then ferry across the Gulf of Finland to Tallin in Estonia. Better still, cross into Russia via Vyborg and on to St Petersburg (make sure you have the appropriate visas) then cross into Estonia. Visit Latvia and Lithuania before returning to London via Poland and northern Germany.

Eastern Europe

In the days of Communism and closed borders, Eastern Europe (the former Eastern bloc) was one of the least visited parts of the continent, particularly among first-time travellers. That situation is changing rapidly – the Czech Republic is firmly on the tourist trail and countries like Romania, Bulgaria and Croatia are increasingly being added to tourist itineraries. Travel in Eastern Europe is cheaper than in Western Europe and you will almost certainly encounter old ways and traditional lifestyles that are fast being diluted by western modernism. In mid-1999, parts of Eastern Europe – especially Yugoslavia, Bosnia-Hercegovina, Kosovo and northern Albania – were not recommended for independent travellers. Seek up-to-date consular advice before venturing into these areas.

This route begins in beautiful Prague, the most touristed of Eastern Europe's cities, but a good introduction to the east. Spend some time in the Czech Republic before taking the train to Warsaw in Poland. Don't miss a visit to Kraków, Poland's glorious royal city, and the nearby former Nazi concentration camps of Auschwitz-Birkenau. From there you can cross the Tatra Mountains into Slovakia and on to its capital, Bratislava. From there head south-east to the Hungarian capital of Budapest and explore the towns along the Danube Bend. From here you can continue east through Hungary and into Romania. The capital, Bucharest, is in the south-east of the country so you could stop along the way in Transylvania, visiting Brasov and Bran. From Bucharest you can cross into Bulgaria and its capital, Sofia. Check out Plovdiv and the Rila Monastery or possibly the coastal resorts on the Black Sea. From Bulgaria you have the choice of crossing into Macedonia (Skopje), Greece (Thessaloniki) or Turkey (Istanbul).

Another alternative route from Hungary (or Austria) is to visit Slovenia with trips to Ljubljana and Bled, then continue south to Croatia. The capital, Zagreb, is an attractive city but the real highlights are the coastal resorts on the Adriatic Sea and the enchanting walled port city of Dubrovnik.

Southern Europe

For many, this region represents Europe at its alluring best. Sun-soaked beaches, rustic villages, ancient ruins, Roman and Grecian architecture, island-hopping in Greece or bar-hopping in Spain, balmy nights spent sipping wine in outdoor cafes ...

There are any number of starting points for this route. From England (Plymouth) there's a long ferry trip to Santander in northern Spain. Otherwise, you can cross the Channel and travel overland through France into Spain. There are also many cheap charter flights from London to coastal resorts in Spain and Portugal, as well as to Athens and Istanbul – an option well worth considering.

Spain has many attractions – don't miss Barcelona, Madrid and Seville, but Valencia, Granada and San Sebastián are also worthwhile. Keep an eye out for Spain's many festivals. Moving into Portugal, visit the Algarve, Lisbon and Porto. Travelling across the south of France (via Monaco), you can enter Italy. Few people would (or should) pass though Italy without visiting Venice, Florence and Rome. The ruins of Pompeii, near Naples, are worth a day, and a trip south into Sicily will give you a different perspective on this country.

The popular overnight ferry ride from Brindisi (south-eastern Italy) to Patras (via Corfu) will get you to Greece. You can explore the Peloponnese or head straight to Athens and hop on a ferry to the islands. There are many choices here: the Cyclades are the most popular islands among backpackers; Rhodes and Crete are oozing ancient Greek history. You can cross into Turkey overland through northern Greece but it's far more pleasant (and easier) to island-hop across to the west coast – the Greek island of Samos is only one hour by ferry from the Turkish port of Kusadasi. You could spend ages exploring Turkey, but don't miss the bizarre landscape of Cappadocia, a few Mediterranean beaches and the vibrant city of Istanbul.

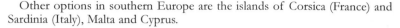

Other options in southern Europe are the islands of Corsica (France) and Sardinia (Italy), Malta and Cyprus.

Thematic Trips

If you have a particular interest you can get a lot more out of your European adventure by featuring it in your plans. This could range from activities such as hiking, cycling, skiing or white-water rafting, to more sedate pursuits such as art appreciation, bird-watching, or wine tasting. Consult the activities section of a good guidebook or search the Internet for detailed options. As well, there are specialised guides available covering Europe's more popular hiking and skiing destinations. The Researching Your Trip section later in this chapter lists resources useful in planning an activity-based trip.

Have a look also at our ecotourism guidelines in the While You're There chapter, to ensure you are sensitive to the preservation of the ecosystems of the places you are visiting, especially while hiking or wildlife spotting.

HIKING

Hiking or trekking is a great way to leave the cities behind and see Europe's many mountains, lakes, national parks and forests. If you're planning on hiking extensively, you'll need to be well prepared with camping equipment and wet-weather gear and, if heading into remote areas, let someone reliable know of your plans. Some of the best (certainly the most scenic) hiking is in the mountain areas such as the Alps of Austria, Switzerland, France and Italy, the Pyrenees in France and Spain, the Tatras in Slovakia and the Highlands of Scotland. Weather can change dramatically and suddenly in these areas, even in midsummer.

You can also make shorter hikes a component of your trip, basing yourself in a particular area and taking day or overnight walks. In some regions, such as England, you can walk from village to village (or pub to pub) for weeks on end, without the need to camp or cook your own food.

Get yourself in shape by walking with a backpack on before you leave home, gradually building up to the distances you expect to cover in Europe. Some good areas for walking in Europe include:

Britain & Ireland – Small and green, Britain and Ireland have excellent infrastructures for walkers and a bed or cosy pub is never too far away. There are many long-distance walking paths (with 'right of way' access over private land) and these can be walked over several days or in short segments. The main thing about walking in Britain is to be prepared for rain, hail, sleet, snow or, with luck, sunshine. Good long-distance walks include: in England, the South-West Coast Path (987km or 613 miles), Cotswold Way (166km), Cleveland Way (177km), Cumbria Way (109km), Pennine Way (417km) and the Dales Way (135km); in Scotland, the West Highland Way (153km); in Wales, the Pembrokeshire Coast Path (304km) and Offa's Dyke Path (285km); in Ireland, the Kerry Way (195km) and Beara Way (159km); and in Northern Ireland, the Ulster Way (898km).

Italy – Northern Italy has the Alps and the spectacular formations known as the Dolomites which have a particularly good network of walking trails. The Sentiero Azzurro, which links the five villages of the Cinques Terres on the Ligurian coast, is a spectacular walk and not too difficult. The Tuscan countryside provides many opportunities for more laid-back walking through patchwork fields, vineyards and ochre-coloured medieval villages. Sardinia island provides good settings for adventurous hikers, and it's usually possible to walk the volcanoes of Etna, Vesuvius and Stromboli.

France – If we told you France has an incredible 120,000km of marked walking trails, you'd have to agree it's a walkers' paradise. The Pyrenees in the far south and the Alps in the south-east provide superb summertime hiking opportunities and there are many mountain huts for accommodation along the way. The famous long-distance footpaths designated by the letters GR *(grande randonnée)*, followed by a number, cross the country in all directions. For more leisurely walking there are plenty of opportunities through the vineyards and historic towns of France's wine-growing regions. Maps, accommodation and guided walking tours are all in abundance in France.

Spain – Again the Pyrenees and the GR *(gran recorrido)* walks feature prominently in Spain. There are many national parks and wilderness areas that provide great hikes, including Picos de Europe in the north and Sierra Nevada in Andalucía. There are numerous 'pilgrim routes' along which devotees and interested walkers tramp long distances to get to various churches. The most famous is the Camino de Santiago (Way of St James).

Switzerland & Austria – The Alps of these Central European countries form a spine that is crisscrossed by fabulous walks, some demanding, others leisurely. Trails are well marked, there are many mountain huts along the way and the scenery is nothing short of spectacular. One of the famous trails is the Haute Route from Chamonix (France) to Zermatt in Switzerland.

Other areas – Other hiking destinations include the mountains that run along the common borders of Poland, Slovakia and the Czech Republic (the Tatras), northern Portugal, the mainland and islands of Greece and Germany's Black Forest. See the country profiles later in this book for more information.

The Internet is loaded with sites specialising in hiking and walking. A few good ones to try include:

www.trailsource.com/hiking
(an excellent guide to over 400 trails around the world, including many in Europe)

http://greentravel.com/europe/trips.htm
(the Green Travel Network gives a lot of background hiking tips and destination information to Europe and the world)

www.mtn.co.uk/walking/walking.htm
(details of various walking trails in Europe with a country by country guide)

www.gorp.com/gorp/activity/europe/Europe.htm
(walking in Europe site with various links to walking sites and information on long-distance paths in Europe)

CYCLING

Whether planning a full cycling tour or just hiring a bike every so often to ride around a town or region, this is a great way to see Europe. With a bicycle you can move at a leisurely pace, stopping whenever you feel like it, but still cover quite a lot of ground.

Europeans love cycling so there are loads of dedicated bike paths all over the continent. This is particularly true of the Netherlands and Belgium. Other good areas for cycle touring include Tuscany in Italy; Dordogne and Provence in France; the Danube Bike Trail in Austria; the Czech Republic; southern Portugal (the Algarve); the Lakes District and southern England in Britain; anywhere in Ireland; and southern Germany. See the Getting Around section in the While You're There chapter for more information on cycle touring.

SKIING

Some of the world's best skiing and most famous ski resorts can be found in the Alps of Austria, Switzerland and France. Skiing is hardly a budget pastime (apart from lift tickets and accommodation, there's all that après ski drinking to consider!), but it is possible to hit the slopes relatively cheaply if you avoid the Alps and head to some of the lesser known mountains in Andorra and Eastern Europe. For cross-country (Nordic) skiing, Scandinavia (particularly Norway) is the place to be.

Ski gear can be hired at even the smallest mountain resorts, so there's no need to lug boots and poles around. The ski season at most resorts is December to March, though at high altitudes and in Scandinavia you may get an extra month either side. For more information, see the individual country profiles on these countries:

Andorra – The surprise package of Europe, this tiny tax-free principality in the Pyrenees offers the cheapest skiing in Western Europe – so it's pretty crowded these days.

Austria – Great Alpine skiing at a price. Tirolean resorts such as Innsbruck and Kitzbühel are popular.

Eastern Europe – This is where to head if your budget is more important than your parallel turns. Resorts in the Krknose Mountains of the Czech Republic, the Tatras of Slovakia and Poland, the Carpathian Mountains in Romania and, to a lesser extent, the Julian Alps in Slovenia, offer skiing at a fraction of the price of Western Europe. The resorts are less developed and the runs are fewer and shorter, but the snow is still cold and slippery.

France – Another trendy Alpine skiing area but again it's not cheap. Chamonix is a spectacular resort.

Switzerland – Perhaps the best (and most exclusive) of the lot, Switzerland is Alps-personified. St Moritz, Klosters, Davos and Zermatt are just a few of the world's great ski resorts.

Other resorts – Italy has fine skiing in its Alps, but you can also ski at small resorts in Scotland, Spain, Turkey, northern Greece, Bulgaria and Germany.

SURFING & WINDSURFING

Opportunities for surfing aren't great in Europe but they do exist, while windsurfing is popular all along the Mediterranean coast. Often you can hire boards and equipment on the beach or in the resort towns. Newquay in north Cornwall is England's chilly but popular surf centre, and the northern coast of Scotland has some good swell (believe it or not, people surf up there!).

Ireland has some good surfing and windsurfing along its west coast. Good areas include Easkey (County Sligo), Barley Cove (County Cork) and Spanish Point (County Clare). The calm, sheltered waters of the Mediterranean aren't much good for surfing, but the Atlantic coast offers more possibilities. In

Spain, the north coast resorts of Santander and San Sebastián are worth trying, while Tarifa in southern Spain is a paradise for windsurfers.

Windsurfing is extremely popular in Greece and you'll see sailboards for hire on just about any beach. Hsrysi Akti on Paros and Vasiliki on Lefkada are the best places to give it a try. The coasts along Italy and Croatia are also great places for windsurfing. Most resorts rent sailboards.

For more information contact *Surfer Magazine*, which publishes *The Surf Report – Journal of World-wide Surfing Destinations*. It will send you a copy for about US$5 per destination. Order at PO Box 1028, Dana Point, CA 92629 or phone on ☎ 1-714-496 5922.

DIVING & SNORKELLING

Although there are no tropical waters around Europe, there are plenty of things of interest under the surface, including caves and grottoes, shipwrecks and antiquities. The best scuba diving and snorkelling is off the coast of Southern Europe. In Greece and Turkey diving is strictly regulated to protect the underwater antiquities, and must be supervised by a registered diving school. You can snorkel practically anywhere though. Croatia is a very popular diving centre, with dive shops and schools all along the Adriatic coast.

Other good diving spots are Malta and Cyprus, parts of Italy, Spain and Portugal. In Britain the main interest is in looking for shipwrecks, though the waters can be murky.

OTHER ACTIVITIES

There are loads of organised adventure activities that you can take part in while in Europe. These include parasailing, canyoning, white-water rafting, hang-gliding, bungee-jumping and ballooning. Most of these activities carry an element of risk – a canyoning tragedy in Switzerland (Interlaken) in 1999 resulted in the death of 21 young travellers when the gorge flooded. Always check the reputation and safety record of the company you use, make sure its equipment is in good condition, and that your travel insurance covers the type of activity you want to try. Also heed local warnings on weather conditions etc.

If you're not an adrenalin junkie, there are more sedate pursuits such as bird-watching and fishing. If you intend to drop a line in the water, make sure you know what the local regulations are. River fishing throughout Europe is subject to all sorts of restrictions and you'll usually have to buy a licence. There may be limits on the type and amount of fish you can take, times when you can fish, minimum weights and so on. In Britain many stretches of river are privately owned and it's extremely expensive to fish there. Fishing tackle shops are often a good source of local information, or contact the national or regional fishing body.

LEARNING A SKILL

Apart from learning a language (see the Language section later in this chapter) you can immerse yourself in all sorts of courses in Europe, whether private or university based. Cooking in France, dancing in Portugal or basket-weaving in Bulgaria are all possibilities.

A good guidebook should list relevant organisations. Otherwise try local universities or advertisements in the local press.

When to Go

Deciding when to go is an important factor in the planning stage. For some there is very little choice. You might have a window of only one or two months. North American students (and teachers) taking summer vacation will be restricted to that busy period between June and August. Travellers taking a year off from work or studies, or Commonwealth citizens on extended working holiday visas, will have more flexibility.

If you do have a choice there are a few things to take into account, including the weather, the timing of special events, and the crowds and higher costs of summer versus the reduced tourist services of the colder months.

For information on specific countries, see the When to Go sections of the country profiles.

WEATHER

Adverse weather will have an impact on outdoor pursuits and can make sightseeing a bit miserable, but generally it shouldn't affect your plans too much. Rainfall is more likely to be a problem than climate, but you can never predict when or where it's going to rain. The summer months are the driest time in southern Europe, but much of Western and Eastern Europe experiences more rainfall in June, July and August. The temperate Atlantic seaboard is relatively wet all year.

Europe is essentially a four season continent: winter, spring, summer and autumn (fall).

Winter

The winter months (December to March) are cold throughout the continent.

In the northern part of Scandinavia (top half of Norway, Sweden and Finland), Arctic winters are extremely cold, nights are very long (almost continuous in midwinter) and snow covers everything from September to May. Unless you're heavily into Nordic skiing or searching for the Aurora Borealis (Northern Lights), this is not the ideal time to visit. Western Europe benefits from the temperate Atlantic climate, while Eastern Europe experiences much colder winters – temperatures in Prague, Warsaw, Sofia and Belgrade regularly drop below freezing.

Mountain areas such as the Alps and Pyrenees are snow-covered from November or December to late March or early April (year-round in high-altitude areas). In southern Europe the climate is mild but it's also the wettest time of year and very little tourist infrastructure is operating in places like Greece.

Spring

This is probably the best period for fine weather in most parts of Europe and the optimum time to travel. From March to June, the northern part of the continent thaws out, days get longer and sunnier and people emerge from their state of hibernation. It's also that beautiful time when flowers bloom (the bulb fields of Keukenhof near Amsterdam are a sight to behold), trees begin to bear fruit and animal and bird life are at their best. In southern Europe the climate is warm and, although not prime beach-going weather, it makes for very comfortable city sightseeing and hiking.

Summer

Summer in Europe can range from gloriously warm to stiflingly hot, from tinder dry to tragically wet. It's not unusual for rain to fall for days on end in an English summer or for the Scottish Highlands to be enveloped in fog. But as a general rule, late June to late August is the time you can expect the finest weather.

In the far north of the continent, the days are exceptionally long – midnight sun days occur roughly between mid-May and late July – and days are often sunny and warm. Further south you can still expect daylight until 9 or 10 pm and temperatures ranging from around 12° to 28°C. All along the Mediterranean coast summers are hot and dry (18° to 30°C) and the beach resorts are packed to the gills. Cities throughout Europe can be quite humid and uncomfortable in summer.

Autumn (Fall)

Temperatures begin to cool down from mid-September, and by November winter is creeping up again. This is a similar month to spring climate-wise, and it can be a great time to travel. In the northern half of the continent, autumn brings the rich colours of brown, orange and yellow as the trees begin to shed their leaves. In southern Europe the days become milder but are still quite warm, and balmy nights are not uncommon in September and even October.

SPECIAL EVENTS

There are countless festivals and special occasions celebrated throughout Europe year-round. They range from ancient religious festivals to contemporary music events, and from village fairs to cultural extravaganzas celebrated with great gusto and much imbibing of alcohol. Many travellers treat festivals serendipitously and may be lucky enough to stumble on an event in progress. Others build them into their travel plans – huge events such as Oktoberfest in Munich and the Running of the Bulls in Pamplona are firmly on the backpacker trail. Some festivals give you a valuable insight into a local culture, while others are simply great party events where outsiders (that's you) are encouraged to join in.

It definitely pays to have some idea of when major festivals are taking place in the countries you intend to visit. You may only have to tweak your plans by a few days here or there to join the party – and it might turn out to be a highlight of your trip. If you're not interested in a particular festival it's worth avoiding that town or city while it's on. Edinburgh is a great place to be during the Edinburgh Festival, but if you happen to turn up there not knowing about it you'll have more chance of meeting Elvis in the Hound & Haggis than getting a bed for the night. Major festivals attract huge numbers of both foreign and domestic travellers, so

Festivals in Europe

There are so many annual festivals in Europe that you would be a very unlucky traveller to spend a couple of months touring in summer and not get to attend one. They range from small-scale traditional village festivals in Switzerland, Britain or Romania, to manic week-long celebrations in Spain and Italy. Festivals can be religious affairs such as Easter and Carnival, traditional events dating back thousands of years, arts or cultural festivals, purely musical events, sporting events, drinkoramas — the list is endless.

Exact dates for festivals may vary from year to year, usually because local authorities decide to alter dates slightly to suit the public. National tourist offices can usually give accurate dates of their own major festivals a year in advance. With some research and planning you can and should try to get to some of these festivals. For the big events, *always* book accommodation well in advance or expect to sleep rough. The following are some of Europe's biggest and best festivals, and a few less well known events.

January/February
La Tamborada (Spain) — The town of San Sebastián dresses up and goes berserk for this event on 20 January.

Carnevale (Italy) — Venice Carnevale is the best known of the many carnivals held in Italy during the 10 days leading up to Ash Wednesday. Venetians don masks and costumes for a continuous street party.

Carnival (Germany) — The carnival season in Germany also leads up to Ash Wednesday with colourful events in Cologne, Munich, Dusseldorf and Mainz, among other cities.

March/April
Comats de Reines (Switzerland) — The start of summer-long cow fighting events in Lower Valais.

Scoppio del Carro (Italy) — The 'Explosion of the Cart' is a colourful event held in the Piazza del Duomo in Florence on Easter Sunday. The festival, in which a cart full of fireworks is set off, dates back to the Crusades.

Feast of St Mark (Italy) — Held in Venice on 25 April, this is one of many feasts to celebrate patron saints around Europe.

Sumar dagurinn fyrsti (Iceland) — First day of summer. The sun may or may not shine but the Icelanders celebrate this day in Reykjavík on the third Thursday in April with great gusto and street carnivals.

Holy Week Festival (Portugal) — There are many colourful parades during Easter week in Braga including the Ecce Homo procession featuring hundreds of barefoot penitents carrying torches.

Las Fallas (Spain) — A week-long party in Valencia in mid-March featuring all-night drinking, dancing and fireworks.

Feria de Abril (Spain) — Another manic week-long party, this time in Seville, in late April that balances the religious peak of Semana Santa (Easter Week).

St Patrick's Day (Ireland) — Parade in Dublin on 17 March.

Festivals in Europe

May/June
Vienna Festival (Austria) – From mid-May to mid-June, this is the biggest of Vienna's many music festivals.

Life Theatre Festival (Lithuania) – Week-long festival in Vilnius.

Constitution Day (Norway) – Biggest national holiday, with displays of traditional costumes.

Bloomsday (Ireland) – Follows Leopold Bloom's Joycean journey around Dublin on 16 June.

Glastonbury Festival (England) – An enormous three day music festival and hippy happening in late June.

Cannes Film Festival (France) – You'll never get a ticket to this exclusive international film festival, but if you want to do some star-spotting, it's on for 10 days in mid-May.

Athens Festival (Greece) – Opera, ballet and classical music from mid-June to the end of September. The major festivities around Greece, however, take place at Easter (March/April).

Holland Festival (Netherlands) – Amsterdam's festival of arts, music, opera, dance and theatre in mid-June.

July/August
Bastille Day (France) – Festivities for this national day on 13 and 14 July are held all over France but the biggest celebration is in Paris with a military parade and fireworks at the Eiffel Tower.

Montreux Jazz Festival (Switzerland) – World-famous jazz music event held in early July on the edge of Lake Geneva.

Salzburg International Festival (Austria) – A huge music and arts festival starting in late July and influenced heavily by Mozart.

San Fermines (Spain) – The famous Running of the Bulls is held in the streets of Pamplona over eight days in early July, amid wild partying.

Festival of Avignon (France) – World-famous event held in Avignon between early July and early August. It features some 300 shows of music, drama and dance staged every day. There's also the fringe festival (Festival Off) held simultaneously.

Il Palio (Italy) – This extraordinary horse race is held in the main piazza of Siena on 2 July and 16 August. Get to it of you can.

Copenhagen Jazz Festival (Denmark) – The acclaimed 10 day jazz festival in early July is the highlight of Denmark's many music events.

Baltika International Folk Festival (Estonia. Latvia and Lithuania shared) – A week-long festival of music, dance and parades in Baltic tradition, held in mid-July.

Edinburgh Festival/Fringe Festival (Scotland) – Premier international arts festival that runs for three weeks from mid-August.

Notting Hill Carnival (England) – Massive Caribbean street carnival in west London (late August).

September/October
Oktoberfest (Germany) – Munich's legendary Bierfest usually starts in late September and goes for a couple of weeks. If you're into beer-drinking and oompah bands, this is a must.

December
Hogmanay (Scotland) – One of the world's great New Year's Eve parties happens in the pubs and streets of Edinburgh.

consider booking accommodation well in advance or look at staying outside the main city or town and day-tripping to the action. Costs may also increase during festivals, so make sure your budget can handle the extra stress. See the boxed text 'Festivals in Europe' for a rundown of some major events.

TRAVEL PERIODS

When planning your arrival, departure and travel within Europe, you will need to take into account peak, off-peak and shoulder travel periods. Peak periods are when the majority of travellers want to fly. These periods usually coincide with the school holidays in your country, and with certain holidays such as Christmas, New Year and Easter. The country you are flying to will also have its peak periods when flights and accommodation will be heavily booked and prices will be higher.

The peak period generally covers late December to early January (Christmas and New Year) and late June to the end of August (summer); the shoulder period is April to early June and September/October (spring and autumn, including Easter); and the low season takes in the remaining months (winter).

If your time in Europe is limited, the shoulder period strikes a good balance between off-peak prices and optimum travel conditions. If you're going for an

---

Giving Thanks for a Turkey Dinner

Some of the best moments in travel come when you least expect them – when you ditch your plans and head in the other direction. While following a fairly well worn path around Turkey we noticed that there was an upcoming traditional festival at a small town named Giresun on the Black Sea coast. It was on the other side of the country but we were headed in that general direction anyway. Giresun is an unassuming place, a working Turkish town with little in the way of sights or even charm. As far as we could tell, we were the only western visitors in town. Within a day we had amassed a small following, led by Deniz, a very mature teenager who spoke some English (nobody else did). We were eagerly shown around town, offered small gifts and saw a part of Turkish life that had nothing to do with beaches, apple tea, ancient ruins or carpet shops. The festival itself was a kaleidoscope of traditional costumes, dancing and singing. It had the sort of vibrancy and spontaneity that larger events often lack.

The following day was Turkey's biggest religious holiday, Kurban Bayrami, when thousands of sheep around the country are ceremoniously sacrificed on the streets. It re-enacts the biblical story of God asking Abraham to sacrifice his son in order to prove his faith, then at the last moment telling him to instead sacrifice a ram that had become entangled in bushes nearby. The slaughter is very solemn and symbolic; the animal is gently restrained and prayers are uttered over its head before a sharp knife is drawn across its throat. There's no wastage – the animals are divided up among families and used for feasting that night. That afternoon we again met Deniz and were promptly invited to have dinner with his family for what would be the equivalent of Thanksgiving or Christmas. It was a great honour, but we were the ones made to feel as if we were bestowing the honour. Over a wonderful meal of freshly sacrificed lamb, Turkish mezes (the soup was a rich brew made from intestines) and raki, we spent an evening in the company of a delightful working-class family, communicating through hastily practised Turkish and Deniz' translations – happy that we'd made the detour to Giresun.

Paul Harding
LP Author, Australia

extended stay, consider flying in the low season when fares are at their cheapest. Undoubtedly the best time to travel in most of Europe is April to June and September/October. The weather is still warm, the crowds are not too thick and most tourist attractions, accommodation and transport services are in full swing.

Bad Travel Times

The single worst time to set foot in most parts of Western Europe and southern Europe is August. This is the month when many Europeans take their holidays, so they pack up the kids and desert the cities in droves. As a result, accommodation prices skyrocket and finding a bed in any popular tourist town or mountain/coastal resort will be very difficult. Trains and buses will also be packed and you might struggle to get a seat on popular train routes in France, Italy, Spain and Portugal. Meanwhile, the cities are full of foreign tourists but many of the shops, businesses and hotels have closed because the proprietors have gone on holiday! OK, it might not be as bad as it sounds, but there's little doubt that July and August are the busiest tourist months in Europe and will require lots of patience and planning in terms of advance bookings.

Getting off the beaten path – away from the beach resorts and inundated tourist towns – is one way to make the best of the high season. Parts of Eastern Europe and Scandinavia will still be relatively deserted in midsummer.

Travel during the Christmas/New Year period can also be quite difficult as domestic tourism again takes over and prices at ski resorts go through the roof. Public transport is usually significantly reduced on major public holidays such as Christmas Day.

Researching Your Trip

Research can be a bit of a drag, especially when you have a thousand other details to attend to, but focused reading, Web exploration, film watching and picking the brains of travel experts and friends can greatly enhance your trip. This is particularly true if you're basing your trip on a particular theme (eg architecture or artworks, history or trekking). Some trips in Europe may require advance arrangements or may only be available at certain times of year – it's no good turning up in the Netherlands expecting to see the place ablaze with tulips in February or July.

GUIDEBOOKS

Travel guides are invaluable tools, particularly when you're travelling in a country for the first time. They'll help you find places to stay and eat, describe popular attractions, provide vocabulary lists, give you an insight into the local culture, and include all the transport options between and within countries. A good guidebook will invariably save you time and money.

Using the information in this book, decide on a rough route before you buy your guidebook(s) and allow yourself plenty of time to read them. If you want to look at detailed guidebooks to the countries you plan to visit, start with your library. They usually carry a range of popular guides and, while they may be out of date, the background information is still very useful. Guidebooks can be quite a weight to lug around, so you'll probably only want to take one or two on the road. You can also pick up new or second-hand guides in many countries along the way, or swap them with fellow travellers on the road.

Selecting a Guidebook

The travel guide market has mushroomed over the past 20 years and there are thousands of titles available. Lonely Planet is a major seller.

Before you buy, ask your friends which books they used – a personal recommendation is often the best. Consider how well the guide caters to your intended budget. Does it cover a range of accommodation and eating styles, or only the cheapest/most expensive of everything? Most guides fit into a particular budget category but you'll probably want one that successfully balances penny-pinching with good value and the occasional splurge.

Consider also how long you plan to spend in each country, as this will influence the level of detail you'll need from a guide. For example, in Lonely Planet's *Europe on a shoestring*, there are 40 countries covered and France merits 81 pages; in the *Western Europe* guide (15 countries), the coverage is expanded to 203 pages; while the detailed *France* guide has 1150 pages! As the focus is sharpened, a greater level of information is provided; recommendations are more expansive; more maps are included; and cultural, historical and artistic issues are given more prominence. The point is, if you think you want to dabble in various corners of Europe, but only want to carry one guide, you'll have to expect the coverage to be less detailed and many out-of-the-way places won't even get a mention. If you intend to spend most of your time in two or three countries, it may be worth taking two or three country-specific guides. If you're just visiting a city, look for Lonely Planet's range of city guides, eg Paris or Amsterdam.

All this will give you plenty to go on. At Lonely Planet we believe we've struck the right balance between background and hard information, with highly detailed maps, full-colour photos and a style of no-nonsense advice that still inspires a sense of adventure.

Specialist Guides

There are many guidebooks on the market aimed at specialist activities, interests and styles of travel. A browse in the travel section of your local bookshop will reveal more subject matter than you could have imagined.

Modes of Transport If you intend to utilise a particular type of transport while in Europe, there'll be a guidebook out there specialising in it.

Europe by Eurail by Laverne Ferguson, *Europe by Train* by Katie Wood & George McDonald, and the *Eurail & Train Travel Guide to Europe* are just a few guides focusing on rail travel. *Moto Europa: The Complete Guide to European Motor Travel* by Eric Bredesen is a comprehensive guide to driving in Europe.

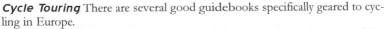

Cycle Touring There are several good guidebooks specifically geared to cycling in Europe.

Europe by Bike by Karen & Terry Whitehill (The Mountaineers, 1993) and *Cycling Europe* by Nadine Slavinski (Bicycle Books, 1992) are two broadly focused books, but they're not particularly user-friendly. You'll probably find country-specific guidebooks more useful. Lonely Planet produces a series of cycling guides including *Cycling Britain* and *Cycling France*, which cover these countries in depth.

Bicycling (☎ 800-666-2806, www.bicyclingmagazine.com) is a leading monthly cycling magazine that covers destinations, training, nutrition, touring, racing, equipment and new technology.

Hiking Lonely Planet publishes a string of walking guides to European countries including: *Walking in Britain*, *Walking in France*, *Walking in Ireland*, *Walking in Spain* and *Walking in Switzerland*. These give detailed route information for both short walks and long treks, as well as accommodation, eating and sightseeing information. Cicerone Press (UK) publishes a list of walking guides to smaller regions such as Tuscany.

Trekking in Europe (AA) covers a range of demanding treks such as the Tour du Mont Blanc through France, Switzerland and Italy and the Bear Trail in Finland. *100 Hikes in the Alps* by Vicky Spring (1992) provides just what it says.

Skiing *The Blue Guide to Skiing in Europe* has extensive coverage of Europe's ski resorts, as does *Ski Europe* by Charles Leocha.

Using Your Guidebook

A guidebook is not intended as a 'bible' to be unquestioningly followed every step of the way. Salty old travellers are often heard to say that the problem with guidebooks is that they create a trail of backpackers, all staying in the same hostels, eating at the same cafes and visiting the same sights 'because they're in the book'. This is where your own judgement and inquisitive nature should come in – making new discoveries (even if it's just a great little restaurant in the backstreets of Budapest) is half the fun of travel. Also, the 'hard' information such as prices and schedules tends to date quite quickly, so don't go into a blue funk if a bus timetable has changed, or a hotel has raised its prices or the standard of its rooms has changed since your guide was published. A good guide will give you all the information and advice you need, but there's no substitute for your own research and for getting up-to-date information from other travellers on the road.

MAPS

If your main method of getting around is public transport, then the regional and city maps in your guidebook should meet your needs. If you plan to hire a car or motorbike, do some independent trekking or an extensive cycling tour, then purchase more detailed maps either at home or once you arrive.

Europe is thoroughly mapped and you won't have trouble picking up fairly detailed maps to every country once you get there. Cities and towns will have maps in English available either free from local tourist offices or for sale in bookshops and newsagencies.

Lonely Planet currently produces detailed colour city maps for Paris, London, Berlin, Amsterdam, Prague, Budapest, Barcelona, Dublin, St Petersburg and Istanbul, with more to come.

A good place to look online is Mapquest Mapstore (www.mapquest.com). Regular shops with good stocks of maps include:

Australia
Mapland
(☎ 03-9670 4383) 372 Little Bourke St, Melbourne, Vic 3000
Nev Anderson Maps
(☎ 02-9878 2809) 30 Fawcett St, Ryde, NSW 2112
The Travel Bookshop
(☎ 02-9241 3554) 20 Bridge St, Sydney, NSW 2001

Canada
World of Maps & Travel Books
(☎ 613-724 6776, ✉ maps@magi.com, www.worldofmaps.com) 118 Holland Ave, Ottawa, Ont K1Y 0X6

New Zealand
Map World
(☎ 03-374 5399, ✉ maps@mapworld.co.nz) PO Box 13-833, Christchurch
Whitcoulls
(☎ 09-356 5400) 210 Queen St, Auckland

UK
The Map Shop
(☎ 06-846 3146) AT Atkinson & Partner, 15 High St, Upton-on-Severn, Worcestershire WR8 OHJ
Stanfords Map Centre
(☎ 020-7836 1321) 12-14 Long Acre, London WC2E 9LP

USA
Hagstrom Map and Travel Center
(☎ 212-398 1222, www.hagstromstore.com) 57 West 43rd St, New York, NY 10036
Rand McNally – The Map & Travel Store
(☎ 212-758 7488, www.randmcnallystore.com) 150 East 52nd St, New York, NY 10022
(☎ 310-556 2202) Century City Shopping Center, 10250 Santa Monica Blvd, Los Angeles, CA 90067
(☎ 415-777 3131) 595 Market St, San Francisco, CA 94105
Traveler's Bookstore
(☎ 212-664 0995) Time Warner Building, 22 East 52nd St, New York, NY 10019
US Library of Congress
(☎ 202-707 5000) Geography & Map Division, 101 Independence Ave, Washington, DC 20540

TRAVEL AGENCIES
Brochures distributed by travel agents can be good sources of information. You can get a good feel for a country's major sights from the full-colour images in these glossy publications. Travel consultants are often widely travelled

and most will be happy to share their experiences with you. Just remember that many consultants work on commission, so don't take up too much of their time if you're not planning to book through them (see also Buying from Travel Agents in the Tickets & Insurance chapter).

INTERNATIONAL TOURIST OFFICES

Most European countries maintain tourist offices in other western countries and these can provide destination information, maps and lists of domestic tour operators. See the Tourist Offices Overseas sections in the country profiles for details or go to Tourism Offices Worldwide Directory (www.towd.com), which has regularly updated links to many tourist office Web sites.

Even if a particular country doesn't have a tourist office in your home country, you can always write to its national tourist office and ask for brochures, calendars of events, accommodation lists and all sorts of other information to be sent to you. You can find the addresses of these offices in guidebooks.

NEWSPAPERS

Many major western newspapers have good-quality weekly or monthly travel sections carrying advertisements for special travel deals and packages. Check out the following papers in your country or access the content on their Web sites:

Australia
Age (www.theage.com.au)
Australian (www.news.com.au)
Sydney Morning Herald (www.smh.com.au)
Canada
Globe & Mail (www.theglobeandmail.com)
Vancouver Sun (www.vancouversun.com)
New Zealand
New Zealand Herald (www.nzherald.co.nz/index.html)
South Africa
Daily Mail & Guardian (www.mg.co.za)
Star (www.star.co.za)
UK
Independent (www.independent.co.uk)
Southern Cross (www.southerncross.co.uk)
Time Out (www.timeout.com/london)
Times (www.the-times.co.uk)
TNT (www.tntmag.co.uk)
USA
Chicago Tribune (www.chicagotribune.com)
LA Times (www.latimes.com)
New York Times (www.nytimes.com)
San Francisco Examiner (www.examiner.com)

BOOKS

There are many good books covering Europe as a whole. These range from history books with dense academic text to humorous travelogues. Here we describe a few worth looking out for.

A Tramp Abroad by Mark Twain is a classic humorous travelogue of Twain's walking tour through Europe in 1878.

Neither Here Nor There by Bill Bryson is a more contemporary humorous account of the author's travels through Europe. *A Merry Dance Around the World* by Eric Newby (Picador, 1996) features extracts from his numerous travel books and includes chapters on Italy, Ireland, the Mediterranean and the Trans-Siberian Railway. *On the Shores of the Mediterranean* by Eric Newby (Lonely Planet) explores the civilisations of the Mediterranean, commencing in Naples.

The World's Most Dangerous Places (Fieldings, 1998) has chapters on Albania and eastern Turkey. *Europe 101: History and Art for the Traveller* by Rick Steves (John Muir Publications, 1996) is a handy, concise guide if you're interested in this field.

For information on books to individual countries, see the country profiles later in this book.

MAGAZINES

Many travel magazines are directly targeted at a particular market and include a combination of holiday and country profiles; comparative pieces on flights, accommodation and cuisine; articles on specialist activities such as hiking, fishing or bird-watching; tips on equipment and clothing; readers letters; competitions; and reams of travel-industry advertisements. Many publications have an e-zine component that you can access on the Web. Also look at the magazines produced by travel organisations, such as STA's *Escape*, Intrepid Travel's *The Intrepid Traveller* or Trailfinders' *Trailfinder Magazine*.

Adventure Magazine
(☎ 800-846 8575) PO Box 461270, Escondido, CA 92046-1270, USA
(a full-colour glossy offering in-depth articles on adventure travel options and practical advice on doing it yourself)

Big World Magazine
(☎ 717-569 0217, ✆ orders@bigworld.com, www.bigworld.com) PO Box 8743, Lancaster, PA 17604-8743, USA
(with its no-frills approach, Big World offers the independent budget traveller a fresh look at the adventures and joys of travel)

Geographical Magazine
(☎ 020-7938 4011, ✆ geogmag@gn.apc.org) 47c Kensington Court, London W8 5DA, England
(the magazine of the Royal Geographical Society [UK], with a focus on cultural, anthropological and environmental issues – beautiful photographs, book and television reviews and some advertising for tour companies make this magazine an excellent read)

Mountain Bike
(www.mountainbike.com)
(information about races, trails, gears and tips for special manoeuvres)

National Geographic
(☎ 1-800-647-5463, www.nationalgeographic.com) Box 98198, Washington, DC 20090-8198, USA
(the magazine of the US National Geographic Society with great photos and excellent background information)

Outside
(☎ 800-678 1131, http://outside.starwave.com) PO Box 54729, Boulder, CO 80322-4729, USA
(for travel by bike, skateboard, kayak or any other means that requires some physical effort – it has a US bias, but includes international destinations)
Traveller Magazine
(☎ 020-7589 3315, ✉ mship@wexas.com, www.travelmag.co.uk) 45-49 Brompton Rd, Knightsbridge, London SW3 1DE, England
(a quarterly with an emphasis on anthropology, exploration and adventure travel, plus travellers' health, book reviews, travel hot spots and advertising for UK-based tour operators)
Travel Unlimited
PO Box 1058, Allston, Mass 02134, USA
(publish details of cheap air fares, special deals and courier options)
Wanderlust
(☎ 01753 620426) PO Box 1832, Windsor, Berkshire SL4 6YP, England
(concise general travel information on both out-of-the-way and routine destinations – has heaps of ads for tours and tour companies)

FILMS

Europe has a diverse film industry, though nothing on the scale of Hollywood. Many films coming out of Europe are arthouse films with English subtitles. Britain pumps out a few good films each year. Documentaries on European culture, politics and nature appear from time to time. For recommended films from individual countries, see the Films sections in the country profiles.

Also check out the Internet Movie Database (www.imdb.com), which allows you to search by location.

USEFUL WEB SITES

The following Web sites are good general resources for deciding which countries you'd like to visit in Europe, and for picking up various bits of up-to-date information. There are many other sites mentioned throughout this book with details on visas, accommodation, plane tickets, activities, health, media and other travel needs. For a full list, see the appendix 'Internet Addresses' at the back of the book. For Internet sites specific to particular countries, see the Online Services sections of the country profiles later in this book.

Lonely Planet
www.lonelyplanet.com
(destination information, health advice, bulletin boards and links to all topics travel-related, use the upgrades to update information given in the profiles of this book)
British Foreign & Commonwealth Office
www.fco.gov.uk
(travel advisories written for Brits, but relevant for most travellers)
Europe For Visitors
http://goeurope.miningco.com/travel/Europe/goeurope
(a useful site with loads of links to all sorts of specialist Europe travel information)

Eurotrip

www.eurotrip.com

(a comprehensive site devoted to budget travel in Europe, including a discussion forum)

Freewheelin' Budget Travel

www.budgetraveler.com

(booking information and details on budget and student travel with an emphasis on Europe)

Frommer's

www.frommers.com

(Arthur Frommer's Budget Travel Online has wide-ranging travel information in a similar style to the books and magazine)

Hiking & Walking Homepage

www.teleport.com/-walking/hiking.html

(excellent information on international trekking spots, tours and clubs)

Internet Guide to Hostelling

www.hostels.com

(details of hostels across the world, with a good travellers news section)

Internet Traveller Information Service

www.itisnet.com

(destination information and advice)

Rail Europe

www.raileurope.com/us

(information on various European rail passes)

Rain or Shine

www.rainorshine.com

(five-day weather forecasts for 800 cities around the world)

Rick Steves

www.ricksteves.com

(gives a lot of Euro-specific travel information for budget travellers)

TNT Magazine

www.tntmag.co.uk

(a good place to look if you intend to spend time in London − travel articles plus loads of travel-related links)

Travelocity

www.travelocity.com

(general travel information, bookings, equipment and links)

Travel World

www.travel.world.co.uk

(links to every European travel-related site you can think of − great place to look for air, rail and bus fares, specialist travel companies and much more)

US State Department Travel Warnings & Consular Information Sheets

http://travel.state.gov/travel_warnings.html

(mildly paranoid warnings about world trouble spots written primarily for American citizens)

World Events Calendar

http://travel.epicurious.com

(huge list of festivals, events and other festivities, which can be searched by theme, country or date)

World Tourism Organization

www.world-tourism.org/ows-doc/wtich.htm

(the United Nations international organisation dealing with travel and tourism policy and development, with members in 138 countries representing local government, tourism associations, airlines, hotel groups and tour operators)

Language

There's no doubt that being able to speak the language of the country in which you're travelling makes life easier, from asking directions on the street to ordering in a restaurant. More importantly, it allows you to get 'inside' a culture. But most of us don't have the time or energy to acquire more than the basics of a foreign language, let alone the several you might need in Europe.

The good news is that English is by far the most common second language in Europe; it is spoken by most locals involved in tourism and business, by many European students and by almost all western travellers. Whatever country you visit, you'll find English more widely spoken in cities than in rural areas.

LEARNING A LANGUAGE

There are numerous 'groups' of languages in Europe, and many are closely related. This can make the job of learning phrases in multiple languages a little easier, and knowledge of one language can be used as a springboard to learn others. For instance, French, Italian, Spanish, Portuguese and Romanian are all Romance languages, descended from Latin. German and Dutch are West Germanic languages closely related to English (believe it or not) and German is also spoken in Austria and parts of Switzerland. Swedish, Danish, Norwegian and Icelandic all bear a strong resemblance to each other. Greek, on the other hand, stands on its own and has its own alphabet.

Balance the difficulty of learning a language against the benefits you will gain from speaking it. There's little point studying a language (specifically for this trip) unless you intend to spend an extended period in that country. But you should make a point of learning a few words and phrases for each country you intend to visit, regardless of how widely English is spoken. The first phrase to learn is 'Do you speak English?', which is a more polite way to begin a question than launching into English on the assumption that everyone should know what you're saying. The basic pleasantries (hello, please, thank you, excuse me and goodbye) will also go a long way. Add a few simple phrases such as 'Where is the … ?', 'How much does this cost?' and so on, plus learn to count to at least 10, and you will find things infinitely easier.

To make headway in really learning a language you will need a textbook, with tapes to assist with pronunciation (for study before departure) and a phrasebook (for use on the road). Good textbook titles include Teach Yourself, Berlitz, Barrons and Routledge.

Set yourself some goals and sit down with the book on a regular basis. Just running your eyes over the words is not only boring, but a waste of time. If you're serious about a language you could supplement your study with private tutoring or language classes. Many local universities offer extension courses and night classes in foreign languages, and community centres also often have foreign-language classes. These places are also useful resources for finding a private tutor; also try the embassy or consulate of the country you plan to visit, look for newspaper advertisements or search the Internet.

Finally, if you intend spending a reasonable amount of time in a particular country, consider starting a language course there after you arrive. This is the fastest way to learn any language since you can put into practice what you learn as soon as you step outside the classroom. Check the local English-language newspaper for listings.

Phrasebooks

Phrasebooks should be compact and have everything written in both English and the local language. Lonely Planet publishes pocket phrasebooks to most of Europe's major languages with an emphasis on useful, current expressions with easy to follow phonetic pronunciations. Words and phrases are written in local script (Cyrillic) for countries like Greece, Russia, Macedonia and Bulgaria.

Lonely Planet also publishes regional pocket phrasebooks for those who are visiting several countries in one region: *Central Europe phrasebook*, *Eastern Europe phrasebook*, *Mediterranean Europe phrasebook*, *Scandinavian Europe phrasebook* and *Western Europe phrasebook*. For example, *Central Europe phrasebook* covers the Czech, French, German, Hungarian, Italian and Slovak languages. Don't forget the language section of your guidebook, which may be all you need for learning the basics if you're on a wide-ranging tour.

Work & Travel

Many travellers plan to supplement or even finance their holiday by working in Europe. The great advantage of mixing work and travel is that you get an inside view of the country you're working and temporarily living in. If this happens to be a non-English speaking country, you will also be able to practice a new language and learn something of the local culture. What often happens, though, is that you'll end up working long hours for relatively low pay, unable to save up quite enough for all the things you planned.

If you want to work legally in Europe, some research and advance planning is essential (see Work Permits later). But many travellers pick up casual 'illegal' work in the hospitality industry, harvesting, labouring, ski or beach resorts and so on. It's risky to turn up anywhere if you don't have reasonable funds to support yourself for at least a few weeks, and preferably a return air ticket. British immigration officials are particularly suspicious of anyone they suspect will work illegally, so don't carry references, CVs etc.

Seasonal work such as fruit picking and work in ski resorts is often taken up before the season begins, so if you turn up too late the best jobs will be gone. In general it's not so easy for foreigners to pick up casual work in Europe. Unemployment rates are high in some regions and because (in theory) any EU citizen can work in any other EU country, casual and seasonal jobs are often taken up by people from elsewhere in Europe.

Weigh up whether you would be better off working in your own country for a few months to save. There's no hassle with work visas, you'll probably receive better pay for casual work, and you'll be able to save more easily – especially if you live with your parents or in a cheap rental situation. Working in Vienna might sound exotic, but not if you're washing dishes for 10 hours a day in a steaming restaurant kitchen and earning the equivalent of US$5 an hour.

Unless you have particular employment plans, the best approach is to plan a flexible trip and seek work along the way – if you pick up a summer bar job on Ios in Greece, that's a bonus.

Working in Britain

Many young Commonwealth citizens (Australians, New Zealanders, Canadians and South Africans) take advantage of Britain's two year working holiday visa to mix work and travel. The visa is available to anyone aged between 17 and 27 and is intended to allow travellers to work on a casual or part-time basis in a variety of industries. As a result, there are thousands of travellers working in pubs, restaurants, factories, offices, households and farms around the country. Many businesses, particularly in London, rely heavily on this temporary workforce so there are many recruitment agencies in the city that specialise in work placements for travellers.

Some of the most lucrative jobs are in accounting, computer programming, banking and secretarial fields where you can earn upwards of £10 (US$16) an hour. Other professional jobs include substitute teaching, nursing, sales and journalism. But if you don't have any qualifications or experience, don't despair – much of the work around is unskilled or semiskilled. You could find yourself packing videos on the night shift one day and filing papers in an office the next. Live-in bar work is extremely popular; it's rare to go into a pub in Earl's Court or Shepherd's Bush and not have your pint pulled by an Australian or some other antipodean. Accommodation and meals are often part of the deal and this is one reason why publicans like to hire travellers – they can afford to pay them less. Busy families regularly employ nannies (au pairs) or other home help (which may also be live-in), tradesmen are often looking for extra labourers, and sporting events and concerts need staff for security, ushering etc.

The first thing you should do is sign up with one or more of the major recruitment companies. Some specialise in particular fields such as nursing temps or secretaries, while others are more general. They will assess you, put you on their list and try to match you with one of the many jobs constantly popping up. These could range from one afternoon of work to a six month placement. You will then be paid directly by the temp agency regardless of where you work. You'll need to provide a telephone contact (such as the number of your hostel). Remember that temp agencies get a lot of feedback from their clients so if you're a good worker, punctual and easy-going, they'll continue to offer you work. Recruitment consultants get cheesed off if you constantly turn down work or pull out of an agreed job at the last minute.

Another source of jobs, including bar work, is the antipodean media. The weekly *TNT Magazine* is the major player, but there's also *Southern Cross*, *New Zealand News UK* and the *SA Times*. These can be picked up free from paper bins outside major tube stations in London. You'll have to get in early and start making phone calls on the day of publication because the jobs go quickly. Other sources include the daily newspapers. The *TNT* Web site (www.tntmag.co.uk) has a list of recruitment agencies.

A word of advice: the working holiday scheme is supposed to be incidental to your travels and, according to its guidelines, no more than half of your trip should be spent in gainful employment. What's more, 'you must not engage in work which represents a continuation of your career'. Immigration officers have the right to refuse entry to the country to anyone they think intends to work outside their visa restrictions. Backpackers have been deported at Heathrow airport for having professional resumes and reference papers in their luggage. Have these 'incriminating' documents posted over to you.

Work Your Way Around the World by Susan Griffith gives good practical advice on a wide range of issues and has a decent section on Europe. *Summer Jobs Abroad* (published by Vacation Work) and *Working Holidays* (published by the Central Bureau for Educational Visits and Exchanges in London) are other good sources.

WORK PERMITS

To work legally in any European country, non-EU nationals (anyone not holding the passport of an EU country) will need to organise a work permit or visa in advance.

Usually this means arranging employment, then obtaining a permit or 'letter of hire' from your employer. In some cases you'll have to cut through reams of red tape and obtain a permit from the consulate in your own country in advance – always contact the embassy or consulate of the country you wish to work in for up-to-date information beforehand.

Sometimes work permits and jobs can be arranged through specialist travel agents (STA Travel has working holiday programs in Britain, France and Spain), and organisations such as BUNAC (the British Universities North America Club; www.bunac.org.uk) can arrange working holidays such as the Work in Britain program for full-time American students.

Commonwealth citizens aged between 17 and 27 (up to your 28th birthday) can get a 'working holiday' visa for Britain, valid for two years. Thousands of young Aussies, Kiwis, South Africans and Canadians take advantage of this every year and form a vast working travellers network centred on London. See the boxed text 'Working in Britain'.

If you have a parent or grandparent who was born in an EU country, you may have certain rights you never knew about. Get in touch with that country's embassy and ask about dual citizenship and work permits – if you go for citizenship, also ask about any obligations, such as military service and residency. Ireland is particularly easy-going about granting citizenship to people with an Irish parent or grandparent, and with an Irish passport, the EU is your oyster. Having a British-born parent or grandparent usually entitles you to a four year work visa for the UK, with an option to apply for residency at the end. Be aware that your home country may not recognise dual citizenship.

ENGLISH TEACHING

It's not as easy as it once was to pick up a job teaching English in Europe. Although there are still plenty of students out there eager to learn English, a proliferation of institutes offering TEFL (Teaching English as a Foreign Language) courses has resulted in stiff competition for teaching jobs.

To get a job teaching English at a school in Europe you will either need to be well dressed and an extremely good bluffer, or you'll need the right qualifications (or both). A recognised TEFL or TESOL (Teaching English to Speakers of Other Languages) certificate will go a long way. A useful credential

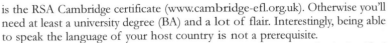

is the RSA Cambridge certificate (www.cambridge-efl.org.uk). Otherwise you'll need at least a university degree (BA) and a lot of flair. Interestingly, being able to speak the language of your host country is not a prerequisite.

It's possible to arrange a job before you arrive in Europe (check classified advertisements in major newspapers), and colleges that offer TEFL courses may be able to help with job placement. But many European schools will prefer to interview candidates in person, so simply doorknocking prospective colleges with your CV in hand might yield results. Being on the spot also allows you to check local newspapers for current job advertisements and telephone books for a listing of language schools.

Don't bother looking for a job in summer when all the schools are shut – August/September is the best time. The other alternative is freelance teaching, where you privately tutor individuals or groups. This requires plenty of front on your part, and a knowledge of the local language will help.

Where to Teach

The most likely place to find English-teaching work is Eastern Europe. A few years ago merely being a native English-speaker was enough to get you a job teaching in the Czech Republic, Slovakia, Hungary, Slovenia or Poland, but that honeymoon period is all but over. Now you'll fare much better with the qualifications described above.

Opportunities abound in the Baltic states (Estonia, Latvia and Lithuania), and in Romania. You could probably line up an English-teaching job in these countries quite easily (even without qualifications) if you have the right work permits. Bear in mind that the pay will probably be quite low.

Spain was once a hotbed of employment for English teachers but now the market is virtually saturated. There are still opportunities in Portugal however. Mainland Greece (outside Athens) is worth trying. You'll have more difficulty in countries such as Italy, France, Germany and Austria, and little chance in Scandinavia.

Teaching Resources

The Internet is awash with English-teaching sites. Some of the best are:

Central European Teaching Program
    www.beloit.edu/~cetp
    (site dedicated to finding teachers for schools in Poland, Hungary, Romania and Latvia)
English Expert Page
    www.englishexpert.com
    (good general information on teaching in Europe and some job listings)
International House
    www.international-house.org
    (good source of information on RSA Cambridge certification)
International TESOL Training Centre
    www.teachandtravel.com
    (information on getting TESOL qualifications and job listings for certificate holders)

TEFL Job Centre
www.jobs.edunet.com
(English-teaching positions all over the world, including Europe)

There are lots of good books about teaching English, including *Teaching English Abroad* by S Griffith and *Now Hiring! Jobs in Eastern Europe* by C Canfield.

BAR & RESTAURANT WORK

The hospitality industry is probably the biggest source of casual employment in Europe (if not the world). With a work permit and a bit of experience you should easily pick up work as a bartender or waiter, but in some circumstances you might not require either. Places that have a booming summer tourist trade, such as the Greek islands and Spanish and Portuguese resorts, sometimes employ travellers for cash-in-hand work. You might not be spinning bottles like Tom Cruise (a la *Cocktail*), but even washing dishes or cleaning up at the end of the night is pretty good if you need the money (and you get to lie on the beach all day). The best way to find this sort of work is to ask around at bars and restaurants and keep an eye on hostel notice boards. The most likely employers will be the English and Irish-style 'pubs' that seem to occupy real estate in every city and tourist resort in Europe. In London, bar and restaurant jobs are advertised in *TNT Magazine* and other free travellers newspapers. In Britain, bar work often comes with accommodation and meals provided. In this way the pubs can utilise their upstairs rooms and pay the overseas bar staff a pittance (as little as UK£2 to UK£3 an hour). The high cost of accommodation in London makes this a pretty good deal though. Remember that for most bar/service work you'll need a good set of clothes.

If you happen to be qualified – say as a chef, silver service waiter or bar manager – don't be afraid to use it. These types of jobs are available and there'll be less competition than for unskilled employment. CVs, references and a work permit will usually be required though.

FRUIT PICKING

Fruit picking or harvesting is possibly one of the easiest forms of casual work to pick up, even if you don't have a permit. Some small-scale farmers, wine-growers and orchardists pay cash in hand and turn a blind eye to the law. They don't want to see your papers any more than you want to show them. In theory, however, you should have a permit; competition for jobs (from other EU workers, for instance) will work against you if you don't have one.

This sort of work is available everywhere, from strawberry and sprout picking in the English Midlands to grape picking in Bordeaux, to plucking olives in Greece. Often the best way to get this work is to approach farmers directly, or to ask around in the nearest town or village, but you might also find advertisements in local papers or on notice boards in youth hostels. Of course, timing is all important here. If you're too early or late in the season there'll be no work. If you turn up in the middle of the harvest, the jobs might all be taken. There are too many types of produce and seasonal variations of harvest in Europe to even begin to list them here, but it's possible to pick something, somewhere, almost year-round. The grape harvest is generally between September and November, while most fruit in Britain is picked from June to August.

SKI RESORTS

If you like to ski, there's nothing better than working at a ski resort where the high accommodation costs and, in many cases, lift passes, are part of the deal.

The best jobs, of course, are ski instructing but you'll need to be qualified, experienced and have contacts to secure these. Then there's restaurant and bar work, helping in ski shops and other stores, reception and office work, cleaning chalets, operating lifts and tows, shovelling snow and so on. Many of these jobs will be filled well before the season begins, but often you'll be able to get work on the spot. You'll need a reasonable amount of money to support yourself while looking for work – it might take weeks to secure a job. The best time to start looking is about a month before the season begins, but you might be extremely lucky (right place, right time …) and get something if you turn up at the start of the season.

TRAVEL WRITING & PHOTOGRAPHY

You may be able to defray some of your travel costs by publishing articles or photos on the places you visit. If you have ambitions of being a photographer, invest in the appropriate equipment (see the Camera section in the What to Bring chapter) and consider taking a course in photography. The field of travel photography is very competitive. Typically, if you submit 100 shots to a photo library, it might accept fewer than 10. However, many magazines and newspapers accept travel articles based on the quality of accompanying photographs, so having good shots to back up your prose is almost essential. Be sure to use slide film, as transparencies are the industry standard.

The same professional approach should be brought to travel writing. Research the potential markets for your stories and even send away for writers' guidelines before hitting the road. When you're on the road, research your material thoroughly and keep good notes. Writing off the top of your head when you get home almost never works. Make sure you record all the necessary practical information (facts, figures etc), but don't neglect the personal insights and descriptions that will give your writing depth and interest. Also look for specific and offbeat angles while travelling – the sharper the focus of your intended articles, the more marketable they are likely to be. Few magazines will accept the ramblings of your two week trip in France, but they could well be interested in your cycling tour around the wineries of the Loire Valley, or a look inside the city of Rouen where Joan of Arc was burned at the stake in 1431.

OTHER WORK

If you have the experience, qualities or inclination, the list of jobs you could get involved in is very long. Possibilities include nannies and au pairs, camp counsellors, busking, factory work or labouring and telemarketing. Another option is asking at youth hostels if they have any work available. Travellers often work short-term as cleaners or receptionists in exchange for free accommodation and a bit of pocket money.

VOLUNTEER WORK

The scope for volunteer work in Europe is broad. Although you won't be paid, the experience you get from helping others can be very rewarding. Getting placed in voluntary work can actually end up costing you money – many organisations charge a sizable fee for placement and living expenses. Most organisations will cover food and lodging expenses, but not your transport from home.

Options in Europe include work camps where volunteers are hired for unskilled labour on community projects, archaeological digs and conservation projects. Research thoroughly the sort of work you're interested in before setting out. Volunteer work can be tough, dispiriting and very uncomfortable, so choose what you're most comfortable with.

A good source of information on available work and placement organisations is *The International Directory of Voluntary Work* (Vacation Work) and *Volunteer Work* (Central Bureau). Community Service Volunteers (www.csv.org.uk) is a good contact in Britain, as is the British Trust for Conservation Volunteers (www.btcv.org.uk). Internet resources include One World (www.one.world.org), or the Directory of International Voluntary Service (www.astro.virginia.edu /-rd7a/morelinks.html).

Below are some international aid organisations and placement organisations to get you started. Also consult country-specific guidebooks and search the Internet.

Australia
Australian Volunteers International
(☎ 03-9279 1788, www.ozvol.org.au) PO Box 350, Fitzroy, Vic 3065

New Zealand
Volunteer Service Abroad
(☎ 04-472 5759, www.tcol.co.uk/comorg/vsa.htm) PO Box 12-246, Wellington 1

UK
International Voluntary Service
(☎ 0131-226 6722) St John's Church Centre, Edinburgh EH2 4BJ
Voluntary Service Overseas
(VSO; ☎ 020-8780 2266, www.oneworld.org/vso) 317 Putney Bridge Rd, London SW15 2PN

USA
Earthwatch Institute
(☎ 800-776 0188, www.earthwatch.org) 680 Mt Auburn St, PO Box 9104, Watertown, MA 02272
Global Volunteers
(☎ 612-482 0915, www.globalvolunteers.org) 375 E Little Canada Rd, St Paul, MN 55117-162
Peace Corps of the USA
(☎ 202-606 3970, www.peacecorps.gov) 1990 K St NW, Washington, DC 20526

MONEY MATTERS ▶▶

If money wasn't a consideration, we'd all be able to swan around Europe without a care in the world. But for most travellers, the daily budget is a constant source of worry – rightly or wrongly, we spend a great deal of time weighing up what we can and can't afford while on the road. Remember that while it's important to stick to a realistic budget, you didn't travel halfway around the world to live on baguettes and cheese, or to stare at the outside of famous museums and galleries without venturing in.

Let's face it, probably more than any other continent, Europe has the uncanny ability to suck the guts out of your budget. You're likely to pass through some of the world's most expensive travel destinations – Scandinavia, Switzerland, France, Britain and Germany among them. But don't panic! Eastern and southern Europe balance these places with good value for money and there are hundreds of things you can do for free all over the continent. With a bit of attention to budget planning you won't have to take out a mortgage for your trip. Bear in mind also, that even if you were at home you'd be spending money.

Travel costs can vary significantly from season to season. If you're travelling during the tourist high season (generally July and August) you can expect to pay up to 50% more than during the low season, especially for accommodation. This mainly applies to popular tourist spots and seasonal destinations such as the Mediterranean coast in summer, or the Alps in winter.

This chapter will give you an idea of how much a trip to Europe will cost. These are rough estimates only – depending on your budget it's possible to spend a little less or a whole lot more. It also covers the best ways of carrying and exchanging money while you're on the road.

Pretrip Expenses

It's worth dividing your travel budget into two parts: what you need to spend before you leave, and what you'll spend once you're on the road. The pretrip expenses will represent a fair portion of your whole budget because the plane ticket will be a major expense (unless you're from the UK). Buying equipment and travel insurance will also make a dent in your savings, but don't try to be too stingy here – you want quality gear that's going to last not only this trip but future trips. And buy the cheapest plane ticket you can find by all means, but make sure you know what you're in for (see the Tickets & Insurance chapter).

PLANE TICKETS

Most travellers will have to fly a long way to get to Europe so there's really no way of doing it cheaply, but you'll certainly do better by shopping around.

The cost of the ticket will essentially depend on three things: the airline, the route and the time of year. The high season for flights into Europe is roughly

April to September and mid-December to mid-January; the low season is mid-January to March and October/November. Remember that the cheaper the ticket, the less comfortable and flexible the flight is likely to be. Assuming that you're flying into London, the most popular gateway to Europe, the following is an example of what you can expect to pay for a discounted return ticket.

from Australia
Sydney - London   A$1350 to A$1850

from Canada
Vancouver - London   C$1300 to C$1450
East coast - London   cheapest to go via New York

from New Zealand
Auckland - London   NZ$1850 to NZ$2500

from South Africa
Johannesburg - London   R1900 to R3000

from the USA
East coast - London   US$400 to US$900
West coast - London   US$500 to US$1050

Online information on air fares can be found at Flight Info.Com (www.flifo .com), Expedia (www.expedia.msn.com/daily/home/default.hts), Travelocity (www.travelocity.com) and STA Travel (www.statravel.com). For Australia, try STA Travel (www.statravel.com.au) and for New Zealand, try Travel Online (www.travelonline.co.nz). See the Tickets & Insurance chapter for more information on buying plane tickets.

TRAIN & BUS PASSES

If you intend to travel through more than a few countries, a rail pass will definitely save you money. The standard pass for people living outside Europe is the Eurail Pass and this must be bought before you leave home (Europeans, including UK residents, can buy an Inter-Rail Pass). The Eurail Pass is divided into several categories ranging in cost from US$458 to US$1558. Assuming you're under 26 years of age and opt for the flexible 15 days in two months ticket, you'll pay US$599.

Another option is the backpackers bus pass offered by Busabout. A 15-days-in-two-months flexipass (under 26/student) costs US$489, but its coverage is not as extensive as the Eurail Pass. See the Getting Around section in the While You're There chapter for more details.

INSURANCE

Good insurance is an absolute necessity. It may cost you a couple of hundred dollars, but if something goes wrong and you're not fully insured, that premium could pale into insignificance. Typical rates for a basic travel insurance package (including health, accidental death, baggage and cancellation insurance) are: one week (US$35), one month (US$115), two months (US$180) and six months (US$400). See the Tickets & Insurance chapter for details on buying insurance.

PASSPORT & VISAS

If you're from Britain or the USA, you can travel in Europe virtually visa-free. Australians, New Zealanders and Canadians require a handful of visas for Eastern European countries, while South Africans get stung by just about every country in the book! If you do have to shell out for visas, costs vary from around US$40 to US$80. A 90 day multiple-entry Schengen visa for South Africans costs around R220 (see the 'Schengen Agreement' boxed text in the Passports & Visas chapter).

New passports cost US$65 (Americans), C$60 (Canadians), A$126 (Australians), NZ$80 (New Zealanders), UK£21 (Brits) and R120 (South Africans).

IMMUNISATIONS

Immunisations (shots) are not really necessary for visiting Europe, but you'll need them if you're planning on travelling in Asia, Africa or South America in the same trip.

There are, however, a few routine vaccinations that are recommended (polio, tetanus, diphtheria and measles), which you may already have had. Others to consider are immunoglobulin or hepatitis A (Havrix) vaccine before extensive travel in southern Europe; a tetanus booster; an immunisation against hepatitis B before travelling to Malta; or a rabies (pre-exposure) vaccination. A round of vaccinations will cost between US$50 and US$100.

EQUIPMENT

The amount you spend on equipment will naturally depend on what you want to take along (and how much you can borrow from friends and relatives). If you're planning on a full camping trip, the costs for gear will be higher than if you intend to backpack around Europe with a knapsack and the clothes you're wearing.

At the very least you should fork out for a decent-quality backpack and daypack, and a good pair of hiking boots. See the Equipment section in the What to Bring chapter for more information. There's a huge price range in equipment, so you'll probably be able to buy things cheaper than the examples listed below, but beware of poor-quality gear.

backpack	US$150 to US$350
camera (compact)	US$50 to US$300
camera (SLR)	US$250 to US$800
hiking boots	US$50 to US$200
pocketknife	US$10 to US$50
sleeping bag	US$80 to US$250
tent	US$100 to US$250
torch (flashlight)	US$10 to US$20

AVERAGE PRETRIP EXPENSES FOR A TWO MONTH TRIP

The following figures are rough estimates to assist in planning for your trip, and assume you are flying from North America. Your actual expenses may vary quite a bit.

gear	US$490
insurance	US$180
passport & visas	US$100
plane ticket (return)	US$600
rail pass	US$460
total	**US$1830**

Daily On-Road Costs

No two people will travel on the same budget: you may choose the masochistic bare-bones backpacking approach, or maybe you can afford to get around in style. Your daily travel expenses will depend on the level of comfort you want, how much you move around, and the cost of living in the countries you visit.

COMFORT LEVELS

Although travellers sometimes make it their mission to get by on as little money as possible, there's a lot to be said for eating out in a decent restaurant, laying down on a comfy bed or booking a couchette on an overnight train every now and then.

Unlike travel in, say, Asia or Africa, it's difficult to really slum it in Europe unless you're prepared to sink to sleeping in train stations or parks. Apart from the obvious dangers involved, that sort of penny-pinching is going to crush the life out of your trip. Travel in Europe can be very trying, particularly if you're on the move a lot. You need to preserve your sanity and health as much as your money, and you will probably have a far more enjoyable time if you're not too hard on yourself. Budget travel shouldn't be a contest to see who can survive the longest time on the least money, so plan your budget with the occasional treat in mind.

MOVING VS STAYING PUT

If you intend to do a lot of independent travelling around the continent, buying a rail pass in advance is a good idea (see the Getting Around section in the While You're There chapter). With a rail pass, long-distance travel won't factor into your daily budget unless you decide to fly somewhere, or travel in a country not covered by the pass (eg Britain or Turkey). However, local transport, ferries and buses will come into the budget.

Staying in one place for a while is cheaper than constantly moving around. You can usually get discounts for stays of a week or more at hostels, buy cheaper daily or weekly public transport passes and suss out the cheapest places to eat and drink. You could base yourself in a town or city and explore the region from there. This is less tiring than the mad dash from country to country that leaves you flopping into a different bed every second night.

COST OF LIVING

The amount you spend will depend very much on where you go. A cup of coffee in Paris could almost buy you dinner and a hotel room in rural Turkey. But don't rob yourself of the chance to see the Swiss Alps or the Norwegian

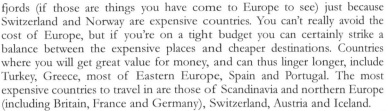

fjords (if those are things you have come to Europe to see) just because Switzerland and Norway are expensive countries. You can't really avoid the cost of Europe, but if you're on a tight budget you can certainly strike a balance between the expensive places and cheaper destinations. Countries where you will get great value for money, and can thus linger longer, include Turkey, Greece, most of Eastern Europe, Spain and Portugal. The most expensive countries to travel in are those of Scandinavia and northern Europe (including Britain, France and Germany), Switzerland, Austria and Iceland.

The major cities in any country are likely to be more expensive than the rural areas. A dorm bed in a central London youth hostel might cost you the same as a cosy B&B in the countryside. The countries of Europe fall roughly into three price categories (see the accompanying table). These figures are a rough estimate of the minimum you can expect to spend each day if you stay in hostels and cheap hotels or pensions, travel on public transport and eat out occasionally. You can easily spend twice or three times these amounts if you require a higher level of comfort. The Money sections of the country profiles later in this book will give you more information on the travel costs of each country. If you camp or stay in dormitories, eat supermarket food, avoid boozy nights, take the cheapest buses or trains and don't buy souvenirs, it's possible to get around on US$20 to US$35 a day – less if you stick to Eastern Europe and parts of southern Europe, but definitely more in Scandinavia. A much more realistic budget would be US$35 to US$50 a day.

inexpensive	moderate	expensive
◂US$35	US$35-US$50	US$50▸
Bulgaria	Albania	Austria
Croatia	Andorra	Britain
Czech Rep	Belgium	Denmark
Hungary	Cyprus	Estonia
Macedonia	Greece	Finland
Netherlands	Italy	France
Poland	Latvia	Germany
Romania	Lithuania	Iceland
Slovakia	Luxembourg	Ireland
Slovenia	Malta	Liechtenstein
Spain	Portugal	Norway
Turkey	Sweden	Switzerland

SAVING MONEY ON THE ROAD

Even after you've set aside the obligatory funds for daily accommodation, food and transport, it's the little things you have to watch out for in your budget. Museum admission, a couple of beers, a newspaper, a roll of film, checking your email, doing your laundry – it all adds up! The good news is that there are many ways to spend less and still get good value from your trip. If you are on a tight budget it's also very important to keep track of your daily spending to avoid any unpleasant surprises, especially if you're using a credit or debit card.

Markets & supermarkets – Buy food from open-air markets and supermarkets. Most hostels and many camping grounds have kitchen facilities so you can cook your own meals. This works out even cheaper if shared between a group. You can also whip up a pretty good lunchtime picnic.

Use student cafeterias & self-serve cafes – If you don't like cooking, try to eat out on the cheap. Avoid restaurants catering to tourists (they're always overpriced) and instead seek out the places where locals eat. If you do eat at a restaurant, ask to see a menu with prices and find out if there are surcharges (eg for sitting at a table, outdoor seating).

Ask for a discount – In the low season you'll be surprised how many hotels and guesthouses will reduce room rates if you ask.

Share lodging costs – At many hotels and hostels, quads (four-person rooms) are cheaper than triples, and triples are cheaper than doubles. In some countries a private triple room at a cheap pension is cheaper than three dormitory beds.

Camp – If you have a tent, you'll save on accommodation. This works better if there are at least two of you because most camping grounds charge for the site, as well as for the number of people.

Take overnight trains – This will save you the cost of a night's accommodation.

Hand-wash your clothes – To save laundry costs use sinks or laundries if such facilities are available.

Avoid taxis – Public transport is efficient and extensive throughout most of Europe, particularly in the cities. Though they're not always cheap, a bus, train or metro ticket will be much cheaper than a taxi.

Walk – One of the best ways to get an appreciation for a city is to see it on foot. Many of the top sights in London and Paris are within walking distance. It's tiring but satisfying and will save you a few dollars on public transport.

Use a phonecard – For calls within Europe, and for the Home Direct service or one of the cut-price carriers for international calls, cards work out cheaper. Also make international calls during off-peak times (after 6 pm and on weekends). Better still, use email rather than the telephone. If you only want to quickly check your email, look for a cybercafe that charges by the minute or in 15-minute blocks.

Attend free events – Concerts and cultural events are often free in summer; ask at the tourist office and check around town for fliers and posters.

Investigate free or half-price entry – Many museums and galleries are free or discounted one day a month, one day a week, or at a certain time of day (eg the Louvre is half-price after 3 pm and on Sunday).

BUDGET BLOWOUTS

For every budget-saving technique there are 10 ways to blow the budget. Usually these are extremely enjoyable blowouts, sometimes they are unwanted but necessary. The following are a few things to try – or to look out for:

Eat out – If you don't make an effort to sample local cuisines, you are denying yourself one of the great pleasures of travel. Every now and again try an upper-end spot. Many restaurants offer set-priced meals and lunch specials that are good value.

Rent a car – This can be good value in the right circumstances, especially if you're travelling in a small group and do not already have a rail pass. In remote or rural regions poorly served by buses and trains, a rental car will save you time and trouble.

Enjoy some nightlife – There's no better way of meeting young local people and other travellers than at pubs, clubs, bars or taverns. It would be criminal not to spend a night downing Guinness while you're in Dublin, or bar-hopping while in Barcelona. Look out for places with no cover charge, and often you'll find drinks specials on weekdays or at certain times of night – just don't overdo it!

Money Carrying Options

If you're coming from the USA, bring US dollars cash or travellers cheques so you don't have to exchange money twice. From elsewhere, British pounds, German marks and French francs are the strongest and most easily exchanged currencies, at least until the euro becomes common currency (see the 'Europe's New Currency' boxed text).

The main options for carrying money are travellers cheques, credit and/or debit cards and cash. Each has advantages, and most experienced travellers carry a combination of all three (see the following sections).

Always keep your money and other valuables where no-one can get them, preferably in a moneybelt worn under your clothing as unobtrusively as possible (see the Moneybelt section in the What to Bring chapter for some advice). You will also need a purse, wallet or change pouch to carry your daily spending money, for convenience and to ensure you don't have to pull out your moneybelt every five minutes. See the Issues & Attitudes chapter for more advice on protecting your valuables against theft.

TRAVELLERS CHEQUES

Tried and true, travellers cheques are still the most popular way to carry money while travelling. The main advantage is that if they are stolen they will be replaced by the issuing bank or agency within a few days (or even on the spot). In most European countries, you'll get a better exchange rate for travellers cheques than for cash, and they make it easier to keep track of your spending than credit cards.

Europe's New Currency

The introduction of a common European currency, the euro, will change the way travellers carry and exchange money over the coming years. The euro was officially introduced on 1 January 1999, but no coins or notes will be circulated until 1 January 2002, so while prices may be quoted in euros you'll still pay in local currency. After that, the French franc, German Deutschmark, Italian lira and Portuguese escudo (for starters) will be phased out in favour of the single currency.

It's all part of the harmonisation of the EU – relaxed borders, the common market and a common currency. But it's not all harmony. Britain, for one, is nationally divided over dumping the pound in favour of the euro and the government has adopted a noncommittal approach. Until coins and notes are issued in 2002, the euro will be paperless. Prices can be quoted in euros and credit card companies can bill in euros. Essentially, the euro can be used anytime it's not necessary to hand over hard cash, so check bills carefully to see if you have been charged in euros or national currency. The euro will have the same value in all member countries and the official exchange rate (January 1999) is roughly €1 = US$1. There will be a confusing six month period during the first half of 2002 when countries will be able to use their old currencies as well as the crisp new euro notes and shiny coins.

While the euro will make travel between these countries that little bit easier as far as changing money is concerned, the homogenising of cash spells the end of those little travel joys – familiarising yourself with all those new notes, fishing in your pocket and pulling out a handful of useless foreign coins, and forcing yourself to spend that last 3000 lira on a cup of coffee before you board the train out of Italy. But never mind – we'll still have Finnish marks, Polish zlotys and Hungarian forints for some time to come.

To facilitate replacement if your cheques are lost or stolen, always keep the purchase agreement of the cheques with you and keep accurate records of the serial numbers of the cheques as you spend them, so you can tell the bank which ones are missing. Keep the purchase record, spending records and the credit card company's emergency contact number in a separate place, so they are not lost or stolen along with the cheques.

Travellers cheques issued by American Express, Thomas Cook and Visa are the most commonly accepted (in that order) and have efficient replacement policies. Amex is probably the best for instant replacement. Other major banks and credit card companies issue travellers cheques, but you may have trouble changing them in out-of-the-way places. It's a good idea to carry large-denomination cheques (say US$100 or US$50) since some places charge a per-cheque cashing fee and this can really add up if you're constantly cashing smaller cheques. If you're moving through quite a few countries though, it pays to also have a book of US$20 cheques for those times when you've only got one day left in a country and need some money to tide you over.

CREDIT CARDS

Plastic cards are becoming more and more popular with travellers and they're readily accepted all over Europe. A credit card is fairly useless for small purchases, but you can certainly use it to pay for meals in restaurants, hotel accommodation, plane or train tickets and large purchases. Many budget travellers use them to get cash advances from local banks, but since not all banks will do this you should definitely have travellers cheques as a backup.

MasterCard and Visa are both widely accepted. MasterCard (also known as Access in Britain) is linked to Europe's extensive Eurocard system. Visa (sometimes called Carte Bleue) is particularly strong in France and Spain. As many local banks are affiliated with either MasterCard or Visa, but not both, get both cards if possible. Charge cards such as American Express and Diners Club are less useful, particularly off the beaten track.

With your PIN number, you can withdraw cash from automatic teller machines (ATMs) in some countries (see the country profiles for details). Only the ATMs in bigger, more touristy areas are linked to international networks. Check your card to see if it matches any of the network stickers displayed on the ATM in question. You can search for ATMs that accept Visa or MasterCard on www.mastercard.com/atm or www.visa.com.

The downside of credit cards is the risk they pose of going into debt. On most cards, including Visa and MasterCard, if you don't pay the account in full each month, you'll be charged interest and the rates are usually exorbitant. The best way to get around this is to put the account in credit before you leave home.

Finally, always check the invoice and the receipt when you buy something with a credit card, and check your account statement when you get home. Credit card fraud is rare, but it does happen (see the Scams & Swindles section in the Issues & Attitudes chapter for further details).

DEBIT CARDS

With a debit card, the money you spend or withdraw is taken straight from your savings or cheque account. If you don't have enough money in your account, you can't make the transaction. Debit cards can be used to withdraw cash from ATMs from Turkey to Iceland, and to make purchases at some stores (with the EFTPOS system). The largest networks in Europe are Cirrus, Plus, Maestro and Eurocard. You can also have your debit card linked to a MasterCard or Visa credit account, giving you the best of both worlds.

A drawback with debit cards is that once money is taken out of your account, it cannot be replaced. If your card is stolen and transactions or withdrawals are made, you won't see that money again. But anyone trying to use the debit card needs to know your PIN number, so keep it safe in your head, not written on a piece of paper stuffed in your wallet. By contrast, if a credit card is stolen, you can request a 'charge back' and have the money returned to you.

CASH

As convenient as it may be, avoid carrying large wads of cash around – if it's stolen or lost you'll never see it again. However, it's a good idea to have some of your travel money in cash, for the following reasons. You might find in some rural areas that you can only exchange cash; you can change a small amount of cash when you don't want to have to cash a big travellers cheque; and if you need to pay for a visa at an Eastern European border you'll need cash – either local currency or US dollars.

But the main reason you should carry some cash – at least US$100 – is for an 'emergency stash'. This money will be a godsend if the unthinkable happens and your moneybelt is lost or stolen with all your travellers cheques, passport and plastic cards. You'll need it to tide you over while you replace the travellers cheques and your passport. Keep this money away from your other valuables, preferably in your main pack (some travellers stitch it into the lining).

INTERNATIONAL MONEY TRANSFERS

If you're going to be away for a long time, or if you happen to run out of money while on the road, you can have more sent by wire from your home country to a local bank. You'll usually have to wait a few days for the transfer to clear and you'll be given your money in local currency, either as cash or travellers cheques. Bring with you the details of your home bank account (account number, branch number, address and telephone number) to speed up the process. Most banks charge a relatively hefty fee for wiring money, so don't do it unless you really have to.

If you intend to spend a lot of time in a particular country (if you're on a working holiday in Britain, for instance), inquire with your bank about having money transferred directly into an account in a bank of that country. Alternatively, you can open an account when you arrive (you'll need to provide a local address and have appropriate ID) and have the money wired over.

RUNNING OUT OF MONEY

This is something no-one likes to think about and it's certainly not something you'll want to experience, but it helps to be prepared. If you realise you are running out of money, take action before you go flat broke or you'll have trouble making arrangements for more. Don't rely on your country's embassy or consulate to help you out if you run out of money – it's not their job and your pleas will fall on deaf ears.

There are two ways to have money sent from home. The first is an international money transfer (see International Money Transfers previously). The second is through a service like Western Union, which specialises in sending cash to all parts of the world. To receive cash this way, you'll have to arrange for someone in your home country to take cash to one of its offices. This is a convenient service, though the rates are significantly higher than those charged by banks for international money transfers. For more information, call Western Union (☎ 0800-833 833 in the UK or ☎ 1-800-325 6000 in the USA). If you have a credit or debit card, the best idea is to get a family member to save your bacon by depositing some money in your account.

Another option if you're running out of money is to find a job. For more details, see the Work & Travel section in the Planning chapter.

Changing Money———————————————

Changing money is one of those little chores that you'll have to attend to every few days or weeks while you're on the road. You can change money at banks, private moneychangers, hotels and sometimes at post offices.

Most European currencies are fairly stable – the Deutschmark and British pound are among the strongest in the world and the euro is currently valued around the same as the US dollar – but a few suffer from high inflation and a volatile exchange rate. The Turkish and Polish currencies are two to watch. For up-to-the-minute exchange rates, check the Oanda online currency converter (www.oanda.com/converter/classic), or the financial sections of newspapers.

Before you change money, check in your guidebook or ask other travellers where the best place is to change money in a particular country. In some countries, banks are the best or only places to change money, while in others you're better off going to a moneychanger (which usually requires less time and paperwork). Also check a local newspaper for the official exchange rate, and compare the exchange rates and commission fees of several places before deciding where to change. You may have to do some calculations here, as the rate offered and the commission charged will vary from place to place. Be sure to ask when cashing travellers cheques if the commission is per cheque or per transaction. If it's per cheque, then you're better off changing a single large-denomination cheque.

If you have American Express or Thomas Cook travellers cheques you can usually exchange them in their respective offices without being charged commission, but often the rates offered are lower than in the banks. Other moneychanging tips include:

- In some Eastern European countries, such as Albania, Yugoslavia and Romania, it's possible to change money on the black market (ie with shady characters on the street), though this is illegal and leaves you vulnerable to arrest or bribery attempts from local police. If you're ripped off, you'll have no legal recourse, and all sorts of scams exist to short-change you. In any case, with the exception of Romania, the currencies in these countries are fully convertible so the black market rate won't be much higher than the official rate.

- You'll usually get the best exchange rates in main cities, so change your money before heading to rural areas where you may find it difficult to change money at all.

- Try not to change at border crossings, where exchange rates are often very low, or change just enough to get you into a major city.

- Each time you change money at a moneychanger or bank, you will be given a slip with the details of the transaction for you to sign. Inspect it carefully. If anything is amiss, you can terminate the transaction immediately.

- Before you sign a travellers cheque, make completely sure that the changer will accept it, as you will probably find the signed cheque difficult to change elsewhere.

- If you're using a credit card for a cash advance, shop around for the best rates and commission fees. Also, check that the figures are correct on the credit card slip before you sign it.

- Always count the bills carefully after your transaction to ensure you haven't been short-changed.

- Take care when changing money. This is one of the few times when you'll have your moneybelt out in public; you'll be particularly vulnerable at street-side moneychangers.

- Try not to change a large-denomination bill or travellers cheque just before leaving a country, as you'll lose on commissions and exchange rates when you reconvert unspent money.

Bargaining & Tipping

Most of Europe, like the rest of the west, doesn't have a practice of bargaining for goods. The notable exceptions are Turkey, Greece and Malta, but even in these countries you'll really only have luck bargaining in markets and for (overpriced) souvenirs. Outside the high season you should also try bargaining for accommodation in these countries (at least ask for a discount).

If you do engage in some bargaining there are lots of implicit rules to be aware of. Most importantly, try to conduct the procedure in a friendly, polite way – getting angry won't result in a better price and will usually just bring the negotiations to a halt. Also, never offer a price unless you're willing to go through with the transaction if that price is accepted.

In many European countries it's common (and the law in France) for a service charge to be added to restaurant bills, in which case no tipping is necessary. In others, simply rounding up the bill is usually sufficient. Tipping is certainly not enshrined in the service industry as it is in North America.

The amount you decide to tip (if any) will depend on the standard of the place you're in. If it's a cheap restaurant or pub, don't bother with a tip. If it's a reasonably nice restaurant or cafe and you were happy with the service, then 5 to 10% is fair. Taxi drivers, porters and guides will probably expect a small tip.

PASSPORTS & VISAS ▶▶

Passports

Your passport is your one indispensable travel document. While you are overseas it's your principal means of identification, as well as your main evidence (via visa stamps or papers) that you have the legal right to be in a country. Always keep your passport safely on your person and try to avoid situations that require you to hand it over for any length of time – whether to a foreign bureaucrat or a hotel proprietor. Photocopy the front page and all pages with prearranged visa stamps on them, and carry these separately from your passport (see the Documentation section at the end of this chapter).

Citizens of the European Union (EU) and those from certain other European countries (eg Switzerland) don't need a valid passport to travel to other EU countries, or even some non-EU countries – a valid identity card will do. However, it's still worth carrying a passport as irrefutable proof of your nationality.

PASSPORT HOLDERS

If you already hold a passport, check its expiry date. If it expires within six months of the date you plan to enter the final country on your itinerary, then get it replaced – some foreign governments require that your passport is valid

---

European Union

The European Union (EU) began its life as the European Economic Community (EEC), which was founded by the Treaty of Rome in 1957. At that stage it was known as the Common Market and was concerned exclusively with economic matters such as the abolition of tariffs between member countries.

The organisation has subsequently broadened its scope far beyond economic measures as it developed into the European Community (1967) and finally the EU in 1993. Since the 1991 Maastricht treaty, the EU has been committed to establishing a common foreign and security policy. A single European currency called the euro came into effect in January 1999 (see the boxed text 'Europe's New Currency' in the Money Matters chapter).

The EEC's founding states were Belgium, France, West Germany, Italy, Luxembourg and the Netherlands. They were joined by Denmark, Ireland and the UK in 1973, Greece in 1981, Spain and Portugal in 1986 and Austria, Finland and Sweden in 1995 – bringing the total membership to 15.

Six more countries – the Czech Republic, Estonia, Hungary, Poland, Slovenia and Cyprus – are expected to be granted full membership within a couple of years, while another seven – Bulgaria, Latvia, Lithuania, Malta, Romania, Slovakia and Turkey – have become candidates for admission. If all 13 were to be admitted, that would increase the total population of the member states from 375 million to more than 580 million. At that stage the EU would truly have become a superstate, governing twice the population of the USA.

for some time after you leave their country (usually three months beyond the date of departure), so the longer the validity of your passport the better. Most passports are valid for 10 years.

Also check how many blank pages you have left for visas and entry and exit stamps. It would be very inconvenient to run out of spare pages when you are too far from an embassy to have a new passport issued or extra pages added.

APPLYING FOR A PASSPORT

If you don't have a passport, applying for one should be your first priority – the process can take anything from a week to several months. You will also have to submit your passport for any visa applications (these can take from three to 14 days each); possibly quote its number to pick up your plane ticket; and present it to buy duty-free goods.

Conditions and requirements for passport issue vary between countries, but most agencies require you to submit the following with the application form:

A fee – This starts at around A$126, NZ$80, UK£21 or US$65 for a standard adult passport of the minimum number of pages, issued within the usual processing time.

Photographs – Two recent head-and-shoulder shots of you taken against a white background; signed and identified on the back.

Proof of any name change – Such as a marriage or deed poll certificate.

Proof of citizenship – Such as a birth, naturalisation or registration certificate.

Passed Your Use-By Date?

The Austrian border looked comfortingly familiar after our long drive from Turkey via Bulgaria, Romania and what was then still Yugoslavia. The immigration officer sneered as Mark handed over our passports but I felt none of the twitchiness borders usually provoke. This was Western Europe, after all – nothing to worry about here.

The guard flicked through the passports and tossed mine back wordlessly, but Mark's clearly bothered him. He stared at the passport, stared at Mark, stared back at the passport and then vanished to confer with colleagues. Minutes passed, then back he came. 'No,' he said. Just no.

Neither of us knew any German so we struggled to understand the problem until finally an exasperated hand indicated the picture of the bearded man in the passport and then Mark's smooth-shaven, look-good-for-the-border face. The passport was nine years old and in that time his appearance had changed drastically.

Mark offered to give a signature for comparison with the one in his passport but the guard turned his back and walked away. Mercifully at the Yugoslav border they let us in again, but we were forced to drive all the way back through what is now Slovenia to approach Austria again via Italy. This time we were as jittery as drug smugglers. I've rarely been so relieved to see a stamp come down on a passport.

And the moral of this tale of wasted time and petrol money? Those humourless individuals who patrol Europe's borders hold all the aces. If they say you're not who you think you are, there's not a lot you can do about it. So if any of your travelling companions come from countries with long-life passports, check their photos carefully and make sure it's not just their mothers who'd recognise them.

Pat Yale,
LP Author, UK

Proof of identity – Someone must vouch for your identity on the application form and on your photographs. This can be either the holder of a current passport from your country who has known you for two years (but is unrelated to you) or a citizen of good standing such as a Justice of the Peace, although this category can somewhat arbitrarily include lawyers, employers, doctors and teachers.

Issuing Period & Rush Jobs

Most agencies will issue your passport within 10 days, assuming you have provided everything they need. If you've left your application until the last moment (or you manage to lose it) then you might need to get a new or replacement passport in a hurry. This process is called expediting, and you'll generally pay plenty for it. In the US there is a US$35 surcharge for the service if you deal directly with the US Passport Agency office and you must prove that your flight leaves within 14 days. Expediting fees can be paid directly to the national issuing agency, or a commercial agency can do it for you for an additional fee, but even then an expedited passport may take a couple of days to get to you. A simple search on the Internet or in the phonebook will give you plenty of options for commercial expeditors.

Issuing Agencies

The government agencies responsible for issuing passports in Australia, Canada, New Zealand, South Africa, the UK and the USA are listed below (you can often submit your application to other authorised agencies such as post offices or banks instead):

Australia
  Passports Australia. Department of Foreign Affairs & Trade
  (☎ 131232, www.dfat.gov.au/passports/passports_faq_contents.html)
Canada
  The Passport Office. Department of Foreign Affairs & International Trade
  (☎ 1-800-567 6868, www.dfait-maeci.gc.ca/passport/paspr-2.htm)
New Zealand
  The Passport Office. Department of Internal Affairs
  (☎ 0800-22 5050, inform.dia.govt.nz/internal_affairs/businesses/doni_pro/fees.html)
South Africa
  Passport Agency. Department of Foreign Affairs
  (☎ 012-314 8911), Private Bag X114, Pretoria 0011
UK
  UK Passport Agency. The Home Office
  (☎ 0870-521 0410, www.open.gov.uk/ukpass/ukpass.htm)
USA
  Passport Services. the State Department
  (☎ 1-900-225 5674, www.travel.state.gov/passport_services.html)

Dual Citizenship

Being able to carry two passports is a very valuable asset, particularly if one happens to be an EU passport (such as a British passport). In this case you can use your home passport to leave and re-enter your own country, and the EU passport to travel unhindered (generally without the need for visas) in Europe.

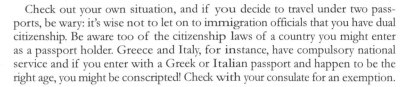
Check out your own situation, and if you decide to travel under two passports, be wary: it's wise not to let on to immigration officials that you have dual citizenship. Be aware too of the citizenship laws of a country you might enter as a passport holder. Greece and Italy, for instance, have compulsory national service and if you enter with a Greek or Italian passport and happen to be the right age, you might be conscripted! Check with your consulate for an exemption.

LOST OR STOLEN PASSPORTS

Losing your passport while you're on the road is a major headache and can lead to interminable bureaucratic hassles, both with the government of the country you're in at the time and with your own embassy or consulate. However, it's not the end of the world, especially if you're reasonably close to a major city where you'll find your country's embassy or consulate.

If you lose your passport, contact your embassy immediately. If your home country does not have diplomatic representation where you are, then contact the embassy in the nearest neighbouring country. Seek advice from the embassy staff on whether you need to notify the local government of the loss, and how to handle it if you do. If your passport is stolen, also inform the local police and get a police report before heading to your embassy.

You'll need some form of identification to satisfy the embassy staff before they'll issue a replacement. You should carry a photocopy of your passport with you, as well as a driver's licence, student card, an old passport, your birth certificate or some other form of ID, including something with your photo on it.

Your embassy should be able to issue a new passport within a couple of days, but you may pay extra for the privilege. If you had visas in the passport that need replacing, you'll have to go to the nearest consulate of that country and reapply – again for a fee.

Visas

Visas are stamps or documents in your passport that permit you to enter a country and stay for a specified period of time. Thankfully, the days of border

The Schengen Agreement

The Schengen Agreement is a system of relaxed border controls between a group of member countries. At the time of writing France, Spain, Portugal, Germany, Belgium, the Netherlands, Luxembourg, Austria, Italy and Greece were Schengen countries, with Denmark, Sweden, Finland, Norway and Iceland expected to join in the future. Travellers from Australia, Canada, Israel, Japan, New Zealand, Norway, Switzerland, the USA and non-Schengen EU countries need only a valid passport to enter any one of these countries (from outside the Schengen area) for up to 90 days. South Africans require a single Schengen visa. You can travel between the member countries without border controls, although authorities reserve the right to make spot checks. When arriving by air, even from another Schengen country, your passport will probably be checked. As of July 1999, Australians need a separate visa for Portugal.

controls in Europe are almost over and most readers of this book will not have to worry about visas. For EU and US citizens the need for tourist visas in Europe is almost nonexistent; Australians, New Zealanders and Canadians need visas for some Eastern European and Baltic countries; South Africans need visas for almost all countries (except Hungary and Slovakia), although things are getting easier with the Schengen Agreement (see the boxed text). The country profiles later in this book have information on visa requirements.

There are no longer passport controls at the borders between most EU countries, but border procedures between EU and non-EU countries can still be fairly thorough. For those who do require visas, it's important to remember that these have 'use-by' dates, and you'll be refused entry after the period ends.

VISA TYPES

There are essentially four types of visas (but each can have varying categories such as length of stay, single or multiple entry etc). They are transit, tourist, business and working holiday visas.

Transit visas are valid for only one or two days and are required if you need to pass overland through a particular country (for which a visa is required) but you don't intend to stay there. Tourist visas allow you to stay for a restricted period, usually between 30 and 90 days, and these can often be extended once you're in the country. A business visa is required if the purpose of your visit is primarily for business or commercial reasons.

The working holiday visa is one that interests many young travellers to Europe. Commonwealth citizens (from Australia, Canada, New Zealand or South Africa) aged between 17 and 27 (up to your 28th birthday) are entitled to a two year working holiday visa to Britain. The visa is activated from the time you enter Britain and is not extendable. It allows you to supplement your holiday with casual work. See the boxed text 'Working in Britain' in the Planning chapter.

HOME OR AWAY?

You generally have the option of obtaining visas in your home country or when you arrive at your destination. In most cases the best advice is to avoid the hassle and get them before you leave home, but if you're not completely sure where you'll be at a particular time during your trip, this might not be practical.

In Eastern European countries and Turkey you can usually get a visa at the border or at the airport on arrival, but not always. Check first with the embassies or consulates of the countries you plan to visit, otherwise you could be kicked off a train or bus at the border. For example, in the Czech Republic (for which Australians need a visa) there are three road border crossings where 30-day visas are issued, but visas are not issued on trains and therefore must be obtained from a consulate in advance.

Visas are *usually* issued immediately by consulates in Eastern Europe, although Bulgarian and Polish consulates may levy a 50 to 100% surcharge for 'express visa service'. Otherwise Bulgarian consulates could make you wait

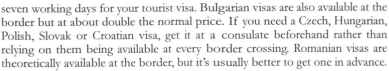

seven working days for your tourist visa. Bulgarian visas are also available at the border but at about double the normal price. If you need a Czech, Hungarian, Polish, Slovak or Croatian visa, get it at a consulate beforehand rather than relying on them being available at every border crossing. Romanian visas are theoretically available at the border, but it's usually better to get one in advance.

Another factor is that not all countries will have an embassy in your home country. See the Embassies sections in the country profiles for contact details.

VISA REQUIREMENTS IN EUROPE

Destination	Aust	Can	Ire	NZ	SA	UK	US
Albania	+	+	+	+	✓	+	+
Andorra	–	–	–	–	–	–	–
Austria	–	–	–	–	✓	–	–
Belgium	–	–	–	–	✓	–	–
Britain	–	–	–	–	–	–	–
Bulgaria	✓	✓	+	✓	✓	–	+
Croatia	–	–	–	–	✓	–	–
Cyprus	–	–	–	–	–	–	–
Czech Rep	✓	–	–	–	✓	–	+
Denmark	–	–	–	–	✓	–	–
Estonia	–	✓	–	–	✓	–	–
Finland	–	–	–	–	✓	–	–
France	–	–	–	–	✓	–	–
Germany	–	–	–	–	✓	–	–
Greece	–	–	–	–	✓	–	–
Hungary	✓	–	–	✓	+	–	–
Iceland	–	–	–	–	✓	–	–
Ireland	–	–	–	–	–	–	–
Italy	–	–	–	–	✓	–	–
Latvia	✓	✓	–	✓	✓	–	–
Liechtenstein	–	–	–	–	✓	–	–
Lithuania	–	–	–	✓	✓	–	–
Luxembourg	–	–	–	–	✓	–	–
Macedonia	✓	✓	✓	✓	✓	✓	✓
Malta	–	–	–	–	–	–	–
Netherlands	–	–	–	–	✓	–	–
Norway	–	–	–	–	✓	–	–
Poland	✓	✓	–	✓	✓	–	–
Portugal	✓	–	–	*	✓	*	*
Romania	✓	✓	✓	✓	✓	✓	+
Slovakia	✓	–	–	✓	*	–	*
Slovenia	–	–	–	–	✓	–	–
Spain	–	–	–	–	✓	–	–
Sweden	–	–	–	–	✓	–	–
Switzerland	–	–	–	–	✓	–	–
Turkey	✓	✓	✓	–	✓	✓	+

✓ tourist visa required
+ 30 day maximum stay without visa
* 60 day maximum stay without visa

PLANNING YOUR VISAS

Bear the following in mind when you're planning your visas:

- Find out whether your visa is activated on entry or on issue. In some countries visas are activated as soon as the stamp appears in your passport so if you wait too long before you enter the country, you'll be left with little time to explore the place.
- The time period can differ depending on whether you arrange the visa at home or on entry. Romania, for example, will give you a six month visa if you apply in your home country, but only 30 days at the border.
- Make sure you know the approved entry and exit points for each of your visas. Some countries may ask you to stipulate which town or airport you plan to arrive at and depart from.

The Visa Requirements in Europe section will give you an idea of which countries you will need a visa for. For further details, see the country profiles. Visa requirements change without notice, so always check with the country's embassy or consulate in your home country. The reasonably reliable Web site, www3 .travel.com.au/everest/index.cgi?E=bevisreq, provides visa requirements by country of origin. A good source of information for South Africans is cargo info.co.za/visa/index.html.

The Application Process

No matter where you apply for your visa, you're likely to face short opening hours, long queues (especially in London) and stone-faced or unhelpful staff. To make this tedious process as hassle-free as possible, consider the following strategies:

- Phone in advance to find out the embassy's opening hours and requirements for costs, photographs, identification and documents.
- Leave yourself plenty of time – your visa may not be processed on your first attempt.
- Arrive early and be prepared to queue. Bring a book to help pass the time.
- Have all your documentation in order and ready to present to the clerk, including your planned entry and departure dates. Make sure you have the correct fee in the appropriate currency – staff sometimes can't or won't provide change.
- When you pick up your visa, be on time and don't leave until you've checked that the dates, length of stay and other details are correct.
- Bring plenty of passport-size photographs with you. Many countries will require two or three photos to process a visa, and you may not be able to find a cheap, instant-photo booth when you need one – though many European cities have them at train stations and post offices.

Other Paperwork
HOSTELLING INTERNATIONAL CARD

Membership of Hostelling International (HI) – also still known as the Youth Hostels Association (YHA) in some countries – is relatively cheap and highly recommended if you intend to stay in hostels during your trip.

While independent backpackers' hostels are springing up around Europe, HI still has the largest single network and you can sometimes use your membership card for other discounts (in lieu of a student or youth card). The

HI card is also useful as a means of identification to avoid producing your passport.

Most HI hostels will allow nonmembers to stay at a slightly higher cost, and some can actually join you up on the spot, usually at a slightly higher cost than joining in your home country. See the Accommodation section in the While You're There chapter for more information.

HI has an excellent Web site (www.iyhf.org) or contact your home country YHA for more information.

Australia
Australian YHA
(☎ 02-9565 1699, fax 9565 1325, ☻ yha@yha.org.au) level 3, 10 Mallett St, Camperdown, NSW 2050
cost: A$49 (for under 18s, A$15)

Canada
HI
(☎ 613-237 7884, fax 237 7868, ☻ info@hostellingintl.ca) 205 Catherine St, Suite 400, Ottawa, Ont K2P 1C3
cost: C$25 (C$12 for under 18s)

Ireland
An Óige (Irish YHA)
(☎ 01-830 4555, ☻ anoige@iol.ie) 61 Mountjoy St, Dublin 7
cost: IR£10 (IR£4 for under 18s)
HI-Northern Ireland
(☎ 01232-315435, fax 439699, ☻ info@hini.org.uk) 22 Donegall Rd, Belfast BT12 5JN

New Zealand
YHA of New Zealand
(☎ 03-379 9970, fax 365 4476, ☻ info@yha.org.nz) 193 Cashel St, 3rd floor, Union House, Christchurch
cost: NZ$34 (NZ$12 for under 18s)

South Africa
Hostels Association of South Africa
(☎ 021-424 2511, fax 424 4119, ☻ info@4244119) 3rd floor, St Georges House, 73 St Georges Mall, Cape Town 8001
cost: R55

UK
YHA of England & Wales
(☎ 01727-855215, fax 844126, ☻ customerservices@yha.org.uk) Trevelyan House, 8 St Stephen's Hill, St Albans, Hertfordshire AL1 2DY
Scottish YHA
(☎ 01786-891400, fax 891333, ☻ info@syha.org.uk) 7 Glebe Crescent Stirling, FK8 2JA
cost: UK£11 (UK£5.50 for under 18s)

USA
American Youth Hostels
(☎ 202-783 6161, fax 783 6171, ☻ hiayhserv@hiayh.org) 733 15th St NW, Suite 840, Washington, DC 20005
cost: US$25 (free for under 18s)

INTERNATIONAL STUDENT & YOUTH CARDS

The International Student Identity Card (ISIC) is the most widely recognised student card in the world. It qualifies the holder for discounts on airline tickets, rail passes, accommodation, shopping and entrance to museums and cultural events. Although the availability and level of discounts varies from country to country, it can save you a small fortune in Europe. The ISIC card is available only to full-time students (there is no age limit) and is issued by accredited travel agencies (such as STA) through the International Student Travel Confederation (ISTC; www.isic.org/index.htm) in Copenhagen, Denmark. You'll need proof of your full-time student status from your university and the card itself costs between US$15 and US$25.

Because of the proliferation of fake ISIC cards that can be picked up in Asia and the Middle East, it's wise to carry your home student card as supplementary proof. If you want to get a student discount from an airline, you may need a letter of proof from your home school or university, so get one and make photocopies before you go.

If you're not a full-time student but are under 25 years of age, you'll qualify for the International Youth Travel Card (IYTC), which is also issued by ISTC. It has similar benefits, but is not as widely recognised.

INTERNATIONAL TEACHER CARD

If you're a full-time teacher at a recognised educational institution, you'll qualify for the International Teacher Identity Card (ITIC). Also issued by ISTC, it offers similar kinds of discounts as the student cards, and is distributed in more than 40 countries and recognised by educational institutions around the world. For further details visit the ISTC Web site at www.isic.org/index.htm.

INTERNATIONAL DRIVING PERMIT

If you plan on driving a car or riding a motorbike while in Europe it's worth getting an International Driving Permit (IDP). These permits are issued only by automobile associations in your home country. To qualify, you normally have to be 18 years of age or over and the holder of a valid driver's licence from your home country. You'll have to supply a couple of passport-type photographs and pay a small fee (eg US$10 in the USA, £4 in the UK, A$10 in Australia).

An IDP is usually only valid for one year. Make sure your permit states that it is valid for motorbikes if you plan to ride one. The IDP is not valid unless accompanied by your home licence, so don't forget to bring it with you.

Contact details for major issuing agencies are:

Australia
   Australian Automobile Association
   (☎ 02-6247 7311, www.aaa.asn.au)
Canada
   Canadian Automobile Association
   (☎ 613-247 0117 ext 2025, www.caa.ca/CAAInternet/travelservices/frames14.htm)
New Zealand
   New Zealand Automobile Association
   (☎ 0800-500 444, www.aa.org.nz)

UK
British Automobile Association
(☎ 0990-500 600, www.theaa.co.uk/membership/offers/idp.html)
USA
American Automobile Association
(☎ 1-888-859 5161, www.aaa.com/vacation/idp.html)

NAME CARDS

You might feel a bit like a travelling salesman, but it can be worthwhile having cards printed with your name, address and email address to give to people you meet along the way. It beats searching for a pen every time you want to give someone your address. Cards can also be useful when dealing with officialdom as they can project an air of credibility (or at least that's what you'll be hoping).

The cheapest and easiest way to get cards printed is by using the instant machines you'll find at airports or train stations.

DOCUMENTATION

The importance of photocopying all relevant documents to provide records shouldn't be understated. Make sure you make two sets of copies of your passport (the page with your personal details plus any visa stamps), airline tickets, rail passes, travel insurance, travellers cheques (receipt and serial numbers), IDP, birth and marriage certificates (if you bring them) and credit cards. Keep one copy in your main luggage (completely separate from the originals) and give the other to a friend or family member at home. If you lose any of the original items, having copies will make them much easier to replace, and they are useful when making out a police report. The copy at home is further insurance, just in case something goes horribly wrong and you lose both sets on the road.

An effective way to store details of vital documents such as passport details and travellers cheques numbers is to use the eKno travel vault. You can access these details by using a password at cybercafes around the world. It's free to join eKno and free to use the travel vault. See the Web site at www.ekno .lonelyplanet.com.

TICKETS & INSURANCE ▶▶

Your Ticket
AIR

Most travellers will fly in and out of Europe and that airline ticket is likely to be the biggest single expense of your trip, especially for long-haul travellers from Australia and New Zealand.

Resist the temptation to leave the purchase of your ticket until the last minute. Although it's possible to get some great deals at short notice, most flights are cheaper if booked well in advance and you're far more likely to get a seat on the flight you want if you shop around with plenty of time to spare.

Buying your ticket early is also a great psychological boost. No matter how much you've told yourself (and others) you're off to Europe, regardless of how far advanced your plans and fantasies are, the deal isn't sealed until you've paid the money and set the date. From that point on you can start getting seriously excited about what lies ahead.

Most of the information in this chapter applies to the international airlines and flights that will transport you to and from Europe.

Airlines

The airline industry has operators catering to the full range of standards and budgets – from respected carriers such as British Airways and Qantas, or top-end outfits like Singapore Airlines, to cut-rate airlines like Russia's Aeroflot.

The adage that 'you get what you pay for' certainly applies to airlines. Cheaper operators have older fleets, which tend to come with greater safety risks, lower levels of comfort and a lower level of reliability, making cancellations and long delays more likely. However, there are many good options in the middle ground, particularly within the European and American carrier markets. It's worth bearing in mind that very few international planes actually fall out of the sky, so if a cheap ticket is more important to you than comfort and the on-board food service, then the choice of airline might not matter so much.

Before you get caught up in the finer details of your route, pick up information on several airlines from a travel agency, and talk to people who have flown recently. Check out the age of the fleet, frequent flyer programs, options for booking, payment and alteration of prebooked tickets, and the cancellation policies of each airline.

Most airlines have a Web site providing information on the routes they fly, their schedules and their frequent flyer programs. A few to try include:

Aeroflot (www.aeroflot.com)
Air France (www.airfrance.com)
Air New Zealand (www.airnz.com)
Alitalia (www.alitalia.com/eng/index.html)

American Airlines (www.americanair.com)
Ansett Australia (www.ansett.com.au)
British Airways (www.british-airways.com)
Canadian Airlines (www.cdnair.ca)
Cathay Pacific (www.cathaypacific.com/index.html)
Continental Airlines (www.flycontinental.com)
KLM (www.klm.com)
Lauda Air (www.laudaair.com)
Lufthansa (www.lufthansa.com)
Qantas (www.qantas.com)
Singapore Airlines (www.newasia-singapore.com, www.singaporeair.com)
Swissair (www.swissair.com)
TAP Air Portugal (www.tap.pt)
United Airlines (www.ual.com)
Virgin Atlantic (www.fly.virgin.com)

Partnerships The airline you choose to fly with will affect your route options, since no airline can fly between all destinations. Access to sectors is jealously guarded and almost always favours the home country airline. To deal with this, most airlines negotiate reciprocal arrangements, or partnerships, with a series of other airlines to allow them access into designated sectors of each other's markets. This allows both airlines to offer a much broader range of flight options, particularly for special fares such as round-the-world (RTW) tickets. If you opt for a single, multisector fare with a particular airline, you will probably fly part of the route with partner airlines, so also check them out beforehand.

Frequent Flyer Programs Most airlines offer frequent flyer programs that can earn you free flights or other benefits (such as upgrades). Rewards are based on the number of kilometres you fly with that airline (or its partners), although you can also gather points by using associated travel services such as designated car rental companies or hotel chains.

Points generally must be used within five years from the time of your flight, and most airlines will allow you to redeem them for members of your family. The downside is that to earn more points you're locked into one airline, or a group of airlines, which may not always have the cheapest fares or most convenient flight schedule. With some airlines, membership is free but most charge a joining fee, and some are even introducing annual maintenance fees.

Obviously you'll want to sign up with the airline that will carry you the greatest distance during your trip, but it also makes sense to choose one of your home country's carriers so you can use your frequent flyer points for domestic travel on your return. Unless you intend to make quite a few flights, you won't rack up enough points to redeem anything more than a domestic flight anyway. A single long-haul flight, say from Sydney to London on Qantas, will give you enough points for several interstate flights in Australia.

Various rules govern frequent flyer flights. Most flights will have only a few seats allocated for 'freebies', so book well in advance. Many airlines also have blackout periods where no free seats are available (eg Christmas).

When you receive your frequent flyer member number, keep a record of it with your other travel documents, as you must quote it every time you book a ticket or use an associated service, in order to get your points credited to your account.

Tickets & Restrictions

There is a bewildering variety of tickets and deals on the market and all are governed by complicated rules and restrictions. Common restrictions include:

Cancellation or change penalties – Cancelling your ticket or altering your route once it's booked may incur financial penalties (most travel insurance policies will protect against unavoidable cancellations).

Directional limits – RTW tickets normally allow you to travel only in one direction.

Minimum or maximum limits – You may have to be away a minimum of 14 days or a maximum of 12 months, for example.

Refund policy – Some refunds can only be made through the travel agency where the ticket was purchased, which is not much good to you once you're in Europe, unless you go through a well known agency with worldwide offices (such as STA).

Seasonal limits – A ticket may only be available in off-peak or shoulder periods (see the When to Go section in the Planning chapter for details).

Stopover limits – There may be a maximum number of stopovers attached to your ticket, or no stopovers at all if it's a very cheap ticket.

The basic ticket is a full-price one-way or return ticket between two cities. Airlines typically offer 1st class (coded F), business class (coded J) and economy class (coded Y) tickets. Once the discounting starts, the conditions become ever more complicated and restrictive as the price drops. Some of the common deals are outlined below.

Discount Return Tickets If Europe is the only continent you plan to visit, then a plain old return ticket to a major gateway such as London, Paris, Frankfurt or Athens is probably your best option. This assumes you intend to return to your starting point to fly home. For more flexibility, you may be able to include one or more stopovers at cities en route to your destination. Stopovers can last several weeks, allowing you to explore one region before you resume your journey. This might be useful if you intend to explore a couple of areas in depth, but not so important if you're planning an around-Europe trip by train or bus. A good example is Icelandair's flight from North America to Oslo, Stockholm, Copenhagen or Luxembourg with a free stopover in Reykjavík, Iceland's capital. This gives you the chance to visit a fascinating country you might not be able to afford to visit as a stand-alone destination.

Open-Jaw Tickets These are return tickets that allow you to fly to one destination, but return home from another, thus saving you backtracking and time. Open-jaw tickets are generally more expensive than standard return fares, but can allow you to see a lot more of a region, especially if the distance between the two cities on your ticket is great. For example, if you can arrange a ticket that arrives in London and departs from Istanbul or St Petersburg, you can explore between those cities without needing to return to London.

One-Way Tickets These tickets tend to be more expensive than half the cost of a return ticket, but are useful if you are unsure of your itinerary or return date. Knowing you have no deadlines or constraints can be a very liberating option. The drawback is that many countries require an onward ticket before they'll even let you in, let alone grant a visa if one is required. However, if you know which route you'll use to leave the country (be it by train, bus or air) and you can prove you have the cash reserves to keep you solvent during your stay, you should be able to get past most officials – check beforehand with the consulate of the country you plan to fly into.

The one-way ticket is particularly useful to Australians, New Zealanders and South Africans on a two year working holiday visa, as most return tickets are valid for a maximum of only one year.

RTW Tickets If you plan to travel to more than one continent, an RTW ticket is a very good deal. This fare gives you a limited period (usually 12 months) to circumnavigate the globe, and you can only go in one direction (which means no backtracking). There'll be a predetermined number of stopoffs, but these can often be increased for an extra charge per stop. There are loads of RTW combinations so you should find something that appeals, and the fares are usually much cheaper than paying for the individual sectors.

Group Tickets You may be able to get a discount if you ostensibly travel with a 'group'. These groups can be brought together by a travel agent for the sole purpose of selling a block of cheap fares, and there's certainly no need to stay with your group once you've touched down. These fares do tend to be restrictive and inflexible. Once your departure date is booked it may be impossible to change, or you may be restricted to only 60 days away.

APEX Tickets Advance Purchase Excursion (APEX) tickets also lock you into a fairly rigid schedule, but they're generally the cheapest 'standard' (ie non-discounted) fare. APEX tickets must be purchased at least two or three weeks before departure; they do not permit stopovers and may enforce minimum and maximum stays, as well as fixed departure and return dates. There are also usually stiff cancellation fees. Unless you have a definite return date, it's often best to purchase an APEX ticket on a one-way basis only.

Student. Teacher & Youth Fares Some airlines offer discounts of up to 25% for holders of student, youth or teacher cards (see the Other Paperwork section in the Passports & Visas chapter). These discounts are generally only available on ordinary economy class fares. You wouldn't get one, for instance, on an APEX or RTW ticket since these are already discounted. As a result, you could probably find a cheaper discounted ticket if you shop around.

Courier Flights Courier flights are a great bargain if you travel ultralight, are willing to be restricted, and are lucky enough to find one. The way it works is that an air freight company takes over your entire checked baggage allowance. You are permitted to bring along a carry-on bag, but that's all. In return, you get a steeply discounted ticket.

There are other restrictions – courier tickets are sold for a fixed date and schedule, so changes can be difficult or impossible. If you buy a return ticket, your schedule will be even more rigid, ie you might have to return a week or two later; and don't expect any refunds.

Booking a courier ticket takes some effort. They are limited in availability, and arrangements have to be made a month or more in advance. You won't find courier flights on all routes – major routes such as New York or Los Angeles to London offer the best possibilities. Courier flights are occasionally advertised in the newspapers, or you could contact air freight companies listed in the phonebook. One possibility (at least for US residents) is to join the International Association of Air Travel Couriers (IAATC; ☎ 561-582 8320, www.courier.org/index.html). Check out *The Courier Air Travel Handbook* by Mark I Field for detailed information.

Tickets to Avoid

Back-to-Front Tickets These tickets are return fares purchased in your destination city, rather than your home city. For example, if you are living in Sydney (where tickets are relatively expensive) and you want to fly to London (where tickets are cheaper), theoretically you could buy a ticket by phone using your credit card and get a friend to mail it to you in Sydney. The problem is that the airlines have computers, will know that the ticket was issued in London and will probably refuse to honour it. Be careful that you don't fall foul of these back-to-front rules when purchasing plane tickets by post or on the Web.

Second-Hand Tickets You'll occasionally see advertisements on youth hostel notice boards and sometimes in newspapers for second-hand tickets, meaning that somebody purchased a return ticket or one with multiple stop-overs, and now wants to sell the unused portion of the ticket.

The prices offered can look very attractive, but these tickets are usually worthless, as the name on the ticket must match the name on the passport of the person checking in. You might reason that the seller of the ticket can check you in with their passport, and then give you the boarding pass. On most international flights, however, immigration officials will check that the boarding pass matches the name in your passport, and will stop you from boarding the flight.

Buying Your Ticket

As you can see, buying your ticket can be a bewildering business. The best idea is to pick the brains of good travel agents – youth-oriented travel agents such as STA and Flight Centre International are used to selling flight-only deals (as opposed to packages), so they're good places to start asking questions. Have a reasonably clear idea of your route and the amount of time you wish to be away, as these will greatly affect the type of ticket you purchase and its cost.

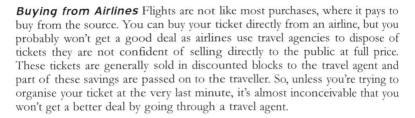

Buying from Airlines Flights are not like most purchases, where it pays to buy from the source. You can buy your ticket directly from an airline, but you probably won't get a good deal as airlines use travel agencies to dispose of tickets they are not confident of selling directly to the public at full price. These tickets are generally sold in discounted blocks to the travel agent and part of these savings are passed on to the traveller. So, unless you're trying to organise your ticket at the very last minute, it's almost inconceivable that you won't get a better deal by going through a travel agent.

Buying from Travel Agents The air travel market is highly lucrative and has attracted a swag of commercial service providers, from respectable travel agency chains to 'bucket shops' specialising in discounted tickets. The former group is 'bonded' to a national association that imposes ethical constraints on their members, including the all-important guaranteed refund if the agent goes into liquidation before you've picked up your ticket. Bucket shops, by contrast, are generally unbonded so you run the risk of losing your money, though they are likely to offer better deals.

If you buy your ticket from an unbonded agency, it's safer to pay by credit card, as the card company will cover the loss if the agency goes bust. If you do pay by cash, make sure the ticket is handed over straightaway; don't agree to pick it up tomorrow or next week. Since you may have to wait for the airline to actually issue the ticket, arrange to leave a small deposit and pay the balance when you pick it up. If you are suspicious of an agency, and they insist on full cash payment in advance, go somewhere else.

Whichever travel agent you go to, don't be satisfied with someone who tries to sell you the first flight that pops up on the computer (unless it's a great deal!). A good travel agent will ask what you're looking for, will have a sound knowledge of your destination and will show some enthusiasm and imagination in searching through the complex flight options. If you're not satisfied with the service, try somewhere else.

Many travel agencies provide a range of services in addition to booking tickets, such as booking your first night's accommodation, arranging travellers cheques, travel insurance, immunisations and visas (although it is generally less expensive to take care of these things yourself). If all you are interested in is a ticket at the lowest possible price, then go to an agency specialising in discounted tickets. Otherwise, you may need to seek out a full-service agency.

Some good, reputable bonded travel agencies include:

Australia
   Flight Centre
   (☎ 13 1600, www.flightcentre.com)
   STA Travel
   (☎ 1300 360 960, www.sta-travel.com)
Canada
   Travel CUTS
   (☎ 1-800-667 2887, www.travelcuts.com)

New Zealand
   STA Travel
   (☎ 0800-100 677, www.sta-travel.com)
UK
   STA Travel
   (☎ 020-7581 4132, www.sta-travel.com)
   Trailfinders
   (☎ 020-7938 3366, www.trailfinder.com)
USA
   Council Travel
   (☎ 1-800-226 8624, www.counciltravel.com)
   STA Travel
   (☎ 1-800-781 4040, www.sta-travel.com)

Buying Online The Internet boom has created a new market for plane tickets. You can find astonishing bargains on the Web if you spend a lot of time online (the really amazing deals do not last long), but equally you can spend an awful lot of time tracking down the ticket you want, when you could have found a cheaper option in half the time through a travel agent.

Nevertheless, a few hours of Web surfing can help you find out what you can expect in the way of budget fares. This can be a good start for negotiating with your travel agent. Try looking at:

Buzz (www.buzzaway.com)
Expedia (expedia.msn.com/daily/home/default.hts)
Flifo (www.flifo.com)
Travelocity (www.travelocity.com)

Getting a Good Deal A good place to start your search for a bargain is in the weekend newspapers or travel magazines (see the Researching Your Trip section in the Planning chapter). Often you'll see what seem like ridiculously cheap advertised fares, but when you call the agent tells you those flights are fully booked 'but we have another one that costs a bit more …', or that only two seats are left which they will hold for only two hours, or that you must fly within the next month. Don't panic! If it doesn't suit you, just try somewhere else. Together with the Web sites listed under the previous Buying Online entry, you will get a good idea of the bargains available (always check the conditions and restrictions).

Try to buy your ticket as early as possible, preferably more than three months before you plan to depart. Most of the really good deals will be quickly snapped up, while others may require full payment well in advance of your departure date. Here are a few tips to help you get the cheapest fare available:

- Decide whether you're prepared to accept a roundabout journey to reach your destination. Talented travel agents may get you a dirt-cheap fare, which is made up of several flights (rather than one direct flight), transiting in different countries over a few days. This is a pretty exhausting way to travel, and you'll spend many empty hours in

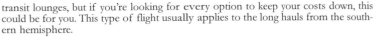

transit lounges, but if you're looking for every option to keep your costs down, this could be for you. This type of flight usually applies to the long hauls from the southern hemisphere.

- Be flexible about your departure date. If you were planning to leave in the high season, see if you can delay or bring forward your departure date by a couple of weeks to take advantage of deals in the shoulder season. Alternatively, if you're planning to be away for several months, consider leaving in the low season, when fares are likely to be cheaper and special deals will be available.
- Be prepared to alter your itinerary to take advantage of a particularly good deal. If you're set on visiting a place that cannot be accommodated by the deal, check out the options for taking a separate sector air fare, or an even cheaper train, boat or bus ride.

Once you've decided on a fare type, get a quote from your travel agent and take it to several other agencies to see if they can beat it. The travel industry is not a level playing field – some airlines have preferred agents and send their best deals through them, so different agencies don't necessarily have access to the same flights and deals. Also check out the payment options – most fares only require full payment around six weeks before departure, so many travel agents will request a small, nonrefundable deposit to ensure that you're a serious buyer.

Your Arrival Time If you can, get a flight that will arrive during daylight hours. If you arrive at lunchtime or early in the afternoon, you'll have time to clear customs and immigration, change some currency, get into the city centre and arrange your first night's accommodation before night falls. You can do all this even if you arrive after dusk, but more services will be open during daylight hours, and arriving in a strange city in the middle of the night can be quite daunting. A morning arrival is ideal because you should have less trouble finding accommodation if you haven't already booked it.

It's generally easier to adapt to a new time zone if you arrive during the day – most people find they can manage to stay awake several hours longer than usual, but it can be difficult to fall sleep when your body is convinced it's another six or seven hours till bedtime.

If you are unable to obtain a flight that will arrive during daylight hours, you should give some thought to prebooking your first night's accommodation, even if you want to remain flexible after that. If not, you can try to make arrangements from the airport on your arrival. For more advice on your arrival, see the Touchdown chapter.

Taking a Bike or Surfboard

If you plan to take a bike, surfboard or any other bulky specialised equipment with you, you'll need to notify the airline when you book your ticket. Most airlines are surprisingly easy-going about accommodating extra gear, as long as they've been given enough notice. They'll probably charge you a nominal fee (often as little as US$10), normally to cover the packing materials. Remind the airline of your extra requirements when you reconfirm your ticket, and get to the airport a little earlier so you can pack your equipment well before the rush – it will be better stored in the luggage compartment if it's not last on the plane.

Bikes Most airlines won't make you take a bike to pieces, as their packages are generally big enough to take the whole bike. You will have to loosen the nut on the stem (to turn your handlebars 90°), remove the pedals and any attachments such as lights, bottles and speedos. If you're particularly attached to your bike, bring some bubblewrap to protect it from denting or scratches. Alternatively, you can put your bike into your own package and turn up with it ready to go.

Surfboards Believe it or not, you can go surfing in Europe, but whether it's worth lugging a board all the way there is another question entirely. Airlines are unlikely to have special packaging for surfboards, so look into getting a travel board cover. It's also a good idea to wrap your boards in foam or bubblewrap to prevent damage.

LAND

Although tickets for land travel in Europe can often be purchased within Europe, there are advantages in purchasing some tickets before you leave home. In some instances, as with Eurail passes, the tickets must be purchased outside Europe, unless your passport shows that you've been in Europe for less than six months. (Even if it does, the ticket will cost more than if you'd bought it before you left home.) For details see the Getting Around section in the While You're There chapter.

SEA

Tickets for sea travel are usually purchased within Europe. Again, see Getting Around in the While You're There chapter for details.

Travel Insurance

A good travel insurance policy is essential. With any luck it will only be for peace of mind, but if something does go wrong it will save your sanity as well as your savings.

Depending on your policy, it can protect you against medical costs through illness or injury, ticket loss, cancellation penalties on advance-purchase flights, theft or loss of possessions, and the cost of additional plane tickets if you are so sick that you have to fly home.

Hospitals and medical services throughout Europe, particularly Western Europe and Scandinavia, are excellent but if you fall very sick or are involved in an accident, the cost could make your entire travel budget look like peanuts.

You may already have personal medical insurance in your own country, either private or government funded, so check whether it applies internationally. You also might be automatically covered if you hold a valid International Student Identity Card (ISIC) or International Teacher Identity Card (ITIC) – ask at the place where you purchased the card (for details on these cards see the Other Paperwork section in the Passports & Visas chapter). It would still pay to check the full extent of the cover and back it up with supplementary cover if need be.

BUYING YOUR INSURANCE

Travel insurance policies are offered by travel agencies and student travel organisations, as well as general insurance companies. Have a good look at what's available – some policies are very cheap, but only offer minimal coverage. Read the small print carefully to avoid being caught out by exclusions.

If you're planning an extended trip, for work or study, consider whether you want full cover for the whole trip, or only while you're actually travelling. Further insurance cover can be arranged once you're in Europe – London, for instance, has dozens or youth and student travel agencies specialising in this area. Remember that the longer your period of cover, the cheaper it becomes per month.

Here are some tips on buying your insurance:

- Try to buy your travel insurance as soon as you've settled on your departure date and itinerary. If you buy it the week before you fly out you may find, for example, that you're not covered for delays to your flight caused by industrial action.

- Credit card companies may provide limited insurance if you pay for your airline ticket with their card. You may be able to reclaim the payment if the operator/travel agency doesn't deliver. Ask your credit card company what it's prepared to cover.

- See whether you can extend your policy if you decide to stay away for a longer period than you anticipated, and whether you can get a cheaper family policy if you're travelling with your partner or a friend.

- Most policies will have a ceiling on the value of possessions to be insured, especially in the case of hi-tech items such as still cameras and video equipment. Make sure you value these items and ask the insurer if they will be fully covered. It's a good idea to leave details of such items (purchase receipts or valuations, serial numbers, make and model and date of purchase) at home.

- An 'excess' (an agreed amount of money you must cough up for each claim) will be imposed by almost all policies. Find out the amount, because in some situations it may be cheaper and quicker for you to bite the bullet and pay all expenses out of your own pocket.

- Find out whether your policy obliges you to pay on the spot and redeem the money later, or whether the company will pay the providers direct. If you have to claim later, make sure you keep all documentation. If you have a medical problem, some policies will ask you to call back (reverse charges) to a centre in your home country where an immediate assessment of your problem will be made.

- Be upfront with the insurance company about any pre-existing medical condition you may have. If you gloss over a problem in the quest for a cheaper deal, the company will have grounds not to honour your claims.

- Some policies specifically exclude 'dangerous activities', which can include scuba diving, motorcycling, skiing, mountain climbing and even trekking. A locally acquired motorcycle licence may not be valid under some policies. Also check that the policy covers ambulances or an emergency flight home, especially if you plan to trek or cycle in remote areas.

HEALTH

Travel in Europe can expose you to some health problems, but the most you are likely to have to worry about are sunburn, foot blisters, insect bites and an upset stomach from eating and drinking too much.

Before You Go

INFORMATION SOURCES

Part of your preparation for this trip should be to get information and advice on any health risks at your destination and how to stay healthy on the road. You can get this information from your family doctor, travel health clinics or national and state health departments. The Internet is also a great reference source.

Specialist travel health clinics are probably the best places to go for advice, but unless you will be travelling well off the usual tourist routes, a trip to your family doctor should be all that is necessary. If you need to pack them, most clinics sell health-related travel essentials such as insect repellent, mosquito nets, and needle and syringe kits.

UK

MASTA (Medical Advisory Services for Travellers; ☎ 0891-224 100), at the London School of Hygiene & Tropical Medicine, Keppel St, London WC1E 7BR, doesn't have a travel clinic but provides information and travel health products.

USA & Canada

To find a travel health clinic in your area, you could call your state health department, or try the Centers for Disease Control & Prevention (CDC; ☎ 888-232 3228, fax 232-3299, www.cdc.gov) in Atlanta, Georgia. It's the central source of travel health information in North America and can advise you on travel medicine providers in your area. CDC publishes an excellent booklet, *Health Information for International Travel* (☎ 202-512 1800 or order it from the Superintendent of Documents, US Government Printing Office, Washington, DC).

Health Canada (fax 613-941 3900, www.hc-sc.gc.ca/hpb/lcdc/osh) is a government department that provides information and general health advice for travellers.

Australia & New Zealand

The Travellers Medical and Vaccination Centre has a network of clinics in most major cities – use the phonebook to find your nearest clinic or check out its Web site (www.tmvc.com.au).

Internet Resources

For general travel health information, try these two sites:

Shorelands

www.tripprep.com

(well organised site is easy to navigate and has lots of good general travel health information, as well as handy country profiles including US State Department travel advisory information)

Travellers Medical and Vaccination Centre

www.tmvc.com.au

(Australian-based site has lots of useful information, and good sections on travelling while pregnant and with children)

Books

For more information on travel health issues, you could consult one of the many publications available. Here are some suggestions to get you started:

Travellers' Health

Dr Richard Dawood, Oxford University Press, 1995

(comprehensive and authoritative)

Bugs, Bites & Bowels

Dr Jane Howarth-Wilson, Cadogan

(practical, down-to-earth guide, full of anecdotes from the author's experience)

IMMUNISATIONS

Immunisations help protect you from some diseases you may be at risk of catching on your travels. No jabs are necessary for travel in Europe, but they may be an entry requirement if you are coming from an infected area (yellow fever is the most likely requirement). If you are travelling to Europe with stops in Asia, Africa or South America, check with your travel agent or the embassies of the countries you will be visiting in Europe.

It's best to make your first appointment for advice on immunisations about six to eight weeks before you go. This is because you usually need to wait one to two weeks after a booster or the last dose of a course before you're fully protected, and some courses may need to be given over a period of several weeks.

You'll need to get individual advice on which immunisations to have, as this depends on various factors, including your destination, the length and type of trip, any medical conditions you have, which ones you've had in the past, and any allergies you have.

Whatever your travel plans, you'll need to be up-to date with your 'routine' immunisations, including tetanus (often given together with diphtheria), polio and some 'childhood illnesses'. In addition, you'll probably need some of the following immunisations.

Hepatitis A

Travellers planning long stays off the usual tourist routes in Eastern, Central or southern Europe and Turkey should be protected against this common viral infection of the liver. Protection is either with hepatitis A vaccine or immunoglobulin. Although it may be more expensive, the vaccine is recommended as it gives good protection for at least a year (longer if you have a booster). Immunoglobulin needs to be given as close as possible to your departure date.

A combined hepatitis A and typhoid vaccine has recently become available – good news if you're not keen on needles (see the Typhoid entry later).

Hepatitis B

Protection against this serious liver infection is recommended for long-term travellers to Eastern Europe and Turkey. It is also recommended if needle-sharing or sexual contact with a local person is a possibility. This immunisation is given routinely to children in some countries, including Australia and the USA, so you may already be protected. If you need both hepatitis A and B immunisations, a combined vaccine is available.

Immunisations Details

If you're an adult, you will probably have had the full course of an immunisation before, usually as a child. With most immunisations, it takes two to three weeks to build up maximum protection.

vaccine	full course	booster	comments
tetanus, usually given with diphtheria	three doses given at four-week intervals (usually in childhood)	every 10 years	full course usually given in childhood
polio	three doses given at four-week intervals (usually in childhood)	every 10 years; usually given orally	full course usually given in childhood
hepatitis A vaccine	single dose	booster at six to 12 months	gives good protection for at least 12 months; with booster, protects for more than 10 years
hepatitis immuno-globulin	a single injection; needs to be given as close to travel as possible	gives protection only for two to six months, depending on dose	because it's a blood product there's a theoretical risk of HIV and hepatitis B or C
typhoid	single injection, or three or four oral doses	injection: every three years; oral: every one to five years	the new vaccine causes few side effects
hepatitis B	two doses one month apart plus a third dose six months later	three to five years	more rapid courses are available if necessary
rabies (pre-exposure)	three doses over one month; booster at six to 12 months	two to three years	the old vaccine was extremely unpleasant as it had to be injected into the stomach, but the new vaccine is injected under the skin, and has few side effects
tick-borne encephalitis	two or three injections over 10 days; booster at 12 months	three years	available from hospital emergency departments in 'at risk' countries

Rabies

Although rare, rabies does exist in many European countries, with the exception of the UK, Ireland, Portugal, Monaco and Malta. With rabies, you have the choice of having the immunisation either before you go or, if you are bitten by a potentially rabid animal, at that time. If you have a pretrip immunisation, you will need to have a course of three injections over a month, which gives you some (but not complete) protection against the disease. If you then get bitten by a suspect animal, you will still need to have two boosters to prevent rabies developing.

Rabies vaccination is generally recommended only if you'll be travelling through rural areas for more than three months or if you'll be handling animals. Children are at particular risk of being bitten, so they may need to be vaccinated even if you're going for a short time; discuss this with your doctor.

Tick-Borne Encephalitis

Tick-borne encephalitis (TBE) can occur in most forest and rural areas of Europe, especially in eastern Austria, Germany, Hungary and the Czech Republic. Consider a vaccination against this tick-transmitted disease if you plan to do extensive hiking between May and September.

The vaccine is available as a series of two or three injections and can be administered quickly; it takes about 10 days to get the three shots.

The TBE vaccination is only available in Europe. If you are coming from Australia, New Zealand or the USA, it's easy and inexpensive to get your shots from hospital emergency departments when you are in Europe.

Typhoid

You'll need vaccination against typhoid only if you intend to really rough it in remote areas of Eastern European countries, including Albania, Croatia and Romania, and Turkey. Typhoid vaccination is available as an injection or as tablets (oral form), although availability of the oral form may be limited. The old injectable typhoid vaccine can produce some pretty unpleasant reactions (fever, chills, headache), but the new injection causes few side effects. The oral form can sometimes give you an intestinal upset.

Malaria Prevention

Except in remote areas of Turkey, malaria is unknown in Europe. There is no risk of malaria in the main tourist areas in the west and south-west of Turkey, but malaria is officially present in the south-east of Turkey. The highest danger is in the muggy agricultural area called Cukurova, north of Adana. If you plan to spend lots of time in rural areas and camp out in this part of Turkey, you will need to think about taking some malaria tablets. Get the latest advice from your doctor or travel health clinic before you go.

TRAVEL INSURANCE

However lucky (or poor) you're feeling, you don't want to be without travel insurance. See the Tickets & Insurance chapter for more information.

PRETRAVEL CHECK-UPS

A medical check-up prior to travel is a good idea to make sure there are no problems waiting to happen. If you've had any niggling problems, now is the time to get them checked out. This goes for your teeth too – make sure you get a dental check-up before you go.

Remember to get any prescription medicines you need from your doctor before you go. If you take any medicines regularly, you'll need to take sufficient supplies with you, as well as a record of your prescription.

If you wear glasses, consider taking a replacement pair, and take a copy of your prescription with you, in case you need to have a pair made up while you are away.

MEDICAL KIT

A medical kit is an essential piece of equipment you should take on your trip. For information on what to include in a medical kit, see the Equipment section in the What to Bring chapter.

FIRST-AID COURSE

Everyone should be familiar with basic first-aid techniques. It you will be travelling well off the beaten track, or are planning some extended hiking, you should consider doing a basic first-aid course before you leave. Contact your local first-aid organisation for details of courses available.

Travellers with Special Needs

You don't have to be able-bodied or in perfect health to travel, but make sure you know what to expect and be prepared to take extra precautions.

Whatever your plans, you'll need to get advice from your doctor or specialist on problems you may encounter when you're travelling and what to do about

Taking the Waters

In Europe there are hundreds of mineral springs whose waters, taken externally or internally, are said to be excellent for all sorts of ailments. The water often tastes quite odd, ranging from rotten eggs to rust, due to mineral content, but you can convince yourself it's doing you a power of good.

Locals and foreigners – mostly elderly – take the cure at a number of thermal baths, with Eastern Europe offering the most choice. The most affordable baths are in Hungary, the Czech Republic and on the Black Sea in Romania.

Among the best are the spas of Karlovy Vary and Mariánské Láznê in the Czech Republic; the Turkish baths of Budapest, the spa town of Harkány and the thermal lake at Hévíz in Hungary; and Dolenjske Toplice and Rogaska Slatina in Slovenia.

Don't be tempted to put off having a thermal bath until you reach the town of Spa in Belgium, as you will be disappointed. Spa was for centuries the luxurious retreat for royalty and the wealthy who came to drink, bath and generally cure themselves in the mineral-rich waters which bubble forth here. But Spa had its day in the 18th and 19th centuries and today it is a rather run-down reminder of what once was.

Leonie Mugavin
Lonely Planet, Australia

them. Take with you a written summary of your medical problems and any treatment you are currently on or have received in the past – you may need to ask your doctor for this before you go.

Check that your travel health insurance covers you for pre-existing illnesses.

Everyday Health

Looking after your general day-to-day health is the best way to stay healthy on your trip. Travelling can be stressful, you will be eating new food, probably at strange hours, taking in lots of second-hand smoke, drinking more than you usually do and probably getting less sleep as well. The idea is to stay well on your trip, rather than treat yourself when you are sick.

SUN

Getting burnt by the sun is probably the main hazard you'll face in Europe. Overexposure to the sun has well known long-term consequences (such as skin cancer) as well as painful short-term consequences (sunburn), so it's worth taking steps to avoid getting fried. Cover up and wear a hat to protect your face and neck from sunburn. Take high-protection factor sunscreen with you as it's not cheap to buy in Europe and use it on exposed areas. You'll also need to protect your eyes with UV-blocking sunglasses (wraparounds are a good idea). The sun is generally at its fiercest between 11 am and 3 pm, so it makes sense to spend this time as most locals do: resting in the shade or indoors.

HEAT

Remember to give yourself a chance to get used to the heat. If you are coming from a cool climate and arriving anywhere along the Mediterranean, especially in summer, you're probably going to feel hot and easily exhausted for a few days. After this, your body will have made adjustments to cope with the heat, and you'll probably find your capacity for activity is about back to normal. Many people find they sweat heavily in the heat. You'll need to drink plenty of fluids to replace the amount you're sweating out – cool bottled water is best, but any not-too-sweet soft drinks or fruit juices are OK. Some other points to consider are:

- Because your feet swell in the heat, especially at first, take footwear that is a little too big rather than small.
- Help your body out by not doing too much during the heat of the day, and avoid large heavy meals and excess alcohol during the hottest part of the day.
- Learn to recognise the symptoms of heat exhaustion and heatstroke, which are the most serious consequences of heat exposure.

FOOD

Travelling usually means you're eating out three meals a day for perhaps weeks on end, and at some point you are likely to encounter a suspect Turkish kebab or a Polish dumpling reheated one time too many.

Restaurants popular with locals and travellers should generally be fine. In some of the Eastern European countries, be careful with food that has been cooked and left to go cold, as is often the case in old-style self-service res-taurants in Poland, the Czech Republic, Slovakia and Hungary. Salads and fruit are generally fine to eat throughout Europe, but take care in more remote parts of Turkey or southern Europe. As autumn approaches, mushroom picking is very popular in many European countries, but make sure you don't eat any that haven't been identified as safe for eating.

Your stomach's natural defences can cope with small amounts of con-taminated foods – if you're not sure about something, don't pig out on it!

If you're on a long trip, or you're budgeting hard, you'll need to take care that your diet is balanced and that you don't lose a huge amount of weight. Consider taking multivitamins with you in case you get run-down.

WATER

Although in most of Europe you can generally rely on tap water, in Eastern Europe, southern Italy, Greece and Turkey it is best to stick to bottled or purified water. Never assume that water from rivers, streams or lakes is safe, because even in relatively unpopulated areas it can be contaminated by animals or hikers. Run-off from fertilised fields is also a concern in agricultural areas. Water from fountains or rustic-looking roadside springs could also cause a few problems. Ice is only as safe as the water it's made from, so it's best to avoid this too.

How you deal with the water issue depends on where you are and what sort of travelling you're doing. Drinking bottled water is one obvious option.

The simplest and most effective way to make water safe to drink is to boil it, which kills all disease-causing bugs. You just need to bring it to a rolling boil for a few minutes and then let it cool.

The Mediterranean Diet

How is it that the French, with their high consumption of cheese, oil, creamy sauces and red wine, appear to live longer than their exercise-conscious, fat-conscious, diet-conscious western counterparts? The answer it seems is not just what the French are eating, but how they eat it.

In recent years the diet of the French, or more broadly the common diet of Mediterranean countries, has become increasingly popular as the model for healthy eating. The Mediterranean diet consists mainly of vegetables, fruit, pulses, cereals, nuts and oils, espe-cially olive oil. Add to this oily fish and red wine and you have a diet that is said to reduce the incidence of cancers and heart disease.

What is said to be so good about this Mediterranean diet, as opposed to a western diet, is its high intake of fruit, vegetables, carbohydrates, olive oil and a low emphasis on red meat and saturated fats. While medical experts have long believed in the health benefits of a diet high in fruit and vegetables, it is the Mediterranean style of cooking and eating with olive oil, espe-cially cold pressed virgin olive oil, that is said to have the most beneficial health affects.

The antioxidant properties of red wine are also thought to help in the prevention of heart disease and cancer. Many health experts now expound the medicinal benefits of a couple of glasses of red wine a day with food cooked and eaten the Mediterranean way. Excellent.

Leonie Mugavin
Lonely Planet, Australia

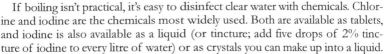

If boiling isn't practical, it's easy to disinfect clear water with chemicals. Chlorine and iodine are the chemicals most widely used. Both are available as tablets, and iodine is also available as a liquid (or tincture; add five drops of 2% tincture of iodine to every litre of water) or as crystals you can make up into a liquid.

Water purifiers are a third choice but they tend to be fairly expensive. Consider purchasing a filter if you are planning a long trip off the usual tourist path, when a filter could be more cost-effective than buying bottled water.

PERSONAL HYGIENE

Many health problems can be avoided by simply taking good care of yourself. This includes always washing your hands before you eat and after using the toilet. Washing your hands frequently can also help to prevent colds and upper-respiratory tract infections.

INSECT BITES

Mosquitoes can be a nuisance in southern and Eastern Europe, but can almost drive you insane during the summer months in northern Europe. Finland with its many lakes is particularly notorious. There are many insect repellent products on the market, but unfortunately none are very effective against the ravenous hordes of mosquitoes that home in on you 24 hours a day. You could still try an insect repellent or ask a local what they recommend. Antihistamine cream can be used to relieve the itching but most people get used to mosquito bites after a few days and the itching and swelling become less severe.

Midges, small flies related to mosquitoes, are common in northern Europe and Scotland and parts of England during the summer. Try mosquito repellent to keep these blood-suckers at bay.

You should always check all over your body if you have been walking through a potentially tick-infested area as ticks can cause skin infections and other more serious diseases, such as Lyme disease and tick-borne encephalitis. (See the Medical Problems section later for more information about these diseases.)

If a tick is found attached, press down around the tick's head with tweezers, grab the head and gently pull upwards. Avoid pulling the rear of the body as this may squeeze the tick's gut contents through the attached mouth parts into the skin, increasing the risk of infection and disease. Smearing chemicals on the tick will not make it let go and is not recommended.

Permethrin is an effective insecticide that can be applied to clothes and mosquito nets, but not to skin. If you're planning on hiking through tick-infested areas (forests and pastures), consider treating your clothes, particularly trousers and socks, with permethrin before you go.

CUTS & SCRATCHES

Wash well and treat with an antiseptic any cuts and scratches. Where possible avoid bandages, which can keep wounds wet. Whatever your travel plans, you'll be doing a lot of walking in Europe so look after your feet. If you do get blisters, soak your feet in hot salty water and leave the blisters to heal themselves.

Jellyfish occasionally inundate the Mediterranean beaches. Their stings are painful but not dangerous. Calamine lotion or antihistamines can help reduce the reaction and relieve the pain.

ACCIDENTS & INJURY

You may be surprised at the apparent disregard for traffic laws in some places (particularly in Italy and Greece). Some basic safety tips are:

- Drinking and driving is best avoided wherever you are.
- Use a seat belt if possible.
- If you're riding a motorcycle or moped, wear a helmet and protective clothing.
- If you're driving, try not to speed, and avoid travelling at night.

Even strong swimmers can get taken by unexpectedly strong currents. Try to follow these safety rules:

- Avoid alcohol when swimming.
- Beware of strong currents at the seaside – check the local situation and don't swim alone.
- Don't dive into shallow water.

SAFE SEX

While it's true that sexually transmitted infections (STIs), including HIV/AIDS and hepatitis B, are a risk anywhere if you're having casual sex, it seems that you're more likely to throw caution to the wind when you are away from home, and are therefore more at risk. Opportunities for casual sex tend to be greater while you're travelling.

Avoiding casual sex altogether is the safest option; otherwise, use a condom. Condoms are widely available in Europe but in some Eastern European countries (eg Poland) condoms won't be on display. You may prefer to take a familiar, reliable brand with you. Rubber condoms disintegrate in the heat, so take care to store them deep in your pack and check them carefully before use.

ALCOHOL & DRUGS

Drinking is almost a national pastime in many parts of Europe. From the well known Belgian beers, Polish vodka and Italian chianti to home-made plum brandy, you won't have to go too far to find a drink. Try every new (or familiar) drink you want to, just don't try them all at once.

Always treat drugs with a great deal of caution. There are lots of drugs available in Europe, sometimes quite openly (eg in the Netherlands) but that does not mean they are legal. Throughout the 1990s, the war in the former Yugoslavia forced drug traders to seek alternative routes from Asia to Western Europe, sometimes crossing through Hungary, Slovakia, the Czech Republic and Poland. These countries, desperately seeking integration into the 'new' Europe, do not look lightly upon drug use. Even a little dope can cause a great deal of trouble in some places. Overdose is always a risk – never take drugs when you are on your own.

Women's Health
BEFORE YOU GO

Some issues you might want to discuss with your doctor before you go include: how travel will affect your method of contraception or hormone replacement therapy; the possibility of taking emergency contraception (the 'morning after pill') with you; stopping your periods temporarily; or taking emergency treatment for cystitis or thrush with you, if you are prone to these.

If you are on the oral contraceptive pill, a touch of diarrhoea or vomiting can reduce the effectiveness of the pill, so this is worth bearing in mind. Take a plentiful supply of your medication with you, as it may be difficult to get your familiar brand.

If you're planning on travelling while you're pregnant, discuss this with your doctor as early as possible.

EVERYDAY HEALTH

You may find that your periods stop altogether when you're away – a result of the physical and mental stresses of travelling (but have a pregnancy test done if you think you may be pregnant). However, you're just as likely to find that travelling brings on the worst period of your life, at the most inconvenient time. If you suffer from premenstrual stress (PMS) be prepared for it to be worse while you are away and take plentiful supplies of any painkiller or other remedy you find helpful.

Hot weather can make thrush (yeast infection) more likely when you're travelling. If you know you are prone to thrush, it's worth taking a supply of medication with you.

Get any symptoms like an abnormal vaginal discharge or genital sores checked out as soon as possible. Some STIs don't cause any symptoms, even though they can cause long-term fertility and other problems, so if you have unprotected intercourse while you're away, be sure to have a check-up when you return home.

Medical Services

You will be able to find good medical care throughout Europe. Local pharmacies or neighbourhood medical clinics are good to visit if you have a small medical problem. Hospital casualty wards will help if it's more serious.

If you need to get medical help while travelling, the tourist office should be able to provide you with names of local doctors who speak your language.

Upmarket hotels can often recommend a doctor, and may even have a doctor attached to the staff.

Medical Problems

Here's a rundown of some of the main health problems that occur in Europe. For more in-depth information on any of these problems, try any of the information sources listed at the beginning of this chapter. Just remember you

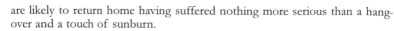

are likely to return home having suffered nothing more serious than a hang-over and a touch of sunburn.

ALTITUDE & CLIMATIC EXTREMES
Effects of Altitude
You may suffer a little light-headedness in the high mountain regions of Italy, Austria, Switzerland and France. The higher you go, the thinner the air and the easier you need to take things (and the quicker you get drunk!).

Altitude sickness can occur above 3000m, but very few treks or ski runs in the Alps reach heights of 3000m or more – Mont Blanc is one exception – so altitude sickness is not likely. Headache, nausea and loss of appetite, difficulty sleeping and lack of energy are all signs to heed, but rest and simple painkillers generally work. If mild symptoms persist or get worse, descend to a lower altitude.

Heat Exhaustion & Heatstroke
Heat can cause a range of conditions from heat cramps and fainting to heat exhaustion and potentially fatal heatstroke. Even if you don't feel too bad, heat and dehydration can affect your physical performance and mental judgement.

In summer in countries such as Turkey, Greece, Portugal, Spain and Italy, even if you are just sightseeing or spending the day at the beach, you can lose an astonishing 2L of sweat in an hour, more if you're doing strenuous physical activity. Sweat contains water and salts, which you need to replace, so drink a lot more than you would in a cool climate, even when you have acclimatised. An adult needs to drink about 3L of fluid a day in a hot climate, or 5L or more if doing a strenuous physical activity such as hiking or cycling. Take a water bottle with you everywhere and drink from it frequently.

Prolonged exposure to high temperatures and inadequate fluid intake can cause heat exhaustion and, more seriously, heatstroke. Symptoms of heat exhaustion are headache, dizziness, nausea and feeling weak and exhausted. You may get muscle aches or cramps. If you notice these symptoms in yourself or your travel companions, rest in a cool environment and drink lots of cool fluids.

With heatstroke, sweating stops and body temperature rises dangerously, which can be fatal. Symptoms include a severe, throbbing headache, confusion and lack of coordination. This is an emergency situation; you will need some medical help pronto.

Hypothermia
The weather in Europe's mountain areas can be extremely changeable at any time of the year. Even if you're just on a half-day trip, skiers and hikers should always be prepared for very cold and wet weather. Be prepared with appropriate equipment if you are planning on sleeping out.

Hypothermia occurs when the body loses heat faster than it can produce it and the core temperature of the body falls. It is surprisingly easy to progress from very cold to dangerously cold due to a combination of wind, wet clothing, fatigue and hunger, even if the air temperature is above freezing. It is best to dress in layers; silk, wool and some of the new artificial fibres are all good insulating materials. A hat is important, because a lot of heat is lost through the head. A strong, waterproof outer layer (and a space blanket for emergencies) is essential. If you are out hiking or skiing, carry basic supplies, including food containing simple sugars to generate heat quickly and fluid to drink.

Symptoms of hypothermia are exhaustion, numb skin (particularly toes and fingers), shivering, slurred speech, irrational or violent behaviour, lethargy, stumbling, dizzy spells, muscle cramps and violent bursts of energy. Irrationality may take the form of sufferers claiming they are warm and trying to take off their clothes.

To treat mild hypothermia, first get the person out of the wind and/or rain, remove their clothing if it's wet and replace it with dry, warm clothing. Give them hot liquids – not alcohol – and some high-kilojoule, easily digestible food. Do not rub victims: instead, allow them to slowly warm themselves. This should be enough to treat the early stages of hypothermia. The early recognition and treatment of mild hypothermia is the only way to prevent severe hypothermia, which is a critical condition.

INFECTIONS
Diarrhoea
Simple things like a change of diet or the climate can send you rushing to the toilet. Even if it's relatively mild, you're probably going to feel a tad sorry for yourself for a day or so as it passes through your system, so it's worth building a few rest days into your travel schedule to allow for this.

If you get it, diarrhoea usually strikes about the third day after you arrive and lasts about three to five days. It's caused by a whole heap of factors, including jet lag, new food, a new lifestyle and new bugs.

Be kind to yourself and your body, excuse yourself from sightseeing duties for a day or so, relax and recover before you start travelling again. The most important aspects of treatment are to prevent dehydration by replacing lost fluid, and to rest. You can drink most liquids, except alcohol, very sugary drinks or dairy products. Oral rehydration sachets can be useful but aren't essential if you're young and otherwise healthy. If you feel like eating starchy foods, potatoes, pasta and bread are thought to help fluid replacement.

Antidiarrhoeals ('stoppers' or 'blockers') are of limited use as they prevent your system from clearing out the toxin and can make certain types of diarrhoea worse, although they can be useful as a temporary stopping measure, for example if you have an 18 hour train journey ahead of you.

Hepatitis A
This common infection is transmitted through contaminated food and drinking water. Taking care with what you eat and drink is the best preventative. Symptoms are fever, sometimes intestinal symptoms, and jaundice (yellowing of the skin and whites of the eyes). It can leave you feeling weak for some time after, but has no other long-term effects.

Hepatitis B

This viral infection of the liver is spread through contact with infected blood, blood products or body fluids, for example through sexual contact, unsterilised needles or contact with blood via small breaks in the skin. Other risk situations include tattooing or body piercing with contaminated equipment. The best prevention is to avoid risk situations. The symptoms of hepatitis B are similar to hepatitis A but are more severe, and the disease can lead to long-term problems such as chronic liver damage, liver cancer or a long-term carrier state.

HIV/AIDS

You're at risk wherever you go if you don't take measures to protect yourself. Any exposure to blood, blood products or bodily fluids is a risk. The disease is spread in Europe mainly through sexual contact and dirty needles, but tattooing and body piercing can be as potentially dangerous as intravenous drug use.

Lyme Disease

Lyme disease is an infection transmitted by ticks that can be acquired throughout forested areas of Europe. The illness usually begins with a spreading rash at the site of the bite and is accompanied by flu-like symptoms. If untreated, symptoms disappear, but over subsequent weeks or months, serious medical problems set in. As the response to treatment is best early in the illness, seek medical attention should you develop any symptoms.

Rabies

Rabies is a fatal viral infection but is rare in most European countries. Many animals can be infected, such as dogs, cats, foxes and bats, and it is their saliva which is infectious. Once symptoms have appeared, death is inevitable, but the onset of symptoms can be prevented by a course of injections with the rabies vaccine, which you need whether or not you have been immunised previously. Avoid contact with animals.

Tetanus

This disease is caused by a germ that lives in soil and in the faeces of horses and other animals. It enters the body via breaks in the skin. The first symptom may be discomfort in swallowing, or stiffening of the jaw and neck; this is followed by painful convulsions of the jaw and whole body. The disease can be fatal. It can be prevented by vaccination.

Tick-Borne Encephalitis

Ticks can carry tick encephalitis, a virus-borne cerebral inflammation. In this case, blotches appear around the bite, sometimes pale in the middle. Headache, stiffness and other flu-like symptoms, as well as extreme tiredness, appearing a week or two after the bite, can progress to more serious problems. Medical help must be sought. A vaccine is also available.

Typhoid

This vaccine-preventable disease is transmitted through contaminated food and water, and is a risk where hygiene standards are low. Symptoms are initially similar to flu, with headache, aches and pains and a fever. Abdominal pain, vomiting and either diarrhoea or constipation can occur. Serious complications such as pneumonia, perforated bowel or meningitis may develop. It can be effectively treated, but medical help must be sought.

When You Return

If you were away for a short time only and had no serious health problems, there's probably no need to get a medical check-up when you return, unless you develop symptoms. If you become sick in the weeks following your trip, be sure to tell your doctor that you have been away and which countries you have visited.

If you've been on a long trip or are concerned that you may have been exposed to a disease, such as an STI, a medical check-up is advisable. See also the Coming Home chapter for a discussion of post-holiday blues.

WHAT TO BRING ▶▶

You've probably heard this tip before: *don't bring too much*. But how much is too much? To some extent this depends on what type of trip you're planning. If it's purely a backpacking trip – short or long – then bring as little as possible because you won't enjoy carting half a wardrobe and your vanity unit around Europe all summer. At the same time, travellers who try to get around for months on end with a pocket-sized pack and the clothes they're wearing are stretching things a bit. A medium-sized backpack (about three-quarters full, not bursting at the seams), and a small day-pack with your camera and other important gear is all you need.

If you're planning on spending a bit longer in Europe, either working or studying, then it might be worth bringing more clothing and personal items and leaving the excess in storage when you actually hit the road.

This chapter contains suggestions for equipment and clothing to consider taking, plus some tips on packing and recording your trip.

Equipment
BACKPACKS

Years ago backpacks were associated with penniless hippy travellers, but now they reign supreme among travellers of all ages and budgets – unless you're a business traveller or a masochist, leave the suitcase at home!

Your backpack will be your constant companion on the road and central to your comfort and convenience. This is one item you should be prepared to spend some decent money on – after a few weeks hauling it around on your back, piling it on and off trains and daily unpacking and repacking it, you won't regret the extra expense. A good-quality backpack will last you many years.

Thankfully, the days of external-framed, canvas rucksacks – desperately uncomfortable, heavy and cumbersome – are long gone. Modern backpacks are miracles of design; they can be customised to your back length and are constructed from highly durable fabrics. There are two principal backpack designs – toploaders and travel packs.

Toploaders

Toploaders are essentially a fabric tube. They are generally more comfortable, hardwearing and watertight than travel packs (they have fewer seams), but are far less convenient because you have to haul everything out to reach the stuff packed at the bottom. If you plan to do a lot of trekking or rafting, the comfort and waterproofing qualities will come to the fore. If, however, you're going to stay mostly in hostels or guesthouses, then you can't go past the travel pack.

Travel Packs

The chief advantage of the travel pack is the zip that runs all the way around the edge and top, allowing you to completely open up the main compartment. This means dead simple packing and access to your stuff. The double zips also make it easy to lock the pack with a couple of padlocks. A zippered flap (which is stowed at the base) can be used to hide and protect the harness when you put your pack on planes, buses, trains or in taxis. A travel pack also has side handles and a detachable shoulder strap, making it easy to carry in crowds or other cramped spaces. Many travel packs have a day-pack that can be zipped onto the back of the main pack so you can carry the whole lot together. The only problem here is that this is a weak point where the seams may come undone after a while and some travellers find the actual day-pack to be too small to be useful (see Day-Packs later).

Buying a Pack

It's sensible to go for a recognised brand; Macpac (www.macpac.co.nz), Karrimor (www.karrimor.co.uk), Kelty (www.kelty.com) or REI (www.REI .com) all have ergonomic designs and are made from the latest hi-tech fabrics, which will protect your stuff from showers (if not a downpour) and allow your skin to breathe during long-distance walks. Prices start at around US$150 and

---

The Trojan Alternative

On my first solo trip to the UK and Europe, I disembarked at Gatwick airport proudly bearing the latest in boy scout-issue backpacks. However, it soon dawned on me that this was not going to be a happy relationship: the external frame rubbed cruelly against my back, the aluminium plumbing gouged into my shoulder blades, and carrying the whole cumbersome edifice engendered excruciating pain – and I'd only got as far as Victoria station. But there, in a small luggage accessory kiosk, I spied my salvation – a set of luggage wheels. To these, after handing over the requisite pounds, I lashed my pack.

There is hardly a moor in that green and fair land that myself and my trusty wheel-borne backpack didn't trundle over, nary a youth hostel up whose stairs we didn't rumble. Admittedly, I received some odd looks (ranging from astonishment to abject scorn) from some members of the backpacking fraternity. A backpack on wheels is, I suppose, a contradiction in terms. Nevertheless, faced with a choice between multiple sessions of physiotherapy and the derision of my fellows (bowed under the weight of their well thumbed Penguin Classic editions of Camus and Nietzsche), I'd make the same choice again.

Years later, while working with the Tibetan community in northern India, I noted with interest a couple who disembarked from a dilapidated bus. This tall, sun-burnished, lean limbed pair had definite traveller cred: long dreds, stylish grunge gear and a 'don't mess with us: we've crossed the Khyber Pass' attitude. I watched as they strode off up the road towards the Hotel Tibet, heads held high, eyes focused on the mountains, as with studied ease they pulled behind them their matching silver Samsonite suitcases on wheels – and I felt vindicated.

Michelle Coxall
LP Author, Australia

disappear into the stratosphere, but consider the following points as you check out the various options:

Capacity – Resist the temptation to buy the biggest pack in the shop – it will only encourage you to pack more stuff you probably don't really need. Have a good idea of what you plan to take with you before you buy your pack, and then purchase the smallest pack for the job; you can always post things home and a smaller pack will compel you to travel light. A 60L pack generally allows enough space for equipment, clothes and purchases over a three month trip; if you're carrying a tent you might want to go for a slightly larger one. However, many seasoned travellers swear by a 40L pack – think small and work up from there.

Fabric & Stitching – Look for durable material and double stitching at weight-bearing places. Also ensure the zippers are strong. If the pack looks a little lightweight or flimsy, go up to the more expensive model.

Fitting – Always try on your pack before you purchase it. Most decent packs have an adjustable internal frame that you can fit to the length of your back. Most companies now have gender-specific models, which are designed to accommodate the different hip and spine shapes of men and women. These can add another dimension to your comfort level.

Straps & Padding – Good packs will be amply padded at the shoulders and hips, as well as lightly padded down the back. The hip pads are the most important as the bulk of the weight is carried there, not on the shoulders. Straps and buckles should be strong and reliable – there's nothing worse than a pack with a broken strap while you're on the road.

Versatility – Look for packs with multiple compartments – a bottom section is ideal for your sleeping bag or dirty laundry and will also protect more fragile items in the main compartment, while front and side pockets are good for regularly needed items such as toiletries, waterproof gear, torch (flashlight), journal, novel, guidebook and map. Loops are useful as tie-down straps for carrying a sleeping bag, towel or tent outside your pack.

Securing Your Pack

Theft is always a risk, particularly if you sleep on overnight trains, lose sight of your luggage when travelling on buses or leave it in a hostel room or tent. Most travel packs have double zippers on all openings that can be padlocked together. If not, find a strong place in the fabric above the zip where you can make a couple of holes; thread a small padlock through the holes and attach the zip fastener – not enough to stop a determined thief with a knife, but a deterrent nonetheless. It's also worth packing a light chain or combination bicycle cable to attach your pack to the luggage rack of trains and ferries so you can sleep with an easy mind. Another option (for the really security conscious) is a pack lock (such as Pacsafe) – a wire mesh cover that slips over the pack and can be locked to a fixed object.

DAY-PACKS

A day-pack is extremely useful and will probably be your constant companion while on the road. Some travellers don't use them, preferring to wander around unencumbered by anything that might make them look like a tourist, but even if you only carry a camera and guidebook around, a day-pack is unbeatable.

Most of your everyday items will be carried in it – apart from the camera and guidebook, it might contain maps, water bottle, sunscreen, pens, your journal etc – so comfort and quality are again the keys. Make sure the shoulder straps and back section are padded and that the fabric is strong and durable. Some backpacks have detachable day-packs, thus saving you the expense of buying a separate unit. However, these are often too small and of basic design, so make sure it will be big enough to take all your bits and pieces. An overstuffed day-pack is a pain to carry, as it lacks a solid frame and will end up tiring your shoulders and back.

MONEYBELT

Your moneybelt is a vital piece of equipment, as it's the safest way of carrying your cash, travellers cheques, credit/debit cards, passport, ticket and other important items. It is crucial to select a moneybelt that can be worn unobtrusively beneath your clothing – keeping your valuables in a bumbag or otherwise exposed over your clothing is simply asking for trouble. Bumbags (moonbags, fannypacks, whatever) are seriously losing favour even for carrying nonvaluable day-to-day items (how they ever became so fashionable is a mystery). All they do is target you as a tourist with something worth stealing.

The most common types of moneybelts are worn either around the waist (safest option) or the neck. Neither design is particularly easy to access, so don't keep your ready cash in it or you'll be fishing in it every five minutes and attracting attention. A small wallet or purse kept in your front pocket with enough local currency to get you through the day is the way to go.

Think about the fabric too. Plastic sweats horribly and leather is heavy and retains perspiration. Cotton is probably the best bet as it's the most comfortable and can be washed, though it's less durable. If you use a cotton moneybelt, put your ticket, passport and other documents in a plastic bag so they don't deteriorate from your sweat.

Check out the belt's clasp or attachment. Your moneybelt is one item that you want to be secure at all times. The best clasps are the durable locking buckles similar to the ones on your backpack – they're easy for you to undo, but not easy for a snatch thief. Velcro is useless and those simple thread-and-tighten buckles you'll find on some cheap moneybelts are a pain to get on and off. Your moneybelt should have at least two zippered compartments – one to keep the documents you won't often need (airline ticket, insurance papers) and one for your travellers cheques, passport and credit card that you will dip into more regularly.

Finally, consider taking a waterproof container for your documents and money which you can wear when swimming, diving or snorkelling – you'll find this is especially useful if you're travelling alone, as otherwise you'll be forced to leave all valuables in a hotel or somewhere safe when you go swimming.

SLEEPING BAG

Whether to take a sleeping bag or not is a matter of personal choice. Most travellers do, and it is recommended even though it's a relatively bulky item. If you plan to do any camping you will need one, and it certainly comes in handy for travelling deck class on ferries, spending a few hours in an airport or train station, or if you're travelling in a cold climate and the accommodation heating is not all it could be (as may be the case in Eastern Europe). Go for a bag that is lightweight, easy to pack up into a small space and warm enough for the conditions you'll be travelling in.

A sleeping sheet is required if you're staying in HI hostels. Basically two sheets sewn together, it will also give you some protection from insects and dodgy beds. You can buy them ready-made from your local YHA but it's easy enough to make one yourself. If you don't have one, HI hostels will hire you one, but this gets expensive after a while.

MEDICAL KIT
You can buy prepared kits (conventional, as well as homoeopathic) from many travel health clinics, mail order companies and homoeopathic practitioners, or you can make one up yourself. Use a container that's waterproof and squash-proof – although the soft, zip-up bags similar to toiletry cases are good.

The following is a list of items you should consider including in your medical kit – consult your pharmacist for brands available in your country.

Antibiotics or any other regular medication – Antibiotics are useful if you're travelling well off the beaten track, but they must be prescribed and you should carry the prescription (and that of any other regular medication you use) with you. If you are allergic to commonly prescribed antibiotics such as penicillin or sulfa drugs, carry this information with you when travelling.
Antifungal cream or powder – For fungal skin infections and thrush.
Antihistamine – Useful as a decongestant for colds; for allergies, such as hay fever; to ease the itch from insect bites or stings; and to prevent motion sickness. Antihistamines may cause sedation and interact with alcohol so take care when using them.
Antiseptic (such as povidone-iodine) – For cuts and grazes.
Aspirin or paracetamol (acetaminophen in the USA) – For pain or fever.
Bandages, Band-Aids (plasters) & other wound dressings – For minor injuries.
Calamine lotion, sting relief spray or aloe vera – To ease irritation from sunburn and insect bites or stings.
Cold & flu tablets, throat lozenges & nasal decongestant.
Insect repellent, sunscreen, lip balm & eye drops.
Loperamide or diphenoxylate – 'Blockers' for diarrhoea.
Multivitamins – For long trips, when dietary vitamin intake may be inadequate.
Prochlorperazine or metaclopramide – For nausea and vomiting.
Rehydration mixture – To prevent dehydration, eg due to severe diarrhoea; particularly important when travelling with children, but is recommended for everyone.
Scissors, tweezers & a thermometer – Note that mercury thermometers are prohibited by airlines.
Water purification tablets or iodine – See also Everyday Health in the Health chapter.

OTHER USEFUL EQUIPMENT
We consider most of the following items to be very useful, if not essential. Bear in mind that all of these things can easily be purchased in Europe:

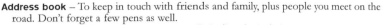
Address book – To keep in touch with friends and family, plus people you meet on the road. Don't forget a few pens as well.

Alarm clock – You don't want to miss your flight/bus/train/other appointment. Travel alarm clocks are tough, light and cheap.

Batteries – Bring spares for your equipment (camera, personal stereo, alarm clock, torch etc) and put new batteries in each before you depart.

Contraception – Condoms can be found all over Europe in pharmacies (drugstores) or vending machines in public toilets, but it won't hurt to bring a supply with you. If you use the pill, then bring enough to cover your whole trip as it may be difficult to get on the road.

Eye wear – Sunglasses are indispensable for both comfort and protection of your eyes. If you wear prescription glasses or contact lenses, take the prescription with you, along with extras such as a case and contact lens solution.

Padlocks & a chain – Apart from securing your backpack, you'll often need your own padlock for hostel lockers etc. Bring a couple of small but sturdy padlocks for your pack and a larger one for lockers. Combination padlocks mean you don't have to look after keys, but you do have to remember combinations – either way, a small hacksaw blade will get you out of a sticky situation! Chains are useful for attaching your backpack to the luggage rack on trains.

Pocketknife – A Swiss army knife (or good-quality equivalent) has loads of useful tools, particularly scissors, bottle opener, can opener and straight blade.

Sunscreen – You're likely to spend long hours in the sun and, apart from the long-term risk of melanoma, sunburn is painful.

Tampons or pads – These are readily available in Europe, but keep a supply for when you're off the beaten track.

Toilet paper – Never leave home without some! Public toilets in Europe range from ultra-modern, self-cleaning, coin-operated comfort machines to pitiful holes in the ground. A roll of toilet paper is handy for those (frequent) times when none is supplied.

Toiletries – Most items are widely available in Europe, but take any speciality products with you. Make sure you have plastic toothbrush and soap containers to keep them clean and dry.

Torch (flashlight) – Most helpful to find stuff late at night in a dorm, to avoid mishaps in outside toilets in the middle of the night, if you're camping or if the electricity packs it in. It's handy, too, for exploring caves and ruins. The Maglite range is almost indestructible, and even the small models throw out a fair bit of light.

Towel – For swimming, as well as for showers in hostels or camping grounds. Don't take a beach towel as it'll take ages to dry, weigh a tonne and get very whiffy. A quick-drying travel towel (made from a chamois-like material or one of the new micro-fibres) is OK, as is the all-purpose sarong (though it doesn't dry you very well). A small bath towel also does the job.

Travel guides. maps and phrasebooks – See Researching Your Trip in the Planning chapter for more information.

Nonessential Equipment

None of the gear listed here is really essential to your travels, but some things will no doubt suit your style of travel and others will make life more pleasant. Again, resist the temptation to take something just for the sake of having it:

Binoculars – Quite the luxury item really, but if you take them, you'll find them infinitely useful, particularly if you have a speciality interest such as bird-watching. Compact, lightweight travel binoculars are the best choice.

Books – A decent-sized book can while away a few hours in train stations, on long bus journeys, or simply when you want a few hours out. They're easy to swap with other travellers or at bookshops. Hostels also often have book exchanges.

Calculator – A pocket calculator is handy for currency conversions and any other mathematical problems you might have on the road. Forget the gimmicky electronic currency converters available in travel shops – a calculator is better.

Camping gear – Only lug this around if you plan to do a lot of camping. Tents, stoves, sleeping mats and cooking gear are bulky and heavy. Camping gear is readily available in most countries.

Compass – Essential for hiking and unbelievably useful for orientating yourself in big cities when you're not sure which way is up on your map. It doesn't have to be expensive – a cheap pocket compass available from camping stores will do.

Earplugs – You'll never regret these if you spend a lot of time in cities, stay near a mosque or sleep in a 20 bed dorm with 16 snorers and three early morning bag rustlers.

Games – Chess, backgammon, Scrabble, dominoes, Chinese chequers, snakes and ladders … whatever your favourite, it's likely there's a travel edition out there somewhere. The king of travel games is a simple set of playing cards – everyone should pack these, and you'll be surprised how many card games you learn on the road.

Glue stick – The glue on stamps and envelopes can be very dodgy. It's also useful to affix tickets and mementos in your journal.

Inflatable pillow – This will allow you to sleep more comfortably on long trips. Many international airlines supply these for you to keep (along with a little pair of socks, a toothbrush and an eye mask – ask your airline before you buy one).

Lighter/matches — For campfires, mosquito coils, candles and cigarettes.

Organiser – In this hi-tech age, an electronic organiser can take the place of your address book, calculator, alarm clock and whatever other functions it happens to perform. The downside is that it will be a target for thieves and if it happens to melt down, you might lose all those precious addresses.

Personal stereo/radio – Good for whiling away idle hours. Short-wave radios can keep you in touch with news from home.

Plug – These are rarely supplied in cheaper accommodation. Double-sided rubber or universal plastic plugs will fit most bath and basin plug holes.

Sewing kit – Needle, thread, a few buttons and safety pins to mend clothing, tears in your backpack, tent or sunglasses. This is surprisingly useful.

Travel journal – See Recording Your Trip later in this chapter.

Washing detergent – For cleaning your clothes in your room. Some hostels and hotels get cranky if you use their sink for washing clothes but most have laundry facilities.

Washing line – A piece of string will do the job, but there are relatively cheap lines on the market with suckers, hooks or both on each end which make them more versatile.

Water bottle – You can just refill a standard plastic bottle, but a more sturdy model will last a lot longer and be more suitable for purifying water on a regular basis.

Specialised Equipment

Diving, snorkelling, surfing, windsurfing, skiing, trekking or cycling equipment can be hired in any place in Europe where these activities are available, so there's really no need to bring your own equipment along. If you plan to undertake any of these activities seriously, look into the rental options in the places you plan to visit – you may feel better taking your own gear. A bike, in particular, is worth carting over if you plan a cycling holiday.

Adventure activities, such as caving, mountaineering, canyoning, parasailing and hang-gliding, are generally done as part of an organised tour led by a guide, with all equipment supplied.

Clothing

When it comes to clothes, pack light. Everything you could possibly need will be readily available in Europe's cities when you get there, so it's better to pack too little than too much. The old adage that you should lay out all the clothes you think you'll need, then take half of them, still rings true. The main things you should leave behind are heavy jumpers or jackets and more than one pair of shoes or boots. Still, the type of travelling and the climatic zones you intend to travel in will have a big influence on the clothes you pack.

DAY-TO-DAY

For regular pieces of clothing like trousers, skirts, shorts, shirts and underwear, natural fibres are definitely the go. While synthetics will dry faster and wrinkle less, they don't breathe very well, will stick to your skin and make you sweat. So look for cotton and linen articles – either pure or blends – and steer clear of nylon, rayon and lycra.

Jeans are OK for travelling in. They're casual and hardwearing although they take longer to dry than, say, cotton pants or cargo pants. It's a good idea to have something presentable to wear at special occasions or when dealing with police, clearing customs or other officials – this doesn't mean a suit or evening dress, but a decent shirt and pants or skirt will lift you out of the perceived backpacking stereotype. European nightclubs and gaming venues often have dress codes, which might include (for men) a collar, long pants and shoes, so if clubbing is a priority for you, make room in your pack.

KEEPING COOL

This is not a fashion statement but a matter of practicality. Western and Mediterranean Europe in high summer can be a steaming, humid pressure cooker. The crowded, choking cities you're wading through are no place for tight-fitting, sweaty duds and ill-fitting shoes. The good news is that it's easier to travel light in summer. Look for lightweight, loose-fitting clothes; light colours will keep you cooler than dark ones, but are harder to keep clean.

Shorts and T-shirts or short-sleeved shirts are the answer. Shorts

Clothing Checklist

- light jacket
- long pants/skirts/dress
- long-sleeved shirts
- sarong
- shoes/boots/sandals/thongs (flip flops)
- shorts (can double as swimwear)
- short-sleeved shirts
- socks/underpants/bras
- something presentable
- specialist clothing, such as hat, gloves, thermals, woollen socks
- sweater
- swimwear
- waterproof jacket
- wide-brimmed hat

aren't commonly worn by local men (and certainly not by women) away from beach areas in Europe, but they're not exactly frowned upon and as a traveller you won't stick out too much. Dress-style or hiking shorts (knee-length with pockets) are the best. In Muslim countries such as Turkey you should be a bit more conservative – women should cover up shoulders and below the knee. See the boxed text 'Dressing Appropriately' in the Issues & Attitudes chapter. Long-sleeved shirts are also useful, as they will keep the sun off you, allow you easier access to religious sites and are versatile in Europe's changeable climate.

Don't forget a wide-brimmed hat or cap – a cap won't protect your neck or ears, but let's face it, they're more popular. A sarong is a brilliantly versatile item as it can function as a full-length dress, skirt, sleeping sheet, beach towel, shade cloth or rope.

If you'll be travelling all over the continent or spending time in northern or Eastern Europe, bear in mind that the weather can be very unpredictable – fine one day, miserable the next – so you'll need a light sweater and waterproof jacket. Summer evenings can also be cool in the north and in Scandinavia.

KEEPING WARM

If you visit Europe in winter, you'll need to revise your wardrobe as it can get bitterly cold, even in the south.

Layers are the key here. It's better to have a T-shirt, long-sleeved cotton shirt and light sweater that can be peeled off than a thick, bulky jumper. Several layers of natural fibres, topped by a good-quality jacket, will give you all the versatility you need. Thermal underwear (such as a spencer or a lightweight, cycling-style, thin silk T-shirt) is also a good idea. Consider two pairs of socks – cotton under wool. If you get too hot you can ditch the woollies, while the cotton will absorb your sweat and prevent the irritation caused by damp wool on bare skin. Also bring waterproofs (a good-quality Gore-Tex jacket might be adequate), gloves and a woolly hat.

SPECIALISED CLOTHING

If you're engaging in specialist activities such as trekking or cycling, this is where synthetics come into their own. Hi-tech fabrics such as Gore-Tex are light, pretty well waterproof and have a one-way design to their knit so your sweat can escape, while keeping you protected from external water. This makes them ideal cold-weather gear. Fleecy jackets don't have the waterproofing abilities of Gore-Tex, but are lighter and smaller to pack.

FOOTWEAR

Whether you're visiting museums in Paris or hiking through the Alps, you will do a lot of walking in Europe. Pack a sturdy pair of walking shoes or boots, and make sure you wear them in properly before leaving.

If you intend to do any trekking or long-distance walking, leather boots are definitely the best. A good-quality pair will have sturdy soles, some waterproofing and plenty of ankle support. A clean pair of boots with long

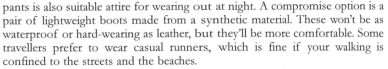

pants is also suitable attire for wearing out at night. A compromise option is a pair of lightweight boots made from a synthetic material. These won't be as waterproof or hard-wearing as leather, but they'll be more comfortable. Some travellers prefer to wear casual runners, which is fine if your walking is confined to the streets and the beaches.

For summer travel, particularly in southern Europe and beach areas, rubber-soled sandals are also worth having. They're cool, comfortable and give your feet a breather from socks and boots, and they're relatively light to pack. Finally, a cheap pair of rubber thongs (flip-flops) is handy for wearing in hostel showers.

Shoes are quite heavy, so try to limit yourself to two pairs – something sturdy enough for day-to-day use, plus a pair of sandals and/or thongs.

Why Backpackers Wear Hiking Boots in Bars

I liked wearing boots. I thought they were cool, they made me look taller, and I could wear odd socks without anyone noticing. So naturally I took my boots with me – the brown ones for around town, the black ones for going out at night, and an expensive pair of lightweight brand-name hiking boots for serious walking. Then I added a few changes of jeans, some shirts, a thin sweater, two thick sweaters, a warm jacket, a waterproof jacket, a sleeping bag, camera, books and so on. I could barely walk with all this stuff in my backpack, but I knew that everything I had was essential.

In less than two weeks I was near crippled from walking the streets in leather-soled boots, and my pack was no lighter – in fact it was getting heavier. It was time to redefine my idea of 'essential'. By that stage my bag was filled mostly with unwashed clothing, and I realised I was travelling the world with 15kg of dirty laundry. Worse still, it was obvious that the few remaining clean garments were completely useless. Facing the fact that I was in little danger of eating in a fancy restaurant, I sent my good shirts home by surface mail.

A sweater has been defined as a garment a child wears when its mother feels chilly, and by extension it's something a traveller packs when they're going somewhere cold. But a thick sweater is not a great travel accessory – it's bulky, hard to wash, and just not versatile enough. If the weather is really cold, you should be wearing every garment you have, and your bag will be almost empty. But you can't wear two thick sweaters at once, or even a thick one and a thin one. Don't tell your mother, but one thin sweater is enough.

There's an important packing principle here – everything you carry should be mutually compatible. If you can't wear shirt A with jacket B, leave one of them at home. That's why the footwear is so problematic – you can only wear one pair at a time. But shoes and boots are bulky in your bag, and expensive to pack and post home, which is why my calf-length brown boots were ultimately abandoned on a lonely train station, standing straight but empty, as I walked away in my black boots, now too scuffed to wear in the classy nightspots I wasn't going to anyway. And what about the brand-name hiking boots? I'd bought them in Australia, but they were made in Taiwan for an American company. They didn't last a week.

So if you're planning a trip that includes trekking as well as some nightlife, or if you'll be walking city streets as well as strolling on beaches, you'll need something versatile from the ankles down. You'll have to decide which is more difficult – dancing in hiking boots or climbing a volcano in high heels.

James Lyon
LP Author, Australia

Packing

BACKPACK

When packing, it's important to realise that weight is just as important as bulk. Even if your pack is only half-full, if you have many heavy items it will be just as uncomfortable to carry as one that's bursting at the seams. Also try to have plenty of spare room in your pack when you depart – you'll certainly pick up extra clothes, souvenirs and other material on the road. Here are a few tips for packing your backpack:

- Try not to leave your packing until the night before you depart. Have a trial run, and spend a couple of hours toting your backpack around your local area. If you can't comfortably maintain the load for any length of time, then have a rethink about your selection of clothes and equipment.

- Pack your heaviest items as close to your spine as possible, preferably in the centre and top portions of the pack. This will prevent the pack pulling backwards at your shoulders.

- Remember that your pack is unlikely to be treated with kid gloves by others, particularly when you're travelling on planes. Pack to protect your belongings.

- Make the most of any compartments. Putting your sleeping bag, dirty clothes or other soft items in the bottom compartment will provide a soft, protective layer for other more fragile items. These items are also relatively light, allowing you to store heavier items higher in the pack.

- Use plastic bags to prevent water damage and also to compartmentalise your belongings for easier access.

- Keep any items with hard points or angles away from your back. Wrap them in clothes for your comfort and their protection.

- Give some thought to which items you'll need most regularly. Place these near the access points (eg side pockets) of the pack if possible.

DAY-PACK

After a few days sightseeing, you'll quickly work out what you want to regularly carry with you in your day-pack. Here's a list to start with:

- book, journal, postcards and pens
- camera and film

Floss It

For the cost of a crummy cigar, you can buy a vacation-saving item. It's called dental floss, and its uses are innumerable. Got a fishhook but no line? Four words: green waxed dental floss. Need to secure a mosquito net? Reach for the dental floss. Forgot to pack a clothesline? You're in luck if you've packed dental floss. Tear in your jeans, rip in your pack? A little dental floss and a sewing needle, and life goes on.

Dental floss comes in 50m and 100m lengths and is sold in nifty little cases complete with in-built cutters. It's cheap, it's light, it's strong and it's outrageously useful. Some say dental floss can even remove decay-causing material from between teeth and upper gums. Now in cinnamon, mint and grape flavours. No kidding.

Scott Doggett
LP Author, USA

- guidebook
- hat
- personal stereo
- pocketknife
- sunscreen
- sweater
- water bottle

Recording Your Trip
CAMERA

Few people are blasé enough to travel halfway around the world for the trip of a lifetime and not take a camera with them. Those amazing sights, rowdy nights, impossibly unpredictable situations and the people you meet will all demand to be photographed for posterity. And someone is bound to demand to see the photos when you get home.

But there is a case to be made for not taking one. Firstly, a camera costs a lot of money; and secondly, it can be a hassle on the road if you're constantly worrying about whether it gets stolen, lost or damaged. A camera can also come between you and the places you've travelled so far to enjoy. If you're constantly wondering if you should be taking a shot of a particular scene or are fumbling to get your camera out of your pack, you may not fully enjoy the sights for yourself.

If you're travelling with a friend you could consider sharing a camera, especially since you're likely to be taking photos of the same scenes.

If you decide to take a camera (as most people do), the one you choose will depend on the type of photos you want to take. If you plan to use your photos for professional purposes (see the Work & Travel section in the Planning chapter), or just want to take high-quality, creative shots, you'll need a single-lens reflex (SLR) camera. If you just want to take decent shots to show your friends and remember your trip by, you'll do fine with an automatic, point-and-shoot camera. If you're torn between the quality of an SLR and the convenience of a point-and-shoot camera, consider buying a high-quality compact with a built-in zoom; there are numerous models on the market.

Weight is another important consideration. SLRs and their lenses are heavy – usually several times the weight of point-and-shoot cameras – and take up a lot of luggage space. This can be a liability if you intend doing a lot of walking.

The more you spend on your camera, the more you'll worry about it on the road. A good SLR with a few decent lenses can cost upwards of US$1000. Having one along is almost like travelling with a child – when it's with you, you'll be worried about it; when it's not with you, you'll be twice as worried. A good insurance policy that covers the cost of your kit should allay these fears – after a while it's the used film, not the camera, that becomes priceless.

As well as the following information, check out the Photo.net Web site (www.photo.net/photo) for information on all aspects of photography.

SLR Cameras

The main advantage of an SLR camera is it allows you to take creative shots by shooting with the camera on its manual setting (perhaps using the built-in light meter as a guide). Many SLRs also have automatic settings, which are ideal for most situations but which can be fooled by unusual lighting or focusing situations. SLRs also allow you to use different lenses, thus vastly increasing your creative range. Some modern SLRs have lightweight plastic bodies, but these are significantly more fragile than those with metal bodies. If you've never used an SLR camera before, seriously consider whether you need one. If you decide you do, buy it well before you leave and learn how to use it.

With an SLR, you'll also need to consider the following:

Camera case − This will protect your camera and can be used to keep it handily outside your backpack. It doesn't need to be a full camera case − a compact case that goes into your day-pack will do the trick and be less conspicuous.

Lenses − Zooms save space and weight. A 24-100mm and an 80-200mm should be sufficient for most situations. If you prefer fixed lenses, you'll need three or four to cover the same situations.

Lint-free lens paper.

Silica gel packets − These will keep the moisture out of your film and equipment.

Skylight (UV) filters for each of your lenses − These protect your lenses and screen out excess ultraviolet light (which makes pictures look dull).

Spare camera battery (or batteries) − These are readily available in Europe, but you never know when you'll need one.

Point-and-Shoot Cameras

Point-and-shoot cameras take the worry out of travel photography. They also make shots of people or sudden experiences easier since they focus almost instantaneously. They're usually small enough to carry in your pocket, so you can whip them out for every Kodak moment. Point-and-shoot cameras range from cheap disposables to top-of-the-range models with precision lenses and a wide range of features. Since there are so many models on the market, it makes sense to ask at a trustworthy camera shop for a recommendation. A case will protect your camera and some silica gel will keep it moisture-free. You'll also need spare batteries and lint-free paper to clean the lens.

Film

Film is widely available in Europe but it's best to pick up supplies in the cities, particularly if you use slide or black-and-white film. Costs vary slightly from country to country, so if you see cheap film it may be worth stocking up (film in Scandinavia is expensive). Avoid buying film from tourist sites such as under the Eiffel Tower or on the Charles Bridge in Prague − it may have been poorly stored and will certainly be more expensive than in the shops. It's also worth picking up a few rolls duty-free at the airport before you arrive in Europe, although the selection of slide film is often limited.

Film comes as slide or print; colour or black and white; and fast or slow. If you have an SLR and professional aspirations, take slide film. Otherwise most people use colour print film, as it's cheaper, easier to have developed and the result is easier to view. Some people like the artistic effects they can achieve with black and white film, but you'll have trouble getting it developed on the road. You will achieve sharper results with slower film (around 100 ASA or lower), but you won't be able to use it in low light without a flash. With 400 ASA or higher you can shoot in much lower light (eg at dusk or on a very overcast day) without the need for a flash. In Britain and northern Europe, where the sky is often overcast, 200 to 400 ASA is preferable. In sunny southern Europe, go for 100 ASA. If the quality of your photographs is important, carry a range of different film speeds (note that the faster the film, the grainier the image).

Treatment of film is an important consideration. The sooner you expose your film after purchase the better. Heat can also damage film – a day in the hot glove compartment of a car is usually enough to fry a roll. Store your film in as cool a place as possible, and always out of direct sunlight.

When flying, always carry your film with you to protect it from the high-energy X-ray machines used in some airports to inspect checked-in baggage. The metal detectors used to check your carry-on baggage are usually film-safe. If you're concerned, simply take out your film and ask that it be hand-checked. To make this easier for the airport staff, you may want to store your film in a small bag or plastic container.

Developing Film

You should have film developed as soon as possible after exposing it to prevent deterioration, though in practice film lasts months in the canister without suffering. You can send process-paid slide film (eg Kodachrome) to your home country for developing. In any European city and most towns you'll find photo labs that will process your film in a couple of hours and the results will generally be every bit as good as you'd get at home. Costs vary from country to country, so check the price and if it seems a bit high, wait until you get to a cheaper country. Slide film (E6 processing) is trickier to get developed; most labs will have to send it away so you may have to wait a day or two before you can pick it up. Once you have the film developed, consider sending the slides or prints back home, as they will probably be destroyed after a few months sitting in your pack.

Photo Restrictions & Etiquette

Exercise some discretion with your camera as it can be an obtrusive. Apart from asking before taking close-up photos of people (see Avoiding Offence in the Issues & Attitudes chapter for advice on etiquette), avoid taking photos of military installations or soldiers in countries such as Turkey, or in the Balkans or Eastern Europe. If in doubt, ask someone. Many museums and galleries have a ban on photography or flash photography. Respect these rules as they are usually designed to protect fragile ancient frescoes and paintings from exposure to light (and sometimes to sell more postcards).

VIDEO

Video cameras can give a fascinating living record of your holiday that can never be captured on still film, and these days a high-quality video is no bigger than your average SLR camera. But the above drawbacks to carrying a camera apply even more to a video – they are very expensive, can be more obtrusive and are fragile pieces of equipment that must be well looked after.

Most of Europe uses the PAL (phase alternation line) system which is not compatible with the NTSC system used in North America and Japan. France (loving to be different) uses the incompatible SECAM system. Australia and New Zealand use the PAL system. Film is not always available, and you'll need a range of plug converters, plus a transformer, to recharge the batteries. If you decide that a video camera is worth having along, here are a few tips:

- As well as filming the obvious – sunsets, sights and spectacular views – remember to record some of the everyday details of life. Often the most interesting things occur when you're actually intent on filming something else.

- Remember that, unlike still photography, video 'flows'. This means you can shoot scenes of a winding road from the front window of a vehicle to give an overall impression that isn't possible with ordinary photos.

- Remember to follow the same rules regarding people's sensitivities as you would when taking photographs – having a video camera shoved in your face is probably even more annoying and offensive than a still camera. Always ask permission first.

- Video cameras have amazingly sensitive microphones, and you might be surprised by how much sound is picked up. This can be a problem if there is a lot of ambient noise – filming by the side of a busy road might seem OK when you do it, but viewing it back home might simply give you a deafening cacophony of traffic noise.

TRAVEL JOURNAL

Even if you've never kept a diary before it's amazing how inspired you'll be to put pen to paper when you start travelling. Apart from being bombarded by experiences, stories, people, sights and events, there will be plenty of times when you're alone with your thoughts – while waiting for a train or sitting on the beach or savouring the view from a mountain – and you'll want to write.

A travel journal doesn't have to be a daily account of what you did and saw, but an occasional record of your thoughts and experiences. The beauty of a travel journal is that it's not only a record of a remarkable episode in your life, but a time capsule of your thoughts, expectations and aspirations. In years to come you can revisit the person that you were, in a way unmatched by photographs. And, if you're blessed with good writing skills, a journal can serve as a blueprint for professional travel articles or books. There are plenty of good travel journals on the market, including a new one from Lonely Planet.

CASSETTE RECORDINGS

Apart from being a great way to send a long letter to friends and family without cramping your wrist, cassettes can provide you with an audio record of your trip. Professional dictaphones with miniature cassettes are compact, but cassettes won't be widely available outside cities.

Senior Travellers

You've worked hard all your life and now you're in retirement – what better way to pass some time than with travel? With an excellent transport infrastructure, and good accommodation, Europe is a very popular destination among senior travellers. Whether you're undertaking relaxed sightseeing in Rome, or walking the Pennine Way in Britain, if you're reasonably fit you can travel independently without too many problems. Alternatively, there are many organised tours catering to the senior market. Trafalgar Tours (www.trafalgartours.com) offers a range of European coach tours and Walking the World (www.walkingtheworld .com) is a US company specialising in outdoor adventure tours for over 50s.

DISCOUNTS

Senior travellers are entitled to many discounts in Europe, particularly on public transport, museum admission fees, public swimming pools, spas and guided tours. The minimum qualifying age is generally 60 or 65 for men and slightly younger for women, and you should always carry proof of age. Pension cards will also get you a discount.

For a small fee, European residents aged over 60 can get a Rail Europe Senior Card as an add-on to their national rail senior pass. It entitles the holder to reduced European fares.

From your home country you may be entitled to all sorts of interesting travel packages and discounts (on car hire, for instance) through organisations and travel agents that cater for senior travellers. Start hunting at your local senior citizens advice bureau.

Tips for Senior Travellers

- Travel as lightly as possible. You can buy almost anything you need on the road.
- Research your trip thoroughly. A good guidebook will have a special section for senior travellers listing the difficulties and facilities of the country you intend to visit. The Internet is still a little short on information for seniors, but see what you can find.
- Try to do most of your sightseeing and local travel during off-peak periods, as negotiating streets and public transport during busy times can be a nightmare.
- Be prepared for long journeys. If you can, take trains (which are more comfortable and safer) instead of buses. Bring a pillow if you have a bad back and find out if there are toilets on board.
- Be flexible. If you find that your original itinerary was too ambitious, don't be afraid to change it.
- You may want to start your travels in a country that is easier to travel around, such as England or France, before tackling a country like Croatia or Turkey.
- Don't be afraid to give things a try. You'll be surprised what you can do in Europe, and a little effort and enthusiasm can go a long way.

HEALTH CONSIDERATIONS

Travel can be taxing at the best of times, so it pays to give some thought to your level of fitness and health before setting out. It's a good idea to arrange a full physical examination in your home country. Unless you're joining a full-on organised tour, you'll do a lot of walking – so get some miles in before you depart to strengthen those leg muscles. Be aware of the likely weather conditions for the time of year you plan to travel – parts of Europe can get extremely cold in winter. As with any traveller, a good travel/health insurance policy is essential. Most prescription medication is easily obtainable in Europe, but if you are on a particular medication, you may want to bring enough to last the entire trip (be sure to bring the proper documentation, such as prescription slips, so you don't have any problems at customs).

Gay & Lesbian Travellers

Europe offers some of the world's best (and possibly worst) travel experiences for gay and lesbian visitors. There are lively and open gay and lesbian scenes in Scandinavia and most of Western Europe, while in parts of Eastern Europe and southern Europe the situation is underground and it's harder to make contact.

Gay and lesbian travellers are unlikely to encounter serious difficulties anywhere in Europe. However, public displays of same-sex affection are frowned upon or greeted with open curiosity in some countries, particularly outside major cities. Hostility towards gays is not unheard of, even in supposedly tolerant countries such as Britain and Germany – use discretion and common sense when in public and you're unlikely to run into any trouble. Also, while hand-holding between men is a common display of friendship in parts of southern Europe, women walking around hand in hand might draw puzzled stares.

Whatever country you're in, the capital city is usually the best place to plug into the local gay and lesbian community. Most cities have a club or organisation catering to gays and lesbians and often you'll find nightclubs, bars and cafes that are either exclusively gay and lesbian or frequented by gays and lesbians. Most cities have gay publications (such as *The Pink Paper* and *Gay Times* in London) with local contacts and nightlife listings.

LAWS

Homosexuality is legal, except in Romania and northern Cyprus. In some countries homosexuality has only recently been legalised (Albania passed a law in 1995 and Ireland decriminalised homosexuality in 1993) and official attitudes remain highly conservative. Bulgaria allows homosexuality 'provided it does not cause public scandal or entice others to perversity'! In Turkey, homosexuality is legally frowned upon – while not strictly illegal, laws banning 'lewd behaviour' are often used to suppress it. The age of consent for homosexuals varies from country to country, from as young as 14 (Iceland) to 21 (Bulgaria).

Denmark, Greenland, Hungary, Iceland, Norway and Sweden allow gay and lesbian couples to form 'registered partnerships' that grant the rights of matrimony except church weddings, adoption and artificial-insemination services.

GAY-FRIENDLY COUNTRIES

Northern Europe is generally more liberal than southern Europe, which is more liberal than Eastern Europe. The Netherlands and Denmark are probably two of the most tolerant countries in the world for gay men and lesbians, while Romania, Lithuania and Turkey are among the least tolerant.

But it's not so much which countries are gay-friendly, as which cities. Some of the best gay cities in the world are in Europe: London, Amsterdam, Berlin (home of the gay liberation movement, begun 100 years ago) and Paris. Other major gay centres are Copenhagen, Manchester and Barcelona, plus the resort of Sitges (south-west of Barcelona), and the Greek islands of Mykonos and Lesvos.

Many capital cities have a Gay Pride March and festival, usually on the last weekend in June. Berlin's 'Love Parade' is probably the biggest in Europe.

RESOURCES

A good guidebook will give contact details for the main gay and lesbian organisations in each country and should have special listings of meeting places and tolerant hotels. The *Spartacus International Gay Guide* (Bruno Gmünder, Berlin) is a good male-only international directory of gay entertainment venues in Europe and elsewhere. For lesbians, *Women's Travel in Your Pocket* (Ferrari Publications, London) is a good international guide.

In the larger cities, some English-language newspapers and magazines carry listings for gay and lesbian organisations and meeting places.

Internet resources include:

Queer Resources Directory
www.qrd.org
(a lot of the general information here is outdated but it has links to every country in Europe)

Copenhagen Gay Life
www.copenhagen-gay-life.dk
(find out what's going on in one of Europe's hottest gay cities)

Travellers with a Disability

Travel, by its very nature, provides its share of problems for people with disabilities. But much of Europe is very well equipped to deal with disabled people and in less developed areas you'll find the local people willing to help you out.

The first thing you should do is contact your national support organisation (see Resources later). It may have a travel department that can help with specific countries you plan to visit. They often have complete libraries devoted to travel, and can put you in touch with travel agents who specialise in tours for the disabled. Another good source of information is the national tourist offices of the countries you intend to visit. They will be able to put you in touch with local support organisations and may well have booklets indicating hotels and public transport services that cater to disabled people. If you're travelling independently, the easiest option is to hire a car and travel with a partner or friend.

105

ACCESSIBILITY

Scandinavia leads the world in terms of facilities for disabled people. For instance, by law every new restaurant in Finland must have a special toilet for the handicapped. There are wheelchair ramps to practically all public buildings, and most department stores, shopping centres and many private shops and some train carriages are fitted with special lifts for wheelchairs. Some city buses are also accessible by wheelchair. The picture is similar in most of Western Europe: countries such as Germany, Austria, Switzerland and the Netherlands are highly user-friendly. As well as ramps in public buildings to assist people, train timetables are often published in braille and special hearing loops are provided in banks and ticket offices. France, Britain and Belgium are moving forward but many hotels, guesthouses and buses are still difficult to access.

It's a different story in Eastern Europe and parts of southern Europe, though things are slowly improving. Perhaps the most restrictive places are countries such as Estonia, Romania and Poland where there are few facilities for the disabled, streets are cobbled or uneven and hotels may lack lifts. In Greece it's tough enough for able-bodied people to negotiate the terrain around ancient sights, let alone someone in a wheelchair.

Spain, Portugal and Italy are not as difficult to get around, though you may find budget hotels and city transport lack wheelchair access.

RESOURCES

A good guidebook should list support organisations in each country that you intend to visit, but your best bet is to contact your home organisation.

Tips for Travellers with Disabilities

- Research the specific challenges and facilities for disabled travellers in the country you'd like to visit. A good guidebook will have a section on travel for people with disabilities and will give contact numbers for local organisations that can assist. The Internet is useful for researching your trip (see the Resources section in this chapter).
- Consider travelling with a companion who can help with day-to-day affairs and arrange for assistance if necessary.
- Consider travelling to one of Europe's more accessible countries, such as France or Germany, before tackling a more challenging one like Albania.
- Depending upon the nature of your disability, you may want to bring a folding stool to use in squat toilets.
- Don't be afraid to ask locals for assistance. People are usually more than willing to help out. If someone is particularly helpful, give them a tip.
- Don't be afraid to try new things. You'd be surprised what you can do with a little imagination and improvisation.
- Don't feel that you have to travel as a part of a group tour. It is quite possible to travel independently and this can be far more rewarding.
- Consider hiring a private car for sightseeing. You may want to hire a personal assistant for some parts of your travel.
  - Ask for ground floor rooms in hotels.

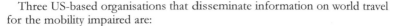
Three US-based organisations that disseminate information on world travel for the mobility impaired are:

Access Foundation
(☎ 01-516-887 5798) PO Box 356, Malverne, NY 11565
Mobility International USA
(☎ 01-541-343 1284, www.miusa.org) PO Box 10767, Eugene, OR 97440
Society for the Advancement of Travel for the Handicapped
(SATH; ☎ 01-718-858 5483, http://ath.org/index.html) 26 Court St, Brooklyn, NY 11242

Abilities magazine (☎ 01-416-766 9188, fax 762 8716), PO Box 527, Station P, Toronto, Ont, Canada M5S 2T1, carries a column called 'Accessible Planet', which offers tips on foreign travel for people with disabilities.

The Global Access Web site (www.geocities.com/Paris/1052) has lots of information for travellers with disabilities, as well as links to related sites.

In the UK, the Royal Association for Disability & Rehabilitation (RADAR; ☎ 020-7250 3222, fax 7250 0212, www.radar.org.uk), 12 City Forum, 250 City Rd, London EC1V 8AF, produces three holiday fact packs (costing UK£2 each) which cover planning, insurance and useful organisations, transport and equipment, and specialised accommodation. RADAR also produces the useful *European Holidays & Travel Abroad: A Guide for Disabled People* (UK£5), which gives a good overview of facilities available to disabled travellers in Western Europe, and a guide to places further afield called *Long-Haul Holidays* (in odd-numbered years). *Accessible Holidays in the British Isles* (£7.50) also includes Ireland.

Australians and New Zealanders can contact the National Information Communication Awareness Network (NICAN; ☎ 02-6285 3713, fax 6285 3714, www.nican.com.au), PO Box 407, Curtin, ACT 2605.

Travelling with Children

Travel with children can be difficult in any part of the world. It can also be tremendously rewarding, both for you and your children. The difficulties you will encounter in Europe are pretty similar to those you would encounter going on a trip in your own country: boredom on long journeys, inadequate facilities for children and the need to keep the tykes constantly entertained, especially if you're traipsing through museums and churches. You shouldn't have any particular health problems with children in Europe, nor should you have trouble finding appropriate foods – a fast-food outlet is never far away if they tire of the local cuisine. Youth hostels in Europe generally welcome children (HI places in Bavaria actually *prefer* them), so you should have little trouble finding accommodation.

Successful travel with young children requires planning and effort. Don't try to overdo things and make sure the activities include the kids as well – balance that day at the Louvre with a day at Disneyland Paris. Include children in the trip planning; if they've helped to work out where you will be going, they will be much more interested when they get there.

Most car-rental firms in Europe have children's safety seats for hire at a nominal cost, but it's essential that you book them in advance. The same goes for highchairs and cots (cribs): they're standard in most restaurants and hotels, but numbers are limited. The choice of baby food, formulas, soy and cow's milk, disposable nappies (diapers) and the like is as great in the supermarkets of most European countries as it is at home, but the opening hours might be different – run out of nappies on Saturday afternoon and you're in for a messy weekend.

Most tourist sights, hotels and public transport services have a reduced rate for children under 16, and children under four or five often travel for free.

CHILD-FRIENDLY PLACES

Most of Europe is very child-friendly. You can usually find public parks for kids, even in the middle of cities, and commercial facilities are numerous. In many parts of Europe, domestic tourism is largely dictated by children's needs, particularly in summer, so there are theme parks, water parks, circuses and so on. Many museums have a children's section with toys and activities, or 'hands on' displays. This is certainly true of Scandinavia and Western Europe.

In Italy and Greece, the islands and beaches will be appealing to children and you might be surprised how much they enjoy exploring ancient ruins.

Travelling with your offspring in Eastern Europe and southern Europe can be more tiring than elsewhere – public transport tends to be slower and more crowded, and accommodation and restaurant facilities are often of a lower standard. However, these regions are very family orientated and the locals love kids, so you'll be well received wherever you go.

RESOURCES

Check out the good Travellers Medical and Vaccination Centre site (www.tmvc .com.au/info7.html) for health tips. For an in-depth look at the issues, get your hands on Lonely Planet's *Travel with Children*.

Tips for Travel with Children

- Consider travelling in an easier country such as Germany before heading to a more difficult one such as Albania. This will give you an idea of how your children hold up to the stresses of travel.
- Bring your children's favourite toys and games to keep them amused on long rides.
- Buses can be very overcrowded and often move at excessive speeds. It's best to take trains or taxis instead.
- Children are particularly vulnerable to food-borne illnesses. Be careful about what your children eat.
- Bring wide-brimmed hats and plenty of sunscreen. Sunglasses are also a good idea to protect the eyes from glare and dust.
- Make sure your child is fully immunised for the countries you plan to visit.
- If your children are old enough, consider getting a language cassette. Helping them learn greetings and a few other words of the local language, which they can practise while travelling, can considerably enliven and enrich a journey.
- Children's multivitamins can be a useful supplement to their diet on the road. Seek advice from your paediatrician.

TAKEOFF

You've saved the money, researched your route, packed your bags, said goodbye to your friends and family; now you're ready for the best part – the trip itself. Before you start cruising around Europe, however, there is one last hurdle to clear: the long flight there. This chapter provides some tips for dealing with the organised chaos of airports, the formalities of reconfirming your ticket and the intricacies of customs and immigration.

Before You Fly

Ideally, the following should be taken care of well before the day of your flight.

SPECIAL NEEDS & REQUESTS

If you have special needs of any sort – a broken leg, you're vegetarian, travelling in a wheelchair, taking the baby, terrified of flying – you should let the airline know as soon as possible so they can make arrangements. Remind the airline when you reconfirm your booking, and again when you check in at the airport. It may be worth ringing several airlines to find out how each can handle your particular needs. Airports and airlines can be extremely helpful with a little advance notice.

Most international airports will have ramps and lifts, and accessible toilets and phones for wheelchair-bound passengers. Most will also provide an escort from the check-in desk to the plane if needed. Aircraft toilets, however, are likely to present a problem; you should discuss this with the airline at an early stage. Guide dogs will often have to travel away from their owner in a specially pressurised baggage compartment with other animals, although smaller guide dogs may be admitted to the cabin. All guide dogs will be subject to quarantine laws (such as six months in isolation) when entering or returning to countries currently free of rabies, including the UK, Japan and Australia. Deaf travellers can ask for airport and in-flight announcements to be written down.

Children under two generally travel for 10% of the standard fare (free of charge on some airlines) if they don't occupy a seat, but they don't get a baggage allowance. Skycots, which will take a child up to about 10kg, should be provided if requested in advance. Children aged between two and 12 can usually occupy a seat for half to two-thirds of the full fare, and do get a baggage allowance. Pushchairs can often be taken aboard as hand luggage.

RECONFIRMING YOUR FLIGHT

Don't assume that just because you have a ticket, you're on the plane. Most airlines require that you reconfirm your international flight at least 72 hours prior to departure, though to be on the safe side it's worth reconfirming between three and five days beforehand, and even reconfirming twice. Some airlines or travel agents will tell you not to worry about reconfirming, but you should do it anyway.

You may be given a number when you reconfirm. This is proof that you reconfirmed, and will be useful for getting a refund or a new ticket if for some reason you are bumped from your flight (see the Glossary at the end of this book for details on this and other air travel terminology). A few airlines will allow you to make a seat selection when you reconfirm, so ask if this is possible. If you have any dietary restrictions or preferences, this is the best time to remind the airline.

CARRY-ON LUGGAGE

Your carry-on luggage should contain all your breakable and valuable belongings – luggage handlers are not generally known for their care and attention. A 5kg weight limit is enforced by many airlines, but most day-packs will meet this criteria. If you exceed the limit, you will probably have to transfer some items to your main luggage. The following is a list of standard items to consider carrying with you on the plane:

- A bottle of water. The air in the cabin can be very dry and you can't always rely on cabin crew to keep you supplied with drinks. Moisturiser is also a good idea.
- Any medication you take regularly, plus aspirin or paracetamol for headaches, and cough drops.
- A pen for filling in immigration and customs forms.
- Basic toiletries.
- Earplugs in case you have difficulty sleeping.
- Exposed and unexposed film. Your main luggage will receive a higher dose of X-rays, which could spoil your film.
- Fragile electronic equipment such as camera, personal stereo, alarm clock or binoculars, plus your pocketknife.
- Games, novel, guidebook, travel journal or whatever else you need to keep yourself entertained.
- Passport, tickets, insurance papers, identification and money should be with you at all times, preferably in your moneybelt.
- Something warm for your torso and feet, as the cabin can get quite cool. Light blankets are supplied on international flights.

DUTY-FREE ALLOWANCES

Most countries allow you to import 200 cigarettes (or an equivalent amount of other tobacco products) and 1L of liquor without paying duty (import tax), although some countries allow twice this amount. You will have to pay duty on arrival on anything that exceeds these limits, or the items may be confiscated. There are no longer duty-free sales between EU countries, so if you land in Italy, then fly to London, you will not be able to buy duty-free on the second leg.

All countries in Europe prohibit the import of firearms and ammunition, narcotics, pornography and fireworks.

If you have to bring medication with you, be sure to have a note from your doctor explaining why you need it, and the original prescription slip. Some countries have particular rules – Greece, for instance, will not allow codeine (a common painkiller) without a doctor's certificate.

Buying Duty-Free

Once you've cleared customs and immigration, you'll have the chance to indulge in some last-minute buying in the duty-free shops. Possible purchases include liquor, cigarettes, perfume and electronic goods. You can also do some duty-free shopping on board the plane, though the prices on most airlines are nothing special. Watch that you don't exceed the duty-free allowances of the country to which you're heading.

Departure Day

A lot of the following may seem obvious, but you'd be surprised what you can forget in the frenzied moments leading up to departure. You could even use these sections as a predeparture checklist.

DRESSING FOR YOUR DESTINATION

If you're travelling long-haul to Europe (from Australia, New Zealand or South Africa) bear in mind that you'll be arriving in the opposite season. This will be most noticeable if your departure is right in the middle of summer or winter but it's still not a big deal – you can always do a quick change in the airport on arrival and Europe's weather is rarely predictable enough to dress appropriately for, anyway!

It's more important to dress comfortably for the flight. Loose-fitting clothing is best but make sure you have something warm, particularly at night. A decent pair of socks will allow you to take off your shoes without freezing

---

Flight Day Checklist

- Make sure you have your house key for when you return.
- Make sure you've reconfirmed your flight (better late than never).
- Turn off the gas and electricity in your home.

Check that you have the following essentials:

- address book
- backpack
- camera
- day-pack
- medications you might need
- moneybelt (with all your credit cards, travellers cheques, cash)
- passport
- plane ticket
- visas you've already received
- wallet/purse

---

your feet. If it's likely to be very cold when you arrive, remember to take a jacket on board with you.

BEING ON TIME

You'd be surprised how many people somehow contrive to be late for their flight, often from being stuck on the freeway in a traffic jam. Some cities seem to organise nonstop traffic jams around their airports specifically for this purpose. If possible, take a train; if you're travelling by road, leave plenty of extra time.

The airline will probably tell you to arrive at least two hours prior to departure. Even if you are still reeling from the previous night's going-away party, heed this advice. Dashing around with heavy bags at the last minute is highly stressful and you'd be surprised how quickly those two hours evaporate. Having all your bags packed the night before is a huge help.

NAVIGATING THE AIRPORT

Packed with people, cluttered with luggage, and riddled with endless departure and arrival gates, airports can be confusing places. Luckily, most display plenty of signs indicating where to head for check-in and pointing you on to immigration and your departure gate. If you do get lost, don't waste time trying to figure things out – ask someone. Many large airports have information desks where you can pick up a floorplan or airport map.

READY MONEY

It's a good idea to change some money before you leave, though airports at most major European gateway cities have 24-hour exchange booths. You can do this at a local bank, or at the airport on the day of your flight. Change just enough to get to your hotel and to pay for the first night's accommodation and dinner, as the rate of exchange will usually be better when you get there.

CHECK-IN

Once you've arrived at the airport, make your way to the international departure terminal and the check-in counter of your airline. Make sure you've tagged your backpack with your name, address, telephone number, airline and flight number. You may want to add a contact address in the country you're headed to. Prepare your backpack for the baggage handlers by tying all pieces of loose webbing, closing all pockets securely, placing all liquids (like shampoo) in plastic bags and making sure your film and camera are in your day-pack.

You'll need both your passport and ticket on hand for check-in. At this time, you'll be asked to make your seat selection (see Best Seats later) and you should remind the airline of any dietary preferences. The agent will then issue your boarding pass.

Also make sure the agent places the appropriate destination tag on each piece of luggage. If you are changing flights en route, ask whether you must collect and recheck your bags yourself. Finally, take your baggage claim slip (this may be attached to your ticket) and you're off.

Best Seats

Unless you're flying business or 1st class, you'll have to fight it out in economy (also known as cattle class for obvious reasons). To make your flight a little more comfortable, try asking for an exit row seat. These seats are usually above the wing and have twice the legroom of normal economy class seats, though they are often next to the service area, so they can be noisy.

The next best choices are aisle seats (which give you room to stretch your legs and easy access to the bathroom) or window seats (if you like to view the scenery). Often, however, these seats will be taken, and you'll find yourself in the middle of a row between a screaming child and a talkative insurance salesman. If this happens, order a beer and call for the earplugs.

INSPECTION & IMMIGRATION

Inspections for departing passengers are usually brief. Your bag will be X-rayed and you will have to walk through a metal detector which invariably seems to go off with a shrill beep. It's usually keys, coins, a belt buckle or something similarly harmless. Things you cannot take on board include weapons, spray cans, explosives and other flammable substances (including lighters). Anything that looks like a weapon will be given close scrutiny. But pocketknives are usually OK.

Immigration formalities are similarly brief when leaving your home country. Usually, the inspector will simply look at your passport and wave you through, and possibly place a departure stamp in your passport.

Surviving the Flight

While some people look on flying as a necessary evil of travel, others see it as a great adventure. In any case, the flight needn't be a claustrophobic endurance test. This section outlines some ways to help the time pass a little more quickly and comfortably. For a list of items to bring with you on the flight, see Carry-On Luggage earlier in this chapter.

ALCOHOL

International flights are a little like wedding receptions – the booze is usually free and plentiful. But drinking too much during the flight can be a very bad idea. The atmosphere inside the cabin will be very dry, and consuming alcohol will hasten the dehydration you are already suffering just by breathing. Worse still, you may end up with a raging hangover halfway through the flight or on landing. If you're going to drink (as most do), it's a good iodea to alternate your drinks with plain water.

SLEEP

Trying to sleep on a plane is not much different to trying to sleep on a bus. Some find it easy to nod off, others find it impossible. You'll be given a pillow and blanket and your seat will recline to about 45°, but that's about the only concessions to comfort. If you can't sleep you'll need something to keep you from going insane – a good book, your language tapes, the in-flight magazine, or the in-flight movies (which often run virtually nonstop).

Sleeping pills aren't a good way to help you sleep on a flight; they may leave you feeling groggy at the other end and make arriving in a strange city difficult.

THE BEST MEALS

Airline food is a favourite subject of ridicule among travellers. Still, you can generally get a decent meal if you know what to ask for. Many travellers request vegetarian or vegan meals because these are often better prepared than regular meals (though there are some glaring exceptions to this). Some travellers go one step further and request Hindu meals, which are often delicious. You will have to request special meals when you book your flight, and again when you reconfirm. The nationality of the airline you fly with will have a bearing on the type of food served – usually it's something resembling that country's cuisine (well, usually it's something resembling food …).

TRANSIT BREAKS

Many airports have facilities to help you pass lengthy transit breaks as agreeably as possible. There may be a day room where you can take a nap or shower, and decent restaurants or cafes offering a civilised (but expensive) bite to eat. Ask at the airport information counter; probably anything's better than sitting on the floor watching the minute hand slowly moving round.

SCARED OF FLYING?

If you've flown before and found the experience unsettling or worse, or have never flown and suspect that you'll suffer from fear of flying, there are some

---

Stay Away from the Prawns!

Call me crazy, but I love airline food. I'd hardly call anything served on a plane 'gourmet', but it's the great sense of anticipation; the ritual of opening all those plastic containers and peeling back the foil on the lukewarm main meal to see what surprising morsels await. Even when I think I'm not hungry, the sight of the meal trolley trundling down the aisle is enough to make me start salivating Homer Simpson-style (the food service always starts at least 10 rows away). When it arrives you usually have the choice of chicken or fish, or perhaps an ethnic dish. Chicken's always a safe bet. The fish is a real lottery. As well as the main plastic box, there'll be a secondary box containing an entree or a pathetic salad, another with a mysterious-looking dessert or some cubes of fruit, some individually wrapped crackers and cheese (a highlight), a bread roll, butter, orange juice, a coffee cup … just like being in hospital! Which brings me to an important point. A friend of mine, on his first long-haul flight (with an airline that will remain nameless), was reckless with his food selection, choosing the prawn cocktail. A day after touchdown he was rushed to a London hospital suffering severe stomach cramps and nausea, was diagnosed with salmonella poisoning and proceeded to spend the first week of his holiday on a drip! When he was well enough to eat, it was back to 'airline' food. And his first meal? Tandoori chicken.

Paul Harding
LP Author, Australia

steps you can take to make the flight as painless as possible. First, if you are really terrified of flying, seek out the appropriate counselling before travelling, rather than trying to overcome your fear by yourself.

If you suffer from only mild fear of flying, try to prepare yourself mentally for the flight before boarding. Some people find that aisle seats are more relaxing than window seats, others vice versa. Whatever the case, make sure you ask for the seat which allows you to feel most comfortable.

Attempting to drown your fears with alcohol is not a good idea as you will merely be replacing an unpleasant mental condition with an unpleasant physical one. If you feel that you might need something to calm your nerves, speak to your doctor beforehand about getting a mild tranquilliser prescribed.

Finally, some turbulence during the flight is nothing to worry about. Veteran pilots point out that planes can withstand infinitely more stress than most people imagine. While it may be disconcerting, you probably have more to fear from the mystery meat in your dinner than from the shaking of the wings.

TOUCHDOWN

▶▶

If you're coming from the east coast of North America, your flight to Europe won't be overly long and exhausting. Coming from the west coast or from the southern hemisphere, you will have endured a lengthy flight. Either way (with the exception of South Africans) you'll have crossed numerous time zones and will probably emerge in a strange city tired and disorientated. But this is also one of the most exciting parts of your trip, so take it easy, get through the airport formalities and prepare to savour new experiences.

Immigration

On arrival you'll have to take care of passport formalities before collecting your baggage and proceeding through customs. Usually you'll be given an embarkation/disembarkation card and a customs form to fill out on the plane, or you can pick these forms up in the immigration hall. The disembarkation card goes to the immigration officer upon arrival. For information on items you may have to declare on your customs form, see the Duty-Free Allowances section in the Takeoff chapter.

Immigration formalities usually take very little time, as long as your passport is in order and contains any visas you were required to get before arrival. Immigration authorities in some countries (such as Britain) are getting tougher on people they suspect might outstay their visa or work illegally; dress neatly and carry proof that you have sufficient funds to support yourself. A credit card and/or an onward ticket will help. Even travellers with a two year working holiday visa have been refused entry because they happened to be carrying papers (like references) that suggested they intended to work in a professional capacity.

After handing over your passport to immigration, you may be asked a few simple questions, such as how long you intend to stay in the country, and what is the purpose of your visit.

BAGGAGE COLLECTION

Once you've passed through immigration, you're free to collect your baggage from the luggage carousel. Monitors in the baggage collection area will tell you which baggage conveyor corresponds to your flight. Your backpack may take a while to appear: be patient and don't panic. If the worst happens, and your baggage does not materialise, report the problem to the baggage office. Fortunately, baggage loss is fairly rare, but it does happen and this is where clearly labelled baggage tags will help.

CUSTOMS

At customs you will probably have to choose the green channel (no goods to declare) or the red channel (goods to declare). If you choose the green channel you can stroll straight through, but of course there are regular random baggage checks. This is routine and nothing to worry about – the inspector will ask you to open your bags and do a cursory check. Drug sniffer dogs are also occasionally used in airports – never try to enter any country with illegal drugs of any sort.

If you go through the red channel you'll be required to show what it is you're declaring and you may be asked to pay excess duty if you've bought too much duty-free. The inspectors will generally have a quick riffle through your bags for good measure.

On Your Way

Once you've collected your luggage and you're out in the arrivals hall, sit down, take stock and make sure you have everything. Check your backpack and day-pack, and make sure your passport and other documents are securely tucked away in your moneybelt.

If you didn't change money before setting out, you can do this at an exchange booth or bank in the arrivals hall. In some countries, you get a poor exchange rate at the airport, in others the rate is as good as in town. If you have the right cards there are also ATMs in most airports (see the Money Matters chapter). Try to change enough for the first couple of nights, especially if you arrive on a Friday or a weekend when the banks will be closed. Also be sure to get some small bills (useful for public transport fares).

LEFT LUGGAGE

The left-luggage facilities at the airport will allow you to leave your bags in safe storage to pick up when you depart. This can be handy if you're alone and have to spend a few hours waiting at the airport, or if you're making a brief stopover and want to explore the city unencumbered.

Left luggage can be fairly expensive, so it's really not worth leaving your luggage there overnight.

GETTING INTO TOWN

If you need information on how to get from the airport to your hotel, or to a part of town where you can look for accommodation, try the public information counter in the arrivals lobby. It's a good idea to research local transport options in your guidebook before setting out, so that you have a good idea of the cost of taxis or buses.

Most European airports – especially in the larger cities – are located well outside the city centre, so a taxi ride will be too exorbitant for most budget travellers unless you can split it between a group. Fortunately, almost all airports are linked to the city centre by frequent and efficient public transport (usually bus and train). London's Heathrow airport, for instance, has a tube station accessible from each terminal from which you can get into the heart of central London in about an hour, as well as the new Heathrow Express rail link that can whisk you to Paddington station in just 20 minutes. Airports in Paris and Frankfurt are also connected by metro to the city centre. Buses are another option. Many airports or national airlines run buses into the city (these are sometimes free if you flew with the national carrier), or you can catch normal city buses that call in at the airport.

If you take a bus or train, make sure you're familiar with where it stops and where you want to get off, particularly if you've got prebooked accommodation. Your guidebook will help here, or you could phone your hostel or hotel from the airport and ask for directions – when you get off the bus or emerge from the underground station onto a crowded street, it helps to know where you're going.

Your First Night

Ideally, you already know where you want to spend your first night in Europe – if not the exact hostel or hotel, at least the general area. If you haven't prebooked your first night's accommodation, your best bet is to consult your guidebook and make a few phone calls from the arrivals hall of the airport. This way you can find out if there is a bed or room available, check current prices and any other details you need to know, and ask directions. If you ring a few places and they're all full, don't panic – there are plenty more, even if you have to pay a bit more than you'd like. Often the airport will have an accommodation booking desk that can help, though they usually deal with mid-range and top-end hotels.

For your first few days in the city, it's nice to be in the thick of things – close to the sights – and popular budget accommodation will often be found within walking distance of the city centre. In some cities, such as Berlin, the few convenient hostels fill up fast and need to be booked well in advance in summer.

If the worst comes to the worst and you arrive late at night (or very early in the morning) without a clue where to stay, you can either stay in the airport until morning (use the luggage lockers to secure your baggage), or use your credit card for a room at the airport hotel.

Coping with Jet Lag

What day is it today? Did I leave home this morning or yesterday morning? Why am I wide awake at 3 am? These are the sorts of questions you might be asking yourself the night you arrive and for your first few days in Europe. Or you might find yourself falling asleep at 4 pm the first few days. For some travellers jet lag is a mild inconvenience, but for others it can be quite unpleasant and disorientating.

Jet lag is caused by the discrepancy between your body clock (which is in tune with the day/night cycle of your home country) and the day/night cycle of the country in which you've just landed. Within a few days of arrival, your body clock will fall into sync with the local day/night cycle. Until this occurs, you may find yourself prowling your room in the wee hours and feeling groggy at high noon.

There's not a lot you can do to prevent jet lag. Try to get your body into its new time cycle by going to bed in the evening and waking up in the morning, just as locals do. The longer you stick to napping during the afternoon and staying up all night, the longer you'll suffer from jet lag.

Some travellers use sleeping tablets to help them sleep on their first night. Other travellers report that melatonin works (available from health-food shops). Still others rely on the tried-and-true method of a glass of warm milk and a good book. Following are a few more tips for dealing with jet lag:

- Avoid drinking alcohol while you're on the plane and during your first few days in the country. As unlikely as this scenario might seem to some, a hangover only makes jet lag worse.
- Try to rest as much as possible before your departure.
- Avoid overeating, especially fatty foods, as these will make you feel bloated and slow you down, thus adding to the feeling of jet lag.

ISSUES & ATTITUDES ▶▶

Most of Europe is very much a modern western society, so it's unlikely you'll suffer the sort of culture shock or be affected by affronting issues of poverty and begging that you might encounter in developing countries.

But there are exceptions, and it would be a mistake to arrive expecting everything to be just like home. Europe is a real melting pot of cultures, lifestyles, religions, standards of living and political leanings. Despite the EU and the move towards a common currency, each country is unique, shaped by history, language and customs – which is what makes travelling on the continent so interesting. There are also inherent dangers in travelling that you should be aware of.

This chapter covers some important issues such as avoiding offence and protecting yourself and your gear from scam artists and thieves. We also cover the issue of ecotourism. Used wisely, the information in this chapter will be handier than your Swiss Army pocketknife and will ensure that your trip is a good and a safe one.

Culture Shock

Culture shock describes the confusion and disorientation travellers feel when they are exposed to new environments. The culture throughout most of Europe is likely to be similar to your own (broadly described as 'western'), so culture shock is not going to be a big problem, even for first-time travellers. Any depression you might suffer in the first few days is most likely to be homesickness!

Still, you will probably be faced with a strange language (except in Britain and Ireland), crowded cities with unfamiliar transport systems and perhaps unusual food. And if your first experience of the continent is in Eastern Europe or parts of southern Europe (including Turkey), you may encounter strange local customs, conservative attitudes and elements of poverty. Although not recommended at the time of writing, if you venture into the war-ravaged Balkans (parts of Bosnia, Croatia or Albania) you will almost certainly find destruction and upheaval that would shock anyone. (See the country profiles for more information on travelling in these areas.)

The impact of culture shock will vary, depending on your previous cross-cultural experiences, your language proficiency and your prearrival knowledge of the new culture. If you're feeling stressed out by a lack of anything familiar, take time to ease yourself into the travel experience; catch up on your sleep (on top of everything else, you're probably jet lagged) and don't try to cram in too much sightseeing in your first few days. The best advice is to start your trip in an 'easy' country such as Britain, and to travel with a friend or with other travellers you've hooked up with.

POVERTY & BEGGING

Poverty is certainly not confined to developing countries, but you probably won't be affected by it much while travelling in Europe. Parts of former Communist Eastern Europe are very poor though and, as a western tourist, you will often be viewed as being very wealthy.

Like anywhere else in the world, beggars can be found all over Europe, from homeless men in London's tube stations to Romanian women cradling babies

---

Bosnia: Expect the Unexpected

Bosnia isn't exactly the place where one expects to find a helping hand. Roofless houses, NATO troops, landmines and other assorted scars of war far outnumber tourists or semblances of civil society. But Bosnia also is a haven for the unexpected – and so I found, in a quaint old Turkish town called Travnik.

Travnik, the seat of Bosnia's 18th century Turkish viziers, lies about a two hour bus ride from Sarajevo along winding roads. The centrepiece of the town, high on a hill overlooking the valley, is an ancient medieval fort. This fort was spared from the fighting that ravaged Bosnia.

Bosnia's 'sights' fill me with intrinsic wariness. Why? Every piece of grass in Bosnia is at risk for mines. So when I paid the old crone guarding the entrance one Deutschmark for admission, I self-consciously inquired, *'Ima li mine?'* (Are there mines?). When the answer came back, *'Nema mine'*, I gingerly stepped in.

It was a beautiful day – the spring sun danced over the fresh grass, and I had a fantastic view of Travnik's beautiful setting. I luxuriated in the solitude, away from the pandemonium of the bus station or the market. But all of a sudden, from behind me, I unexpectedly heard a voice. 'Can you take a picture of us?' said a young, black-haired Bosnian woman, in perfect English, standing beside her tall, lanky companion.

I was doubly startled – first to have my solitude interrupted, and second to be addressed in English. (Not that I look Bosnian, but still …) I gladly took the photo, and soon we fell to talking.

The young woman, Zaggie, turned out to be an interpreter for the NATO troops, as was her companion. He was stationed in Travnik, but she was in Banja Luka – the next town on my itinerary. Within a few minutes of our acquaintance, Zaggie had already insisted that I drive with her to Banja Luka. She turned a deliberately deaf ear to my weak protests about taking the four hour bus, so after a tasty lunch of local fish, we hopped into Zaggie's battered red Golf and were off.

Getting into a car with a stranger is always an adventure. In Bosnia, no adventure can be complete without a taste of Bosnia's ethnic politics. To make a long story short, Zaggie's Golf had Serb licence plates in a Muslim and Croat-controlled part of the country. Zaggie was adamant that she should be able to go wherever we wanted, regardless of ethnicity. Inevitably, we were stopped by a police officer wanting to make trouble. But we both lavished on him our sweetest smiles and, to our amazement, he let us proceed without a fine.

Upon arriving in Banja Luka, we drove straight to Zaggie's house. There the kindness continued: Zaggie's mother, sister and aunt force-fed us tasty Bosnian pastries and Turkish coffee, and insisted I stay with them during my two day visit. Zaggie then insisted on driving me around, in her tiny Golf, to all the sights in Banja Luka. It was a travel writer's absolute dream.

It was a strange but classic day in Bosnia (a country full of contradictions): on visiting a fort, I expected mines. Instead I found myself enveloped by wonderful hospitality and lasting friendship.

Kate Galbraith
LP Author, UK

in Bucharest. As a tourist you might find yourself getting extra attention from beggars, but obviously whether or not you give anything is a purely personal decision. Some travellers feel that giving to beggars only encourages them to hassle future travellers. Others feel it is a superficial interaction with no long-lasting benefit. In contrast, you may feel that giving away a little of your money to someone in need is the least you can do.

Donations

A different solution if you are troubled by the plight of beggars is to donate money to local aid organisations or schools, where you can be sure the money will be put to good use. You could also make a donation to an international aid organisation, such as Oxfam International (www.oxfaminternational.org).

Avoiding Offence

When travelling in foreign countries, it's only natural that you worry about committing some dreadful *faux pas*. Fortunately, this is a lot easier said than done. You'll find in Europe that if you abide by the rules of common decency and good manners that apply in your own country, you will almost never go wrong.

For country-specific do's and don'ts, see the society and conduct sections of your guidebooks.

PHOTO ETIQUETTE

Wherever you go in Europe there'll be fabulous photo opportunities, and often the best pictures involve people. Locals going about their business in a

Temper Tantrums

Figuratively speaking, running into brick walls is one of those things that happens whenever you go travelling and the trick is learning how to keep flexible. Unless you are a born nomad, leaving an environment of familiarity tends to heighten all kinds of emotional responses to otherwise mundane details. That's why it's called a trip. One extreme and common expression of this heightened emotional response is aggravated impatience, or just plain losing it. This condition is usually a result of not knowing the rules of the game that everyone else is playing. It inevitably occurs at the exact moment when time is of the essence, like when you are trying to catch a plane that only flies once a week or a train which required strategic planning to get a ticket.

No matter how much you read about the virtue of patience, it can be very, very difficult to maintain when you are on a trip. Patience is not a heightened emotional response; it's a long, disciplined exercise in controlling emotions. Therefore, in times of imminent failure to get anywhere, instead of losing your temper, try collapsing in a heap and bursting into tears. Of course, this usually works more effectively for women. Opening the tear ducts should not be overused, but it can be very effective in moments of great need, like when you need that ticket come hell or high water. But patience is always something to keep in mind, even if you can't quite put it into practice. Sycophancy and smiles can go a long way to opening doors that might offer a solution. Remember, it's help you're after, not territory.

Marie Cambon
LP Author, Canada

tiny Portuguese fishing village, old men playing chess outside a cafe in Sicily, women dancing in brightly coloured costumes during a traditional festival in Bulgaria or sangria-soaked Spaniards going mad during one of their frenzied fiestas – they all make great candid shots. But the camera can be a very obtrusive instrument. Some people simply don't want their photograph taken (especially at close range), while others will do anything to edge themselves into the frame (especially children). Don't let the temptation to take a great picture override the respect you should show to the local people. The following are some basics tips to make sure that both you and your subject come away happy from your interaction:

- If you are taking a picture of a person at close range, ask their permission. Obviously, you lose some spontaneity by asking permission, but there are ways around this: bring a long (telephoto) lens and take photos from a distance; take two pictures – the first posed and the second when the person has relaxed; or use humour to relax the person.
- Do not take photos of private or sacred events unless you are absolutely sure it is OK to do so (by asking permission). This includes weddings, funerals and religious services.
- If you are photographing a religious ceremony or similar event, take care not to bother the participants and onlookers with the sound of your camera or the light of your flash.
- Check whether it is OK before taking photographs inside religious structures. Many, such as London's Westminster Abbey and the Sistine Chapel in Rome, ban flash photography.
- People whose pictures you take may sometimes ask you to send them copies; don't promise to do so unless you really intend to follow through. It's too easy to get home and forget all about it.

RELIGIOUS CONSIDERATIONS

Christianity – in one form or another – is the predominant religion in Europe. Followers range from Roman Catholics and Protestants to Lutherans and the Eastern Orthodox religions of Eastern Europe and Greece. Throughout history, wars have been fought and societies have been divided over religion, and there are still some areas where religious (usually accompanied by political) differences stand out. The most obvious spots are Northern Ireland and the Balkans. As a traveller you're unlikely to be affected by religion in anything but a positive way, visiting the many magnificent cathedrals or attending a religious festival, for instance – but it would be unwise to openly discuss contentious religious or political issues in sensitive areas. Common sense dictates that you wouldn't decry the merits of Catholicism over Protestantism (or vice versa) in a Belfast pub. Discretion is always the best policy.

Muslim Sensibilities

The only European countries (covered by this book) with anywhere near a majority Muslim population are Turkey (99%) and Albania (70%). In both cases the population is mostly Sunni Muslim, but you generally won't find the sort of religious fervour and fundamentalism that characterises some nations further east. In rural and eastern Turkey you may encounter a growing section of 'born again' or strict Muslims, and everywhere you'll hear the tinny sound of the *ezan* (call to prayer) resonating from speakers perched in the minarets of the country's ubiquitous mosques.

Regardless of how modern and 'European' these nations may appear, the following of the Islamic religion is very strong and visitors should respect this, especially when entering mosques. Everyday dress is also a consideration, particularly for women. In Turkey and many parts of southern and Eastern Europe, revealing clothing (singlets or sleeveless shirts, skimpy skirts or tight shorts etc) is either very offensive or just asking for trouble.

Here are a few rules to be aware of when visiting a mosque in any country:

- Remove your shoes before entering. If you really want to show respect, wash your hands, feet and face at the washing basins provided.
- Dress respectfully. Men should wear trousers and shirts, women long skirts or trousers and loose, long-sleeved blouses, with their hair covered by a scarf. In many mosques, robes and scarves are available if you need them.
- Women cannot enter the main prayer hall.
- Non-Muslims of either sex may not be permitted to enter some mosques, especially during prayer times.
- Never walk between a Muslim and Mecca when they are praying.
- Always ask permission before taking photos and do not take pictures during prayer times.

CULTURAL SENSITIVITY

Locals who are used to tourists usually overlook their odd or bemusing ways, but no-one wants to push the stereotype of the 'ugly tourist'. These people tend to shout a lot, whine about how things are better/cheaper/more efficient in their country, and show total disregard for local sensibilities. If you witness such an outburst you'll probably be thoroughly embarrassed, especially if the offender is from your country, and even more so if you realise it's you. A few things to consider:

Greetings & Handshakes

Greetings are an important part of meeting people in Europe. Appropriate and polite greetings create a good first impression, whether you're meeting a poor family, a shopkeeper or a local official.

Another thing to look out for is understanding simple body language. In Albania and Bulgaria, for instance, people nod their heads up and down for 'no' and side to side for 'yes' – the exact opposite of what you'll be used to. In Turkey, 'yes' is signified by a forward nod, while 'no' is indicated by an upward movement of the head and raised eyebrows. Nodding the head from side to side means 'I don't know'.

It helps to learn the appropriate form of address for men and women in each country and to use them in formal situations. A good guidebook will fill you in on social conduct and how to avoid offence.

- Don't assume that everyone you meet will speak English or understand it. To launch into English while asking directions of a stranger in Europe is impolite, even if it turns out that person does speak English. This is perhaps why the French have a reputation (not always deserved) for completely ignoring tourists. Learn the phrase for 'Do you speak English?' in each country you're travelling in and start with that.

- If you ask a question in English and are met with blank stares, don't repeat the question slowly and loudly *in English* – it's extremely rude.

- It's always best to blend in rather than stand out. Aggressive queue-jumping is a part of life in some Eastern European countries. But resist the urge to spit the dummy and start lecturing an old lady about the etiquette of queuing.

- Try to follow some common local customs. For instance, in many European countries it's customary to greet shopkeepers (in the local language) when you enter a store and to say goodbye when you leave. If you're invited to someone's home, bring a gift such as flowers or a bottle of wine.

Women Travellers

For the most part, travelling by yourself is a richly rewarding and usually safe experience. As a woman you face subtle discrimination in your everyday life anyway, and will probably be perfectly familiar with the behaviour you encounter on the road. This won't necessarily make it any easier to deal with, especially if you're feeling lonely or homesick. As with all travel, care and precautions are essential.

Dressing Appropriately

In most parts of Europe, dressing casually (as you would at home) is perfectly normal and acceptable. Dressing to suit the climate is the norm for travellers, and local people will rarely be surprised at the eccentric dress sense of tourists. In many parts of Western Europe and Italy, particularly in the cities, you'll notice that 'dressing up' and flaunting the latest fashions are a high priority, so in certain company you might find yourself feeling uncomfortably scungy. Certainly, shorts are uncommon as a standard form of dress in most parts of Europe, except on children or for sporting/outdoor activities. You might find you're not being taken seriously while standing in line at the Romanian consulate in your best pair of hiking shorts.

But there are certain dress considerations. Long pants or knee-length dresses should be worn when sightseeing in churches, mosques, monasteries or synagogues anywhere in Eastern or southern Europe. Singlets (sleeveless tops) are also inappropriate. In predominantly Muslim countries such as Turkey, immodesty in dress, particularly by women, is frowned upon. In general terms, the further you get from the cities, the more conservative the dress codes are. In some areas locals may take matters into their own hands if they feel sufficiently scandalised, by either making overt sexual advances or becoming violent.

Women should also carry these conservative dress attitudes over to other southern European countries, particularly Italy, but also Greece and Spain. Here, local men in rural areas might see women revealing too much leg, stomach or cleavage as promiscuous and fair game, if only for a little cat-calling and leering. In short, it's easy to save yourself hassle, ignominy and possible hazard simply by dressing appropriately. Avoid figure-hugging clothes and keep the bikinis and bare chests for the beach. Apart from making good practical sense, you'll be showing a level of respect for local cultures that will make your trip more fulfilling and will go some way to lessening resentment against travellers as a whole.

If you're a lone female, or a woman travelling with a female friend, consider how to deal with the most common forms of harassment – lewd looks, touching and unwanted advances. Researching the culture you're planning to travel in can help you avoid much of this.

Attitudes towards women vary in Europe. In Mediterranean Europe, particularly rural Spain, southern Italy, Greece and Turkey, women are likely to receive unwanted attention from men who think that staring and calling out to a woman is to pay her a flattering compliment. In Muslim countries, a western woman without a male companion will receive constant attention from males.

Relatively conservative dress will help limit this attention. Away from beach resorts, sleeveless tops and tight shorts are best avoided and it's a good idea to take note of what the local women in your age group are wearing. Clothes that expose the thighs, shoulders or breasts are considered improper in some countries, and beach wear should be reserved for the beach. While it may appear unfair to tailor your dress to the perceptions of others, a little sensitivity can not only protect you from harassment, but will show respect to the people of the country you are visiting. Wearing sunglasses is a good way to avoid unwanted eye contact (which is often a cue for wolf whistles and leers) and in some countries, fair-haired women will benefit from wearing a head scarf. Marriage and family are highly respected in southern Europe so a wedding ring (worn on the left ring finger) might help. Talking of 'my husband', as well as showing photos of family and friends from home, will also earn respect.

Women should take extra care not to find themselves alone on empty beaches, alone in dark streets or in any other situation where help might not be available. Never hitchhike alone in these areas.

Above all, try to stick to your own moral code. As an outsider, some people may feel that it's OK to touch or bully you. Assertive behaviour is often the best reaction – don't allow yourself to be pushed around or made to feel like a victim. If you are clear about your rules, others will soon get the message. Remember, you're travelling to see and experience new cultures, and you can't do that if you're entirely protected and afraid to meet people's eyes.

Ecotourism

In some parts of the world, ecologically sound tourism is one of the most contentious issues in the travel industry. The philosophies of ecotourism probably won't affect you much if you're travelling through cities and towns in Europe. But if you plan to trek in national parks, visit remote areas such as the Norwegian fjords, or travel through rural Eastern Europe, you should be aware of responsible travel practices. As a traveller, much of the responsibility rests on you to ensure that whatever activities you engage in protect and support the environment and communities of the areas you visit.

Ecotourism is usually defined as travel that conserves the natural environment, while benefiting the wellbeing of local people in a sustainable way. It was born as a backlash against destructive travel practices, particularly in the more remote regions of the world. There are many travel companies

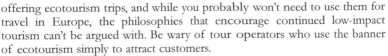

offering ecotourism trips, and while you probably won't need to use them for travel in Europe, the philosophies that encourage continued low-impact tourism can't be argued with. Be wary of tour operators who use the banner of ecotourism simply to attract customers.

A number of organisations have developed useful guidelines for ecotourism, including Conservation International's Ecotravel Center (www.ecotour.org/ecotour.htm) and the Ecotourism Association of Australia (www.wttc.org). For more information on ecotourism and lists of reliable ecotour operators, check out their Web sites.

ECOTOURISM GUIDELINES

- Leave only footprints and take only photographs. This is a cliché, but it sums up the most important tenet of ecotourism: do not leave garbage in the places you visit and do not take any natural or historical souvenirs (especially plants or antiquities).
- Learn about the culture and environment of the places you plan to visit, so you are familiar with the specific problems facing a region.
- Learn about local and international conservation groups working in the area and support their efforts.
- Patronise environmentally friendly and locally owned businesses.
- Never buy products made from endangered species.
- If possible, use environmentally friendly methods of transportation or walk from place to place.
- Stick to designated trails and camping spots.
- Avoid polluting water sources. Use established toilets, or go at least 50m from rivers or lakes.
- Try to minimise all aspects of your energy consumption.
- Produce as little garbage as possible by using recyclable containers. If your garbage won't be disposed of properly, carry it out yourself.

Hazards & Safeguards

Travelling in Europe is generally quite safe. Violent crime is rare and the threat from terrorists and religious fanatics is virtually zero. But travelling anywhere makes you vulnerable for two main reasons: you tend to cover a lot of ground, meet many new people and encounter more unfamiliar situations than you would at home; and because you're carrying your valuables (camera, cash etc) around with you all day every day. The main threats facing travellers are pickpockets, bagsnatchers and scam artists but there's no need to become paranoid. Most crimes committed against travellers are opportunistic thefts; if you use your common sense, you will have very little to worry about. The same is true of other potential hazards in Europe. Natural disasters, political unrest, unexploded landmines and terrorism are far less of a worry than you might think from reading the news. If you heed the warnings and do not deliberately expose yourself to danger, you'll have little to fear except random acts of fate. (To be on the safe side, do not travel without adequate travel insurance covering both medical expenses and loss of baggage – see the Tickets & Insurance chapter for details.)

A good guidebook will have a detailed section on the hazards particular to each country and how to avoid them. Update your information through newspapers, magazines and the Internet just before visiting a country. The Researching Your Trip section in the Planning chapter lists useful Web sites. The following are not intended to spook you – just to raise your awareness.

THEFT

Stories of theft abound on the backpacker trail in Europe. From the Vespa-riding bagsnatcher in Rome to the traveller who awoke with a headache and no possessions on the overnight train from Barcelona to Lisbon, some of these tales seem to have entered the realm of urban myth. Thefts do happen, but you will almost never be the victim unless you are careless or foolish. Try to keep your wits about you all the time. Trying not to look *too* much like a tourist will also help make you less of a target – don't wear a bumbag or wander around looking lost (even if you are) with a camera strung around your neck. And always look after your moneybelt – if it is stolen, it will mean several days wasted replacing your passport and travellers cheques, and cancelling your credit cards. One Lonely Planet author carries a 'decoy' wallet with some expired credit cards and Monopoly money in his back pocket – it's always the

Holiday Romances

If you've seen Julie Delpy and Ethan Hawke killing time in Vienna in the film *Before Sunrise*, you might well be planning a holiday romance yourself. And while losing yourself in the arms of a mysterious lover at the same time as losing yourself on the streets of a strange city has enormous romantic appeal, there are a few things to consider. If you're going to be spontaneous these days, it's important to plan. And there's more to consider than just the price of a bottle of red wine and the easy spread of sexually transmitted diseases.

Lots of travellers, and especially those travelling alone, set out with the intention of seeing a bit of love action while away from home. But few contemplate the variety of motivations and enormous list of repercussions such play might carry with it.

Many travellers find part-time love with other travellers. This is hardly surprising; you're unlikely to find a native Frenchman in a Paris youth hostel. You might even hook up with someone you've just met in order to cut costs on a day trip or taxi fare, then end up beginning a beautiful – if necessarily short – friendship. People travel with different itineraries, and after a couple of days in the City of Lights, you'll be off to the French Riviera to catch a tan and he'll be heading to Somalia to unload grain for the Red Cross. Now if you never really liked him anyway – maybe you've just always wanted to kiss a Welsh guy – there's no problems. Unless he likes you. Or unless you start to miss him. Or unless he's stolen your day-pack. The liberation of travel is quickly eclipsed by affairs of the heart, and where that troublesome organ is concerned, all other care can fly out the bus window.

Breaking up is hard to do. It's almost inevitable, though, when travelling. And the longer you drag out travel together, the harder the parting is likely to be. It's important to remember that although you may share intimate secrets with your new pal, you probably won't tell them everything, and they'll keep things from you too. They might have a partner they're planning to return to, they might be homesick for the Vladivostok coast or they might simply be after some quick, disposable sex. If you're just after sexual experience and conquest, you might

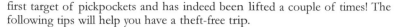

first target of pickpockets and has indeed been lifted a couple of times! The following tips will help you have a theft-free trip.

- Always keep your passport, plane tickets, travellers cheques, most of your cash and important travel documents in your moneybelt, underneath your clothing. The only time you shouldn't be wearing your moneybelt is when it's in a secure hostel or hotel safety deposit box or when you're sleeping (in which case it should be under your pillow). For more details, see Money Carrying Options in the Money Matters chapter.
- Don't carry large amounts of cash around. Change only what you need to get you through three to four days.
- Don't flash your cash, valuables or camera around. If possible, do not let people see that you are wearing a moneybelt, and carry a small amount of day-to-day cash in a purse or wallet in your front pocket.
- When swimming, diving or snorkelling, bring your important documents and money with you in a waterproof container, or leave them in the safety deposit box of your hostel or hotel (if you're confident it's safe).
- When you're in a restaurant or bar, secure your pack with a lock or strap or lean it against you so that you'll know if someone is trying to take it.
- Have a small padlock for using on hostel lockers, and to lock your luggage to overhead racks on long-distance buses or trains.
- Be very wary of accepting drinks or food from strangers. In some countries in Europe, thieves have been known to put drugs in drinks or food and then rob the unconscious victim (see Druggings later).

Holiday Romances

be in luck. But all can end in disaster if the people you meet have more serious intentions, attach stronger cultural importance to physical relationships or if you plunge headlong into love. If anyone's going to get hurt, the best advice is to skip the encounter and head to the French Riviera as you'd planned.

If you're looking to hook up with a local in a new country, many of the same pleasures and risks can be expected. Again, discovering your intended partner's expectations is the first step to carnal bliss. Are they aware of your travel plans? Are they aware that you need to marry a local in order to stay? Are they aware of the 'Love Checklist' in your back pocket with a gap next to 'Spain'? Are you aware of local customs and expectations of a sexual partner? A night of passion is all well and good, but you don't want to wake up the next morning buried to your waist and being force-fed raw lobster in the first of a 12-step marriage ceremony. As with new relationships at home, establishing the ground rules is the best way to avoid nasty or upsetting confusion.

If sex (always safe sex) is one of the reasons you're travelling, remember that it carries different connotations in different cultures. Learn a little about where you are before heading for someone's pants. There are plenty of girls on the road looking for a little short-term affection and plenty of guys at local bar who'd love to show a traveller their etchings, which means there's no need to take advantage of someone who is playing by different rules.

There is, of course, a chance that you may actually find the love of your life on the road. My parents met while my mother was on holidays. But their blossoming relationship meant that my father-to-be had to pack his bags, leave his job, family and friends and chase her halfway around the world. Not everyone is happy to throw it all away just to give it a go with someone they've just met. Are you?

John Ryan
Lonely Planet, Australia

- Don't close the door of a taxi or pay the driver until your baggage has been unloaded. Also be careful of unregistered taxis and never fall asleep in the back of a taxi or on public transport.
- Don't give your hotel name or room number to strangers, as they might follow you back and try to rob you.
- Be careful of your valuables while you're taking a shower. If you're not sure that your room is safe, bring them into the bathroom with you. Remember that it's not just locals who may steal your belongings – unfortunately there are quite a few travellers around who pay for their trips by ripping off other travellers.
- Pickpockets usually work in teams. If you feel that people are jostling or crowding you for no reason, stand back and check discreetly to see that your valuables are still on you. Innocuous-looking Gypsy children in tourist areas in France, Spain and Italy tend to be a particular threat.
- Don't walk alone at night or in unfamiliar areas. If you find yourself in an unsavoury spot, or if you think you're lost, flag down a taxi.
- Be especially careful when boarding and riding buses and trains. You're at your most vulnerable to pickpockets at these times. If the bus or train is really crowded, try to keep your hands unobtrusively over your wallet and moneybelt.
- Take care when using lockers in public places such as train stations. Check that they are secure and don't let a stranger help you find or load things into a locker (they may have a key or the combination).
- Never leave any valuables in a tent or car – not even in the boot. Thefts from cars are common throughout Europe and the sight of a bag or jacket on the back seat is all the invitation a passing thief will need to smash a window.
- It's difficult to keep your wits about you when you're drinking. If you know you're going to have a big night out, try to store your valuables and most of your cash in a secure hostel or hotel safety deposit box.
- Take extra care at major festivals such as Munich's Oktoberfest or Pamplona's San Fermines. Many thieves and pickpockets attend these events specifically to relieve tourists of their belongings. Not only do the crowds make it difficult to catch a bagsnatcher, but most people at these parties are affected by alcohol.

SCAMS & SWINDLES

Each year Lonely Planet receives hundreds of letters from travellers who have been duped by predatory scam artists. New swindles constantly appear, but the

Check Your Pockets

Theft isn't the only way of parting with your possessions. For many travellers it's difficult to get through a trip without the loss of a pair of sunglasses, a towel, five pens, a toothbrush, a pocketknife and a key ring. They may be little things, but they usually need to be replaced, which is a hassle. I've had to hacksaw through two padlocks (on separate trips) just to get into my backpack after losing the keys. It's called carelessness and, if you're anything like me, it's something you'll need to train yourself against. Always check around your room and the bathroom before you leave a hostel or hotel; check around the seats of trains and buses when you get off, particularly after long trips; and check your pockets when you get up after sitting down. At the same time, it's also worth checking that your moneybelt is secure and your day-pack has all its contents intact. Good luck!

Paul Harding
LP Author, Australia

best advice is to keep your wits about you, and approach all situations with a healthy dose of scepticism.

You're more likely to come across certain scams in some countries than others. In Turkey, for instance, there's a good chance you'll spend some time inside an Istanbul carpet shop. You may not be 'scammed' but high-pressure sales tactics might result in you paying a lot of money for a carpet you really didn't want. In Eastern Europe you're more likely to encounter corrupt border officials than in Western Europe where border controls have virtually been dropped.

Many scams take the form of an offer from a businessperson or local who befriends you. If you're offered a deal that seems too good to be true, then it almost certainly is. Some scams are listed below, but there are others which prey on a traveller's gullibility or carelessness.

Card scams – These are more common in Asia than Europe, but are still worth being aware of. The drill here is that you're invited by a very friendly local to visit his relative's house. Once you get there, you find that a card game is under way. Your friend may coach you on how to win big and you'll be invited to join the game. Invariably, you'll be allowed to win a few hands, then you'll start losing until you have no more money to play with. At this point, your friend or another player will offer to lend you some cash. Needless to say, you'll quickly lose this and then find yourself in debt to a complete stranger. Of course, the game was rigged from the start.

Carpet scams – These may occur in Turkey or Morocco; someone (usually a shop owner) convinces you that if you buy his carpets, you can resell them for a profit back home. Of course, if this was true, he wouldn't be cutting you in on the deal. Unless you are a carpet expert, steer clear of these deals. Also be wary of the shop owner offering to ship the carpet to your home. If it arrives at all it may be a different (inferior) carpet to the one you paid for.

Credit card scams – There are various credit card scams out there and most are pretty simple. For example, a shop owner takes your card out to the back of the shop and runs off three or four purchase slips with it and then uses the one you sign to forge the signature on the others. Never let your credit card out of your sight and carefully watch what is done with it.

Lady at the bar scam – This one can happen anywhere from Soho in London to the Omonia area of Athens, but usually occurs in the 'seedier' parts of town and solo males are always the victims. You enter a bar or are befriended by a young man who takes you to a bar. A lady will pull up a seat next to you and start chatting. When you go to leave you will be handed an outrageous bill for her drinks and you may have no recourse but to pay up.

Druggings

Though it may run counter to your generous nature, it is unwise to accept food and drinks from strangers. Travellers are especially vulnerable on trains and buses. The typical ploy involves someone you've just met offering to buy or share a drink or snack. Your new 'friend' may seem offended if you do not accept their small token of friendship; if you acquiesce, you may wake up 10 hours later with a throbbing headache and a missing backpack.

Gassings have also been reported on a handful of overnight international trains. The usual scenario involves the release of a sleep-inducing gas into a sleeping compartment in the middle of the night. Once the gas takes effect, the perpetrator searches the victims for moneybelts and whatever valuables are lurking in their luggage. The best protection against gassings is to lock the door of your sleeping compartment (use your own lock if there isn't one) and to lock your bags to luggage racks. Most importantly, never sleep alone in a train compartment.

'Hello my Friend!'

After a few months in Europe you will recognise the type – a nice man (rarely a woman) who speaks good English, is very friendly, and goes out of his way

---

Not-so-Great Train Robberies

While travelling around Europe you'll probably hear all sorts of 'horror stories'. A backpacker relieved of his travellers cheques and passport by a light-fingered Gypsy child in Madrid; another caught out by a Vespa-riding bagsnatcher who disappeared without trace into a crowded Naples street; or even the unlucky traveller whose moneybelt vanished while he was taking a shower at a Munich youth hostel.

It's not that these things happen with alarming regularity as such, but that they make the best stories. They inspire empathy, sympathy and sometimes even wonder (if the incident was dramatic enough). Any traveller who suffers an unsavoury incident feels compelled to tell everyone else he or she meets, and those travellers in turn tell others, and so the story grows. Thefts and scams *do* happen and first-time travellers are often targeted because they're usually the most vulnerable. Your best defence is to be wary and aware at all times (without dissolving into paranoia) especially in crowds and even more so if you're alone. I have given generously to the pickpocketing and bagsnatching fraternity on my travels (almost always through my own stupidity). And just to prove a point about those stories, here's one of mine …

Having travelled from Greece to Brindisi in Italy, three friends and I boarded a late-night train for the trip to Naples. We were surprised but relieved to find the carriage half-empty (it was mid-June) so we split into two compartments for a much-needed lie down. When we woke the next morning we discovered some of our packs had been riffled in the night and one girl had had the contents of her moneybelt lifted (passport, travellers cheques, cash) – while she was wearing it! Frantic, we reported the thefts to the utterly dispassionate conductor (who waved us away with the words 'no Eengleesh, no Eengleesh …'), then spent half an hour searching the train before it lurched into Naples. Standing on the platform in stunned disbelief, we happened to notice someone open the toilet door on the end of our carriage, peer out, then quickly close it. It was too suspicious. While two of us guarded the carriage the others dashed off to the station police. Three of Italy's finest promptly arrived, revolvers drawn, yelling instructions at the toilet door in Italian. It was like something out of a low-budget movie and I was half-expecting gunshots to start ringing out at any minute. They started kicking at the door and eventually a cowering Italian teenager emerged, along with a bag containing all our pilfered belongings and a few other items from his night's work. With the help of a translator we spent an hour making a report and were invited to return the following week for his court appearance. But we had other places to be, so we'll never know how the young thief was dealt with. It turned out that the Brindisi-Rome overnight train that we were on is notorious for theft, but in the end we were the lucky ones: we came away with all our belongings *and* a good story.

Paul Harding
LP Author, Australia

to be helpful. The actual scam varies from country to country, but all share one common feature – lulling you into a false sense of trust. At some point your new friend will gently suggest something that, under normal circumstances, you would not do. Maybe you need to visit the toilet – your new friend will kindly offer to watch your bags. Maybe you're tired and need help lifting your bags – your new friend (or perhaps an accomplice) will create a diversion and grab a camera or a day-pack.

In some cases your new friend is less a thief and more a hustler. It's late and you don't have a hostel or hotel reservation. Coincidentally your new friend knows this great hotel just across town. This ploy could involve an exorbitant taxi fare and an inflated hotel price, with your new friend scoring hefty commissions from the taxi driver and hotel owner.

There is no limit to the number of scams out there. Don't be paranoid, and don't cut yourself off from the people you meet on the road, 99% of whom are honestly interested in striking up a friendship. Yet it pays to be suspicious of overly friendly people, especially on long-distance trains and buses (after all, most people are less than friendly after 10 hours on a train). Never allow strangers to watch your bags and never allow a situation to evolve in ways that make you feel uncomfortable. If your new friend is genuine, they will certainly understand if you say 'no' to taking a taxi at 1 am in a strange town to an unfamiliar hotel.

Black Markets

The black market is a thing of the past in most European countries. With the passing of communism most countries have begun the transition to free-market economics. In the process currencies have been freed from government controls (the main reason that black markets exist) and are now fully convertible.

Black markets still exist in some countries, but the rates on offer are only marginally better than bank rates. Moreover, many black market money-changers will not hesitate to dupe foreign travellers.

'Can I see some ID?'

In some countries, especially in Eastern Europe, you may encounter people claiming to be from the tourist police, the special police, the super-secret police ... or whatever. Unless they're wearing a uniform and have a good reason for accosting you (eg you're robbing a bank or the like), treat their claims with suspicion.

A common scam runs like this: someone asks you to change money. You say no, and seconds later an 'undercover' police officer 'arrests' the moneychanger. The officer then asks to check your passport and money, in case it's counterfeit – then runs away!

Needless to say, never show your passport or cash to anyone on the street. Simply walk away. If they flash a badge, politely offer to accompany them to the nearest police station.

NATURAL DISASTERS

There's not a lot you can do about the forces of nature and getting caught up in a natural disaster is usually a case of being in the wrong place at the wrong time. However, careful research and keeping abreast of the news regarding weather conditions will keep you safe. Although natural disasters such as earthquakes in Turkey or floods in Italy will make headline news, these are rare and isolated events. Here are some basic safety pointers:

Earthquakes – These are not terribly common in Europe, although Turkey seems to suffer one every 10 years or so (two disastrous quakes struck northern Turkey in 1999) and Italy and the Balkans have suffered major quakes in recent years. If one strikes while you're indoors, take shelter in a doorway or under a strong table. Do not run outside as this exposes you to falling debris. If you're outside, get away from buildings or other things that can collapse on you.

Floods – Europe has no monsoon (rainy) season but rivers occasionally swell and flood, particularly in mountain areas. Be very careful when crossing flooded streams. If you're camping near a river and heavy rain sets in, move to higher ground even if you must do so in the middle of the night (better yet, do not camp in areas that can be reached by rising waters).

Freak weather conditions – Weather is rarely predictable in some parts of Europe. In northern and Eastern Europe especially, bitterly cold snaps or sudden heat waves seem to seriously affect daily life. Britain is notorious for extremes of weather affecting society – during heat waves water restrictions are rushed in, and if a few flakes of snow fall, the public transport systems shut down!

DRUGS

Drugs are freely available in some parts of Europe, but nowhere are they legal and in most countries the penalties for possession are very severe. Amsterdam is famous for its tolerance of soft drugs (cannabis) and availability of harder drugs (heroin, LSD, ecstasy), but even here these drugs are *not legal*. Possession of soft drugs for personal use (up to 5g) is unofficially tolerated in the Netherlands – larger amounts will put you in the persecuted dealer category, and anything harder will be treated just as seriously as anywhere else. Although border checks in Western Europe have generally been done away with, you can expect random checks when going from the Netherlands to Germany, Britain, Denmark or France. Possession is illegal in these countries (as it is elsewhere in Europe) and will attract a fine and possibly a court appearance, depending on the amount. Authorities in some countries, such as Greece, are very severe on drugs – even possession of a small amount of cannabis could land you in a very unpleasant jail.

Big cities such as London, Berlin, Amsterdam and Copenhagen have thriving club scenes where 'recreational' drugs such as ecstasy are widely used.

The dangers involved in attempting to buy any drugs are that the dealer may be the police or a police informer, or may simply rip you off. Being under the influence of drugs can also make you a target for thieves.

For information on the potential health risks of drug use, see Alcohol & Drugs in the Health chapter.

RACISM

As a whole, Europe is a fairly tolerant region and as a traveller you're unlikely to encounter any racial problems. Unfortunately though, racism persists in some countries, particularly where there has been a lot of immigration.

Germany, Britain and France are three countries where right-wing-style racial violence manifests itself. It usually occurs in cities or poor suburbs and is almost always directed against immigrants, such as North African Muslims in France, Turks in Germany and West Indians in Britain. Elsewhere you'll no doubt encounter strong national pride, but little racial intolerance.

OTHER DANGERS & ANNOYANCES

There are a few other hazards you may (but probably won't) come across in Europe, as well as a host of mild day-to-day annoyances, ranging from clouds of cigarette smoke in a restaurant to crazy bus drivers. If these things bother you, your best defence is to be aware of them and either avoid them or steel yourself for the experience.

Smoking – In many European countries, particularly on the Mediterranean (France, Portugal, Spain, Greece and Turkey) the majority of people seem to chain-smoke. Many restaurants and public transport services have smoking bans, but often these are completely ignored.

Queues – You'll find a stark contrast between east and west in regard to the orderliness of queues. In Britain queuing is almost a national obsession and nothing is guaranteed to raise the ire of the locals more than pushing in. In Romania, locals will squash together in queues and elbow their way to the front. Generally though, queuing is just like everywhere else in the western world.

Unsafe drivers – Southern Europe is notorious for the insanity of its drivers. Portugal has the highest number of accidents per capita in Europe, while road laws and speed limits are frequently flouted in Italy, Greece and Turkey. And it's not simply the drivers of vehicles in which you travel that you must be wary of; take care when crossing roads, walking around cities, driving a hire car and riding a bicycle.

Touts – Although they'll often help you find a decent place to stay, touts are occasionally a pain in the neck. They can usually be found wherever there's a concentration of tourist or backpacker accommodation, but are really only pushy when things are quiet. Train and bus stations and ferry terminals (Greece) are the most likely places to be accosted by touts. If they have flyers, see what sort of accommodation they have to offer, find out the cost and (perhaps most importantly) how far away it is – you don't want to end up miles out of town. If it looks OK, there's no reason not to go with them, but don't let them carry your bags and don't get pushed into going anywhere you don't want to go.

Land mines – In Croatia, Bosnia and Yugoslavia, unexploded land mines are a grim reminder of ongoing conflicts. Fortunately, most land mines are in areas off limits to travellers. Avoid restricted areas and never trek into an area about which you are unsure.

IF YOU DO GET INTO TROUBLE ...

If the worst happens and you're the victim of a crime or some other disaster, try to take decisive steps to set things right as quickly as possible. As long as you are physically in one piece, the simple fact that you are taking action will go a long way towards making you feel better. You can always enlist the assistance of another traveller or trustworthy local, and you may be surprised how helpful others can be when you're in need.

If something has been stolen or you've been the victim of any other crime, immediately report it to the police. Even if you've lost your passport, you will need a police report so you can get a new passport. A report will also be necessary for replacing travellers cheques or claiming on insurance. Someone in the police station should be able to speak English. If not, an interpreter should be organised or your embassy may be able to write a report to give to the police.

In the case of lost or stolen passports, you should go to your country's embassy or consulate, which can issue you a new passport, advise you about local laws, put you in touch with English-speaking lawyers or doctors, and contact friends or relatives back home in the case of an emergency. They will not, however, lend you money, get you out of jail or pay to fly you home.

Two Weeks in a Greek Jail

Corfu is a busy island, especially from May to August. By late September most tourists are gone, and the island reverts to its winter tranquillity. But four months of tourism takes its toll. Once-patient hoteliers and restaurant staff become slightly less accommodating, and people in the street give you a 'we've had enough of you' look. Into this walked me – 21 years old and indestructible.

The trouble began in the early afternoon. I had hooked up with three English women who were on Corfu for some autumn sun. We parked ourselves in a taverna and started in on the ouzo. By late afternoon we were all quite drunk.

After leaving the restaurant a man approached. He stood directly in front of me, hands behind his back and stared. As I tried to walk around him he began yelling. At first I tried to ignore him. I thought he was the town loco out to harass the last of the tourists. I didn't want any trouble. I just wanted to get back to my hotel and deal with the impending hangover.

I had 10 minutes to catch the last bus to where I was staying. As I pushed past the man he reared up and punched me on the side of the head. There was a flash of light, then pain and finally fury. I turned on my attacker and let him have it. I think I got one, maybe two punches in before I found myself face down in the street. What I didn't know at the time, but found out later, was that the man who hit me was a police officer.

What ensued was a horrific experience involving a trip to the mental ward of the local hospital, followed by two weeks (as far as I can tell) in a squalid little cell in a Greek prison. Scenes from *Midnight Express* kept playing through my head like a loop tape. I was convinced I was going to end up being the plaything of some hairy-backed jailer.

No-one spoke English, and I was by myself. I had no idea what was happening. Nobody even knew where I was. I hadn't spoken to my family or friends in months.

After what felt like an eternity, the nightmare ended as quickly as it started. A man entered the cell one morning and said I could go. Just like that. He spoke passable English but wouldn't answer any questions. He escorted me out of the building and set me free.

To this day I have no idea why it all happened in the first place. I was drunk, but I wasn't causing a disturbance. I now put it down to stress caused by a summer of loud, drunk tourists. Sixteen years have passed, and I have worked as a photographer and writer in some insane places. But whenever I've had to deal with small men with big authority, and even bigger guns, I always remember the lesson I learned in Greece.

Doug McKinlay
LP Author, UK

WHILE YOU'RE THERE ▶▶

You've survived the plane trip and you're ready to hit the road. Now it's time to get into the nitty-gritty of finding suitable accommodation, eating on the run, getting around on public transport and, once all that's done, enjoying yourself and seeing the sights.

With a good guidebook and a bit of advance knowledge about what to expect in each country, these tasks can be made a little easier, giving you more time to relax and enjoy the trip. This chapter covers the various types of accommodation in Europe, how to eat well on the road, and the modes of transport you're likely to use.

Accommodation

Where you're going to sleep each night is one of the biggest issues you'll face while travelling, and in Europe accommodation is often your biggest single daily expense. The cheaper you sleep, the cheaper your overall trip will be – which is why many travellers lug a tent around. Consider staying in different types of accommodation, depending on the country, location, local standards and, of course, your budget. After sleeping in rock-hard camping grounds or noisy dormitories for a couple of months, a night in a comfy bed and a room to yourself can be luxurious enough to lift your spirits and recharge your batteries. And remember that a hostel dorm bed is not always the cheapest or best-value option; with a group, you can often find that a shared room in a cheap guesthouse costs around the same per person.

Also look out for unusual or atmospheric accommodation. In London there's a converted barge on the Thames where you can sleep in a four bed cabin for £12 a night; in Turkey you can stay in a cave hotel cut into the soft volcanic rock at Cappadocia; or in Spain you can bed down in an ancient monastery. It's easy to settle for the characterless hostel next door to the train station, but a little research and initiative could result in an unexpectedly memorable experience.

TYPES OF ACCOMMODATION

Accommodation throughout northern and Western Europe is of a reasonably high standard in all budget ranges, although you can come across the occasional grimy dive anywhere. In southern and Eastern Europe, standards can vary wildly.

The cheapest places to stay are camping grounds, followed by hostels and student dormitories. Depending on which country you're in, guesthouses, B&Bs (bed & breakfast), private rooms and pensions also offer comfort and good value. Hotels are rarely cheap anywhere in the northern half of Europe.

Camping

Camping is immensely popular in Europe (especially among European travellers) and provides the cheapest accommodation there is, often at very well equipped sites.

There are two main drawbacks to camping. The first is that you usually need your own tent, which means carrying a lot of equipment. This is not always the case: many camping grounds hire out bungalows or caravans (although you may find this is no cheaper than staying in a hostel) and some, such as on popular Greek islands, have on-site tents for hire. If you're travelling in a group of two or more, carrying the equipment won't be so bad and it will also keep the overall camping costs down. The second problem is that camping grounds are almost always located some distance from the centre of large cities, so you have to spend time and money getting in to see the sights or to eat out every day. Both these problems can be solved if you have your own transport. Many travellers buy a campervan and cruise around Europe in groups of four or more, staying almost exclusively at camping grounds – see the Getting Around section later in this chapter for more information.

Official camping grounds usually charge per tent or site, per person and per vehicle. The costs vary from as little as US$2.50 a night in parts of Eastern Europe to US$18 a night in Scandinavia. National tourist offices should have booklets or brochures listing camping grounds all over their country. A useful document to have is the Camping Card International (CCI), which can be used instead of a passport when checking into a camping ground and includes third-party insurance (up to US$1.75 million for damage you may cause). Many camping grounds offer a small discount if you sign in with one. CCIs cost US$8 to US$12 and are issued by automobile associations, camping federations and, sometimes, on the spot at camping grounds.

Free Camping One of the advantages of camping is the ability to not only get right off the beaten track, but also to experience some free wilderness camping. However, it's difficult to pitch a tent outside designated camping grounds in some places because the population density of Western Europe makes it hard to find an isolated spot. It may also be illegal without permission from the local authorities (the police or local council office) or from the landowner.

In some countries, such as Austria, the UK, France, Germany and Denmark, free camping is illegal on all but private land (with permission), and in Greece it's illegal altogether. This doesn't prevent hikers from occasionally pitching their tent for the night, and you'll usually get away with it if you have only a small tent, are discreet, stay only one or two nights, take the tent down during the day and do not light a campfire or leave rubbish. At worst, you'll be woken up by the police and asked to move on. Norway, on the other hand, has an 'everyman's right' rule dating back 1000 years. This allows you to pitch a tent anywhere in the wilderness for two nights as long as you camp at least 150m from the nearest house and leave no trace of your stay.

Hostels

Hostels offer the cheapest (secure) roof over your head in Europe, and they're no longer the domain of noisy students or penniless backpackers. Europe's hostels are used by budget-conscious travellers of all ages – they're great places to meet people and usually offer a reasonable standard of facilities (see the boxed text 'Life in a Hostel'). Occasionally, especially in summer, you may be forced to stay in a 'sleep in' or grotty hostel whose only aim is to cram in as many people as possible. It may be an unpleasant experience but it's certainly not the norm.

Many hostels accept reservations by phone or fax, but usually not during peak periods; they'll often book the next hostel you're heading to for a small fee. You can also book many hostels through national hostel offices. Popular

Life in a Hostel

You've probably heard of youth hostels, but if this is your first trip, the closest you've come to staying in one is most likely your high school camp. If you're travelling around Europe on a budget, hostels will often be your first choice of accommodation. So what are they like? Is that image of 200 camp beds in a basketball stadium true? Once upon a time, YHA hostels (which were pretty much the only ones around) were rather uninviting places, fit only for students and penniless backpackers. They had rules such as curfews, daytime lockouts, huge dormitories and a general ban on fun. You were expected to do chores such as cleaning the toilets for the privilege of paying such a pittance for a bed. Thankfully those days are long gone and hostels are now frequented by all sorts of travellers and are regarded as a very important part of the accommodation hierarchy.

Hostels vary in character from modern, purpose-built places or homely traditional lodgings to the faceless tower blocks you'll still encounter in Eastern Europe and some large cities. A proliferation of independent hostels (not connected to the HI/YHA organisation) has added to the variety. Basically you'll get a bed in a dormitory (usually sex-segregated and usually bunk beds) plus use of communal bathroom/shower facilities. Dorms are often four to six-bed these days, although some are much bigger, and many hostels have double and single rooms. Good hostels will also have a fully equipped kitchen where you can prepare your own meals, and these are a great place to meet other travellers while you're sharing pots, pans and recipes. There should also be a common room with lounge chairs and perhaps a TV or sound system, a laundry and, increasingly, Internet and email access. You'll also find notice boards, local information and a pay phone. Some modern hostels have a bar, cafe or restaurant (usually instead of a kitchen).

Apart from the relatively low cost, the best thing about staying in hostels is the likelihood of meeting other travellers from all over the world. Even if you're the quiet type you'll soon be chatting with the people sharing your room. The drawbacks are the lack of privacy, and being woken at 5 am by the incessant rustling of a guy stuffing his dirty socks into a plastic bag as he rushes off to catch an early train. While most of the rules in hostels have been relaxed, some basic regulations remain to prevent complete anarchy. Clean up after yourself, particularly in the kitchen. Nothing is guaranteed to piss off your hostel manager and fellow travellers more than leaving your dirty dishes in the sink or an exploded soufflé in the microwave. Respect the sleeping by keeping quiet around the rooms in the evening and on no account should you spend half an hour in the shower.

hostels can be heavily booked in summer and limits may even be placed on how many nights you can stay. The price of a bed can vary quite a lot depending on the country, the location and the standard – in London a youth hostel association (YHA) hostel in a prime location near St Paul's Cathedral costs almost twice as much as a private hostel in Earl's Court or Paddington. Generally, a dormitory bed costs from US$3.50 to US$8 in Eastern Europe and from US$12 to US$25 in Western and northern Europe. Prices in southern Europe fall somewhere in between. Some hostels offer breakfast with the room price – if you don't want it, ask for a discount. Some hostels, particularly outside cities, close during winter.

The two types of hostels you'll find are the official ones affiliated with the worldwide YHA/HI organisation, and independent hostels that are privately run.

YHA/HI Most European countries have a network of hostels that are part of the YHA. These associations are affiliated with Hostelling International (HI), although many European countries still have the old International Youth Hostel Federation (IYHF) logos. In practice it makes no difference: IYHF and HI are the same thing and the domestic YHA almost always belongs to the parent group.

Technically, you must be a YHA or HI member to use affiliated hostels (see the Other Paperwork section in the Passports & Visas chapter for details on membership). If you don't have a membership card you can often stay by paying an extra nightly fee that will be subtracted from the cost of future membership. Stay enough nights as a nonmember and you're automatically a member. Bavaria in Germany is one of the few places hanging onto a strict age limit (27 years old) for hostelling members.

YHA/HI hostels are run by employees of the national association, so standards of management and cleanliness are usually quite high. In the past these hostels also imposed strict rules and regulations and even chores. With changing attitudes to budget travel and competition from independent hostels, the rules are mercifully being cut back; many hostels are now open all day (though some, such as in Sweden, still have daytime lockouts), and 'wardens' with a sergeant-major mentality are an endangered species.

Private Hostels The biggest growth in hostelling in recent years has been in the private hostel market (also called 'independent' or 'backpackers' hostels). There are a few privately run hostelling organisations in Europe, and hundreds of unaffiliated hostels owned and run by individuals. Unlike some HI hostels, they have fewer rules (eg no curfew, no daytime lockout) and are usually full of independent travellers rather than noisy groups of European school children. These hostels range from small, cosy places in a converted house to large impersonal places in the middle of large cities. The main drawback with private hostels is that facilities vary greatly (unlike HI hostels, which must meet minimum safety and cleanliness standards), but again, competition has resulted in some great independent places.

If you like a good party while you're travelling, private hostels are often the best places to meet like-minded travellers, and in some cases the hostel *is* the party. The Bauhaus International Youth Hostel in Bruges (Belgium) and the International Youth Hotel in Salzburg (Austria) are two well known places with thumping music, in-house bars and backpackers dancing on the tables. Private hostels usually charge around the same as their YHA/HI counterparts.

University Accommodation

Some university towns rent out student accommodation during summer holiday periods (June to mid-August). This is very popular in France, the UK and in many Eastern European and Baltic countries, as universities become more accountable financially.

Accommodation will sometimes be in single rooms (more commonly in doubles or triples) and may have cooking facilities. Inquire directly at the college or university, at student information services or at local tourist offices. In Finland and Norway, this sort of accommodation is usually affiliated with the national YHA.

B&Bs, Guesthouses & Pensions

There's a huge range of accommodation in Europe above the hostel level (but below hotel level in terms of price). These mid-range places vary in character and style (and name) from country to country, but are often comfortable, home-style places run by families – a great alternative to hostels if you're travelling as a couple or group of three or four.

In Britain and Ireland the best bargain in this field is bed and breakfast accommodation, known simply as B&B. Here you get a room (usually a double but some have singles) and breakfast in a private home. The best part of the deal is the breakfast: at a good B&B it will be a full cooked English breakfast (sausages, eggs, bacon, toast, mushrooms, black pudding, the works) and in some places you help yourself to as much as you want – enough to get you through to tea time! In some areas (such as the Lakes District) every other house will have a B&B sign out the front.

In other countries, similar private accommodation – though often without breakfast – may go under the name of pension, guesthouse, *Gasthaus* or *Zimmer frei* (in Germany), *chambre d'hôte* (in France), *domatia* (in Greece) and so on. Although the majority of guesthouses are simple affairs, there are more expensive ones where you'll find en suites (attached bathroom) and other luxuries.

Hotels

Another step up you'll find hotels. At the bottom end of the hotel bracket these may be no more expensive than B&Bs or guesthouses, and at the other extreme they extend to luxury five-star properties with price tags to match.

In some areas hotels may be the only form of public accommodation (as opposed to private homes with rooms to let) available, but these are likely to be places not frequented by tourists. Although hotel categorisation varies between countries, they are usually star-rated from one (or none) to five. You'll often find inexpensive hotels clustered around the bus and train station areas, so these are good places to start if you're in a hurry to find a place. In some large cities these are also the seediest parts of town.

With cheap hotels, perhaps more so than other types of accommodation, you should check the room before you agree to take it (see the Inspecting the Room section later). Also ask about discounts — cheaper rates are often available for groups, for stays of longer than one night or on weekends. If you think a hotel room is too expensive, ask if there's anything cheaper; hotel owners may try to steer you into more expensive rooms. In France and Britain it is common practice for business hotels (usually more than two stars) to slash their rates by up to 40% on Friday and Saturday nights when the business trade is dead. Save your big hotel splurge for the weekend. Hotels are usually poor value for solo travellers — even if they offer single rooms they may not be much cheaper than a double room.

Another form of hotel accommodation is the pubs of Britain and Ireland. Many pubs have a few cheap rooms upstairs, usually with shared bathroom facilities. These can be noisy because of bar activity, but they can be great fun in small towns and villages where you're at the hub of the community.

Private Homes

In some parts of Europe, private homes are the best places to stay. Not only are they reasonably priced, but you get to mix directly with local families in a unique way. Private homes are particularly popular in Albania, Croatia, Slovenia, Macedonia, Portugal (where they are known as *quarto particular*), Denmark, Norway and the Baltics. Often these are not much different from private guesthouses, but as you'll be staying in a family home, you may well be the only guest.

There are several ways to find private rooms. Some cities have agencies that will find them for you, or the tourist office may have a list. In both cases (certainly in the former) you'll probably pay some sort of commission or fee for the service. Another way is to ask around or look out for signs advertising rooms for rent. At some tourist areas, home owners or touts will be at bus and train stations looking for guests. When deciding on a private room, first check its location — it may be a good hike from the centre of town.

Other Types of Accommodation

The places listed previously are the standard types of accommodation you'll find all over Europe, but there are many more if you're prepared to look for them. Some options include:

Canal Boats & Yachts – In countries such as Britain, France and the Netherlands it's possible to hire a converted barge or canal boat for a week or more of drifting along the waterways in the countryside. If you have a group this can be reasonably affordable as the boats are equipped for sleeping and cooking. Likewise, it's not beyond the realms of budget possibility to charter a yacht for sailing the waters around Turkey, Greece or Croatia if you have a group.

Farmstays – In many rural parts of Europe you can stay on farms. This usually means a bed in a farmhouse, cooked meals and activities such as horse riding. These are usually working farms, so as well as getting to sample the country lifestyle, you can enjoy fresh produce and maybe get to milk a cow.

Monasteries & Castles – Throughout Europe you'll find historic buildings such as castles that have been converted into accommodation. These are rarely cheap though. Monasteries, still inhabited by monks, are usually more affordable. While the amenities may be basic, the locations are often spectacular and you can't beat them for atmosphere. Portugal and Spain are good places to look.

Mountain Huts – Also called *refuges* or *gîtes d'étapes* (in France), these basic timber huts can be found in mountain areas such as the Alps or Pyrenees, and along hiking trails all over Europe. Some have wardens but most are empty and require advance booking and payment. They're usually run by the national parks department or mountaineering association, but are open to anyone. Very basic huts, such as those in Andorra, are free. Inside most refuges you'll find a fireplace, bunk beds, running water and, in the better ones, cooking equipment. Huts on popular routes are likely to be full during summer months, so book ahead.

Rental Accommodation – If you intend to spend a while in a particular area (if you're working or studying, for example), renting private accommodation is the cheapest way to go. There's plenty of rental accommodation available in cities, but the closer to the city centre, the more expensive it will be. Check local newspapers, student notice boards or ask the tourist office to direct you to a rental agency.

FINDING THE RIGHT PLACE

Finding a place for the night can be a withering task, especially when you've just staggered off an overnight train or bus. You might spend hours tramping around a hot, crowded city, or go through a frustrating process of phoning around for a bed, battling the language barrier and cursing the fact that you didn't make a booking. Getting settled and dumping your bags is essential to enjoying the rest of the day, but a good night's sleep is important for your sanity so it's worth getting stuck into the task and finding a clean, comfortable room.

Using an accurate, up-to-date guidebook and talking to fellow travellers are the best ways to find good budget accommodation. A decent guidebook will have listings of several kinds of accommodation in different parts of town. You'll soon discover if these write-ups are accurate and if they cater to your personal taste. The obvious drawback is that places raved about in guidebooks may well be full, or their popularity may have caused standards to slip.

Heading straight to the tourist office is another good idea, particularly as it will often be located conveniently close to transport terminals. Train and bus stations and airports in large cities often have their own tourist information counters. A good tourist office will provide reliable information and should have a list of places in all budget categories. What's more, they can make bookings (sometimes for a fee), give you a map, and advise you how to get there by public transport. Unfortunately, not all tourist offices are good and some are so ridiculously busy that the staff won't have much time for you.

Another option is to use private accommodation agencies, but these will always charge a fee or commission and they usually deal only with top-end accommodation or private rooms. Tourist offices, travel agents or your guidebook should be able to direct you to these services.

Touts are another common way of finding accommodation – whether you're getting off a ferry at a Greek island or joining the stampede out of Amsterdam Central station, they're likely to by lying in wait. Although they *should* be treated with a healthy dose of suspicion, as often as not they can be a blessing. Touts usually materialise at transport terminals in major cities or resorts where tourists congregate and they'll zero in on anyone lugging a backpack. They'll often have flyers or photographs of their accommodation and may even have transport to get you there. It helps to have an idea of local accommodation prices before you agree to anything, because this is a good time to negotiate the rate, especially outside peak season. Above all, be cautious if you're on your own and make sure the place isn't miles from anywhere – you might find you don't like it and will have to return to town.

When searching for accommodation, it pays to be a little choosy. If there is a range of options and you have the time, check out a few before making up your mind. This is easiest when you have a travelling partner; one of you can stay with the bags while the other searches for a room.

Also, try to time your arrival for before noon, or even earlier, when there will probably still be some rooms available. If all the rooms are taken, you can ask to be put on a waiting list, or try a different part of town. If you cannot find the accommodation you want, you may have to shell out for something in a different price bracket, if only for one night.

Inspecting the Room

Before paying for a room you should ask to have a look at it. Sometimes you'll wonder why you bother – one hostel dormitory in Europe will look much like another and you may be more interested to see if the communal bathroom is clean and the kitchen has all the necessary pots and pans. But there's always a chance the hostel, hotel or pension that looks so nice in the lobby is really a complete dump, and you won't have much option to back out once you've paid the money and signed the guestbook. If the first room you see is not to your liking, ask to see another – this will often yield good results. One thing you should be looking for is value for money. If you're paying peanuts, don't expect too much, but if you're paying good money and the room is not clean and comfortable, you can probably do better. When you inspect a room, you should check the following:

Is it clean? – Have a close look at the toilet, under the bed and between the sheets.

Does everything work? – Check the lights, the fan or air-con, the hot and cold water taps, the toilet and shower. If you are near the sea, make sure the taps run fresh water.

Is it safe and secure? – Check for fire exits, ladders, and windows and doors that open and close properly. Does it have a good lock on the door, or a place to mount your own padlock? Make sure the windows are barred or lockable and that any other doors leading into the room are locked or sealed.

Is it likely to be quiet? – There may be a busy street, market, mosque or bar nearby. Rooms on the upper floors near the back of the hotel tend to be the quietest.

Are there any holes in the walls or ceilings? – In some cheaper hotels, you might find holes in some rooms or bathrooms that are used to spy on guests. If possible, move to another place, or plug the holes with toilet paper.

Is it comfortable? – Give the bed a try!

Negotiating a Rate

Accommodation prices in Europe are usually fixed, but in parts of southern and Eastern Europe you may be able to negotiate a lower price in the low season (winter) or the few months either side of summer. This is especially true in Greece, Turkey and most of the seaside resort towns in Croatia, Spain and Portugal. If you're angling for a reduction, try not to come across as rude or demanding. Simply asking: 'Do you have any discounts?' or 'Is that your best price?', while keeping a smile on your face, is the best tactic.

Whether you can negotiate or not, many places in Europe will have a variation in high and low-season prices. In large cities such as London, Berlin and Paris, accommodation prices will generally remain static all year.

Find out whether there are any taxes or surcharges to be added onto the quoted rates before you agree to the room. Many local authorities in France, for instance, charge a 'tourist tax', which will go onto your nightly accommodation, while some places in Europe add a surcharge for stays of only one night.

An Antidote To Paranoia

My wife and I were doing a spot of island-hopping in Greece, and had caught the ferry from Chios to Samos. There had been an announcement on the ferry as we came into Samos, but it was incomprehensible. We got off the ferry thinking that we had arrived at Samos town, the island's capital and main town. We hadn't realised that the ferry stops at two places on the island, Karlovasi (a small town on the north-west coast) and then Samos town.

When we disembarked, I was surprised at the smallness of the town, but there were nevertheless a couple of touts attempting to persuade us to stay at their premises. One of them looked a bit dubious. He was on a motorbike, and the combination of a baseball cap and a thin moustache gave him a sinister aspect. We brushed him off as we made our way to the tiny accommodation bureau. There, the pickings were slim, and what was available was unsatisfactory. We emerged to look further around the town, and were accosted again by the motorcycling tout. 'I have these rooms,' he said. 'Only 7km away … like paradise … '. We were getting desperate, so I asked how we could see them. Could I come with him on the back of his bike? 'The bike is too small,' he replied with surprising diplomacy. 'I take your wife.' I was *very* doubtful about this proposition, but I looked at my wife, and she paused, but then nodded. So I stayed with our luggage while she went off on the pillion.

I waited … and waited … and waited. After almost an hour, when I was on the verge of attempting to find a police station, the bike returned, with my wife intact and smiling. 'It really is a paradise,' she said.

So we caught a taxi there, and I was just as impressed as my wife. It was a beautifully constructed clifftop apartment with a private patio, a great view out to sea, and an attractive taverna in the middle distance. We immediately agreed to take it for a week. First impressions can indeed be misleading!

Graham Fricke
Lonely Planet, Australia

Checking In

Whether you're staying in a camping ground or top-class hotel, you'll have to fill out a straightforward form or sign the guestbook, usually with your name, address, nationality, date of birth and passport number.

You may be asked to show your passport but there's no reason for anyone to keep it, so don't hand it over. If the passport is being asked for as security against your bill, offer some other form of ID or just go somewhere else. It's not uncommon to be asked to pay up front, especially at hostels and other budget places, but make sure you get a receipt. You may also have to pay a small key deposit, which is refunded in cash when you check out – if nothing else it gives you an extra reason to look after your room key!

Security

You should never leave valuables like your passport, visas, credit cards, cash, travellers cheques and camera in your room when you go out. If you don't want to carry your valuables around, ask to leave them in a safety deposit box at the hotel. Many hostels and camping grounds will have lockers for your bags; if possible use your own padlock.

In hostel dormitories, nearly every traveller leaves their main pack unattended in the room. This is usually OK – most of them are full of smelly old clothes anyway – but it's best not to leave your good shirts or whatever lying around. Keep your stuff inside the pack and padlock it when you're not around.

Food

One of the pleasures of continental travel is indulging in the various national foods, from snack stalls selling mussels and *pommes frites* in Brussels or pizza in Naples to a splurge restaurant meal in Paris or tapas in Madrid.

Backpackers on a tight budget usually consider eating to be one area where they can keep costs down. As a result the daily diet consists of bread, cheese, a jar of mustard and some bananas, with an occasional trip to McDonald's thrown in! This is fine for a while, but you should really make an effort to eat out a few times in every country and to seek out the best-value food and unique local specialities. In Mediterranean and Eastern Europe, you should be able to eat out regularly.

A lot of the food you'll encounter in Europe will be familiar, but few regions in the world offer such a wide variety of cuisines in such a small space. In some countries, particularly the 'cold' regions of northern and Eastern Europe, the food tends to have a reputation as being bland and stodgy. Germany is known as a meat, potatoes and dumplings society, Britain (or at least England) is big on Sunday roasts and fish and chips, and you're in trouble if you don't like meat and fish in Scandinavia. On the other hand, the Italians gave us pasta and pizza, the French came up with omelettes and those wonderful soft cheeses, Austria gave us the Wiener schnitzel and croissant, Spain invented paella and we have Germany to thank for pretzels and Black Forest cake.

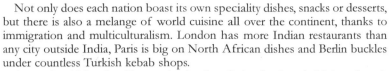

Not only does each nation boast its own speciality dishes, snacks or desserts, but there is also a melange of world cuisine all over the continent, thanks to immigration and multiculturalism. London has more Indian restaurants than any city outside India, Paris is big on North African dishes and Berlin buckles under countless Turkish kebab shops.

A good guidebook will contain details of the food and drinks of each country, plus a section explaining proper eating etiquette (if appropriate) and types of eating places. Most important is a section listing the names of some common dishes, written in both English and that country's language. A guide to local eateries, such as Lonely Planet's *Out to Eat – London* can be great for tapping into budget eateries and bars.

The staff at your hostel or guesthouse should be able to recommend a good place to try local food, and they should know where the best-value places are. Another good idea is to eat where the locals do. If everyone in town crowds into a particular spot at lunchtime, then it's a pretty sure sign that the food is good.

TYPES OF EATING PLACES

Going out to eat in Europe doesn't only mean sitting down at restaurants and cafes. As pleasant an eating experience as they may be, they're also the most expensive. Instead you might find yourself in an English pub, a Greek taverna, a Swiss university Mensa, an Italian trattoria or an Icelandic petrol station! The following are a few of the eateries you can expect to find:

Restaurants – European restaurants can range from cheap places with laminex tables and dubious cleanliness, to classy joints with silver service and bow-tied waiters. The former may or may not serve good local food; the latter will blow a small inheritance! In many countries restaurants will have a menu (with prices) posted outside. Check this to see if the food and the prices are to your liking before going in – in France it's considered extremely rude to leave a restaurant without eating once you're seated. If possible avoid restaurants catering to the tourist crowd – they will probably charge more than places frequented by locals and the food may be substandard.

Cafes – Many parts of Europe (eg France, Austria, Italy and the Netherlands) can be described as having a 'cafe society'. Locals and visitors alike love nothing more than to spend a few hours over coffee or tea, socialising, reading the paper or just watching the world go by. In summer, tables and chairs usually spill out onto the pavement (alfresco-style). Most cafes are open from breakfast through to early (or sometimes late) evening and many serve full meals from a limited menu. Others may only serve coffee and snacks and provide reading matter for patrons. Cafes in Germany and France often serve alcohol as well as hot drinks.

Coffee shops & tearooms – A coffee shop is much like a cafe but is less likely to serve meals or alcohol. At a coffee shop you can sometimes pay less by standing at a high table or bar with your drink rather than taking a seat. In Vienna, the coffee houses are an integral part of city life and shouldn't to be missed. Amsterdam's coffee shops are another thing altogether – they serve coffee, but mainly sell smoke. Tearooms are another variation of the coffee shop, ranging from an outdoor Turkish tea garden to a Devonshire tearoom in England. They serve tea, coffee, scones, cakes and pastries.

while you're there – food

Cafeterias – These include cheap self-service cafeterias, supermarket cafeterias and student cafeterias (known as Mensas in Switzerland and Austria). The decor and furniture are usually plain and the food can be bland but they're good for a cheap, filling meal.

Pubs – The great British pub is still a good place for a hearty meal although in many towns and cities they seem to be going more upmarket. Other parts of Europe also have pubs that are primarily for drinking but serve meals for lunch and dinner.

Wine bars – These are more upmarket drinking establishments where you can get a reasonably priced meal and enjoy a nice atmosphere. Wine cellars like *Heuringen* in Austria and *Weinstubl* in Germany often feature live music.

Takeaways – There are endless varieties of takeaway shops throughout Europe and they're usually great value for a quick feed. In Britain you can get good fish and chips and curries to go; in Turkey it's kebabs; in Greece it's gyros or souvlaki; and in Belgium and the Netherlands it's pommes frites with mayonnaise.

Fast food – Not too many surprises here. In most European cities you can find McDonald's, KFC, Wendy's, Pizza Hut and local variations on the hamburger joint. You know what you're getting and they're always a good option for using the toilet.

MARKETS & SELF-CATERING

Self-catering – buying your own food or ingredients and preparing it yourself – is undoubtedly the cheapest way to eat in Europe. Hostels and camping grounds often have kitchens with cooking facilities so this is a great way to eat cheaply every so often.

Every town or city in Europe has a well stocked supermarket where you can pick up everything you need. Better still, seek out a produce market. Most towns will have one somewhere (although it might only operate on certain days of the week) and in rural villages the market is often a focal point of daily life. This is the best place to buy fresh fruit and vegetables, as well as breads, cheeses, condiments and more.

VEGETARIAN OPTIONS

Generally vegetarians will have nothing to worry about in Europe. Most restaurants will have a few vegetarian dishes and in the larger cities you should have no trouble weeding out a specialist vegetarian restaurant. Your biggest gastronomic hurdle will be most of Eastern Europe where meals, including soups and snacks, tend to be meat heavy. The Scandinavians are more fond of fish than broccoli but lunchtime restaurants often have a salad bar. In parts of southern Europe (such as Sicily) many of the local dishes are vegetarian anyway.

ORDERING MEALS

In tourist areas and main cities and towns you'll find that most restaurants have menus in English as well as the local language, but inevitably there will be places where you can't read the menu and the staff don't speak English. Fortunately, you needn't starve to death or enrol in an intensive language course. Here are a few ordering tips:

- Point at the food on display. A lot of restaurants prepare their food in advance so it's simply a matter of pointing at whatever appeals to you.

- Use your guidebook. A good guidebook will have a section with common dishes written in both English and the local language.
- Learn a few key phrases from your guidebook, eg 'What do you recommend?', 'I'll have that' or 'Do you have any set meals?', and memorise the names of some common dishes.
- Ask someone at your hostel or guesthouse to write down the names of some dishes, to use when ordering.

Drinks

For so many backpackers this is a subject very close to the heart. A few alcoholic drinks at the end of a hard day's sightseeing is part of the unwinding process, and nights out on the town are key factors in the travelling social life. This fits in well with European society because in many countries drinking is an integral part of the local social life; the pub crawls in Reykjavík (Iceland) and Dublin (Ireland) are legendary, Spanish fiestas are a haze of sangria and *cerveza* (beer) and the French would hardly dream of eating a meal without a glass of wine.

But let's not dwell on alcohol! A strong coffee in an Italian cafe or a cuppa (tea) in an English garden are equally social pastimes. Major soft drink brands, plus a few local varieties, are available all over Europe, as are fruit juices and flavoured milk drinks.

Tap water is safe to drink throughout most of Europe, but if you're unsure (or you simply don't like the taste), bottled water is available everywhere. An important tip while travelling, particularly in summer, is to drink plenty of water. It can be very hot and humid in European cities between June and September and constant travelling quickly drains your energy. It's a good idea to always carry a small bottle of water, and if you're hiking carry a large bottle.

ALCOHOLIC DRINKS

Europe has undoubtedly the widest variety of alcoholic beverages of any region in the world, so it's worth mentioning a few here. The main drawback with drinking (apart from hangovers) is the cost – it will seriously eat into your travel budget if you go out regularly. Buying alcohol in supermarkets and partying at your camping ground or hostel is a cheap option but it also cuts you off from the local experience – there's nothing quite like sitting around the fireplace at a cosy English pub or joining the locals at a Greek *ouzeria*.

Drinking is much cheaper in some parts of Europe than others. Eastern Europe is generally the cheapest, while Scandinavia is easily the most expensive. Spain, Greece and Turkey are very reasonably priced for most drinks and Italy is good value for wine.

Beer – Europe has the world's heartiest beer drinkers. The Czech Republic has the world's highest beer consumption per capita – mainly Budvar (the original Budweiser but no relation to the American brand) and Pilsen. Most countries brew at least one beer and often you can tour the breweries, such as the Heinekin Museum in Amsterdam. Bavarian beer halls in Germany are an experience not to be missed and Belgium brews an astonishing 350-plus varieties.

Spirits, aperitifs & liqueurs – There's a wide range of aperitifs (drinks preceding a meal), spirits and liqueurs consumed in Europe. France is the home of brandies (such as Cognac) and well known liqueurs such as Cointreaux and Grand Marnier. The aniseed-based ouzo is popular in Greece, while the Turkish equivalent is called raki. Germany has its schnapps, a strong digestive liqueur made from apples, pears, plums or wheat. Bulgarians and Hungarians swear by their plum brandies. And, of course, Portugal is the place to taste the original port, a fortified wine that's great with coffee at the end of a meal.

Wine – You only need to hear the names of the famous wine regions to know how much we owe to Europe in this department. The Moselle and Rhine regions in Germany, and Champagne, Burgundy, Loire Valley and Bordeaux in France are some of the best places to indulge in some wine tasting. Italy produces such popular wines as chianti (Tuscany), Frascati (Rome) and grappa. Some of Europe's cheapest wines, particularly reds, come from Bulgaria and Romania, and they're not half-bad.

Sightseeing

Europe is the epitome of sightseeing. Everywhere you go you'll be confronted by amazing or famous 'sights' – many people travel to Europe just to see the celebrated buildings, awesome monuments, museums and ancient ruins. Who would go to London and not want to see St Paul's Cathedral or Big Ben? Or skip the Louvre and the Eiffel Tower while in Paris?

Some days it will be a chore to motivate yourself to get out there and see the sights. The summer heat and crowds in Europe's cities can really sap your energy and the quickest route to travel burnout is to treat sightseeing like a race to see everything in the quickest possible time. The truth is, you won't be able to see everything unless you plan to spend at least a week or more in cities and several days in towns. Even then sightseeing takes a bit of planning. Try working out the following day's schedule over dinner or drinks. Peruse your guidebook, chat to travellers and helpful locals, and create an itinerary that caters to your interests and your own pace. The following are some tips for successful city sightseeing:

Work out a realistic itinerary – It's difficult to know how much time you'll want to spend at each sight but you'll soon get a feel for the balance between cramming too much in and getting bored. Europe's major museums and galleries (eg the Louvre or British Museum) would take days, weeks or months to see in any depth, but combine the crowds with those endless masterpieces and you'll probably be ready to leave after a couple of hours. Again, pick the artworks and paintings you most want to see and head for them first.

Prioritise sights – Using your guidebook, tourist office literature and tips from other travellers, work out the things you most want to see and how long it will take to see them. If your time is limited and you stop to check out a few minor sights, you could miss the things you really came for.

Explore areas – It's a good idea to divide large cities into areas, then explore the sights of a particular area on foot, or devise a walking route that takes in the sights you want to see. A good guidebook will often have walking routes included.

Check opening times – If you can enter it, it probably has an opening and closing time. Some sights, including museums and galleries, close on certain days of the week or public holidays. Some places close for lunch; churches and mosques may be out of bounds on certain religious days. Check with the tourist office or your guidebook to avoid wasted trips. Also check whether there are any times when sights offer free or reduced admission, and try to visit places in the early morning or late afternoon when there are fewer people around.

Allow for rest – Whether taking a day or two off and just laying on the beach, or regularly stopping in cafes or parks during the day, allow plenty of time for rest and relaxation.

If the prospect of negotiating another day's sightseeing is simply too overwhelming, many local travel agencies, tourist offices and sometimes hostels offer day tours of various sights. Some might be designed for elderly package tourists and will bore you to tears, but others are tailor-made for backpackers. Either way they can be quite worthwhile if led by a knowledgeable guide, and will make organising your sightseeing far less strenuous.

Many important or historical sites have their own guided tours. Sometimes these are long, boring and relatively expensive, other times they are free and well worthwhile. If you have no literature and there are no labels indicating what you're looking at, a guide can really bring an historic building or a museum to life.

Simply strolling around, stopping now and then for a drink in a local cafe and soaking up the atmosphere can be a pleasant change to dashing madly about town trying to squeeze in just one more tourist sight before sundown. As an independent traveller, you can take whichever approach suits you from day to day.

GETTING OFF THE BEATEN TRACK

It's easy to spend months in Europe hopping from city to city and never getting off the beaten track – many people do. But in most countries you don't

---

Top 10 Tips for First-Time Travel in Europe

Travel light – You can always buy things you need on the road if need be.

Don't try to do too much – You'll have other opportunities to see the places you miss this time round.

Get off the beaten track – Even if you spend most of your time on the tourist trail, try to get somewhere that few foreigners visit at least once.

Get out of the cities – It's all too easy to tramp from one city to the next, and yet some of the most beautiful sights are in rural areas.

Splurge once in a while – Don't get too hung up on penny-pinching. When you're feeling run-down, treat yourself to a fantastic meal, a night on the town, or a bed in a nice hotel.

Avoid high summer – Travel early (April/May/June) or late (September/October) to avoid those interminable crowds and humid temperatures.

Try some unusual foods – Eating exotic cuisines is part of the fun of travel, and Europe has some great culinary traditions.

Learn a few words of the language of the countries you visit – With language, a little can go a long way.

Seek advice from other travellers – There's nothing like a first-hand account from someone who's just been there and done that.

Give yourself a break from time to time – If you've just spent two months dashing from city to city, why not spend a week lying on a Greek beach to recover?

have to go too far to get away from the tourist trail. Some of your most enriching travel experiences will happen away from the popular spots – stumbling on a traditional festival in a Bulgarian village, being invited in for dinner by a Turkish family or trekking to an isolated Portuguese farming community. Of course, the further you get from the tourist trail the harder things get. There may be no cheap accommodation (although you should be able to find a camping ground), public transport may be less extensive, guidebooks and tourist offices will be less useful, and the language barrier will probably increase. But that's all part of the challenge!

The easiest way to get off the beaten track is with your own transport (see Getting Around later in this chapter), but trains and buses will also take you to some very out-of-the-way places. Probably the best way to escape the tourist trail – while taking in some great scenery – is to go hiking. There are many fantastic national parks, forests, mountain areas, moors and glaciers in Europe that are both spectacular and ideal for extended walking trips. Some remote areas, such as Norway's fjords or the islands around Stockholm or Scotland are not completely off the tourist trail but are sufficiently removed to give you the feeling that you have the place all to yourself. Follow common sense if you're going into remote areas: make sure you're well equipped, don't go alone, let someone know when you depart and when you're likely to return, check weather conditions and heed any local warnings.

Travelling in the less 'popular' countries will separate you from most of the tourists. Almost anywhere in Eastern Europe will have fewer visitors than Western or southern Europe. The Baltic states are only just opening up to tourism, and tiny Luxembourg and Liechtenstein are often overlooked.

Craft & Souvenir Highlights

Eastern Europe
- amber jewellery (Poland, Czech Republic)
- folk music (Hungary, Czech Republic)
- embroidery (Romania, Croatia)
- glass and crystal (Czech Republic)

Mediterranean Europe
- carpets (Albania, Turkey)
- ceramics (Greece, Italy, Spain)
- filigree silverwork (Ioannina in Greece)
- leather goods (Greece, Italy, Spain)
- shoulder bags (Greece)
- silk (Albania)
- silver, copper and woodwork (Albania)

Scandinavian & Baltic Europe
- amber jewellery (Lithuania, Latvia)
- glassware (Finland)
- pewter and silverware (Norway)
- pottery and ceramics (Baltic states)
- woollen garments (Iceland)

Western Europe
- knitwear and tartans (Scotland)
- porcelain (Germany)
- pottery (Ireland)
- scarves, lingerie (France)
- swiss knives (Switzerland)
- watches (Switzerland)

Shopping

Europe is a shoppers' paradise. You can find anything you want; from *haute couture* fashions in Paris to imitation Loch Ness monsters in Scotland.

There are two basic categories of souvenirs for sale: those produced for tourists and those produced for locals. Tourist crafts will cost more, but you'll probably have a broader range of choices. Still, the quality of the goods won't be any better, so you'll save money and have more fun shopping in local shops and markets than in the souvenir malls sprinkled throughout big cities. Also bear in mind that when you buy in markets, more profit usually goes directly to the artisan.

Some countries are better for shopping than others. Shopping around and consulting your guidebook for advice will help you learn to discern between good and shoddy workmanship. Markets are often the best places to shop, and some are world-renowned (eg Camden Market in London, Porta Portese in Rome, Christkindmarkt in Nuremberg). Guidebooks often list the best markets and you should try to visit them if only for the experience. See the boxed text 'Craft & Souvenir Highlights' for country-specific shopping highlights.

Try to price different items that appeal to you before buying. Browse at shops and markets to get an idea of price ranges and ask other travellers what they've been paying. Being an informed shopper will help you save money. If possible, do your shopping as near to the end of your trip as is practical. By this time you'll have a good idea of what a reasonable price is, and you won't risk blowing your budget.

One of the biggest pains about shopping is toting around all that loot. If you do leave your shopping to the end of your trip you can avoid lugging it around with you. Alternatively, consider shipping your purchases home. This can be a safe, reliable and cheap option (see the Staying in Touch chapter for more details), but always attend to the shipping yourself even if a shop promises shipping and handling in the price. Another option is to keep your goods in the luggage storage of a trustworthy guesthouse or at the airport (although the latter can be quite expensive), returning later to collect your things.

Big-time shoppers should remember that there is a baggage limit on your plane flight and if you exceed it, you'll have to pay a fee. Also consider what can be easily carried and stored in the tight spaces of a plane and always carry ceramics and glassware on the plane with you.

You will not find many bargains in Europe, especially Western Europe. But if you do want to buy souvenirs or gifts, you should check out the possibility of obtaining refunds of VAT (Value Added Tax) or other taxes before you embark on a purchasing spree. Keep records and fill out the paperwork and you may save yourself a worthwhile amount.

Getting Around

Given Europe's highly developed infrastructure, there is no shortage of ways to get from A to B. Roads – from English country lanes no more than a car width to six lane German autobahns with no speed limit – connect towns, cities and villages across the continent. The world's most comprehensive rail network spreads out like a web, and regular air services zip in all directions daily. Ferries ply the coastal waters while a variety of river boats will take you up the Rhine or down the Danube. Then there's self-powered transport – walking trails or bicycle touring.

Some journeys you make in Europe will be memorable, others will be dull. It's worth researching the transport options of the countries you intend to visit through a good guidebook and the Internet (see Researching Your Trip in the Planning chapter for a list of resources) and by talking to other travellers. You might find you can take a pleasant journey instead of a horrific one simply by using a different mode of transport, or by paying a little more.

AIR

Air travel is usually the most expensive mode of transport. There are exceptions though: some of the charter companies operating out of Britain, for example, offer short-hop flights to the continent for less than the cost of a train ticket! Flying lacks the flexibility of ground transport, and you may not always be able to find the deals when you want them.

But for longer journeys, jumping on a plane can save you from a difficult and boring trip. Consider this scenario: your starting point is London, you have a two month Eurail Pass and you want to travel through Europe, including Turkey (where Eurail is not valid) and Greece (where bus and ferry travel is a better alternative). You can pick up a discounted one-way flight to Istanbul for under UK£100, travel for as long as you want in Turkey and Greece, then start your two month Eurail Pass when you get to Italy. Likewise, if you wanted to travel only in France, Spain and Portugal, you could fly from London to Lisbon or the Algarve for around UK£80, then return by bus and train. Air travel is also useful if you suffer from seasickness and want to reach, say, Malta, Cyprus, Ireland or Iceland without spending the journey with your head in the toilet.

Since 1997, air travel within the EU has been deregulated. This 'open skies' policy allows greater flexibility in routing, and potentially greater competition and lower prices. Air travel is still dominated by the large state-run and private carriers, but these have been joined by a new breed of no-frills small airlines, such as the UK-based Go (a subsidiary of British Airways) and EasyJet, which sell budget tickets directly to the customer. London is probably the best place in Europe for picking up cheap, restricted-validity tickets through 'bucket shops' (travel agents specialising in discounted flight-only tickets). Amsterdam, Athens and Istanbul are other good places for bucket-shop tickets.

In the UK, Trailfinders (☎ 020-7937 5400) and STA Travel (☎ 020-7361 6161) can give you details of tailor-made flights. Look up Europe By Air (www.europebyair.com) for more on domestic flights within Europe. For more tips on flying, see the Takeoff chapter.

BUS

International bus travel in Europe tends to take second place to the relative comfort and romance of going by train. In some countries bus travel is

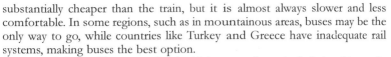

substantially cheaper than the train, but it is almost always slower and less comfortable. In some regions, such as in mountainous areas, buses may be the only way to go, while countries like Turkey and Greece have inadequate rail systems, making buses the best option.

Some of the problems associated with bus travel, particularly local buses in southern Europe, include insane drivers, plumes of cigarette smoke wafting around your face and the proximity in which you're forced to sit with a robust and possibly odorous stranger. But bus travel is a good way of getting to some out-of-the-way places or to tourist sights just outside the main cities.

Another excellent option for independent travellers are the hop-on hop-off buses that operate on set circuits around Europe and in Britain and Ireland.

International Buses

Europe's biggest network of international buses is provided by a group of bus companies operating under the name Eurolines (www.eurolines.com; this Web site has links to each of the national bus networks). Eurolines representatives can often be found at the main bus or train station in each country's capital city. These buses are modern and about as comfortable as standard buses get, with reclining seats, video movies, toilets etc, and they're smoke-free.

If you intend to do a lot of bus travel between major cities it makes sense to look at buying a pass, but the Eurolines passes are neither as extensive nor as flexible as rail passes. The standard pass covers 48 European cities and you get unlimited travel in any direction (seats are only guaranteed if you make an advance booking). There are no refunds for cancellations or lost tickets.

Eurolines also has seven circular explorer routes, always starting and ending in London. The popular London-Amsterdam-Paris route costs UK£69.

Hop-On Hop-Off Buses

In the last five years or so, the market for a bus service specifically for budget travellers spawned the 'hop-on hop-off' style of bus service. These buses run on set circuits around a particular region, stopping at major points to drop off and pick up travellers. You buy a pass and follow the circuit, getting on and off when you please, but you must continue in one direction – there's no backtracking.

The advantages of this type of travel are that you'll meet a lot of travellers (everyone on board is likely to be a fellow backpacker) and the buses are very safe (no night drives, your luggage won't be nicked etc). The downside is that you might feel a bit like you're on tour, and any side trips you want to make away from the circuit will have to be organised independently. In summer the buses are often oversubscribed, so you'll need to prebook each sector to avoid being stranded. The buses turn up every second day in summer, less frequently between November and April.

The main company operating in Europe at present is the London-based Busabout (www.busabout.com), which has a pretty comprehensive set of routes. There are several colour-coded circuits covering most of Europe's main cities as far apart as Lisbon, Oslo and Rome. If you buy some 'add-ons' on top of your pass you can get as far as Warsaw, Kraków, Budapest, the Greek islands, Istanbul and Morocco. The passes give you unlimited travel in a set amount of time, ranging from 15 days to 'unlimited' (which means the summer or winter operating period − about six months). There's also a Bedabout scheme, which gives you prearranged accommodation in tents, bungalows or hostels.

Similar hop-on hop-off services (using smaller buses) operate in Britain and Ireland under names such as the Stray Travel Network, Haggis Backpackers, Go Blue Banana, Hairy Hog and Explorer Britain.

TRAIN

Rail travel is still the classic way of getting around Europe. It's probably the mode most favoured by foreign independent travellers, but also by the many Europeans journeying around their own countries.

Europe's rail network is extensive, its trains are mostly fast, comfortable, frequent and (usually) on time. These factors may vary from country to country, as do the fares. France and Germany have excellent train systems but they are very expensive to travel in. In Spain, Portugal, Italy and much of Eastern Europe, trains are more crowded but much cheaper. In Britain it's often better (and cheaper) to take the bus, while Scandinavia and Switzerland have some spectacular train trips that are worth the high cost.

Which Transport Pass?

When looking at bus or rail passes, you'll want to consider the length of your trip, the amount of distance you want to cover and, of course, the cost. The table below gives the basic high-season costs of the main passes. Eurail, Inter-Rail and Europass are for trains, Busabout and Eurolines are for buses. The first of the two prices is the youth (under 26) or student fare, the second is the adult fare (on trains this means 1st class travel).

Standard Pass	Eurail	Inter-Rail	Europass	Busabout	Eurolines
15 days (unlimited)	$388/554	–	–	$285/395	–
21 days	$499/718	$264/380 (one zone)	–	$380/495	–
30 days	$623/890	$380/513 (three zones)	–	$465/635	$329/379
30 days	–	$430/580 (all zones)	–	–	–
60 days	$882/1260	–	–	$690/875	$409/449
90 days	$1089/1558	–	–	$850/1145	–
Flexipass					
10 days in two months	$458/654	–	$363/528	$349/439	–
15 days in two months	$599/862	–	$513/728	$489/639	–
21 days in two months	–	–	–	$659/819	–
30 days in two months	–	–	–	$869/1099	–

Note: all prices are in US dollars, although Inter-Rail passes are only available from within Europe.

If you intend to travel extensively through Europe by train then you should really consider the benefits of a rail pass against paying as you go. Likewise, it might be worth getting hold of the *Thomas Cook European Timetable*, which gives a complete listing of train schedules and indicates where supplements apply or where reservations are necessary. It's updated monthly and is available from Thomas Cook outlets in the UK and Australia, or in the USA from Rail Europe.

The *European Planning & Rail Guide* is an informative annual magazine; send US$1 (US$3 from outside the USA) to BETS (☎ 734-668 0529, fax 665 5986), 2557 Meade Court, Ann Arbor, MI 48105-1304, USA.

Remember that European trains sometimes split en route in order to service two destinations, so even if you know you're on the right train, make sure you're also in the correct carriage.

Types of Trains

Many international trains in Europe are of the old, rickety compartment variety. A corridor runs up one side of each carriage (usually patrolled by a grim-faced, mustachioed conductor), and each compartment has a pair of facing bench seats that supposedly seat six people but will probably contain eight on popular routes in summer. The compartments have cushioned seats, overhead luggage racks, large windows and closable (but not always lockable) doors. On shorter routes, or in certain countries (such as Britain), the carriages may be modern and open with rows of seats facing forward (known as coach seating).

Most trains have 1st class and economy class carriages. First class has more comfortable seating, air-conditioning and is rarely crowded. But economy is perfectly comfortable and is a good place to meet other travellers and local commuters. Types of trains include:

Express trains – Fast trains or those that make few stops are identified by the symbols EC (EuroCity) or IC (InterCity). The French TGV, Spanish AVE and German ICE trains are even faster. Supplements can apply on fast trains, and it is a good idea (sometimes obligatory) to make seat reservations at peak times and on certain lines.

Overnight trains – If you don't like the idea of sleeping bolt upright in your seat with somebody else's head on your shoulder, you can usually get a choice of couchette or sleeper. Reservations are advisable as sleeping options are allocated on a first-come, first-served basis. Couchettes are bunks numbering four in 1st class or six in 2nd class (per compartment) and are comfortable enough, if lacking a bit in privacy. A bunk costs a fixed price of around US$28 for most international trains, irrespective of the length of the journey. Sleepers are the most comfortable option, offering beds for one or two passengers in 1st class, and two or three passengers in 2nd class. Charges vary depending on the journey, but they are significantly more expensive than couchettes. Most long-distance trains have a dining or buffet (cafe) car or an attendant who wheels a snack trolley through carriages. Prices tend to be steep.

Security

Stories occasionally surface about train passengers being gassed or drugged and then robbed. Be wary of accepting food or drinks from 'friendly' strangers on long-distance trains – if you're travelling alone it's safer to risk appearing rude by declining than to end up being a victim. If possible, lock compartment doors from the inside, chain your luggage to the rack and keep your moneybelt well hidden beneath your clothing. If you're travelling in a group on an overnight train, you could take it in turns having one person stay awake. See the Hazards & Safeguards section in the Issues & Attitudes chapter for more information.

Rail Passes

Things to consider when deciding which rail pass to buy – or indeed whether to buy a rail pass at all – include how much train travel you intend to do, over what period or time and in which countries. If you plan to do a few long trips in Western Europe or Scandinavia over a reasonably short period, then a pass will definitely save you money. If you're hanging around Greece, Italy and Spain all summer, then it probably won't. If you're uncertain where you want to go, but you know you want to see a fair bit of Europe in a two or three month period, a pass will give you flexibility. The other major advantage of a pass is that you won't have to queue up to buy tickets – for an economy seat on most trains, you just climb on board.

If you do get a pass, there are some simple strategies for making the most of it. By planning a rough route before setting out, you can work out when to start using the pass (the period of validation begins with your first train trip). For instance, there's no point getting a one month unlimited travel pass, validating it, then hanging out in Berlin for three weeks. Time your static periods for before and after the period of your pass. If you have a pass that gives limited days over a one or two month period (such as the Eurail flexipass), don't waste a day of travel by taking a short trip in Italy that might only cost US$20 – you're better off paying for it and saving your travel days for a long trip. Shop around too, as pass prices can vary between different outlets. Once purchased, take care of your pass, as it cannot be replaced or refunded if it's lost or stolen.

Eurail These passes can only be bought by residents of non-European countries, and should be purchased before arriving in Europe. (They can be purchased within Europe, as long as your passport proves you've been there for less than six months, but the outlets are limited, and the passes will be more expensive than getting them in your home country.) Eurail passes are valid for unlimited travel on national railways and some private lines in Austria, Belgium, Denmark, Finland, France (including Monaco), Germany, Greece, Hungary, Ireland, Italy, Luxembourg, the Netherlands, Norway, Portugal, Spain, Sweden and Switzerland (including Liechtenstein). Britain, Turkey and most Eastern European countries are not covered. Eurail is also valid on some ferries between Italy and Greece, and between Sweden and Finland. Reductions are given on some other ferry routes and on river/lake steamer services in various countries. Eurail passes offer reasonable value to people aged under 26 (travelling on 2nd class trains), and the 'flexipass', which gives you a chosen number of days travel (10 or 15) within a two month period, offers a bit of flexibility. If you're over 26 you pay for 1st class travel so it's

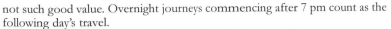
not such good value. Overnight journeys commencing after 7 pm count as the following day's travel.

You must fill out in ink the relevant box in the calendar before starting a day's travel; not validating the pass in this way earns a fine of US$50, plus the full fare. Tampering with the pass (eg using an erasable pen and later rubbing out earlier days – many a traveller has tried it) costs the perpetrator the full fare plus US$100, and confiscation of the pass.

Inter-Rail Inter-Rail passes are available to European residents of six months or more (passport identification is required). There's no flexipass version of Inter-Rail (all travel is unlimited over consecutive days) but it's considerably cheaper than the Eurail version and covers more of the continent (ie most of Eastern Europe as well). The Inter-Rail pass is split into zones. Zone A is Ireland (and Britain if purchased in continental Europe); B is Sweden, Norway and Finland; C is Denmark, Germany, Switzerland and Austria; D is the Czech Republic, Slovakia, Poland, Hungary and Croatia; E is France, Belgium, the Netherlands and Luxembourg; F is Spain, Portugal and Morocco; G is Italy, Greece, Turkey, Slovenia and Italy-Greece ferries; and H is Bulgaria, Romania, Yugoslavia and Macedonia. The normal Inter-Rail pass is for people under 26, though travellers over 26 can get the Inter-Rail 26+ version.

Europass Also for non-Europeans, the Europass gives unlimited travel on freely chosen days (from five to 15) within a two month period. Youth and adult versions are available, and purchasing requirements and sales outlets are as for Eurail passes. They are cheaper than Eurail passes because they cover only France, Germany, Italy, Spain and Switzerland.

Euro Domino There is a Euro Domino pass (called a Freedom pass in Britain) for each of the countries covered in the Inter-Rail pass, except Macedonia. Adults (travelling 1st or 2nd class) and youths under 26 can choose from three, five or 10 days validity within one month.

National Passes If you intend to travel extensively within one country, check which national rail passes are available. These can sometimes save you a lot of money, but you need to plan ahead as some passes (such as Britrail for Britain) can only be purchased prior to arrival in the country concerned.

Great Trains & Train Journeys

Train travel doesn't only have to be a way of getting from A to B. Many of Europe's old trains have an air of romance (others have an air of old socks), but if you look around, you'll find some of the world's great train journeys in Europe. In some parts of Eastern Europe (such as Poland), you'll still find a few steam-hauled narrow gauge passenger trains, while Wales is famous for its little steam trains that now mainly run for tourists and rail buffs. In the Swiss Alps and the Norwegian fjords you'll find some of the world's most scenic rail

Major International Rail Routes & Eurail P

untries

COUNTRIES WHERE
EURAIL PASSES ARE VALID

journeys. If you're filthy rich, take the *Orient Express* or the *Royal Scotsman*. If not, consider these:

Diakofto to Kalavryta – This rack-and-pinion railway runs through the spectacular Vouraikos gorge in the Peloponnese, Greece. The original steam engines have been replaced by diesel, but the view during this one hour ascent makes the trip worthwhile.

Ffestiniog – One of the great little railways in Wales, this is a 22km narrow gauge line winding up into the Snowdonia National Park. The steam train leaves from Porthmadog on the coast for the trip to Ffestiniog Blaenau.

Glacier Express – Switzerland's most famous train ride and one of the most spectacular in the world, this starts in Zermatt (in the shadow of the Matterhorn) and ends in St Moritz eight hours later. It's expensive though and, being a private line, rail passes are not valid.

Jungfraubahn – The highest railway in Europe, this train crawls to the top of Switzerland's Jungfrau, slicing through the Eiger and the Mönch. Even with the Eurail discount, the fare is as steep as the track.

Oslo to Bergen – This 470km trip in Norway is a fine scenic ride through snowcapped mountains and stunning fjords. The side trip on the Flåm line, which hairpins down the Flåm Valley, is another must.

TGV Express – France's famous ultramodern high speed trains can reach speeds of over 500km/h, but usually travel at about 300km/h. There are five services out of Paris, including the Eurostar to London (via the Channel Tunnel).

West Highland line. Scotland – Leaving from Glasgow and chugging up through the beautiful Scottish Highlands to Fort William and Mallaig, this is one of Britain's most scenic train trips.

CAR & MOTORCYCLE

Travelling with your own vehicle is the best way to reach remote places, and it gives you almost unlimited flexibility. You can go where you want, when you want and, with a group, you can travel relatively cheaply. Unfortunately, the independence you enjoy tends to isolate you from the whole travelling experience – not only from local people but from other travellers. Cars are also inconvenient and positively frightening in big city centres, where it's generally worth ditching your vehicle and relying on public transport. Apart from coming to grips with heavy traffic and strange road rules, you'll never find anywhere to park.

Paperwork & Preparations

Proof of ownership of a private vehicle should always be carried (Vehicle Registration Document for British-registered cars) when touring Europe. Although your home licence may be valid in most European countries, it's well worth getting an International Driving Permit (IDP) from your motoring organisation (see the Other Paperwork section in the Passports & Visas chapter). Third-party motor insurance is a minimum requirement in Europe. Most UK motor insurance policies automatically provide this for EU countries and some others. Get your insurer to issue a Green Card (which may cost extra), an internationally recognised proof of insurance, and check that it lists all the countries you intend to visit. You'll need this in the event of an accident outside the country where the vehicle is insured. Also ask your insurer for a

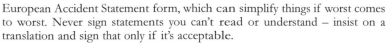

European Accident Statement form, which can simplify things if worst comes to worst. Never sign statements you can't read or understand – insist on a translation and sign that only if it's acceptable.

Taking out a European motoring assistance policy – such as the AA Five Star Service or the Royal Automobile Club (RAC) Eurocover Motoring Assistance – is a good investment. Check with your national motoring organisation as it may be cheaper to arrange international coverage before leaving home. Also ask your motoring organisation for details about free services offered by affiliated organisations around Europe.

Some things you should have while driving in Europe include a sticker showing your vehicle's country of registration; a warning triangle to be used in the event of breakdown (compulsory almost everywhere); a first-aid kit (compulsory in Austria, Slovenia, Croatia, Yugoslavia and Greece); a spare bulb kit (compulsory in Spain); and a fire extinguisher (compulsory in Greece and Turkey).

Road Rules

With the exception of Britain, Ireland and Malta, driving is on the right-hand side of the road. Vehicles brought over from any of these countries should have their headlights adjusted to avoid blinding oncoming traffic at night. Britain's RAC publishes an annual *European Motoring Guide* (UK£4.99), which gives an excellent summary of regulations in each country, including parking rules. Motoring organisations in other countries have similar publications.

Take care with speed limits, as they vary from country to country. You may be surprised at the apparent disregard for traffic regulations in some places (particularly in Italy and Greece), but as a visitor it is always best to be cautious. Many driving infringements are subject to an on-the-spot fine in all countries except Britain and Ireland. Always ask for a receipt. European drink-driving laws are particularly strict. The blood-alcohol concentration (BAC) limit when driving is between 0.05 and 0.08%, but in certain areas – Gibraltar and some Eastern European countries – it can be 0.00%.

Roads & Hazards

Road conditions vary across Europe, but main roads are generally very good. The fastest routes are four or six-lane dual carriageways/highways, ie two or three lanes either side (motorway, autobahn, autostrada etc). These tend to skirt cities and plough through the countryside in straight lines, often avoiding the most scenic bits. Some of these roads incur tolls, often quite hefty (eg in Italy, France and Spain), or have an annual charge for visitors (Switzerland and Austria), but there will always be an alternative route you can take.

Road surfaces on minor routes are not so reliable in some countries (eg Greece, Romania and Ireland), although normally they will be more than adequate. These roads are narrower and progress is generally much slower. To compensate, you can expect better scenery and plenty of interesting villages en route.

Driving in Eastern Europe and southern Europe is considerably more dangerous than it is in Western Europe. Driving at night can be especially hazardous as the roads are often narrow and winding, and horse-drawn vehicles, bicycles, pedestrians and even domestic animals may be encountered at any time. Extra care should also be taken on winding mountain roads and on any roads in winter when 'black ice' can send you skidding like a toboggan, or fog will reduce visibility to a matter of inches.

If you're parking your car or van anywhere, never leave anything of value in it. In places like France and Italy theft from cars is rife.

Renting a Car or Motorcycle

The big international firms – Hertz, Avis, Budget Car, Eurodollar, and Europe's largest rental agency, Europcar – will give you reliable service and a good standard of vehicle. You may have the option of returning the car to a different outlet at the end of the rental period.

With these companies you will get cheaper deals if you prebook well in advance. If you want to rent a car on the spot, look for national or local firms, which can often undercut the big companies by up to 40%. Be wary of dodgy deals where they take your money and point you towards some clapped-out wreck, or where the rental agreement is bad news if you have an accident or the car is stolen. When booking, ask in advance if you can drive a rented car across borders. In the USA try Auto Europe (☎ 800-223 5555, www.autoeurope.com), which has low long-term rental rates.

No matter where you rent, make sure you understand what is included in the price (unlimited or paid kilometres, tax, injury insurance, collision damage waiver etc) and what your liabilities are. We recommend taking the collision damage waiver, though you can probably skip the injury insurance if you and your passengers have decent travel insurance. The minimum rental age is usually 21 or even 23, and you'll probably need a credit card. Note that prices at airport rental offices are usually higher than at branches in the city centre.

Motorcycle and moped rental is common in some countries, such as Italy, Spain, Greece and the south of France, but take care – it's all too common to see inexperienced riders leap on bikes and very quickly fall off them again.

Leasing

Leasing a vehicle has none of the hassles of purchasing and can work out considerably cheaper than hiring over longer periods. The Renault Eurodrive Scheme provides new cars for non-EU residents for a period of between 17 and 170 days. Other companies with comparable leasing programs include Peugeot and Citroen. Check out the options before leaving home.

Buying a Car or Motorcycle

The purchase of vehicles in some European countries is illegal for nonresidents of that country. Britain is probably the best place to buy: second-hand prices are usually good and, even when buying privately, you won't have the language difficulties that can get in the way of negotiations.

Bear in mind that you will be getting a car with the steering wheel on the right in Britain. If you want left-hand drive and can afford to buy new, prices are reasonable in the Netherlands and Greece (without tax), France and Germany (with tax), and Belgium and Luxembourg (regardless of tax). Paperwork can be tricky wherever you buy, and many countries have compulsory roadworthiness checks on older vehicles.

Camper Van Touring

Touring Europe by camper van (picture the VW Kombi) has long been a classic trip, especially for rampaging groups of Aussies and Kiwis. The advantages are obvious: it's large enough to comfortably carry a group of three or four plus luggage, so you save money on fuel, tolls, purchase or rental of the van etc; you can camp or sleep in the van, saving on accommodation costs while providing some security; and you have mobile cooking facilities. Buying or hiring a van when you get to Europe is the way to go, and London is a good place to start looking. London's free weekly *TNT Magazine* (www.tntmag.co.uk) has advertisements for vans to buy and rent, or seeking travellers wanting to join a group in a van tour. The Van Market in Market Rd, London N7, is a great place to go and get an idea of what's available and how much they cost. Private vendors congregate here on a daily basis. Some second-hand dealers offer a 'buy-back' scheme for when you return from the continent, but buying and reselling privately will be more worthwhile if you have the time.

Camper vans usually feature a fixed high-top or elevating roof and two to five bunk beds. Apart from the essential camping gas cooker, professional conversions may include a sink, fridge and built-in cupboards. You will need to spend from at least UK£2000 (US$3200) for something reliable enough to get you around Europe for any length of time. Getting a mechanical check is a good idea before you buy. The eternal favourite for budget travellers is still the VW Kombi; they aren't made any more but the old ones seem to go on forever, and getting spare parts isn't a problem. Remember to set some money aside for emergency repairs.

A disadvantage of camper vans is that you are in a confined space for much of the time. (Four adults in a small van can soon fry each other's nerves, especially if the group has been formed at short notice.) Another problem is that they're not very manoeuvrable around town, and you'll often have to leave your gear unattended inside (many people bolt extra locks onto the van). They're also relatively expensive to buy in spring and hard to sell in autumn.

Motorcycle Touring

Europe is made for motorcycle touring, with good-quality winding roads and stunning scenery. Just make sure your wet-weather gear is up to scratch.

Crash helmets for rider and passenger are compulsory everywhere in Europe. Austria, Belgium, France, Germany, Luxembourg, Portugal and Spain also require that motorcyclists use headlights during the day; in other countries it is recommended.

On ferries, motorcyclists rarely have to book ahead as they can generally be squeezed in. Take note of the local custom about parking motorcycles on pavements (sidewalks). Though this is illegal in some countries, the police usually turn a blind eye as long as the vehicle doesn't obstruct pedestrians. Don't try this in Britain though.

BICYCLE TOURING

A tour of Europe by bike might seem like a daunting prospect, but a surprising number of people do it. Few forms of transport can give you such a sense of freedom and closeness to nature as the bicycle and, because you'll be moving relatively slowly, you really appreciate your surroundings. Is there any better way of coming to grips with the continent than cycling through the vineyards and chateaux of the Loire Valley in France, or along the Algarve coast in Portugal? Some countries are made for cycling. The Netherlands and Belgium are pancake-flat and have almost as many dedicated bike paths as roads.

But as romantic and bucolic as tackling Europe by bicycle sounds, it's definitely not to be taken lightly and, if this is to be your main means of transport, it will take a bit of planning. One organisation that can help in the UK is the Cyclists' Touring Club (CTC; ☎ 01483-417 217, ✆ cycling@ctc.org.uk), Cotterell House, 69 Meadrow, Godalming, Surrey GU7 3HS. It can supply information to members on cycling conditions in Europe as well as detailed routes, itineraries, maps and cheap specialised insurance. Membership costs UK£25 a year, UK£12.50 for students and people under 18, or UK£16.50 for senior citizens. Check its Web site at www.ctc.org.uk. Michelin maps indicate scenic routes, which can help you construct good cycling itineraries. Lonely Planet's cycling guides include *Cycling Britain* and *Cycling France*.

A primary consideration on a cycling tour is to travel light, but you should take a few tools and spare parts, including a puncture repair kit, tyre levers and pump and an extra inner tube. Panniers are essential to balance your possessions on either side of the bike frame. A bike helmet is also a very good idea (and compulsory in some countries). Take a good lock and always use it when you leave your bike unattended. If you get tired of pedalling or simply want to skip a boring transport section, you can put your feet up on the train. On slower trains, bikes can usually be transported as luggage. Fast trains can rarely accommodate bikes: they might need to be sent as registered luggage and may end up on a different train from the one you take. This is often the case in France and Spain. British Rail is not part of the European luggage registration scheme, but Eurostar is: it charges UK£20 to send a bike as registered luggage on its routes. You can transport your bicycle with you on Eurotunnel through the Channel Tunnel. With a bit of tinkering and dismantling (eg removing wheels) and a bike bag, you'll be able to get your bike on a train as hand luggage and save yourself the nightmare (and extra expense) of working out which trains take bikes.

The European Bike Express is a coach service where cyclists can travel with their bicycles. It runs in the summer from north-east England to France, Italy

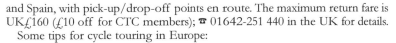

and Spain, with pick-up/drop-off points en route. The maximum return fare is UK£160 (£10 off for CTC members); ☎ 01642-251 440 in the UK for details. Some tips for cycle touring in Europe:

• Make sure your bike has very low gearing; once you add a couple of panniers to a bike that easy hill will look (and feel) like the Alps.

• Cycling requires energy (lots of energy!) so eat, drink and be merry (after you've finished riding for the day, of course). And carry plenty of water during the day.

• There's lots to see in Europe so plan on riding between 45 and 80km per day.

• Get a cycle computer for your bike (so you can see how far and how fast you're going) and learn how to fix a puncture, adjust your brakes and gears, and replace a broken spoke.

• Get fit before you start your cycle tour. Start training at least six weeks before you leave and build up to a point where you can ride 60km on a fully loaded bike without expiring.

Rental

You don't necessarily have to get ready for a Tour de France to enjoy a bit of cycling in Europe. Bikes and equipment (such as panniers) can easily be hired throughout most of Europe on an hourly, half-day, daily or weekly basis. Many train stations have bike-rental counters. An option is to store most of your luggage in a long-term locker or at a reliable hostel, then take off on a hired bike to explore, say, Holland, Tuscany or Cornwall before continuing on with more conventional travel. Sometimes it's possible to return the machine to a different outlet so you don't have to retrace your route.

Buying a Bike vs Bring Your Own

For major cycling tours, it's best to have a bike you're familiar with, so consider bringing your own rather than buying on arrival. If you do decide to buy, there are plenty of places where you can find high-quality bikes in cycle-mad Europe, but you'll need to visit a specialist bicycle shop for a machine capable of withstanding European touring. CTC can provide a leaflet on purchasing.

Free Copenhagen Bikes

The city of Copenhagen operates a generous scheme, called Bycykler (City Bikes), by which anyone can borrow a bicycle for free. It's motivated in part by an effort to control motor vehicle traffic in the heart of the city. Sponsors, who paint the bikes with their logos, include private businesses, the local tourism office and the city council. In all there are some 2500 bikes available during summer and autumn (14 April to 1 November).

Although the bicycles are not streamlined and are certainly not practical for long-distance cycling, that's part of the plan – use of the cycles is limited to the city centre. To deter theft and minimise maintenance, the bicycles have a distinctive design that includes solid spokeless wheels with puncture-resistant tyres. The bikes can be found at 150 widely scattered street stands in public places, including train stations.

If you're able to find a free bicycle, you deposit a 20kr coin in the stand to release the bike. When you've finished with the bicycle you can return it to any stand and get your 20kr coin back.

Cycling is very popular in the Netherlands and Germany, and these are good places to pick up a well equipped touring bicycle. European prices are quite high (certainly higher than in North America), but non-Europeans should be able to claim back VAT on the purchase.

If you want to bring your own bicycle to Europe, you should be able to take it along with you on the plane relatively easily (see the Bikes section in the Tickets & Insurance chapter). You can either take it apart and pack everything in a bike bag or box, or simply wheel it to the check-in desk, where it should be treated as a piece of luggage. You may have to remove the pedals and turn the handlebars sideways so that it takes up less space in the aircraft's hold; check all this with the airline well in advance, preferably before you pay for your ticket. If your bicycle and other luggage exceed your weight allowance, ask about alternatives or you may suddenly find yourself being charged a fortune for excess baggage.

HITCHING

Hitching is never entirely safe in any country in the world, and we don't recommend it. Travellers who decide to hitch should understand that they are taking a small but potentially serious risk. People who do choose to hitch will be safer if they travel in pairs and let someone know where they plan to go.

A man and woman travelling together is probably the best combination. Two or more men won't go far; two women together will make good time and should be relatively safe. A woman hitching on her own is taking a big risk, particularly in parts of southern Europe.

Some countries are better than others for hitchhiking. Britain and Ireland are good, as is Germany where hitching is an accepted practice, but you'll find things more difficult in Spain, Italy and Greece. In some Eastern European countries such as Albania, Romania and sometimes Poland, drivers expect riders to pay the equivalent of the bus fare. In Romania traffic is light, motorists are probably not going far, and almost everywhere you'll face small vehicles overloaded with passengers. Some general tips are:

- Don't try to hitch from city centres or close to a major intersection: take public transport to suburban exit routes.
- Hitching is usually illegal on motorways (freeways) – stand on the slip roads, or approach drivers at petrol stations and truck stops.
- Never hitch where drivers can't stop in good time or without causing an obstruction.
- Look presentable and cheerful and make a cardboard sign indicating your intended destination in the local language.
- Don't even think about hitchhiking at night. At dusk, give up and think about finding somewhere to stay.
- If your itinerary includes a ferry crossing (for instance, across the Channel), it might be worth trying to score a ride before the ferry departs rather than after, since vehicle tickets sometimes include a number of passengers free of charge. This also applies to Eurotunnel via the Channel Tunnel.

It's possible to arrange a lift in advance by checking notice boards at hostels, in colleges, or by contacting car-sharing agencies. Such agencies are popular in France (Allostop Provoya, Auto-Partage) and Germany (Mitfahrzentralen).

WALKING

It may be slow, but there's no better way of taking in your surroundings than on foot. For some this will be restricted to city sightseeing; for others the entire trip may be one big hike.

There are many options for short walks or overnight hikes that won't require you to lug your backpack around, but you'll still need to be reasonably fit. Start taking walks from home at least six weeks before your trip (with or without a pack) to build up some endurance.

In summertime many of the walking trails in popular areas will be crowded, so time your walks for spring and autumn but check first whether accommodation and transport will be available. Some other tips for walking include:

- Take a day-pack and a pair of light, comfortable walking boots – useful for travelling, invaluable for walking. Ask about walks in the area at local tourist information offices or park visitor centres. Many carry useful leaflets in more than one language.
- Be prepared with sun protection and plenty of water if it's hot, or warm and water-proof clothing in cool climates.
- Take all your litter with you when you leave: if you carried it in, you can carry it out.
- Carry a compass – invaluable for map reading and a great help if you get lost.

For more information on walking in Europe, see the Thematic Trips section in the Planning chapter.

SEA TRAVEL

You mightn't consider sea travel to be your primary way of getting around Europe, but if you're making an extensive trip you'll almost certainly use the ferries at some stage. Some of the most enjoyable trips you will make in Europe might be by boat – crossing by steamer from Stockholm to the surrounding islands, navigating the Greek islands among a sea of sleeping bags on deck class, or cruising the Mediterranean coast by chartered yacht.

Several different ferry companies compete on all the main ferry routes, and major crossings (such as the English Channel) have frequent services. Most sea ferries take vehicles as well as passengers, but you usually won't have access to the vehicle once you're on board. If you visit Britain, you'll probably use ferries to get to mainland Europe and back (although the Channel Tunnel can whisk you under the waves in a fraction of the time these days), but you don't have to settle for the short English Channel hop between France and Britain. Consider the 24 hour crossing from Plymouth to Santander in northern Spain, or the overnight ferries from Newcastle to Bergen (Norway), Gothenburg (Sweden) or Hamburg (Germany).

Scandinavia provides plenty of opportunities for ferry travel with boats regularly plying the Baltic and North seas. Steamers pull out of Stockholm regularly to the many islands of its eastern archipelago. Finland is best reached by ferry from Stockholm (Sweden), Tallin (Estonia) or Travemünde (Germany). Croatia is the one country in Eastern Europe with significant (and affordable) sea routes. A boat trip along Croatia's heavily indented coast is one of the scenic highlights of Eastern Europe.

The classic European ferry travel is cruising the Greek islands in the Mediterranean and Aegean seas. Dozens of ferries link these islands in summer but services are drastically reduced in winter. The Italy-Greece overnight crossing is very popular and you can continue island-hopping all the way to the west coast of Turkey. The *Thomas Cook Guide to Greek Island Hopping* gives comprehensive listings of ferry times, routes and sightseeing.

On most ferries you can choose between deck class, where you can take a seat inside or roll your sleeping bag out on the floor, or the more expensive option of a cabin which must be booked in advance. Most ferries have a snack bar selling expensive (and usually lousy) food, so it's worth bringing supplies of your own for crossings of any more than a few hours. Some of the overnight ferries in northern Europe are like floating nightclubs with bars, casinos and duty-free shops on board. The Scandinavian ferries in particular have cheaper alcohol on board than the locals can get at home, so many young people treat a trip like a night out on the town – avoid weekend ferries unless you want to join the party!

RIVER TRAVEL

There are many opportunities for river travel in Europe but usually it's more a choice than a necessity. Some river trips in Europe are stunningly scenic, romantic or unusual; others are a very laid-back way to see the sights, but they are rarely cheaper than land transport.

Major cities are often dissected by famous rivers and these make great sightseeing trips. In London you can take a boat down the Thames to Greenwich or in the other direction to Kew Gardens and Hampton Court. In Paris you can cruise the Seine; in Turkey you can ferry up the Bosphorous to the mouth of the Black Sea. The Danube flows through Vienna and Hungary, the Tiber splits Rome, and Lisbon's Rio Tejo has launched many a seafaring explorer.

Canal boat travel (on barges, longboats or gondolas) is popular in some cities such as Venice, Amsterdam and Bruges, and in rural France and England. There are numerous extended river cruises that, while perhaps not cheap, can give you a new perspective on Europe. Some cruises (such as the Rhine River cruise) are free or discounted with Eurail or Inter-Rail passes. Some of Europe's great river trips include:

Danube (Austria) – A steamer ride on the 'blue' Danube can be taken from Vienna, but the stretch of the Danube Valley from Krems to Melk is the most scenic. If you have the money (deck prices start at UK£1780) you can take a 12 day cruise on the *Swiss Pearl* all the way from Vienna to Amsterdam, linking up with the Rhine in Germany.

Danube (Hungary) – The Danube Bend between Esztergom and Szentendre (just north of Budapest) is perhaps the most beautiful part of the Danube's entire 3000km length. A ferry ride here is relatively cheap, passing mountain peaks, resorts and river towns.

Douro (Portugal) – The Rio Douro (River of Gold) runs from the Spanish border to the sea at Porto in northern Portugal. You can cruise all the way from Barca de Alva through dramatic gorges to lush port-wine country at Porto.

Moselle (Luxembourg) – Like the Rhine, the Moselle cuts through wine-growing country and is a region of lush valleys and quaint little villages. The Moselle Valley in

Luxembourg is one of Europe's smallest wine regions and a cruise along here is a pleasure.

Rhine (Germany) – This ferry trip from Mainz to Cologne passes through vine-covered valleys dotted with classic German castles. The most scenic section is Mainz to Koblenz (the entire trip is free with Eurail).

CITY TRANSPORT

It's inevitable that you'll use inner-city public transport in Europe. In the big cities, walking (or even cycling) is simply not viable if you want to see all the sights or even if you just want to get from one area to another. The good news is that most city transport services are excellent.

The bad news is that public transport can be overcrowded (avoid morning and afternoon weekday rush hours) and relatively expensive. If you're in a city for a few days or longer, it's always cheaper to buy a day pass, week pass or book of tickets rather than to pay as you go. Some other tips to consider:

- Get hold of a route map. The public transport services in most cities publish a transport map for local train, bus and metro routes. These can be picked up at tourist offices, newsagents and bus, train or metro terminals and are invaluable.
- Make sure you have plenty of small change before boarding buses and trams that require you to pay the driver – often they will only accept exact change. Better still, buy a ticket in advance.
- Cities are often divided into transport zones, which should be shown on the route map. When you buy a ticket, make sure it corresponds to the zone(s) you intend to travel in – if you cross into zone 3 and you only have a zone 2 ticket, you can be fined.
- Watch your bags closely when on crowded trains or buses. These can be a haven for pickpockets. Buses that are popular with tourists are particularly bad – bus No 64 in Rome, from the train station to the Vatican, is notorious for theft.
- In countries where English isn't widely spoken, have your stop or destination written in the local language by the owner of your hostel or guesthouse, to show to a local passenger so they can tell you when to get off.
- Transport day passes are often cheaper if purchased after 9 am on weekdays (after the morning rush hour), giving you another reason to avoid those early crowds.

Bus

There are public buses in every city and town and they vary from modern and comfortable to slow-moving rust buckets.

In busy cities, buses can be interminably slow because of the heavy traffic, but they do give you an opportunity to see the city at ground level (as opposed to underground level). In fact, grabbing an upstairs window seat on a London double-decker bus is a great, cheap way to do a bit of sightseeing. The hardest thing, of course, is figuring out the local bus system. It's rarely simple because buses take circuitous routes and more than one bus will run on similar or overlapping routes. The destination on the front of the bus is usually where the vehicle is going (eventually) and there will also be a number (something ridiculous like 1134Ev), which will hopefully correspond to something on your route map.

In some cases you will have to pay the driver as you get on, in others there will be a conductor on board. On some services (such as in Amsterdam) you have to buy strip tickets and validate them in a machine (usually a small box with a slit opening) on board. Most cities have reduced night bus services that start up when the metro and regular bus services shut down.

Outside cities, local buses are the main way of getting around and between towns. A good guidebook will give bus numbers to the main tourist sights.

Taxi

Taxis in Europe are metered and rates are usually high. There might also be supplements for things like luggage, the time of day, the location and extra passengers. Lower fares make taxis more viable in some countries, such as Spain, Greece, Portugal and Turkey. In some Eastern European countries beware of unregistered taxis or taxi drivers trying to rip you off. Check that the taxi has a working meter and ask for an estimate of the fare beforehand.

Metro, Tram & Local Train

Probably the easiest, quickest and most convenient way of getting around large cities is the underground train system. In France and numerous other countries it's called the Metro, in Germany, Austria and Switzerland it's the U-Bahn, in England it's the tube (officially known as the Underground) and in Norway it's the T-bane. Whatever it's called, you descend into the bowels of a city, board a small train which darts off into a tunnel, and some time later you emerge in a completely different part of the city.

Some metros are large and confusing (Paris and London), some have only two or three lines (Prague and Rome), but they all work the same way. They have a series of lines which are designated by name, number or letter, and each train runs on only one line. If you need to change lines you'll have to get off at an intersecting station and find the appropriate platform. Keep an eye out the window to see which stop you're at, although most services now have a recorded voice which tells you where you are, what the next stop will be and, in London, to 'mind the gap' on your way out. Some metro systems work on the ticket validation system where you buy the ticket at a kiosk in advance then validate (punch) it on board the train. Effectively this means you could ride around for free, but inspectors regularly patrol the trains and if you're caught riding without a ticket, or with an unvalidated ticket, you'll cop a hefty fine and be subjected to open ridicule. In Germany this system works well because no-one wants to be publicly disgraced on a crowded train.

Some cities still have old trams (street cars), which are a quaint way to travel. You'll find them in Poland, Portugal, Croatia and Romania and they're much the same as travelling on a bus. In Eastern Europe they can be very crowded and require some practice to board successfully. Another form of transport you might encounter is the trolleybus, which is a cross between a tram (with the overhead wires) and a bus.

Finally, many cities, including those with metro systems, have local trains which run above ground and often serve outer suburbs.

There are few places in Europe where you won't be able to phone home, post a letter, send a fax, or – in the cities and tourist areas at least – send an email to family and friends. Even in former communist Eastern Europe, once a black hole of archaic, unreliable phone lines and unpredictable post, the services are moving well into line with the efficiency of Western Europe. But while you're having a great time on the road, it's all too easy to forget about keeping in touch. Home seems a long way away and there may be a temptation to put that call off until the next town or send that postcard next week. Meanwhile, people at home are wondering about you all the time.

It's only fair to ease your parents' minds with the occasional phone call or postcard, and to let your friends know you're still thinking about them (even if you're not!). And don't underestimate the extent to which hearing familiar voices will cheer you up when you're in an unfamiliar place. There's no better way of appreciating the experiences you're having than relating them to someone at home. If something goes wrong on the road, the best way to pick yourself up is to listen to a few comforting words from the people who care.

It does cost some money to keep in touch with home, particularly by phone, so factor it into your budget. Some tips on staying in touch include:

- Give those at home a general itinerary, so they'll have an idea where you are at different stages of your trip.
- Call friends and family before heading out on long treks or trips into remote areas where you may be out of touch for a while (and call again to let them know you're OK when you get back).
- Ask someone at home to save the letters you send them. This is almost as good as keeping a diary and they make great reading when you get home.
- Work out ideal times to call family and individual friends to minimise the chance of calling when they're not home. It's best not to make definite calling times or schedules in case you forget to make the call and people start to worry.
- If you get tired of writing the same news to everyone, write up one good, detailed letter or email and send copies to everyone, with some personalised information at the end.
- If your personal stereo has a record function, you can send back audio letters on cassette tapes.
- Include a few photos that you've had developed on the road to add spice to your letters and help people visualise what you're experiencing.

Telephone

A phone box or telecommunications centre will never be far away in Europe.

In most countries public phones all have International Direct Dialling (IDD) access, or you can go through international or domestic operators. When you call other European countries, engaged signals and ringing tones may sound different from those at home.

Remember that there'll probably be a significant time difference if you're calling from Europe to another continent, so check this before calling home unless you want to drag someone out of bed at 3 am (see the back inside cover of this book for time zone information). This time difference can work in your favour as most countries have off-peak calling times which are significantly cheaper than peak calls. Off-peak is usually outside business hours (ie 6 or 8 pm to 8 am on weekdays and any time on weekends).

For country-specific details of telephone services, see the Post & Communications sections of the country profiles later in this book.

WHERE TO CALL FROM

Throughout Western and northern Europe (including Scandinavia) you can make international calls from almost any pay phone (call box). The situation is the same in most of Eastern and southern Europe, although in some rural areas and small towns you may have to visit a telecommunications centre and make an operator-assisted call. Most new public phones throughout Europe now accept phonecards and it can be difficult to find phones that accept coins.

Public cardphones can always be found at the post office (either inside or outside, or both). In some Eastern European countries (eg Slovenia or Poland) it's often better to make an operator-assisted call from the post office or a telephone centre (which may be attached to or inside the post office). Usually you make a timed call from a booth then pay the cashier afterwards. In some countries, notably Britain, there are independent telephone centres that undercut the national telephone company, making them cheaper for international calls.

You can also make international phone calls from hotel lobbies or your hotel room, but these will always be more expensive than from a public phone.

TYPES OF CALLS

There are numerous ways of making calls from public (or private) phones:

Direct (person-to-person) – This is the easiest and usually the cheapest way to call. Direct calls can be made from international pay phones and private phones in countries that have IDD facilities. You simply dial the International Access Code (IAC) for the country you are calling from (usually 00 in Europe), then the country code (eg 61 for Australia, 1 for the USA and Canada), then the area code and number of the party you want to reach. Many of the new pay phones have displays showing how much credit you have left on your phonecard or telling you to insert more money.

Operator assisted – Direct-dialling is rapidly replacing the need for this service, but in some rural areas in Eastern Europe you may find this is the best way to make an international call, particularly where there are still the old analogue phones in place or if you don't have a phonecard. A number will be provided to get through to the local operator, but if language is a problem you may be better off using the Home Country Direct system (see later).

Reverse charge (collect) – The operator will place these calls for you. They can be pretty expensive, so make sure the other party understands how much their bill is likely to be. Reverse-charge calls can be made from some pay phones, hotel phones and telephone offices. A better option is to make a quick direct dial call and get the home party to call you back, but this may not be possible from phone boxes because they don't always display the number. If you can't do it from a phone box, try the post office.

Home Country Direct – By dialling a specific number you can bypass local operators entirely and speak directly to an operator in your home country, who can then arrange a credit card or reverse-charge call. The Home Country Direct service allows you to dial a toll-free number from most European countries. The USA offers the most comprehensive service, while calls to Canada, Australia and New Zealand are available from all but a handful of Eastern European countries. Home Country Direct numbers will be listed in most guidebooks, or call the telephone company. Calls can be made free of charge from public phones, but a small fee may be charged from hotels or telephone centres.

Credit card – Public phones where you can swipe your credit card and have the call billed to it are becoming more common in Europe. These calls may be charged at a higher rate so beware. Often they accept both credit cards and phonecards.

PHONECARDS

Plastic phonecards with a magnetic strip (variously known as *teletarges*, *telekartes*, *cartela telefonica* etc) are superseding coins as the preferred way to make public phone calls throughout Europe. Most phones will accept them, and the cards are readily available at post offices, newsagents, tobacconists or general stores. The obvious advantage of the phonecard is that you don't need to search for change to make a local call and you don't need a pocketful of coins to make an international call. They also make good souvenirs, as they often have a scene from the country printed on them.

The cards come in various denominations of local currency; a card purchased in one country cannot be used in another country, so it pays to use up the credit before moving on.

Apart from the official phonecards, in some countries (such as Britain) you can get special prepaid phonecards that can offer international calls up to 10 times cheaper than the national company. You dial a toll-free number, then an account number before dialling the number you want and the cost is deducted from what's on your card.

Another product available in some areas is the Country Card. These are available from post offices or telephone centres, and give you a 15 to 20% discount on calls to certain countries. Country Cards in the Netherlands, for example, are now available for the USA, Canada, Australia, New Zealand and South Africa.

International Phonecards

There's a range of international phonecards on the market. Lonely Planet's eKno communication service is designed specifically for independent travellers and offers low cost international calls from over 60 countries, plus email and global voicemail, where friends and family can leave you messages for free. You can currently access the eKno service from all Western European and Scandinavian countries plus Poland and Hungary, and new countries are being added all the time. The easiest way to join eKno is online, visit www.lo nelyplanet.com and follow the links to eKno. Alternatively, call one of the following local toll-free access numbers. To contact eKno's 24-hour Customer Service team dial the access number for the country you are in, then press 0.

country	access number
Austria	0800-291-018
Belgium	0800-77888/75711
Cyprus	0809-6248
Denmark	8088-3550/2823
Finland	0800-114-009/112-010
France	0800-900-850/909-118
Germany	0800-634-8086/182-7153
Greece	00800-161-220-30287/125-282
Hungary	06800-14141/13568
Iceland	800-8336
Ireland	1800-555-180/557-457
Italy	800-875-801/683
Luxembourg	800-29240/29148
Monaco	0800-913-588
Netherlands	0800-023-3971/022-3605
Norway	800-16607/15794
Poland	00800-451-1263/111-2804
Portugal	800-812-993/819-734
Spain	900-931-951/971-537
Sweden	0200-214-883/0207-94782
Switzerland	800-897-306/837-798
Turkey	00800-151-0788/142-030-266
UK	800-376-2366/169-8646

• Always check the Web site for the latest access numbers.

Post

Postal services in Europe are generally as efficient and reliable as you'd expect, even in Eastern Europe. There are some exceptions, such as Poland, Italy and Greece, which can be relatively slow, but you can still expect your mail to get through eventually.

Post offices in main cities or towns are usually the best places to do business, especially if you're posting parcels or picking up mail. In some countries post offices can get very crowded, often with people paying bills. If you only need to post a letter or postcard, buy stamps at a newsstand or general store to avoid queuing at the post office (you'll need to know the international postal rates).

RECEIVING MAIL WHILE YOU'RE ON THE ROAD

The most common way to receive mail while you're on the road is to have it sent poste restante (see later), although email is fast making this obsolete for travellers just wanting to pick up messages.

If you have an American Express card or American Express travellers cheques, you can also have mail (but not parcels) sent to American Express offices along your route. When you buy your cheques ask for a booklet listing Amex offices worldwide – most European capitals have one.

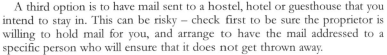

A third option is to have mail sent to a hostel, hotel or guesthouse that you intend to stay in. This can be risky – check first to be sure the proprietor is willing to hold mail for you, and arrange to have the mail addressed to a specific person who will ensure that it does not get thrown away.

Finally, for important or valuable items, or if you need something in a hurry, you can use an international courier service like Federal Express or DHL (for a hefty price).

Poste Restante

Poste restante is a worldwide system whereby you can have mail sent to a specified post office for collection (in North America it's known as general delivery). If you give people at home a rough itinerary, or tell them in advance to send mail to a particular post office, you can pick it up along the way. Most post offices will hold mail for a month (some only hold it for two weeks), and you'll need your passport or similar identification to collect it. Although most post offices have this service, it's best to use the main post office in a capital city or large town if you can. Letters sent poste restante should be clearly marked with your last name written first (in block letters and underlined), and with the appropriate post code (zip code) if you know it:

> SMITH, Mike
> c/o Poste Restante
> Main Post Office
> Paris 75008
> France

Mail sent to capital cities will usually find its mark even if the post code isn't given. Unless the sender specifies otherwise, it will always go to the city's main post office (GPO in the UK and Ireland).

Letters are usually filed alphabetically under your family name, but may occasionally be misfiled under your first name, so check there too. Some countries (such as France) charge a small fee for collecting poste restante mail.

You can have packages sent poste restante, but avoid having anything important sent, and definitely don't have anything illegal sent (drugs, pornography, weapons etc) as it will probably be inspected and you will be charged with illegal importation.

SENDING LETTERS & POSTCARDS

Sending letters or postcards from Europe is no different to sending them from your own country – pop them through the slot at any post office or any street post box. There may be separate slots for domestic and international mail, or for mail within/outside Europe, so be sure to check. Write 'airmail' or 'par avion' on the envelope to ensure it goes by airmail – surface (sea) mail takes months and is only useful if you want to ship large items back home.

Mail usually takes four to six days to reach North America from Europe and a week or more to reach Australia and New Zealand, but these times can vary from country to country. Postal rates also vary considerably. Books, magazines and printed matter can be sent at a cheap rate but not if you include a letter with it – the package must be handed to the post office unopened for inspection.

SHIPPING THINGS HOME

If your backpack starts to get a bit heavy, the best way to lighten the load is to start chucking things out – or have a few things shipped home.

If it's a relatively small parcel you could send it airmail from the post office, which is quicker and more reliable than surface mail, but as the weight goes up the cost becomes prohibitive. Surface mail takes four to six weeks to reach North America and from three to six months to reach Australasia! You'll probably have to parcel the goods yourself before taking them to the post office, although city post offices often have special packaging materials such as padded bags and boxes. Leave the package open so that it can be inspected by postal staff.

If you have a lot of stuff to ship home, a cheaper option is to use one of the commercial shipping agents. In cities such as London there are dozens of agents specialising in worldwide shipping and catering to travellers who have been hanging around so long they've accumulated crate-loads of possessions. Look for advertisements in the daily newspapers, or (in London) in travellers magazines such as *TNT Magazine*. The goods are generally sent in cardboard cartons or tea chests which you pack yourself, and you can have them sent to the port in your home country or, for an extra charge, to your home (door to door). When choosing a shipping agent, check that it's a reputable operator, preferably a member of the International Association of Removers – fly-by-night companies have been known to disappear, leaving you to somehow retrieve your possessions.

ADDRESS BOOKS

Whatever you do, don't leave home without your address book and make sure that all the addresses in it are current. Since this may be lost or damaged during your travels, you should copy the entire book before setting out and leave the copy at home. An address book is important not just for sending mail home but also for collecting the addresses of people you meet along the way.

Fax

You can send and receive faxes from post offices in main cities and towns anywhere in Europe. Travel agencies also usually have a fax service.

Many businesses and hotels have fax machines, so they can be useful for making bookings or receiving confirmations, but generally email is a much better method of communication.

Email

Email is *the* way to keep in touch on the road, not only with family and friends back home, but also with other travellers you meet during your trip. It's cheaper than the telephone, quicker than conventional (snail) mail, easier than

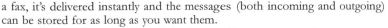

a fax, it's delivered instantly and the messages (both incoming and outgoing) can be stored for as long as you want them.

But the true beauty of email is that, as Internet access becomes more widespread, anyone can pick up messages from just about anywhere. Being on the road no longer isolates you from anyone, which is why you'll see Internet cafes humming with backpackers sending messages all over the continent while receiving messages from all over the world. You can walk into an Internet cafe in Madrid, pick up a message from a friend you last saw in Prague, then send an email to another former travelling companion who is soon to read it in Oslo!

Internet cafes (often called cybercafes) are constantly popping up all over Europe, particularly where travellers congregate. In some Eastern European countries the capital may be the only place you'll find them at this stage, but that is rapidly changing. Many of these places have forgone the cafe part and are simply computer/communications centres where you can access email and surf the Internet. You'll find some travel-related businesses with a single computer terminal. At other cybercafes you can still kick back with a coffee and a bit of cake. Costs vary from US$3 to US$8 per hour online. In some countries (such as Denmark) you can find free Internet access at the public library (though access policies vary and you'll probably have to book in advance), while others have Internet access at post offices or telecommunications centres.

France & the Internet

France's relationship with *l'informatique* (the whole sphere of computer use) in general and the *les autoroutes de l'information* (the information superhighway) in particular has been marked by a certain *technophobie* (technophobia) tinged with Gallic reticence. On the one hand, France is the country that created the world's first online service for the masses, France Télécom's popular but primitive and expensive Télétel (Minitel) system. On the other hand, it was President Jacques Chirac who, when told how simple it is to use an *ordinateur* (computer) – 'you just click on the mouse' – replied famously, 'Qu'appelez-vous la souris?' (What is it that you call a mouse?). And this in December of 1996! At the end of the 1990s, though, the Gallocentric view that *le Cyberespace* is an irrelevant Anglophone fad has given way to a national computer and Internet literacy campaign – this despite the selfish, short-term interests of the many powerful French companies who make vast sums of money charging by the minute for Minitel access.

France's linguistic patriots have been waging a rearguard action to save the French language from an invasion of Internet terms from English, the uncontested lingua franca of cyberspace (85 to 90% of Web sites are in English, as opposed to just 2% in French). A lively linguistic debate, with as yet inconclusive results, has ensued. A mouse is either *une souris* or, often tongue in cheek, *un mulot* (field mouse). The Internet remains *l'Internet* (often without the definite article) for now, but the World Wide Web – *le Web* for most people – is also known as *la toile* (spider's web) or, absurdly – in order to avoid that quintessentially un-French letter, the 'W' – the *oueb* or (as in *Le Monde*) the *ouèbe*. A Web surfer is either an *internaute* or a *surfeur*.

To collect your *courier électronique* (email) you'll need to access *(accéder à)* what the locals call *un fournisseur d'accès* (access provider). Before an email address (whose French accents can, in general, safely be ignored), you often see the notation *mél*, short for *message électronique*, which is supposed to look like *tél*, written before phone numbers.

Even more conveniently, many youth hostels, hotels and travel agents now provide Internet access specifically for travellers.

FREE EMAIL ACCOUNTS

Free Internet-based email accounts are so easy and convenient to use that it's difficult to imagine why anyone wouldn't want one. You can set up an account on any Internet-capable computer back home; if you don't have a computer, do this at a local Internet cafe. You should make it a priority to set up an account before you leave home so that you can hand out your email address to friends. If you don't get around to it, you can always do it at any Internet cafe in Europe and simply email your friends from there.

With a free email service such as HotMail (www.hotmail.com), Yahoo! Mail (www.yahoo.com), Mail Excite (www.excite.com) or eKno (www.ekno .lonelyplanet.com), you register and receive an email address (and password), where people can send emails. The emails are stored on the service's computer, and you can access them from anywhere in the world. Most Internet cafes and communication centres will have popular free email services listed on the 'bookmarks' or 'favourites' menus of Internet programs – simply pull down the menu, select your service and read your messages. You can also send emails with these services.

Using Your Existing Account

Major Internet service providers (ISPs) such as AOL (www.aol.com), CompuServe (www.compuserve.com) and IBM Net (www.ibm.net) have dial-in nodes throughout Europe so you can access your account with a local call (from major cities); it's best to download a list of the dial-in numbers before you leave home.

You can usually configure your Internet-based email service to access your home account. You need to know the POP or IMAP server name and your password – look under the 'options' menu of the free email service for instructions on how to gain access. Another option for accessing your home account is to use an Internet service like Mailstart (www.mailstart.com). All you need is your user name and the password you normally use to log on to your home server, and Mailstart will download your new messages.

Using Internet Cafes

To have email sent to Internet cafes, you'll need to find Internet cafes willing to hold email for travellers in the cities you plan to visit. Try The Internet Cafe Guide (www.netcafeguide.com) to search for such Internet cafes. Make sure that the sender puts your name in the subject box (last name in capital letters) of the message so that it can be filed properly. Just like regular poste restante, you should check under your first name as well, in case your message was misfiled. Of course, you have very little privacy with this method, so tell people not to send sensitive information. The ease and convenience of setting up your own email account makes this method a complicated waste of time.

TAKING YOUR OWN COMPUTER

The idea of taking along a laptop or notebook computer goes against all the rules of travelling light and it's not a great idea if you're backpacking and using public transport in Europe.

However, if part of your trip involves working or studying in Europe, it mightn't be a bad idea. Unless you know what you're doing, travelling with a portable computer is fraught with potential problems. A good investment is a universal AC adaptor for your appliance, so you can plug it in anywhere without frying the innards if the power supply voltage varies. You'll also need a plug adaptor for each country you visit, often easiest bought before you leave home. Most of Europe uses the standard round two-pin plug.

Secondly, your PC-card modem may or may not work once you leave your home country and you won't know for sure until you try. The safest option is to buy a reputable 'global' or 'world' modem before you leave home, or buy a local PC-card modem if you're spending an extended time in any one country.

Keep in mind that the telephone socket in each country you visit will probably be different from that at home, so ensure that you have at least a US RJ-11 telephone adaptor that works with your modem. You can almost always find an adaptor that will convert from RJ-11 to the local variety. For more information on travelling with a portable computer, see www.teleadapt.com or www.warrior.com.

Media

When you're on the road it can be difficult to keep track of newsworthy events from home (especially if you're from Australia or New Zealand!), but it's easy to keep up with the world media in Europe. Some travellers like to lose themselves for a while and would be quite happy not to open a newspaper for the entire trip, but for those who do like to follow world events there's more than enough English-language media to occupy those idle hours.

RADIO

With a good radio, you can tune into world news services like BBC World Service and Voice of America (VOA). Check their Web sites for the frequencies of local stations and for scheduling information (www.bbc.co.uk/world service, www.voa.gov). These services often also broadcast features and music.

Close to the English Channel you can pick up British radio stations, particularly BBC's Radio 4. There are also numerous English-language broadcasts or even rebroadcasts on local AM and FM radio stations in Europe.

Radio Canada International's half-hour English-language broadcasts, including relays of domestic CBC programs such as the World at Six, often come in loud and clear. Although Radio Australia (www.abc.net.au/ra) directs most of its broadcasts to the Asia-Pacific region, it can sometimes be picked up in Europe.

TELEVISION

Most hotels and guesthouses have TV sets, and many hostels have TV rooms. These will invariably have cable or satellite connections, otherwise you'll have to get familiar with the local stations. This is fine in Britain and Ireland, but might be a challenge elsewhere (we hear the Italian game shows are a hoot though). Sky TV can be found in many hotels throughout Western Europe, as can CNN, BBC Prime and other networks. Pubs and bars often screen major sporting events. You can also pick up many cross-border TV stations, including British stations close to the Channel.

NEWSPAPERS & MAGAZINES

Capital cities in a handful of European countries have locally produced English-language newspapers, such as the *Copenhagen Post*, the *Turkish Daily News* and the *Athens News*. These are fine for reading up on national news. In major cities you'll find the *International Herald Tribune* on the day of publication and relatively expensive editions of some of the world's larger newspapers, most commonly the *New York Times* and *USA Today*. A swag of respected newspapers (and not-so-respected tabloids) are published in London. Papers like *The Times* and *Guardian* can be found on the continent as well as in Britain.

The *European* is a weekly paper that is also widely available, and it includes a mixture of world and European news, sport and business. Good magazines for keeping up with news events include the *Economist*, *Time* and *Newsweek*. As with anywhere else in the world, newspapers and magazines can be bought from stands in the street, at bus and train stations, or at newsagents.

THE INTERNET

The Internet is a great source of up-to-date news while you're on the road. The beauty of it is that you can look up the site of the daily newspaper closest to your home town as most major newspapers maintain Web pages on which they post the day's top stories. See the appendix 'Internet Addresses' at the back of this book for online news service addresses.

COMING HOME ▶▶

This is the part of the trip that no-one wants to talk about. Coming home can certainly be an anticlimax after you've spent the previous few weeks, months (or even years) living footloose and fancy-free in exotic lands. For many the homecoming itself is eagerly anticipated and exciting – the chance to see family and friends again and regale them with the tales of your trip – but the realities of normal life soon kick in. It's enough to make you want to turn right around and get on the next plane to anywhere. But it doesn't have to be that bad. If you approach your homecoming in the right frame of mind, your travel experiences can be the springboard to a positive new stage of your life.

Post-Holiday Blues

One of the hardest aspects of returning home is that your friends and family may not be particularly interested in hearing about your experiences So what if you spent a night near Dracula's castle in Transylvania and ran with the bulls in Pamplona? Though these were incredible experiences for you, when you try to relate them, their eyes glaze over and they cut you off with the latest gossip about your friends. Try not to let this lack of appreciation get you down, and don't automatically disown your friends as a bunch of small-minded bores. In fact, make an effort not to become a travel bore yourself.

The reality is that much of the world you experienced in Europe is so far removed from their daily lives that it's difficult for them to really comprehend your stories. Plus, there may be an element of jealousy floating around about the good times you've had. This is where travelling with friends from home can be a bonus – you can spend many nights reminiscing about the good times and weaning yourselves off the travel experience.

Even worse than the inability to communicate is the simple realisation that the good times are over and now you're back to the daily grind. Life on the road is challenging, exciting, unpredictable and fulfilling while life back home can appear bleak, boring and dreadfully lacking in meaning. The best way to fight the blues caused by this disparity is to be realistic – you cannot travel all the time, so you are going to have to get on with your regular life. Don't be tempted by the notion of perpetual travel as a way of escaping from 'real' life, as this can be a trap in the long run. Eventually, everyone has to return home.

There may in fact be a physiological component to your post-holiday blues. You may feel depressed, tired, emotionally unbalanced or even unable to sleep. Many of these symptoms may be chemical in nature and are quite similar to Seasonal Affective Disorder (SAD). This disorder effects millions of people each year during autumn and winter, and is thought to result from physiological changes caused by lack of sunlight. A very simple way to combat your post-holiday blues may be to do as the SAD people do, and get out in the sunshine and do some exercise. Some people also recommend a good daily intake of vitamins B and C, and still others prescribe the herbal remedy St John's wort (thought to act as a natural antidepressant). Whatever you do, it's best not to sit around moping and wishing you were back on the road.

Making the Transition

To ease yourself into life back home, it helps to give the end of your trip some serious thought while you're still on the road. You'll have a lot of free time while travelling to think about what you want to do when you get back. Ideally, your time on the road can recharge your batteries, give you a new perspective on the world and realign your priorities. If you simply avoid thoughts of home while you're on the road, you'll be in for a big shock when you arrive home.

When you do arrive home, you may find that you are suffering from post-holiday blues (discussed previously), or you may find that you are infused with a kind of manic energy. Either way, you'll want to get started on your new life as quickly as possible, and implement the changes you've decided to make. Most of all, try to apply some of what you've learned to your daily life. By doing so, you'll feel that your travel was not just a fleeting holiday, but a meaningful step in your life. The cliche that 'travel broadens the mind' will develop real meaning.

Remembering Your Trip

Within a few days of coming home, your trip can seem as though it never happened at all. To prevent the memories from sliding into oblivion, try some of the following techniques:

Make a photo album – Choose the best prints from your trip and put them in chronological order. If you've taken slides, putting them in the proper order is essential for giving slide shows.

Maintain contacts – You should try to keep in touch with the people you met along the way. This includes both locals and fellow travellers. Also, if you've promised anyone copies of your pictures, then send them as soon as you can – if you let a few months go by, you'll never get around to it. You can also send thank-you letters to some of the local people who went out of their way to help you, whether guesthouse owners, tour guides, or just people you met on the street.

Research the cultures – Deepen your interest in some of the countries you visited. Take a course at your local university or search out some books at the library. You'll find your study, whether it be languages, history, art or Italian cooking, is much more meaningful once you've encountered the real thing.

Study a language or two – If a country particularly interested you, try to improve your facility with its language. Whether it's just for your own interest or because you'd like to go back some day, studying a language is one of the best ways to become better acquainted with another culture.

Read your journal – If you kept a journal during your trip, revisit your record. Even more than the pictures, the words you wrote while you were there can bring your trip alive again months, or even years down the track. And, if you find that your journal reads like the best travel novel you've ever read, then you can always write up some of the better passages and send them off to magazines as potential travel articles. Who knows, it may be the start of a career as a travel writer.

learn a bit of the local lingo and you'll make pals in no time

top left: a soldier dutifully stands guard at st james's palace, london *(neil setchfield)*
top right: fresh as a daisy (or a tulip) in traditional costume, netherlands *(leanne logan)*
bottom: chat to a friendly stall holder at the market, italy *(alan benson)*

walk it, cruise it, ski it ... just get out into the countryside

top left: take a drive through southern ireland's lush countryside *(oliver strewe)*
top right: fields of wild flowers smother a dormant vineyard in spain *(mason florence)*
bottom: autumn on lemmenjoki river is simply stunning, finland *(john borthwick)*

top: don't forget your mittens. ben nivas, fort william. scotland *(gareth mccormack)*
bottom left: petra tou romiou – the birthplace of aphrodite. cyprus *(chris christo)*
bottom right: frolic in the wild flowers of the loire valley. france *(diana mayfield)*

explore medieval villages by day and boogie in vibrant cities by night

top: wander through the cobbled, picturesque streets of rovinj, croatia *(jon davison)*
bottom left: the twin steeples of gothic tyn church, prague, czech republic *(jonathon s.*
bottom right: nestled in volcanic rock, a cliff·top church in santorini, greece *(tamsin w.*

top left: o la la ... guess where? *(john hay)*
top right: get on your bike and see the sights in denmark *(glenda bendure)*
bottom: a calm and serine dusk in venice, italy *(christopher groenhout)*

marvel at grandiose monuments and immerse yourself in ancient civilisatio

top: wonder at the mysteries of stonehenge, england *(bryn thomas)*

bottom: you can catch a glimpse of the acropolis from almost everywhere in the city athens, greece *(juliet coombe)*

top left: the teatro romano at merida, once the biggest city in roman spain *(oliver strewe)*
top right: crumbling ruins of girnigoe castle, nossltead, scotland *(neil wilson)*
bottom: the hauntingly beautiful ampitheatre of termessos, turkey *(neil wilson)*

stock up on gloriously fresh produce. get a bottle of plonk ... and enjoy

top left: munch on a sweet cherry in spain *(oliver strewe)*
top right: coming to a bottle near you .... france *(sally dillon)*
bottom: stuffed with feta and herbs. zucchini flowers are a treat. italy *(alan benson)*

It may not be high on most back-packers' itineraries, but Albania is an eye-opener. It manages to combine sunny Mediterranean charm with Soviet-style efficiency and an odd blend of religions, cultures and landscapes.

Albania only shed its communist skin and opened up to the outside world in 1990, following more than 40 years of dictatorship under Stalinist leader Enver Hoxha. Its political history is one of invasions, blood vendettas and even a strange Chinese-style cultural revolution in the 1960s. Despite the social and economic upheavals that accompanied the first steps into democracy (civil anarchy erupted in 1997 after many Albanians lost their savings in fraudulent financial schemes), Albania is embracing the outside world and the relatively few foreign travellers who venture in — don't be surprised if you're viewed with great curiosity almost everywhere (except perhaps in Tirana). Infrastructure is gradually improving, opening the countryside up to visitors.

Warning

In mid-1999, the situation in Albania became unstable when the Kosovo refugee crisis saw displaced ethnic Albanians spill over the border. As a result, increased criminal activity and roving gangs have been reported. It's advisable to travel with a local guide outside Tirana and not to travel at night.

The area close to the border with Kosovo, especially Bajram Curri and Tropoje, should be avoided altogether. This situation is likely to improve in the near future.

WHEN TO GO

The best month to visit is September, when it's still warm, the days are long and the fruit and vegetables are in good supply. The sun shines longest from

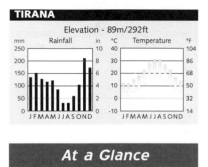

At a Glance

Full Country Name: Republic of Albania (Shqipëri)
Area: 28,748 sq km
Population: 3.3 million
Capital City: Tirana (pop 400,000)
People: Almost entirely ethnic Albanian, with Greek, Vlach, Macedonian and Gypsy minorities
Language: Albanian (Shqip)
Religion: 70% Sunni Muslim, 20% Albanian Orthodox, 10% Roman Catholic
Government: Republic
Currency: Albanian lekë = 100 quintars
Time Zone: One hour ahead of GMT/UTC; clocks are turned ahead one hour at the end of March and back at the end of September
International Telephone Code: 355
Electricity: 220V/50Hz

May to September, and July is the warmest month, but even April and October can be pleasant. Winter can be uncomfortable, as many hotel rooms are not heated.

Itineraries

Two Days
If you're making a flying visit to Albania, skip Tirana and head straight to the museum town of Gjirokastra, about 170km south of the capital. If you're coming from Greece (which is more than likely) this is the first major town after the Kakavija border crossing. From there you can head south to the coastal town of Saranda and the nearby archaeological ruins of Butrint. If you arrive on the ferry from Corfu, you'll visit Saranda and Butrint first.

One Week
With a bit more time to spend, you can do the two-day places, plus a stop in Tirana for its museums and cultural attractions. You'll also be able to take in Durrës, before heading south to Fier/Apollonia, and across to Berat, with its 14 century citadel. Finally, you may still have time to fit in Pogradec, on the shores of Lake Ohrid, or Korça, Albania's carpet and rug-producing centre. Korça is only 28km west of the Kapshtica border crossing into Greece.

Two Weeks
In two weeks you can see a fair slice of Albania. Follow the one week itinerary but spend a few days in Tirana getting used to the local culture and making onward travel plans. Kruja is only 32km north and can be visited on a day trip by local bus. Further north of Tirana is Lezha, where you'll find the tomb of 15th century resistance leader, Skënderbeg. Depending on the political situation, you can continue on to Shkodra near the Yugoslav border. Also try to make it across to the hill town of Kukës, which can be reached from Shkodra but is best approached from Tirana.

HIGHLIGHTS
The best of Albania lies in its historical legacies such as the Onufri Museum in Berat Citadel and the museum town of Gjirokastra, as well as the natural attractions of the Adriatic coast and the inland lakes.

Tirana
Capital of Albania since 1920, Tirana is compact and pleasant enough to explore on foot.

The National Museum of History is the largest and finest museum in Albania, while the Archaeological Museum has a fantastic selection of objects from prehistoric times to the Middle Ages. There are plenty of restaurants and bars in the capital, and you can see opera and other cultural performances at the Palace of Culture on central Skënderbeg Square.

Ancient Towns & Ruins
Durrës, a commercial port 38km west of Tirana, is an ancient city founded by the Greeks in 627 BC. Here you'll find Roman ruins and Byzantine fortifications, as well as sandy beaches to the south-east of the city.

Butrint, 18km south of Saranda, is a real gem if you're into ancient world ruins. Virgil claimed that the Trojans settled Butrint, but no evidence of this has yet been found, despite archaeologists poring over the site. Among the ruins are a Greek theatre and baths.

Gjirokastra is a strikingly picturesque museum town, perched on the side of a mountain above the Drino River. Dominating the town is the 14th century citadel, now a museum of armaments.

Berat, Albania's second most important museum town, is sometimes

ALBANIA HIGHLIGHTS & ITINERARIES

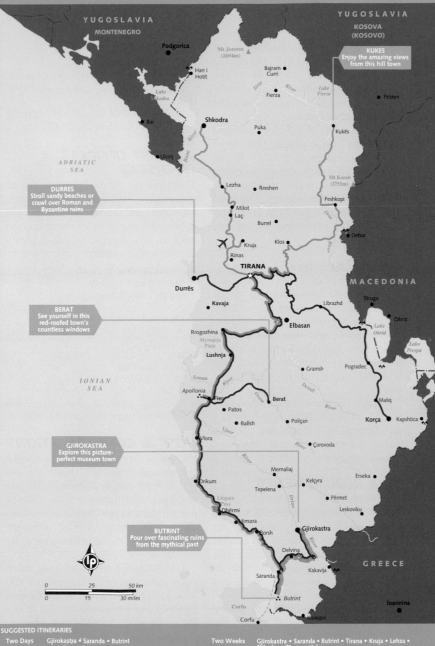

YUGOSLAVIA
MONTENEGRO

YUGOSLAVIA
KOSOVA
(KOSOVO)

Podgorica

Mt Jezerce
(2694m)

KUKES
Enjoy the amazing views
from this hill town

Han i
Hotit

Bajram
Curri

Fierza

Drin River

Lake
Fierza

Prizren

Bar

Lake
Shkodra

Shkodra

Puka

Kukës

Ulcinj

Buna River

ADRIATIC
SEA

Lezha

Rreshen

Mt Korab
(2751m)

DURRES
Stroll sandy beaches or
crawl over Roman and
Byzantine ruins

Milot

Peshkopi

Drin River

Laç

Burrel

Debar

Kruja

Klos

Rinas

TIRANA

Durrës

Kavaja

Librazhd

Struga

MACEDONIA

Ohrid

Elbasan

Lake
Ohrid

Lake
Prespa

BERAT
See yourself in this
red-roofed town's
countless windows

Rrogozhina

Myzaqeja
Plain

Lushnja

Seman River

Gramsh

Pogradec

IONIAN
SEA

Apollonia

Fier

Osum River

Berat

Devoll River

Maliq

Patos

Poliçan

Korça

Kapshtica

Ballsh

GJIROKASTRA
Explore this picture-
perfect museum town

Vlora

Vjosa River

Çorovoda

Drikum

Memaliaj

Kelçyra

Erseka

Tepelena

Përmet

Leskoviku

BUTRINT
Pour over fascinating ruins
from the mythical past

Llogara
Pass

Dhërmi

Drino River

Himara

Gjirokastra

Borsh

Delvina

GREECE

Kakavija

Saranda

Corfu

Butrint

Ioannina

Corfu

Konispol

0   25   50 km
0   15   30 miles

called 'the city of a thousand windows' for the many windows in its red-roofed houses. Along the ridge above the gorge is a 14th century citadel sheltering small Orthodox churches and the superb Onufri Museum.

Shkodra is one of the oldest cities in Europe and the traditional centre of the Gheg cultural region. In 500 BC an Illyrian fortress was already guarding the crossing west of the city where the Buna and Drin rivers meet. The road to Kosovo also begins here, so it may be a risky place to visit until the refugee crisis subsides.

Lakes & Beaches

Perched high above Lake Fierza, just below the bald 2486m summit of Mt Gjalica, Kukës has possibly the most beautiful setting of any town in Albania. Further south, a bit less than half of Lake Ohrid is in Albania (the rest is in neighbouring Macedonia) and the beautiful scenery here makes the lakeside resort of Pogradec worth a visit.

Albania has some fine beaches, and you could easily spend a month just travelling the Adriatic and Ionian coasts, hopping from one stunning, sun-soaked spot to another.

VISA REQUIREMENTS

Travellers from Australia, New Zealand, Canada, the USA and European Union (EU) countries do not need visas. Citizens of other countries can obtain an Albanian visa at the border for a price equivalent to what an Albanian would pay for a tourist visa in those countries.

Upon arrival you will fill in an arrival and departure card. Keep the departure card with your passport and present it when you leave.

Albanian Embassies

UK
(☎ 020-7730 5709, fax 7730 5747) 38 Grosvenor Gardens, London SW1 0EB
USA
(☎ 202-223 4942, fax 628 7342) 1511 K St NW, Washington, DC 20005

TOURIST OFFICES OVERSEAS

There are no official Albanian tourist offices overseas (or in Albania for that matter). You should be able to get some information from the following sources, or you could try travel agents in your home country:

Australia & New Zealand
The Albania Society
PO Box 14074, Wellington
UK
Albania Society of Britain
(☎ 020-8540 6824) 7 Nelson Rd, London SW19 1HS
USA
Jack Shulman
(☎ 718-633 0530) PO Box 912, Church St Station, New York, NY 10008
(for Albanian books, maps, videos and folk-music cassettes by mail order)

POST & COMMUNICATIONS

Postage is inexpensive and the service surprisingly reliable. There are no public mailboxes in Albania; you must hand in your letters at a post office in person. Letters sent to poste restante, Tirana, should reach you, although mail is liable to be first opened by curious postal workers.

Long-distance telephone calls made from main post offices cost about 150 lekë (about US$1) a minute to Western Europe, and a three minute call to the USA is 840 lekë. Phonecards are available from post offices and street kiosks.

Faxes can be sent from the main post office in Tirana, or from major hotels (though they will charge more). Internet access is currently available only in Tirana.

MONEY
Costs

Travelling in Albania is not expensive by European standards, but prices in Tirana are considerably higher than in the rest of the country, so budget travellers should see the sights, then head for the hills. If you are on a tight budget, you could get by out in the country on US$25 to US$40 a day (more if you hire a guide), but you'll need closer to US$55 to US$70 in Tirana. That will give you fairly basic accommodation and three meals a day. Paying for a few more comforts, staying in a better class of hotel and doing some guided trips could raise the budget to US$80 to US$90 a day.

Expect to pay around US$5 to US$10 for a budget meal and twice that for a moderate restaurant meal. A private room will cost from US$5 to US$10 (from US$20 in Tirana), and a moderate hotel room from US$40 to US$60.

Changing Money

Every town has a free currency market that usually operates on the street in front of the post office or the state bank. Look for the men standing around with pocket calculators in hand; they'll give you about the same rate as a bank without the 1% commission, although some banks will change US dollar travellers cheques into US dollars cash without a commission. Transactions on the street are legal, but count your notes before walking away. US dollars are the favourite foreign currency, but you can pay for everything in lekë. Credit cards are only accepted in major hotels and travel agencies, and there were no ATMs at the time of research.

ONLINE SERVICES

Lonely Planet's Destination Albania page can be found at www.lonelyplanet .com/dest/eur/alb.htm. Other useful Web sites to point your browser at are the Albanian WWW Home Page (www .albanian.com) or the United Nations Development Project site (www.tirana .al). Excite Travel has an informative site (www.excite.com/travel/countries /albania).

BOOKS

Ismail Kadare's *The Palace of Dreams* is a vision of totalitarianism with echoes of Kafka and Borges. *Albania – From Anarchy to a Balkan Identity* by Miranda Vickers & James Pettifer looks behind former President Enver Hoxha's isolationist policies and examines the momentous events that led to the transition to a parliamentary government. Anton Logoreci's *Albanians* is a well balanced and readable account of Albanian history up to 1987. *Biografi* by Lloyd Jones is a fanciful story set in the immediate post-communist era, involving the search for Hoxha's alleged double. A clear, insightful interpretation of the collapse of communism throughout the late 1980s is Timothy Garton Ash's *We the People*. June Emerson's *Albania – The Search for the Eagle's Song* is a picture of what it was like to visit Albania just before 1990.

Journeys in Albania – The Accursed Mountains by Robert Carver is an inspiring travelogue published in 1990.

FILMS

A film worth checking out is *Lamerica*, a brilliant and stark look at Albanian post-communist culture. Despite its title, it is about Albanians seeking to escape to Bari, Italy, in the immediate post-communist era.

ENTERING & LEAVING

Numerous European airlines fly into Rinas airport, 26km north-west of Tirana. The cheapest way to enter the country is by bus from Greece or Macedonia. Ferries travel to and from Albania from Italy and Greece (Corfu).

Airport departure tax is US$10, which is payable in dollars or lekë. There's also an 'entry tax' of US$5 (except for US citizens), whether you enter by land, sea or air. Departure tax from Albanian ports is US$2. Private cars departing from Albania pay US$5 road tax per day for each day spent in the country.

ANDORRA

Pint-sized Andorra would probably still be a quiet backwater squashed between France and Spain if not for its growing popularity as a skiing and duty-free shopping haven.

Andorra comprises just a few hundred kilometres of mountainous landscapes and meandering rivers – some of the most dramatic scenery in the Pyrenees. Winter skiing is the big drawcard but during the warmer months there are good hiking opportunities in the remote countryside, away from the overdevelopment and heavy traffic that plague the capital, Andorra la Vella.

There's relatively little of cultural or historical interest in Andorra, merged as it is between Spanish and French. Its princedom status continued for seven centuries until 1993, when it became a democracy. But the French and Spanish princes, who formerly ruled the co-princedom, remain joint heads of state, exercising ceremonial functions.

WHEN TO GO
The ski season begins around December and lasts through March, though many resorts buffer nature's contributions with man-made snow that prolongs the season well into spring. Hiking season begins when the snowfall lets up and continues through until October. Andorra's village festivals take place between July and September. Hotels are at their fullest in July and August and from December to March.

HIGHLIGHTS
Skiing & Hiking
Skiing is justifiably a big attraction, as Andorra has the finest inexpensive skiing and snowboarding in the Pyrenees – much cheaper than the more famous Alps to the north-east. Pas de la Casa-Grau Roig and Soldeu-El Tarter are the best resorts based on size, elevation and number of lifts, but they are also more expensive than Andorra's smaller ones. Ski (lift) passes cost from US$18 to US$28 per day and ski-gear rental is

At a Glance

Full Country Name: Principality of Andorra
Area: 450 sq km
Population: 64,000
Capital City: Andorra la Vella (pop 22,000)
People: Spanish (61%), Andorran (30%), French (6%)
Language: Catalan, Spanish, French
Religion: Roman Catholic
Government: Constitutional democracy
Currency: French franc (FF) and Spanish peseta (pta)
Time Zone: One hour ahead of GMT/UTC in winter, and two hours ahead from the last Sunday in March to the last Sunday of September
International Telephone Code: 376
Electricity: 125V or 220V, both at 50Hz

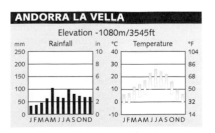

ANDORRA LA VELLA
Elevation -1080m/3545ft

Rainfall

Temperature

J F M A M J J A S O N D

around US$10 a day. Contact Ski Andorra (☎ 864389) for more information.

The tranquillity of Andorra's beautiful, relatively unspoiled back country makes for some great hiking. The north-westerly parish of Ordino has especially good trails. The GR11 trail, which traverses the Pyrenees from the Mediterranean to the Atlantic, passes through the southern part of Andorra. Hikers can sleep for free in the numerous *refugis* (shelters) along the major trails. The best time for hiking is from June to September, when daytime temperatures are well above 20°C.

Itineraries

Two Days

Being such a tiny place it would be easy to spend only a short time in Andorra, as long as you don't plan on hiking or skiing.

Spend a day in Andorra la Vella checking out the Casa de la Vall, Andorra's seat of parliament, and relaxing in the Caldea spa complex in Escaldes. Unfortunately, the capital itself is a rather uninspiring conglomeration of developments and duty-free shops – something reminiscent of a (very) tiny Hong Kong! From here, head 14km north to Llorts, where you can get a taste of a pristine Andorran mountain town.

One Week

Spend a couple of days in Andorra la Vella, then head up to Llorts or El Serrat, where you can do several good hikes in the Ordino-Arcalis region. On the way back, stop at the larger village of Ordino. From here, if you're well prepared, you can hike east along the GR-11 trail to Encamp, about 6km away. During winter you could spend most of this time checking out the ski resorts of Soldeu-El Tarter, Ordino-Arcalis, Arinsal or Pal.

Two Weeks

With two weeks you can do all of the above at your own pace and explore a good slice of the Andorran Pyrenees.

Caldea

In the Les Escaldes suburb east of Andorra la Vella, Caldea is an enormous complex of pools, hot tubs and saunas enclosed in what looks like a futuristic cathedral. Fed by natural thermal springs, the spa complex centres on a 600 sq metre (6450 sq ft) lagoon kept at a constant 32°C. You can further soak up the serenity with a hydromassage or a dip in the Turkish baths, both of which are included in the three hour entrance ticket.

Llorts & Encamp

The tiny hamlet of Llorts (pop 100) is set amid fields of tobacco and backed by near-pristine mountains. It's one of the most untouched places in the country and is a good base for hiking. There's a popular three hour walk up the valley west of town along the de l'Angonella River, which leads to the Estanys de l'Angonella, a group of lakes. The village also has Andorra's most beautiful camping ground.

The town of Encamp has one of Andorra's few museums, the Museu Nacional de l'Automòbil, which exhibits about 100 cars dating from 1898 to 1950, as well as scores of antique motorcycles and bicycles. Encamp's nearby resorts, Soldeu-El Tarter and Pas de la Casa-Grau Roig, have some of the best skiing in Andorra.

VISA REQUIREMENTS

Visas are not required for Andorra, but you must carry your passport or national identity card.

Andorran Embassies

Andorra doesn't have any diplomatic missions abroad, but Spain and France have embassies in Andorra la Vella.

ANDORRA HIGHLIGHTS & ITINERARIES

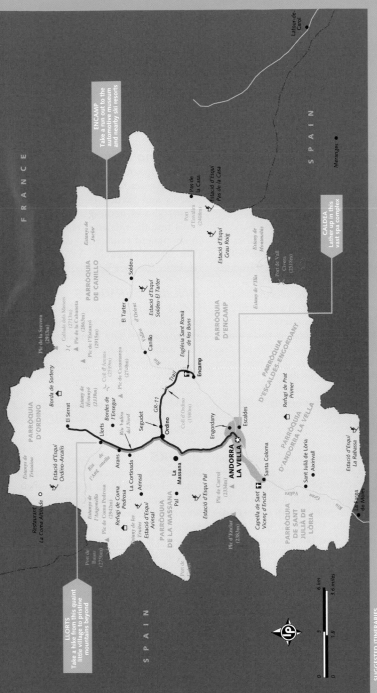

LLORTS
Take a hike from this quaint little village to pristine mountains beyond

ENCAMP
Take a run out to the automotive museum and nearby ski resorts

CALDEA
Lather up in this vast spa complex

FRANCE

SPAIN

Latour-de-Carol

Estanys de Juclar

Pas de la Casa

Estació d'Esquí
Pas de la Casa

Estany de Montmalús

Estació d'Esquí
Grau Roig

Port de Vall
Creus
(2518m)

Estany de l'Illa

Merangs

Pic de Serrera
(2913m)

Callada dels Meners
(2713m)

Pic de la Cabaneta
(2863m)

Pic d'Estanyó
(2915m)

Pic de Casamanya
(2740m)

Vall d'Orient

Soldeu

El Tarter

Estació d'Esquí
Soldeu-El Tarter

Canillo

Església Sant Romà
de les Bons

Encamp

PARRÒQUIA
DE CANILLO

PARRÒQUIA
D'ENCAMP

Estanys de
Tristaina

Estació d'Esquí
Ordino-Arcalís

Borda de Sorteny

El Serrat

Estany de
l'Estany
(2339m)

Bordes de
l'Ensegur

Llorts

Segudet

Ordino

Coll d'Ordino
(1980m)

GR-11

Trail

Trail

Coll d'Arenes
(2539m)

Riu Valira
del Nord

PARRÒQUIA
D'ORDINO

Restaurant
La Coma Altitude

Port de
Rialb
(2720m)

Estany de
l'Angonella
(2942m)

Pic de Coma Pedrosa
(2942m)

Refugi de Coma
Pedrosa

Arans

La Cortinada

Arinsal

Estació d'Esquí
Arinsal

Pal

Estació d'Esquí Pal

Estany de les
Truites

La Massana

PARRÒQUIA
DE LA MASSANA

Pic de Carroi
(2334m)

ANDORRA
LA VELLA

Santa Coloma

Capella de Sant
Vicenç d'Enclar

Sant Julià de Lòria

Aixirivall

Riu d'Enclar
(2383m)

Port de
Cabús

Engordany

Escaldes

PARRÒQUIA
D'ESCALDES-ENGORDANY

Refugi de Prat
Primer

PARRÒQUIA
D'ANDORRA LA VELLA

PARRÒQUIA
DE SANT
JULIÀ DE
LÒRIA

Estació d'Esquí
La Rabassa

Riu Gran Valira

La Farga
de Moles

SPAIN

FRANCE

SPAIN

N

0   3   6 km
0   1.8   3.6 miles

SUGGESTED ITINERARIES

Two Days ● Andorra la Vella ● Llorts

One Week ● Andorra la Vella ● Llorts or El Serrat ● Ordino ● Encamp

TOURIST OFFICES OVERSEAS

There are no Andorran tourist offices overseas. You can contact the National Tourist Office (☎ 820214), Carrer del Doctor Vilanova, Andorra la Vella.

POST & COMMUNICATIONS

Andorra has no postal system of its own; France and Spain each operate separate systems with their own Andorran stamps, which are needed only for international mail.

Postal rates are the same as those of the issuing country, with the French being slightly cheaper, so you're better off routing your mail (except letters to Spain) through the French postal system. Poste restante to Andorra la Vella goes to the French post office.

Public phones take pesetas or phonecards, known as *teletarges* (a three minute call to the USA costs 330 pta, or about US$2). Andorra does not have reverse-charge call facilities. There are at least two public Internet cafes with email facilities in Andorra la Vella.

MONEY
Costs

If you're camping and eating at markets, a tight belt could see you get by on US$10 to US$15 per day. A more realistic budget, allowing a warm bed, a few restaurant meals and local transport would be US$40 to US$60 per day. Hiking is free, but skiing and staying at the resorts will push your budget up beyond US$60 to US$70 a day.

Count on $US10 to US$20 for a budget room, US$3 to US$5 for a cheap meal and from US$15 for a good restaurant meal. Service charges are usually included in most bills, but porters and waiters expect a further tip of 10%.

Andorra's very low tax regime has made it famous as a duty-free bazaar for electronic goods, cameras and alcohol. While today's prices no longer justify a special trip, you can still find prices 30% below those in Spain and France if you shop around.

Changing Money

Andorra has no currency of its own, so locals trade mainly in Spanish pesetas and French francs. Prices are almost always quoted in pesetas, and you'll find the exchange rate for francs in shops and restaurants is seldom in your favor. There are ATMs at most banks in Andorra la Vella.

ONLINE SERVICES

Lonely Planet's Destination Andorra page can be found at www.lonelyplanet .com/dest/eur/and.htm. Try the official tourism page (www.turisme.ad /angles/angles.htm) or AndorraWeb (http://andorraweb.com/aw), which includes a discussion board. For a list of ski resorts, go to the resorts list (www.skiin.com/static/country/static /andorra-main.en.html).

BOOKS

Approach to the History of Andorra by Laidia Armengol Vila is a solid work.

For something heavier, try *Fragmentation and the International Relations of Micro-States* by Jorri Duursma. *Andorra* by Peter Cameron is a darkly comic novel set in a fictitious Andorran mountain town.

ENTERING & LEAVING

You can only enter Andorra by road, making train or bus connections from France or Spain. Coming from France you cross Port d'Envalira (2408m) – the highest pass in the Pyrenees.

AUSTRIA

Once the centre of the mighty Habsburg empire, Austria oozes both historical charm and stunning natural scenery.

These days it is one of Europe's most popular year-round destinations, with the winter sports in the alpine resorts giving way to spring and summer crowds visiting the lakes, the Danube Valley and cities no less captivating than Vienna and Salzburg. It's not the cheapest destination in Europe but days spent marvelling at the Gothic and Baroque architecture in Vienna or walking in the mountains near Innsbruck cost little, and all around you the country moves to the rhythm of its unrivalled musical tradition.

WHEN TO GO

The summer high season is in July and August, when crowds and prices will be at their highest. It can be uncomfortably hot in the cities over summer and many famous institutions close down. Consequently, June and September are also busy months. During winter you'll find things less crowded in the cities and the hotel prices are lower (except over Christmas and Easter). Winter sports are in full swing from mid-December to late March with the high season over Christmas, New Year and February. Alpine resorts are very quiet from late April to late May and in November. Spring in the Alps is in June, when the Alpine flowers start coating the mountains with colour.

HIGHLIGHTS

If you only visit one place in Austria, it should be Vienna, the glorious legacy of the Habsburg dynasty, which controlled much of Europe for over 600 years. It offers awe-inspiring public buildings, art treasures culled from the old empire, and music – don't miss a trip to the opera or a classical music performance.

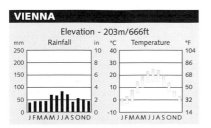

At a Glance

Full Country Name: Republic of Austria
Area: 83,854 sq km
Population: 8.1 million
Capital City: Vienna (pop 1.64 million)
People: 97% Germanic origin, 2% Slovene and Croat, 1% Turkish
Language: 97% German, plus some Turkish, Slovene and Croat
Religion: 88% Roman Catholic, 6% Protestant
Government: Federal Republic
Currency: Austrian Schilling (AS) = 100 groschen
Time Zone: One hour ahead of GMT/UTC; clocks go forward one hour on the last Saturday in March and back back on the last Saturday in October
International Telephone Code: 43
Electricity: 220V, 50Hz

Salzburg, birthplace of Mozart and a Baroque masterpiece, comes in a close second.

Palaces, Churches & Castles

Top of the many fine sights in Vienna is St Stephen's Cathedral, with its Romanesque Tower of Heathens and 136m Gothic Südturm (south tower). The Hofburg (Imperial Palace) nearby was the home of the Habsburgs and is a monumental repository of Austria's cultural heritage. Another famous Baroque palace in the capital is the Schönbrunn Palace, once home to Maria Theresa and later to Napoleon. It also contains the Mirror Room, where Mozart played his first royal concert and the Napoleon Room, which strangely contains a stuffed crested lark.

Salzburg has a wealth of churches, plazas, courtyards and fountains, all dominated by the 11th century Hohensalzburg Castle, which stands on a rock outcrop about 120m above the city. The Baroque Hellbrunn Palace, 4km south of Salzburg's old town, was built in the 17th century and the grounds contain ingenious trick fountains and water-powered figures. Also worth a look is the Mirabell Palace, particularly for its manicured gardens (featured in *The Sound of Music*).

In Innsbruck, the Schloss Ambras is a fine Renaissance Castle, and the impressive Hofkirche contains the mausoleum of Emporer Maximilian I.

Music & Festivals

Music is the pulse of Austria, particularly in Vienna and Salzburg. If classical music is an interest, take in an opera performance at the lavish Staatsoper in Vienna (no performances during July and August), or try the Volksoper. Orchestral concerts are held in Vienna's Musikverein, or the Konzerthaus.

In Salzburg, Mozart concerts are regularly played at numerous venues, including the Mozarteum. If you want the hills to come alive, Sound of Music tours get a real workout here, too. The Summer Music Festival in Vienna and the Salzburg International Festival, both held in July and August, are Austria's major cultural festivals. There are many minor events held throughout the country year-round: Linz hosts the Bruckner Festival in September, and how could you miss the Giant Chocolate Festival in Bludenz if you are there in July?

Coffee Houses & Wine Taverns

Coffee houses are an integral part of Viennese life and a must if you're visiting the city. The coffee isn't particularly cheap, but the custom is to linger and soak in the atmosphere. Wine taverns *(heuringen)* have a fabulous ambience with oompah bands, congenial wine consumption and relatively cheap food. They are found in the wine-growing suburbs around Vienna and, as there are usually several close together, it's easy to do some Heuringen-hopping on foot.

Skiing & Hiking

Like Switzerland, the Austrian Alps are famous for their pricey ski resorts. Vorarlberg (St Anton) and Tirol (Innsbruck) are the most popular areas, but there is also skiing in Salzburg province (Saalbach/Hinterglemm), Upper Austria and Carinthia. Kitzbühel and Lech are the jet-set resorts. Cross-country skiing is cheaper and takes place just about anywhere there's sufficient snow and a shortage of buildings. The Arlberg region comprises several linked resorts and is considered to have some of the best skiing in Austria. St Anton is the largest and least elitist of these resorts, but even here budget travellers can kiss their savings goodbye amid the easy-going atmosphere and vigorous nightlife.

There are thousands of kilometres of well signposted hiking trails to explore in the Alps and there are some 500 mountain huts scattered around the eastern Alps. The Kaisergebirge mountains in northern Tirol are a favourite with mountaineers.

Out in the Country

Set at an elevation of 1640m, the Eisriesenwelt Caves near Werfen are the largest accessible ice caves in the world. They comprise more than 40km of explored passageways and 30,000 cubic metres of ice. The similarly stunning Dachstein caves are at Obertraun, south-east of Salzburg. Both cave systems are open between May and October.

The 50km Grossglockner Road, Austria's No 1 panorama, passes through the Hohe Tauern National Park where there are dramatic views of numerous peaks, including the mighty Grossglockner (3797m). The Grossglockner Road is open to traffic between May and November. Start the journey in Zell am See and end in Heiligenblut.

A river cruise on the not-so-blue Danube is a must, especially for Strauss lovers – the most picturesque stretch is between Krems and Melk.

The Salzkammergut lakes area, just east of Salzburg, comprises a pleasant and popular string of scenic lakeside resorts with plenty of boating and watersports on offer.

VISA REQUIREMENTS

European Union (EU), US, Canadian, Australian and New Zealand citizens do not require visas for stays of up to three months. Nationals of African and Arabic countries generally require a visa – also valid for up to three months. For South Africans, Austria is part of the Schengen Agreement.

Austrian Embassies

Australia
(☎ 02-6295 1533, fax 6239 6751) 12 Talbot St, Forrest, Canberra, ACT 2603

Canada
(☎ 613-789 1444, fax 789 3431) 445 Wilbrod St, Ottawa, Ont KIN 6M7

New Zealand
Consulate: (☎ 04-801 9709, fax 385 4642) 22-4 Garrett St, Wellington
(does not issue visas or passports; contact the Australian office for these services)

UK
(☎ 020-7235 3731, fax 7235 8025) 18 Belgrave Mews West, London SW1 8HU

USA
(☎ 202-895 6700, fax 895 6750) 3524 International Court NW, Washington, DC 20008

TOURIST OFFICES OVERSEAS

Branches of the Austrian National Tourist office include:

Australia
(☎ 02-9299 3621, fax 9299 3808, ✆ oew syd@world.net) 1st floor, 36 Carrington St, Sydney, NSW 2000

Canada
(☎ 416-967-3381, fax 967-4101, ✆ anto .tor@sympatico.ca) 2 Bloor St East, Suite 3330, Toronto, Ont M4W 1A8

UK
(☎ 020-7629 0461, fax 7499 6038, ✆ oew lon@easynet.co.uk) 14 Cork St, London W1X 1PF

USA

(☎ 212-944 6880, fax 730 4568,
✉ antonyc@ibm.net) PO Box 1142,
New York, NY, 10108-1142
(☎ 310-477 2038, fax 477 5141,
✉ antolax@ ix.net.com) 11601 Wilshire
Blvd, Suite 2480, Los Angeles, CA 90025

Some offices aren't open to personal callers, so phone first.

POST & COMMUNICATIONS

Post office hours vary but a few main post offices in big cities are open 24 hours a day. Stamps are also available in tobacco *(tabak)* shops. Poste restante is *Postlagernde Briefe* in German. Mail can be sent care of any post office and is held for a month (address it to 'Postamt', followed by the postcode).

Telephone calls are expensive, though much cheaper during off-peak hours (nightly from 8 pm to 6 am). International direct dialling is nearly always possible; otherwise, dial ☎ 09 for the operator. Post offices invariably have telephones but be wary of using telephones in hotels, as they can cost several times as much as public phones. Phonecards *(Telefon-Wertkarte)* will save you a bit of money and are available for AS50, AS95 and AS190. Faxes can be sent from the post office.

There are Internet cafes in most cities such as Vienna, Salzburg, Graz and Innsbruck, and access is available at the library in Vienna.

MONEY
Costs

In tourist areas, budget travellers can get by on about US$25 a day if they camp or stay in hostels, travel on a rail pass, self-cater or stick to student cafes

---

Itineraries

Two Days
For a fleeting visit, spend your time in Vienna checking out the central sights, visiting a few coffee shops and heurigen and taking in a show at the opera or concert hall. Alternatively, if you're a fan of Mozart and Julie Andrews and you're coming to Austria from Munich (only two hours to the west), you might want to stop in Salzburg. Here you should definitely visit the Hohensalzburg Castle, wander the Baroque streets in search of something that isn't connected with Mozart, and down a few mugs of dark beer at the Augustiner Bräustübl, an atmospheric beer hall and brewery run by monks.

One Week
With a week you can afford to spend a few more days in Vienna (that's if you can afford it!), further exploring the city's historical, architectural and cultural attractions. Travel across to Salzburg for a couple of days and take a day trip to either Werfen (for the ice caves and fortress) or the Salzkammergut lakes.

Two Weeks
Two weeks will give you time to more easily fit in some skiing or hiking, or to get ensconced in Vienna if the mood takes you. Spend up to five days in and around Vienna, including a cruise on the Danube, possibly from Krems to Melk. Give yourself three days in Salzburg (with a day trip to Werfen); two days at the Salzkammergut lakes staying at either Bad Ischl, Hallstatt, or St Gilgen; two days in Innsbruck and two days at an alpine resort such as St Anton.

One Month
With a month you can visit all of the previous places at a more leisurely pace, and add a tour of the south, taking in the university city of Graz, Hohe Tauern National Park and the Styrian wine routes, Klagenfurt and Lienz.

AUSTRIA HIGHLIGHTS & ITINERARIES

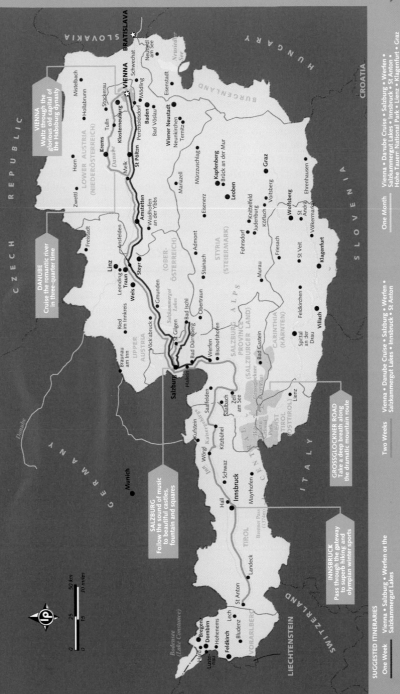

VIENNA
Waltz through the glorious old capital of the Habsburg dynasty

DANUBE
Cruise the romantic river in three-quarter time

SALZBURG
Follow the sound of music to beautiful castles, fountain and squares

INNSBRUCK
Pass through the gateway to superb hiking and olympian winter sports

GROSSGLOCKNER ROAD
Take a deep breath along the dramatic mountain route

SUGGESTED ITINERARIES

One Week Vienna • Salzburg • Werfen or the Salzkammergut Lakes

Two Weeks Vienna • Danube Cruise • Salzburg • Werfen • Salzkammergut Lakes • Innsbruck • St Anton

One Month Vienna • Danube Cruise • Salzburg • Werfen • Salzkammergut Lakes • Innsbruck • St Anton • Hohe Tauern National Park • Lienz • Klagenfurt • Graz

and only have the occasional drink. Staying in a cheap pension and eating out more will require about US$50 a day – add US$10 for a room with private bathroom. To stay in a mid-range hotel, have a cheap lunch, a decent dinner, some money to spend on evening entertainment and not be too concerned about how expensive a cup of coffee is, a daily allowance of at least US$80 would be needed.

Expect to pay from US$7 to US$15 for camping or a hostel bed, from US$45 for a cheap double room, US$6 to US$10 for a budget meal and US$10 to US$20 for a moderate restaurant meal.

Hotel and restaurant bills include a service charge, but it is also customary to tip in restaurants and cafes. Round up smaller bills and add an extra 5 to 10% to larger ones. Taxi drivers will expect around 10% extra.

Changing Money

Exchanging travellers cheques and cash is rarely a problem in Austria. Changing cash attracts a negligible commission but the exchange rate is usually 1 to 4% lower than for cheques. Banks charge a whopping AS100 (US$9) for travellers cheques. American Express is the best place to change, especially if you have its cheques. Post offices have low commissions but poor exchange rates. After hours, train stations usually have a currency exchange counter that remains open till late.

A surprising number of Austrian shops and restaurants refuse to accept any credit cards but Bankomats (ATMs) are common in Austria, even in small villages; you can withdraw cash from credit and debit accounts 24 hours a day.

ONLINE SERVICES

Lonely Planet's Destination Austria page can be found at www.lonelyplanet .com/dest/eur/aus.htm. The Vienna Tourist Board is at www.info.wien.at and the Austrian National Tourist Office is at www.austriatourism.at. A site aimed at the English-speaking community in Vienna is www.austriaguide .com/info. The City of Salzburg site includes an Austrian Beer Guide (www .salzburginfo.at)! The Austrian Federal Railways site (www.oebb.at) has train information and timetables.

BOOKS

Austrian fiction reached a monumental peak with Robert Musil's three-volume, unfinished *The Man Without Qualities*, which depicts Austria in the early years of the 20th century as the Habsburgs' power waned.

Cutting Timber by Thomas Bernhard is an incisive and scintillatingly dismissive portrait of Austrian society. Peter Handke's bleak and beautiful writings include *The Goalkeeper's Anxiety at the Penalty Kick* and *The Left-Handed Woman*.

Austria has proved fertile turf for foreign writers: Graham Greene set *The Third Man* in a rather spooky Vienna; Christina Stead's *The Salzburg Tales* is a Chauceresque novel about gatherers at the Salzburg Festival in the 1930s who tell each other stories; John Irving's *Setting Free the Bears* is a finely spun tale about releasing the animals from Vienna's zoo.

Mozart & the Wolf Gang by Anthony Burgess is a learned but enjoyable celestial fantasy in which the great composers discourse on music and Mozart. *Mozart and Vienna* by HC Robbins Landon focuses on Wolfgang's Vienna years.

FILMS

Perhaps the most famous film set in Austria is *The Third Man* (1949), with Orson Welles as the mysterious Harry Lime. Set in post-war Vienna, it's a dark film that was made famous as much by Welles' improvised dialogue and the zither score by Anton Karas as by the plot itself.

Equally renowned is *The Sound of Music*, set in and around Salzburg. Julie Andrews plays the nun who becomes a nanny and then a mother for the singing Von Trapp family. It is set during during WWII.

ENTERING & LEAVING

Vienna is Austria's main air transport hub, but there are international airports at Linz, Graz, Salzburg, Innsbruck and Klagenfurt. If you're visiting Austria from outside Europe, it may be cheaper to fly to a European 'gateway' city and travel overland from there. Technically there's no departure tax when flying out of Austria, but you pay a 'passenger service charge' of around US$15, which is included in the ticket price.

Austria has excellent rail connections to all major European destinations. Buses are generally slower, cheaper and less comfortable than trains. Fast, well maintained *autobahnen* (motorways) fan out to all surrounding countries. Major border crossing points are open 24 hours a day.

Fast hydrofoils skim along the Danube between Vienna, Bratislava and Budapest during spring and summer but they're not exactly cheap. Steamers ply the Danube between Vienna and the German border town of Passau from May to late September.

Surprisingly little is commonly known about Belgium, though it spawned some of Western Europe's first great towns, the first masters of oil painting (the Flemish school), and was the scene of one of history's most tragic battles. Positioned between France, Germany and, across the North Sea, Britain, Belgium has long been one of Europe's punching bags. Napoleon was defeated at the Battle of Waterloo near Brussels in 1814, and there are still grim reminders among the poppies in Flanders of the bloody battles of WWI.

These days, however, the history and the new European Union (EU) bureaucracy combine to draw tourists, businesspeople and politicians in large numbers. And the things you may know about Belgium – fabulous beer and chocolates – are here in abudance. The Belgians themselves are modest and confident, but rarely strive to impress.

WHEN TO GO

April to September is the warmest time of the year in Belgium, but be prepared for grey skies and soggy streets no matter when you go. July and August are the warmest, busiest and wettest months, so May, June and September are better times to visit. The Ardennes is generally cooler than the rest of the country with snow from November to March.

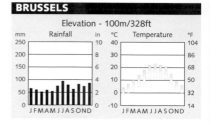

BRUSSELS

Elevation - 100m/328ft

HIGHLIGHTS

For a tiny country, Belgium packs quite a lot in. The capital, Brussels, is an unpretentious mix of grand edifices and modern life – as the headquarters of the EU and NATO, it's packed to the rafters with bureaucrats and Eurocrats. Medieval Bruges is a 'living museum' split by canals and cobbled streets, while Flanders Fields near Ypres is a poignant reminder of the massacre that was WWI. And let's not forget those Belgian waffles, chocolates and beers …

At a Glance

Full Country Name: Kingdom of Belgium
Area: 30,518 sq km
Population: 10.2 million
Capital City: Brussels (pop 970,000)
People: 55% Flemish (of Teutonic origin), 33% Walloons (French Latin) and about 10% foreigners
Language: Flemish, French and German. Most Belgians also speak English
Religion: More than 75% Roman Catholic
Government: Constitutional parliamentary monarchy
Currency: Belgian franc (Bf) = 100 centimes
Time Zone: One hour ahead of GMT/UTC; clocks go forward one hour on the last Sunday in March and back again on the first Sunday in September
International Telephone Code: 32
Electricity: 220V, 50Hz

Museums & History

In Brussels, don't miss the Horta Museum, an introduction to the Art Noveau style led in Belgium by Victor Horta. Beer-drinkers should check out the Brewery Museum inside one of the guildhouses on the impressive Grand Place. Though it's hardly an historical museum, Tintin fans should not go past the Belgian Comic Strip Centre.

Bruges has a richly ornate 13th century centre that is a museum in itself. Here you'll find Belgium's oldest town hall and the Church of Our Lady, which contains Michelangelo's sculpture, *Madonna and Child*. A highlight of the town is Begijnhof, a 13th century grassy square enclosed by whitewashed homes that are now inhabited by Benedictine nuns. If possible, steer clear of Bruges in midsummer when the crowds can smother the age-old ambience.

Named after the famous poem, In Flanders Fields Museum at Ypres is a must before or after a tour through the quiet fields, where more than 300,000 Allied soldiers died during WWI. You'll also want to see the memorial Menin Gate, inscribed with the names of 55,000 troops who have no graves.

Antwerp has some excellent museums. First stop for most is Rubens' House, and you'll find more works by the Flemish master in the cathedral and the Royal Museum of Arts.

Pubs & Beers

No trip to Belgium would be complete without sampling its national beverage. Even if you don't normally drink beer, the tasty fruit beers may appeal. You can visit several breweries around Brussels and Bruges, and there are some wonderfully atmospheric pubs to try. In Brussels, head straight to Falstaff, a trendy Art Noveau showpiece. There is a cosy beer house in Bruges, 't Brugs Beertje, which boasts over 300 types of beer. Antwerp has some 2500 bars and cafes, most of which serve the sweet local liqueur, Élixir d'Anvers. The Oud Arsenaal is a popular local bar with the cheapest beers in town.

There are more beer varieties in Belgium than you could possibly sample in one trip. The most noted are the traditional abbey-brewed Trappist beers – dark in colour, grainy and potent. Wheat beers such as Hoegaerden are light and refreshing, while the sweet beers mixed with cherries or raspberries are another taste altogether. Look out for popular brews Duvel, Westmalle Triple, Palm and Timmermans Gueuze.

Hiking

The Ardennes is an area of deep river valleys and high forest, often overlooked by travellers to Belgium. It's a good place to go rambling along a network of forest trails, particularly around La Roche and in Hautes Fagnes National Park further east.

Namur is the best base to begin exploration – it's on the railway line to Luxembourg – though La Roche and Champlon are closer to the best hiking areas. Liège is the northern gateway to the Ardennes and, along with Spa, is a good base for trips into Hautes Fagnes.

VISA REQUIREMENTS

Travellers from Australia, Canada, New Zealand, Japan, the USA and many other countries need only a valid passport (no visa) to enter Belgium for up to 90 days. EU citizens can enter on an official identity card. Belgium is part of the Schengen Agreement.

Belgian Embassies

Australia
(☎ 02-6273 2501) 19 Arkana St, Yarralumla, Canberra, ACT 2600

Canada
(☎ 613-236 7267/9) 80 Elgin St, 4th floor, Ottawa, Ont K1P 1B7

Itineraries

Two Days
Spend one day in Brussels looking around one of Europe's finest central squares, the pentagonal Grand Place. Take in some of the terrace cafe life (sample the famed Brussels mussels), the Royal Palace and as many museums as possible before taking the one hour train ride west to Bruges. Here you should wander through the medieval Markt and Burg areas, climb the belfry for a panoramic view, visit a bar or brewery, sample a few praline chocolates, and check out the Begijnhof. That should do.

One Week
Spend two days exploring Brussels and one day in Bruges, then make a trip to Ypres and Flanders Fields. From there take the train to Antwerp, the diamond capital of Europe and once home to Pieter Paul Rubens. As well as Rubens' House, there are several museums and a throbbing nightlife.

From there (especially if you're heading to Germany or Luxembourg), whip down to the Ardennes for fresh air and easy hiking. Namur and La Roche are on the main rail lines.

Two Weeks
With two weeks you can have a good look around Brussels over three days (including a trip to Waterloo), at least two days in Bruges, and a day in Ypres and Flanders Fields. From there, head to Ghent for a day. It's medieval Europe's second largest city after Paris and boasts the excellent Fine Arts Museum and good views from its belfry. Continue on to Antwerp for two days, perhaps taking a cruise on the Scheldt River. The remainder of your time can be spent exploring the Ardennes (including the towns of Liège and Namur) and Hautes Fagnes National Park.

New Zealand
(☎ 04-472 9558) 1-3 Willeston St, Wellington

UK
(☎ 020-7470 3700) 103-105 Eaton Square, London SW1W 9AB

USA
(☎ 202-333 6900) 3330 Garfield St NW, Washington, DC 20008

TOURIST OFFICES OVERSEAS

France
(☎ 01 47 42 41 18, fax 01 47 42 71 83) 21 Blvd des Capucines, 75002 Paris

Germany
(☎ 0211-86 48 40, fax 13 42 85) 47 Berliner Allee, 40212 Düsseldorf

The Netherlands
(☎ 023-534 44 34, fax 534 20 50) 3 Kennemerplein, 2011 MH Haarlem

UK
(☎ 020-7629 3977, fax 7629 0454) 29 Princes St, London W1R 7RG

USA
(☎ 212-758 8130, fax 355 7675) 780 Third Ave, Suite 1501, New York, NY 10017-7076

POST & COMMUNICATIONS

Post offices have reliable poste restante, though it can attract a f15 fee (often waived).

Phone boxes accept f5 and f20 coins, or f200, f500 and f1000 Telecards (Belgacom phonecards) available from post offices and newsagents. Phonepass and the phonecard cards (used in normal public phones but valid only for international calls to some countries) are sold from various agents such as Thomas Cook. These phonecards are better value than Telecards. International calls can be made from public boxes, the post office or telephone centres. A three minute call to the USA costs f91 (US$2.50).

Faxes can be sent from telephone offices, and there are cybercafes for

BELGIUM HIGHLIGHTS & ITINERARIES ▶▶

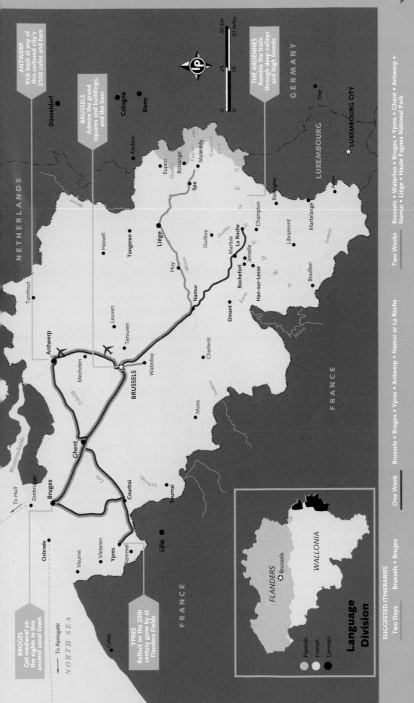

ANTWERP
Kick back at any of this cultured city's 2500 cafes and bars

BRUSSELS
Admire the grand squares and buildings, and the beer

THE ARDENNES
Ramble the trails through deep valleys and high forests

BRUGES
Get medieval on the sights in this ancient canal town

YPRES
Reflect on the 20th century gone by at Flanders Fields

GERMANY
NETHERLANDS
LUXEMBOURG
FRANCE
NORTH SEA

Düsseldorf
Cologne
Bonn
Aachen
Eupen
Botrange
Malmédy
Spa
Hasselt
Tongeren
Liège
Durbuy
La Roche
Champlon
Martelange
Libramont
Bastogne
Arlon
Trier
LUXEMBOURG CITY

Turnhout
Leuven
Tervuren
Namur
Huy
Marloie
Rochefort
Jemelle
Han-sur-Lesse
Dinant
Bouillon
Charleroi
Mons
BRUSSELS
Waterloo
Antwerp
Mechelen
Ghent
Bruges
Zeebrugge
Oostende
Veurne
Vleteren
Ypres
Kemmel
Courtrai
Tournai
Lille
Calais

To Hull
To Ramsgate
Westerschelde

0   25   50 km
0   15   30 miles

Language Division

Flemish
French
German

FLANDERS
WALLONIA
Brussels

SUGGESTED ITINERARIES

Two Days Brussels • Bruges

One Week Brussels • Bruges • Ypres • Antwerp • Namur or La Roche

Two Weeks Brussels • Waterloo • Bruges • Ypres • Ghent • Antwerp • Namur • Liège • Haute Fagnes National Park

email/Internet access in the larger towns and cities.

MONEY
Costs

Being so small, Belgium is cheap to get around, and camping grounds and hostels are plentiful. Budget hotels, however, are rare and in summer everything is heavily booked. Travelling modestly, you could survive on US$25 per day, a little more if you're hanging around Brussels. If you want to indulge more in restaurants and try some of Belgium's beer and chocolates, it will be around US$45 per day.

Expect to pay from US$8 to US$10 for a hostel bed, from US$30 for a cheap hotel room, US$7 to US$10 for a budget meal and US$10 to US$25 for a moderate restaurant meal.

Changing Money

Banks are the best place to change your money, charging up to US$4 commission on travellers cheques. Out of hours, there are the less generous exchange bureaux. All major credit cards are widely accepted. Tipping isn't obligatory, and haggling is not common.

ONLINE SERVICES

Lonely Planet's Destination Belgium (www.lonelyplanet.com/dest/eur/bel .htm) will get you off to a good start. The Belgium Tourist Office's official Web site (www.visitbelgium.com) has events listings, country information and photos of major cities. Discover Belgium (www.discoverbelgium.com) has transport and accommodation information, plus links to other Belgium-related sites. Also try the Belgium Travel Network (www.trabel.com).

BOOKS

The Sorrow of Belgium by Bruges-born Hugo Claus is one of the few pieces of local literature translated into English. It describes wartime Belgium through the eyes of a Flemish adolescent.

Live & Work in Belgium, the Netherlands and Luxembourg, by Vacation Work Publications, is handy if you're planning to settle in for a while. Lieve Joris is a Flemish author who writes about cultures in transition in Africa, the Middle East and Eastern Europe. Her *Gates of Damascus*, published by Lonely Planet, is about daily life in Syria.

FILMS

If It's Tuesday This Must Be Belgium (1969), starring Suzanne Pleshette, is actually about a whirlwind trip around Europe, but naturally features a bit of Belgium. *Between the Devil and the Deep Blue Sea* (1995) is a fine drama starring Stephen Rea.

ENTERING & LEAVING

Belgium has two international airports, the main one being Zaventem, 14km north-east of Brussels. Deurne, close to Antwerp, may have cheaper flights to London. If you're in Europe already, a bus or train is the best option. Belgium Railways has frequent international services, with Brussels being the central hub. Two companies that operate car/passenger ferries to and from Britain are: North Sea Ferries (overnight from Zeebrugge to Hull) and Oostende Lines/Sally Ferries (six boats daily between Ostend and Ramsgate).

There's a departure tax of around US$16 if you're flying out of Brussels, but this is often included in your ticket.

BRITAIN

At one stage of its history this small island ruled half the world's population and had a major impact on much of the rest. For those whose countries once lay in the shadow of its great empire, a visit may almost be a cliche, but it's also essential: a peculiar mixture of homecoming and confrontation.

Britain is still one of the most beautiful islands in the world. Though small in area, the more you explore the bigger it seems to become. Visitors are often fooled by this magical expansion and try to do too much too quickly. Covering it all in one trip is impossible. The UK comprises England, Wales, Scotland and Northern Ireland (see the Ireland profile for information on Northern Ireland).

Sometimes in summer it can feel as if the whole world has come to Britain. But it's certainly possible to avoid the rush. Don't spend all your time in the big, tourist-ridden towns; rather, pick a small area and spend at least a week or so wandering around the country lanes and villages.

WHEN TO GO

Anyone who spends an extended period in Britain will soon sympathise with the locals' conversational obsession with the weather. Although in relative terms the climate is mild, and some find the weather perfect, grey skies can make for an utterly depressing atmosphere. Even in midsummer you can go for days without seeing the sun, or you get a freak 'heatwave' where the

mercury nudges 30°C – expect the unexpected.

July and August are the busiest months, and should be avoided if possible. The crowds in London and popular towns like Oxford, Bath and York have to be seen to be believed. You are just as likely to get good weather in spring and autumn, so May/June and September/October are the best times to visit, although October is getting too late for the Scottish Highlands. Easter is another time to avoid popular holiday places like the Lake District, Edinburgh and Cornwall. If you intend to be in Edinburgh for the festivals in August or for New Year's Eve, book accommodation well in advance.

At a Glance

Full Country Name: Great Britain, or the United Kingdom (UK)
Area: 244,820 sq km
Population: 56.7 million
Capital City: London (pop 10 million)
People: Anglo-Saxons, Celts, Scots, Welsh, Irish, West Indians, Pakistanis, Indians
Language: English, Welsh, Scottish Gaelic
Religion: Church of England, Methodist, Baptist, Catholic, Muslim, Presbyterian Church of Scotland
Government: Parliamentary democracy
Currency: British pound (£) = 100 pence (also Scottish pound at the same value)
Time Zone: GMT/UTC; clocks go forward one hour in late March and back again in late October
International Telephone Code: 44
Electricity: 240V, 50Hz

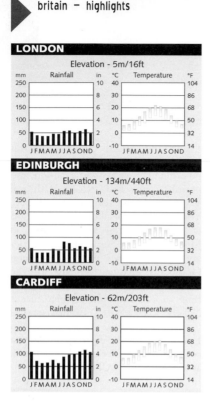

LONDON
Elevation - 5m/16ft

EDINBURGH
Elevation - 134m/440ft

CARDIFF
Elevation - 62m/203ft

HIGHLIGHTS

Planning a trip around Britain can be bewildering for the first-timer (or the second or third-timer for that matter). The country may be small but its long history as an influential world power has left it with a rich heritage of medieval castles and cathedrals, historic cities and towns, stately homes and elegant gardens. Added to this are the natural attractions: the national parks, beautiful coastal regions, and the spectacular highlands and islands of Scotland. The following touch on some highlights.

London

Britain's capital is one of the world's truly great cities and, despite high costs and the occasional gloominess of the place, it should not be missed. Indeed, 'Cool Britannia' has made London a swinging place again in recent years, so try to catch a band or a theatre production and enjoy some of the nightlife as well as taking in all that sightseeing.

Royalty is still the biggest drawcard among tourists. You won't want to miss Buckingham Palace (and the Changing of the Guard), Westminster Abbey, St Paul's Cathedral and the Tower of London (with the crown jewels). Then there's the Houses of Parliament, Big Ben, Trafalgar Square, Piccadilly Circus, Hyde Park, Covent Garden and some fine museums and galleries. A boat trip on the River Thames to Greenwich, Hampton Court Palace or Kew Gardens is a must.

Historic Cities & Towns

Bath, in south-west England, is blessed with superb Georgian architecture and Roman ruins, but is also inundated with tourists. Beverley, in Yorkshire, is an unspoilt, little visited market town with two superb medieval churches. The famous university towns of Cambridge and Oxford are delights to visit.

Edinburgh is undoubtedly another of the world's greatest cities, with a dramatically situated castle and an extraordinary architectural heritage. Once a great port and industrial city, Liverpool boasts a superb legacy of Victorian and Edwardian architecture, a strong cultural identity, vibrant nightlife and plenty of Beatles connections.

The Scottish university and golfing town of St Andrews has a ruined castle and harbour on a headland overlooking a sweeping stretch of sand. Shrewsbury, near Wales, is an interesting town of half-timbered architecture and curious medieval streets. Whitby, the home of explorer Captain James Cook, is an atmospheric fishing port on magnificent coastline in North Yorkshire. The ancient English capital of Winchester, south-west of London, is rich in history and sports a great cathedral. York is another proud city with a spectacular cathedral and medieval walls, and many excellent museums.

Cathedrals & Churches

Britain has many fine cathedrals and churches, most of which can be visited free. Some of the best are Canterbury Cathedral in Kent County south-east of London, Westminster Abbey and St Paul's Cathedral in London, Durham Cathedral, York Minster, Winchester Cathedral, Wells Cathedral in Somerset, Ely Cathedral in Cambridgeshire, King's College Chapel in Cambridge, Lincoln Cathedral, Rievaulx Abbey in North Yorkshire, Salisbury Cathedral in Wiltshire, and St David's in Pembrokeshire, Wales.

Museums & Galleries

Some of the world's greatest museums and art galleries are in Britain – and not only in London. The British Museum, the Victoria & Albert Museum, the National Gallery and the Tate Gallery, all in London, are must-sees (all but the V&A are free). Others worth visiting include the Burrell Collection in Glasgow, York Castle Museum, Ironbridge Gorge in Shropshire, the Imperial War Museum in London and the HMS *Victory* and *Mary Rose* in Portsmouth. The *Victory* is the world's oldest commissioned warship, and was Admiral Nelson's

flagship at the Battle of Trafalgar. The *Mary Rose* was Henry VIII's flagship.

Castles & Historic Houses

Britain's long history of defence and battle has left a legacy of hundreds of impressive castles. The following are some of the best.

Leeds Castle in Kent is an extraordinarily beautiful and justly famous castle set in the middle of a lake and only marred by the crowds. Since 1078 the Tower of London has been a fortress, royal residence and state prison. It is now home to the stunning British crown jewels and the snappily dressed Beefeaters.

Edinburgh Castle dominates the city and has a truly spectacular cliff-top setting. It's also home to the Scottish crown jewels. Also in Scotland, Stirling Castle was the favoured royal residence of the Stewarts. Windsor Castle, the royal residence with restored state rooms and the beautiful St George's Chapel, makes an easy day trip from London. Other castles worth seeking out are Alnwick (Northumberland), Caerlaverock (Scotland), Caernarfon (North Wales), Conwy (North Wales) and Dover Castle (Kent).

There are many stately homes and palaces with interesting historical backgrounds. The childhood home of Winston Churchill, Blenheim Palace (in Oxfordshire), is an enormous baroque-style private house built by Sir John Vanbrugh in 1704. Another Vanbrugh masterpiece, Castle Howard, has a dramatic setting in superb landscaped gardens just north of York.

Henry VIII's Hampton Court Palace, just outside London, was established in 1514 and served as a royal residence until the 18th century. It's an enormous, fascinating complex surrounded by beautiful gardens. Ightham Mote (Kent) is a small moated manor house that has scarcely changed for 500 years.

Knole House, also in Kent and surrounded by parkland, is an enormous house dating from the 15th century and virtually untouched since the 17th century. The Royal Pavilion in Brighton is an exotic fantasy, combining Indian, Chinese and Gothic elements, built by George IV in 1815.

Prehistoric Remains & Roman Sites

Stonehenge is Britain's most famous stone circle and a site of pilgrimage for many, although some are disappointed by its proximity to the motorway and the fact that you can't walk among the stones. The extensive remains at Avebury in Wiltshire are more impressive.

Callanish Standing Stones on the Isle of Lewis in Scotland is a cross-shaped avenue and circle on a dramatic site.

On Orkney, the Ring of Brodgar is a well preserved stone circle, part of a ceremonial site that includes standing stones and a chambered tomb. Also on Orkney, Skara Brae is the extraordinarily well preserved remains of a village inhabited 3000 years ago.

There is plenty of evidence of the Roman occupation of Britain – Bath is a prime example. For Roman ruins, check out the evocative Hadrian's Wall – a monumental attempt to divide Scotland and England; Fishbourne Palace, near Chichester – Britain's only Roman palace, with beautiful mosaics; and remote Chedworth Villa in Gloucester.

Islands & Coastline

Britain has thousands of kilometres of rugged coastline and many interesting islands where, in some cases, time seems to have stood still.

Brighton is a tacky but vibrant seaside resort south of London, and nearby Beachy Head has spectacular chalk cliffs backed by rolling downland

Sustrans & the National Cycle Network

Sustrans is a civil-engineering charity whose goal is the creation of a 10,460km network of cycle paths that will pass through the middle of most major towns and cities in Britain.

When Sustrans announced this objective in 1978 the charity was barely taken seriously, but increasingly congested roads have now made the public reconsider the exalted place of the car in modern Britain. The government's massive road building program has been cut back and £42 million was donated to Sustrans by the Millennium Commission to ensure that 4025km of routes are open by the early 2000. The whole network will be complete by 2005.

Half the network is to be on traffic-free paths (including disused railways and canal-side tow-paths); the rest of the system along quiet minor roads. Cyclists will share the traffic-free paths with wheelchair users and walkers. Many useful sections are open now – the 26km path between Bath and Bristol, for example, is the ideal way to visit these two places. In 1996 Lôn Las Cymru, the Welsh National Cycle Route stretching north-south across the country, was opened. The Scotland National Cycle Route runs 684km from Carlisle to Inverness.

Maps are available from Sustrans covering all the routes (free for the shorter paths, £3.99 to £5.99 for map-guides for the national routes). For more information, contact Sustrans (☎ 0117-929 0888), 35 King St, Bristol BS1 4DZ, or visit its Web site (www.sustrans.org.uk).

Itineraries

Three Days
Spend your time in London visiting the main sights (see Highlights – London). Also make a day trip to either Greenwich, Hampton Court Palace or Kew Gardens, all of which can be reached by boat on the Thames – a fine way to see some of this great city.

One Week
Spend two days in London and take a day trip to Greenwich or Hampton Court Palace. Also visit Windsor and Eton, Oxford, Bath and Wells.

Two Weeks
If you want a snapshot of the country, follow the one week itinerary plus Salisbury (and Stonehenge), Avebury, Cambridge, York and Edinburgh. Alternatively, concentrate on a particular area:

South England After London and Windsor, visit Kent (Leeds Castle), Brighton and Winchester, then travel across to Devon and Cornwall, working your way around this spectacular coast and up to Bath. There are many resorts and fishing villages along the way; some are tourist traps (like Land's End), others are quaint (Polperro, St Ives); yet others are historically interesting (Plymouth, Tintagel, Falmouth). Try to avoid this part of Britain in July and August, when it might be better to head into the less visited interior of Devon and Cornwall such as Bodmin Moor and Dartmoor National Park.

Central England & Wales After visiting Oxford and Bath, continue west into Wales, stopping briefly in the capital, Cardiff, before seeing the Brecon Beacons National Park and then the coastal village of St David's. Continuing up the coast to North Wales, visit Porthmadog and take the train through Snowdonia National Park to Ffestiniog, Conwy and Llandudno. From there you can loop back down to Shrewsbury in England or continue up to Liverpool.

North England After visiting London, Windsor and Oxford, head up to touristy Shakespeare country at Stratford-upon-Avon, then to Liverpool and Blackpool on the west coast. From there you can cross over to York and explore the Yorkshire Dales, possibly with a trip to Scarborough or Whitby. Cross back over to the Lake District, where you can base yourself for a couple of days (avoid weekends) at Keswick or Windermere.

Scotland Though small, Scotland requires at least two weeks to explore the main sights. Starting in Edinburgh, you can do a loop that takes you up to Inverness, across to the Isle of Skye, down to Fort William and Glencoe, to the port of Oban with trips to Mull and Staffa, then down to Glasgow and back to Edinburgh. This trip takes in some of Scotland's highlands and islands. You will need more time to get up to the remote and wild north of Scotland, to the Orkney islands and Outer Hebrides, and to explore the Borders area south of Edinburgh, or east Scotland around Perth, St Andrews and Aberdeen.

One Month
For an overview of Britain, take in the following circuit: London, Cambridge, York, Edinburgh, Inverness, Isle of Skye, Fort William, Oban, Glasgow, the Lake District, Liverpool, Chester, Stratford-upon-Avon, the Cotswolds, Bath, Wells, Avebury, Salisbury and Oxford.

Alternatively, combine two or more of the previous itineraries, or pick one area and explore it in much more depth.

Two Months
With two months you could cover the one month itinerary, but stay put for a week or so in one place. Explore Snowdonia (North Wales) or the remote Scottish islands, and perhaps attempt a long-distance walk like the West Highland Way. If you are fit, you might even consider hiring a bicycle and riding between Bath and Bristol (only about 10km), or for part of the route between Inverness and Carlyle.

YORK
Choose among the grand Gothic cathedral, medieval walls and many museums

EDINBURGH
Arrive in August for the peak of festivals, or any time for Edinburgh Castle

CALLANISH STANDING STONES
Step back a millennium prior to Egypt's pyramids at this huge stone Celtic cross

100 km
50 miles

SHETLAND ISLANDS
Lerwick
Foula

NORTH SEA

ORKNEY ISLANDS
Stromness
John o'Groats
Wick
Thurso

To Shetland Islands (See inset)

Ullapool

Isle of Lewis
Callanish Standing Stones

OUTER HEBRIDES
North Uist
South Uist
St Kilda

Isle of Skye
Kyle of Lochalsh

North West Highlands
North Minch

Inverness
Loch Ness
Aviemore
Elgin
Moray Firth
Spey

Peterhead
Aberdeen
Dee
Braemar
Grampians
Montrose
Arbroath
Dundee
Perth
St Andrews

Fort William
Glencoe
Oban
Loch Linnhe
Loch Lomond
Stirling

SCOTLAND

Firth of Forth
Kirkaldy
EDINBURGH
Motherwell
Galashiels
Lammermuir Hills
Dunbar

Glasgow
Kilmarnock
Ayr
Sanquhar
Dumfries

Southern Uplands
Jedburgh
Cheviot Hills
Berwick-upon-Tweed

Northumberland National Park
Ashington
Newcastle Upon Tyne
Sunderland
Hartlepool
Saltburn-by-the-Sea
Whitby
Scarborough

Carlisle
Durham
Darlington
Middlesbrough

Pennines
Eden
Tyne
Tees
North York Moors National Park

Keswick
Workington
Lake District National Park
Windermere

INNER HEBRIDES
Rum
Coll
Tiree
Colonsay
Mull
Jura
Islay
Arran

Frith of Clyde
North Channel
Stranraer
Isle of Man

ATLANTIC OCEAN

Larne
BELFAST
Derry
NORTHERN IRELAND

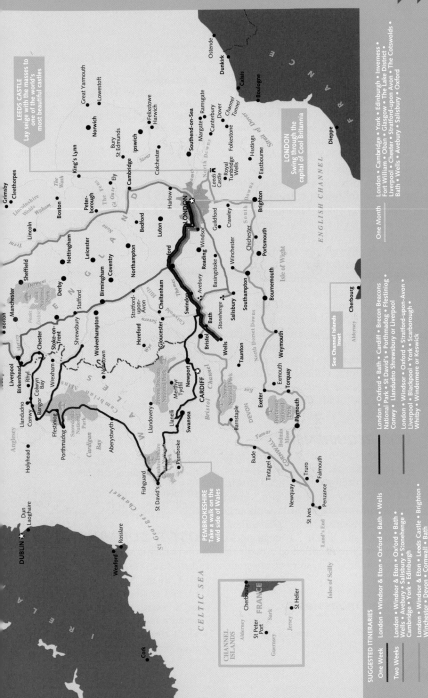

SUGGESTED ITINERARIES

One Week — London • Windsor & Eton • Oxford • Bath • Wells

Two Weeks — London • Windsor & Eton • Oxford • Bath • Wells • Avebury • Salisbury • Stonehenge • Cambridge • York • Edinburgh

—— London • Windsor & Eton • Leeds Castle • Brighton • Winchester • Devon • Cornwall • Bath

London • Oxford • Bath • Cardiff • Brecon Beacons National Park • St David's • Porthmadog • Ffestiniog • Conwy • Llandudno Shrewsbury or Liverpool

London • Windsor • Oxford • Stratford-upon-Avon • Liverpool • Blackpool • York • Scarborough • Whitby • Windermere or Keswick

One Month — London • Cambridge • York • Edinburgh • Inverness • Fort William • Oban • Glasgow • The Lake District • Liverpool • Chester • Stratford-upon-Avon • The Cotswolds • Bath • Wells • Avebury • Salisbury • Oxford

LEEDS CASTLE
Lay seige with the masses to one of the world's most beautiful castles

LONDON
Swing through the capital of Cool Britannia

PEMBROKESHIRE
Take a walk on the wild side of Wales

rich in wild flowers. The stretch of coast from Land's End to St Ives in Cornwall provides a landscape littered with historical reminders and relics. Tintagel Head near Newquay is a surf-battered headland topped by a ruined castle, believed to be King Arthur's birthplace. Scarborough is a classic English seaside resort in North York-shire with a superb location. The coast-line from here to Saltburn is dotted with beautiful fishing villages.

In North Wales, Llandudno is an old-style seaside resort with great Vic-torian architecture, while in South Wales, St David's to Cardigan is a stretch of unspoilt coastline in Pem-brokeshire Coast National Park.

Virtually the entire Scottish coast is spectacular, and some of the most stunning cliffs in Britain are to be found in Orkney and Shetland islands.

The best of Britain's islands are in Scotland. Try not to miss Skye, Harris, Staffa and Iona. Others are Colonsay, with fine sandy beaches and a mild climate, and wild and remote Jura Island.

VISA REQUIREMENTS

European Union (EU) citizens may live and work free of any immigration controls. Citizens of the USA, Canada, Australia, New Zealand and South Africa can stay six months without a visa. Australians, New Zealanders, Canadians and South Africans under the age of 28 are entitled to a two year working holiday visa, subject to certain conditions.

British Embassies
Australia
(☎ 02-6270 6666) Commonwealth Ave, Canberra, ACT 2600

Canada
(☎ 613-237 1530) 80 Elgin St, Ottawa, Ont K1P 5K7
New Zealand
(☎ 04-472 6049) 44 Hill St, Wellington 1
South Africa
(☎ 021-461 7220) 91 Parliament St, Cape Town 8001
USA
(☎ 202-462 1340) 3100 Massachusetts Ave NW, Washington, DC 20008

TOURIST OFFICES OVERSEAS

There are more than 40 British Tourist Authority (BTA) offices worldwide. They include:

Australia
(☎ 02-9377 4400, fax 9377 4499) Level 16, The Gateway, 1 Macquarie Place, Circular Quay, Sydney, NSW 2000
Canada
(☎ 416-925 6326, fax 961 2175) 111 Avenue Rd, Suite 450, Toronto, Ont M5R 3JD
New Zealand
(☎ 09-303 1446, fax 377 6965) 3rd floor, Dilworth Building, corner Queen and Customs Sts, Auckland 1
South Africa
(☎ 011-325 0343, fax 325 0344) Lancaster Gate, Hyde Park 2196, Craighall 2024
USA
(☎ 1800-462 2748) 625 N Michigan Ave, Suite 1510, Chicago, IL 60611 (personal callers only)
(☎ 1800-GO 2 BRITAIN) 551 Fifth Ave, Suite 701, New York, NY 10176-0799

POST & COMMUNICATIONS

A post office is never far away in Britain, and mail can be sent poste restante to any of them. An airmail letter to the USA or Canada will generally take less than a week; to Australia or New Zealand it takes around a week.

Since British Telecom (BT) was pri-vatised, several companies have started competing for its business. However, most public phone booths are still operated by BT. The familiar red phone booth survives only in conservation areas such as Westminster in London. Phonecards are widely available from all sorts of retailers, including post offices and newsagents; some public phones only take cards, others take cards and coins and even credit cards. Note that as of Easter 2000, the telephone area code for London changed to 020.

Most hotels now have faxes. Some shops also offer fax services, advertised by a sign in the window. To collect your email, there's a growing number of cybercafes throughout the country.

MONEY
Costs

Britain isn't the most expensive European country in which to travel, but it's right up there, especially in London.

In the capital you will need to budget about US$35 for bare survival (dorm accommodation, a one day travel card and the most basic sustenance). Even moderate sightseeing or nightlife can easily add another US$25 to this. If you stay in a hotel and eat restaurant meals you could easily spend US$90 a day without being extravagant. Once you get out of the big smoke, the costs will drop, particularly if you have a transport pass and if you cook your own meals. You'll still need at least US$30 a day, and if you stay in B&Bs, eat one sit-down meal a day and see the sights, you'll need about US$65 a day.

At decent restaurants, you should leave a tip of around 10% unless the service was unsatisfactory. Some restaurants add a service charge. Taxi drivers expect to be tipped about 10%, especially in London.

Changing Money

Travellers cheques are widely accepted in English banks, and you might as well buy them in pounds sterling to avoid changing currencies twice. Exchange bureaux in London frequently levy outrageous commissions and fees, so make sure you establish any deductions in advance. The bureaux at the international airports are exceptions to the rule, charging less than most banks and cashing sterling travellers cheques for free. Cashpoints (ATMs) are very common in Britain: most are linked to major credit cards as well as the Cirrus, Maestro and Plus cash networks, but if a machine swallows your card it can be a nightmare. Most banks insist on chopping it in half and sending it back to your home branch – very helpful.

ONLINE SERVICES

Britain is second only to the USA in its number of Web sites, and there are plenty of sites to interest cyber-travellers. An increasing number of towns, attractions, even B&Bs, have their own Web sites. Lonely Planet's Destination England page can be found at www .lonelyplanet.com/dest/eur/eng.htm.

The BTA site (www.bta.org.uk) has plenty of information and links to its offices worldwide. The UK Travel Guide has a useful site (www.uktravel .com). Knowhere: A User's Guide to Britain (www.knowhere.co.uk) is a great site with listings and inside information on more than 500 towns in Britain. There is another action-packed London site with listings, a restaurant guide, what's on and more: www.londontown.com. There's also the site of the *Sunday Times* newspaper: www.sunday-times.co.uk.

The Scottish Tourist Board has a site at www.holiday-scotland.net. For up-to-date information on all of Edinburgh's festivals, try www.go-edinburgh-co.uk. For the Edinburgh Fringe Festival, try www.edfringe.com.

If you're interested in Wales, the Wales Tourist Board has a site at www.tourism.wales.gov.uk.

BOOKS

Bill Bryson's highly entertaining and perceptive *Notes from a Small Island* is a recent travelogue covering Britain. *The Kingdom by the Sea* by Paul Theroux and Jonathan Raban's *Coasting* were both written in 1982 and so are now a little dated, but they're nonetheless very readable. Older but still readable is John Hillaby's *Journey Through Britain*, which describes a walk from Land's End to John o'Groats in 1969, great for measuring the changes that have taken place over the last 30 years.

Dervla Murphy's *Tale of Two Cities* (1987) offers a veteran travel writer's view of life among Britain's ethnic minorities in Bradford/Manningham and Birmingham/Handsworth.

For a look behind the razzamatazz of Cool Britannia, Nick Danziger's *Danziger's Britain* should be required reading, though it paints a depressing picture of late 20th century Britain. *Falling Towards England* by Clive James humorously recounts the Australian presence in 60s London and is classic stuff from the acclaimed expat. *A Traveller's History of England* by Christopher Daniell offers a quick introduction to English history.

For a left-looking analysis of Britain's position at the close of the 20th century,

try either *The State We're In* or *The State to Come* both by *Observer* editor Will Hutton. One of the striking things about the 1997 election was the arrival of 100-odd female MPs in a House of Commons previously even more dominated by men. Linda McDougall's *Westminster Women* examines the difference their presence is likely to make.

Windrush – The Irresistible Rise of Multicultural Britain by Mike & Trevor Phillips traces the history of black Britain and the impact of immigrants on British society.

FILMS

Notting Hill (1999), with local star Hugh Grant alongside Julia Roberts, is the biggest film (in box office terms) ever to come out of Britain. It has some good scenes of Portobello Rd and London in general. The same people brought us that other Hugh Grant hit *Four Weddings and a Funeral*.

The Full Monty, a tale of unemployed Sheffield steelworkers turned male strippers, was a simple story that turned into a worldwide hit. Less hyped but in some ways an even better film is *Brassed Off*, the sad story of a colliery band attempting to keep going while the South Yorkshire pit on which they depend for work closes down.

A world away from such gritty social realism were a spate of adaptations of Jane Austen novels that hit the screens during the 1990s. *Pride and Prejudice* was made for television but *Emma* and *Sense and Sensibility* were feature-length films. Filming took place all around England; see if you can recognise Montacute in Somerset, Lacock in Wiltshire and Lyme Park in Cheshire.

The French Lieutenant's Woman, based on the John Fowles novel of the same name, made great play with the landscape around Lyme Regis in Dorset. *Howard's End*, the Merchant-Ivory adaptation of the EM Forster novel, looked as if it was set in the Home Counties but actually strayed as far afield as Ludlow in Shropshire. The seedy side of Edinburgh and its drug culture is depicted in *Trainspotting*, while Mel Gibson's *Braveheart* portrays the inspiring story of William Wallace and features plenty of Scottish (but also Irish) countryside.

ENTERING & LEAVING

London is one of the most important international air-transport hubs in the world and the main gateway to Britain, although there are airports at Manchester, Newcastle, Bristol, Edinburgh, Glasgow and Cardiff. Departure tax on international flights is US$34 (US$17 if you're flying to an EU country).

Two rail services operate through the Channel Tunnel, linking Britain with mainland Europe: Eurostar is a high-speed passenger service between London, Paris and Brussels; Eurotunnel has a shuttle service (Le Shuttle) for cars, motorbikes and buses between the English port of Folkestone and the French port of Calais.

A cheaper option is a bus or train connection with a short ferry or hovercraft ride thrown in. The boat trip on the shortest routes (from Dover or Folkestone to Calais or Boulogne) takes about 90 minutes; the hovercraft takes about 35 minutes. Ferries go to France, Belgium, Germany, the Netherlands and Scandinavia from a number of southern and eastern British ports; to Spain from Portsmouth and Plymouth; and to Ireland from a handful of western English ports.

BULGARIA

While Bulgaria struggles with economic and social difficulties in the post-communist era, for visitors this little known country comes as a pleasant surprise.

The landscape is green and lush, and because Bulgaria gets relatively few western tourists, those who do come are rewarded with a warm welcome. Bulgarians still manage to be helpful and friendly despite the economic difficulties thrust upon them by a decade of upheaval. Bulgaria is a safe country, and although bureaucracy can sometimes be frustrating, most Bulgarians will go out of their way to smooth the path for those travellers who come. There's plenty to see and do, and prices can seem ridiculously cheap, especially in ski and beach resorts that would cost you a small fortune in Western Europe.

You certainly don't need wads of cash to appreciate Bulgaria's dramatic mountains, haven-like monasteries, churches, mosques, Roman and Byzantine ruins, or the excellent coffee you'll be offered wherever you go.

Cyrillic script and Turkish mosques are constant reminders that Bulgaria has one foot firmly in the east. Bulgaria has been liberated by Russia twice (in 1878 and 1944) and this close historical relationship has in the past made it one of the Soviet Union's most dependable allies. After five centuries of Turkish rule, Bulgarian culture reappeared in the 19th century as writers and artists strove to awaken national consciousness.

WHEN TO GO

Bulgaria has a temperate climate, but winters are cold and damp and the Rodopi Mountains are often subjected to heavy snowfalls. Summer is generally warm and dry. Average daily temperatures in Sofia are above 15°C from May to September, above 11°C in April and October, above 5°C in

At a Glance

Full Country Name: Republic of Bulgaria
Area: 110,912 sq km
Population: Nine million
Capital City: Sofia (pop 1.1 million)
People: 85% Bulgarian, 8.5% Turkish, 2.6% Gypsy, 2.5% Macedonian
Language: Bulgarian; Turkish and Romany are spoken by minorities
Religion: 80% Bulgarian Orthodox, 13% Muslim
Government: Democracy
Currency: Bulgarian lev (plural: leva) = 100 stotinki
Time Zone: Two hours ahead of GMT/UTC; clocks go forward one hour at the end of March and back at the end of September
International Telephone Code: 359
Electricity: 220V, 50Hz

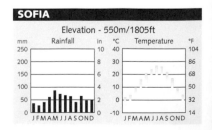

March and November, and below freezing in December and January.

There are cultural and folk festivals held throughout the year.

HIGHLIGHTS

The capital, Sofia, is likely to be your first stop in Bulgaria and although an industrial city, it's surprisingly quiet and clean. As well as plenty of information services you'll find numerous galleries and museums, including the National Museum of History and the Foreign Art Gallery. If you have time though, you should get out of the city and consider the following:

Mountains & Monasteries

South and south-east of Sofia, the high country comprises mountain ranges strung together over several hundred kilometres. There is good hiking in the Rila Mountains and cheap hostels are scattered around this area. Even if you don't have time for hiking, the Rila Monastery is well worth a visit. It was established in AD 927 and helped keep Bulgarian culture alive during five centuries of Turkish rule.

The Rodopi Mountains are home to Bulgaria's most isolated and ethnically diverse communities, and include the spectacular gorges of Tregrad and Yagodino. The traditions of Bulgaria's Slavic people are strongest in the Rodopi: wild pagan festivals take place in many villages, and folk music still features in the local culture. In this area you'll find the fascinating Bachkovo Monastery, founded in 1083 by two Byzantine aristocrats.

Historic Towns

Clinging to the cliffs on the banks of the Yantra River, Veliko Târnovo is not to be missed if you're in northern Bulgaria. Among the sights in this medieval town are a ruined citadel and the remains of a royal palace. In central Bulgaria, Koprivshtitsa is a carefully preserved museum village representative of Bulgaria's 19th century National Revival. It's smothered with architectural monuments, set among cobbled streets and red-tile houses. Plovdiv is a larger but equally interesting town.

Black Sea Coast

The resorts of the Black Sea coast are Bulgaria's summer playground – packed to the gills and enjoying a carnival atmosphere in July and August, but dead from mid-September to the end of May. Despite the crowds, there are inviting beaches and bays all along this coast and it's not hard to find a quiet place to relax.

Varna is the biggest resort town and erupts with an outstanding summer music festival from mid-June to mid-July. Nesebâr is big with tourists these days, but it's a beautiful medieval town and well worth a visit. Sozopol is another picturesque town and is well set up to cater for independent travellers.

Wining & Dining

Eating out can be one of the pleasures of visiting Bulgaria, partly because it's so cheap. A night out at a good-quality restaurant will cost half to two-thirds less than in Western Europe, so you can afford to splurge! Folk-style *mehanas* (taverns) serving traditional Bulgarian dishes make an interesting night out and many offer live music.

Bulgaria is one of the world's five leading exporters of wine, both red and white, and again it is very cheap. If you're not a wine drinker, try Bulgarian beer for good value, or the lethal plum brandy, *slivova*.

VISA REQUIREMENTS

Visa requirements have eased up in recent times, so it's not the hassle it once was to get into Bulgaria. Nationals of the USA and the European Union (EU) are admitted without a visa for stays of less than 30 days. Most other travellers must shell out for Bulgaria's expensive entry documents – either a single or double entry visa or a transit visa. Travellers on package tours are the exception – if the Bulgarian authorities

know where you're going to be, there's generally less red tape.

There is a US$23 'border tax' required of all arrivals other than citizens of the EU, Iceland, Norway, Switzerland, the USA and most Eastern European countries. Be sure to have this amount ready in cash when you arrive in the country.

Bulgarian Embassies

Australia
(☎ 02-9327 7581, fax 9327 8067) 4 Carlotta Rd, Double Bay, NSW 2028

Canada
(☎ 613-789 3215, fax 789 3524, ✉ mail mn@storm.ca) 325 Stewart St, Ottawa, Ont K1N 6K5

Greece
(☎ 01-647 8105) Str Kallari 33, Psyhiko, Athens
(☎ 031-829 210) N Manou 12, Thessaloniki

UK
(☎ 020-7584 9400, fax 7584 4948) 187 Queen's Gate, London SW7 5HL

USA
(☎ 202-387 7679, fax 234 7973) 1621 22nd St NW, Washington, DC 20008

TOURIST OFFICES OVERSEAS

UK
(☎ 020-7491 4499) 19 Conduit St, London W1R 9TD

USA
(☎ 212-822 5900, fax 338 6830) 20 East 46th St, Suite 1003, New York, NY 10017

POST & COMMUNICATIONS

Stamps and envelopes are available at all post offices and REP kiosks. Mail addressed c/o poste restante, Sofia 1000, Bulgaria, can be picked up at the main post office.

It's easy to telephone Western Europe and North America from Bulgaria. Direct dial international telephones are

---

Itineraries

Two Days
In two days you won't get much further than Sofia, particularly if you want to have a good look at its museums and cathedrals, but it is possible to make a day trip to the Rila Monastery if you start early.

One Week
Spend a couple of days in Sofia. If you want to head towards the Black Sea coast, travel east to Veliko Târnovo, then on to the summer beach centre of Varna and (if time permits) down to the ancient town of Nesebâr. If you'd prefer to go hiking in the mountains, head south from Sofia to the Rila Monastery, then down to the interesting village of Melnik (and the Rozhen Monastery) or across to Plovdiv and up to Koprivshtitsa.

Two Weeks
In two weeks you can spend time in Sofia before heading south to enjoy the Rila Mountains (including the one day walk from Complex Malyovitsa to Rila Monastery). From there go to Melnik, then Plovdiv and on to Koprivshtitsa. From there you can travel across to the Black Sea coast via Veliko Târnovo and Madara, and spend a few relaxing days in Varna, Nesebâr and maybe Sozopol.

BULGARIA HIGHLIGHTS & ITINERARIES ▶▶

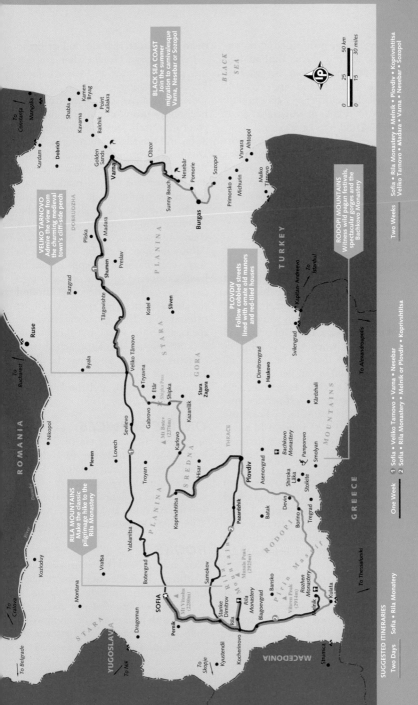

BLACK SEA COAST
Join the summer migration to carnivalesque Varna, Nesebar or Sozopol

VELIKO TARNOVO
Admire the view from the charming medieval town's cliff-side perch

RODOPI MOUNTAINS
Witness wild pagan festivals, spectacular gorges and the Bachkovo Monastery

PLOVDIV
Follow cobbled streets lined with ornate old manors and red-tiled houses

RILA MOUNTAINS
Make the classic pilgrimage hike to the Rila Monastery

SUGGESTED ITINERARIES

Two Days   Sofia • Rila Monastery

One Week   Sofia • Veliko Tarnovo • Varna • Nesebar
            1 Sofia • Veliko Tarnovo • Varna • Nesebar
            2 Sofia • Rila Monastery • Melnik or Plovdiv • Koprivshtitsa

Two Weeks   Sofia • Rila Monastery • Melnik • Plovdiv • Koprivshtitsa
            Veliko Tarnovo • Madara • Varna • Nesebar • Sozopol

found in all large post offices. You pay the clerk as you leave. BulFon and Betcom phonecards can be used all over the country and are available from telephone offices. A one minute call to the USA or Australia costs about US$1.80.

Faxes can be sent from most post offices, but operator-connected faxes can turn out to be very expensive, if they turn out at all. Sofia has a couple of places where you can access the Internet.

MONEY
Costs
Despite the introduction of a 22% value-added tax in 1996, you'll still find that all forms of transport (including taxis), souvenirs, admissions, food and drink are cheap. Anything you can get for the same price as a Bulgarian will be cheap, but when there's a higher tourist price (as there is for almost all accommodation), it can get expensive.

Camping or sleeping in hostels, self-catering or eating in self-service restaurants will allow you to keep the budget under US$20 a day. Add a few restaurant meals and other luxuries, and you can expect to spend more like US$30 to US$40.

It is common practice to round up restaurant bills, and waiters may indeed keep the expected change anyway. The same applies to taxis with meters. With nonmetered taxis, you should agree on the fare beforehand.

Changing Money
Cash is easily changed in Bulgaria at numerous small exchange offices for no commission. Travellers cheques, on the other hand, are a bit of a hassle, because many banks refuse to change

them and those that do deduct up to 5% commission. Hotel exchange counters give low rates and deduct about 5% commission.

Cash advances on credit cards are becoming more common, although you cannot rely on this service outside Sofia and the Black Sea resorts. ATMs are also appearing in Sofia and on the Black Sea coast. Cirrus, Maestro, Visa and MasterCard can be used to draw cash from your account.

The lev is now a freely convertible currency and there are no problems changing excess leva back into dollars. Although there is no black market as such, you may still be approached by hustlers looking for your spare foreign cash to exchange, especially around the train station in Sofia. You'll be offered up to 10% above the bank rate for cash on the street, but these transactions should be approached with extreme caution. You may be given counterfeit leva, be short-changed or otherwise cheated, and the law won't be on your side.

ONLINE SERVICES
Start your Internet tour of Bulgaria with Lonely Planet's site (www.lonely planet.com/dest/eur/bul.htm). Other sources include Bulgaria on the Internet (pisa.rockefeller.edu:8080/Bulgaria) and the All about Bulgaria site (www.cs .columbia.edu/radev/bulginfo.html).

BOOKS
Exit into History by journalist Eva Hoffman chronicles her trips through Eastern Europe, including Bulgaria.

Nagel's Encyclopaedia-Guide Bulgaria is packed with history and descriptions of Bulgaria's monuments and attractions. *The Bulgarians from Pagan Times to the*

Ottoman Conquest by David Marshall Lang brings medieval Bulgaria to life. The maps, illustrations and lucid text make this book well worth reading. RJ Crampton's *A Short History of Modern Bulgaria* is outdated but useful for background information up to 1987.

ENTERING & LEAVING

Balkan Bulgarian Airlines has flights to most European capitals, the major Asian hubs and some cities in North America, but it's a notoriously unreliable airline. Before buying a return air ticket to Bulgaria from Western Europe or North America, check the price of the cheapest package tour to the Black Sea resorts. This could be cheaper and you can just throw away the hotel vouchers if you don't care to sit on the beach for two weeks. Travellers from Australasia will usually have to connect through more popular European destinations. Buses and trains are the easiest way to get to Bulgaria from Europe and Turkey, with frequent services from Greece, Yugoslavia, Macedonia, Albania, Istanbul, Prague and Western Europe. There are no buses to Romania, and the train from Greece is usually a hassle (take the bus).

When you enter Bulgaria by car, you must state which border crossing you'll be using when you leave and pay a road tax accordingly. Route restrictions apply if you're only in transit through Bulgaria. A regular car ferry crosses the Danube from Vidin to Calafat in Romania. Crossing the 'Friendship Bridge' from Romania to Ruse in Bulgaria can be painfully slow, though outbound travellers are not usually delayed.

CROATIA

Before 1991, Croatia (then part of Yugoslavia) was shaping up as the new Costa del Sol. Planeloads of tourists were hitting the Adriatic shores in search of sun, cheap living, medieval quaintness and perhaps a spot of naturism. The violent break-up of Yugoslavia changed the face of Croatia, but its charms have largely remained intact. Most of the areas popular with travellers emerged unscathed or have been restored since the war, but reminders of the country's painful history abound and everyone has a story to tell.

There is an aura of medieval Croatia in the cobbled streets of Rovinj and the recently restored other-worldliness of Dubrovnik's Stari Grad (Old Town). The country is also home to some of Europe's finest Roman ruins, including the immense palace of Diocletian in Split. The weather and the beaches are as good as they always were and Croatia is a safe place to visit: the good news is that the tourists haven't returned in such numbers yet.

Warning

On 15 January 1998, the formerly Serb-held area of Eastern Slavonia on the Croatia-Yugoslavia border was transferred from the United Nations to the Government of Croatia. A UN transitional administration controlled the area for two years and managed to

At a Glance

Full Country Name: Republic of Croatia
Area: 58,540 sq km
Population: Five million
Capital City: Zagreb (pop: one million)
People: 78% Croats, 12% Serbs, Slavic Muslims, Hungarians, Slovenes
Language: Croatian, German, Serbian
Religion: Roman Catholic, Eastern Orthodox
Government: Parliamentary democracy
Currency: Croatian kuna (KN)
Time Zone: One hour ahead of GMT/UTC; clocks go forward one hour at the end of March and back again at the end of September
International Telephone Code: 385
Electricity: 220V, 50Hz

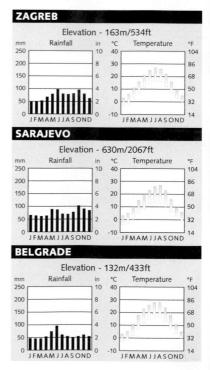

successfully demilitarise and stabilise it. But there continue to be isolated incidents of violence and civil unrest, and hundreds of antipersonnel mines remain scattered in the region.

WHEN TO GO

May to September are the best months to visit Croatia weather-wise, though July and August can be busy along the Adriatic coast. September is probably the optimum month, since by then the crowds have thinned out, off-season rates apply and fruits such as figs and grapes are abundant. In April and October it may be too cool for camping, but the weather is usually fine along the coast, and private rooms are plentiful and inexpensive. You can swim in the sea from mid-June to late September.

HIGHLIGHTS
Historic Towns

All along the Adriatic coast are white-stone towns with narrow, winding streets enclosed by defensive walls. Each town has its own flavour. The hilly fishing village of Rovinj looks out over the sea, while medieval Korcula sits on its own island, separated from the mainland peninsula by a narrow channel. Zadar retains echoes of its original Roman street plan, while Hvar (also on an island) and Trogir are traditional medieval towns. But none can match the exquisite harmony of Dubrovnik, with its fascinating fortified old town and impressive harbour. The ancient city, substantially rebuilt after shelling in 1991, displays a blend of medieval and Renaissance architecture.

Museums & Galleries

Art museums and galleries are easier for a foreign visitor to enjoy than historical museums, which are usually captioned in Croatian only. In Zagreb the Museum Mimara contains an outstanding collection of Spanish, Italian and Dutch paintings as well as

Yugoslavia & Bosnia Hercegovina

The one area of Europe you probably won't want to enter is Yugoslavia and, to a lesser extent, Bosnia Hercegovina.

Although the Serb army has withdrawn from Kosovo and the military crisis is all but over, localised crime and instability make the whole Federal Republic of Yugoslavia pretty much a no-go zone, including the republics of Montenegro and Kosovo. NATO forces commenced bombing raids in Kosovo, around Belgrade and in other parts of the Serbian Republic on 24 March, 1999, after the peace talks over the disputed territory broke down. NATO claimed the Serbs had violated the ceasefire signed the previous year; the Serbs continued to attack ethnic Albanians, maintaining that Kosovo was theirs anyway. Thousands of ethnic Albanians and Serbs were killed in the fighting.

At the turn of the decade Yugoslavia was a beach-haven bonanza about to happen, the next big thing in tourism. But the declaration of independence by Bosnia, Croatia, Slovenia and Macedonia led to four years of civil war that changed the face of this region. Many of the old towns of Yugoslavia and Bosnia were destroyed, along with their appeal to travellers. Travel in Bosnia is now reasonably safe and citizens of the USA, UK, Canada and Ireland can enter without-out a visa. However, over a million land mines are estimated to remain in Bosnia, including the suburbs of Sarajevo. Travel in the Republika Srpska region should also be avoided.

It will be a while before the Federal Republic of Yugoslavia is fit for independent travel and visas are required of anyone wishing to enter.

an archaeological collection, exhibits of ancient art from the Far East and collections of glass, textiles, sculpture and furniture. The Strossmayer Gallery, also in Zagreb, is worthwhile for its exhibits of Italian, Flemish, French and Croatian paintings.

The Meštrovic Gallery in Split is worth a detour to see, and in Zagreb the Meštrovic Studio gives a fascinating insight into the life and work of this remarkable sculptor.

Castles

The palace of the Roman emperor Diocletian in Split has been named a World Heritage Site by UNESCO. Despite a weathered facade, this sprawling imperial residence and fortress is considered the finest intact example of classical defence architecture in Europe.

Just outside Zagreb is an impressive circle of castles. To the north is Veliki Tabor, a fortified medieval castle in the process of restoration, but the most impressive is Trakošcan, beside a long lake. Medvedgrad, west of Zagreb, was built by bishops in the 13th century. The Varazdin Castle in northern Croatia has recently been restored and hosts an annual music festival. Trsat Castle in Rijeka offers a stunning view of the Kvarner Gulf.

Itineraries

Two Days
If you only have a short time in Croatia, try to spend it in Dubrovnik, exploring the fortified old town. If you're coming from the north (Slovenia or Hungary), this would mean travelling all the way down the Adriatic coast.

One Week
With a week to spare you could spend a couple of days in Zagreb, with its numerous museums, galleries and churches. During July and August, Zagreb is virtually devoid of people – they've all gone to the coast for their holidays. From there, travel down to the harbour town of Split in the heart of Dalmatia. Here you can visit Diocletian's Palace and enjoy nearby islands and beaches. The final two or three days should be spent in Dubrovnik.

Two Weeks
Visit Zagreb, with a day trip out to Samobor, then head east to the pretty peninsula town of Rovinj. From there, head down the coast and explore all of the Dalmatia region, including Split, Hvar, Brela and Dubrovnik.

One Month
With a month to spare you can undertake the two week itinerary and fit in some specialist activities. If you enjoy walking or outdoor activities, stop at Plitvice Lakes National Park or Paklenica National Park, both in the Zadar region and about 140km and 200km south of Zagreb respectively.

If you like the idea of exploring the coast by boat, the route from Rijeka to Dubrovnik, stopping off at the many islands and cities, is one of the great journeys in Central Europe. You can combine a through-ticket on the large Jadrolinija ferry with trips on local ferries to visit fishing villages, Roman ruins, sprawling resorts and remote islands. Your boat may stop at rustic Dugi Otok before docking at Zadar, where you can spend a few days exploring the town centre and then visit Pag, Mali Lošinj or Cres islands. Your next stop will be Split, where you could easily spend a week taking day trips to Brac, Vis and Šolta islands, relaxing on the beaches of Makarska or poking around in the ancient cities of Trogir and Salona. Hvar Island is next, with the architectural treasure of Hvar town, and a wealth of beautiful coves and bays to explore. Continue on to the walled town of Korcula and lush Korcula Island before arriving in Dubrovnik.

CROATIA HIGHLIGHTS & ITINERARIES

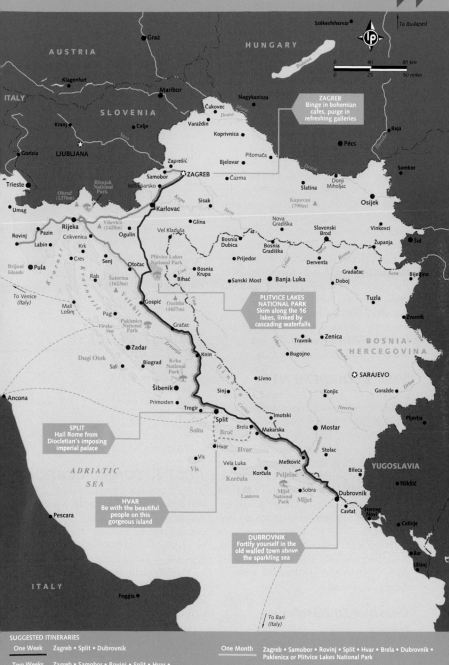

To Budapest

Székesfehérvár

AUSTRIA

Graz

HUNGARY

Klagenfurt

Nagykanisza

Maribor

ITALY

Kranj

SLOVENIA

Čakovec

Baja

Gorizia

Celje

Varaždin

Koprivnica

Pécs

LJUBLJANA

Zaprešić

Pitomača

Sombor

Trieste

Risnjak National Park

Samobor

ZAGREB

Bjelovar

Čazma

Donji Miholjac

Osijek

Umag

Obruč (1376m)

Jastrebarsko

Čazma

Slatina

Slavonski Brod

Vinkovci

Karlovac

Sisak

Kaparan (790m)

Rovinj

Pazin

Rijeka

Viševica (1428m)

Vel Kladuša

Glina

Nova Gradiška

Slavonski Brod

Vinkovci

Labin

Crikvenica

Krk

Ogulin

Bosnia Dubica

Bosnia Gradiška

Derventa

Županja

Šid

Cres

Senj

Otočac

Plitvice Lakes National Park

Bihać

Bosnia Krupa

Prijedor

Sanski Most

Banja Luka

Doboj

Gradačac

Bijeljina

Brijuni Islands

Pula

Rab

Šatorina (1623m)

Velebit

Gospić

Ozeblin (1657m)

PLITVICE LAKES NATIONAL PARK
Skim along the 16 lakes, linked by cascading waterfalls

Tuzla

Zvornik

To Venice (Italy)

Mali Lošinj

Pag

Paklenica National Park

Gračac

Knin

Travnik

Zenica

BOSNIA-HERCEGOVINA

Virsko Sea

Dugi Otok

Zadar

Biograd

Sali

Krka National Park

Šibenik

Primosten

Trogir

Split

Brač

Hvar

Bugojno

Livno

Sinj

Imotski

Brela

Makarska

SARAJEVO

Konjic

Goražde

Pljevlja

Ancona

SPLIT
Hail Rome from Diocletian's imposing imperial palace

Šolta

Mostar

Stolac

ADRIATIC SEA

Vis

Vis

Vela Luka

Korčula

Korčula

Pelješac

Mljet National Park

Metković

Sobra

Mljet

YUGOSLAVIA

Bileća

Nikšić

HVAR
Be with the beautiful people on this gorgeous island

Lastovo

Dubrovnik

Pescara

Cavtat

Herceg Novi

Cetinje

DUBROVNIK
Fortify yourself in the old walled town above the sparkling sea

Bar

Ulcinj

ITALY

Foggia

To Bari (Italy)

ZAGREB
Binge in bohemian cafes, purge in refreshing galleries

SUGGESTED ITINERARIES

One Week   Zagreb • Split • Dubrovnik

Two Weeks   Zagreb • Samobor • Rovinj • Split • Hvar • Brela • Dubrovnik

One Month   Zagreb • Samobor • Rovinj • Split • Hvar • Brela • Dubrovnik
Paklenica or Plitvice Lakes National Park

Beaches & Natural Wonders

Whether rocky, pebbly, gravelly or (rarely) sandy, Croatian beaches are often on the edge of a pine grove and slope into crystalline water that always seems to be the right temperature. Croatia's spectacular 1778km coastline is indented with wide bays and cosy coves, and there are 1185 islands dotting the Adriatic Sea. The 140 islands of the Kornati archipelago are a sailor's haven. The Brijuni islands were Tito's paradise, and lush islands such as Korcula, Hvar, and Rab could easily become anyone's Shangri-la.

The Velebit mountain range includes the distinctive karst formations of Paklenica National Park, with its great opportunities for hiking and rock climbing. Plitvice Lakes National Park has been named a World Heritage Site for its 16 lakes linked by crashing, tumbling and trickling waterfalls.

VISA REQUIREMENTS

Citizens of the USA, Canada, Australia, New Zealand, Israel, Ireland and the UK don't need a visa for stays of up to 90 days. Citizens of Singapore must apply in Jakarta for a 90 day visa and South Africans must apply for a 90 day visa in Pretoria. The price is roughly 148KN and you may have to show a return ticket. Contact Croatian embassies or travel agencies for information.

If you want to stay in Croatia longer than three months, the easiest thing to do is to cross the border into Italy or Austria and return.

Croatian Embassies

Australia
(☎ 02-6286 6988) 6 Bulwarra Close, O'Malley, Canberra, ACT 2606

(☎ 03-9699 2633) 9-24 Albert Rd, South Melbourne, Vic 3205
(☎ 02-9299 8899) 379 Kent St, Level 4, Sydney, NSW 2000
(☎ 08-9321 6044) 68 St George's Terrace, Perth, WA 6832
Canada
(☎ 613-230 7351) 130 Albert St, Suite 1700, Ottawa, Ont K1P 5G4
(☎ 905-277 9051) 918 Dundas St E, Suite 302, Mississauga, Ont L4Y 2B8
New Zealand
(☎ 09-836 5581) 131 Lincoln Rd, Henderson, Auckland
UK
(☎ 020-7387 0022) 21 Conway St, London W1P 5HL
USA
(☎ 202-588 5899) 2343 Massachusetts Ave NW, Washington, DC 20008
Yugoslavia
(☎ 11-668063) Cakorska 1a, 11000 Belgrade

TOURIST OFFICES OVERSEAS
UK
Phoenix Holidays
(☎ 020-8563 7979) 2 The Lanchesters, 162-164 Fulham Palace Rd, London W69 ER
USA
(☎ 201-428 0707) 300 Lanidex Plaza, Parsippany, NJ 07054

POST & COMMUNICATIONS

The Croatian post office, HPT Hrvatska, offers a wide variety of services – from selling stamps and phonecards to sending faxes. Mail sent to poste restante, 10000 Zagreb, Croatia, is held at the post office next to Zagreb train station, which is open 24 hours a day. A good coastal address to use is c/o Poste Restante, Main Post Office, 21000 Split, Croatia.

To make a phone call from Croatia, go to the main post office. There are few coin-operated phones, so you'll need a phonecard, which can be bought at any post office and most tobacco shops and newspaper kiosks.

There are currently cybercafes for Internet and email access in Zagreb, Rijeka and Korcula, but more will open – ask at local tourist bureaus and travel agencies.

MONEY
Costs

Budget accommodation is in short supply in Croatia, but transport, food, and concert and theatre tickets are reasonably priced. It's not difficult to travel around Croatia on US$35 a day if you stay in hostels or private rooms – even less if you camp. Eating only things such as bread, cheese, yoghurt and canned fish or meat will help to cut costs (cooking facilities are seldom provided). Double that if you want to travel in comfort.

Expect to pay US$10 to US$12 for a hostel bed, US$15 to US$30 for a cheap private room (double) and US$25 to US$50 for a hotel. A budget meal will cost you around US$4 to US$8 and a moderate restaurant meal US$8 to US$20.

If you're served well at a restaurant, round up the bill unless a service charge has already been added.

Changing Money

There are numerous places to change money, all offering similar rates. Exchange offices charge commission but some banks do not. Banks are the only places you can change kuna back into hard currency. You can get a cash advance on your credit card at banks throughout the country, though Visa cards are not accepted by all banks. Post offices allow cash withdrawals on

MasterCard and Cirrus, and major towns have bankomats (ATMs).

ONLINE SERVICES

Cultural and historical Web sites are proliferating madly as Croats in the country and abroad aim to tell the world about their new country.

Lonely Planet's Destination Croatia (www.lonelyplanet.com/dest/eur/cro.htm) has country information, pictures and links. The National Tourist Board's Web site (www.htz.hr) has good links to other sources such as bus, train and plane information, contact information for tourist offices throughout the nation and abroad, and practical information on accommodation and outdoor activities. Another site (www.dalmatia.net) has a grab bag of cultural, political, practical and entertainment information, as well as links to other sites. Another colourful site (http://islands.zesoi.fer.hr) is dedicated to Croatia's islands in the Adriatic.

BOOKS

Anatomy of Deceit by Jerry Blaskovich tells the story of Croatia's recent war through the eyes of a physician who worked with the Croatians. *Croatia – A Nation Forged in War* by Marcus Tanner tries to adopt a more objective viewpoint. For more tales of misery, try *The Yugoslav Auschwitz and the Vatican*, edited by Vladimir Dedijer. It tells the story of Croatia's Serb massacres and the involvement of the Catholic Church in the horrors of WWII. Barisa Krekic's *Dubrovnik – A Mediterranean Urban Society* is a collection of works written about the town's history from 1300 to 1600. *Fording the Stream of Consciousness*, edited by Dubravka Ugresic, is a collection of writing.

FILMS

A Story from Croatia (1990) is a film set in the former Yugoslavia before the break-up. *Tajne Nikola Tesna* (The Secret of Nikola Tesna; 1980) follows the life of a famous Croatian scientist.

ENTERING & LEAVING

Flights connect Zagreb to a swag of European cities. Croatia's international airport is 17km south-east of Zagreb. The departure tax is US$8. Buses run between Zagreb and several cities in Hungary and Germany, as well as to Amsterdam (the Netherlands) and Antwerp (Belgium). Trains connect Zagreb to Italy, Germany, Austria, Hungary and Romania, while ferries link Croatia to Greece and Italy. Travellers with their own vehicle can use four border crossings between Hungary and Croatia, 29 between Slovenia and Croatia, 23 between Bosnia and Croatia and seven between Yugoslavia and Croatia.

With its perfect Mediterranean climate, beach resorts, orchards and vineyards, ancient Greek and Roman ruins, monasteries and castles, Cyprus could easily be described as a visitors' paradise. But tempering that picture is the political unease that has divided the island since the Turkish invasion of 1974.

Cyprus is a country divided. The Green Line, running right through Lefkosia, separates the Greek southern part (Republic of Cyprus) from the Turkish northern part (Turkish Republic of Northern Cyprus). However, despite the UN guards and tough-looking border patrollers, people on both sides of the border are friendly.

Most people tend to visit the Republic of Cyprus (from where you can day-trip to the North), and as a result there's a rather strong tourist resort feel, with plenty of hotels and chips-with-everything tavernas. But Cyprus also presents an infinite variety of natural and architectural delights. Two high mountain ranges tower above a fertile plain. Landscapes are dotted with ancient Greek and Roman ruins, frescoed Orthodox monasteries and crusader castles.

Cyprus is the legendary birthplace of Aphrodite and, being close to Greece, Turkey, Jordan, Israel and Egypt, it is a useful stepping stone for those travelling between east and west.

WHEN TO GO

The shoulder seasons (April/May and September/October) are the most pleasant times, climatically, to visit

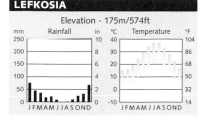

Cyprus. Summer (June to August) can be very hot, and winter is sometimes wet but still pleasant.

HIGHLIGHTS
Republic of Cyprus

A visit to Lefkosia, the walled capital divided by the Green Line, is essential if

At a Glance

Full Country Name: Republic of Cyprus/ Turkish Republic of Northern Cyprus

Area: 9251 sq km

Population: 911,000

Capital City: Lefkosia (formerly Nicosia; pop 48,220)

People: Greek 78%, Turkish 18%

Language: Greek, Turkish

Religion: Greek Orthodox, Muslim

Government: Democracy

Currency: Cyprus pound (CY£)/Turkish lira (TL)

Time Zone: Two hours ahead of GMT/ UTC; clocks go forward one hour on the last weekend in March and back again on the last weekend in October

International Telephone Code: 357 (for North Cyprus dial: 90 [Turkey], then 392 [North Cyprus])

Electricity: 240V, 50Hz

Itineraries

Cyprus isn't the sort of place you just pass through, so if you make the effort to get here, chances are you'll stay at least a week.

One Week
Republic of Cyprus Spend two days in Lefkosia, visiting the archaeological museums and perhaps taking one of the free walking tours of the old city. From there, head down to Lemesos and work your way along the ancient coastal sites to Paphos. Here you can spend at least a day visiting the archaeological sites, including the Paphos Mosaics and the Tombs of the Kings. The rest of your time should be spent exploring the many tiny villages and monasteries of the Troodos Massif, including Pedhoulas, Kakopetria, Platres and Omodos.

North Cyprus Spend one day in North Lefkosia visiting its museums and mosques and wandering the quiet back streets. From there you can head east to the well preserved walled city of Famagusta. Half a day is enough to inspect the classical remains at Salamis. The remainder of your time can be spent in the attractive port of Kyrenia, and visiting the castles in the nearby Kyrenia Mountains.

Two Weeks
Republic of Cyprus Follow the one week itinerary, but spend extra time in Lefkosia and make one or two trips into North Cyprus. Also add trips to the beach resort of Polis and the Akamas Peninsula for more beaches and hiking opportunities. While in Lemesos you could stop and have a steam bath and/or massage at the hammam.

North Cyprus Follow the one week itinerary, but spend longer in North Lefkosia and have a Turkish bath in the Büyük *hammam*. Spend some time exploring the near-deserted Karpasia Peninsula and its archaeological sites.

you want to appreciate the island's situation. It is more Cypriot in character than the tourist-oriented coastal towns. There are several good museums in Lefkosia, including the Byzantine Museum and the archaeological Cyprus Museum. You can usually cross the border into North Cyprus on a day visit via the checkpoint at the Hotel Ledra Palace, but you can't go the other way (ie from North Cyprus to the Republic).

Nine of the frescoed Byzantine churches in the Troodos Massif are on UNESCO's World Heritage List and they really are special. The Kykkos Monastery is the best known, but try to visit the small Church of Archangelos and St Nicholaos of the Roof. Also in the Troodos there are good hiking trails and traditional wine-making villages, particularly around Omodos.

The renowned Paphos Mosaics date back to the 3rd century and are on most people's must-see list. The Tombs of the Kings, near Kato Paphos, are six centuries older than the Roman mosaics and are fascinating to explore.

Of the coastal resorts, Polis is relatively unspoilt by tourism and is close to the wild, remote hiking region of the Akamas Peninsula.

North Cyprus
North Lefkosia, swarming with soldiers but also crammed with Ottoman architecture and cottage industries, is worth a day or two – don't leave without being pummelled to oblivion in the steamy Büyük *hammam* (Turkish bath).

With the Byzantine castle at one end, Kyrenia's cafe-lined waterfront must be one of the most beautiful in the Mediterranean. In the mountains behind Kyrenia are a number of interesting castles.

CYPRUS HIGHLIGHTS & ITINERARIES

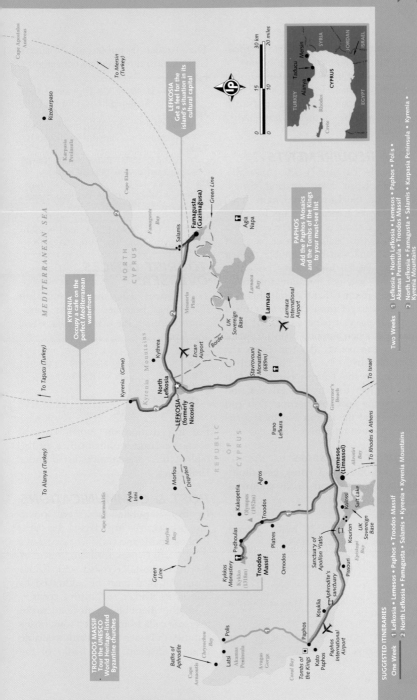

SUGGESTED ITINERARIES
One Week — 1 Lefkosia • Lemesos • Paphos • Troodos Massif
2 North Lefkosia • Famagusta • Salamis • Kyrenia • Kyrenia Mountains

Two Weeks — 1 Lefkosia • North Lefkosia • Lemesos • Paphos • Polis •
Akamas Peninsula • Troodos Massif
2 North Lefkosia • Famagusta • Salamis • Karpasia Peninsula • Kyrenia •
Kyrenia Mountains

TROODOS MASSIF
Tour the UNESCO
World Heritage-listed
Byzantine churches

KYRENIA
Occupy a cafe on the
perfect Mediterranean
waterfront

LEFKOSIA
Get a feel for the
island's situation in its
cultural capital

PAPHOS
Add the Paphos Mosaics
and the Tombs of the Kings
to your must-see list

Salamis, the site of Cyprus' most important classical city, boasts a gymnasium with an incredible number of upright marble columns, and a fully restored Roman amphitheatre. North Cyprus also has some of the island's best beaches.

VISA REQUIREMENTS

Nationals of the USA, Australia, Canada, Japan, New Zealand, Singapore and the European Union (EU) can stay in Cyprus for up to three months without a visa. If you have a North Cyprus stamp in your passport you can still visit the Republic, but it will be deleted by customs on entry, and this will not prevent you from visiting Greece either. Despite this, it is advisable to get immigration to stamp a separate piece of paper instead of your passport when entering North Cyprus.

You can usually day-trip from the Republic to the North. This involves walking to the Turkish checkpoint at the border crossing in Lefkosia and purchasing an entry permit. You can then spend the day in North Cyprus but you must return by 5 pm.

Cypriot Embassies

The Republic of Cyprus has diplomatic representation in 26 countries, including:

Australia
(☎ 02-6281 0832) 30 Beale Crescent, Deakin, Canberra, ACT 2600
Greece
(☎ 01-723 2737) Irodotou 16, 10675, Athens
UK
(☎ 020-7499 8272) 93 Park St, London W1Y 4ET
USA
(☎ 202-462 5772) 2211 R St NW, Washington, DC 20008

The Turkish Republic of Northern Cyprus has representative offices in:
Canada
(☎ 905-731 4000) 328 Highway 7 East, Suite 308, Richmond Hill, Ont LB4 3P7
Japan
(☎ 03-203 1313) 4th floor, 6th Arai Blog-1-4, Kabohi-cho, Shinytku-ku, Tokyo 160
Turkey
(☎ 312-437 6031) Rabat Sokak No 20, Gaziosmanpasa 06700, Ankara
UK
(☎ 020-7631 1920) 26 Bedford Square, London WC1B 3EG
USA
(☎ 212-687 2350) 821 United Nations Plaza, 6th floor, New York, NY 10017

TOURIST OFFICES OVERSEAS

The Cyprus Tourism Organisation (CTO) has branches in most European countries, the USA, Russia, Israel and Japan.

UK
(☎ 020-7734 9822, fax 7287 6534) 213 Regent St, London W1R 8DA
USA
(☎ 212-683 5280, fax 683 5282) 13 East 40th St, New York, NY 10016

For information on North Cyprus, contact a Turkish tourist office, or the diplomatic representatives listed under Embassies.

POST & COMMUNICATIONS

In the Republic there are poste restante services in Lefkosia, Larnaca, Paphos and Lemesos.

In North Cyprus, mail can be sent to North Lefkosia, Kyrenia and Famagusta. All mail must be addressed to Mersin 10, Turkey, *not* North Cyprus.

In the Republic, you can make overseas calls from all telephone boxes but they only take phonecards available from newsagents, some banks or the

Republic's telephone company (CYTA). At peak times, a three minute call to the USA will cost CY£2.90, but only 21 cents during off-peak (10 pm to 8 am, and on Sunday).

In North Cyprus, most public telephone boxes only take phonecards bought at a Turkish Telecom administration office; the old system of *jetonlar* (tokens) has almost been phased out. A peak three minute call to the USA will set you back UK£1.35, and off-peak UK£0.90. In the Republic you can send faxes from the post office, and in the North from the Turkish Telecom administration offices or from main-street shops in both regions.

There are Internet cafes in all main towns in the Republic of Cyprus and several in the North. The majority stay open late (usually closing in the early hours of the morning) and have become real social centres for travellers and locals alike.

MONEY
Costs
Compared with elsewhere in Europe, Cyprus is moderately cheap. You'll need to budget around US$35 a day if you're going to stick to public transport, stay in very cheap rooms and live mostly on food from shops rather than eating out. Closer to US$70 a day will let you stay in a mid-range place, eat out twice a day, and get around in a hire car. In the North it's a different story. Although costs are generally lower, it's harder to travel on a budget here because there really aren't many budget-travel facilities. If you can find them, however, rooms are cheaper here (good places will cost you around US$15 a night), you can get a decent feed for US$12 and car rental is cheap. For US$50 a day you should be

able to live in relative luxury. All over the island, things are cheaper in winter.

A 10% charge is tacked onto most restaurant bills in the Republic, so you needn't bother tipping unless the service is something special. In the North, service is only added to the bill in flasher places.

Changing Money
Banks throughout Cyprus will exchange all major currencies in either cash or travellers cheques. Most shops and hotels in North Cyprus will accept Cyprus pounds and other hard currencies.

In the Republic you can get a cash advance on Visa, MasterCard, Diners Club, Eurocard and American Express at one or more banks, and there are plenty of ATMs. In North Cyprus, cash advances are given on Visa cards at the Vakiflar and Kooperatif banks in North Lefkosia and Kyrenia.

ONLINE SERVICES
Lonely Planet's Destination Cyprus (www.lonelyplanet.com/dest/eur/cyp .htm) covers the island.

The Cyprus Home Page (http://kypros .org/cyprus) has information on tourism, sports and news. The Cyprus Tourism Organisation has a site (www .cyprustourism.org) and Cosmosnet (www.cosmosnet.et/azias) has some great links including a chat room. Cyprus Mail (www.cynew.com) is a good place for online news. Cyprus Visitors Directory has a site (www .cyprusvisitor.com).

Top sites for North Cyprus include Cyprus Internet Communications (www .cypnet.com/cyradise) and the Turkish Republic of Northern Cyprus site (www .trncwashdc.org).

BOOKS

The Cyprus Revolt by Nancy Cranshaw is one of the most up-to-date guides to the political situation in Cyprus, while *30 Hot Days* by Mehmet Ali Birand tells it from the Turkish perspective. *Cyprus, from the Stone Age to the Romans* by Vassos Karageorghis is a good introduction to the island's history.

Journey Into Cyprus, written in 1972 by Colin Thubron, is the classic Cyprus travelogue.

ENTERING & LEAVING

The Republic has airports at Larnaca and Paphos, handling flights from most of Europe and the Middle East. North Cyprus has an international airport at Ercan, but only Turkish airlines fly there, so you'll probably arrive via Turkey. By sea, you can get to Greece, Rhodes and Israel from the Republic's port in Lemesos. If you want to go to the Greek islands, you'll have to change at Athens. To get to Turkey you'll have to leave from North Cyprus. There are ferries from Famagusta to Mersin, Kyrenia to Tasucu and (during the peak season) Kyrenia to Alanya. Departure tax from the Republic is CY£11 by sea and CY£7 by air.

CZECH REPUBLIC

In 1989 Czechoslovakia opened its doors after the Communist government was thrown out by the people in the 'Velvet Revolution'. This was followed four years later by the 'Velvet Divorce', when the Czech Republic and Slovakia were officially separated – for the second time in a century. Since then visitors and expats have been revelling in the accessibility of this top tourist destination.

Despite the procession of tourists into the capital, the Czech Republic is still a fascinating corner of Europe and an excellent introduction to the east. While Prague shakes with excitement, almost everything outside this astonishing city is still well off the beaten tourist track and unspoiled. Medieval castles, fairy-tale chateaux, spa towns, and great mountain hiking are all waiting for travellers willing to wander out of Prague's pubs and off the beaten path.

Adjoining Austria, Germany, Poland and the Slovak Republic, the Czech Republic consists of Bohemia in the west and Moravia in the east.

WHEN TO GO

May, June and September are the prime visiting months, with April and October as chillier and sometimes cheaper alternatives (though many sights are also closed). Don't completely discount winter, though – Prague is especially beautiful under a mantle of snow and the Krkonoše Mountains have some of the cheapest skiing in Europe.

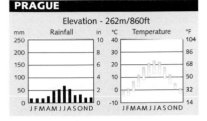

PRAGUE

Elevation - 262m/860ft

Most Czechs take their holidays in July and August. Hotels and tourist sights become crowded, and hostels are crammed with students, especially in Prague (Praha) and the resorts in the Krkonoše and Tatra mountains. From October or November until March or April, most castles, museums and other tourist attractions outside the main cities close down.

At a Glance

Full Country Name: Czech Republic
Area: 78,864 sq km
Population: 10.3 million
Capital City: Prague (pop 1.2 million)
People: Czech with minorities of Moravians, Slovaks, Poles, Germans and Romanies (also known as Gypsies)
Language: Czech
Religion: 40% Roman Catholic, 10% Protestant
Government: Parliamentary democracy
Currency: Czech crown (Kc)
Time Zone: One hour ahead of GMT/UTC; clocks go forward one hour at the end of March and back again at the end of October
International Telephone Code: 420
Electricity: 220V, 50Hz

Itineraries

Two Days

Spend a short trip in Prague, visit the magnificent castle and St Vitus Cathedral, explore the quiet back lanes of Hradcany, battle the crowds on Charles Bridge, watch the hourly performance of the astronomical clock in the Old Town Square, and enjoy the nightlife or a cultural performance.

One Week

Spend two or three days in Prague, then travel east (75 minutes by bus) to the beautiful historic town of Kutná Hora. From there head to Ceské Budevjovice in southern Bohemia. This is the original home of Budvar (Budweiser – no relation to the American brand) beer and it's great fun sampling mugs of the brew in local pubs. From there it's only one hour by train to Ceský Krumlov, one of Europe's most beautiful towns and a great place to end your trip to the Czech Republic.

Two Weeks

Spend at least three days in Prague and add a day trip to the castles at either Konopište or Karlštejn. Visit Kutná Hora, then detour to the picturesque town of Telc before continuing to Ceské Budejovice and Ceský Krumlov. From there it's just a short trip into the Šumava Protected Landscape Area, where you could easily spend a few days walking in the forests and mountains. Finish the trip with a day soaking in the Bohemian spas at Karlovy Vary.

One Month

You can cover the two week itinerary and continue from Karlovy Vary to the attractive church town of Litomeøice in northern Bohemia and up to the Krkonoše Mountains for some skiing or hiking. You could also get down to Moravia in the south-east of the country. The Moravian Slovácko region is a rich repository of traditional folk culture, particularly during the summer music festival – Straznice is a good base. The Moravian Karst, near Brno, is also worth visiting for its caves.

HIGHLIGHTS
Prague

The Czech Republic's biggest attraction is undoubtedly the Gothic beauty of Prague – although many architectural styles, including Romanesque, Renaissance and baroque combine to paint the face of this beguiling city. The historical core of the city – Hradcany (the Castle District) and Malá Strana (the Small Quarter) west of the river, Staré Mesto (the Old Town) and Václavské námesti (Wenceslas Square) to the east, and Charles Bridge in between – covers about three sq km and is easily explored on foot.

Also high on Prague's attraction list is its entertainment: music from classical to modern jazz and rock, opera and ballet, avant-garde theatre, excellent museums, dozens of art galleries, and wonderful bars and beer halls. Prague's greatest distraction, however, is that it is now one of Europe's most popular tourist destinations, and when choked with summer crowds it could be argued that the best time to visit Prague is during winter, when a thin veil of snow laces the city and there's hardly a visitor in sight.

Castles & Chateaux

The castle at Ceský Krumlov is the second largest in the Czech Republic (after Prague's) and it dominates the town from a hill overlooking a horseshoe-shaped bend of the Vltava River. Krivoklat Castle was built in the late 13th century as a royal hunting lodge, and contains an exemplary late-Gothic chapel, impressive halls and the requisite prison and torture chambers. Half the pleasure of visiting Krivoklat is getting there – by train up the wooded Berounka Valley. Karlštejn, only 40

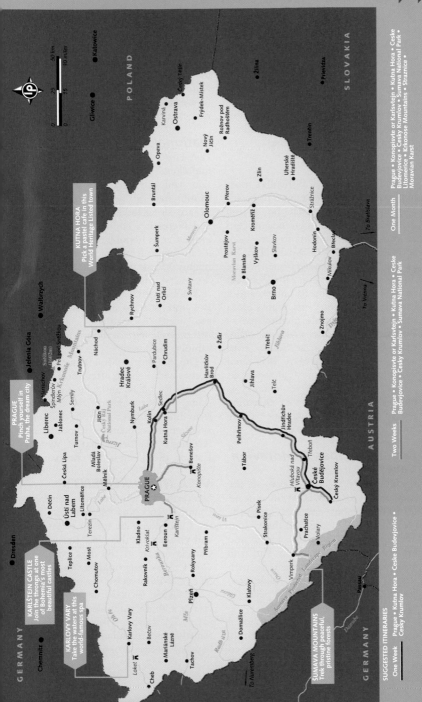

KARLSTEIN CASTLE
Join the throngs at one of Bohemia's most beautiful castles

KARLOVY VARY
Take the waters at this world-famous spa

PRAGUE
Pinch yourself in Praha, the dream city

KUTNA HORA
Pick a pastel cafe in this World Heritage Listed town

ŠUMAVA MOUNTAINS
Trek through peaceful, pristine forests

SUGGESTED ITINERARIES

One Week Prague • Kutna Hora • Ceske Budejovice • Cesky Krumlov

Two Weeks Prague • Konopiste or Karlstejn • Kutna Hora • Ceske Budejovice • Cesky Krumlov • Sumava National Park

One Month Prague • Konopiste or Karlstejn • Kutna Hora • Ceske Budejovice • Cesky Krumlov • Sumava National Park • Litomerice • Krkonose Mountains • Straznice • Moravian Karst

minutes from Prague, is one of the most beautiful castles in Bohemia – and the one most crowded with tourists. The French-style castle of Konopište was once owned by Archduke Franz Ferdinand and is set in the attractive wooded grounds where he used to indulge his passion for hunting.

Historic Towns

Kutná Hora was once Bohemia's most important town after Prague. Today it's a shadow of its old self, but is still dressed up with enough magnificent architectural monuments to have been added to UNESCO's World Heritage List in 1996. With a pastel-hued square dotted with cafes, medieval alleys with facades from Gothic to cubist, and a cathedral to rival St Vitus, Kutná Hora is certainly as densely picturesque as Prague. For a truly macabre sight, there is a cemetery at Sedlec containing a Gothic ossuary decorated with the bones of some 40,000 people.

Telc, in the south of the country, is one of the country's most charming towns. It boasts a Renaissance castle and a stunning town square.

Bohemian Spas & Moravian Caves

Karlovy Vary is the oldest of the Bohemian spas and is world famous for its regenerative waters. It's also the most beautiful of the 'big three' spas (the others are Mariánské Lázne and Františkovy Lázne). Karlovy Vary still manages a definite Victorian air, with elegant colonnades and boulevards complementing the many peaceful walks in the surrounding parks.

The Moravian Karst is a beautiful heavily wooded hilly area north of Brno, carved with canyons and honeycombed with some 400 caves, created by the underground Punkva River. Other caves to be visited in this area include Katerinska, Balcarka and Sloupsko-Sosuvske. Traces of prehistoric humans have been found in these caves.

National Parks & Mountains

For large, tranquil forests, largely unpolluted and undamaged by acid rain, you can't go past the Šumava Mountains, stretching for about 125km along the border with Austria and Germany. The oldest mountains in the Czech Republic, the Šumava are ideal for walking or trekking. The mighty Vltava rises in the Šumava, as do several other major rivers.

The Ceský Ráj National Park in East Bohemia is a maze of low hills and sandstone 'rock towns'. The area offers excellent walking trails and camping facilities.

The Krkonoše Mountains, on the border with Poland, offer good opportunities for hiking and winter downhill skiing. The best resorts are at Spindleruv mlyn and Pec Pod Snezkou and, although the standard of runs, lifts and facilities is well below that of Western Europe, the skiing is dirt cheap.

VISA REQUIREMENTS

Nationals of all Western European countries and New Zealand can visit the Czech Republic for up to 90 days, and citizens of the UK, Ireland and Canada for up to 180 days, without a visa. US passport holders can stay for 30 days without a visa. Australians need a visa (A$56 for a 30 day single entry visa or a 90 day multiple entry visa).

Czech tourist visas are readily available at consulates, or at three highway border crossings – one from

Germany and two from Austria – and at Prague's Ruzynév airport. Visas are never issued on trains.

Czech Embassies & Consulates

Australia
(☎ 02-6290 1386, fax 6290 0006) 38 Culgoa Circuit, O'Malley, ACT 2606
Consulate: (☎ 02-9371 8877, visa information: ☎ 9371 8878, fax 9371 9635) 169 Military Rd, Dover Heights, NSW 2030 (visas are only issued at the consulate)

Canada
(☎ 613-562 3875) 541 Sussex Drive, Ottawa, Ont K1N 6Z6
(only in-person visa applications are accepted)

New Zealand
Consulate: (☎ 04-564 6001) 48 Hair St, PO Box 43035, Wainuiomata, Wellington (visa applications must be made to the Czech consulate in Sydney, Australia)

UK
(☎ 020-7243 1115) 26 Kensington Palace Gardens, London W8 4QY
(the visa office, ☎ 020-7243 7943, is next door at number 28)

USA
(☎ 202-374 9100) 3900 Spring of Freedom St NW, Washington, DC 20008
Consulate: (☎ 310-473 0889) 10990 Wilshire Blvd, Suite 1100, Los Angeles, CA 90024

TOURIST OFFICES OVERSEAS

Canada
(☎ 416-367 3432) Exchange Tower, 2 First Canadian Place, 14th floor, Toronto, Ont M5X 1A6

UK
(☎ 020-7291 9924) 96 Great Portland St, London W1N 5RA

USA
(☎ 212-288 0830) 1109-1111 Madison Ave, New York, NY 10028

POST & COMMUNICATIONS

Postal services are fairly efficient and inexpensive, though it's safest to mail international parcels from main post offices in large cities.

You can buy stamps in post offices and also from street vendors and newsagents. Most larger post offices have a window for poste restante, though the most reliable services are at the main post offices in Prague.

Blue coin telephones accept only 2, 5, 10 and 20 Kc coins and can be used to make local, long-distance and international calls. A more convenient and common alternative is a *telekart* (phonecard), good for local, long-distance and international calls. Cards are sold in post offices, newsagents and the main telephone bureau.

You can make international telephone calls at main post offices; operator-assisted calls cost US$3 a minute to New Zealand; US$2.50 a minute to Australia, Canada, the USA and Japan; and US$1 a minute to most of Europe.

Email is possible from Internet cafes in Prague and Brno.

MONEY
Costs

Food, transportation and admission fees are fairly cheap for western travellers; it's mainly accommodation in the cities that makes the Czech Republic one of the most expensive countries in this part of Europe. Outside Prague your costs will drop dramatically.

By staying at cheap hostels and camp sites, sticking to self-catering, pubs and stand-up cafeterias, and going easy on the beer and wine, you might get away with US$15 per day in summer. In a private home or better hostel, with meals at cheap restaurants, and using public transport, you can get by on US$25 to US$30.

In Prague, add a third to half again, even more if you want to be close to the centre. A disappointing side of the Czech concept of a 'free market economy' is the official two price system in which foreigners pay around double the local price for most hotel rooms, bus tickets, museum and concert tickets, and sometimes international airline tickets.

A tip of 5 to 10% is appreciated in any tourist restaurant with table service.

Changing Money

Travellers cheques are easily cashed throughout the Czech Republic. Eurocheques are cashed free of charge at Komercní banks, and there are American Express and Thomas Cook offices in Prague that will change their cheques at bank rates free of charge. Private exchange offices (which open longer hours than banks) charge commissions of up to 10%. US dollars and German marks are the most sensible currencies to use: they're as welcome as crowns in touristy parts of the republic.

Upper-end hotels and restaurants in major tourist centres accept some credit cards, usually American Express, Visa or MasterCard (Access) and sometimes Eurocard, Diners Club or JCB.

ATMs (bankomat) are everywhere, even in smaller towns, and you generally get an excellent rate of exchange. Nearly all ATMs in the Czech Republic accept Eurocard. Equally common are MasterCard/Cirrus and Visa/Plus ATMs.

ONLINE SERVICES

Lonely Planet's Destination Czech Republic (www.lonelyplanet.com/dest /eut/cze.htm) is loaded with country information.

EU Net (www.eunet.cz) provides regional information, travel tips, and links to related Web pages at its Czech site. Stay on top of Czech news stories courtesy of the *Prague Post* (www .praguepost.cz). The CTK news service (www.ctknews.com) is also good.

The Czech Ministry of Foreign Affairs has an excellent site (www .czech.cz) packed with country and travel information, and lots of links. Central Europe Online (www.ceo.cz) is a popular site with lots of links to Czech and Slovak servers. Another site (www.travel.cz) has a hotel reservation service. Two sites (www.czweb.com, www.jobs.cz) focus on Czech business and jobs in the republic.

BOOKS

The Europe-based journalist Timothy Garton Ash's *We the People – The Revolutions of 1989* features gripping first-hand accounts of the revolutions that swept away the region's old guard.

Several books by the dissident-turned-president, Václav Havel, offer an 'inside' view. *Disturbing the Peace* is a collection of recent historical musings. *Letters to Olga* is a collection of Havel's letters to his wife from prison in the 1980s, and *Living in Truth* is a series of absorbing political essays. *The Reluctant President – A Political Life of Vaclav Havel* is a biography by Michael Simmons.

Milan Kundera is one of the Czech Republic's best known authors-in-exile, who wrote about life under the Communist regime. His best novel is probably *The Joke*. Other good reads are *Cowards* by Josef Skvorecký, *The Ship Named Hope* by Ivo Klima and anything by Bohumil Hrabal. Jaroslav

Hasek's *The Good Soldier Svejk* is a classic WWI comic novel about the trials of the republic's literary mascot, written in instalments from Prague's pubs. Bruce Chatwin's *Utz* is a quiet, absorbing novella about a porcelain collector in Prague's old Jewish quarter.

One of the masters of 20th century fiction, Franz Kafka wrote in German but was born in Prague; *The Castle* is a macabre homage to the town.

FILMS

Prague has been a backdrop for several Hollywood films; *Amadeus* was shot there, as were *Kafka* and *Mission Impossible*. *The Unbearable Lightness of Being* (1988) is an existential love story set in Prague in 1968, as the Soviet tanks roll in.

As far as Czech films go, look out for the internationally acclaimed *Kolja* (1996), which managed to score the two big film prizes of 1997 – the best foreign film awards at the Cannes Film Festival and the US Academy Awards. it is about a Russian boy being brought up by a Czech bachelor. Films critical of the post-invasion regime were made during 1969 and 1970, but were promptly banned from public screening. The most outstanding of these were *Spalovacv mrtvol* (The Cremator of Corpses) by Juraj Herz, *Zert* (The Joke) by Jaromil Jireš, *Ucho* (The Ear) by Karel Kachyna and *Nahota* (Nakedness) by Václav Matejka. In the post-communist era, Zdenek Sverák is the only director who has consistently managed to make good and entertaining films. His 1994 hit *Akumulátor* was the most expensive Czech film to be produced to date.

ENTERING & LEAVING

Scheduled international flights arrive at Prague, which is connected worldwide by at least two dozen international carriers, including CSA (Ceske Aerolinie), the old state-run airline. Departure tax is 350Kc, which is normally included in the price of the ticket.

The easiest (if not the cheapest) way to get to the Czech Republic from Western Europe is by train, with some 18 rail crossing points. By road, visitors can enter the republic at more than 30 points (and the list is growing all the time), but if you require a visa, there are only three official border crossings.

DENMARK

With little to get angry about in Scandinavia's cosiest and most PC community, post-Viking Danes have had to file down their horns and make their mark in a more civilised fashion. The Danes have responded by inventing Lego, being the European Union's cagiest member, producing some talented upstart soccer players and baking delicious pastries.

Denmark's capital, toe-tapping, toy-town Copenhagen, is probably Scandinavia's most exciting nightlife centre and the cost of a beer here won't kill you as much as it will further north.

Among the historic treasures you'll find around the country are 2000-year-old 'bog people', Neolithic dolmens and Viking ruins. Denmark also has wonderful white-sand beaches, Scandinavia's warmest waters and scores of unspoilt islands to explore. The country is largely flat which, combined with an extensive network of cycle routes, makes it a great place to explore by bike.

WHEN TO GO

Considering its northern latitude, Denmark has a fairly mild climate all year round. Still, the winter months – which are cold and with short daylight hours – are certainly the least hospitable. Many tourist destinations come alive in late April, when the weather beings to warm up and the daylight hours start to increase. By October they again become sleepers.

May and June can be delightful months to visit: the weather is comfortable and you'll beat the rush of tourists. Autumn can be pleasant, but it's not nearly as scenic.

At a Glance

Full Country Name: The Kingdom of Denmark
Area: 42,930 sq km
Population: 5.2 million
Capital City: Copenhagen (pop 1.4 million)
People: 97% Danish, 3% foreign nationals
Language: Danish; English and German are widely spoken
Religion: Lutheran
Government: Constitutional monarchy
Currency: Krone
Time Zone: One hour ahead of GMT/UTC. Clocks go forward one hour on the last Sunday in March and back on the last Sunday in October
International Telephone Code: 45
Electricity: 220V, 50Hz

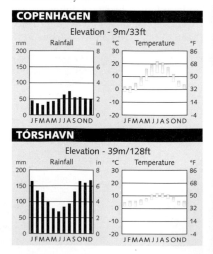

The high tourist season is July and August. There are open-air concerts, lots of street activity and basking on the beach. Other bonuses for travellers during midsummer are longer hours at museums and other sightseeing attractions. The last half of August can be a particularly attractive time to travel, as it still has summer weather but far fewer crowds. The Copenhagen Jazz Festival is held over 10 days in July and attracts plenty of visitors.

HIGHLIGHTS

Lively Copenhagen is the first stop on most people's itinerary. It combines some of the country's finest museums and historic castles with 24 hour nightlife and free tours of the Carlsberg Brewery. Other Danish highlights include:

Castles

Denmark has castles aplenty, some with lofty turrets and towers, some with dungeons and others just misnamed manor houses. The most strikingly set is Egeskov Castle, surrounded by a moat and formal gardens in the Funen countryside. For the most elaborately decorated Renaissance interior, Frederiksborg

Faroe Islands

This tiny archipelago in the North Atlantic Ocean, roughly midway between Scotland and Iceland, is seldom visited by budget travellers. Those who do will find a starkly beautiful landscape, a strong Norse culture and some of the friendliest people in the Scandinavian region.

There are 18 Faroe islands, which form an independent nation within the Kingdom of Denmark. Visa requirements and currency are the same as for Denmark. The population is just over 44,000, of which almost 16,000 people live in the capital Tórshavn on the main island of Streymoy. The islanders speak Faroese, a language closely related to Icelandic, though Danish is widely spoken, as well as some English. The islands see a lot of rain, so bring your wet-weather gear and be prepared for anything. The best time to come is between June and August.

The main reasons to visit the Faroes (apart from a desire to really get away from it all) are for hiking and fishing, and to observe the nesting sea bird colonies. An age-old Faroese tradition that most westerners find outrageous is the *grindadráp* – a mass hunt and slaughter of migrating pilot whales.

Tórshavn is a relaxed and engaging 1000-year-old town set around a small peninsula. There are plenty of historic buildings, a ruined fort and a couple of local museums. Around the islands, some of the best sights are the sheer cliffs that harbour colonies of sea birds such as puffins (which are netted and eaten by the locals), guillemots, fulmars, razorbills and kittiwakes. A boat trip to the cliffs of Vestmanna (on Streymoy), a hike to the Enniberg cliffs (on Viðoy) and anywhere along the coast of Fugloy Island provide spectacular sights.

Villages worth visiting include picturesque Gjógv (on Eysturoy Island), Kirkjubøur on Streymoy and Viðareiði on Viðoy Island. The westernmost island of Mykines is the jewel, with turf-roofed houses, an isolated lighthouse and zillions of sea birds.

Costs in the Faroes are similar to Iceland, but transport costs are lower because of the short distances. If you're camping or staying in hostels and self-catering, you can get by on US$35 a day. Triple that if you want to stay in hotels.

Atlantic Airways has flights from Copenhagen (Denmark), Glasgow and Aberdeen (Scotland) and Reykjavík (Iceland), roughly between May and October. Smyril Line has a weekly ferry from Denmark, Norway and Shetland (Scotland), which stops at Tórshavn before continuing to Iceland.

Castle in Hillerød is unequalled. In Copenhagen the king of castles is Rosenborg, where the dazzling crown jewels are on display.

The most well known castle in Scandinavia is Elsinore Castle (Kronborg Slot), at Helsingør, north of Copenhagen. Shakespeare used it as the setting for *Hamlet*, but historically its primary function was to collect shipping tolls.

Historic Towns

Half-timbered houses (with a timber frame and interstices filled in with brick or plaster), cobblestone streets and ancient churches are thick on the ground in Denmark, but a few places are unique. Ribe, the oldest town in Denmark, has an exquisite historic centre encircling a 12th century cathedral.

The tiny fortress island of Christiansø, off Bornholm, retains its ramparts and 17th century buildings, with almost no trace of the 20th century. And Ærøskøbing on Ærø has a town centre of 18th century houses that's arguably the most picturesque in Denmark.

Museums

Denmark has several open-air folk museums with period buildings. The most impressive is Den Gamle By in Århus, which is set up as a provincial town, while the folk museum in Odense has the most engaging natural setting.

The best preserved bog people – intact Iron Age bodies found preserved in peat bogs – are at the Silkeborg Museum in Silkeborg and the Moesgård Prehistoric Museum in Århus. In Zealand, top art museums are Ny Carlsberg Glyptotek in Copenhagen and Louisiana in Humlebæk.

Viking Sites

The Danish countryside has a number of Viking sites, including fortresses

---

Itineraries

Two Days
Buy a Copenhagen Card and explore the capital's palaces, museums, parks and gardens. Don't miss the city's amusement park, Tivoli, and a stroll down the Strøget pedestrian mall.

One Week
After spending a couple of days exploring Copenhagen, head for North Zealand's castles (Frederiksborg and Kronborg) and beaches (Hornbaek, Gilleleje and Tisvildeleje). From there you can travel south to Roskilde and its cathedral, and across to the Viking fortress of Trelleborg. You should still have time to explore some of the sights in southern Zealand such as historic Køge, Ringsted or the hamlet of Vallø.

Two Weeks
Having covered the areas listed under One Week, take the train across to the island of Funen, stopping off at Odense (birthplace of Hans Christian Andersen) and Egeskov Castle before heading down to Ærø, an idyllic little island of fishing villages and patchwork farmland. If you still have time, travel west to Jutland, Denmark's largest island, and head up to the lively university city of Århus, with its fine open-air folk museum.

One Month
With a month you can do the two week route and add travel around Jutland, including visits to Skagen, medieval Ribe and the Danish Lake District (Silkeborg).

You should also take a ferry from Copenhagen to the island of Bornholm and cycle around the many bike paths. If you have time, it's worth the further one hour boat ride to the tiny 17th century fortress island of Christiansø.

DENMARK HIGHLIGHTS & ITINERARIES

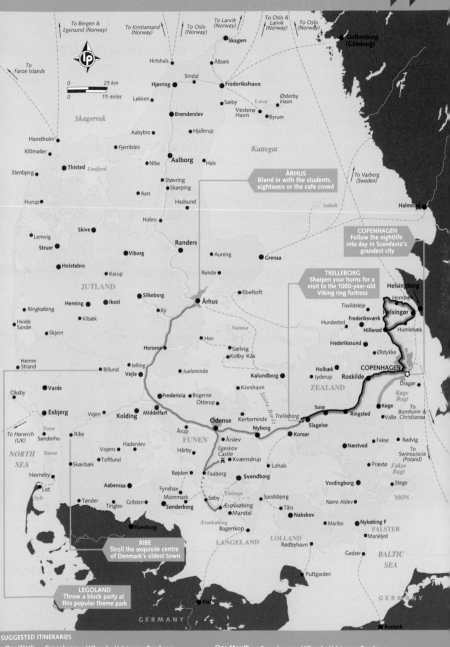

ÅRHUS
Blend in with the students, sightseers or the cafe crowd

COPENHAGEN
Follow the nightlife into day in Scandavia's grandest city

TRELLEBORG
Sharpen your horns for a visit to the 1000-year-old Viking ring fortress

RIBE
Stroll the exquisite centre of Denmark's oldest town

LEGOLAND
Throw a block party at this popular theme park

SUGGESTED ITINERARIES

One Week   Copenhagen • Hillerød • Helsingør • Beaches • Roskilde • Trelleborg

Two Weeks   Copenhagen • Hillerød • Helsingør • Beaches • Roskilde • Trelleborg • Odense • Egeskov Castle • Ærø • Århus

One Month   Copenhagen • Hillerød • Helsingør • Beaches • Roskilde • Trelleborg • Odense • Egeskov Castle • Ærø • Ribe • Silkeborg • Århus • Skagen

dating back to around AD 980. Their circular earthen-work walls remain intact and surround the faint remains of house sites where timbered stave-style structures once stood. Best preserved are the Trelleborg fortress in southern Zealand, 7km outside Slagelse, and the Fyrkat fortress in Jutland, 3km outside Hobro in Jutland; both have reconstructed Viking houses.

There are Viking ships on display at the Viking Ship Museum in Roskilde (west of Copenhagen) and the Bangsbo Museum in Frederikshavn (northern Jutland). The impressive Lindholm Høje, outside Aalborg, contains the largest plot of Viking and Iron Age graves in Scandinavia.

In summer, Viking festivals and open-air Viking plays can be found at several locations, including Frederikssund in Zealand and the Fyrkat fortress.

Festivals

Denmark is big on music festivals, which run almost nonstop all year and cover a broad spectrum of music from jazz, rock, blues and gospel to Irish, classical, country and Cajun. Beginning with Midsummer's Eve bonfires in late June, some of the most popular are the Roskilde Festival, northern Europe's largest rock music festival, held in late June or early July; the Midtfyns Festival in Ringe (early July); the Copenhagen Jazz Festival, held over 10 days in early July; and the Tønder Festival, one of northern Europe's largest folk festivals (end of August).

The nine day Århus Festival, beginning on the first Saturday in September, turns that city into a stage for nonstop revelry, and incorporates a Viking festival.

VISA REQUIREMENTS

Most western nationals, including Americans, citizens of EU countries, Australians, Canadians, New Zealanders, Malaysians, Singaporeans and most South Americans do not need a visa.

Danish Embassies

Australia
(☎ 02-6273 2195/3864) 15 Hunter St, Yarralumla, Canberra, ACT 2600

Canada
(☎ 613-562 1811, fax 234 7368) 47 Clarence St, Suite 450, Ottawa, Ont K1N 9K1

Ireland
(☎ 01-475 6404, fax 478 4536) 121 St Stephen's Green, Dublin 2

Japan
(☎ 03-3496 3001, fax 3496 3440) 29-6 Sarugaku-cho, Shibuya-ku, Tokyo 150

New Zealand
Contact the Danish embassy in Australia

UK
(☎ 020-7333 0200, fax 7333 0270) 55 Sloane St, London SW1X 9SR

USA
(☎ 202-234 4300, fax 328 1470) 3200 Whitehaven St NW, Washington, DC 20008

TOURIST OFFICES OVERSEAS

UK
(☎ 020-7259 5959, fax 7259 5955, @ dtb.london@dt.dk) 55 Sloane St, London SW1X 9SR

USA
(☎ 212-885 9700, fax 885 9710, @ info@goscandinavia.com) PO Box 4649, Grand Central Station, New York, NY 10163

POST & COMMUNICATIONS

You can receive mail c/o poste restante at any post office in Denmark, but it's usually held for only two weeks. International mail sent from Copenhagen is generally out of the country within 24 hours.

Denmark has an efficient phone system. Phonecards *(telekort)* are more convenient than pumping in coins. Cards can be bought at post offices and many kiosks, especially at train stations. Card phones are found in busy public places side by side with coin phones; direct dial international calls can be made from both.

Faxes can be sent from hotels and larger post offices. Many public libraries in Denmark have Internet access, though access policies vary; sometimes you need to book in advance. Larger post offices usually have Internet computers in the lobby that can be accessed with a phonecard. As most families in Denmark have their own computers, cybercafes are not particularly popular.

MONEY
Costs

By anything other than Scandinavian standards, Denmark is certainly an expensive country. Part of the blame lies with the 25% tax, included in every price from hotel rooms to shop purchases. Still, your costs will depend on how you travel and it's possible to see Denmark without spending a fortune.

If you take advantage of Denmark's extensive network of camping grounds or stay in hostels and prepare your own meals, you might get by on US$30 a day. If you stay in modest hotels and eat at inexpensive restaurants, you can expect to spend about US$65 to US$75 a day. Car rental is expensive in Denmark; if you want wheels, it might be worth hiring a car in Germany for about one-third of the price, and taking it across the border.

Expect to pay around US$10 to US$12 for a cheap bed, US$6 to US$8 for a budget meal and US$15 to US$40 for a moderate restaurant meal.

Restaurant bills and taxi fares include service charges in the quoted prices. Further tipping is unnecessary, although rounding up the bill is not uncommon when the service has been good. Bargaining is not a common practice in Denmark.

Changing Money

All common travellers cheques are accepted at major banks in Denmark, but bank fees for changing money are hefty, so it's best to change a reasonable amount at a time. Post offices will change foreign cash and they are open on Saturday mornings, which can be handy. Most major banks have ATMs that give cash advances on credit cards. There are also 24-hour cash exchange machines in Copenhagen.

ONLINE SERVICES

Lonely Planet's Destination Denmark (www.lonelyplanet.com/dest/eur/den .htm) has country information. The Danish foreign ministry site (www .denmark.org) has a wealth of information, including updated weather and exchange rates, plus links to many other Danish sites. Welcome to Denmark (www.denmark.dt.dk) is the official tourist office homepage. Copenhagen NOW (www.copenhagen.now.dk/eng lish.html) is a good source of information on the capital.

BOOKS

The Viking World by James Graham-Campbell gives an outline of Viking history, while *Denmark – A Modern History* by W Glyn Jones is one of the more comprehensive and insightful accounts of contemporary Danish society. *The Concept of Dread* by philosopher Søren Kierkegaard is considered to be the first work of depth psychology ever written. *A Kierkegaard Anthology* by Robert Bretall has a broad selection of major works by Kierkegaard.

Pelle the Conqueror by Martin Andersen Nexø is an intriguing novel about the harsh reality of life as an immigrant in 19th century Denmark. *Smilla's Sense of Snow*, a crisp 1994 bestseller by Peter Høeg, was made into a slightly mushier movie. *Tales Told for Children* by Hans Christian Andersen includes such classic stories as 'The Tinderbox' and 'The Princess and the Pea'.

FILMS

Babette's Feast (1988), directed by Gabriel Axel, won the Academy Award for Best Foreign Film. It was an adaptation of a story written by Danish author Karen Blixen, whose novel *Out of Africa* was turned into an Oscar-winning Hollywood movie three years earlier.

In 1989 Danish director Bille August won the Academy Award for Best Foreign Film as well the Cannes Film Festival's Palme d'Or award for the film adaptation of *Pelle the Conqueror.*

August also directed *Smilla's Sense of Snow* (1997), which starred Julia Ormond and Gabriel Byrne. Up-and-coming Danish directors include Lars von Trier, whose best known film to date is *Breaking the Waves* (1996), and Thomas Vinterberg, whose film *Festen* (The Celebration) won the jury prize at the 1998 Cannes Film Festival.

ENTERING & LEAVING

Most overseas flights to Denmark arrive at Copenhagen international airport. A few international flights, mostly coming from other Scandinavian countries or the UK, land at small regional airports in Århus, Aalborg, Esbjerg and Billund. There are daily bus and rail services between Germany and Denmark's Jutland Peninsula. It's also possible to arrive from Norway and Sweden by ferry. Other boat options are the daily (high season) and weekly (iceberg bashing) ferries running from Germany (Kiel and the island of Sylt), Iceland (Seyðisfjörður), Norway (Oslo and Larvik), Sweden (Gothenburg, Kalmstad, Helsingborg, Limhamm, Malmö and Varberg), Poland (Swinoujscie) and the UK (Harwich). There are no departure taxes when leaving Denmark.

ESTONIA

Estonia (Eesti), the most northerly of the three Baltic states, is just 80km across the Gulf of Finland from Helsinki and is socially and economically creeping closer week by week. Only fully independent since August 1991, Estonia's transition from a Soviet socialist republic to western-style economy has been little short of miraculous. This relatively smooth transition to capitalism and independence makes visiting Estonia less of a culture shock and a good starting point for a trip through the Baltic states.

Estonia's past lingers in the medieval heart of Tallinn, which is a highlight of any visit to the Baltic region. The Estonians struggled for centuries to retain their identity and a rich folk culture is the result. Even eating will be a new and challenging experience – blood sausages and blood pancakes are served in most traditional Estonian restaurants, and no-one quite knows what the sickly sweet and very strong Vana Tallinn liqueur is made from!

Although lifestyle indicators now approach western levels, Estonia is still a relatively cheap destination for budget travellers.

WHEN TO GO

Given the severity of Estonian winters (December to March) and the dampness of its autumns, the best time to visit the country is in late spring (April and May) and summer (June to early September). July and August are the warmest months, with daily highs reaching 30°C. If you're keen on

TALLINN

Elevation - 44m/144ft

| mm | Rainfall | in | °C | Temperature | °F |

skiing, skating or ice fishing, though, winter is a great time to go.

HIGHLIGHTS
Tallinn

Tallinn's Old Town, with its winding, cobbled streets and gingerbread facades, is a definite high point of any trip to Estonia. There are several good museums to visit, and an evening stroll along the Pirita tee to watch the sun set over the bay is a must. It's worth making the side trip to Keila-Joa, 30km west of Tallinn. This small

At a Glance

Full Country Name: Republic of Estonia
Area: 45,200 sq km
Population: 1.5 million
Capital City: Tallinn (pop 443,000)
People: 62% Estonian, 30% Russian, 3% Ukrainian
Language: Estonian
Religion: 23% Christian (Lutheran and Russian Orthodox); the majority of Estonians have no religious convictions
Government: Independent republic
Currency: Eesti kroon (EEK)
Time Zone: Two hours ahead of GMT/UTC
International Telephone Code: 372
Electricity: 220V, 50Hz

village has a picturesque waterfall beside a 19th century manor house.

Islands

The virtually untouched islands of Hiiumaa and Saaremaa are two spots of remarkable solitude and beauty. Here you can retreat into nature, stroll through pretty fishing villages or take a boat trip to Estonia's even lesser explored islands (Vormsi and Ruhnu). The tiny island of Kihnu, with its traditionally dressed locals and thriving folklore tales, is another

---

Itineraries

Two Days

Two days could easily be spent in Tallinn, exploring the Old Town, Pirita and taking a trip out to the waterfall at Keila-Joa. Alternatively, spend one day in Tallinn and the other in the Lahemaa National Park (Viitna or Võsu), only 70km east of Tallinn, or Estonia's second city, the historic university town of Tartu.

One Week

Spend two days in Tallinn, then spend a day or two exploring Lahemaa National Park. From there you can travel south to Tartu for a day, then spend the rest of the week visiting Saaremaa Island, particularly Kuressaare and the Sörve Peninsula. You might even have time to slip across to Hiiumaa Island.

Two Weeks

Two weeks is ample time to see a good slice of Estonia. Spend two or three days in Tallinn, a couple of days in the Lahemaa National Park, two days in Tartu, a day in Pärnu with a trip out to Soomaa National Park for a paddle in the bogs, and the rest of the time exploring the islands of Saaremaa, Hiiumaa and Kihnu. If you have more time, you could visit Estonia's highest point, Suur Munamägi, and the Setumaa area bordering Russia in the far south-east of the state.

---

place island-lovers should not miss out on.

National Parks, Bogs & Beaches

In northern Estonia, the Lahemaa National Park has numerous walking trails and (unusually for a national park) some quaint coastal fishing villages to visit. The baroque Palmse Manor is a showpiece here.

Soomaa National Park, an area of wetlands primarily made up of four peat bogs, is in south-west Estonia, between the towns of Pärnu and Viljandi. The bogs are split by tributaries of the Pärnu River, and the only way to explore this area is by paddling in traditional Estonian dugout canoes.

Estonia mightn't be synonymous with lazing on a beach, but Pärnu has a beautiful white-sand beach and is a buzzing resort town in summer. There are also beaches along the coast west of Tallinn.

VISA REQUIREMENTS

Travellers from Australia, New Zealand, Japan, the USA and most northern, Central and Eastern European countries do not require a visa to enter Estonia.

Estonian Embassies & Consulates

Australia
 (☎ 02-9810 7468, fax 9818 1779, @ eest ikon@ozemail.com.au) 86 Louisa Rd, Birchgrove, NSW 2041

Canada
 (☎ 416-461 0764, fax 461 0448, @ est consu@ inforamp.net) 958 Broadview Ave, Toronto, Ont M4K 2R6

USA
 (☎ 202-588 0101, fax 588 0108, @ info@ estemb.org, www.estemb.org) 2131 Massachusetts Ave NW, Washington, DC 20008

ESTONIA HIGHLIGHTS & ITINERARIES ▶▶

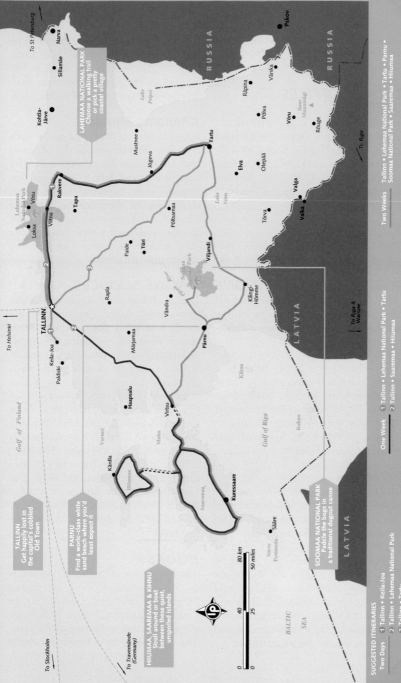

TALLINN
Get happily lost in the capital's cobbled Old Town

PÄRNU
Find a world-class white sand beach where you'd least expect it

HIIUMAA, SAAREMAA & KIHNU
Stroll around or boat between these quiet, unspoiled islands

SOOMAA NATIONAL PARK
Paddle the bogs in a traditional dugout canoe

LAHEMAA NATIONAL PARK
Choose a walking trail or pick a pretty coastal village

SUGGESTED ITINERARIES

Two Days 1 Tallinn • Keila-Joa
2 Tallinn • Lehemaa National Park
3 Tallinn • Tartu

One Week 1 Tallinn • Lehemaa National Park • Tartu
2 Tallinn • Saaremaa • Hiiumaa

Two Weeks Tallinn • Lehemaa National Park • Tartu • Pärnu •
Soomaa National Park • Saaremaa • Hiiumaa

Consulate: (☎ 212-247 7634/1450, fax 262 0893) 630 5th Ave, Suite 2415, New York, NY 10111

TOURIST OFFICES OVERSEAS

Estonia boasts a wide network of tourist information offices coordinated by the Estonian Tourist Board (☎ 372-6411 420, fax 6411 342, ✆ info@turism.ee) Pikk 71, EE0001 Tallinn, Estonia. Their representatives overseas include:

Canada
Orav Travel
(☎ 416-221 4164, fax 221 6789) 5650 Yonge St, North York, Ont M2M 4G3

POST & COMMUNICATIONS

Postal services in and out of Estonia are reasonably reliable. Stamps can be bought at post offices, tourist information offices and hotels.

Public telephones accept phonecards, which are available from post offices, hotels and street kiosks. There are reasonably priced public fax services in the main cities, mainly at post offices and in all major hotels.

There are cybercafes for email and Internet access in Tallinn.

MONEY
Costs

Budget travellers can find bargains in Estonia: camp site cabins and hostel beds are around US$8 per person, and decent meals can be found for under US$5, so you should be able to get by on as little as US$25 a day. Travellers on a more generous budget should expect to spend between US$40 and US$75 a day, though you can shave that figure considerably by self-catering and staying outside of the larger towns.

It's fairly common to tip waiters 5 or 10% by rounding up the bill. Some bargaining goes on at flea markets but savings are not likely to be more than 10 or 20% below the initial asking price.

Changing Money

It's difficult to find places to cash travellers cheques outside the big cities and towns, but Eurocheques can be cashed in most banks, and you can change cash in every town. Cash dispensing ATMs accepting Visa and MasterCard/Eurocard are widespread in cities and larger towns. Credit cards are widely accepted in hotels, restaurants and shops.

ONLINE SERVICES

Lonely Planet's Destination Estonia (www.lonelyplanet.com/dest/eur.est.htm) is a good place to start your search. For hotel, restaurant, bar, nightclub and theatre listings in Tallinn, as well as a calendar of events and transport schedules, try www.inyourpocket.com. Another site (www.ciesin.ee/NEWS/index.html) has news about the Baltics, Central and Eastern Europe, and links to English-language media sources, including the Baltics On-line.

The site of the Estonia Country Guide is www.ciesin.ee/ESTCG. The homepage of the Estonian Tourist Board (www.tourism.ee) has plenty of colourful information and lots of hot links.

BOOKS

Among the Russians by Colin Thubron is an Englishman's account of driving throughout the pre-glasnost Soviet Union and includes Tallinn. It captures the gloomy, resigned mood of the time. *The Christening* by Denise Neuhaus brilliantly captures the paranoia of Soviet-era Tallinn.

The Czar's Madman by Jaan Kross, Estonia's most celebrated novelist, uses historical tales to address contemporary themes. *The Baltic States – The Years of Independence, 1917-40*, by Georg von Rauch, and *The Baltic States – Years of Dependence, 1940-80*, by Romualdas Misiunas & Rein Taagepera, are both weighty historical tomes.

Clare Thomson's *The Singing Revolution* traces the path of the Baltic states towards independence as she travelled through the region in 1989 and 1990.

ENTERING & LEAVING

There are flights between Tallinn and Amsterdam, Copenhagen, Helsinki, Kiev, London, Minsk and Stockholm. There are no departure taxes when leaving Estonia.

Bus is the cheapest mode of transport to and from Estonia, and Eurolines links Tallinn with Western and Scandinavian Europe. While public buses get priority over private vehicles at border crossings, Estonian border guards take perverse pleasure in not only stamping every Western passport but also inviting travellers to their offices so they can key your passport data into their computers.

The daily *Balti Ekspress* between Tallinn and Warsaw is a good option for train buffs. Numerous ferries sail directly between Estonia and Finland, Sweden and Germany.

FINLAND

Finland and its capital, Helsinki, are often viewed as a quick stopover on the way through to St Petersburg (see the boxed text in this profile). But when the nights are long in Finland (and they can be very, very long) there's much more to do than huddle inside with a vodka or two. You can ski across vast frozen lakes or relax in a sauna, beating yourself ever so gently with a fragrant branch of birch leaves to loosen the travel grime. During the months of the midnight sun, coastal regions, including the Turku archipelago and Åland islands, are a sailing and fishing paradise. Inland, the largest unspoilt wilderness in Europe attracts thousands of trekkers every year.

In the south, Helsinki has more than 30 art galleries and museums, while in the north, Santa Claus kicks back 364 days a year. Where else in the world can you take a reindeer tour or an icebreaker cruise, then hit the green for some midnight golf?

Despite its size – this is Europe's seventh largest country – Finland has just over five million inhabitants. It is eight times the size of the Netherlands but has less than a third of its population. This is a land of considerable wilderness, lakes and islands but it's the people that make Finland such an unforgettable place to visit – you might find Finns a bit aloof or hesitant at first, but that never lasts.

WHEN TO GO

Whatever time of year you visit Finland, there's something happening. Most museums and galleries are open year-round, and there is as much to do in the depths of winter as there is at the height of summer. Nevertheless, travel will be more rewarding in the warmer months, any time from May to September. As well as the advantages of warm weather, summer is the time of the midnight sun. Winter north of the Arctic Circle is a chilly confluence of strange bluish light and encroaching melancholy. Despite snowfalls from November, it stays

At a Glance

Full Country Name: Finland
Area: 338,000 sq km
Population: 5.16 million
Capital City: Helsinki (pop 891,000)
People: 98% Finns, 0.7% Samis, Gypsies
Language: Finnish and Swedish (English is widely spoken in tourist establishments)
Religion: 93% Lutheran, some Orthodox
Government: Democratic republic
Currency: Finnish markka (mk)
Time Zone: Two hours ahead of GMT/UTC; clocks are turned forward one hour in early April and back again in late October
International Telephone Code: 358
Electricity: 220V, 50Hz

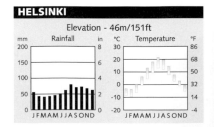

HELSINKI
Elevation - 46m/151ft

pretty sludgy until late winter; skiing isn't great until February, the coldest month, and you can ski in Lapland right through to June.

HIGHLIGHTS

Finland, the land of lakes, is an ideal country to visit if you enjoy the great outdoors. There's plenty to see and do, whether you're travelling under the midnight sun or by the eerie glow of the aurora borealis. A must while you're in Finland is to let off some steam in a sauna – the best of all saunas is the 60 person smoke sauna in Kuopio.

Museums & Galleries

Kiasma in Helsinki is the daring new national museum of contemporary art, while the bulk of the national art collection is at Ateneum. Retretti at Punkaharju is also a noteworthy art venue. Helsinki's Mannerheim Museum, preserving the home of Finland's great independence-era leader CGE Mannerheim, is intimate and intriguing. Seurasaari, near Helsinki, and Luostarinmäki in Turku are two of the best open-air history museums in the country. For experiencing the northern culture, Arktikum in Rovaniemi and Saamelaismuseo in Inari are top-class.

Castles & Manor Houses

Olavinlinna, at Savonlinna, is the mightiest and best preserved of the northern medieval castles and is superbly set between two lakes. It's home to a world-class opera festival in summer. Less imposing are the castles of Turku and Hämeenlinna, each with extensive museums. Åland has the smaller Kastelholm castle. There are many manor houses in Finland; Louhisaari in Askainen is one of the most stunning.

Historic Towns

Quite a number of towns in Finland qualify as 'medieval' – though due to the ravages of war and fire few actually look their age. Turku, founded around 1200, is the oldest city in Finland but its oldest buildings date from the 18th century. Porvoo, Rauma, Hamina and Naantali have picturesque old town quarters, and Hanko is the place to see late 19th century Russian villas.

Churches

Finland boasts the largest wooden church in the world, in Kerimäki. The Tampere cathedral is the most noteworthy example of national romantic edifices. The medieval churches of Åland are particularly attractive and easy to visit, as they are along popular bicycle routes.

Outdoor Activities

Finland may not have the rugged mountains of Norway, but it does have some fine ski centres, particularly in Lapland. Better yet, these centres offer hundreds of kilometres of cross-country skiing trails, and some are illuminated for winter cruising. Other winter activities unique to Finland include ice-fishing, dog sledding, reindeer sleigh safaris, snowmobile touring and snowshoeing. Bring your woolies!

In summer, there's superb trekking in northern Finland, and many of the wilderness huts along the trails are well maintained and free of charge. The Lakeland is the place to take an idyllic cruise on an old steamer ferry, or rent canoes and kayaks and explore the riverways on your own. Cycling is best in Åland, where distances are short and the scenery very pretty.

VISA REQUIREMENTS

Most western nationals, including Americans, citizens of European Union (EU) countries, Australians, Canadians, New Zealanders, Malaysians, Singaporeans and most South Americans do not need a visa for stays of up to three months.

Finnish Embassies

Australia
  (☎ 02-6273 3800) 10 Darwin Ave, Yarralumla, Canberra, 2600 ACT

Canada
  (☎ 613-236 2389) 55 Metcalfe St, Suite 850, Ottawa, Ont K1P 6L5

Ireland
  (☎ 01-478 1344) Russell House, St Stephen's Green, Dublin 2

Japan
  (☎ 03-3442 2231) 3-5-39 Minami-Azabu, Minato-ku, Tokyo 106

UK
  (☎ 020-7235 9531) 38 Chesham Place, London SW1X 8HW

USA
  (☎ 202-298 5800) 3301 Massachusetts Ave NW, Washington, DC 20008

TOURIST OFFICES OVERSEAS

Australia
  (☎ 02-9290 1950, fax 9290 1981) Level 4, 81 York St, Sydney, NSW 2000

Canada
  (☎ 800-346 4636) PO Box 246, Station Q, Toronto, Ont M4T 2M1

Japan
  (☎ 03-3501 5207, fax 3580 9205) Imperial Hotel, Room 505, 1-1-1 Uchisaiwai-cho, Chiyoda-ku, Tokyo 100-0011

UK
  (☎ 020-7930 5871, ☎ 7321 0696, @ mek .lon@mek.fi) 3rd floor, 30-35 Pall Mall, London SW1Y 5LP

USA
  (☎ 212-885 9700, fax 885 9710) PO Box 4649, Grand Central Station, New York, NY 10163-4649

POST & COMMUNICATIONS

Stamps can be bought at bus or train stations and R-kioski newsstands as well as at the post office *(posti)*. Letters posted to Australia take less than a week, to North America almost two weeks. There is poste restante at the main post offices in cities.

The vast majority of Finnish pay phones accept plastic phonecards, but a few older public phones accept coins. Phonecards can be purchased at post

---

Itineraries

Two Days
Spend a day in Helsinki, visiting the Kiasma Museum of Contemporary Art and/or the Mannerheim Museum, strolling down Pohjoisesplanadi to the market square and enjoying a boat trip to the island fortress of Suomenlinna. On day two, go to the medieval town of Porvoo (by historic ferry in summer).

One Week
Buy a Helsinki Card and spend two days exploring Helsinki. From there you can head west to Turku, Finland's oldest town, then do a loop of the Lakeland via Tampere, Kuopio, Savonlinna and Lappeenranta, with a stop in Porvoo on the way back to Helsinki. Alternatively, you could go straight up to Lapland (Rovaniemi or Sodankylä) for some Nordic skiing or midnight sun activity, then head back down to explore the lakes.

Two Weeks
With two weeks you can cover the one week route and add a few days in the Åland islands. After Helsinki, travel across to Turku, then take the ferry over to Åland, where you can enjoy cycling, camping and a unique culture more akin to Swedish than Finnish. Returning to the mainland, you can head up to Lapland via Tampere, then down to the lakes of eastern Finland. You'll need more than two weeks to explore these areas in any depth.

FINLAND HIGHLIGHTS & ITINERARIES

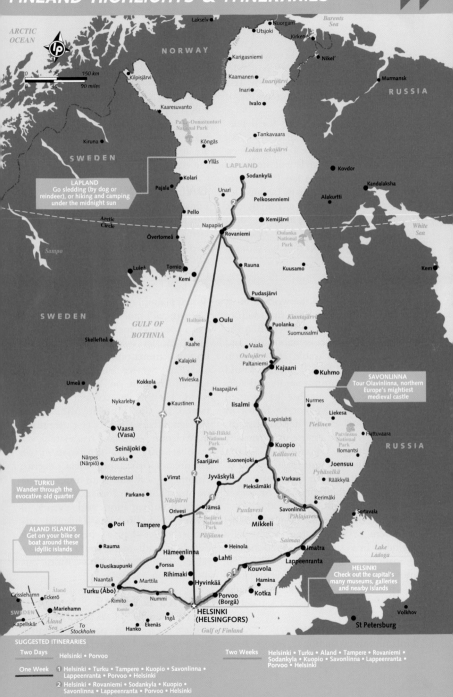

LAPLAND
Go sledding (by dog or reindeer), or hiking and camping under the midnight sun

SAVONLINNA
Tour Olavinlinna, northern Europe's mightiest medieval castle

TURKU
Wander through the evocative old quarter

ALAND ISLANDS
Get on your bike or boat around these idyllic islands

HELSINKI
Check out the capital's many museums, galleries and nearby islands

SUGGESTED ITINERARIES

Two Days — Helsinki • Porvoo

One Week —
1 Helsinki • Turku • Tampere • Kuopio • Savonlinna • Lappeenranta • Porvoo • Helsinki
2 Helsinki • Rovaniemi • Sodankyla • Kuopio • Savonlinna • Lappeenranta • Porvoo • Helsinki

Two Weeks — Helsinki • Turku • Aland • Tampere • Rovaniemi • Sodankyla • Kuopio • Savonlinna • Lappeenranta • Porvoo • Helsinki

offices, shops and R-kioski newsstands. There are several different pay telephone networks in Finland – the Tele company has the widest network of card phones.

Faxes can be sent from local telephone offices (usually adjacent to the post office in big cities). Tourist offices, hotels and some hostels will also send and receive faxes for a fee. Cybercafes are rare in Finland, perhaps because it's possible to use Internet terminals free of charge in most public libraries. Most town libraries have at least one terminal, and bigger ones may have three.

MONEY
Costs

Finland was declared the world's most expensive country in 1990, right before it was hit by recession. Since then the markka has been reasonably low and prices are more bearable. If you're on a tight budget, US$25 a day would cover hostel accommodation and self-catering, but no alcohol or bottled drinks. Then you've got to factor in transportation costs, depending on your itinerary. For a more user-friendly holiday, a budget of around US$50 a day is a minimum, and for a few more luxuries, such as your own bathroom, taxis and a restaurant meal or two a day, you'll need about US$100 a day.

Tipping is generally not necessary anywhere. Service charges are usually included in restaurants' listed prices. Bargaining will get you nowhere in most shops, but if you're after trekking equipment or used bikes, you might get a 10% discount if you ask nicely.

Changing Money

Finland's three national banks have offices all over the country, but they will charge you slightly more for exchanges than private exchange bureaux. Travellers cheques are expensive to change. Many Finnish ATMs will accept foreign cards on the Visa or Plus system, but if they don't take your plastic, rest assured that credit cards are accepted in establishments all over the country.

ONLINE SERVICES

Finland may well have more Web sites per capita than any other country – virtually all of the city tourist offices have them, and so it seems, does every other person, place and thing in Finland.

Lonely Planet has a site at www.lonelyplanet.com/dest/eur/fin.htm. The official Finnish Tourist Board also has a site: www.mek.fi. For the Finnish Youth Hostel Association (SRM), look up www.srmnet.org. Consult the Forest and Park Service site (www.metsa.fi) for information on Finnish national parks. There is an excellent site maintained by the Finnish Ministry of Foreign Affairs at http://virtual.finland.fi. Welcome to Finland has a site (www.publiscan.fi) with information on culture, sports and local events. Another good site with information on travelling in Finland, including regional information and events, is www.travel.fi/fin. The Helsinki city tourist office has a site (www.hel.fi/english) with maps, transport timetables, listings and loads more city information.

BOOKS & FILMS

Matti Klinge's *A Brief History of Finland* is a good paperback introduction. *Blood, Sweat and Bears* by Lasse Lehtinen is a parody of a war novel, dealing with Soviet relations. *Sami – Europe's Forgotten People* by N Valkeapää is a detailed look at Finland's once nomadic people.

There aren't many English translations of Finnish literature, but you should be able to find *The Kalevala* (translated by Keith Bosley). Notable Finnish authors such as Mika Waltari *(The Egyptian* and *The Dark Angel)* and Väinö Linna *(The Unknown Soldier)* are also available in English.

Leningrad Cowboys Go to America is a 1989 Finnish road film. There are several annual film festivals in Finland, the Midnight Sun Festival in Sodankylä being one of the most interesting.

St Petersburg

Beautiful St Petersburg is Russia's most European city. Founded on the banks of the Neva River in 1703 by Peter the Great, the city was built mostly by European architects and was spared the harshness of Stalinist reconstruction and the intimidating character of Moscow.

St Petersburg was renamed Leningrad shortly after the formation of the USSR in 1924, but the original name was reinstated in 1991 following the failed Moscow putsch that led to the final break-up of the Soviet Union. St Petersburg (pop 4.83 million) is Russia's cultural centre, with a long history of writers, artists and performing arts (notably ballet and opera). For art lovers, the Hermitage, one of the world's great art museums, and the Russian Museum are not to be missed.

The stunning Winter Palace dominates the city's historic heart, while the Admiralty and the golden dome of St Isaac's Cathedral add to the architectural excellence. A stroll along Russia's most famous street, 4km-long Nevsky Prospekt, is a good way to get a feel for the city, and an evening spent in its lively bars and clubs offers another perspective. Across the Neva is Petrograd Side, where you'll find the Peter & Paul Fortress, St Petersburg's oldest building, and the stunning Cathedral of Saints Peter & Paul within. Further west, Vasilevsky Island offers some of the best views of the city.

St Petersburg's northerly latitude means freezing winters (and a frozen Neva) and long (almost continuous) summer days. May to August is the most pleasant time to visit.

As with any part of Russia, you need a visa to enter St Petersburg. A tourist visa requires written confirmation of hotel reservations; these can usually be arranged through travel agencies or the HI St Petersburg Hostel.

The currency in St Petersburg is the unstable Russian rouble, although prices are often listed in US dollars (the most accepted foreign currency). Costs in the city are not as low as in the neighbouring Baltic states – you'll need at least US$30 a day if staying in a hostel and eating moderately, more like US$50 to US$60 if you stay in a cheap hotel and enjoy some nightlife.

St Petersburg is connected by air to many European cities and many destinations within Russia. Long-distance trains depart from one of the four major stations to Moscow, Helsinki, south to Belarus and west to the Baltics and beyond. Buses also serve the routes to the Baltics and south and east to Moscow.

For cyber-info on the city and Russia generally, Lonely Planet has a Web site at www.lonely planet.com/dest/eur/rus.htm. A great general starting point for St Petersburg information, including links to the *St Petersburg Times*, is www.spb.ru. Glasnet (www.glas.apc.org) has connections to ecological resources and information from all over the world, religious sights, helpful and educational resources and Russia Cams. The Hermitage has a great site (www.hermitage-museum .com) showing current exhibitions and press releases.

For good up-to-date visa information, try www.russianembassy.org. The Moscow Ministry of Foreign Affairs Web site is at www.mid.ru/eng/bod.htm.

ENTERING & LEAVING

Finnair and SAS have scheduled flights to Helsinki from most major cities in Europe, as well as from New York, San Francisco, Cairo, Bangkok, Singapore, Beijing, Sydney and Tokyo. Twenty-two other international airlines offer regular flights to Helsinki. There are no departure taxes when leaving Finland.

Land crossings into Finland from Sweden and Norway are hassle-free, and are serviced by frequent buses and trains. Land crossings from Russia are a little more problematic, but border crossings are becoming more relaxed all the time. If you stick to the main tourist corridors (eg Helsinki-St Petersburg), you won't have any trouble, but make sure you have a Russian visa before you roll up at the frontier. You can buy a Trans-Siberian Railway ticket in Helsinki for the Chinese border via Moscow. Beware of sharks offering discounted tickets on this service; it's almost certain you'll be ripped off.

Baltic ferries run from Sweden, Estonia and Germany to Helsinki, Turku, Vaasa and Pietarsaari. The ferries are impressive seagoing craft and have been compared to hotels and shopping plazas; they actually make more money from duty-free shops than they do from passenger tickets!

FRANCE

The largest country in Western Europe, France is also the region's most diverse. It stretches from the rolling plains of the north to the jagged ridges of the Pyrenees, and from the rugged coastline of Brittany to the icy crags of the Alps. It's a country of familiar romantic images – of wine and chateaux, the Eiffel Tower and exclusive beach resorts, baguettes and cafes.

With an excellent train network, you can go skiing one day and sunbathing the next. France's cities and towns are especially alluring. In Paris, celebrated for centuries for its stunning architecture and romantic *joie de vivre*, as well as in other cities, you'll see people strolling along grand boulevards, picnicking in parks and watching the world go by from cafe terraces. Although the ubiquity of Levis and Le Big Mac flusters the country's cultural purists, anything from a year in Provence to a weekend in Paris will explain why half the world grows dreamy over stalking the streets of Cyrano or picnicking Manet-style *sur l'herbe*. Geographically France is on the western edge of Europe, but with the unification of Europe, it is at the crossroads politically: between England and Italy, in the middle of Belgium, Germany and Spain. Of course, this is just how the French have always viewed their nation – at the very centre of things.

WHEN TO GO

Weather-wise, France is at its best in spring ('April in Paris', remember?), with the beach resorts beginning to

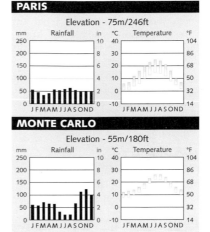

PARIS

Elevation - 75m/246ft

MONTE CARLO

Elevation - 55m/180ft

At a Glance

Full Country Name: French Republic
Area: 551,000 sq km
Population: 58.3 million
Capital City: Paris (pop 13 million)
People: 92% French, 3% North African, 2% German, 1% Breton, 2% other
Language: French (also Flemish, Alsatian, Breton, Basque, Catalan, Provençal and Corsican)
Religion: 90% Roman Catholic, 2% Protestant, 1% Muslim, 1% Jewish, 6% unaffiliated
Government: Democracy
Currency: French franc (FF)
Time Zone: One hour ahead of GMT/UTC; clocks are turned forward one hour on the last Sunday in March and back again on the last Sunday in September
International Telephone Code: 33
Electricity: 220V, 50Hz

pick up in May. Autumn is also pleasant but the days are fairly short and the temperatures get chilly towards the end, even along the Côte d'Azur. Winter is great for snow sports in the Alps, Pyrenees and other mountain areas, though you should avoid the Christmas school holidays. Mid-July to the end of August is when most city dwellers take their annual five weeks vacation to the coasts and mountains, and the half-desolate cities tend to shut down a bit accordingly – except Paris, which will be packed with tourists.

HIGHLIGHTS

France has a wealth of wonderful places to visit – the following list touches on a few of its highlights.

Paris

Perhaps the world's most beautiful city, you'll be familiar with the famous images of Paris long before you get there, but that won't make them any less impressive.

You could spend weeks just strolling around the city streets, admiring the architecture, joining the locals in cafes, and studying the great works in the many fine galleries and museums. Traffic aside, Paris is a great city for walking: you can wander along the Left Bank of the River Seine from Notre Dame to the Eiffel Tower, then cross the river to the Arc de Triomphe and walk down the Champs Élysées to Place de la Concorde and on to the Louvre. Stop in a cafe on the Boulevard Saint Michel before exploring the student-oriented Latin Quarter. As well as these sights, don't miss Sainte Chapelle, Invalides, and the Sacré Cœur at Montmartre.

Museums & Galleries

Every city and town in France has at least one museum, but a good number of the country's most exceptional ones are in Paris. In addition to the rather overwhelming Louvre (*Mona Lisa*, *Venus de Milo* etc – not to be attempted in a single visit), Parisian museums that should not be missed include the Musée d'Orsay (late 19th and early 20th century art), the Pompidou Centre (modern and contemporary art), the Musée Rodin, and the Musée National du Moyen Age (Museum of the Middle Ages) at the Hôtel de Cluny. Other cities known for their museums include Nice, Bordeaux, Strasbourg and Lyon.

The Bayeux Tapestry, in the museum of the same name in Bayeux, northern France, offers a fascinating 'living' history. The Musée de l'École de Nancy, in Nancy, boasts a heady collection of Art Nouveau pieces.

Beaches

The Côte d'Azur – the French Riviera – has some of the best known beaches in the world (St Tropez, Nice, Cannes), made popular by the rich and famous. You'll also find lovely beaches further west on the Mediterranean coast, as well as on Corsica, along the Atlantic coast (such as at Biarritz) and even along the English Channel in Brittany (Dinard). The northern beaches of Normandy are interesting from an historical viewpoint – it was here that the WWII D-Day landings took place.

Historic Towns & Cities

Dijon, with its elegant medieval and Renaissance centre, is a vibrant university town and a good base for exploring the Burgundy region. Although a commercial and industrial centre, Lyon is a striking city with outstanding museums, a dynamic cultural life and superb cuisine – like Paris, it's a great place to stroll around and absorb the ambience.

The ochre-red village of Roussillon in Provence is interesting; the whole village is built from the local reddish stone. The spa resort of Vichy, in the Massif Central, is a great place to slip into the curative waters and feel some of France's faded *belle epoque* charm. Grasse, the perfume-making centre near Cannes, is as fragrant a town as you'll ever visit – you can tour three of the 40 perfumeries that give Grasse its overpowering aroma. Other interesting towns worth visiting include Avignon

Itineraries

Three Days
Spend your time in Paris exploring the major sights and a few of the top museums. You can also spend a day at Versailles visiting the famous palace and gardens, or even take a day trip to Chartres for its magnificent cathedral.

One Week
Spend two or three days in Paris, plus a trip to Versailles, and then visit a nearby area such as the Loire Valley (Tours or Blois), Champagne (Reims or Épernay), Alsace (Route du Vin) or Normandy (Rouen, D-Day beaches, Bayeux).

Two Weeks
With two weeks you can begin to explore some different areas. A possible whirlwind trip giving an overview of the country might include Paris and Versailles, Rouen, Mont Saint Michel, Bayeux, Saint Malo, Bordeaux, the Côte d'Azur (using Nice as a base with visits to Cannes and Monaco), the French Alps (Chamonix, Annecy or Chambéry), Dijon and the Loire Valley or Champagne. This is not really going to allow you time to draw a breath and would be better done over a month, or divided up.

Northern France The main areas to explore here are the northern provinces of Normandy and Brittany, and the wine regions of Burgundy, Alsace, Champagne and the Loire Valley.

After spending a few days in Paris, travel down to Dijon in Burgundy, then head up into Alsace where you can get on the Route du Vin near Colmar and sample some Alsatian wines on the way to Strasbourg. Travel west to the refined city of Nancy in Lorraine, then on to Épernay or Reims in Champagne – the two most important centres of champagne production in France. Reims is also historically important as the site of many French coronations. Crossing into Normandy, you can explore Rouen, Bayeux and Mont Saint Michel, then on to the beaches of Saint Malo or Dinan in Brittany. Make a quick stop in Nantes before heading east into the Loire Valley, where you can finish the trip exploring the chateaux around Blois and Tours, and the wine cellars, such as those around Chinon.

Southern France This route takes in the wine regions of Bordeaux and Languedoc-Roussillon, picturesque Provence, the Côte d'Azur and the French Alps.

From Paris travel via Chartres to Nantes, then down the Atlantic coast to Bordeaux, where you can spend a couple of days exploring the region's wineries. Travel via Toulouse to the Mediterranean coast, visiting Carcassonne and Nîmes and Avignon in Provence. Spend a couple of days on the Côte d'Azur (Nice, Cannes, Monaco) and some time in the Alps (Chamonix, Annency or Chambéry), and finish the circuit with either Lyon or Dijon.

One Month
With a month you could combine the itineraries and try to see a bit of everything, or spend more time in particular regions. Add a few days hiking in the Pyrenees (from Cauterets or Vallée d'Aspe) or in the Alps, or spend some time in more remote areas such as the Basque Country or the island of Corsica.

FRANCE HIGHLIGHTS & ITINERARIES

EPERNAY
Let it all go to your head at Champagne central

DIJON
Get medieval on the sights in this ancient canal town

PARIS
Take in the wonders of the City of Light, and stroll through nearby Versailles

LOIRE VALLEY
Sample superb scenery, magnificent chateaus - oh, and wine too

CHAMONIX
Walk up or slalom down the slopes

THE PYRENEES
Cycle, hike or ski
around this romantic
mountain range

CÔTE D'AZUR
Be among the beautiful
people beaching on the
famed French Riviera

SUGGESTED ITINERARIES

Three Days Paris • Versailles or Chartres

One Week Paris • Versailles • Loire Valley, Champagne,
Alsace (Route du Vin) or Normandy

**Two Weeks to
One Month** 1 Paris • Dijon • Colmar • Strasbourg • Nancy •
Champagne • Normandy • Brittany • Nantes •
Chinon • Tours • Blois

2 Paris • Chartres • Nantes • Bordeaux • Toulouse •
Carcassonne • Nîmes • Avignon • Cannes • Nice •
Monaco • French Alps • Lyon or Dijon

(Provence), Strasbourg (Alsace) and Lille (in far northern France).

Castles & Chateaux

The royal palace at Versailles is the largest and most grandiose of the hundreds of chateaux all over the country. Many of the most impressive, including Chambord, Cheverny, Chenonceau and Azay-le-Rideau, are in the Loire Valley around Blois and Tours. Others in this area are Château de Chaumont and Château Amboise.

The Renaissance-style Château de Sully is in Burgundy, while the Château des Comtes de Foix is an imposing 10th century castle in the Pyrenees.

Churches & Cathedrals

The cathedrals at Chartres, Strasbourg and Rouen are among the most beautiful in France, and of course, Notre Dame and Sacré Cœur in Paris are must-sees. The Basilique Saint Sernin is the largest and most complete Romanesque structure in France, while the magnificent Cathedrale de Sainte-Marie in Auch is a fantastic sight. The abbey at Mont Saint Michel is also impressive.

Wine Regions

French wines are world famous and the names of the regions alone – Champagne, Burgundy, Beaujolais – conjure up images of fine drops. Other well known wine districts are Bordeaux, the Loire Valley, Alsace, Rhône and Languedoc-Roussillon.

For travellers, one of the best places to experience French wines at their source is the Route du Vin (Wine

Monaco

Synonymous with millionaire playboys tethering their yachts just long enough for a quick flutter in the Monte Carlo casino, Monaco is more a stunningly extravagant town than a country.

Most of the people who live here come from somewhere else, drawn by the sun, glamorous lifestyle and – most importantly – tax-free income. Even if your budget doesn't run to a single casino chip, Monaco is still worth a visit for its sheer decadence and spectacular setting. Historically, the principality has been under the rule of the Grimaldi family for most of the period since 1297, with Prince Rainier III in charge since 1949.

Only 1.95 sq km in area and sandwiched between France and the Mediterranean Sea, the two main areas of interest are Monaco Ville (the old city, just south of the port) and Monte Carlo, home of the casino and famous as the scene of the annual Formula One Grand Prix (north of the port).

Monaco Ville, perched up on a 60m-high rocky outcrop, affords great views over the port and Monte Carlo, and contains most of Monaco's major sites. At the Prince's Palace you can visit the state apartments and see the daily changing of the guard, while the outstanding Museum of Oceanography is the best aquarium in France. The cathedral here is unremarkable except for the much-visited grave of Princess Grace (former actress Grace Kelly) who died in 1982.

If you have a decent set of clothes you can wander into Monte Carlo's most famous attraction, the casino. If you want to get into the gaming rooms to watch the high-rollers, however, you must be at least 21 and pay the entry fee of 50FF (about US$8). A good way to while away an hour or two is to sit on the marina sipping a coffee or beer and watching the luxury yachts come and go.

Accommodation in Monaco is expensive, but you don't need to stay here: Nice is a 20 minute train ride away, as are numerous other towns along the Cote d'Azur. There are no border controls and the currency is French.

Route) in Alsace. This 120km route winds its way through picturesque villages such as Molsheim, Obernai and Kayserberg, as well as roadside *caves* (wine cellars) where you can sample the local viticulture. The vine-covered Côte d'Or in Burgundy is another great spot for wine tasting, particularly around Beaune, and in the Loire Valley you can combine visits to wine cellars with visits to the spectacular French chateaux (eg around Chinon).

Hiking & Skiing

France is one of the finest countries in Europe for hiking, with a staggering network of marked walking trails, many of them traversing the Alps and the Pyrenees.

Of the 400-plus ski resorts in France, some of the most favoured areas are Chamonix, Les Trois Vallées (The Three Valleys), Les Arcs and Alpe d'Huez, and around Grenoble.

VISA REQUIREMENTS

Nationals of the European Union (EU), the USA, Canada, New Zealand, Australia and Israel do not require visas to visit France as tourists for up to three months. Except for people from a handful of other European countries, everyone else must have a visa. France is part of the Schengen Agreement.

French Embassies & Consulates

Australia
(☎ 02-6216 0100, fax 6273 3193) 6 Perth Ave, Yarralumla, Canberra, ACT 2600
Consulate: (☎ 03-9820 0944/0921, fax 9820 9363) 492 St Kilda Rd, Level 4, Melbourne, Vic 3004
Consulate: (☎ 02-9262 5779, fax 9283 1210) St Martin's Tower, 20th floor, 31 Market St, Sydney, NSW 2000

Canada
(☎ 613-789 1795, fax 789 0279) 42 Sussex Drive, Ottawa, Ont K1M 2C9
Consulate: (☎ 514-878 4385, fax 878 3981) 1 Place Ville Marie, 26th floor, Montreal, Que H3B 4S3
Consulate: (☎ 416-925 8041, fax 925 3076) 130 Bloor St West, Suite 400, Toronto, Ont M5S 1N5

Ireland
(☎ 01-260 1666, fax 283 0178) 36 Ailesbury Rd, Ballsbridge, Dublin

New Zealand
(☎ 04-472 0200, fax 472 5887) 1-3 Willeston St, Wellington

South Africa
(☎ 021-212 050, fax 261 996) 1009 Main Tower, Cape Town Center, Heerengracht, 8001 Cape Town
(January-June)
(☎ 012-435 564, fax 433 481) 807 George Ave, Arcadia, 0132 Pretoria
(July-December)

UK
(☎ 020-7201 1000, fax 7201 1004) 58 Knightsbridge, London SW1X 7JT
Consulate: (☎ 020-7838 2000, fax 7838 2001) 21 Cromwell Rd, London SW7 2DQ
(for visa information ☎ 020-7838 2051)

USA
(☎ 202-944 6000, fax 944 6166) 4101 Reservoir Rd NW, Washington, DC 20007
Consulate: (☎ 212-606 3688, fax 606 3620) 934 Fifth Ave, New York, NY 10021
Consulate: (☎ 415-397 4330, fax 433 8357) 540 Bush St, San Francisco, CA 94108

TOURIST OFFICES OVERSEAS

Australia
(☎ 02-9231 5244, fax 9221 8682, **@** frencht@ozemail.com.au) 25 Bligh St, 22nd floor, Sydney, NSW 2000

Canada
(☎ 514-288 4264, fax 845 4868, **@** mfrance@mtl.net) 1981 McGill College Ave, Suite 490, Montreal, Que H3A 2W9

Ireland
(☎ 01-703 4046, fax 874 7324) 35 Lower Abbey St, Dublin 1

South Africa
(☎ 011-880 8062, fax 880 7722, ✆ mdfsa@frenchdoor.co.za) Oxford Manor, 1st floor, 196 Oxford Rd, Illovo 2196

UK
(☎ 0891-244 123, fax 020-7493 6594, ✆ piccadilly@mdlf.demon.co.uk) 178 Piccadilly, London W1V 0AL

USA
(☎ 212-838 7800, fax 838 7855, ✆ info@francetourism.com) 444 Madison Ave, 16th floor, New York, NY 10022-6903
(☎ 310-271 6665, fax 276 2835, ✆ fgtola@juno.com) 9454 Wilshire Blvd, Suite 715, Beverly Hills, CA 90212-2967

POST & COMMUNICATIONS

Postal services in France are fast, reliable and expensive. Poste restante mail goes to the town's main post office.

You can dial direct from any phone in France to almost anywhere in the world. Almost all public phones now require phonecards *(télécartes)*, which are sold at post offices, tobacconists' *(tabacs)*, Paris metro ticket counters and supermarket check-out counters.

Virtually all French post offices can send and receive domestic and international faxes, telexes and telegrams. Email can be sent and received at cybercafes all over the country, and a new service set up by La Post provides public Internet access centres at 1000 post offices around France. France Telecom has also been sponsoring 'Internet stations' where you can surf the Internet, send emails and take free beginners' courses on how to use the Net at slightly cheaper access rates than commercial cybercafes.

MONEY
Costs

The land of the US$5 *cafe au lait* is not exactly Europe's cheapest destination, but that doesn't mean you have to break the bank to visit. Devoted scrimpers can get by on around US$40 a day, though it means a whole lot of brie-and-baguettes in the park. If you're camping and cycling around, or spending a lot of time in one region, you could squeak by on a little less. For a more well rounded culinary experience and a comfy bed or two, a minimum of US$80 is in order.

Leaving a *pourboire* (tip) is done at your discretion – restaurants and accommodation places add 10 to 15% to every bill, but most people leave a few coins if the service was satisfactory.

Changing Money

Travellers cheques are almost universally accepted, especially in larger towns and tourist centres. Banks and exchange bureaux give better exchange rates for travellers cheques than for cash; Banque de France offers the best rates in the country. France's ATMs accept all the major international credit and bank cards, and credit cards also get a better exchange rate on purchases.

ONLINE SERVICES

Lonely Planet's France site is at www.lonelyplanet.com/dest/eur/fra.htm. There is an official tourism site (www.francetourism.com) with all manner of information on and about travel in France. Guide Web has a good site (www.guideweb.com), but only for selected regions. Maison de la France has a site at www.maison-de-la-france.fr and the Paris Tourist Office has a site at www.paris-promotion.fr. The Real France site (www.realfrance.com) provides 'inside' information on arts and crafts, nature, leisure, food, restaurants, wine, museums, sights, events, hotels, guesthouses and chateaux). If you're after information about ski resorts, services and snow conditions, try www.skifrance.fr. There is also a 'queer resources directory' (www.france.qrd .org) for gay and lesbian travellers.

BOOKS

The historiography of France is vast. Of the general studies, the best is Alfred Cobban's *A History of Modern France*, a very readable three volume set that covers the period from Louis XIV to 1962. For the dynamics of political history, check out Simon Schama's *Citizens*, an influential and truly monumental work that examines the first few years after the storming of the Bastille in 1789. John Ardagh's *France Today* is an exhaustive review of all aspects of modern-day French society. On women's position in society, see Simone de Beauvoir's *The Second Sex*, a pioneering work that helped inspire the modern feminist movement. A very tasty – indeed, the definitive – region-by-region introduction to French cuisine is Waverly Root's *The Food of France*. First published in 1958, it has recently been reissued in paperback.

Emergent (and readable) voices in French literature include Annie Ernaux and Daniel Pennac (urban crime fiction). France has long attracted writers of the first rank from around the world. These included Ernest Hemingway, who wrote *A Moveable Feast*, a portrayal of bohemian life in Paris between the world wars; and Gertrude Stein, whose *The Autobiography of Alice B Toklas* memorably recounts the author's years in Paris. Henry Miller also set a number of his 'sexy' novels in Paris, including the *Tropic of Cancer* and *Tropic of Capricorn*. A penetrating and poignant look at down-at-heel Paris in the late 1920s is read George Orwell's *Down and Out in Paris and London*. More recently, Peter Mayle's *A Year in Provence* and *Toujours Provence* are bestselling accounts that take a witty, patronising and very English look at the French.

Classic works of travel literature about France include Henry James' *A Little Tour in France* and Laurence Sterne's *A Sentimental Journey*, a digressive and fanciful account of his 1765 coach tour through France and Italy.

FILMS

France's place in the film history books was ensured by those cinematographic pioneers, the Lumière brothers, who invented 'moving pictures' and organised the world's first paying public movie screening in 1895.

Et Dieu Créa la Femme (And God Created Woman; 1956) brought sudden stardom to Brigitte Bardot, the young director Roger Vadim and the little fishing village of St Tropez. Modern French cinema has a reputation for being intellectual, elitist and, frankly, boring. But French films aren't always so pat and serious. Light social comedies like *Trois Hommes et un Couffin* (Three Men and a Cradle; 1985) and *Romuald et Juliette* (1989) by Coline Serreau have been among the biggest hits in France in recent years. Luc Besson achieved success as a director with *Subway* (1985) and *The Big Blue* (1988), then the more commercial *Nikita* (1990) and *Léon* (1995).

Gérard Depardieu, more than any other French actor, has reached worldwide audiences. Among his most powerful roles were with Catherine Deneuve in François Truffaut's *Le Dernier Métro* (1980), *Jean de Florette*

(1986; directed by Claude Berri) and *Cyrano de Bergerac* (1990), directed by Jean-Paul Rappeneau. Philippe Noiret, a veteran of over 100 French films, found international acclaim in 1989 as the Sicilian movie-loving projectionist in *Cinema Paradiso*.

ENTERING & LEAVING

Air France, France's national carrier, and scores of other airlines link Paris with every part of the globe. Other French cities with direct international air links include Bordeaux, Lyon, Marseille, Nice, Strasbourg and Toulouse.

Paris is the country's main bus and rail hub, with services to/from every part of Europe. Buses are slower and less comfortable than trains, but they are cheaper. The completion of the Channel Tunnel in 1994 has meant travel between England and France –

on the silent, ultramodern Eurostar rail service – is now quick and hassle-free. The 'Chunnel' also has high-speed shuttle trains that whisk cars, motorbikes and coaches from England to France.

By sea, the quickest passenger ferries and hovercrafts to England run between Calais and Dover, and Boulogne and Folkestone. There are numerous routes linking Brittany and Normandy with England; Saint Malo is linked by car ferry and hydrofoil with Weymouth, Poole and Portsmouth, while Roscoff has ferry links to Plymouth. Ferries also ply the waters between France and Ireland (Cherbourg-Cork), the Channel Islands, Sardinia (Marseille-Porto Torres), Italy (Corsica-Genoa) and North Africa (Marseille-Algiers, Marseille-Tunis, Sète-Tangier).

GERMANY

Germany still manages to conjure up images of merry stein-waving Bavarians clad in *lederhosen*, fairy-tale castles and medieval villages. Its strong culture shines through, even though this is one of Europe's most modern, progressive and economically successful nations.

Situated in the heart of Europe, Germany has had a greater impact on the continent's history than any other country. From Charlemagne and the Holy Roman Empire to Otto von Bismarck's Reich, two world wars and the fall of the Berlin Wall, no other country has moulded Europe the way Germany has – for better or worse. Germany's reunification in 1990 was the beginning of yet another chapter. Though it's now one country, the cultural, social and economic differences of the formerly separate Germanys will take years to disappear altogether. Nevertheless, the integration of the two is proceeding about as smoothly as might be expected.

Much of Germany's history and culture is easily explored by visitors today, with museums, soaring cathedrals and a heavy emphasis on festivals and culture. Infrastructure is extremely well organised, there is plenty of accommodation and the beer, food and wine are all excellent.

Germany is also a land of great physical beauty, from the Bavarian Alps and the majestic, castle-lined Rhine River to windswept North Sea islands and the enchanting Black Forest.

WHEN TO GO

The German climate is variable, so it's best to be prepared for all types of weather throughout the year, though May to October has the most reliable conditions. This coincides, naturally enough, with the standard tourist season (except for skiing). The shoulder periods at either end of this

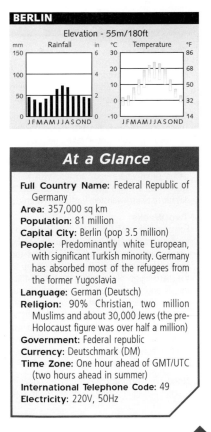

At a Glance

Full Country Name: Federal Republic of Germany
Area: 357,000 sq km
Population: 81 million
Capital City: Berlin (pop 3.5 million)
People: Predominantly white European, with significant Turkish minority. Germany has absorbed most of the refugees from the former Yugoslavia
Language: German (Deutsch)
Religion: 90% Christian, two million Muslims and about 30,000 Jews (the pre-Holocaust figure was over half a million)
Government: Federal republic
Currency: Deutschmark (DM)
Time Zone: One hour ahead of GMT/UTC (two hours ahead in summer)
International Telephone Code: 49
Electricity: 220V, 50Hz

season can bring fewer tourists and surprisingly pleasant weather.

Popular tourist areas such as the Rhine Valley can get pretty crowded in July and August, and getting a bed in Munich around the end of September – for the beginning of Oktoberfest – means booking well in advance.

HIGHLIGHTS
Berlin

Germany's most vibrant and historically interesting city, once-divided Berlin is again the national capital and a hip place to be. The wall came down in 1989 but the differences between modern west Berlin and industrial east Berlin remain evident.

Berlin is Germany's 24 hour 'party' city, and hardly a month goes by without some old power station or underground bunker being turned into a thumping new nightclub. But there are plenty of things to do and see in the daylight hours. Start with a stroll down the Kurfürstendamm, Berlin's major street, lined with shops, cafes and buskers. The bombed tower of the Kaiser

Itineraries

Two Days
If you have to pick one city to visit, make it Berlin. There is more to do in Berlin than any other city in Germany and it's the best place to appreciate Germany's turbulent past.

One Week
Spend three days in Berlin, including a day trip to Potsdam. From there take the train to Munich for a couple of days of Bavarian culture, and visit an Alpine resort like Berchtesgaden (from where you can also visit Kehlstein, Hitler's 'Eagle's Nest'). Also consider a day trip to Neuschwanstein Castle from Munich.

Two Weeks
For a snapshot of Germany, follow the one week itinerary and include an exploration of the vibrant university town of Freiburg and the nearby southern Black Forest. Continue up to the charming city of Heidelberg, with its Gothic-Renaissance castle. From there you can detour to Trier, Germany's oldest town with scatterings of Roman ruins. Travel up the Rhine Valley from Mainz to Cologne, stopping at a few of the wine villages along the way. In Cologne you can marvel at Germany's finest cathedral.

Alternatively, explore in greater depth:

Northern Germany Start with a few days in Berlin including a trip out to Potsdam with its numerous Prussian palaces. Head north to historic Stralsund on the Baltic Sea coast – from here you can easily explore the islands of Rügen and Hiddensee. Continue west via Rostock to Warnemünde, one of eastern Germany's most popular beach resorts and a pleasant village. Stop at the medieval city of Lübeck – once capital of the Hanseatic League of traders – on the way to the pulsating port of Hamburg. Heavily bombed in WWII, Hamburg is a modern city with a stylish shopping area and a world-famous red light district, the Reeperbahn.

Bremen is another harbour city worth visiting, and from here you can follow the Fairy-Tale Road for a couple of days towards Hanover and Göttingen in the Harz Mountains. Highlights of this road include Hamelin, home of the Pied Piper legend, and Bodenwerder, birthplace of legendary Baron von Münchhausen. Alternatively, visit the Frisian Islands in the North Sea.

Central Germany From Berlin travel south to Dresden, a nonindustrial city that was heavily fire-bombed in WWII. Its position on the Elbe River (where you can take a paddle steamer ride) makes it a pleasant diversion, and there are a number of interesting towns and palaces in the vicinity. If you're interested

Wilhelm Memorial Church stands starkly among the malls at the eastern end. Check out Checkpoint Charlie – or at least the museum that tells the story – as well as the Brandenburg Gate and Charlottenburg Palace. Other areas to explore are Museumsinsel (an island with five museums), Unter den Linden, the Scheunenviertel neighbourhood and the huge city park, Tiergarten.

Historic Towns

Time stands still in many parts of Germany. Some of the best towns in which to relive the 'days of yore' include Rothenburg ob der Tauber, Goslar and Regensburg. Meissen and Quedlinburg have a story-book atmosphere, Weimar holds a special place in German culture, and Bamberg and Lübeck are two of Europe's true gems. The old district *(Altstadt)* remains the heart and highlight of many large cities.

Castles

With castles of all periods and styles, Germany is a great place to indulge in

Itineraries

in the life of Protestant reformist Martin Luther, pay a visit to Wittenberg where he did most of his work in the 16th century. Weimar is worth a visit for its refined architecture and proximity to the former Buchenwald concentration camp. From here you can visit the wonderful towns of Quedlinburg, Wernigerode and, on the edge of the Harz Mountains, medieval Goslar. Alternatively, explore the Thuringian Forest from Erfurt and Eisenach (birthplace of Bach).

Continuing west, you can drop down to the banking and commerce centre of Frankfurt, then across to Mainz for a tour up the Rhine Valley to Cologne (by boat, bus or car). The stretch from Mainz to Koblenz is the most picturesque section of the Rhine River.

Southern Germany Start with a few days in Munich, home of the famous Oktoberfest and capital of Bavaria. At any time of year the Hofbrauhaus beer hall will be pumping and cosmopolitan Munich has plenty to offer in the way of museums and architecture. Also pay a visit to the well preserved remains of the Dachau concentration camp. From Munich, head into the Bavarian Alps. Berchtesgaden is one of the finest Alpine resorts and is a base for visiting Kehlstein. Other resorts further west include Garmisch-Partenkirchen and Mittenwald. Visit Füssen, near the Austrian border, for easy access to the famous Neuschwanstein and Hohenschwangau castles. This is also the start of the Romantic Road, which passes through some of Germany's most beautiful towns on its way to Würzburg. Augsberg is another good base for exploring this route.

You may want to pass through Stuttgart on the way to Freiburg and the Black Forest. Head back up to Heidelberg and across to Trier or up to the Rhine Valley.

One Month

If you have a month in Germany, combine parts of the previous itineraries or spend more time in areas of interest, by exploring Berlin in depth, hiking in the Harz Mountains or sampling wines along the Rhine and Moselle rivers. Another alternative is to explore the Bavarian Forest north-east of Munich. Zweisel is the best base.

Two Months

With two months you could cover most of Germany, or cover some areas in greater depth. Additional places worth considering include: a comprehensive tour of the Romantic Road and the German Wine Road, Münster, the Ahr Valley, Mainz, Worms, Speyer, Bamberg, the Moselle Valley and the Thuringian Forest.

GERMANY HIGHLIGHTS & ITINERARIES

BALTIC SEA

POLAND

Szczecin (Stettin)

Pasewalk

Frankfurt an der Oder

Lübben

Cottbus

Bautzen

Görlitz

Dresden

BERLIN

Potsdam

Lutherstadt Wittenberg

Leipzig

Halle

Dessau

Magdeburg

SAXONY

BRANDENBURG

Brandenburg

Rheinsberg

Neustrelitz

Neubrandenburg

MECKLENBURG–WESTERN POMERANIA

Greifswald

Binz

Sassnitz

Rügen Island

Hiddensee Island

Stralsund

Barth

Rostock

Warnemünde

Wismar

Schwerin

Poel Island

Puttgarden

Kiel

Flensburg

Husum

Westerland

North Frisian Islands

East Frisian Islands

NORTH SEA

Norddeich

Emden

Groningen

NETHERLANDS

Emmerich

Mönchengladbach

Düsseldorf

Solingen

Wuppertal

Hagen

Bochum

Essen

Duisburg

Oberhausen

Gelsenkirchen

Recklinghausen

Hamm

Dortmund

NORTH RHINE-WESTPHALIA

Münster

Osnabrück

Rheine

Bad Bentheim

Bielefeld

Lake Steinhude

Oldenburg

BREMEN

Bremen

Bremerhaven

Wilhelmshaven

Cuxhaven

Weser River

Aller River

LOWER SAXONY

Hamelin

Hildesheim

Hanover

Braunschweig

Wolfsburg

Celle

Bordenwerder

Goslar

Bad Harzburg

Wernigerode

Quedlinburg

Harz National Park

THURINGIA

Göttingen

Kassel

SAXONY-ANHALT

Salzwedel

Stendal

Lüneburg

HAMBURG

Hamburg

Lübeck

Neumünster

SCHLESWIG-HOLSTEIN

DENMARK

Elbe River

Oder River

Ems River

Stettiner Haff

SAXONY

Leine River

Elbe River

100 km

60 miles

50

30

0

0

LÜBECK
Pay a visit to the Queen of the medieval Baltic cities

BERLIN
Discover what really happened to all those Cold War bunkers

HARZ MOUNTAINS
Take a break from Bad Hangover in a relaxing spa town

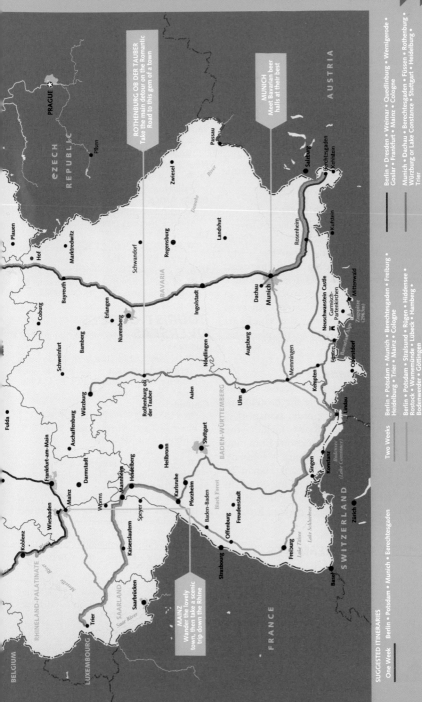

ROTHENBURG OB DER TAUBER
Take the main detour on the Romantic Road to this gem of a town

MUNICH
Meet Bavarian beer halls at their best

MAINZ
Wander the lovely town, then take a scenic trip down the Rhine

PRAGUE ★

CZECH REPUBLIC

Plzeň

BELGIUM

LUXEMBOURG

RHINELAND-PALATINATE

Koblenz

Trier

Saarbrücken

SAARLAND

Kaiserslautern

FRANCE

Strasbourg

Basel

SWITZERLAND

Zürich

Fulda

Frankfurt-am-Main

Wiesbaden

Mainz

Darmstadt

Worms

Speyer

Mannheim

Heidelberg

Karlsruhe

Baden-Baden

Offenburg

Freudenstadt

Black Forest

Pforzheim

Freiburg

Lake Schluchsee

Lake Titisee

Singen

Konstanz
(Lake Constance)

Bodensee
(Lake Constance)

Aschaffenburg

Würzburg

Schweinfurt

Bamberg

Coburg

Bayreuth

Erlangen

Nuremberg

Rothenburg ob
der Tauber

Aalen

BADEN-WÜRTTEMBERG

Heilbronn

Stuttgart

Ulm

Nördlingen

Augsburg

Memmingen

Kempten

Lindau

Oberstdorf

Füssen

Neuschwanstein Castle

Garmisch-
Partenkirchen

Zugspitze
(2964m)

Bavarian Alps

Mittenwald

Hof

Plauen

Marktredwitz

Schwandorf

Zwiesel

Regensburg

Danube River

Landshut

Ingolstadt

BAVARIA

Dachau

Munich

Rosenheim

Kufstein

Salzburg

Berchtesgaden

Kehlstein

AUSTRIA

Passau

Danube River

SUGGESTED ITINERARIES

One Week — Berlin • Potsdam • Munich • Berechtesgaden

Two Weeks — Berlin • Potsdam • Munich • Berechtesgaden • Freiburg • Heidelberg • Trier • Mainz • Cologne

Berlin • Potsdam • Stralsund • Rügen • Hiddensee • Rostock • Warnemünde • Lübeck • Hamberg • Bodenwerder • Göttingen

Berlin • Dresden • Weimar • Quedlinburg • Wernigerode • Goslar • Frankfurt • Mainz • Cologne

Munich • Dachau • Berechtesgaden • Füssen • Rothenburg • Würzburg or Lake Constance • Stuttgart • Heidelburg • Trier

fairy-tale fantasies. If you're into castles you won't be disappointed. Make sure you pay a visit to Heidelberg, Neuschwanstein Castle (that's the Disney fantasy), Burg Rheinfels on the Rhine River, Burg Eltz on the Moselle, medieval Wartburg Castle in Eisenach, Renaissance Wittenberg Castle, baroque Schloss Moritzburg near Dresden and Romantic Wernigerode Castle.

Museums & Galleries

Germany is a true museum-lover's dream. Munich has the huge Deutsches Museum, and Frankfurt's Museumsufer (Museum Embankment) has enough museums for any addict. The Dahlem Museum complex in Berlin and the New Masters Gallery in Dresden are among the chief art museums. Stuttgart is the place for motor museums.

Theme Roads

Germany has several scenic theme routes. Car is generally the best way to explore them, but public transport is available. Theme roads include the very touristy but picturesque Romantic Road in Bavaria (Würzburg to Füssen), the Fairy-Tale Road from Hanau to Bremen, the German Wine Road in the Rhineland-Palatinate, the Black Forest Road and the Vineyard Road in Saxony-Anhalt.

VISA REQUIREMENTS

European Union (EU) citizens can enter on an official identity card. Americans, Australians, Canadians, New Zealanders and Japanese need only a valid passport for stays of up to 90 days. Germany is part of the Schengen Agreement.

German Embassies

Australia
(☎ 02-6270 1911) 119 Empire Circuit, Yarralumla, Canberra, ACT 2600

Canada
(☎ 613-232 1101) 1 Waverley St, Ottawa, Ont K2P 0T8

Japan
(☎ 03-3473 0151) 5-10-4 Minami-Azabu, Minato-ku, Tokyo 106

New Zealand
(☎ 04-473 6063) 90-92 Hobson St, Wellington

South Africa
(☎ 012-344 3854) 180 Blackwood St, Arcadia, Pretoria 0083

UK
(☎ 020-7824 1300) 23 Belgrave Square, London SW1X 8PZ

USA
(☎ 202-298 8140) 4645 Reservoir Rd NW, Washington, DC 20007-1998

TOURIST OFFICES OVERSEAS

Australia
(☎ 02-9267 8148, fax 9267 9035) c/o German-Australian Chamber of Industry & Commerce, PO Box A980, Sydney South, NSW 2000

Canada
(☎ 416-968 1570, fax 968 1986) 175 Bloor St East, North Tower, Suite 604, Toronto, Ont M4W 3R8

Japan
(☎ 03-3586 5046, fax 3586 5079) 7-5-56 Akasaka, Minato-ku, Tokyo 107

South Africa
(☎ 011-643 1615, fax 484 2750) c/o Lufthansa German Airlines, 22 Girton Rd, Parktown, Johannesburg 2000

UK
(☎ 020-7495 0081, fax 7495 6129) Nightingale House, 65 Curzon St, London W1Y 7PE

USA
(☎ 212-661 7200, fax 661 7174) Chanin Building, 122 East 42nd St, 52nd floor, New York, NY 10168-0072
(☎ 312-644 0723, fax 644 0724) 401 North Michigan Ave, Suite 2525, Chicago, IL 60611

(☎ 310-575 9799, fax 575 1565) 11766 Wilshire Blvd, Suite 750, Los Angeles, CA 90025

POST & COMMUNICATIONS

You'll often find main post offices in Germany located at or near the main train station. Letters sent to destinations within Europe or to North America take four to six days and to Australasia five to seven days. Mail can be sent poste restante to the main post office in most cities, but they hold mail for only two weeks.

Making phone calls in Germany is simple, but rates are extraordinarily high thanks to the monopoly still enjoyed by Deutsche Telecom. Most public phones in Germany accept only phonecards nowadays. Cards are sold at post offices and occasionally at tourist offices, news kiosks and public transport offices.

Most of the main post offices have handy public fax-phones that operate with a phonecard. You can keep in touch via email at the many Internet cafes that have sprung up in Germany – there are dozens in cities like Berlin.

MONEY
Costs

With the monetary restructuring caused by reunification now easing, inflation has fallen and the Deutschmark is relatively stable against most other European currencies. Prices have almost reached western levels in the cities of eastern Germany, but food and accommodation are generally affordable by Western European standards.

Cheap travel in Germany is difficult because long-distance public transport is expensive and budget accommodation is lacking, especially in the east.

If you've got a rail pass and restrict yourself to cheap takeaways and self-catering, it's possible to get by on less than US$35 a day. If you want to eat at restaurants most days, travel freely by public transport, occasionally stay in a hotel and have a few beers, count on US$60 to US$80 a day.

Tipping is not widespread in Germany. Service charge is included in most restaurants, but it's normal to round up the bill. Taxi drivers expect a small tip – 10% is considered generous.

Changing Money

The easiest places to change cash in Germany are banks or foreign-exchange counters at airports and train stations, particularly those of the Reisebank. Travellers cheques are widely used and accepted in Germany, especially if issued in Deutschmarks.

Post offices often have money-changing facilities, and rates for cash – but not for travellers cheques – tend to be better than at banks. Credit cards are not always accepted outside major cities in Germany, but are handy in emergencies. Hotels and restaurants often accept MasterCard, Visa and American Express. ATMs are widespread.

ONLINE SERVICES

There's a bewildering amount of information on all aspects of Germany (culture, institutions etc) on the Internet. Most towns have their own Web site. Most of the sites listed here are in English and provide useful links.

Lonely Planet has a site at www .lonelyplanet.com/dest/eur/ger.htm. There is a site run by the German Information Center in New York and the German Embassy in Washington (www.germany-info.org) that is packed with useful general information and links to just about everything, be it language or exchange programs, German media, the postal-code directory, political foundations, business, law and, of course, travel. For a great site with information about the country, language, cities and even such practical matters as rail passes, try www.webfoot.com/travel/guides/germany/germany.html. For English news from *Deutsche Welle*, try www.dwelle.de/english. For German and international phone numbers online (in German) try www.dino-online.de/seiten/go01t.htm. There are a number of German-language search engines: www.web.de, www.yahoo.de, www.dino-online.de. The nonprofit Goethe Institut language and cultural centres have a site (www.goethe.de), with information on German-language courses in Germany and around the world. An online version of Munich's street magazine is at www.munichfound.com.

BOOKS

A Concise History of Germany by Mary Fulbrook is an accessible introduction to the country's complex past. For more cultural detail and insights into the German character, dip into Gordon Craig's *The Germans*. The landmark history of Hitler's reign is William Shirer's *The Rise and Fall of the Third Reich*.

For a treatment of the effects of Nazism on the postwar German psyche, pick up *The Tin Drum* by 1999 Nobel Prize winner Günter Grass. Other German authors worth checking out are Heinrich Böll (another Nobel Prize winner) and the playful post-modernist Walter Abish. The most popular author currently writing in German is probably Patrick Süskind.

His 1985 novel *Perfume* is the extraordinary tale of a psychotic 18th century perfume maker. Mark Twain's *A Tramp Abroad* is recommended for his comical observations of German life. And if you've never read Johann Wolfgang von Goethe's *Faust*, make your visit to Germany the excuse to read it!

FILMS

Fritz Lang's *Metropolis* (1926) stands out as an ambitious cinema classic. It depicts the revolt of a proletarian class that lives underground. The Marlene Dietrich classic *Der blaue Engel* (The Blue Angel; 1930), directed by Joseph von Sternberg, tells the story of a pedantic professor who is hopelessly infatuated with a sexy Kabarett singer, played by Dietrich.

Bernhard Wicki's *Die Brücke* (The Bridge; 1959) is an exceptional and highly recommended film about a group of young boys who faithfully try to defend an insignificant bridge against advancing Americans in the last days of the war.

Der geteilte Himmel (Divided Heaven) is a 1964 adaptation by Konrad Wolf of a novel by the East German writer Christa Wolf. *Nackt unter Wölfen* (Naked Among Wolves; 1963), directed by Frank Beyer, has a concentration-camp plot. When a child is smuggled into Buchenwald it presents moral dilemmas for other inmates by endangering a resistance movement.

Wim Wenders won a Golden Palm at Cannes for *Paris, Texas* (1984) and followed up with *Der Himmel über Berlin* (English title: Wings of Desire; 1987), starring Peter Falk, based on two angels who move through divided Berlin. Detlev Buck's 1993 *Wir können*

auch anders (English title: No More Mr Nice Guy) is arguably the best film to emerge since reunification. It is a comic road movie about two innocent brothers from the backwoods of Schleswig-Holstein who set off for the wilds of eastern Germany to claim an inheritance.

ENTERING & LEAVING

The main arrival/departure points for flights in Germany are Frankfurt, Munich and Berlin. Frankfurt is Europe's busiest airport after Heathrow. An airport departure tax of around US$5 is included in ticket prices. If you're already in Europe, it's generally cheaper to get to and from Germany by bus or train. Train travel is more expensive, more comfortable, but less flexible than catching a bus. Germany is served by an excellent highway system connected to the rest of Western Europe. Roads from Eastern Europe are being upgraded but some border crossings are a little slow, especially from Poland.

Ferries run from Germany's northern coast (Hamburg, Kiel, Sassnitz and Travemünde) to Scandinavia, the UK and St Petersburg.

GREECE

Greece is a mecca for sun and sea worshippers but it also oozes classical history. To travel through Greece is to journey through Europe's greatest ages from the Mycenaean and Minoan to the classical, Hellenistic and Byzantine. The country's enduring attraction is its archaeological sites: the Acropolis in Athens needs no introduction, but you cannot wander far in Greece without stumbling across a broken column, a crumbling bastion or a tiny Byzantine church.

And where else in Europe can you spend the summer months lazily island-hopping from one dazzling whitewashed village to the next? Greek culture is a unique blend of east and west, inherited from the long period of Ottoman rule and apparent in its food, music and traditions. The mountainous countryside is a walker's paradise crisscrossed by age-old donkey tracks leading to stunning vistas.

The magnetism of Greece is also due to less tangible attributes – the dazzling clarity of the light, the floral aromas that permeate the air, the spirit of place. And then again, many visitors come to Greece simply to get away from it all and relax in one of Europe's friendliest and safest countries.

WHEN TO GO

Spring and autumn are the best times to visit Greece. Winter is pretty much a dead loss outside the major cities, as most of the tourist infrastructure goes into hibernation from the end of November to the beginning of April. However, there are initiatives to extend services, so this may slowly change. Conditions are perfect between Easter and mid-June, when the weather is pleasantly warm in most places but not too hot, beaches and ancient sites are relatively uncrowded, public transport operates on close to full schedules and accommodation is cheaper and easier to find than in the mid-June to end of August high

At a Glance

Full Country Name: Hellenic Republic
Area: 131,944 sq km
Population: 10.66 million
Capital City: Athens (pop approx 3.1 million)
People: 98% Greek with minorities of Turks, Slavic-Macedonians and Albanians
Language: Greek
Religion: 97% Greek Orthodox
Government: Multiparty democracy
Currency: Greek drachma (dr)
Time Zone: Two hours ahead of GMT/UTC; three hours ahead during daylight savings from the last Sunday in March to the last Sunday in September
International Telephone Code: 30
Electricity: 220V, 50Hz

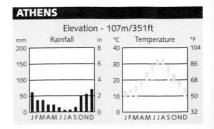

ATHENS
Elevation - 107m/351ft
Rainfall — Temperature

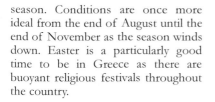

season. Conditions are once more ideal from the end of August until the end of November as the season winds down. Easter is a particularly good time to be in Greece as there are buoyant religious festivals throughout the country.

HIGHLIGHTS

Greece boasts many highlights, but for most visitors they can be divided into three categories: history, islands and hiking.

Ancient Sites & Monuments

Greece is full of them, but some are more famous and imposing than others. The Acropolis in Athens is at the top of most people's must-see list. Many people find Athens itself to be a traffic-clogged, polluted and unappealing city, but wandering up to the Parthenon is still an awesome experience. The Acropolis is visible from almost everywhere in the city. Also in Athens is the Ancient Agora (marketplace) where Socrates spent a fair bit of time. Delphi, in Central Greece, is a stunning site and includes the Sanctuary of Apollo.

In the Peloponnese, Olympia (birthplace of the Olympic Games) is a highlight, with its immense Temple of Zeus. Other ancient sites here include Mycenae, Epidaurus and Mystras. Thessaloniki, Greece's second largest city, has some magnificent Byzantine churches and a scattering of Roman ruins. Many of Greece's islands are also repositories of historic monuments and civilisations. Particularly worth a visit are the archaeological sites on ancient Delos and Santorini, and the many Minoan sites on Crete (Europe's earliest advanced civilisation).

Islands

Where do you start? There are countless islands in the Ionian, Aegean and Mediterranean seas and plenty of ferries plying between them in summer. For many travellers the main attractions are beaches and partying, for others it's the archaeological sites and traditional villages, while some are looking for complete solitude. The following is a rundown of the main island groups:

Cyclades Easily the most popular islands with backpackers and young travellers, a handful of these are the archetypal Greek islands of sun, sand and all-night raging. Ios is the real party island with little to do except dance on the tables all night and lie on the beach all day (heaven!). Paros is a little more refined but still good fun, and it has some interesting sights. Mykonos is classier again – the most sophisticated and expensive of the 'resort' islands. Santorini is the most interesting of this group. Partially formed when a volcano exploded and sank into the sea, it's a good mix of stunning coastline, archaeological sites and nightlife. Naxos is a lush island where you can escape the hordes, and uninhabited Delos is the archaeological jewel. There are other, less visited islands in the Cyclades such as Anafi and Milos.

Dodecanese Strung along the south-western coast of Turkey, these islands are among the furthest from mainland Greece. Rhodes, the largest and most famous of the Dodecanese, has a mighty fortified old town, a fascinating history and plenty of water sports. Kos is the next most popular island with the package tourists, boasting plenty of beaches and bars. Patmos also gets busy, while Kastellorizo is a good place to sample traditional Greek island life. Volcanic Nisyros offers some stunning moonscapes, while Tilos is quiet but has some excellent beaches.

North-Eastern Aegean Less visited than the Cyclades and Dodecanese, these islands are also much closer to Turkey than mainland Greece, and two of them – Samos and Chios – are major stepping stones between the two countries. Samos, reputedly the birthplace of Pythagoras, is an important centre of Hellenic culture and an enjoyable island to explore. Lesvos was once the home of Sappho, one of the great poets of ancient Greece, and is now visited by many lesbians paying homage to her. Parts of Samothraki remain untouched and this is a walker's paradise. It also has ancient sites such as the Sanctuary of the Great Gods.

Ionian Corfu is undoubtedly the most well known of this group and is a popular stopover on the ferry ride between Italy and Greece. You can explore Old Corfu town and there are some good beaches around Paleokastritsa and Agios Gordios. Zakynthos is a beautiful island, unfortunately

Itineraries

Coming up with an itinerary for Greece is difficult. Some travellers want to concentrate on island-hopping, others prefer to explore the mainland. Remember that when visiting the islands you can be at the mercy of ferry schedules, so plan ahead, book during busy times and allow extra contingency time.

Two Days
Visit Athens, exploring the Acropolis and taking a walking tour of the Plaka district, the central city area below the Acropolis. Also visit the National Archaeological Museum. In the evening visit a *rembetika* (a kind of blues) club and dine out beneath the Acropolis. It might be possible to include a day trip to the ancient site of Delphi (three hours from Athens).

One Week
With a week you can spend two or three days in Athens visiting the ancient sites and museums, then four days touring the Peloponnese (Corinth, Mycenae, Olympia and Sparta). Or, spend those four days in the Cyclades – choose between Ios, Paros or Mykonos for partying, and Santorini or Naxos for exploration.

Two Weeks
With two weeks you can just begin to explore, combining some mainland travel with a small amount of island-hopping. Spend two or three days in Athens, and visit Delphi on the way to the Epiros region in Northern Greece. Here you should not miss the Zagoria area and Vikos Gorge, particularly the village Monodendri. Spend the rest of your time in the Peloponnese or Cyclades islands as for the one week itinerary, allowing two days for travel.

Alternatively, split your travels:

Mainland Spend two or three days in Athens, then cross to Corinth in the Peloponnese. Visit Nafplio and use it as a base to visit the ancient sites of Epidaurus and Mycenae. Head south to Sparta and visit the ruins of Mystras from there, then travel across the Taÿgetos Mountains to Kalamata. Make your way up the west coast to ancient Olympia; visit the site early in the morning and continue north around the coast through Patras to Diakofto where you can ride the rack-and-pinion railway up to Kalavryta.

You can then cross by ferry to Northern Greece and travel up to Ioannina. Continue north to the Zagoria region and Vikos Gorge.

more sullied than most by package tourism. Kefallonia is the largest of the Ionian islands and boasts a mountain range and colourful wild flowers. Lefkada is also worth a visit for its traditional villages and people.

Crete The largest of all the Greek islands, Crete also receives the most tourists. Fertile, blessed with a fine climate and home to ancient sites of the Minoan civilisation, Crete shouldn't be missed. You can escape the summer crowds by sticking to the west coast, exploring the mountainous interior or staying in the villages of the Lassithi Plateau.

Hiking

There are some fine opportunities for hiking in Greece, particularly on the mainland. Much of the terrain is mountainous and ideal for serious trekking, while the islands have many less demanding trails that link villages and bays. The region of Zagoria and the dramatic Vikos Gorge are among the best places for hiking. The village of Monodendri is the starting point for walks into the gorge. The massive rock columns of Meteora, topped by 14th century monasteries, are best explored on foot. Kardamyli, a tiny village in the Peloponnese, has some excellent hiking around the Vyros Gorge and Taÿgetos

Itineraries

You could also cross to Mt Olympus or make your way back down to Athens, stopping at Meteora and Delphi.

Islands If you're coming from Italy, spend a couple of days on Corfu; otherwise, this itinerary starts from the mainland port of Piraeus.

Start with a couple of days exploring Santorini, then party on Ios and/or Paros and Mykonos (depending on your tastes). Sail south to Crete for a few days of hiking, water sports and surveying the ancient sites. Continue east to Rhodes, where you can wander the medieval city, then base yourself in Kos and take day trips to Nisyros and Tilos. From here you can either make the long ferry ride back to Athens, or the very short hop to Bodrum in Turkey.

One Month

With a month in Greece you can combine the mainland and island itineraries, or explore each area in more depth. On the mainland, for instance, you could spend some time on the Peloponnese, including some trekking around Kardamyli. Also allow at least four days in Zagoria, with some time spent hiking, and continue up to Kastoria and Thessaloniki in the north.

The possibilities for island-hopping are endless and a month is the minimum time required for a decent look around – combined with a reasonable amount of lazing on beaches, of course. Spend more time in the Cyclades, including Naxos and a day trip to Delos. Spend up to a week on Crete and a week in the Dodecanese, including Rhodes, Kos, Nisyros, Tilos and (if solitude appeals) Kastellorizo. Continue on to the North-Eastern Aegean islands of Samos, Chios, Lesvos and maybe Samothraki. Other options are the Saronic Gulf islands close to Athens, and the Sporades further north. You'll be hard pressed to cover this lot in a month, though!

Two Months

With two months you've got a good chance of combining some in-depth mainland travel with island-hopping. You may be able to include the Ionian islands in your itinerary, especially if you come across from Italy. Also spend a bit longer in and around Athens to get a better feel for the capital. Try not to make these two months July and August, or you'll have a complete nightmare of a time getting around and finding accommodation, as it's uncomfortably hot and crowded.

GREECE HIGHLIGHTS & ITINERARIES

ZAGORIA
Hike past fairy-tale stone villages to trek the Vikos Gorge

OLYMPIA
Before the Olympics became a circus, there was the Temple of Zeus

CRETE
Hang out in Hania's harbour cafes or go Minotaur-spotting around Knossos

SUGGESTED ITINERARIES

Two Days — Athens • Delphi

One Week
1 Athens • Corinth • Mycenae • Olympia • Sparta
2 Athens • Ios, Paros, Mykonos, Santorini or Naxos

BULGARIA
Smolyan
▲ Mt Falakro (2111m)
Drama
Xanthi
Kavala
Komotini
THRACE
Alexandroupolis
Edirne
Didymotiho
TURKEY
BLACK SEA
Istanbul
Izmit

THRACIAN SEA
Thasos
Samothraki
Gökçeada
Gallipoli
Bandırma
Bursa
SEA OF MARMARA

Karyes
Mt Athos ▲ (2033m)
Athos Peninsula
Myrina
Limnos
NORTH-EASTERN AEGEAN ISLANDS
Çanakkale
Balıkesir

DELPHI
ee the awe-inspiring
etting for the mother
of all fortunetellers

SPORADES
Agios Efstratios
Piperi
Kyra Panagia
Alonnisos
Skantzoura
Skyros
Lesvos
Ayvalık
Mytilini
Uşak

Kymi
Psara
Inousses
Manisa
Izmir

EVIA
AEGEAN SEA
Chios
Chios
Çeşme

ATHENS
See the glory of ancient
Greece in the Acropolis and
its crowning Parthenon

Nea Styra
Karystos

DELOS
Check out the
remarkable remains of
Apollo's home town

Kuşadası
Aydın
Denizli

Gavrio
Kea
Andros
Gyaros
Tinos
Ikaria
Samos
Agathonisi
Arki
Farmako
Milas
TURKEY

Syros
Kythnos
Renia
Delos
Mykonos
Fourni Islands
Lipsi
Patmos

Serifos
Paros
Naxos
Donoussa
Leros
Kalymnos
Bodrum

Sifnos
Antiparos
Naxos
Amorgos
Kos
Kos
Datça
Marmaris

Kimolos
Iraklia
Sikinos
Ios
Astypalea
Nisyros
Symi
Rhodes

Milos
Folegandros
Santorini (Thira)
Anafi
Sirna
Tilos
Alimia
Rhodes
Kastellorizo

CYCLADES
Thirasia
Lindos
DODECANESE
Katavia
Saria

SEA OF CRETE
Karpathos
Kassos
Pigadia

Akrotiri Peninsula
Hania
CRETE
Rethymno
Mt Ida ▲ (2456m)
Iraklio
Agios Nikolaos
Sitia

Hora Sfakion
Matala
Ierapetra
Gavdos

Mountains. For more serious walkers, the ascent of Mt Olympus (abode of the gods) takes two days, with accommodation available at refuges.

Of the islands, the best hiking can be found on Crete, but Samothraki, Lesvos, Samos and Naxos also have rewarding walks.

VISA REQUIREMENTS

Nationals of Australia, Canada, European Union (EU) countries, Israel, New Zealand and the USA are allowed to stay in Greece for up to three months without a visa. South Africans require a Schengen visa.

Greek Embassies

Australia
(☎ 02 6273 3011) 9 Turrana St, Yarralumla, Canberra, ACT 2600

Canada
(☎ 613-238 6271) 76-80 Maclaren St, Ottawa, Ont K2P OK6

Ireland
(☎ 01-767 254/255) 1 Upper Pembroke St, Dublin 2

Japan
(☎ 03-340 0871/0872) 16-30-3 Nishi Azabu, Minato-ku, Tokyo 106

New Zealand
(☎ 04-473 7775) 5-7 Willeston St, Wellington

South Africa
(☎ 021-24 8161) Reserve Bank Bldg, St George's Rd, Cape Town

UK
(☎ 020-7229 3850) 1A Holland Park, London W11 3TP

USA
(☎ 202-667 3169) 2221 Massachusetts Ave NW, Washington, DC 20008

TOURIST OFFICES OVERSEAS

Australia
(☎ 02-9241 1663) 51 Pitt St, Sydney, NSW 2000

Canada
(☎ 416-968 2220) 1300 Bay St, Toronto, Ont MSR 3K8
(☎ 514-871 1535) 1233 Rue de la Montagne, Suite 101, Montreal, Que H3G 1Z2

Japan
(☎ 03-3505 5911) Fukuda Bldg West, 5th floor, 2-11-3 Akasaka, Minato-ku, Tokyo 107

UK
(☎ 020-7499 9758) 4 Conduit St, London W1R ODJ

USA
(☎ 212-421 5777) Olympic Tower, 645 5th Ave, New York, NY 10022
(☎ 312-782 1084) 168 North Michigan Ave, Suite 600, Chicago, IL 60601
(☎ 213-626 6696) 611 West 6th St, Suite 2198, Los Angeles, CA 92668

POST & COMMUNICATIONS

Post offices are easily identifiable by the yellow signs outside. Mail can be sent poste restante to any main post office. After one month, uncollected mail is returned to the sender.

The Greek telephone service, operated by OTE, is modern and efficient. Public telephones all use phonecards, which are widely available from outlets such as *periptera* (street kiosk), corner shops and tourist shops. Direct-dial long-distance and international calls can be made from public phones and OTE offices. Reverse charge (collect) calls can be made from an OTE office. Main city post offices have fax machines.

Greece was slow off the mark in entering cyberspace, but now Internet cafes are springing up everywhere, even on the islands where tourists are naturally the main clientele.

MONEY
Costs

Greece is no longer dirt cheap. A rockbottom daily budget of US$20 would mean walking or hitching, staying in youth hostels or camping, staying away from bars, and only occasionally eating in restaurants or taking ferries. Of course, you could spend less if you do nothing but lie on a beach all day, but where's the fun in that? Allow at least US$35 a day if you want your own room and plan to eat out regularly. If you really want a holiday – comfortable rooms and restaurants all the way – you will need closer to US$45 per day.

It's around US$7 for a hostel bed or US$25 to US$30 for a cheap double room, US$3 to US$8 for a budget meal or US$8 to US$18 for a restaurant meal.

In restaurants, the service charge is included in the bill but it is the custom to leave a small tip; rounding up the bill is usually sufficient. Bargaining is not as widespread in Greece as it is further east, though it's always worth bargaining over the price of hotel rooms, especially if you are intending to stay a few days or in the low season.

Changing Money

Banks will exchange all major currencies in either cash or travellers cheques; the commission is lower for cash. All post offices have exchange facilities, and they're often quicker and charge less commission than banks. Credit cards are only accepted in larger, more expensive establishments. Visa, Master-Card (Access) and Eurocard are the most widely accepted. Most banks have ATMs where you can access your debit account through the Maestro and Cirrus networks, and there are also 24-hour banknote exchange machines.

ONLINE SERVICES

Lonely Planet has a Web site, Destination Greece, at www.lonelyplanet.com /dest/eur/gre.htm. Another site (www .gogreece.com) is an excellent all-round site with classifieds, cultural information, travel news and chat rooms. If you intend to do a lot of ferry travel, you should consult www .greekferries.gr. It has schedules for all domestic and international ferries as well as travel and accommodation information. A University of Pennsylvania site is devoted to ancient Greek history: www.museum.upenn.edu/Greek _World/index.html. Another site (www .geocities.com/westhollywood/2225 /guide.html) offers a guide to gay and lesbian travel in Greece. Plus Odysseas has a site (http://Odysseas.com) with plenty of travel information and links to online reservation services. There is an official site for the 2004 Olympic Games to be held in Athens: www .athens2004.gr.

BOOKS

Homer (9th century BC), author of the *Iliad* and the *Odyssey*, was the greatest ancient Greek writer. The world's first travel writer was Pausanias who, in the 2nd century BC, wrote *The Guide to Greece*. Umpteen editions later, it is now available in English in paperback.

The Greek Myths by Robert Graves is one of the best collections of the ancient myths. *Greek Art* by John Boardman is a concise yet comprehensive introduction to ancient and Byzantine art.

A Traveller's History of Greece by Timothy Boatswain & Colin Nicholson is a good general historical reference tracing times from the Neolithic era to the present day. *Eleni* by Nicholas Gage conveys the strength of feeling which still festers in most

Greeks on the subject of the civil war, although it is unashamedly right-wing and anticommunist.

The most celebrated contemporary Greek author is Nikos Kazantzakis. His novels, which include *The Last Temptation* and *Zorba the Greek*, are full of larger-than-life drama. Mary Renault's novels provide an excellent insight into ancient Greece: *The King Must Die* and *The Bull from the Sea* are vivid tales of Minoan times. *Captain Corelli's Mandolin* by the irrepressible Louis de Bernières is a captivating WWII-era love story set on a Greek island.

Home Time and *Milk* by Australian author Beverley Farmer are evocative collections of stories focusing on the experiences of foreigners who endeavour to make their home in Greece. *The Mule's Foal* by Australian Vogel Prize winner Fotini Epanomitis is a magical account of the life and times of her Greek forebears. Patricia Storace's *Dinner with Persephone* is a thoughtful but lacerating account of a year in Athens confronting Greek machismo, sexism and rudeness. The book examines the country's stunted modern identity, and is guaranteed to erase any Shirley Valentine fantasies you may be harbouring.

FILMS

Greece's most acclaimed film director is Theodoros Angelopoulos, whose films include *The Beekeeper*, *Alexander the Great*, *Travelling Players*, *Landscapes in the Mist* and *The Hesitant Step of the Stork*. All have received awards at both national and international festivals.

Shirley Valentine (1989) is the story of a downtrodden British housewife who leaves her husband and flies off to the Greek islands in search of romance.

ENTERING & LEAVING

Greece has 16 international airports and has air links to every major city in Europe. In addition, there are direct flights to and from the USA, Canada, Australia and various Asian cities. There are also frequent flights to and from Istanbul and Sofia. Cheap charter flights are available from London, Amsterdam, Frankfurt and Paris to Athens, Thessaloniki and some of the islands. However, conditions apply; if you take a side trip to Turkey, you may not be allowed to use the return portion of your charter-flight ticket.

By land, there are road connections from Turkey, Bulgaria, Albania and Macedonia. There are also trains from Macedonia and Turkey. Travelling to Greece on an Inter-Rail or Eurail pass does not necessarily entail travel through Macedonia, however, as the ferry crossing from Italy is often included in the ticket. Alternatively, take trains through Hungary and Bulgaria to avoid the trouble spots.

There are ferries from Brindisi, Bari and Otranto in Italy, and from various Aegean ports in Turkey. There are also boats from Israel and Cyprus.

HUNGARY

Firmly entrenched in the Communist Soviet bloc until the late 1980s, Hungary is now an independent republic making its own decisions. Its central position and experience in welcoming travellers makes Hungary an ideal place to enter the post-Soviet world. The majority of travellers arrive in picturesque Budapest, which has a lively arts, cafe and music scene, and is host to a range of cultural and sporting festivals. To venture outside the capital is to travel through plains, resort-lined lakes, baroque towns and rustic villages. Hungary's other attractions include sampling its quality wines, 'taking the waters' in a relaxing thermal spa, or bird-watching in some of the best spots in Europe.

While some of Hungary's neighbours may have more dramatic scenery or older and more important monuments, travel here is essentially hassle-free and, by western standards, is still a bargain destination with very affordable food, lodging and transport.

WHEN TO GO
Though it can be pretty wet in May and June, spring is glorious in Hungary. The Hungarian summer is warm, sunny and unusually long, but the resorts are very crowded in late July and August. Like Paris and Rome, Budapest comes to a halt in August (called 'the cucumber-growing season' here because that's about the only thing happening).

Autumn is beautiful, particularly in the hills around Budapest and in the

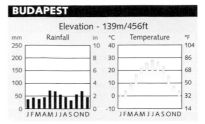

Northern Uplands. November is one of the rainiest months of the year, and winter is cold and often bleak, and museums and other tourist sights are often closed.

HIGHLIGHTS
Historic Towns
Many of Hungary's historic towns, including Eger, Győr, Székesfehérvár and Veszprém, were rebuilt in the baroque style during the 18th century.

At a Glance

Full Country Name: Republic of Hungary
Area: 93,000 sq km
Population: 10.4 million
Capital City: Budapest (pop two million)
People: 90% Hungarian, 5% Gypsy, 2% German, 1% Slovak
Language: Hungarian
Religion: 68% Roman Catholic, 21% Reformed (Calvinist), 6% Evangelical (Lutheran), 5% other
Government: Parliamentary democracy
Currency: Hungarian forint (Ft)
Time Zone: GMT/UTC plus one hour (winter); plus two hours (summer)
International Telephone Code: 36
Electricity: 220V, 50Hz

Sopron and Kőszeg are among the few Hungarian towns with a strong medieval flavour. The greatest monuments of the Turkish period are in Pécs.

Itineraries

Two Days

Visit Hungary's beautiful capital, Budapest, split by the Danube River and full of interesting sights. Try to take in Castle Hill and what remains of medieval Buda, St Stephen's Basilica and the National Museum, and take a thermal bath at one of the numerous bathhouses.

One Week

Spend two or three days in Budapest, then explore the Danube Bend, including the art town of Szentendre, Visegrád and historic Esztergom. If you're heading to Austria, stop in Sopron, another historically important town close to the border. If you're heading towards Croatia, stop in Pécs, a large, fortified city with a lively student atmosphere.

Two Weeks

Spend at least three days in and around Budapest, then explore the Danube Bend. From there you can travel down to the north shore of Lake Balaton, basing yourself at Keszthely or the spa town of Balatonfüred. The lake has popular sandy beaches and water sports, but gets a bit crowded in July and August. From there, travel west to the 'jewellery box' town of Kőszeg, with one of the most picturesque town squares in Hungary. If you have time, continue to Sopron, Pécs, Kecskemét or Eger.

One Month

Follow the two week itinerary and include visits to the central Hungarian town of Kecskemét, famous for its apricot brandy, and the northern Hungarian town of Eger, famous for its many wine cellars and potent Bull's Blood red wine. Also make a stop at Győr, on the Danube between Budapest and Vienna, and the cultured city of Szeged in the south of the country.

Kecskemét has wonderful examples of Art Nouveau architecture.

Castles & Palaces

Hungary's most famous castles are those that resisted the Turkish onslaught in Eger, Kőszeg and Szigetvár. Though in ruins, the citadel at Visegrád evokes the power of medieval Hungary. Those at Siklós, Sümeg, Hollókó and Boldogkőváralja have dramatic locations. Among Hungary's finest palaces are the Esterházy Palace at Fertöd, the Festetics Palace at Keszthely, the Széchenyi Mansion at Nagycenk and the Bishop's Palace at Veszprém.

Museums & Galleries

The following museums stand out not just for what they contain but for how they display it: the Christian Museum in Esztergom (Gothic paintings), the Storno Collection in Sopron (Romanesque and Gothic furnishings), the Zsolnay Museum (Art Nouveau porcelain) and the Csontváry Museum in Pécs, the Palóc Museum in Balassagyarmat (folklore collection), the Ferenc Móra Museum in Szeged (Avar finds), the Imre Patkó Collection (Asian and African art) in Győr, and the Applied Arts Museum (furniture) and the Hungarian Commerce & Catering Museum (antique cookware) in Budapest.

Churches & Synagogues

The following is just a sampling of Hungary's most beautiful houses of worship: the baroque Minorite church in Eger, the Gothic Calvinist church in Nyírbátor, the Art Nouveau synagogue in Szeged, the baroque cathedral at Kalocsa, Sümeg's Church of the

HUNGARY HIGHLIGHTS & ITINERARIES ▶▶

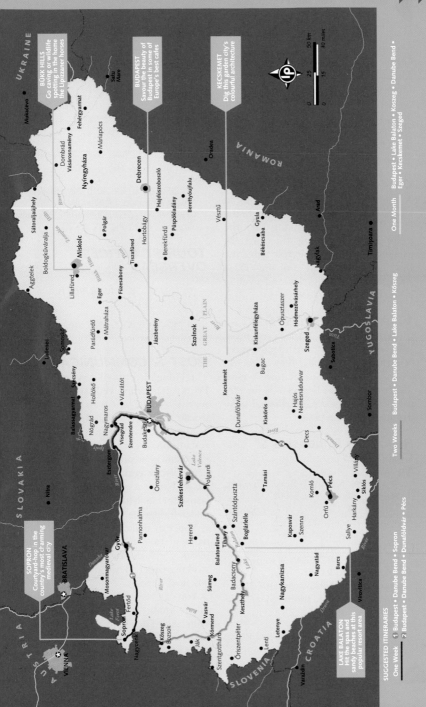

BÜKK HILLS
Go caving or wildlife spotting in the home of the Lipizzaner horses

BUDAPEST
Savour the beauty of Budapest in some of Europe's best cafés

KECSKEMÉT
Dig this garden city's colourful architecture

SOPRON
Courtyard-hop in the country's most charming medieval city

LAKE BALATON
Hit the spas and sandy beaches at this popular resort area

UKRAINE

Mukacevo

Satu Mare

Fehérgyarmat
Dombrád
Vásárosnamény
Máriapócs
Nyíregyháza

Sátoraljaújhely
Oradea
ROMANIA
Debrecen
Hajdúszoboszló
Boldogkőváralja
Miskolc
Polgár
Berettyóújfalu
Sárospatak
Berekfürdő
Aggtelek
Püspökladány
Lillafüred
Hortobágy
Vésztő
Szécsény
Eger
Tiszafüred
Arad
Parádfürdő
Füzesabony
Gyula
Hollókő
Mátraháza
Jászberény
Kiskunfélegyháza
Békéscsaba
Vácrátót
Szolnok
Hódmezővásárhely
THE GREAT PLAIN
Nógrád
Opusztaszer
Nagylak
Balassagyarmat
Nagymaros
Kecskemét
Szeged
Timişoara
Bugac
Subotica
Esztergom
Visegrád
BUDAPEST
Szentendre
Dunaújváros
Hajós
Nemesnádudvar
Oroszlány
Kiskőrös
Sombor
Dunaföldvár
YUGOSLAVIA
Lake Velence
Székesfehérvár
Polgárdi
Decs
Pannonhalma
Tamási
Győr
Herend
Szántódpuszta
Pécs
Komló
Mosonmagyaróvár
Sümeg
Balatonfüred
Boglárlelle
Orfű
Villány
Tihany
Kaposvár
Siklós
Fertőd
Badacsony
Szenna
Harkány
Keszthely
Sopron
Nagykanizsa
Sallye
Nagycenk
Kőszeg
Vasvár
Nagyatád
Barcs
Bozsók
Körmend
Jak
Letenye
Virovitica
Szentgotthárd
Lenti
Őriszentpéter
Varaždin
SLOVENIA
CROATIA
Drava

VIENNA
AUSTRIA
BRATISLAVA
SLOVAKIA
Nitra

SUGGESTED ITINERARIES

One Week ■ 1 Budapest • Danube Bend • Sopron
■ 2 Budapest • Danube Bend • Dunaföldvár • Pécs

Two Weeks ■ Budapest • Danube Bend • Lake Balaton • Kőszeg

One Month ■ Budapest • Lake Balaton • Kőszeg • Danube Bend •
Eger • Kecskemét • Szeged

50 km
25
0
40 miles
15
0

Ascension (for its frescoes), the Gothic Old Synagogue in Sopron, the Abbey Church in Tihany and the Minorite church in Nyírbátor (for their carved wooden altars), the Romantic Nationalist Szolnok Synagogue (now the Szolnok Gallery), the Romanesque church at Öriszentpéter and Pécs Synagogue.

Outdoor Activities

Among the top outdoor activities in Hungary are bird-watching in the Hortobágy region, hiking in the Zemplén Hills, riding the narrow-gauge railway from Miskolc into the Bükk Hills, canoeing on the Tisza River, caving in Aggtelek and cycling in the Danube Bend area.

VISA REQUIREMENTS

Citizens of the USA, Canada and most European countries don't require visas. Nationals of Australia, New Zealand and Asian countries require visas, which are valid for between 30 and 90 days. South Africans are allowed a 30 day stay without a visa.

Hungarian Embassies & Consulates

Australia
> (☎ 02-6282 3226) 17 Beale Crescent, Deakin, Canberra, ACT 2600
> *Consulate:* (☎ 02-9328 7859) Edgecliff Centre, Suite 405, 203-233 New South Head Rd, Edgecliff, NSW 2027

Canada
> (☎ 613-230 2717) 299 Waverley St, Ottawa, Ont K2P 0V9
> *Consulate:* (☎ 416-923 3596) 102 Bloor St West, Suite 1005, Toronto, Ont M5S 1M8

Ireland
> (☎ 01-661 2902) 2 Fitzwilliam Place, Dublin 2

Japan
> (☎ 03-3798 8801) 2-17-14 Mita, Minato-ku, Tokyo 108

South Africa
> (☎ 012-433 030) 959 Arcadia St, 0132 Pretoria
> *Consulate:* (☎ 021-641 547) 14 Fernwood Ave, Newlands, 7700 Cape Town

UK
> (☎ 020-7235 2664) 35/b Eaton Place, London SW1X 8BY

USA
> (☎ 202-362 6730) 3910 Shoemaker St NW, Washington, DC 20008
> *Consulate:* (☎ 212-752 0661) 223 East 52nd St, New York, NY 10022

TOURIST OFFICES OVERSEAS

UK
> (☎/fax 020-7871 4009) PO Box 4336, London SW18 4XE

USA
> (☎ 212-355 0240, fax 207 4103) 150 East 58th St, 33rd floor, New York, NY 10155

POST & COMMUNICATIONS

The Hungarian postal service (Magyar Posta) has improved somewhat in recent years, but post offices are usually still crowded and English may not be spoken. Mail addressed to poste restante in any town or city will go to the main post office. Since the family name always comes first in Hungarian usage, have the sender underline your last name, as letters are often misfiled under foreigners' first names.

You can make domestic and international calls from most public telephones, which are usually in good working order. Buy a phonecard from any post office.

You can send telexes and faxes from most main post offices around Hungary. There are several Internet cafes in Budapest, and some hostels offer email services.

MONEY
Costs

Hungary remains a bargain destination for foreign travellers. If you stay in hostels, dormitories or camping grounds and eat at self-service restaurants or food stalls, you could get by on US$15 a day. If you prefer private rooms, eat at medium-priced restaurants and travel 2nd class on trains, you should manage on about US$25 a day without scrimping. Expect to pay US$5 to US$8 for a budget room and US$3 to US$5 for a cheap meal.

Hungary is a very tip-conscious society and virtually everyone routinely tips waiters, hairdressers and taxi drivers – even doctors, dentists and petrol-station attendants! – about 10%. Bargaining is not the done thing in Hungary, but you can try a little gentle haggling in flea markets or with individuals selling folk crafts.

Changing Money

You can exchange cash and travellers cheques at banks and travel agents, usually for a commission of 1 to 2%. Post offices almost always change cash, but rarely cheques. ATMs accepting credit and debit cards can be found throughout the country, but it's always useful to carry a little foreign cash, preferably US dollars or Deutschmarks, in case your plastic doesn't work. Credit cards can be used in upmarket restaurants, shops, hotels, car rental firms, travel agencies and petrol stations.

ONLINE SERVICES

Lonely Planet's Destination Hungary (www.lonelyplanet.com/dest/eur/hun .htm) has loads of useful information and links. Tourinform maintains a site (www.hungary.com/tourinform) with plenty of tourist information. The Hungarian Tourist Office produces a standard site at www.hungarytourism.hu. The Hungarian Home Page (www.fsz .bme.hu/hungary) has good regional information on towns and history. Another site (www.globewalker.com) is dedicated to Budapest; it has information on places to stay and eat, entertainment and sights.

BOOKS

There is no shortage of books on Hungary and things Hungarian. Historical accounts include the lightweight *Hungary – A Brief History* by István Lázár. If your passion is politics, try Charles Gati's *Hungary and the Soviet Bloc*, a dry but definitive treatise on Hungarian foreign policy from 1944 to 1986, or Sándor Kopácsi's *In the Name of the Working Class*, a thoroughly readable account of the events leading to the 1956 uprising. For clear, insightful interpretations of what led to the collapse of Communism in 1989, try *We the People* or *The Uses of Adversity* by Timothy Garton Ash.

Two classic travelogues on the country are Patrick Leigh Fermor's *Between the Woods and the Water*, which traces his 1933 walk through Hungary en route to Constantinople, and Brian Hall's tempered love affair with the still-Communist Budapest of the 1980s described in *Stealing from a Deep Place*. British-based writer Tibor Fischer's *Under the Frog* is an immensely readable black comedy about basketball and the 1956 revolution.

FILMS

The scarcity of government grants has severely limited the production of quality Hungarian films, but a handful are still produced every year. For classics, look out for anything by Oscar-winning István Szabó *(Sweet Emma, Dear Böbe)*, Miklós Jancsó *(The Red and the White)* and Péter Bacsó *(The Witness, Live Show)*. György Szomjas' *Junk Film*, Lívia Gyarmathy's *The Joy of Cheating*, Gábor Dettre's *Diary of the Hurdy-Gurdy Man*, György Molnár's *Anna's Film* and Marcell Iványi's award-winning *Wind* are more recent films showing the great talent of their directors.

ENTERING & LEAVING

Malév Hungarian Airlines, the national carrier, flies direct to Budapest from the USA and more than 30 European countries. Hungary is connected to all of its seven neighbouring countries by road and rail. Volánbusz (which means 'steering wheel bus' – presumably as opposed to those without steering wheels) runs regular transport services to nearly 20 European countries, while Magyar Államvasutak (MÁV) has express rail services that run as far as London, Stockholm, St Petersburg, Istanbul and Rome. Motorists can choose from 60 or so border crossings into the country, although 15 are restricted to citizens of Hungary and the neighbouring countries. You can also walk or cycle across the border (many border guards frown on this, particularly in Romania, Serbia and Croatia) or take the hydrofoil that plies between Budapest and Vienna from April to early November.

The country with the chilly name is becoming one of the hottest destinations in Europe. Nowhere on earth are the forces of nature more evident than here, where glaciers, hot springs, geysers, active volcanoes, icecaps, tundra, snowcapped peaks, vast lava deserts and waterfalls vie for the visitor's attention. On the cliffs that gird much of the coastline are some of the world's most crowded sea-bird colonies, and in the summer, the lakes and marshes teem with nesting waterfowl.

Superimposed on this wilderness is a tough and independent society, descendants of the farmers and warriors who fled the tyranny of medieval Scandinavia to settle a new and empty country. With them they brought a rich history, literature and folklore tradition, typified by the sagas. However, tempering Iceland's appeal is, the fact is its prices are the most expensive in Europe. That doesn't mean it can't be visited on a shoestring, but it does mean that budget travellers will have to spend some time camping, and on foot or bicycle in order to fully appreciate the country without needing to get on intimate terms with their bank manager.

Iceland is the least densely settled country in Europe. With a land mass more than double that of the Netherlands, it has less than a fiftieth of Holland's population. Its ratio of less than three people per square kilometre contrasts with that of say, Malta, which has more than 1200 people per square kilometre – the visitor to Iceland has plenty of room to move.

WHEN TO GO

Every year on 15 August, someone puts on the brakes and Icelandic tourism grinds to a halt. Hotels, youth hostels and camping grounds shut down and buses stop running. Many late-summer travellers are disappointed to find that all the most popular attractions are practically inaccessible by 15 September, and by 30 September

REYKJAVÍK

Elevation - 18m/59ft

At a Glance

Full Country Name: Republic of Iceland
Area: 103,000 sq km
Population: 272,000
Capital City: Reykjavík (pop 170,000)
People: 97% Icelanders
Language: Icelandic (as well as English and German)
Religion: 95% Evangelical Lutheran, 3% other Protestant denominations, 1% Roman Catholic, and some followers of Ásatrú (an ancient Norse religion)
Government: Democratic republic
Currency: Icelandic króner (Ikr)
Time Zone: GMT/UTC; in summer time (late March to late October) it's GMT minus one hour
International Telephone Code: 354
Electricity: 220V, 50Hz

Itineraries

Three Days
Spend a day in Reykjavík, visiting the National Museum, the Volcano Show and the old town. For a unique cultural experience, Reykjavík is the place to join the beautiful youth on a Friday night pub crawl through the city's 'in' bars and clubs. Spend the next two days doing a tour of the Golden Triangle, taking in Þingvellir, Gullfoss and Geysir.

One Week
Head straight to northern Iceland, spending a day or two in urban Akureyri before exploring spectacular Lake Mývatn and the surrounding volcanic and geothermal areas. You can also go whale-watching (in season) at Húsavík, 50km north-east of Akureyri. It is sometimes possible to combine these itineraries, starting with Reykjavík and the Golden Triangle, then heading up to Akureyri. Bear in mind that weather may affect your travel plans and many interior roads are only open from July to September.

Two Weeks
Combine the previous itineraries, and include a trip to Vestmannaeyjar (there's a summer ferry from Þorlákshöfn just south of Reykjavík to the main island of Heimaey). From Mývatn you could also head north into the Jökulsárgljúfur National Park.

One Month
With enough money you could easily spend a month or more exploring Iceland, particularly if you're well prepared for camping and trekking. Cover the two week itinerary and include the four day trek from Þórsmörk to Landmannalaugar, which will take you to the Fjallabak Reserve (you can also do this walk in reverse). From there, visit Skaftafell National Park to the east. If you have time left over, visit Snæfellsnes (of *Journey to the Centre of the Earth* fame) and continue further north to the wild Westfjords Peninsula.

it seems the country has gone into hibernation. Although it's safe to predict that the situation will change in coming years as tourism builds, but for now it's a good idea to plan your trip with this in mind. May, June and July are the driest months, but you can expect rain, gales and fog at any time.

HIGHLIGHTS
Iceland's main draw for visitors is undoubtedly its natural beauty, clean air and wide untrampled spaces.

Lakes, Mountains & Islands
Most of Iceland's geological phenomena are represented at Mývatn in northeast Iceland, and the region offers some of the country's best weather. The centrepiece is a lovely blue lake teeming with bird life, while Krafla, a few kilometres from the lake, is Iceland's most awesome lava flow. The Blue Lagoon, south of Reykjavík, is not a lake – it's actually a pale blue pool of effluent from a power plant – but swimming in it is an ethereal experience.

Landmannalaugar is a remote oasis in central Iceland. It's an area of incredible mountains of variegated rhyolite, lava flows, hot springs, and lots of trekking routes.

Vestmannaeyjar, off the south central coast, is a group of 16 islands with some of the most geologically active spots in the world. As well as illustrating Iceland's volcanic history, they are known for their bird life and relaxed atmosphere.

National Parks
Skaftafell National Park in south-east Iceland has green moorlands, numerous waterfalls and rugged snowcapped peaks and glaciers.

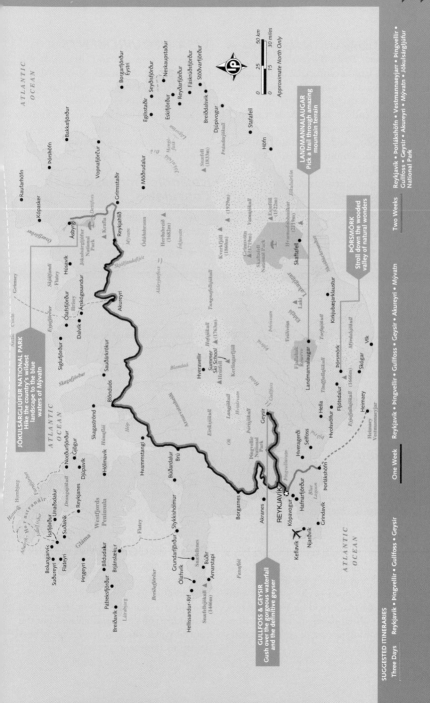

JÖKULSÁRGLJÚFUR NATIONAL PARK
Hike the country's wildest landscape to the blue waters of Mývatn

LANDMANNALAUGAR
Pick a trail through amazing mountain terrain

ÞÓRSMÖRK
Stroll down the wooded valley of natural wonders

GULLFOSS & GEYSIR
Gush over the gorgeous waterfall and the definitive geyser

SUGGESTED ITINERARIES

Three Days Reykjavík • Þingvellir • Gullfoss • Geysir

One Week Reykjavík • Þingvellir • Gullfoss • Geysir • Akureyri • Mývatn

Two Weeks Reykjavík • Þorlákshöfn • Vestmannaeyjar • Þingvellir • Gullfoss • Geysir • Akureyri • Mývatn • Jökulsárgljúfur National Park

ATLANTIC OCEAN

Approximate North Only

0   25   50 km
0   15   30 miles

At Jökulsárgljúfur National Park in north-east Iceland you'll find the country's largest canyon, lush vegetation, bizarre basalt formations, springs and fabulous waterfalls; Dettifoss, at the southern end of the park, is Europe's most powerful waterfall.

Þingvellir, Iceland's third national park, is the country's most important historical site – it was here that the first Alþing (parliament) was established in AD 930. History aside, Þingvellir is a truely stunning area of canyons, caves, streams, springs and waterfalls, all flanked by snowcapped peaks.

Golden Triangle

Gullfoss and Geysir in south central Iceland are Iceland's most visited tourist attractions. Gullfoss is a much photographed two tiered waterfall, and Geysir contains the country's best examples of spouting hot springs (after which all geysers are named). Although it no longer spouts forth, nearby Strokkur does the job for tourists.

Þingvellir makes up the third part of the Golden Triangle (also called the Golden Circle).

Trekking

Trekking is a popular activity in Iceland and the best way to see the natural attractions. Lónsöræfi, in south-east Iceland, is a vast trekking area offering numerous remote routes and spectacular rhyolite scenery. Þórsmörk, in south central Iceland, is a popular valley characterised by beautiful woodlands, glaciers, braided rivers and rugged peaks studded with hoodoo formations. The four day trek from Landmannalaugar to Þórsmörk or on to Skógar (six days) is Iceland's premier walk.

VISA REQUIREMENTS

Western Europeans and citizens of the USA, Canada, Australia, New Zealand, Hong Kong, Singapore and at least two dozen other countries do not require visas. Tourist stays are granted for up to three months, and can be easily extended at local police stations. South Africans will need a visa.

Icelandic Embassies & Consulates

Denmark
(☎ 031-159604, fax 930506) Dantes Plads 3, DK-1556 Copenhagen V
UK
(☎ 020-7730 5131, fax 7730 1683) 1 Eaton Terrace, London SW1 8EY
USA
(☎ 202-265 6653, 265 6656) 2022 Connecticut Ave NW, Washington, DC 20008
Consulate: (☎ 212-686 4100, fax 532 4138) 370 Lexington Ave, New York, NY 10017

TOURIST OFFICES OVERSEAS

UK
Icelandair
(☎ 020-7388 4499, fax 7387 5711) 3rd floor, 172 Tottenham Court Rd, London W1P 9LG
USA
(☎ 212-949 2333, fax 983 5260) 655 Third Ave, New York, NY 10017
(☎ 212-967 8888, fax 330 1456) 610B Fifth Ave, Rockefeller Centre, New York, NY 10020

POST & COMMUNICATIONS

The Icelandic postal system is both reliable and efficient, and rates are comparable to those in other Western European countries. Poste restante is available in all cities and villages but the central post office in Reykjavík is best set up to handle it.

Public telephone offices normally occupy the same buildings as post offices. Iceland has coin and cardphones; cards are sold at post and telephone offices.

Public fax services are provided at most telephone offices, and there's at least one Internet cafe in Reykjavík.

MONEY
Costs

Because just about everything must be imported, food, accommodation and transport prices in the North Atlantic are high. In fact, Iceland is generally considered second only to Japan in its ability to deplete travellers' means. If you can happily drop US$200 a day you won't encounter any problems, but those with finite means may have to put in some effort not to break the budget. If you're willing to give up some comforts and sleep in youth hostels, eat at snack bars and travel on bus passes, you'll probably be able to keep expenses down to an average of about US$40 to US$45 per day. Bringing a private vehicle to Iceland (from Europe), especially a campervan, will give you a bit more comfort while still keeping you within a reasonable budget.

Expect to pay from US$15 to US$45 for a hostel bed or cheap room (camp sites are around US$5), US$5 to US$10 for a budget meal and US$15 to US$25 for a restaurant meal.

Changing Money

Foreign-currency travellers cheques, postal cheques and banknotes can be exchanged at any bank. A commission of about US$2.50 will be charged, regardless of the amount changed. Major credit cards are accepted at most places. Icelanders are plastic mad and use cards even for buying groceries and other small purchases.

Tipping is not obligatory: finer restaurants will automatically add a service charge to the bill making further tipping unnecessary.

ONLINE SERVICES

Lonely Planet's Destination Iceland site (www.lonelyplanet.com/dest/eur.ice.htm) has a detailed country profile and pics. For daily news from Iceland on Iceland, see www.centrum.is/icerev. Another site (www.bok.hi.is) contains the catalogue of the National Library and Archives, as well as other information. An Icelandic travel information site (www.travelnet.is) has tours, transport information and other useful bits. The Eye on Iceland site (www.eyeoniceland.com) is packed with contributed information, including articles and restaurant reviews.

BOOKS

Some of the best reading available is to be found in the great sagas or historical novels of medieval Iceland, such as *Hrafnkels Saga*, *Egils Saga* and *Grettis Saga*. These are normally found in bookshops under the names of their translators, usually Magnús Magnússon, Hermann Pálsson, or both.

The works of Halldór Laxness, the country's Nobel Prize-winning author, have also been translated into English, and include *The Atom Station*, *The Fish Can Sing* and *Independent People*.

Another book that Iceland-bound travellers may enjoy is Jules Verne's *Journey to the Centre of the Earth*, which features descriptions of Reykjavík and Snæfellsjökull, the volcano that served as the gateway to the centre of the earth.

Iceland Saga by Magnús Magnússon is a valuable introduction to the country's history and literature.

Look out also for *Letters from Iceland* by WH Auden & Louis MacNiece, an irreverent and thoroughly facetious collection of poems, letters and narrative concerning the two poets' journey. Another travel classic, though in a more contemporary vein, is *Last Places – A Journey to the north* by Lawrence Millman. This collection of side-splittingly funny experiences tells of the author's four month trip from Scotland to Newfoundland via the Faroes, Iceland and Greenland.

FILMS

The movie version of Jules Verne's *Journey to the Centre of the Earth* (1959) begins its journey in an Icelandic volcano.

Iceland (1942), set in Reykjavík, is a fairly corny musical/romance where a US marine falls for a local girl and struggles with Icelandic customs. A better film is *Cold Fever* (1994), a road movie about a Japanese man who heads into a remote part of Iceland to find the place where his parents died. *Börn Natturunnar* (Children of Nature; 1991) is an Icelandic drama about an elderly man who leaves his remote home to live in Reykjavík.

ENTERING & LEAVING

Icelandair, the national carrier, has regular and direct flights to Europe and the USA. Flying to Iceland is expensive: plan as far in advance as possible, shop around for cheap fares and purchase airline tickets at least 30 days prior to departure. If you're travelling between the USA and Europe (Copenhagen or Luxembourg), you may be able to make a limited stopover in Iceland.

A pleasant way to travel between Europe and Iceland is by ferry, although it takes a bit more time and is still not cheap. A ferry service operates from late May to early September out of Esberg in south-western Denmark (passengers are required to spend two nights in the Faroe Islands en route). There's also a coastal ferry between Greenland and Denmark, via Iceland, from mid-December to mid-January, and another from Iceland to Norway during the second week in September and returning the first week in October. Between June and August there's a ferry to Iceland from Lerwick in the Shetland Islands, off the north-east coast of Scotland.

IRELAND ▶▶

It's said that Ireland, once visited, is never forgotten, and for once the blarney rings true. The Irish landscape has a mythic resonance, due as much to the country's tangible history as its claim to being the home of the fairies and the 'little people'. Sure, the weather may not always be clement, but the dampness ensures there are 50 shades of green to compensate – just one of the reasons Ireland is called the Emerald Isle.

Although the 'Troubles' aren't over in the North, the recent referendum clearly signalled a willingness for peace, and a genuine resolution may be in sight. If the country isn't quite the paradise that its misty-eyed emigres tend to portray, Ireland is still one of Western Europe's most lightly populated and least 'spoilt' countries. Its long history is easy to trace, from Stone Age passage tombs and ring forts, through ancient monasteries and castles, down to the great houses and splendid Georgian architecture of the 18th and 19th centuries. And when you raise a pint of Guinness in a pub in Galway or Derry, you'll see that Ireland is home to some of the most gregarious and welcoming people in Europe.

Just to get the terminology out of the way, Ireland refers to the island as a whole; the Republic of Ireland refers to Eire or the South; and Northern Ireland is referred to as the North. The Republic of Ireland is an independent country; the North is part of the United Kingdom.

WHEN TO GO

The weather is warmest in July and August and the daylight hours are long, but the crowds will be greatest, the costs the highest and accommodation hardest to come by. In the quieter winter months, however, you may get miserable weather, the days are short and many tourist facilities will be shut. Visiting Ireland in June or September has a number of advantages: the weather can be better than at any other time of the year, it's less crowded and everything is open.

At a Glance

Full Country Name: Republic of Ireland; Northern Ireland (part of the UK)

Area: 84,421 sq km total (70,282 sq km in the Republic; 14,139 sq km in the North)

Population: 5.2 million (3.6 million in the Republic; 1.6 million in the North)

Capital City: Dublin (pop 1.5 million); Belfast (NI; pop 500,000)

People: Irish

Language: English, Gaelic (around 80,000 native speakers)

Religion: 95% Roman Catholic, 3.4% Protestant in the Republic; 60% Protestant, 40% Roman Catholic in Northern Ireland

Government: Democracy

Currency: Irish pound (or punt; I£)

Time Zone: GMT/UTC; clocks go forward one hour for daylight savings from late March to late October

International Telephone Code: 353

Electricity: 220V, 50Hz

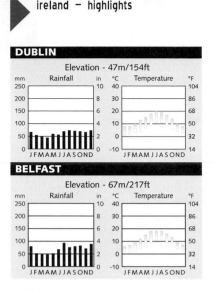

DUBLIN
Elevation - 47m/154ft

BELFAST
Elevation - 67m/217ft

HIGHLIGHTS
Scenery, Beaches & Coastline
The scenery is one of Ireland's major attractions. Highlights include the stunning green scenery around the Ring of Kerry and the Dingle Peninsula, the barren stretches of the Burren, and the beautiful lake areas in the south and north.

Favourite stretches of Ireland's 3200km coastline include the wildly beautiful Cliffs of Moher, the Connemara and Donegal coasts, and the wonderful Antrim coast road of Northern Ireland. Also in Northern Ireland, the Causeway Coast and the basaltic columns known as the Giant's Causeway shouldn't be missed. There are fine beaches (and marginally warmer water) along the south-east coast.

Museums, Castles & Houses
Trinity College Library, with the ancient Book of Kells, is on every visitor's must-see list, but Dublin also has the fine National Museum and National Gallery. Belfast has the excellent Ulster Museum and, just outside the city, the extensive Ulster Folk & Transport Museum.

Ireland is littered with castles and forts of various types and sizes and in various stages of ruination. The Stone Age forts on the Aran Islands are of particular interest, but there are other ancient ring forts all over Ireland. Castles are numerous and prime examples are Dublin Castle, Charles Fort at Kinsale and Kilkenny Castle, not forgetting Blarney Castle and its famous oft-kissed stone!

The Anglo-Irish aristocracy left a good selection of fine stately homes, many of which are open to the public: Castletown House, Malahide House, Westport House, Bantry House and Mt Stewart, and the beautiful gardens at Powerscourt Estate.

Religious Sites
Stone rings, portal tombs or dolmens and passage graves are reminders of an earlier pre-Christian Ireland. The massive passage grave at Newgrange is the most impressive relic of that time. Early Christian churches, many well over 1000 years old, are scattered throughout Ireland, and ruined monastic sites, many with round towers, are also numerous. Clonmacnois, Glendalough, Mellifont Abbey, Grey Abbey, Inch Abbey and Jerpoint Abbey are particularly interesting monastic sites. The rock-top complex at Cashel is one of Ireland's major tourist attractions, and the beehive huts built by monks on Skellig Michael, off the coast of Kerry, are well worth visiting.

Islands
Lying off Ireland's coast are dozens of islands, some inhabited by humans,

others inhabited only by migrating birds.

The Aran Islands in County Galway and Achill Island in County Mayo are the most touristy, but it's not difficult to find more isolated islands if that's what you're after. A boat trip to the Skelligs is one of the highlights of any visit to Ireland, and their wildlife is fascinating. The Blaskets, off the Dingle Peninsula in County Kerry, are glorious on a fine day. Tory Island, off the Donegal coast, is a wild place and is the home of a group of local artists. County Cork has a number of easily accessible islands, of which Clear Island is famous for its abundant bird life and great scenery, and nearby Sherkin Island has safe sandy beaches to explore.

VISA REQUIREMENTS

For citizens of most western countries no visa is required. UK nationals born in Great Britain or Northern Ireland do not require a passport to visit the Republic.

Irish Embassies

Australia
(☎ 02-6273 3022) 20 Arkana St, Yarralumla, Canberra, ACT 2600
Canada
(☎ 613-233 6281) 130 Albert St, Ottawa, Ont K1A 0L6
South Africa
(☎ 012-342 5062) Delheim Suite, Tulbach Park, 1234 Church St, 0083 Colbyn, Pretoria
UK
(☎ 020-7235 2171) 17 Grosvenor Place, London SW1X 7HR
USA
(☎ 202-462 3939) 2234 Massachusetts Ave NW, Washington, DC 20008
(also, there are consulates in Boston, Chicago, New York and San Francisco)

TOURIST OFFICES OVERSEAS

Bord Fáilte (Irish Tourist Board) and the Northern Ireland Tourist Board (NITB) operate separate tourist offices but produce some joint brochures and publications. They also administer a computerised tourist information and accommodation reservation service known as Gulliver – you can go to a travel agent and access this information and make reservations from anywhere in the world.

Australia
(☎ 02-9299 6177) 5th floor, 36 Carrington St, Sydney, NSW 2000
(has information on Northern Ireland)
Canada
(☎ 416-929 2777) 160 Bloor St East, Suite 1150, Toronto, Ont M4W 1B9
New Zealand
(☎ 09-379 3708) Dingwall Bldg, 87 Queen St, Auckland 1
UK
(☎ 020-7493 3201) Ireland House, 150 New Bond St, London W1Y 0AQ
USA
(☎ 212-418 0800) 345 Park Ave, New York, NY 10154

Tourist information for Northern Ireland is handled by the British Tourist Authority (see the Britain profile), although you may also find offices of the NITB in some locations.

POST & COMMUNICATIONS

Mail to both the North and the Republic can be addressed to poste restante at post offices but is officially only held for two weeks. Writing 'hold for collection' on the envelope may have some effect. Letters sent to North America take about 10 days, Britain and the rest of Europe three to five days and Australia a week to 10 days.

International calls can be made directly from pay phones throughout

Ireland (calls between Northern Ireland and the Republic are international). Telecom Éireann, the Republic's state-owned telecommunications company, has one of the most up-to-date digital telephone systems in the world. In the North, most public phones are owned by the privately run British Telecom (BT), but other companies compete for its business. Phonecards (callcards in the south) are widely accepted.

Faxes can be sent from post offices or other specialist offices. Most hotels also have faxes. You can log onto the Internet at some public libraries, or at one of the growing number of cybercafes.

MONEY
Costs

Ireland can be expensive, but costs vary around the country. If you stay at

---

Itineraries

Three Days

Dublin could easily fill three days of your time, but you could also make a day trip to nearby Powerscourt or Glendalough to the south, or to the historic sites of Newgrange, Mellifont Abbey and Monasterboice to the north. In Dublin, visit Trinity College, the National Museum, Dublin Castle, the Guinness Hopstore and the pubs and restaurants of the Temple Bar district. Other places of interest include St Patrick's Cathedral, Kilmainham Gaol and a walking tour in the footsteps (and drinking haunts) of Dublin's literary greats.

One Week

The South Spend two days in Dublin, then travel south to Glendalough. From there head to Kilkenny, with its famous castle and splendid medieval cathedral, and across to Killarney, one of Ireland's biggest tourist towns. This is the starting point for trips into Killarney National Park and for the incredibly popular (and crowded) 179km Ring of Kerry, which skirts around the Iveragh Peninsula. The circuit can be done in a day by car or bus, or three days by bicycle, but the longer you take, the more you're likely to appreciate it. Assuming you're in a hurry, continue on and spend a day in the attractive fishing port of Dingle (which is fast succumbing to tourism).

The North Start in Dublin and visit Newgrange and Mellifont on the way up to Belfast. Here you should take a 'black taxi'

ride through Falls and Shankill roads for a first-hand history lesson on the Troubles. Belfast is a bustling, clean and modern city with plenty of typically Irish nightlife to keep you amused. From Belfast, take the spectacular coast road all the way around to Derry. This stretch includes the Antrim Coast via Larne, Cushendall and Ballycastle, and Causeway Coast, featuring the Giant's Causeway and Bushmill's Distillery.

Two Weeks

The South Follow the one week itinerary but stop at Cork and Blarney Castle before Killarney. You can also spend longer on the Ring of Kerry and add a couple of days exploring the Dingle Peninsula. After that, continue up to the Burren (stay at the village of Doolin), and maybe also get to Galway.

The North Follow the one week route but include a visit to historic Armagh and continue around the coast, back into the Republic of Ireland, to County Donegal and lively Donegal town.

One Month

With a car or motorcycle you'd have time to explore most of Ireland's main attractions, perhaps combining the previous itineraries and adding a trip to the Aran Islands. This would be more difficult to achieve within a month on public transport. By skipping a couple of places or concentrating on particular areas, you could fit in some walking and cycling too.

REPUBLIC OF IRELAND AND NORTHERN IRELAND

CAUSEWAY COAST
Don't miss Northern Ireland's most romantic gesture, the Giant's Causeway

NEWGRANGE
Travel back in time in the massive Celtic passage tomb

DINGLE PENINSULA
Walk or ride along the less-touristed neighbour of the Ring of Kerry

DUBLIN
Pay your respects to the Book of Kells, and later the Temple Bar district

KILKENNY
Long before South Park, there was Kilkenny Castle

SUGGESTED ITINERARIES

Two Days
1 Dublin • Powerscourt or Glendalough
2 Dublin • Newgrange • Mellifont • Monasterboice

One Week
1 Dublin • Glendalough • Kilkenny • Killarney • Ring of Kerry • Dingle
2 Dublin • Newgrange • Mellifont • Belfast • Derry

Two Weeks
1 Dublin • Glendalough • Kilkenny • Cork • Blarney Castle • Killarney • Ring of Kerry • Dingle • the Burren (Doolin) • Galway
2 Dublin • Newgrange • Mellifont • Armagh • Belfast • Derry • Donegal

a hostel, eat a light pub lunch and cook your own meal in the evening, you could get by on US$25 a day. Once you factor in moving around the country, you'll need to increase the budget a bit. Added extras to watch out for include the awful practice of having to pay an extra pound or two for a bath and the more pleasurable ruin of buying the assembled company a round of expensive pints of Guinness.

Fancy hotels and restaurants usually add a 10 or 12% service charge, and no additional tip is required. Simpler places usually do not add service; if you decide to tip, just round up the bill or add 10%. Taxi drivers don't have to be tipped, but again 10% is reasonable. Tipping in bars is not expected.

Changing Money

Most major currencies and brands of travellers cheques are readily accepted in Ireland, but carrying them in pounds sterling has the advantage that in Northern Ireland or Britain you can change them without exchange loss or commission. Banks generally give the best exchange rates, but change bureaux are open longer hours. Many post offices offer currency exchange facilities and they're open on Saturday mornings. Credit cards are widely accepted, though many B&Bs and some smaller remote petrol stations will only take cash. There's quite a good spread of cash-spewing ATMs in both the North and the Republic.

ONLINE SERVICES

Lonely Planet's Destination Ireland site (www.lonelyplanet.com/dest/eur/ire.htm) offers an insight into the Emerald Isle. Bord Fáilte has a site at www.ireland.travel.ie. The NITB also has a site (www.nitourism.com). Best of Ireland (http://internet-ireland.ie/boi) provides detailed descriptions of various destinations in the country. Ireland Online (www.iol.ie/discover) has information on sights, transport, accommodation, visas and more. Virtual Library: Ireland (www.itw.ie/wwwlib.html) features information on government, arts, media, education, travel and so forth. Hedonist's Guide to Dublin (http://shaw.iol.ie/smytho/dublin) is aimed at young people and takes a fun look at pubs, clubs, cafes, shopping and everything else in the capital.

Aer Lingus, the Irish airline's site (www.aerlingus.ie), gives details of services, flight schedules, special offers and links to related sites.

BOOKS

For a readable and well-illustrated short history pick up *A Concise History of Ireland* by Máire & Condor Cruise O'Brien, or try *The Oxford History of Ireland* edited by RF Foster. Books about Northern Ireland's recent history tend to go out of date before they're published, and are rarely impartial. *Free Ireland – Towards a Lasting Peace* is Sinn Féin President Gerry Adam's latest, though David Thomson's enchanting memoir, *Woodbrook*, provides a more palatable slice of Irish history. Edna O'Brien's *Mother Ireland* is a lovely autobiographical travel book. Eric Newby's *Round Ireland in Low Gear* is a classic from the school of travel masochism. If you're visiting Dublin, be sure to read James Joyce's *Dubliners* or Roddy Doyle's *Barrytown Trilogy*. If you're heading off the beaten track to the Aran Islands, take JM Synge's *The Aran Islands* for company. *Culture Shock!*

Ireland by Patricia Levy is recommended as an up-to-date introduction to aspects of Irish culture. *The Irish Pub Guide* lists and describes a number of pubs across Ireland that are interesting for one reason or another.

FILMS

Ireland and Dublin have made numerous movie appearances and many Irish people have achieved international success in the film industry.

Hollywood came to Ireland in 1952 when John Ford filmed John Wayne as the *The Quiet Man*, wooing Maureen O'Hara in Cong, County Sligo. The 1970 David Lean epic *Ryan's Daughter* with Sarah Miles, Robert Mitchum, Trevor Howard and John Mills was filmed on the Dingle Peninsula in County Kerry. The region has since become 'Ryan's Daughter country'.

The Tom Cruise and Nicole Kidman vehicle *Far & Away* (1991) provided picturesque views of the west coast region, and Dublin's Temple Bar district stood in for late 19th century Boston! *Secret of Roan Innish* (1994) is a mystical tale set off the west coast.

Many films have featured Dublin. John Huston's superb final film was *The Dead*, released in 1987 and based on a story from *Dubliners*. Noel Pearson and Jim Sheridan's *My Left Foot* (1989) tells the true story of Dublin writer Christy Brown, who was crippled with cerebral palsy.

The Commitments (1990), by English director Alan Parker, was a bright and energetic hit about a Dublin soul band.

The troubles have spawned a number of films, including *The Odd Man Out* (1947), *Angel* (1982) and *Cal* (1984). The IRA featured in the British film *The Long Good Friday* starring Bob Hoskins. *The Crying Game* (1992) is perhaps the most intriguing commercial film to feature the IRA. *In the Name of the Father* (1993), filmed in Kilmainham Jail in Dublin, starred Daniel Day-Lewis as Gerry Conlon and Emma Thompson as his lawyer. Beginning with powerful scenes of rioting in Belfast in the early 1970s, it tells the story of the arrest and conviction of the Guildford Four for a pub bombing in England; then of the struggle to clear their names and their release.

Neil Jordan's powerful *Michael Collins* (1996) stars Liam Neeson and Stephen Rea. It follows the life of Collins from the Easter Rising, through the creation of the IRA to the Anglo-Irish war, civil war and his death in 1922 at the hands of his former comrades. *Some Mother's Son* (1996), starring Helen Mirren, deals with events surrounding the hunger strike of 1981 and the election of Bobby Sands as MP for Tyrone & Fermanagh shortly before his death.

ENTERING & LEAVING

Virtually all international visitors to Ireland travel via England. There are flights to Dublin and Belfast from London's four international airports, as well as flights from provincial cities. Several major European cities offer direct flights to Ireland. Airport departure taxes are built into the cost of your ticket. Ferry services operate between Dublin and Holyhead in Wales; Rosslare and Fishguard and Pembroke, also in Wales; Belfast and Liverpool in England; and Belfast and Stranraer in Scotland. Services also link Cork with Swansea in England, and Cherbourg and Roscoff in France.

ITALY

Italy has so many familiar and beautiful images that it sits high on most travellers' European itineraries. Who hasn't wanted to glide along the canals of Venice in a gondola? Or stand in the shadow of the statue of *David*? And there are few experiences as surreal as standing in the immensity of St Peter's Basilica or staring up at the ceiling of Michelangelo's Sistine Chapel (despite the crowds). Even the food – pizza and pasta – is a favourite of just about everyone. As well as age-old Roman ruins and awesome Renaissance art, Italy has tiny medieval hill towns, exquisite countryside, the majestic Dolomites and more beautiful churches than you imagined could exist in one country.

Unified as a nation for the past century only, Italy is a magnificently complex, if unevenly woven, tapestry. After the collapse of the empire, Rome continued to exercise extraordinary power and attract exuberant wealth as the seat of the Catholic Church, but its hold over the rest of the peninsula was far from complete. City-states to the north and feudal kingdoms to the south shared control and together left a legacy of unparalleled diversity. The economic miracles of the past decades have transformed the country, but beneath all the style, fine food and delicious wine, there remains, happily, a certain chaotic air.

You could not hope to experience all the wonders of this country in even a year of travel – but you can certainly give it a try.

WHEN TO GO

Italy is at its best in spring (April-May) and autumn (October-November). During these seasons the scenery is beautiful, the temperatures are pleasant and there are relatively few crowds. Try to avoid August, as this is the time that most Italians take their vacations, and many shops and businesses are closed as a result, but popular holiday spots

At a Glance

Full Country Name: Italian Republic
Area: 301,250 sq km
Population: 57.8 million
Capital City: Rome (pop four million)
People: Italian
Language: Standard Italian and numerous dialects
Religion: 85% Roman Catholic, 5% Jewish and Protestant
Government: Parliamentary republic
Currency: Italian lira (L)
Time Zone: One hour ahead of GMT/UTC; clocks go forward one hour from the last Sunday in March and back again on the last Sunday in September
International Telephone Code: 39
Electricity: 220V, 50Hz

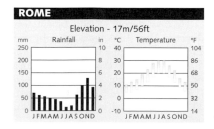

ROME — Elevation - 17m/56ft

are packed. Even Rome seems virtually devoid of locals (but still full of tourists).

The ski season generally lasts from December to late March, swimming is best between June and September, and July and September are the best months for walking in the Alps. The further south you go, the longer you can linger into November and December without feeling the pinch of winter. Italy's multitude of festivals and traditional events may be a factor in planning your visit; Easter, in particular, is celebrated fervently, and every second town has a festive saint's day.

HIGHLIGHTS

The list of highlights in Italy is endless. For most people a basic tour will include Rome, Venice and Florence, but those cities alone have loads of treasures to be explored, and are the ones most likely to be heaving with tourists.

Rome

The Roman Empire once ruled a fair slice of Europe, and the Italian capital is no disappointment when it comes to ancient ruins, and Renaissance architecture. Highlights of ancient Rome include the Colosseum, the Roman Forum, the Pantheon and the Baths of Caracalla. From a more modern era, there's the baroque Trevi Fountain, the Spanish Steps (a famous meeting place) and the Arch of Constantine. The biggest attraction, however, is Vatican City, with the unbelievable St Peter's Basilica and the Vatican Museums.

Rome is a very large, very crowded and chaotic city, but walking is still the best way to see the sights. There are many fascinating *piazzas* (squares) enclosing classical monuments and fountains, and lined with palaces or alfresco cafes. Piazza Navona, Piazza del Popolo, Campo de' Fiori and Piazza Venezia should not be missed. A week is required to do justice to Rome.

Other Towns & Cities

It's difficult to offer highlights without mentioning a few of Italy's great cities. Florence, cradle of the Renaissance and home of Michelangelo, Dante and the Medicis, is overwhelming in its wealth of art and culture. Florence (Firenze) boasts some wonderful palaces and piazzas and should not be missed. The romance of Venice (Venezia) may not always be evident in high summer when tourists are out in force and the canals are a bit on the nose, but there's no denying the beauty of the city. Despite all the waterways and gondolas, the best way to see Venice is on foot. Verona is well worth a side trip from Venice, and not only for its associations with Romeo and Juliet. Verona has a relaxed feel and a wonderful marble Roman amphi-theatre that is now the city's opera house.

Siena, Italy's best preserved medieval town, is a real gem. Its Palazzo Publico (the town hall) is considered one of the most graceful Gothic buildings in the country. Even if you can't afford to shop, Milan – Italy's fashion capital – is still a refined and cultured place to visit. Bologna (home of spaghetti bolognese as well as lasagne) stands out among Italy's beautiful cities, with its porticoed (arcaded) streets and harmonious architecture. Sicily has a completely different character to northern and central Italy, so a visit to its capital, Palermo, is worthwhile. Although in a state of decay since

WWII, enough evidence remains of Palermo's halcyon days to make it one of Italy's most fascinating cities.

Finally, the five villages of the Cinque Terre – Monterosso, Verazza, Corniglia, Manarola and Riomaggiore – squeezed between the mountains and the Mediterranean in Liguria, form part of Italy's most extraordinary countryside.

Museums & Galleries

The Vatican Museums in Rome contain a superb array of art and treasures collected by generations of popes, and the walls of many apartments, corridors and chapels are decorated with frescoes. Also in Rome, the National Museum houses an important collection of Roman and Greek sculpture. Florence is oozing museums and galleries: don't miss the Uffizi Gallery (Botticelli's *Birth of Venus* and da Vinci's *The Annunciation* among many others), the Accademia (housing Michelangelo's real *David* plus many other sculptures), and the Bargello Museum.

The Academy of Fine Arts in Venice has an impressive collection of Venetian art, while the Peggy Guggenheim Collection nearby is dedicated to modern art. The national Archaeological Museum in Naples contains one of the most important collections of Graeco-Roman artefacts in the world.

Ancient Sites

Other than the well preserved sites in Rome, the ruins of Pompeii are the most absorbing in Italy. Buried under a sea of volcanic ash and lava when Mt Vesuvius blew its top in AD 79, Pompeii provides a fascinating 'frozen' insight into how the ancient Romans lived. The site is easily reached from Naples. Nearby, Herculaneum (also engulfed by Vesuvius) is often overlooked by visitors but it's a smaller and better preserved site. Further south on the Amalfi coast, Paestum is the evocative image of three superbly preserved Greek temples. The archaeological park in Syracuse (Sicily) has a Greek theatre, Roman amphitheatre and various other ancient sites.

Cathedrals & Churches

As the home of the Catholic Church, Italy is naturally well endowed with churches.

St Peter's Basilica in Rome must not be missed. Mostly the work of Michelangelo (he designed the soaring dome), it contains his superb *Pieta*, and Bernini's bronze *Baldacchino* over the papal altar. The Pope usually gives a public audience here every Wednesday. St Mark's Basilica in Venice (at the eastern end of the famous piazza) has an elaborately decorated facade, a stunning gold altarpiece and a 99m free-standing bell tower.

Duomo is the Italian name for the fine domed cathedrals you'll find in many cities. Some of the best include the pink, green and white marble creation in Florence, the pinnacled structure in Milan, and the spectacular cathedral in Siena. The Cathedral of San Giovanni in Turin contains the Shroud of Turin, purported to be the cloth used to wrap the crucified Christ but now more or less debunked. St Francis' Basilica in Assisi is a place of pilgrimage for millions of devotees and tourists every year, but the town still retains a certain charm.

VISA REQUIREMENTS

Residents of The USA, Australia, Canada and New Zealand do not need

Itineraries

Whatever it is that attracts you to Italy, remember that you could spend days or weeks in any one city just looking at monuments and galleries. It's very easy to get burnt out if you try to see too much in Italy!

Two Days

Visit Rome. If you start early you'll have time to see St Peter's Basilica and the Vatican Museums in one day, the Colosseum, Roman Forum and a few piazzas on the other.

One Week

Spend two or three days in Rome, then catch the train up to Florence and allow a couple of days for the Uffizi Gallery, Accademia, Duomo and palaces. You could take an afternoon trip out to Pisa to see the famous leaning bell tower, or simply head straight to Venice for two more days of exploration through the narrow streets and canals.

Two Weeks

With two weeks you can begin to explore a bit deeper. Follow the one week itinerary but include a trip to Siena and perhaps Perugia, and a day trip from Venice to Verona. From there you could visit Bologna or Milan. Another option is to head south from Rome to Naples, an energetic and seductive city from where you can easily reach the haunting ruins of Pompeii, Herculaneum and Paestum.

Alternatively, explore part of the country in more detail:

Northern Italy If you're coming to Italy from France, Switzerland, Austria or Slovenia, you can easily start this trip in Milan, Turin, Genoa or Venice. However, we'll start in Rome and work up.

After spending at least three days in Rome, stop in Perugia, capital of the Umbria region and one of Italy's best preserved medieval hill towns. Continue on to the even more attractive historic town of Siena – the Gothic buildings here are various shades of the colour known as burnt sienna. Next, make the short trip to Florence, where you can spend a couple of days exploring the museums and palaces,

and making an afternoon trip to Pisa. If time permits, stop at Bologna next, or head straight to Venice for a couple of days of leisurely sightseeing and canal cruising. Spend a day in Verona before heading across to Milan, or travelling straight to the Ligurian coast to explore the five villages of the Cinque Terre, possibly using Genoa as a base.

Southern Italy Starting with three days in Rome, travel south to the chaotic but seductively dark city of Naples for a day. From here it's an easy trip to the preserved cities of Pompeii and Herculaneum and the ruins of Pasteum. You could spend some time exploring the Amalfi coast (including fashionable Positano or Sorrento), or take a trip to the beautiful island of Capri before continuing south through untouristed Calabria and into Sicily. Spend a couple of days in the capital Palermo, from where you can take a ferry to the captivating Aeolian islands (the best of which are Lipari, Vulcano, Salina and Stromboli); or visit the historic city of Syracuse, with its archaeological park and nearby medieval island of Ortygia. If you have any time left, you can detour to Mt Etna, Italy's (and Europe's) largest and most active volcano. The best bases are Catania or the touristy and expensive resort town of Taormina.

One Month

With a month you can combine the two-week itineraries, or explore each area in more depth.

In northern Italy, for example, you could visit Assisi in Umbria, spend some time in the countryside around Tuscany and spend a few days exploring the Ligurian coast. Also visit Turin, and allow a few days for the Italian Alps – the spectacular limestone mountain range known as the Dolomites. There are some great hiking trails here and several winter ski resorts. Val Gardena and Canazei are popular resorts here.

In southern Italy you could easily spend more time exploring Sicily, including Mt Etna and the Aeolian islands, and perhaps take a ferry ride over to the island of Sardinia.

ITALY HIGHLIGHTS & ITINERARIES

THE DOLOMITES
Ski the spectacular limestone range, or hike the many trails

VENICE
Wander the winding streets of La Serenissima, the Most Serene Republic

FLORENCE
Feast on the amazing fruits of the Renaissance

ROME
Discover why all roads still lead to Rome

SIENA
See the majestic Gothic hues of Italy's best – preserved medieval town

a visa for stays of up to three months. Visitors from the European Union (EU) countries need only a passport or national identity card, and can stay for as long as they like. South Africans need only a Schengen visa.

Italian Embassies & Consulates

Australia
(☎ 02-9392 7900) Level 45, The Gateway, 1 Macquarie Place, Sydney 2000
Consulate: (☎ 03-9867 5744) 509 St Kilda Rd, Melbourne, Vic, 3004

Canada
(☎ 416-977 2569) 496 Huron Street, Toronto, Ontario M5R 2R3

New Zealand
(☎ 04-473 5339) 34 Grant Rd, Thorndon, Wellington

UK
(☎ 020-7312 2200) 14 Three Kings Yard, London W1 2EH

USA
(☎ 212-439 8600) 690 Park Ave, New York, NY 10021-5044
Consulate: (☎ 415-931 4924) 2590 Webster St, San Francisco, CA 94115

TOURIST OFFICES OVERSEAS

Australia
(☎ 02-9247 1308) Alitalia, Orient Overseas Building, Suite 202, 32 Bridge St, Sydney, NSW, 2000

Canada
(☎ 514-866 7667) 1 Place Ville Marie, Suite 1914, Montreal, Que H3B 3M9

UK
(☎ 020-7408 1254 or 0891-600 280) 1 Princes St, London W1R 8AY

USA
(☎ 212-245 4822) 630 Fifth Ave, Suite 1565, New York, NY 10111
(☎ 310-820 2977) 12400 Wilshire Blvd, Suite 550, Los Angeles, CA 90025
(☎ 312-644 0990) 401 North Michigan Ave, Suite 3030, Chicago, IL 60611

Sestante-CIT (Compagnia Italiana di Turismo), Italy's national travel agency, also has offices throughout the world (known as CIT or Citalia outside Italy). Sestante-CIT offices include:

Australia
(☎ 02-9267 1255) 263 Clarence St, Sydney, NSW 2000
(☎ 03-9650 5510) Level 4, 227 Collins St, Melbourne, Vic 3000

Canada
(☎ 514-845 4310) 1450 City Councillors St, Suite 750, Montreal, Que H3A 2E6
(☎ 416-927 7712) 111 Avenue Rd, Suite 808, Toronto, Ont M5R 3I8

UK
(☎ 020-8686 0326) Marco Polo House, 3-5 Lansdowne Rd, Croydon, Surrey CR9 1LL

USA
(☎ 212-697 2497) 342 Madison Ave, Suite 207, New York, NY 10173
(☎ 310-338 8615) 6033 West Century Blvd, Suite 980, Los Angeles, CA 90045

POST & COMMUNICATIONS

Mail sent from Italy is relatively slow. An airmail letter can take up to two weeks to reach the UK or the USA, while a letter to Australia will take between two and three weeks. Postcards will take even longer because they are low-priority mail. Stamps are available at post offices and authorised tobacconists, but you may have to go to a post office to get the correct international mailing rate. In Rome, use the Vatican post office in St Peter's Square; it has an excellent record for prompt delivery but doesn't accept poste restante mail. Poste restante (known as *fermo posta* in Italy) is available at most other post offices.

Telephone rates in Italy, particularly for long-distance calls, are among the highest in Europe. Local and long-distance calls can be made from any public phone, or from a Telecom office in larger towns. Most public phones accept only phonecards or other credit cards. You can buy them at tobacconists and newsstands, or from vending machines at Telecom offices.

You can send faxes from post offices and from some *tabacchi* (tobacco) shops, but again they're relatively expensive. There's a growing number of Internet cafes in Italy, mainly in the larger cities such as Rome, Venice, Florence and Milan.

MONEY
Costs
Those on a tight budget will find eating and sleeping in Italy a little more expensive than expected. Prudent backpackers might squeeze by on around US$35 a day if they stay in hostels, buy sandwiches and pizza slices, avoid indulging in alcohol and don't visit too many museums (the entrance fee to most modern museums is cripplingly expensive). A room in a one or two-star hotel, one sit-down meal per day and occasional visits to museums will cost close to US$80 per day. However, public transport is reasonably priced and wine bought at supermarkets is quite cheap. Italy has more luxury hotels, expensive restaurants and shops to die for than you can shake a Gold Amex card at, so be prepared to stretch your budget if you have no self-restraint.

Service charges are included in your restaurant bill, so you are not expected to tip. It is common practice, however, to leave a small amount. Tipping taxi drivers is not common practice, but your hotel porter will expect a little something.

Changing Money
Banks are the most reliable places to change travellers cheques, and generally offer the best rates; shop around for the lowest commission deals and the shortest queues. Credit cards are widely accepted in Italy. Visa is the easiest card with which to obtain cash advances from banks. ATMs *(bancomats)* are common in cities.

ONLINE SERVICES
Lonely Planet's Destination Italy is a good place to start (www.lonelyplanet .com/dest/eur/ita.htm). There's a great travel site at www.travel.it with information on hostels and hotels, thematic travel and a focus on Rome. Another excellent site (www.chiantinet.it) has lots of information about the Chianti area and links to other sites. Welcome Italy page (www.alfanet.it) has links to information about Rome. Another site (www.italysource.com) has everything from Italian cooking and shopping to travel and culture.

The Florence Art Guide site (www.mega.it/eng/egui/hogui.htm) has plenty of information on this arts and culture capital. For a cool site with everything you need to know about Florence, see http://english.firenzenet. The site of Rome's municipal government, the *comune* (www.comune.roma.it) doubles as a source of information for residents and tourists. The Pope Page (www.catholic.net/RCC/POPE/pope .html) has everything you ever wanted to know about John Paul II, the Vatican and popes through the ages.

BOOKS
Enough books have been published on Italian culture and history to sink a small navy. Vincent Cronin's *Concise History of Italy*, Jerome Carcopino's *Daily Life in Ancient Rome* and Bernard Berenson's *Painters of the Renaissance* are useful places to start.

Venice by James Morris and HV Morton's *A Traveller in Italy* are classic travelogues. The popular historian Christopher Hibbert's many books include the 'biographies' of Rome and Venice and *The Rise and Fall of the House of the Medici*.

Classics include Cicero's *Selected Works*, Livy's *Early History of Rome*, Ovid's *Metamorphoses* and Virgil's *The Aeneid*. You could then progress to Dante's *The Divine Comedy*, Boccaccio's *The Decameron* and Machiavelli's *The Prince*. Modern novels include Giuseppe di Lampedusa's *The Leopard*, Carlo Levi's *Christ Stopped at Eboli*, Umberto Eco's *The Name of the Rose* and absolutely anything by Italo Calvino.

For a spot of Edwardian romance, you can't avoid stepping into EM Forster's *Room with a View*.

FILMS

If you want to get in the mood before heading off to Italy, here are a few suggestions: *Roman Holiday* (Gregory Peck and Audrey Hepburn scootering around Rome), *Three Coins in a Fountain* (three American women get their men at the Trevi fountain), *It Happened in Naples* (Sophia Loren), *Come September* (Rock, Gina, Sandra and Bobby romp around the Amalfi coast), *The Agony & the Ecstasy* (Charleton Heston as Michelangelo), *A Room with a View*, *Stealing Beauty* (dumb film, but a great Tuscan travelogue) and Peter Sellers' *The Pink Panther* (set in Cortina and Rome).

Ingrid Bergman starred in two films set in Italy, *Stromboli* (1949) and *Viaggio in Italia* (Journey in Italy; 1953). Roberto Benini's *Life is Beautiful* (1998) is an entertaining, Oscar-winning story set in Tuscany during WWII.

ENTERING & LEAVING

Visitors travelling to Italy from non-European destinations will find flights are numerous and competitive. Leaving Italy, the departure tax is factored into the cost of your plane ticket. Unless you're pushed for time, train travel is a great way to enter Italy from within Europe. Buses are numerous but can't really compete with the convenience of the train. Ferries connect the country with Greece, Turkey, Tunisia, Malta, Albania, Egypt and Spain.

LATVIA

Those who dub Latvia the 'Switzerland of the Baltics' need a thorough talking to. For a start, a tenth of the country is below sea level, sometimes up to 50m, and Latvia toes a most-un-Alpine line in being the small, flat and largely boggy meat in the sandwich between its Baltic neighbours, Estonia and Lithuania. And hopes of becoming a financial centre were swamped when Bank Baltija went bust, causing a national banking crisis.

Lacking Estonia's close proximity to a western country (Finland) or the fame that Lithuania achieved on its path to independence, Latvia used to be the least known of the Baltic states. But this is rapidly changing, with a dramatic influx of tourists and foreign investors since independence was achieved in 1991 (the first democratic elections were held in 1993). You should probably get along to Latvia before it actually becomes fashionable.

WHEN TO GO
Spring and summer (April through September) are far and away the best times of year to visit. These months see better weather, more daylight, fresher food and plenty of folk festivals cropping up nationwide. The weather during this period is suitable for most outdoor activities – as long as you don't mind the slushy and chilly weeks at either end. Winter weather (from November to late March) can be extreme in Latvia, but this period also sees the most theatre performances and concerts, and is the time for skiing. July/August is the peak tourist season, when hotels are often fully booked.

HIGHLIGHTS
Riga
Cosmopolitan Riga is the biggest and most vibrant of the Baltic capitals. A fascinating mix of Latvian, Russian and German influences, Riga has a well preserved historic old town. It has a castle (home to Latvia's president) and several museums, including a motor museum displaying cars that

At a Glance

Full Country Name: Republic of Latvia
Area: 64,589 sq km
Population: 2.62 million
Capital City: Riga (pop 874,100)
People: 57% Latvian, 30% Russian, 4% Belarusian, 3% Ukrainian, 3% Polish
Language: Latvian, Russian
Religion: Lutheran, Roman Catholic, Russian Orthodox
Government: Republic
Currency: Latvian lats (plural: lati)
Time Zone: Two hours ahead of GMT/UTC
International Telephone Code: 371
Electricity: 220V, 50Hz

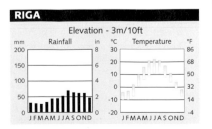

RIGA
Elevation - 3m/10ft

Rainfall / Temperature chart

JFMAMJJASOND

once belonged to Stalin and Brezhnev. Riga's other highlight is its nightlife (bars and clubs) and cultural shows (opera, ballet, classical music). You can afford to make merry here too – Riga champagne is dirt cheap and doesn't taste too bad.

At Salaspils, 15km south of Riga, is the former Nazi concentration camp where an estimated 100,000 Jews were murdered.

Gauja Valley
The Gauja Valley, and the 920 sq km Gauja National Park, is the highlight of rural Latvia and a great place for the outdoorsy types. Siguldu (known locally as the Switzerland of Latvia) is the main gateway and is an easy trip from Riga. One of the best ways to enjoy the valley is to take a canoe trip on the Gauja River from Valmiera; otherwise, there are many hiking

opportunities out of Sigulda as well as a bobsleigh centre, also in Sigulda.

Castles & Palaces
Latvia has its share of historic castles, many of them in ruins. Notable ones include Sigulda Castle, Krimulda Castle, and the imposing Bauska Castle. The nearby 18th century Rundale Palace is the architectural highlight of rural Latvia.

Coastal Areas
Long, sandy beaches attract thousands of sun-lovers to the string of coastal villages and resorts just east of Riga known as Jurmala. Majori and Dzintari are the main towns.

More off the beaten track is the Kurzeme region to the west. Taking your time to explore this coastal tip – the land of the Livs and a world apart from the rest of Latvia – is a magnetic experience.

VISA REQUIREMENTS
All nationalities require a visa except citizens of the Czech Republic, Denmark, Estonia, Finland, Hungary, Iceland, Ireland, Lithuania, Norway, Poland, Sweden, UK and USA.

Latvian Embassies & Consulates
Australia
   (☎ 03-9499 6920) 38 Longstaff St, Ivanhoe East, Vic 3073
Canada
   (☎ 613-238 6014/868, fax 238 7044, ✆ latvia-embassy@magmacom.com, www2 .magmacom.com/latemb) 112 Kent St, Place de Ville, Tower B, Suite 208, Ottawa, Ont K1P 5P2
UK
   (☎ 020-7312 0040, fax 7312 0042) 45 Nottingham Place, London W1M 3FE

Itineraries

Two Days
Visit Riga and then spend a day at Sigulda, walking, bobsleighing or just looking around.

One Week
Spend two days in Riga, including a visit to the former concentration camp at Salaspils, then head west to the beach resort towns of Jurmala. Spend the rest of your time in the Gauja Valley, taking a canoe trip from Valmiera to Sigulda and exploring the Sigulda area.

Two Weeks
With two weeks you should be able to see Riga, Jurmala, and the Gauja Valley (including Valmiera, Sigulda, Cesis and Ligatne). After that, go down to Bauska Castle and Rundale Palace, then west to Kuldiga and Ventspils in the Kurzeme region.

LATVIA HIGHLIGHTS & ITINERARIES

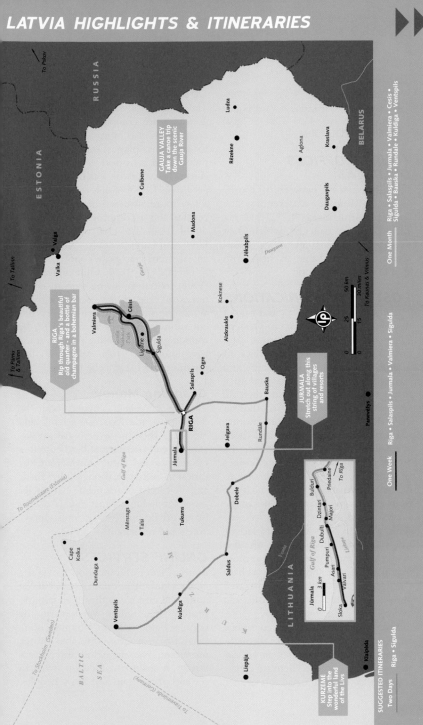

RIGA
Rip through Riga's beautiful old quarter – and a bottle of champagne in a bohemian bar

GAUJA VALLEY
Take a canoe trip down the scenic Gauja River

JURMALA
Stretch out along this string of villages and resorts

KURZEME
Step into the wonderful land of the Livs

SUGGESTED ITINERARIES

Two Days   Riga • Sigulda

One Week   Riga • Salaspils • Jurmala • Valmiera • Sigulda

One Month   Riga • Salaspils • Jurmala • Valmiera • Cesis •
Sigulda • Bauska • Rundale • Kuldiga • Ventspils

USA
(☎ 202-726 6757/8213, fax 726 6785, ✉ latvia@seas.gwu.edu, www.seas.gwu.edu/guest/latvia) 4325 17th St NW, Washington, DC 20011

TOURIST OFFICES OVERSEAS

Latvia has a small network of tourist offices in Europe representing the Latvian Tourist Board (☎ 7327 542, fax 7229 945, www.eunet.lv), which is at Pils laukums 4, LV-1050 in Riga. Travel agents should be able to help with inquiries outside Europe.

POST & COMMUNICATIONS

These days mail service in and out of the three Baltic states is up to Western European standards – letters and postcards take seven to 10 days to North America. Buy your stamps at a post office *(pasts)* and post your mail there, too. There are poste restante services in the central post office in Riga where mail is held for one month.

Telephone services have also been overhauled since the demise of the Soviet Union, with new exchanges allowing direct digital connections to the west. International calls can be made from the new public card phones in the streets. These accept *telekartes* (phonecards) that can be bought from kiosks, shops and post offices. There are also new coin-operated phones, and in more remote areas and some cities, such as Daugavpils, the old token-operated phones from which only local calls can be made are still quite common.

There are reasonably priced public fax services in the main cities throughout the region, mainly at post offices and in all major hotels. There are cybercafes in Riga offering email services.

MONEY

Costs

Travelling in Latvia is pretty expensive, as prices are comparable to those in Scandinavia. Accommodation is likely to be your biggest expense, while public land transport is still relatively cheap. Travellers on a tight budget can get by on US$30 a day, though adding a few more sit-down meals and more comfortable accommodation can easily double that. The cost of a luxurious lifestyle in Latvia is equivalent to that in any Western European country.

There's an 18% value-added tax (VAT) in Latvia, so be sure to check prices to see if it's been included. While tipping isn't compulsory, it's common to tip waiters 5 to 10% by rounding up the bill. There's some bargaining at flea markets, but discounts are likely to be minimal.

Changing Money

Cashing travellers cheques can be difficult outside Riga, Daugavpils and Sigulda, though every town has somewhere to exchange hard currency. US dollars and Deutschmarks are the easiest to exchange, though other Baltic and Western European currencies aren't far behind. Most ATMs accept major credit cards, as do most shops, hotels and restaurants.

ONLINE SERVICES

Lonely Planet's Destination Latvia site (www.lonelyplanet.com/dest/eur/lat.htm) will give you a thorough country profile. The online version of the popular Baltic *In Your Pocket* guidebook (www.inyourpocket.com) has hotel, restaurant, bar, nightclub and theatre listings, a calendar of events, what to see and plane, train and bus schedules.

A good site for news about the Baltics and links to English-language media sources is at www.ciesin.ee/NEWS/index.html.

BOOKS

The Singing Revolution by Clare Thomson traces the path of all three Baltic states towards their new independence through an account of her travels there in 1989 and 1990. *Among the Russians* by Colin Thubron recounts a drive through the pre-glasnost Soviet Union, including Riga. It captures the gloomy, resigned mood of the time. *The Baltic States: The Years of Independence 1917-40* by Georg von Rauch and *The Baltic States – Years of Dependence 1940-80* by Romualdas Misiunas & Rein Taagepera are both weighty historical tomes.

Letters from Latvia by Lucy Addison is the compelling journal of a 79-year-old woman who, at the outbreak of WWII, refused to leave Latvia and endured the German, then Soviet occupations. *The Holocaust in Latvia 1941-1944 – The Missing Center*, by Andrew Ezergailis, provides an insightful and balanced account of this provocative subject and addresses the sensitive issue of Latvian participation in the holocaust.

FILMS

Hundarna I Riga (1995) is a Swedish thriller set largely in Riga. *Cilveka berns* (Child of Man; 1992) is a drama set in a pre-WWII Latvian village.

ENTERING & LEAVING

State-run Air Baltic is in partnership with SAS (Scandinavian Airlines) and links Riga with Copenhagen, Frankfurt, Geneva, Hamburg, Helsinki, Kiev, London, Minsk, Moscow, Paris, Stockholm, Tallinn, Vilnius and Warsaw. There are no direct flights between Riga and North America, Australia or Asia. There is no departure tax (yet).

There are direct buses to Riga from Denmark, France, Germany, Norway, Poland, Sweden, Finland, Russia, Belarus, Estonia and Lithuania. The Berlin-St Petersburg train service passes through Daugavpils in south-eastern Latvia. Trains also link Riga with Moscow, St Petersburg and Minsk, and Daugavpils with Chernivtsi.

If you prefer to suck in the sea air, there are direct ferries to Riga from Travemünde in Germany, Stockholm and Slite in Sweden, and Roomassaare on the Estonian island of Saaremaa.

LIECHTENSTEIN

Nod off and you might miss Liecht-enstein – it's only 6km from east to west as you pass through from Austria to Switzerland. You could even be for-given for thinking it was part of Switzer-land: its currency is Swiss, all travel documents valid for Switzerland are also valid for Liechtenstein, and the only border formalities are on the Aus-trian side. Liechtenstein issues its own postage stamps and, unlike Switzerland, it joined the United Nations in 1990 and the European Economic Area (EEA) in 1995. Apart from that, it's pretty much business as usual in the Alps – skiing, fine wines and clean mountain air. It doesn't take long to see, so if you're passing, why skip one of the world's smallest countries?

WHEN TO GO

You can visit Liechtenstein any time of the year. Summer lasts roughly from

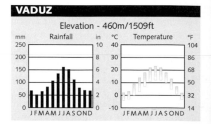

June to September, and offers the most pleasant climate for outdoor pursuits. Unfortunately, you won't be the only tourist during this period, so prices can be high. You'll find much better deals during the shoulder seasons of April to May or late-September to October.

If you're keen on winter sports, resorts in the Alps begin operating in late November and move into full swing around Christmas. They close down when the snow begins to melt in April.

HIGHLIGHTS
Vaduz

Little more than a village, Liecht-enstein's capital won't hold your atten-tion for long, but it's worth visiting for the prince's State Art Collection.

Hiking & Skiing

The mountains of Liechtenstein – the Tirolean Alps in the south-east – are perfect for winter skiing or summer hiking. The Rhine Valley to the west also offers good opportunities for walking. Malbun is the main ski resort, with a variety of runs and six hotels.

At a Glance

Full Country Name: Principality of Liecht-enstein
Area: 160 sq km
Population: 31,500
Capital City: Vaduz (pop 5000)
People: 87.5% Germanic, Italian, Turkish, 12.5% other
Language: German
Religion: Roman Catholic, Protestant
Government: Hereditary constitutional monarchy
Currency: Swiss franc (SwF)
Time Zone: Two hours ahead of GMT/UTC
International Telephone Code: 075
Electricity: 220V, 50Hz

LIECHTENSTEIN HIGHLIGHTS & ITINERARIES

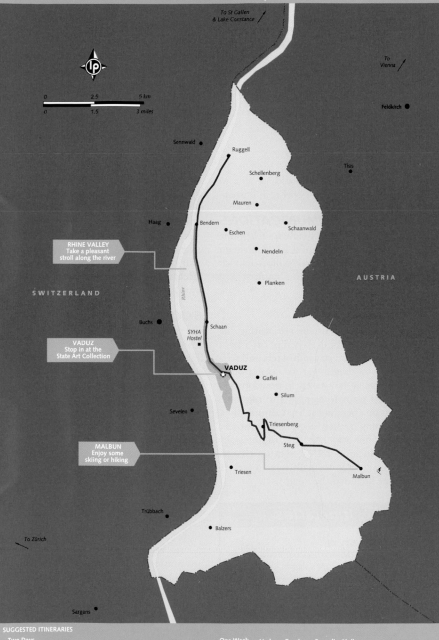

To St Gallen
& Lake Constance

To Vienna

Feldkirch

Sennwald

Ruggell

Schellenberg

Tisis

Mauren

Haag

Bendern

Eschen

Schaanwald

RHINE VALLEY
Take a pleasant
stroll along the river

Nendeln

SWITZERLAND

Planken

AUSTRIA

Rhine

Buchs

Schaan

SYHA
Hostel

VADUZ
Stop in at the
State Art Collection

VADUZ

Gaflei

Silum

Sevelen

Triesenberg

MALBUN
Enjoy some
skiing or hiking

Steg

Triesen

Malbun

Trübbach

To Zürich

Balzers

Sargans

VISA REQUIREMENTS

Citizens of Australia, Canada, Ireland, New Zealand, South Africa, the UK and the USA do not require visas for visits of up to three months.

Liechtenstein has no overseas embassies.

TOURIST OFFICES OVERSEAS

Swiss tourist offices should be able to help with information on Liechtenstein.

POST & COMMUNICATIONS

Liechtenstein shares the Swiss telephone and postal system, but it issues its own postage stamps – many collectors visit Liechtenstein just for the stamps!

MONEY
Costs

Costs in Liechtenstein are among the highest in Europe. If you're on a tight budget and you stay in hostels and self-cater, you could get by on around US$40 a day. If you stay in pensions, eat out and want to sample the nightlife, count on spending at least double that.

Tipping is rarely necessary, as hotels, restaurants and bars are required by law to include a 15% service charge. Even taxi fares normally have a service charge included.

Itineraries

Two Days
In two days you can check out Vaduz and go for a walk in the Rhine Valley or visit a village in the lowlands of Northern Liechtenstein.

One Week
After a week you're practically a local. Do the two day options and head across to Malbun for a few days of skiing or hiking in the Alps.

Changing Money

All major travellers cheques and credit cards are accepted. Commission is not charged for changing cash or cheques, but shop around for the best rates (hotels usually have the worst rates).

ONLINE SERVICES

Lonely Planet has a site, Destination Liechtenstein, at www.lonelyplanet .com/dest/eur/lie.htm. Excite Travel's site (www.city.et/countries/liechtens tein) has some good travel information and loads of useful links. Liechtenstein News (www.news.li) has updates on what's happening in the principality with the royals, jobs, stamps etc. The Liechtenstein government has a site at www.gk.soft.com/govt/en/li.

BOOKS

The majority of books about Liechtenstein focus on company law, and there is precious little to read otherwise. See the Switzerland profile for books that have relevance to the region.

For the history/antique/firearms buffs, there is *Firearms from the Collections of the Prince of Liechtenstein* by Stuart Pyhrr. *Minkus Stamp Catalog – Austria, Liechtenstein, Switzerland* by George Tlamsa is a serious look at Liechtenstein's stamps for the seriously keen.

ENTERING & LEAVING

Liechtenstein has no airport; the nearest is in Zürich, Switzerland. There are no local railways apart from the international line from Zürich to Vienna that stops at Schaan, north of Vaduz. There are normally three buses an hour from the Swiss border towns of Buchs and Sargans to Vaduz, and buses run every half-hour from the Austrian border town of Feldkirch.

Any country that gives pride of place to a memorial statue of singer Frank Zappa has got to be worth a visit. Lithuania is the most vibrant Baltic state, shown not only by its anti-establishment statues but more deeply by its daring and emotional drive for independence in 1990-01.

The southernmost Baltic state, Lithuania owes much to the rich cultural currents of Central Europe: with neighbouring Poland it once shared an empire stretching from the Baltic Sea almost to the Black Sea. The Lithuanian people are regarded as much more outgoing and less organised than their Estonian and Latvian counterparts, and most still practice the Roman Catholicism that sets them apart from their Lutheran Baltic neighbours.

Although compact and less than spectacular, Lithuania boasts attractions ranging from the intriguing Curonian Spit and the strange Hill of Crosses to the urban pleasures of Vilnius, the historic, lively capital. What's more, it's the cheapest of the Baltics. Savouring the unique atmosphere and friendliness of Lithuania's ethnic street carnivals and theatre festivals is another unbeatable highlight for many.

WHEN TO GO

Summer and spring (May through September) are the best times of the year to travel in Lithuania. The majority of foreign tourists come during July and August, when low-budget hotels and hostels can be fully booked. While there's usually a picturesque sprinkling

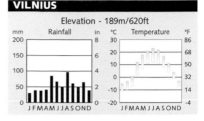

of snow on the ground in winter (November through March), there's also only a few hours of daylight each day.

HIGHLIGHTS
Vilnius

The heart of Vilnius – the largest Old Town in Eastern Europe – is a chocolate box of three storey baroque and classical buildings. Among the sights are the Vilnius Cathedral, several

At a Glance

Full Country Name: Republic of Lithuania
Area: 65,200 sq km
Population: 3.7 million
Capital City: Vilnius (pop 575,000)
People: 80% Lithuanian, 9% Russian, 7% Polish
Language: Lithuanian
Religion: Predominantly Roman Catholic, plus Russian Orthodox, Old Believers and Lutheran
Government: Independent republic
Currency: Lithuanian litu (plural: litas)
Time Zone: One hour ahead of GMT/UTC
International Telephone Code: 370
Electricity: 220V, 50Hz

museums and the Frank Zappa statue. The latter was erected by the Lithuanian Frank Zappa Fan Club in 1995 after a long battle with authorities, who thought the idea preposterous. Vilnius also has its share of bars, western-style nightclubs, opera and ballet.

Curonian Spit

The enchanting coastal region of the Curonian Spit (also known as the Neringa Spit) is a world of windswept sand dunes and pine trees. It's a thin finger of sand stretching 97km south of Klaipeda and separating the Baltic Sea from the Kuršiu Lagoon. Klaipeda is a good base for visits (a regular ferry crosses from here to the northern point). The main settlement on the spit itself is Nida.

Itineraries

Two Days
Spend your time in Vilnius, exploring the Old Town, and make a day trip out to Trakai, with its two lakeside castles.

One Week
Spend two days in Vilnius, then travel west to Klaipeda and spend a couple of days exploring the Curonian Spit. You could also make a stop at the historic town of Kaunas between Vilnius and Klaipeda.

Two Weeks
You could spend two or three days exploring Vilnius, a day in Kaunas, then up to Šiauliai to visit the Hill of Crosses. From there, make a stop at the Zemaitija National Park and the Orvydas Garden before continuing down to Klaipeda and the Curonian Spit.

If you have any more time in Lithuania, include a trip from Vilnius up to the lake-filled Aukštaitija National Park (Ignalina is a good base) for some canoeing and walking.

National Parks & the Hill of Crosses

The 300 sq km Aukštaitija National Park in eastern Lithuania is a remote area that remains blissfully untouched. The park has a labyrinthine scattering of lakes and offers good walking and canoeing.

The fantastical rock and sculpture Orvydas Garden, in Salantai just outside the Zemaitija National Park, is a moving tribute to those that were persecuted under Stalin's regime. Lake Plateliai, in the centre of the park, is good for boating, fishing and camping.

The bizarre Hill of Crosses, near Šiauliai in the north of the country, is a place of pilgrimage for Lithuanians and something worth seeing if you're passing this way. It consists of a two-humped hillock covered in thousands of crosses. The crosses have been placed here since the 14th century for many reasons, though many were planted to commemorate people killed during the 19th century anti-Russian uprisings.

VISA REQUIREMENTS

Lithuania requires visas from most nationalities except citizens of the Baltic states, Australia, Canada, Denmark, Ireland, Italy, Switzerland, the UK and the USA.

Lithuanian Embassies
Australia
(☎ 02-9498 2571) 40B Fiddens Wharf Rd, Killara, NSW 2071
Canada
(☎ 613-567 5458) 130 Albert St, Suite 204, Ottawa, Ont K1P 564
UK
(☎ 020-7938 2481) 17 Essex Villas, London W8 7BP
USA
(☎ 202-234 5860) 2622 16th St NW, Washington, DC 20009

LITHUANIA HIGHLIGHTS & ITINERARIES ▶▶

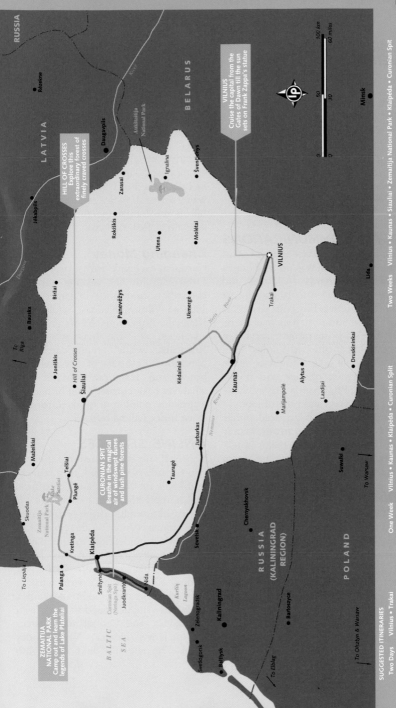

ZEMAITIJA NATIONAL PARK
Camp out and learn the legends of Lake Plateliai

CURONIAN SPIT
Breathe in the magical air of windswept dunes and lush pine forests

HILL OF CROSSES
Explore this extraordinary forest of finely carved crosses

VILNIUS
Cruise the capital from the Gates of Dawn till the sun sets on Frank Zappa's statue

RUSSIA

LATVIA

BELARUS

RUSSIA (KALININGRAD REGION)

POLAND

BALTIC SEA

Rēzekne
Daugavpils
Jēkabpils
Bauska
To Riga
Zarasai
Rokiškis
Utena
Moletai
Ignalina
Švenčionys
Aukštaitija National Park
VILNIUS
Trakai
Lida
Minsk
Biržai
Panevėžys
Ukmergė
Joniškis
Hill of Crosses
Šiauliai
Kėdainiai
Kaunas
Alytus
Lazdijai
Druskininkai
Marijampolė
Jurbarkas
Tauragė
Mažeikiai
Telšiai
Plungė
Zemaitija National Park
Lake Plateliai
Skuodas
Kretinga
Klaipėda
Palanga
Smiltynė
Nida
Juodkrantė
Curonian Spit (Neringa Spit)
Kuršių Lagoon
Zelenogradsk
Kaliningrad
Svetlogorsk
Baltiysk
Chernyakhovsk
Sovetsk
Suwałki
Bartoszyce
Minsk

Neris River
Nemunas River
Dauguva

To Liepāja
To Riga
To Olsztyn & Warsaw
To Warsaw
To Elbląg

0   50   100 km
0   30   60 miles

SUGGESTED ITINERARIES

Two Days Vilnius • Trakai

One Week Vilnius • Kaunas • Klaipėda • Curonian Spit

Two Weeks Vilnius • Kaunas • Šiauliai • Zemaitija National Park • Klaipėda • Curonian Spit

TOURIST OFFICES OVERSEAS

Lithuania has a small network of tourist offices, coordinated by the Lithuanian Tourist Board (☎ 22-622 610, fax 226 819), Ukmerge 20, LT-2600 in Vilnius.

Its representatives overseas include:

USA

Vytis Tours
(☎ 718-423 6161 or toll free 800-778 9847, fax 718-423 3979, ✆ vyttours@ gnn.com) 40-24 235th St, Douglaston, NY 11363

POST & COMMUNICATIONS

These days, mail service in and out of the three Baltic states is up to Western European standards – letters and postcards take seven to 10 days to get to North America. Buy your stamps at a post office and post your mail there, too. There's a poste restante service in the central post office in Vilnius.

International calls can now be made from all private phones and public cardphones. Phonecards are available from news kiosks and post offices.

There are reasonably priced public fax services in the main towns, mainly at post offices and in all major hotels. You can send and receive email from cybercafes in Vilnius.

MONEY
Costs

Lithuania is the cheapest of the Baltic states to travel in, with food in particular being ridiculously cheap. Hostel accommodation is rarely more than US$10 and can go as low at US$2 for a bed in a shared room. This style of accommodation, combined with eating in cheap canteens or cafeterias, or self-catering, and travelling in small bursts by bus or train, can keep daily costs

down to under US$10 a day. If you prefer homestays or mid-range hotel accommodation and eating in quality restaurants, daily costs could easily rise to around US$40 to US$60 a day. Public transport is still very affordable.

Lithuania has a value-added tax (VAT) of 18%, which is automatically included in all accommodation and eating costs. Tipping isn't compulsory in Lithuania, but it's common to give waiters 5 or 10% by rounding up the bill. Some bargaining (but not a lot) goes on at flea markets.

Changing Money

Currency exchange isn't a problem in Lithuania, although cashing travellers cheques is best done in larger cities such as Vilnius, Kaunas, Šiauliai and Klaipeda. Numerous ATMs give cash advances on Visa, MasterCard and Eurocard, while credit cards are common methods of payment in hotels and restaurants. Make sure whatever cash currency you bring in is in pristine condition. Marked, torn or worn notes will be refused.

ONLINE SERVICES

Lonely Planet's Destination Lithuania (www.lonelyplanet.com/dest/eur/lit .htm) will get you started. The official site of the Lithuanian tourist office is at www.ktl.mii.lt/visitors/strukt.htm. The online version of the popular *In Your Pocket* guidebook to the Baltics (www.inyourpocket.com) has hotel, restaurant, bar and theatre listings for Vilnius, a calendar of events, what to see, and plane, train and bus schedules.

Another site dedicated to news from the Baltics, and Central and Eastern Europe is www.ciesin.ee/NEWS/index .html. The site has links to English

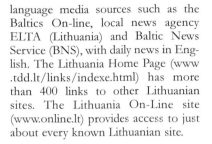

language media sources such as the Baltics On-line, local news agency ELTA (Lithuania) and Baltic News Service (BNS), with daily news in English. The Lithuania Home Page (www .tdd.lt/links/indexe.html) has more than 400 links to other Lithuanian sites. The Lithuania On-Line site (www.online.lt) provides access to just about every known Lithuanian site.

BOOKS & FILMS

The Baltic Revolution by Anatol Lieven is an insightful account of the heady days of the early 1990s, written by the Baltic states correspondent for the *London Times*. *Journey into Russia* by Laurens Van Der Post is an account of the author's travels through Soviet Russia in the 1960s, including a visit to Vilnius. William Palmer's *Good Republic* conjures up the atmosphere of the pre-WWII Baltics, the Soviet and Nazi occupations, and the feel of emigre life.

Bohin Manor by Tadeusz Konwicki is set in Lithuania in the aftermath of the 1863 uprising. It evokes tensions between locals, their Russian rulers and a Jewish outsider, as well as the foreboding and mysterious nature of the Lithuanian backwoods. *Forest of the Gods* by Lithuanian dramatist Balys Sruoga is locally published and available in Vilnius. It is a powerful account of the author's time spent in the Stutthof Nazi concentration camp.

Niekas nonorejo mirti (Nobody Wanted to Die; 1963) and *Trys Dienos* (Three Days; 1991) are two films set in Lithuania.

ENTERING & LEAVING

Frequent flights operate between Vilnius or Kaunas and most European capitals. There are no direct flights between Lithuania and North America, Australia and Asia.

Buses are the cheapest but least comfortable way of reaching Lithuania, with direct buses from Belarus, Denmark, Finland, France, Germany, Norway, Poland, Russia and Sweden. The buses between Poland and Belarus and Lithuania are notoriously subject to long delays: motorists have had to queue for as long as four days at the border between Ogrodniki, Poland and Lazdijai. Lithuanian border guards are pretty nonchalant nowadays – they don't bother stamping passports and have even been known to crack a smile.

The Berlin-St Petersburg train passes through Vilnius. If you're coming from Poland, you can take a direct train from Warsaw to Kaunas, then pick up one of the frequent connections to Vilnius. The direct train from Warsaw to Vilnius passes through Belarus. The daily *Baltic Express*, which links Poland with Estonia, stops at three Lithuanian destinations. Ferries link the west coast port of Klaipeda with Århus, Fredericia and Copenhagen (Denmark), Kiel and Mukran (Germany), and Harwich (England).

LUXEMBOURG ▶▶

Many travellers regard Luxembourg as a nonevent or a novelty – a pocket of greenery somewhere in between Belgium, Germany and France. But that's only the people who haven't been there.

Those who do make the effort to find out what's in Luxembourg will discover a surprisingly diverse little land, from the charming wine-producing Moselle Valley in the east to the deep valleys and quaint towns of the north. History is widely apparent in the many feudal castles, chateaux and abbeys, but these days Luxembourg is a prosperous country at the forefront of the European Union (EU) and international finance.

Luxembourg may not be as big a tourist draw as its neighbours, but its charms are nonetheless unique and its people justly proud of their heritage and homeland. After years of being fought over by European powers, Luxembourg (along with Belgium) was included as part of the United Kingdom of the Netherlands in 1814. Later it was split between Belgium and the Netherlands and eventually, in 1839, the Dutch portion became present-day Luxembourg.

WHEN TO GO
Spring, the best time of year to visit, brings a riot of wildflowers and ushers in celebrations and folk festivals nationwide. From spring to autumn is usually good for outdoor activities, although a fair amount of rain falls at this time. Winter is not as extreme in Luxembourg as it can be in nearby countries, so if you find yourself there during the colder months, you needn't weigh yourself down with polar gear.

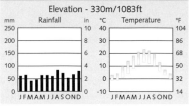

At a Glance

Full Country Name: Grand Duchy of Luxembourg
Area: 2586 sq km
Population: 415,870
Capital City: Luxembourg City (pop 90,000)
People: 70% nationals (Celtic stock, with French and German), 30% resident foreigners (mostly Belgian, French, German, Italian and Portuguese)
Language: Luxembourgish (Letzeburgesch), French, German
Religion: 97% Roman Catholic
Government: Constitutional monarchy
Currency: Luxembourg franc (f)
Time Zone: One hour ahead of GMT/UTC; clocks are turned forward one hour on the last Sunday in March and back again on the last Sunday in October
International Telephone Code: 352
Electricity: 220V, 50Hz

HIGHLIGHTS
Luxembourg City
Often described as Europe's most dramatically situated city, the capital is perched on a promontory overlooking the Pétrusse and Alzette valleys. The

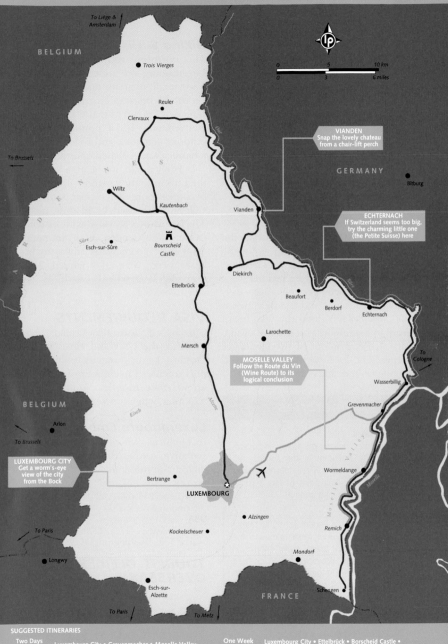

To Liège &
Amsterdam

BELGIUM

Trois Vierges

Reuler

Clervaux

To Brussels

Wiltz

Kautenbach

A R D E N N E S

Sûre

Esch-sur-Sûre

Bourscheid
Castle

Ettelbrück

Mersch

BELGIUM

Arlon

To Brussels

LUXEMBOURG CITY
Get a worm's-eye
view of the city
from the Bock

Bertrange

LUXEMBOURG

Kockelscheuer

To Paris

Longwy

Esch-sur-
Alzette

To Paris

To Metz

Vianden

Diekirch

GERMANY

Bitburg

VIANDEN
Snap the lovely chateau
from a chair-lift perch

ECHTERNACH
If Switzerland seems too big,
try the charming little one
(the Petite Suisse) here

Beaufort

Berdorf

Echternach

Larochette

Sûre

To
Cologne

Wasserbillig

MOSELLE VALLEY
Follow the Route du Vin
(Wine Route) to its
logical conclusion

Grevenmacher

Wormeldange

Alzingen

Remich

Mondorf

Schengen

FRANCE

Moselle Valley

Eisch

Alzette

0   5   10 km
0   3   6 miles

older part of the city and its remaining fortifications are World Heritage listed, but elsewhere this is a modern city.

Luxembourg is made for walking, and one of the highlights is strolling along the pedestrian promenade Chemin de la Corniche at sunset. The Bock Casemates, a honeycomb of tunnels and rock rooms carved under the cliff known as the Bock, can be explored and there are two good museums in town.

Moselle Valley

More than a dozen small towns line the Route du Vin (Wine Road) along the Moselle Valley, one of Europe's smallest and most charming wine regions.

It's easy to spend a couple of lazy days exploring this area and tasting wines at the *caves* (cellars) along the way. From April to September you can sail up the Moselle River on one of two passenger ferries. The local wine festivals begin in August and climax in November.

Itineraries

Two Days
Spend a day walking the streets in Luxembourg City and another day touring the Moselle Valley, using Grevenmacher as your starting or finishing point (it has a youth hostel and a camping ground).

One Week
Spend two days in Luxembourg City, taking time to see the Bock Casemates and the museums. From there, travel north to Ettelbrück and Bourscheid Castle, then spend three days in the north, with visits to Wiltz, Clervaux, Vianden and Diekirch. Spend a day in the Little Switzerland region using Echternach as a base and the final day travelling down the Moselle Valley from Grevenmacher.

Hiking & Historic Towns

The northern and eastern parts of Luxembourg are superb hiking areas. The small area around Echternach, about 40 minutes north-east of the capital, is known as Petite Suisse (Little Switzerland). It's a popular area for outdoor activities, and Echternach has a basilica and a Benedictine abbey.

Further north, in the area known as the Luxembourg Ardennes, the scenery becomes more spectacular, with deep valleys overlooked by historic castles. The towns of Clervaux, with its feudal castle, and Vianden, with an impeccably restored chateaux, make the best bases here. West of Vianden, 1000-year-old Bourscheid Castle is well worth visiting.

VISA REQUIREMENTS

Citizens of Australia, Canada, New Zealand, the USA and virtually all of Western Europe require only a passport to enter Luxembourg for stays of up to three months. South Africans require a Schengen visa.

Luxembourg Embassies

In countries where there is no representative, contact the Belgian or Dutch diplomatic missions.

UK
(☎ 020-7235 6961) 27 Wilton Crescent, London SW1X 8SD

USA
(☎ 202-265 4171) 2200 Massachusetts Ave NW, Washington, DC 20008

TOURIST OFFICES OVERSEAS

UK
(☎ 020-7734 1205) 122-124 Regent St, London W1R 5FE

USA
(☎ 212-935 5896) 17 Beekman Place, New York, NY 10022

POST & COMMUNICATIONS

Mail sent from Luxembourg to Australia, Canada, New Zealand and the USA takes at least a week. There's a small fee (sometimes waived) for collecting poste restante mail.

International phone calls can be made from some post offices, telephone centres or public phones using phonecards.

Faxes can be sent and received at post offices. Email facilities are limited but you'll find a cybercafe in Luxembourg City.

MONEY
Costs

Though Luxembourg is not Western Europe's cheapest destination, a shoestring traveller should be able to get by on about US$30 a day. Travelling in comfort, sleeping in midrange places and letting your belly get the better of your budget you could easily double that.

Expect to pay US$15 for a hostel bed, US$25 to US$30 for a cheap hotel, US$5 to US$7 for a budget meal or US$8 to US$20 for something in a restaurant.

A 15% value-added tax (abbreviated in French as TVA) is slapped on just about everything except for hotel, restaurant and camping ground prices, which are taxed at a much gentler 3%. Tipping is not obligatory.

Changing Money

The Luxembourg franc is pegged to Belgium's, and although the latter is commonly exchanged in both countries, the reverse does not hold true. To avoid a walletful of Luxembourgian mementos, exchange your change before you leave. Banks are the best places to change money, and major credit cards are widely accepted.

ONLINE SERVICES

Lonely Planet's Destination Luxembourg (www.lonelyplanet.com/dest /eur/lux.htm) should be your first stop. The Luxembourg Homepage (www.restena.lu/luxembourg/lux_wel come) has links to many sites relating to all things Luxembourgish. The Luxembourg tourist bureau site (www .luxembourg-city.lu) has the standard tourist information. Luxembourg Central (www.luxcentral.com) is another good site. For up-to-date news, see Luxembourg News at www.news.lu.

BOOKS

The Making of a Nation – From 1815 to the Present Day (Vol XII) by Christian Calmes offers a readable analysis of the history of modern Luxembourg. *The Moon of the Big Winds* by Claudine Muno is a novel about a young man who grows up in a brothel managed by his father. Cathy Clement's *Aleng* is a good read for anyone wanting to bone up on their Luxembourgish.

ENTERING & LEAVING

The international airport, Findel, is 6km east of the capital and is serviced by buses. The national airline, Luxair, flies to a a few European destinations, including Amsterdam, Athens and London.

Buses and trains connect the city to all of Europe's major cities, as well as many neighbouring towns. The major road routes into the Grand Duchy include the A4 to Brussels and Paris, the A31 via Dudelange to France and the A48 via Trier to Germany. During the summer, the touristy MV *Princesse Marie-Astrid* plies the Moselle River en route from Schengen, at the southernmost tip of Luxembourg, to Bernkastel and Trier in Germany.

The Former Yugoslav Republic of Macedonia (FYROM) is at the southern end of what was once the Yugoslav Federation. Its position in the centre of the Balkan Peninsula between Albania, Bulgaria, Serbia and Greece has often made it a political powder keg.

A melding of these cultures, and of Orthodox Christianity with Islam, has produced a fascinating culture and a unique country that deserves more than a passing glance on the way to somewhere else. Macedonia is a land of medieval monasteries, timeworn Turkish bazaars, Orthodox churches and space-age shopping centres. It also has the drone of the local bagpipes, Turkish-style grilled mincemeat and

Balkan *burek* (cheese or meat pie). The country is unbelievably green and breathtakingly gorgeous; its people are hospitable and welcoming.

It could all be one happy playground but for its political instability and grinding poverty. Fortunately, the war in Kosovo and Yugoslavia did not spread here, but the huge influx of ethnic Albanian refugees put significant pressure on the country.

Warning

NATO's bombing of Yugoslavia and Kosovo, and the Serbian response, threatened to push the Balkan war over the border into Macedonia. From mid-1999 the country was swamped by ethnic Albanian refugees, stretching accommodation and other resources to the limit. In early 2000 the situation was considered stable as far as travel to the country is concerned, but you should check the situation before heading off.

WHEN TO GO

There's no bad time to go to Macedonia weather-wise, as the country benefits from being close to the Aegean Sea, which keeps it relatively warm in winter

At a Glance

Full Country Name: The Former Yugoslav Republic of Macedonia
Area: 25,700 sq km
Population: Two million
Capital City: Skopje (pop 600,000)
People: 66% Macedonian Slavs, plus Greek Macedonians, Albanians, Turks, Serbs, Gypsies
Language: Macedonian
Religion: Most Albanians and Turks are Muslim; Slavs are Eastern Orthodox
Government: Emerging democracy
Currency: Macedonian denar (MKD)
Time Zone: One hour ahead of GMT/UTC; clocks go forward one hour at the end of March and back again on the last Sunday in September
International Telephone Code: 389
Electricity: 220V, 50Hz

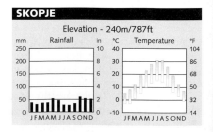

SKOPJE

Elevation - 240m/787ft

Rainfall — Temperature

MACEDONIA HIGHLIGHTS & ITINERARIES

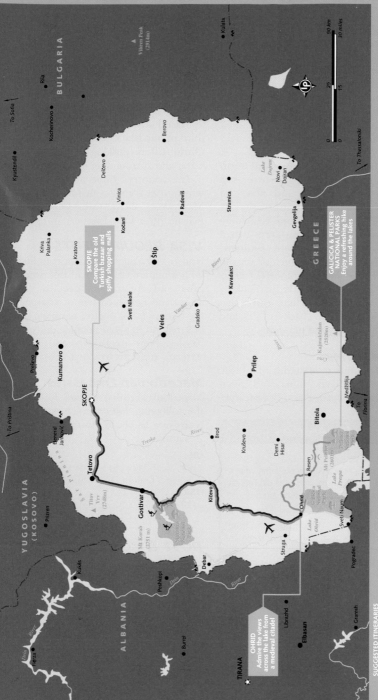

SKOPJE
Compare the old Turkish bazaar and spiffy shopping malls

GALICICA & PELISTER NATIONAL PARKS
Enjoy a refreshing hike around the lakes

OHRID
Admire the views across the lake from a medieval citadel

SUGGESTED ITINERARIES

One Week ▬ Skopje • Ohrid

Two Weeks ▬ Skopje • Ohrid • Galicica & Pelister National Parks

and very nice in summer. July and August are the best months to catch festivals: the Balkan Festival of Folk Dances and Songs is held in Ohrid in early July, while the Ohrid Summer Festival takes place later that month.

HIGHLIGHTS
Skopje
The Macedonian capital, in the north near the border with Kosovo, is a curious mix of old and new. An earthquake devastated parts of the city in 1963 and the resultant rebuilding created a strangely modern urban landscape, complete with futuristic shopping centres. But much of the old city survived and the colourful Caršija (old Turkish bazaar) is particularly worth exploring. There are also Turkish baths dating back to 1499, and several mosques and museums.

Monasteries
The Byzantine monasteries of Ohrid, particularly Sveti Sofija and Sveti Kliment, are worth a visit. Both feature vivid frescoes. The town of Ohrid is Macedonia's tourist mecca.

Lakes & National Parks
Lake Ohrid is simply beautiful and is, without doubt, the most popular place in Macedonia. Bordering Albania (one-third of the lake is actually in Albania), Ohrid offers striking vistas of the water and surrounding mountains.

The country's three national parks, which offer some scope for hiking, are Mavrovo, Galicica (near Ohrid) and Pelister (near Lake Presper).

VISA REQUIREMENTS
British and Yugoslav passport holders do not require visas. Canadians, Americans and Australians need a visa. These can be issued free of charge at the border, but it's better to obtain one beforehand to avoid possible delays or hassles. New Zealanders and South Africans need prearranged visas.

Macedonian Embassies
Macedonian embassies are found in the following countries. There are no embassies as yet in Australia or New Zealand.

UK
(☎ 020-7499 5152) 19a Cavendish Square, London, W1M 8DT 5JJ
USA
(☎ 202-337 3063) 3050 K St NW, Washington, DC 20007

POST & COMMUNICATIONS
There are poste restante services at the main post offices in Skopje and Ohrid.

Long-distance phone calls are cheaper at main post offices than from hotels. Phonecards can be purchased at post offices.

Itineraries

Two Days
Spend your time in Skopje exploring what's left of the old city, including the old Turkish bazaar and the Mustafa Pasha mosque.

One Week
Spend a couple of days in Skopje, then head down the western side of Macedonia to Ohrid. Here you can explore the town and its Byzantine monasteries, and relax around the lake for a few days.

Two Weeks
Cover the one week route and include some hiking in the Pelister and Galicica national parks between Ohrid and Bitola.

You can check email at Internet cafes in Skopje.

MONEY
Costs

Macedonia's hotels are very expensive and will take up most of your budget. If you're able to find a private room, you'll be better off financially and should be able to get by on about US$20 to US$40 a day. If not, count on spending at least US$50 a day for a roof over your head and some food in your belly. Expect to pay US$10 to US$40 for a budget room, and US$2 to US$10 for a cheap meal.

Changing Money

The denar is now a stable currency, but it's worthless outside Macedonia. Travellers cheques can be changed at most banks, with no commission deducted. Small private exchange offices can be found throughout central Skopje and Ohrid, and the rate they offer is generally good.

ONLINE SERVICES

Lonely Planet's Destination Macedonia (www.lonelyplanet.com/dest/eur/mac.htm) is a good starting point. The Macedonia Information Almanac has a site (www.b-info.com/places/macedonia/republic), as does Virtual Macedonia (www.vmacedonia.com/index2.html). The British Foreign & Commonwealth Travel Advice Web site (www.fco.gov.uk/travel/countryadvice.asp) will bring you up to speed on travel-related issues.

BOOKS

A couple of good background books are *Who Are the Macedonians?* by Hugh Poulton, a political and cultural history of the region, and *Black Lamb and Grey Falcon* by Rebecca West, a between-the-wars Balkan travelogue. *Macedonia and Greece – The struggle to Define a New Balkan Nation* by John Shea talks about the renewed conflicts between Macedonia and Greece since the break-up of the former Yugoslavia. *Children of the Bird Goddess – A Macedonian Autobiography*, by Sapurma Kita & Petrovska Pandora, is an oral history spanning the lives of four generations of Macedonian women.

ENTERING & LEAVING

With the demise of JAT Yugoslav Airlines, a number of local carriers have emerged offering direct flights from Skopje to cities in Germany, Switzerland and the Netherlands. There is also an international airport at Ohrid. The airport departure tax is about US$12.

The international bus station in Skopje has buses to and from Sofia, Tirana, Istanbul and Belgrade daily, and to Munich twice weekly. For Croatia, you must travel through Belgrade and Hungary. To and from Albania, you can travel between Skopje and Tirana by bus or walk across the border at Sveti Naum near Ohrid.

Express trains run five times a day between Skopje and Belgrade. Trains run twice a day between Skopje and Thessaloniki. If you're interested in travelling further into Greece, it's best to buy a ticket only to Thessaloniki and get another on to Athens from there. There's no direct rail link between Macedonia and Bulgaria, and the train is not recommended for travel between Sofia and Skopje, as you're forced to change trains in Yugoslavia and a visa will be required.

MALTA

With its megalithic temple ruins, medieval dungeons and classic fortified cities, Malta's known history spans almost 6000 years. The narrow cobblestone streets of its towns are crowded with Norman cathedrals and baroque palaces. The countryside is littered with the oldest known human structures in the world.

To many visitors (particularly Brits and Italians), Malta is a pleasant place for a holiday with a fine climate and some great beaches, so a formidable tourism industry already exists. But the islands are not yet overrun, and the staunchly Roman Catholic culture has helped the Maltese maintain a tightknit community that has kept a lid on runaway development.

The upshot is that travellers can enjoy a refreshing balance of convenience and unvarnished local charm, and can get comfort for considerably less than many comparable Mediterranean destinations. And despite their relaxed disposition, the Maltese like to celebrate. Every village holds an annual *festa* (usually to celebrate the feast day of a patron saint), and these unbridled festivities go on somewhere in Malta virtually nonstop from June to mid-September.

The Maltese archipelago consists of three inhabited islands: Malta, Gozo and Comino. They lie in the Mediterranean Sea, about 93km south of Sicily.

WHEN TO GO

The best time to visit Malta is the lull of February to June, between the rainy season (such as it is) and the hot Mediterranean summer. This is also when rates drop by as much as 40% from the late June to August high season. September and October are also good months to visit. The main reason for visiting in summer is the chance to catch one of the island's festi.

At a Glance

Full Country Name: Republic of Malta
Area: 320 sq km
Population: 405,000
Capital City: Valletta (pop 92,000)
People: Arab, Sicilian, Norman, Spanish
Language: Maltese and English
Religion: 98% Roman Catholic
Government: Constitutional parliamentary monarchy
Currency: Maltese lira (Lm)
Time Zone: One hour ahead of GMT/UTC; clocks are turned forward on the last Sunday in March and back again on the last Sunday in October
International Telephone Code: 356
Electricity: 250V, 50Hz

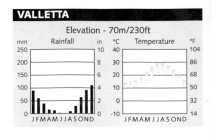

VALLETTA
Elevation - 70m/230ft

HIGHLIGHTS
Valletta

Valletta, the City of the Knights of the Order of St John, is an architectural masterpiece. Beautifully situated on a spit of land, the 16th century fortified city overlooks two harbours. Within its walls you'll find the Grand Master's Palace (now the seat of the Maltese parliament), St John's Co-Cathedral & Museum and the National Museum of Archaeology. Further north are the residential suburbs of Sliema and St Julian's and the nightlife centre of Paceville.

Temples & Historic Sites

The evocative Hagar Qim prehistoric temples on the south coast are without doubt the highlight of a visit to the island. Dating from as early as 3800 BC, Hagar Qim and the other Neolithic temples on Malta (such as the nearby Mnajdra temple) are the oldest known human structures in the world. This megalithic temple complex is adorned with carved animals and idols, sacrificial altars and oracular chambers, all executed with nothing more than flint and obsidian tools.

On Gozo, the imposing megalithic temples of Ggantija are the most spectacular in Malta. The hilltop medieval town of Mdina is another must-see. The fortified city has been around for more than 3000 years and includes the Mdina dungeons, restored subterranean prisons with tableaux depicting their victims.

Diving, Walking & Lazing

With 30m of visibility, warm water and dramatic undersea vistas, Malta has great diving. Gozo has the best spots, including the waters off the north-eastern coast near Marsalforn. St George's Bay, on the south-eastern coast, is another good place for a plunge. Comino also has good dive spots, including a 40m drop-off at Ras I-Irieqa on the south-western tip of the island.

All the islands in the archipelago are excellent for walking. Gozo and Comino are small enough to be covered on foot in a day or less, and nothing is really very far from anything else on Malta.

Despite its rocky coastline, Malta has some fine sandy beaches. Gnejna and Golden bays, on the north-west coast, and St George's Bay have warm waters, but they can be very crowded in summer. Ramla Bay has Gozo's best beach.

The Inland Sea, a secluded pool of clear water and pebbly sand on the western coast of Gozo, has one of the most beautiful beaches in the Mediterranean. Centred around Dwejra Point, the area's outstanding feature is the Azure Window, a giant rock arch in the cliff.

VISA REQUIREMENTS

Visas are not required for visits of up to three months by Australians, Britons, Canadians, New Zealanders, South Africans or North Americans.

Maltese Embassies

Australia
(☎ 02-6295 1586) 261 La Perouse St, Red Hill, ACT 2603

Canada
(☎ 416-207 0922) The Mutual Group Centre, 3300 Bloor St West, Suite 730, West Tower Etobicoke, Ontario

UK
(☎ 020-7292 4800) 36-38 Piccadilly, London W1V OPQ

USA
(☎ 202-462 3611) 2017 Connecticut Ave NW, Washington, DC 20008

TOURIST OFFICES OVERSEAS

The National Tourism Organisation Malta (NTOM) has its main office in London (☎ 020-7292 4900) at Malta House, 36-38 Piccadilly, London W1V OPP. There are also offices in Paris, Frankfurt, Milan, Amsterdam and New York, and representative offices in 16 other cities. Embassies and offices of Air Malta can provide information in other countries.

POST & COMMUNICATIONS

There are post office branches in most towns and villages, and a poste restante service at the main post office in Valletta.

Public telephones are widely available and generally take phonecards only, which you can buy at Maltacom offices, post offices and stationery shops.

Fax and telex services are available at Maltacom offices. The Internet is booming in Malta and there are public Internet cafes in Valletta.

MONEY
Costs

By European standards, Malta is very good value. Around US$25 to US$30 a day will get you pleasant hostel accommodation, a simple restaurant meal, a decent street-side snack and enough cold drinks to keep you going. You can travel in real comfort and style for US$75 to US$100 per day.

Expect to pay US$10 for a hostel bed, US$15 to US$40 for a moderate hotel or guesthouse, US$5 to US$10 for a cheap meal and US$10 to US$25 for a restaurant meal. Restaurants and taxis expect a 10% tip. Bargaining for handicrafts at stalls or markets is essential, but most shops have fixed prices. There's a 15% value-added tax on all consumer items.

Changing Money

Banks are the best place to change money; they almost always offer a significantly better rate than hotels or

---

Itineraries

Two Days

If for some odd reason your time is short on Malta, spend one day in Valletta exploring the walled city, then head down to Qrendi on the south coast, from where you can easily visit the prehistoric temples of Hagar Qim and Mnajdra.

One Week

With a week you can spend two days exploring Valletta and enjoying the weekend nightlife at Paceville before heading down to spend a day at Hagar Qim and Mnajdra. From there, travel north-west to the fascinating medieval town of Mdina, with its cathedral museum and dungeons. Spend the rest of your time on the quieter and less crowded island of Gozo, visiting the Inland Sea and the Ggantija temple complex.

Two Weeks

With a leisurely couple of weeks you can cover the one week route, plus fit in some diving or snorkelling, and lazing on the beaches at Gnejna Bay, Golden Bay and Paradise Bay. Alternatively, step out of Malta's mainstream tourism for a day or two and visit the Cottonera (Vittoriosa, Senglea and Cospicua), just across the Grand Harbour from Valletta. This area offers a glimpse into the island's daily working life, and there's a Maritime Museum with exhibits on Malta's naval history.

If you really want to get away from it all, you could stop over on Comino, the smallest and sleepiest island in the Maltese chain. The only inhabitants are a handful of farmers. It's halfway between Malta and Gozo.

MALTA HIGHLIGHTS & ITINERARIES

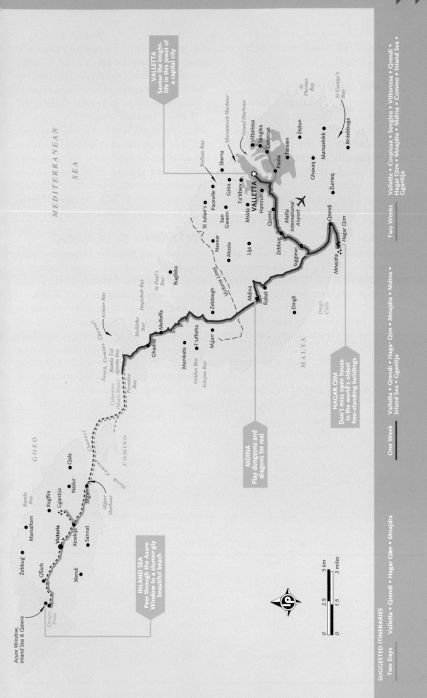

VALLETTA
Savour the knight-
life in this jewel of
a capital city

MDINA
Play dungeons and
dragons for real

HAGAR QIM
Don't miss open house
in the world's oldest
free-standing buildings

INLAND SEA
Peer through the Azure
Window to a stunningly
beautiful beach

MEDITERRANEAN SEA

GOZO

COMINO

MALTA

Azure Window,
Inland Sea & Qawra

Żebbuġ
Għarb
Marsalforn
Xagħra
Nadur
Qala
Victoria
Ġgantija
Mġarr
Xewkija
Samnat
Xlendi

Mellieħa
Ghadira
T'uffieħa
Mġarr
Manikata
Żebbiegħ
Mosta
Naxxar
St Julian's
Paceville
Sliema
Gżira
San Gwann
Ta'Xbiex
Msida
Ħamrun
Sliema
Valletta
Vittoriosa
Senglea
Cospicua
Paola
Tarxien
Żejtun
Għaxaq
Marsaxlokk
Birżebbuġa
Żurrieq
Qrendi
Ħaġar Qim
Mnajdra
Siġġiewi
Żebbuġ
Qormi
Lija
Mdina
Rabat
Dingli

Malta
International
Airport

St Paul's Bay
Buġibba
Bugibba
Golden Bay
Għajn Tuffieħa Bay
Paradise Bay

Marsamxett Harbour
Grand Harbour
Balluta Bay
St Thomas's Bay
St George's Bay

Dingli Cliffs

N

0   2.5   5 km
0   1.5   3 miles

SUGGESTED ITINERARIES

Two Days   Valletta • Qrendi • Ħaġar Qim • Mnajdra

One Week   Valletta • Qrendi • Ħaġar Qim • Mnajdra • Mdina •
Inland Sea • Ġgantija

Two Weeks   Valletta • Cospicua • Senglea • Vittoriosa • Qrendi •
Ħaġar Qim • Mnajdra • Mdina • Comino • Inland Sea •
Ġgantija

restaurants. All major credit cards are widely accepted.

ONLINE SERVICES

Lonely Planet's Destination Malta site (www.lonelyplanet.com/dest/eur/mal .htm) has plenty of useful information. The official site of the NTOM (www .tourism.org.mt) has plenty of standard information. Discover Malta (www .discovermalta.com) has all sorts of stuff, including hotel accommodation, leisure activities and events.

BOOKS

Christopher Marlowe's *Famous Tragedy of the Rich Jew of Malta* is a blank-verse play, first published in 1633, about Christian exploitation of Jews on Malta and the tragic end of one Jew's protest. For the historical background to Marlowe's tale, see *The Jews of Malta in the Late Middle Ages* by Godfrey Wettinger. *The Knights of Malta* by HJA Sire is a recent scholarly account of the 900 year history of the Knights of St John up to

the present day. The story of their 250 year slide from the saviours of Europe to Napoleon's pushovers is told in Alison Hoppen's *The Fortification of Malta by the Order of St John, 1530-1798.*

Ernle Bradford tells the story of Malta during WWII in *Siege Malta, 1940-43*. *The Kappillan of Malta* by Nicholas Monsarrat is the story of a priest's experiences during WWII and other dramatic episodes. *The Battle of Malta* is a memoir of WWII by the Maltese novelist Joseph Attard.

ENTERING & LEAVING

Air Malta has flights between the main island and a host of European cities. It also has flights between Malta and Cairo, Dubai, Damascus and Tunis.

During summer, a ferry service is available between Malta and Sicily and Genoa in Italy. The run between Malta and Catania (on Sicily) takes about three hours. All passengers departing by sea must pay a US$10 departure tax, plus a 15% government levy.

The Netherlands has managed to combine liberal attitudes with one of the most orderly societies on earth, in a community that manages to be radical and sensible without being silly or staid. The Dutch aren't bogged in their cliches, even though bikes, dikes, windmills and blazing flower fields are pretty much the norm outside the major cities.

Most travellers make a beeline for Amsterdam, but the rest of the Netherlands is easy to travel in, the locals are friendly and many speak excellent English. The towns are still surrounded by canals and castle walls; the endlessly flat landscape that inspired the nation's early artists still stretches unbroken to the horizons, and the dikes still occasionally threaten to give way.

WHEN TO GO

Hordes of tourists snap their way around the Netherlands in summer, and there's no denying that this is a good time of year to sit by the canals, in the parks and in alfresco cafes. Spring is the best time to visit, as the bulbs are in bloom – April for daffodils, May for tulips. If you can be in Amsterdam for Koninginnedag (Queen's Day) on 30 April, do it! Rain is spread pretty evenly over the year, so there's not much point trying to avoid Dutch drizzle. Winter can get bitingly cold, but the museums are quiet and if everything freezes over, there's great ice skating on the canals and flood plains.

HIGHLIGHTS
Amsterdam

The exuberant capital is the highlight of any visit to the Netherlands, and not necessarily for its tolerant attitude to drugs either. There's no doubt that this is one of the world's best hang-outs, but before spending too much time in its brown cafes, coffee shops and the

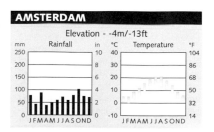

At a Glance

Full Country Name: Kingdom of the Netherlands
Area: 41,160 sq km
Population: 15.65 million
Capital City: Amsterdam (pop 700,000)
People: More than 95% Dutch (Germanic and Gallo-Celtic stock); Indonesian, Surinamese, Moroccan
Language: Netherlandic (Dutch)
Religion: 60% Christian (Roman Catholic and Protestant), 3% Muslim
Government: Constitutional monarchy
Currency: Dutch guilder (Nfl)
Time Zone: One hour ahead of GMT/UTC; clocks go forward one hour on the last Sunday in March and back again on the last Saturday in October
International Telephone Code: 31
Electricity: 220V, 50Hz

AMSTERDAM

Elevation - -4m/-13ft

	Rainfall			Temperature	
mm		in	°C		°F
250		10	40		104
200		8	30		86
150		6	20		68
100		4	10		50
50		2	0		32
0		0	-10		14
	JFMAMJJASOND			JFMAMJJASOND	

Heineken Brewery, immerse yourself in some of Europe's finest museums and galleries, cycle around the canal-lined streets and admire the 17th and 18th century architecture. Wandering around the canal belt and people-watching in Ledseplein are free.

Museum & Galleries

There is no shortage of fine museums and art galleries in the Netherlands, many of them in Amsterdam. The Rijksmuseum houses a huge collection of works by Dutch artists from the 15th to 19th centuries, the Van Gogh Museum has the world's largest collection of Vincent's works, Anne Frank's House is a moving reminder of the Jewish teenager's two years in hiding from the Nazis, the Jewish Historical Museum gives a wider picture of Jewish society and the Holocaust, and Rembranthuis displays sketches in the former home of the Dutch master.

There's also the Mauritshuis in The Hague and the excellent Kröller-Müller Museum near Arnhem.

Flowers & Windmills

Otherwise known as 'Dutch cliches', these things are nonetheless worth

Itineraries

Two Days

Amsterdam is not an easy place to leave and if you've only got two days in the Netherlands this is as far as you'll get. Try to visit the Rijksmuseum and/or the Van Gogh Museum. Other options are Anne Frank House (the queues here can be horrendous), a cruise on the canal, wandering around the red-light district in the evening and a tour of the Heineken Museum. When that's done, you can repair to a smoking coffee shop or a brown cafe. You'll certainly never get bored in Amsterdam.

One Week

Spend two or three days in Amsterdam, then make the short trip west to Haarlem, from where you can visit the Keukenhof gardens. Spend a day in Leiden and The Hague, then take the train to Arnhem and spend a couple of days exploring the Hoge Veluwe National Park (including the Kröller-Müller Museum). If there's any time left, you could stop in Rotterdam between The Hague and Hoge Veluwe.

Two Weeks

Spend at least three days in Amsterdam and two days in Haarlem, with a visit to Keukenhof. From there, head south to the

thriving student town of Leiden for a day, then on to The Hague, the Dutch seat of government and residence of the royal family. Continue south to Delft, where you can visit the Delftware potters, then to the harbour city of Rotterdam and the nearby Kinderdijk windmills.

Next stop is Middleburg in the province of Zeeland. From here you can explore the Delta region – a wild area of quaint villages and islands connected by causeways. Here you'll find the Waterland Neeltje Jans water theme park. From Middleburg, travel up to Arnhem and the Hoge Veluwe National Park. The remainder of your stay (if there's any time left) can be spent in the north of the country, either in Groningen or the island of Schiermonnikoog.

One Month

A month should be long enough to see most of the places of interest in the Netherlands. Following the two week itinerary, you could easily spend more time in the Hoge Veluwe National Park and include a stop in Den Bosch and a side trip down to Maastricht. Also spend more time exploring the north – mud flat-walking around Groningen and hopping between the Frisian islands.

NETHERLANDS HIGHLIGHTS & ITINERARIES

KEUKENHOF GARDENS
Tiptoe through the tulips in style

AMSTERDAM
Bend the rules – Europe's best hang-out

HOGE VELUWE NATIONAL PARK
Cycle, stroll and check out the excellent Kroller-Muller Museum

KINDERDIJK
Sail past a row of lovely windmills on your 'borrowed' bike

SUGGESTED ITINERARIES

One Week
Amsterdam • Haarlem • Lieden • The Hague • Arnhem • Hoge Veluwe National Park

Two Weeks
Amsterdam • Haarlem • Lieden • The Hague • Delft • Rotterdam • Middelburg • Arnhem • Hoge Veluwe National Park • Groningen

One Month
Amsterdam • Haarlem • Lieden • The Hague • Delft • Rotterdam • Middelburg • Den Bosch • Maastricht • Arnhem • Hoge Veluwe National Park • Groningen • Frisian Islands

seeing. Keukenhof gardens are a must if you're around while the tulips and daffodils are in bloom. Expect crowds (a staggering 800,000 visitors over two months), but the colours are amazing. Haarlem is a good base.

There are still many working windmills around the country but the Kinderdijk, outside Rotterdam, offers a picture-postcard string of 19 windmills. The sails are cranked up on the first Saturday of every month and every Saturday in July and August.

Cycling & Walking

With nary a hill in sight and 10,000km of cycling paths, a bike is a great way to travel in the Netherlands. The Hoge Veluwe National Park and Delta region are great areas for cycling or walking. Bikes can easily be hired in Amsterdam. If you don't mind getting your feet dirty, you could investigate the art of *wadlopen* (mud-flat walking) on the tidal mud flats near Groningen.

VISA REQUIREMENTS

European Union residents just need their EU papers to enter. No visas are required for travellers from Australia, New Zealand, Canada, Japan and the USA for visits of up to 90 days. South Africans need only a Schengen visa.

Dutch Embassies

Australia
(☎ 02-6273 3111) 120 Empire Circuit, Yarralumla, Canberra, ACT 2600

Canada
(☎ 613-237 5030) 350 Albert St, Suite 2020, Ottawa, Ont K1R 1A4

New Zealand
(☎ 04-473 8652) 10th floor, Investment House, Ballance & Featherston St, Wellington

UK
(☎ 020-7584 5040) 38 Hyde Park Gate, London SW7 5DP

USA
(☎ 202-244 5300) 4200 Linnean Ave NW, Washington, DC 20008

TOURIST OFFICES OVERSEAS

Canada
(☎ 416-363 1577, fax 363 1470) 25 Adelaide St East, Suite 710, Toronto, Ont M5C 1Y2

Japan
(☎ 03-3222 1112, fax 3222 1114) 5th floor, NK Shinwa Building, 5-1 Kojimachi, Chiyoda-ku, Tokyo 102

UK
(☎ 020-7828 7900, fax 7828 7941) PO Box 523, London SW1E 6NT

USA
(☎ 212-370 7360, fax 370 9507) 355 Lexington Ave, 21st floor, New York, NY 10017
(☎ 310-348 9339, fax 348 9344) 9841 Airport Blvd, Suite 710, Los Angeles, CA 90045
(☎ 312-819 1500, fax 819 1740) 225 N Michigan Ave, Suite 1854, Chicago, IL 60601

POST & COMMUNICATIONS

The Dutch postal service is reliable, and you'll find a poste restante service at post offices around the country. Letters take about a week to the USA and Canada, and six to 10 days to Australia and New Zealand.

Public phones accepting coins and cards are widespread. International calls can be made from public phones, post offices or Primafoon shops. When calling abroad to some countries, it is cheaper to buy a PTT Telecom Country Card, which gives a 15 to 20% discount over ordinary phonecards. Country Cards are available for the USA, Canada, Australia, New Zealand and South Africa. International faxes can also be sent from post offices in some large cities but they are relatively expensive.

Cybercafes for email and Internet access can be found in the major towns and are usually open until 10 or 11 pm.

MONEY
Costs

Although Amsterdam casualties will tell you it's possible to scrape by on only one stolen bike a day, the Netherlands is not really cheap – not many people get by on a tight budget in Amsterdam because there are too many costly entertainment distractions. If you're happy eating chips, sleeping in hostels and walking around, it's possible to hang in there for under US$30 a day. There are a lot of free activities to stretch your budget, especially in Amsterdam in summer. If you prefer a couple of solid meals a day, a comfortable bed with private facilities and travelling by public transport, US$70 a day is a more sensible budget. Money-saving ideas include getting hold of a museum pass if you're an avid museum-goer, and obtaining a bicycle for getting around.

Tipping is not compulsory in the Netherlands, but rounding up the bill is always appreciated in taxis, restaurants and pubs with table or pavement service. If you're eating out in a group, it is common to split the bill, but don't suggest 'going Dutch' as the expression is unknown here. Don't bother trying to bargain, though the Dutch themselves sometimes manage to get away with it at flea markets.

Changing Money

Any post office will change cash or travellers cheques for you, and you'll find exchange bureaux are common in large towns. Banks generally offer the best exchange rates, but the service can be slow. Cash-dispensing ATMs are all over the place: Cirrus access is common and MasterCard is the most widely accepted credit card.

ONLINE SERVICES

Lonely Planet's Destination Netherlands (www.lonelyplanet.com/dest/eur /net.htm) gives a thorough country profile. DDS (De Digitale Stad – The Digital City) has a site at www.dds.nl. The Amsterdam city site (www.amst erdam.nl) has plenty of information on the capital. There is a touristy site at www.visitholland.com with good links to other Netherlands information.

BOOKS

CR Boxer's *The Dutch Seaborne Empire 1600-1800* was first published more than 30 years ago, but it remains one of the most readable accounts on how this small corner of Europe dominated world trade. If you plan to settle in for a while, get hold of *Live & Work in Belgium, the Netherlands and Luxembourg* from Vacation Work Publications.

The famous *Diary of Anne Frank*, an autobiography by a Jewish teenager, movingly describes life in hiding in Nazi-occupied Amsterdam. *The Un-Dutchables* by Colin White & Laurie Boucke takes a humorous look at Dutch life; sometimes it's spot on, and sometimes it's so wide of the mark it becomes slapstick.

There aren't many English translations of Dutch literature. The Dutch Shakespeare, Joost van den Vondel, has been translated but he can be heavy going. Lieve Joris, a Flemish author who lives in Amsterdam, writes about cultures in transition in Africa, the Middle East and Eastern Europe. Her *Gates of Damascus*, published by Lonely Planet, is about life in Syria.

FILMS

The Diary of Anne Frank (1959) is the film based on the book about a Dutch Jewish family in hiding during WWII. Shelley Winters won an Oscar for her performance. *The Amsterdammed* (1988) is a Dutch thriller set in the capital. *In Old Amsterdam* is a documentary that looks at the history and art of the city. There are a couple of films about the life of Rembrandt (both called *Rembrandt*), produced in 1942 and 1999.

ENTERING & LEAVING

The Netherlands has just one main international airport, Schiphol, about 10km south-west of Amsterdam. Although it's one of Europe's major international hubs, flights into London or Brussels are usually cheaper than flights to Amsterdam, and many travellers do the last leg to Amsterdam by train or bus. There are no departure taxes if you are leaving by air. Euro-lines buses connect Amsterdam to most European cities, as well as to North Africa. Eurolines and Citysprint buses travel across the channel to Britain, usually through France (make sure you've got a visa if required). Amsterdam's Centraal station has regular and efficient rail connections to all neighbouring countries, but the bus will always be cheaper unless you've got a Eurail pass or equivalent.

Travelling to the Netherlands by car or motorcycle on those lovely Western European highways is easy. If you're driving from the UK, it's a fair bit cheaper to put your car on the ferry than on the shuttle through the Tunnel, though the latter might save a few hours travelling time from London. Most travellers go overland through Belgium and France to pick up a boat to England, but ferries also run between Hook of Holland and Harwich, UK; Europoort (near Rotterdam) and Hull, UK; Ijmuiden (near Amsterdam) and Newcastle, UK; and Ijmuiden and Kristiansand, Norway.

NORWAY

Norway (Norge) is a ruggedly beautiful country of high mountains, deep fjords and icy blue glaciers. It stretches 2000km from beach towns in the south to treeless arctic tundra in the north. Norway offers incredible wilderness hiking, year-round skiing and some of the most scenic ferry, bus and train rides imaginable. Summer days are delightfully long, and in the northernmost part of the country the sun doesn't set for weeks on end. Conversely, winter nights are endless but the aurora borealis (northern lights) offers a breathtaking lightshow.

In addition to the lure of the spectacular western fjords, Norway has pleasantly low-key cities, unspoiled fishing villages and rich historic sites that include Viking ships and medieval stave churches.

Norway retains something of a frontier character, with even its biggest cities surrounded by forested green belts. Wilderness camping is one of the best ways to see the country and a good way to beat some of Norway's high costs.

WHEN TO GO
Norway is at its best and brightest from May to September. Late spring is a particularly pleasant time – fruit trees are in bloom, daylight hours are long, and most hostels and sights are open but uncrowded.

Unless you're heavily into winter skiing or searching for the aurora borealis of the polar nights, Norway's cold dark winters are not the prime time to visit. Midnight-sun days, when the sun never drops below the horizon, extend from 13 May to 29 July, and from 28 May to 14 July in the Lofoten islands.

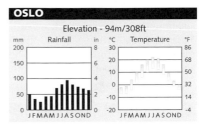

HIGHLIGHTS
Fjords
Nothing typifies Norway more than its glacier-carved fjords, and ferrying

At a Glance

Full Country Name: Norway
Area: 324,220 sq km
Population: 4,326,000
Capital City: Oslo (pop 465,000)
People: 97% Nordic, Alpine and Baltic, with a Lapp minority
Language: Bokmål and Nynorsk
Religion: Christian (93% Evangelical Lutheran)
Government: Constitutional democracy
Currency: Krone (Nkr)
Time Zone: One hour ahead of GMT/UTC; clocks go forward one hour on the last Sunday in March and back again on the last Sunday in October
International Telephone Code: 47
Electricity: 220V, 50 to 60Hz

along these inland waterways is Norway's top sightseeing activity. While the Geirangerfjord has the most spectacular waterfalls, the Nærøyfjord provides the most stunning scenery in the Bergen region.

Although the fjords are scenic from the water, often the most majestic angle is found on the surrounding mountainsides. Many fjord-side villages have hiking trails that lead up to lookouts with picturesque views. In addition, the road from Gudvangen to Voss, and the Trollstigen and Eagle roads between Åndalsnes and Geiranger, have high vantages with breathtaking fjord scenery.

Skiing, Hiking & Fishing

The Norwegians are outdoorsy types and skiing, hiking and fishing are three of their favourite pastimes (they claim to have invented skiing). There are thousands of kilometres of maintained cross-country (Nordic) ski trails and numerous resorts with downhill runs. The Holmenkollen area near Oslo, Geilo and Lillehammer are three of the best spots.

Norway's hiking areas range from easy trails in the 'green zones' near cities to long treks through national forests. The most popular hiking areas are the Jotunheimen and Rondane mountains.

Itineraries

Two Days

If your time is short, visit Bergen (there are international ferries to Bergen from Denmark and the UK), then travel by rail to Flåm and take a combination boat/bus trip back to Bergen. You can see some fjords on route. If arriving from Sweden, take the scenic seven hour train ride from Oslo to Bergen with a side trip to Flåm.

One Week

Spend two days in the capital, Oslo, visiting some of Norway's finest museums, including the Viking Ship, Kon-Tiki and Polarship Fram museums. Also visit the Royal Palace (residence of the King of Norway) and the medieval Akershus Fortress. From there, take the Oslo-Bergen railway with the side diversion to Flåm, where you can take in some of the superb scenery of Sognefjord. After spending a day or two in Bergen, take a three day jaunt through the western fjords – Sognefjord, Nordfjord and Geirangerfjord. Balestrand, Stryn and Geiranger are respectively the best base towns here.

Two Weeks

Follow the one week itinerary, then continue north through Åndalsnes, situated on the edge of Romsdalsfjord, to the pleasant university town of Trondheim and on to the spectacular Lofoten islands. The islands, Norway's prime winter fishing grounds, are peaks of glacier-carved mountains shooting up from the sea. Here you can explore traditional fishing villages, ancient Viking sites and rugged scenery. Bodø is the main departure point for the islands, with regular ferry services to the towns of Stamsund, Svolvær and Moskenes.

One Month

Follow the two week itinerary but, if you like hiking, spend a couple of days on the trails in Jotunheimen National Park. This is Norway's most popular wilderness destination, with 60 glaciers and the country's highest mountain peaks. The town of Bøverdalen, on the edge of the park, has a hostel. After the Lofoten islands, take a coastal steamer cruise, breaking at the lively university town of Tromsø (it has more pubs per capita than anywhere else in Norway), and at Nordkapp in the far north. This is the northernmost town in Europe and the place to bask in the midnight sun. (See the boxed text.)

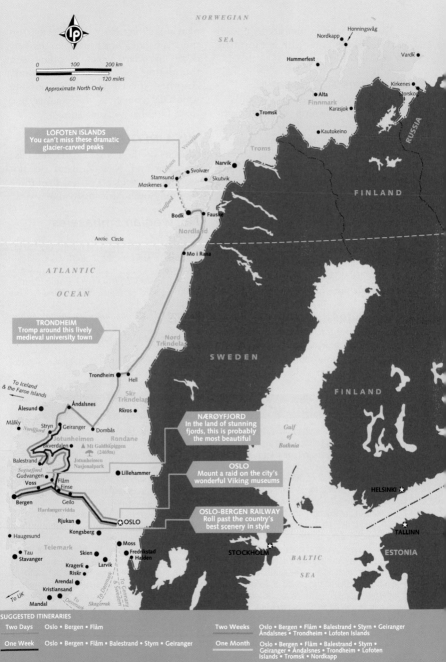

NORWAY HIGHLIGHTS & ITINERARIES

NORWEGIAN SEA

IP

| 0 | 100 | 200 km |
| 0 | 60 | 120 miles |

Approximate North Only

Nordkapp
Honningsvåg
Hammerfest
Vardk
Kirkenes
Alta
Storskog
Tromsk
Finnmark
Karasjok
RUSSIA
Kautokeino

Troms

FINLAND

LOFOTEN ISLANDS
You can't miss these dramatic
glacier-carved peaks

Narvik
Stamsund
Svolvær
Skutvik
Moskenes

Bodk
Fauske

Nordland

Arctic Circle

ATLANTIC

OCEAN

Mo i Rana

TRONDHEIM
Tromp around this lively
medieval university town

Nord
Trkndelag

SWEDEN

FINLAND

Trondheim
Hell
To Iceland
& the Faroe Islands
Skr
Trkndelag

Ålesund
Åndalsnes
Målky
Stryn
Geiranger
Rkros
Nordfjord
Dombås
Jotunheimen
Rondane
Bkverdalen
▲ Mt Galdhkpiggen
(2469m)
Balestrand
Jotunheimen
Nasjonalpark
Sognefjord
Gudvangen
Lillehammer
Flåm
Voss
Finse
Bergen
Geilo
Hardangervidda
Rjukan

Gulf
of
Bothnia

NÆRØYFJORD
In the land of stunning
fjords, this is probably
the most beautiful

OSLO
Mount a raid on the city's
wonderful Viking museums

OSLO-BERGEN RAILWAY
Roll past the country's
best scenery in style

HELSINKI ★

Kongsberg
☆ OSLO
Haugesund
Telemark
Moss
Tau
Skien
Fredrikstad
Stavanger
Kragerk
Larvik
Halden
STOCKHOLM ★
TALLINN ★
Riskr
Arendal
Kristiansand
To Denmark
Sweden
ESTONIA
To UK
Skagerrak
To Denmark
Mandal

BALTIC
SEA

SUGGESTED ITINERARIES

Two Days	Oslo • Bergen • Flåm
One Week	Oslo • Bergen • Flåm • Balestrand • Styrn • Geiranger
Two Weeks	Oslo • Bergen • Flåm • Balestrand • Styrn • Geiranger • Åndalsnes • Trondheim • Lofoten Islands
One Month	Oslo • Bergen • Flåm • Balestrand • Styrn • Geiranger • Åndalsnes • Trondheim • Lofoten Islands • Tromsk • Nordkapp

Norway's salmon runs are legendary and the best place to fish is Finnmark in June and July.

Museums & Churches

Oslo's Bygdøy Peninsula holds a fascinating collection of explorers' ships: the polar *Fram*, Thor Heyerdahl's *Kon-Tiki* raft and three ships built by Vikings a millennium ago. Be sure to visit one of the 29 remaining stave churches, which date to medieval times and incorporate Viking influences. In the 19th century many of the surviving stave churches were moved to open-air folk museums, along with other historic timber buildings. Bygdøy has Norway's largest folk museum, while the one in Lillehammer is the most evocatively presented.

Train Rides

The Oslo-Bergen railway (470km) is Norway's finest: it's a scenic trip passing snowcapped mountains and the wind-swept Hardanger-vidda (Hardanger plateau). Don't miss the side trip on the Flåm line, which hairpins its way down the Flåm Valley, stopping at a thundering waterfall mid-route. Another special train trip, passing waterfalls galore, is the Rauma line from Dombås to Åndalsnes.

VISA REQUIREMENTS

Citizens of the USA, Canada, the UK, Australia and New Zealand do not require visas for stays of less than three months. South Africans require a visa.

Norwegian Embassies

Australia
(☎ 02-6273 3444) 17 Hunter St, Yarralumla, Canberra, ACT 2600
Canada
(☎ 613-238 6570) Royal Bank Centre, 90 Sparks St, Suite 532, Ottawa, Ont K1P 5B
Ireland
(☎ 3531-662 1800, fax 662 1890) 34 Molesworth St, Dublin 2
UK
(☎ 020-7591 5500) 25 Belgrave Square, London SW1X 8QD

Midnight Sun & Polar Night

Because the earth is tilted on its axis, the polar regions are constantly facing the sun at their respective summer solstices and are tilted away from it in the winter. The Arctic and Antarctic circles, at 66° 33' north and south latitude respectively, are the southern and northern limits of constant daylight on the longest day of the year.

The northern half of mainland Norway, as well as Svalbard and Jan Mayan, lie north of the Arctic Circle, but even in southern Norway, the summer sun is never far below the horizon. Between late May and mid-August, nowhere in the country experiences true darkness and in Trondheim, for example, the first stars aren't visible until mid-August. Although many visitors initially find it difficult to sleep while the sun is shining, most people quickly get used to it, even if that simply means joining the locals in their summer nocturnal hyperactivity.

Conversely, winters here are dark and dreary, with only a few hours of twilight to break the long polar nights. In Svalbard, not even a twilight glow can be seen for over a month, and most northern communities make a ritual of welcoming the sun the first time it peeks above the southern horizon. During this period of darkness, many people suffer from SAD syndrome, or 'seasonally affected depression', which results when they're deprived of the vitamin D provided by sunlight. Its effects may be minimised by using dosages of vitamin D (as found in cod liver oil) or with special solar spectrum light bulbs.

USA
   (☎ 202-333 6000) 2720 34th St NW, Washington, DC 20008

TOURIST OFFICES OVERSEAS

Australia
   Royal Norwegian Embassy
      (☎ 02-6273 3444) 17 Hunter St, Yarralumla, Canberra, ACT 2600
UK
      (☎ 020-7839 2650) Charles House, 5-11 Lower Regent St, London SW1Y 4LR
USA & Canada
      (☎ 212-949 2333) 655 Third Ave, New York, NY 10017

POST & COMMUNICATIONS

Norway has an efficient postal service. Mail can be received poste restante at any post office in Norway.

Most pay phones accept coins, and cardphones are often found alongside coin phones. Phonecards *(telekort)* can be purchased at post offices and the ubiquitous Narvesen newspaper kiosks.

Faxes can be sent from many post offices or your hotel. Many public libraries have computers with Internet access but in most cases there are queues of locals waiting to get online, so travellers aren't encouraged to use them for checking email. Some larger hotels, including those of the nationwide Rainbow chain, have credit card accessed Internet computers in their lobbies.

MONEY
Costs

Norway is very expensive, but if you tighten your belt there are ways to take out some of the sting. If you use only camping grounds and prepare your own meals you might squeak by for under US$30 a day. If you stay at hostels, breakfast at a bakery, lunch at an inexpensive restaurant and shop at a grocery store for dinner, you should be able to get by on US$45 a day. If you stay at 'cheap' hotels that include a buffet breakfast, have one meal at a moderately priced restaurant and snack for the other meal, expect to spend US$60 a day. This is still pretty bare-bones – entertainment, alcohol and transport costs are all extra, so having a rail pass (Eurail, Inter-Rail or Scanrail) and staying off the grog will help. A glass of beer in a bar costs US$4 to US$5 but a bottle of wine at a liquor shop costs as little as US$8.

Service charges and tips are included in restaurant bills and taxi fares, so no additional tip is expected. Bargaining is not a common practice in Norway.

Changing Money

Post offices and banks exchange major foreign currencies and accept all travellers cheques. Some banks charge a fee per cheque, so you'll save money by changing travellers cheques in higher denominations. ATMs are widespread and all major credit cards are widely accepted.

ONLINE SERVICES

Lonely Planet's Destination Norway (www.lonelyplanet.com/dest/eur/nor .htm) has updated country information. Norway On-line (www.norway .org) has plenty of general and tourism-related information about Norway. A good guide to the capital is to be found at www.oslopro.no. The official Norwegian Tourist Board Guide is at www.tourist.no.

BOOKS

A Brief History of Norway by John Midgaard covers Norwegian history from prehistoric to modern times. *The Vinland Sagas – The Norse Discovery of America* (translated by Magnússon/Pálsson) tells of the discovery of America before the arrival of Columbus. A good accompaniment to both these works is *The Viking World* by James Graham-Campbell, which traces the history of the Vikings by detailing excavated sites and artefacts. The photos are excellent.

Norwegian works of literature include *Kristin Lavransdatter* by Sigrid Undset, a trilogy that portrays the struggles of a 13th century Norwegian family; *Hunger and Mysteries* by Knut Hamsun, which delves into the troubled aspect of the human character; a number of Henrik Ibsen's classics, such as *A Doll's House*, *Peer Gynt* and *Ghosts*; and the contemporary success, *Sophie's World* by Jostein Gaarder.

Information on wilderness trails, hiking itineraries, sketch maps and trail huts can be found in Erling Welle-Strand's *Mountain Hiking in Norway*. Welle-Strand also wrote *Motoring in Norway*, a concise book describing the country's picturesque motor routes.

ENTERING & LEAVING

International airlines link Oslo with most major European cities. Bergen, Stavanger and Trondheim also have international airports. There is no departure tax when leaving Norway. Trains run daily from Oslo to Copenhagen in Denmark and to Helsingborg and Stockholm in Sweden. There are also trains to Stockholm from Trondheim and Narvik. Numerous highways and secondary roads link Norway with Finland and Sweden. A bus and a catamaran service link Kirkenes in northern Norway with Murmansk in Russia. There are also ferries to and from Denmark, Sweden, the UK, Iceland and the Faroe Islands.

POLAND

Situated in the heartland of Europe, Poland has been both a bridge and a front line between Eastern and Western Europe. Today, free from outside interference, this is still a largely unexplored country that retains much of its traditional way of life. It's a multifaceted nation where the capital and medieval old towns are coddled by contemporary city slickers, but where horse-drawn carts still negotiate country lanes between villages that look as though the 21st century got lost somewhere down the road.

Poland's centuries-old towns and cities shelter a rich architectural and artistic heritage that has survived all the battles fought on Polish soil over the centuries. A huge amount of damage was done during WWII, but the energy and resources that have gone into rebuilding are astonishing – the old quarters of Warsaw (Warzawa) and Gdansk are miracles of loving reconstruction, and the unscathed old royal capital of Kraków is not to be missed. Outside its cities and towns you'll find spectacular mountain ranges along the southern border and white sandy beaches skirting the northern Baltic coast.

Now is a good time to visit Poland – it has improved its tourist infrastructure and developed into a modern, vibrant and progressive state, yet at the same time maintained its traditional culture.

WHEN TO GO

The tourist season runs roughly from May to September, peaking in July and

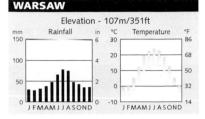

WARSAW

Elevation - 107m/351ft

Rainfall / Temperature chart (months J F M A M J J A S O N D)

August. At this time the Baltic beaches are taken over by swarms of humanity, resorts and spas are invaded by tourists, Masurian lakes are crowded with thousands of sailboats and the mountain trails are full of walkers. The best time to come is either late spring (mid-May to June) or the turn of summer and autumn (September to mid-October). These are pleasantly warm periods and there are plenty of cultural activities going on. Winters are harsh and many

At a Glance

Full Country Name: Republic of Poland
Area: 312,677 sq km
Population: 38.5 million
Capital City: Warsaw (pop 1.75 million)
People: 98% Polish, plus Ukrainian and Belorusian minorities
Language: Polish
Religion: 95% Roman Catholic
Government: Parliamentary democracy
Currency: Polish zloty (zl)
Time Zone: One hour ahead of GMT/UTC; clocks go forward one hour in late March and back again in late September
International Telephone Code: 48
Electricity: 220V, 50Hz

camp sites and hostels are closed, but it's not a bad time for visiting Poland's cities, which are occasionally dusted with an attractive layer of snow.

HIGHLIGHTS
Historic Towns
Of all the cities in Poland, only Kraków has a fully authentic old centre, almost untouched by WWII. This is a classic historic city, listed on the World Cultural Heritage Register and crammed with works of art. The main market square, with its Renaissance cloth hall, and Wawel Castle, are highlights. Kraków is also a good base for visiting nearby places of interest such as Auschwitz and the salt mines at Wieliczka.

Itineraries

Two Days
If time is short, don't miss Kraków, which can be reached directly by train or bus from surrounding countries (eg Germany, Czech Republic or Slovakia). You could easily absorb a day or two just wandering around the streets and the market square, but definitely visit Wawel Castle and Wawel Cathedral and try to make a day trip to either nearby Wieliczka (see One Week) or to the infamous and sobering Nazi death camp of Auschwitz/Birkenau, 60km west of Kraków.

In the evenings, check out Kraków's unique cellar-vaulted pubs.

One Week
Spend one or two days in Warsaw visiting the beautifully restored Old Town, razed during WWII but flawlessly reconstructed from 1949 to 1963. The nearby New Town has some interesting buildings, including the childhood home of Marie Curie. Visit the Royal Castle and the Lazienki Palace (linked by the 4km-long Royal Way).

Spend three or four days in Kraków, with an afternoon excursion to the salt mines at Wieliczka. Here you descend 135m underground into an eerie world of tunnels and chambers and chapels. There are intricate carvings including statues, altars and even a chandelier – all hewn by hand out of solid salt! Also make a day trip out to the disturbing Auschwitz/Birkenau concentration camps, near the village of Oswiecim.

If you still have a day or two left, make a quick trip to Zakopane in the Tatra Mountains. Principally a base for winter skiing or summer hiking, Zakopane is an interesting resort town in itself. Two worthwhile trips that require no exertion are the funicular to the summit of Mt Gubalowka, and the cable car from Kuznice to the summit of Mt Kasprowy Wierch – both offer superb mountain views.

Two Weeks
Follow the one week itinerary and add any of the four following options, depending on your taste: head up to the north via Wroclaw for the cultural trip to the historic centres of Gdansk (birthplace of Solidarity), Malbork and its huge medieval church, and Torun; go wildlife and bird-watching in Bialowieza or Biebrza national parks in the north-east of the country; set a leisurely pace following the pleasant eastern route between Warsaw and Kraków; or spend a full good week hiking in the Tatra and Pieniny mountains.

One Month
With a month you could combine some of the above itineraries and add a trip to the cultured city of Wroclaw in the south-west of Poland. From there you could also visit the Sudeten Mountains to the south, or alternatively the Beskids and Bieszczady in the Carpathian Mountains east of the Tatras – both these ranges provide a good mix of culture and nature.

If you like beaches, head up to some of the Baltic coastal resorts such as Leba and its environs. If you prefer lakes, you could spend some time kayaking or sailing on the Great Masurian Lakes in the north-east.

POLAND HIGHLIGHTS & ITINERARIES

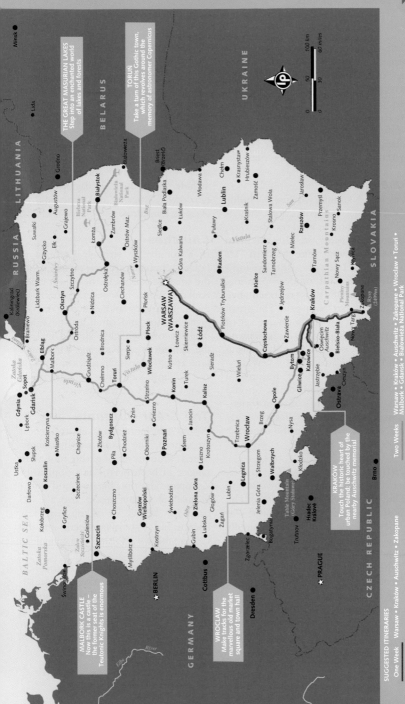

THE GREAT MASURIAN LAKES
Step into an enchanted world of lakes and forests

TORUŃ
Take a turn of this Gothic town, which revolves around the memory of astronomer Copernicus

MALBORK CASTLE
Now this is a castle — the former seat of the Teutonic Knights is enormous

WROCŁAW
Make tracks for the marvellous old market square and town hall

KRAKÓW
Touch the historic heart of urban Poland; be touched by the nearby Auschwitz memorial

RUSSIA
LITHUANIA
BELARUS
UKRAINE
SLOVAKIA
CZECH REPUBLIC
GERMANY
BALTIC SEA

SUGGESTED ITINERARIES

One Week — Warsaw • Kraków • Auschwitz • Zakopane

Two Weeks — Warsaw • Kraków • Auschwitz • Zakopane • Wrocław • Toruń • Malbork • Gdańsk • Białowieża National Park

The damaged historic cores of Poznan, Torun and Wroclaw have been masterfully restored. The old towns in Gdansk and Warsaw were destroyed almost totally in WWII and rebuilt from scratch, with amazing results. Among the smaller urban centres, Zamosc in south-east Poland is a 16th century Renaissance town.

Museums

Warsaw's National Museum holds Poland's largest art collection, though national museums in Kraków, Wroclaw, Poznan and Gdansk are also extensive and worth visiting. The Modern Art Museum in Lódz houses Poland's largest collection of modern painting, while Plock has the most representative collection of Art Nouveau. The small town of Jedrzejów has a unique set of more than 300 sundials. The Auschwitz museum at Oswiecim is a harrowing reminder of the atrocities of WWII.

Anyone interested in traditional rural architecture and crafts should visit some of Poland's *skansen* (open-air museums), in particular those at Sanok and Nowy Sacz in the country's south-east.

Castles & Palaces

There are more than 100 castles in Poland of many different kinds. The imposing Malbork Castle, one-time seat of the Teutonic Knights, is reputedly the largest surviving medieval castle in Europe. Other remarkable castles built by the knights include those in Lidzbark Warminski and Kwidzyn.

For hundreds of years, the mighty Wawel Castle in Kraków sheltered Polish royalty, most of whom are buried in the adjacent cathedral. True castle lovers will also seek out castles in

Pieskowa Skala, Baranów Sandomierski, Niedzica, Ksiaz and Goluchów. All these castles are now museums.

Warsaw contains Poland's two most magnificent royal palaces: the 17th century Wilanów Palace and the 18th century Lazienki Palace. In the countryside, feudal magnates built splendid Renaissance, baroque and rococo palaces, the best of which include those in Lancut, Nieborów, Kozlówka, Rogalin and Pszczyna, all open as museums.

Churches

In a country as strongly Catholic as Poland, churches are everywhere, from the smallest villages to the largest cities. Kraków alone has several dozen of them. Plenty of old churches are of great historic and often artistic value. Any list of highlights should include the cathedrals in Kraków, Torun and Gniezno, St Mary's churches in Kraków and Gdansk, and the Monastery of Jasna Góra in Czestochowa.

The Great Outdoors

Poland's mountains, lakes and coast are superb. The Tatras are the uncontested winners among the mountain ranges, in both height and popularity. Zakopane is the biggest and most popular mountain resort and a good base for hiking or skiing. Far less known but also magnificent are the Góry Stolowe (Table Mountains) in the Sudetes.

There are several lake districts in Poland, of which the Great Masurian Lakes are the largest and most popular. The Baltic coast has sandy beaches along almost its entire length; one of the most beautiful and least polluted stretches is near Leba, with its shifting dunes.

The primeval Bialowieza Forest on Poland's eastern border is home to the largest remaining herd of European bison and other wildlife.

VISA REQUIREMENTS

Citizens of most European Union (EU) countries and the USA can enter Poland without a visa and stay for 90 days. Australians, Canadians, New Zealanders and South Africans still need visas. Border laws are being liberalised, so check with a Polish embassy before you leave.

Polish Embassies & Consulates

Australia
(☎ 02-6273 1208) 7 Turrana St, Yarralumla, Canberra, ACT 2600
Consulate: (☎ 02-9363 9816) 10 Trelawney St, Woollahra, Sydney, NSW 2025

Canada
(☎ 613-789 0468) 443 Daly Ave, Ottawa 2, Ont K1N 6H3
Consulate: (☎ 514-937 9481) 1500 Ave des Pins Ouest, Montreal, Que H3G 1B4
Consulate: (☎ 416-252 5471) 2603 Lakeshore Blvd West, Toronto, Ont M8V 1G5
Consulate: (☎ 604-688 3530) 1177 West Hastings St, Suite 1600, Vancouver, BC V6E 2K3

Japan
(☎ 03-3280 2881) Oak Homes, 4-5-14 Takanawa, Minato-ku, Tokyo 108

UK
(☎ 020-7580 0475) 73 New Cavendish St, London W1N 7RB
Consulate: (☎ 0131-552 0301) 2 Kinnear Rd, Edinburgh E3H 5PE

USA
(☎ 202-234 3800) 2640 16th St NW, Washington, DC 20009
Consulate: (☎ 312-337 8166) 1530 North Lake Shore Drive, Chicago, IL 60610
Consulate: (☎ 212-889 8360) 233 Madison Ave, New York, NY 10016
Consulate: (☎ 310-442 8500) 12400 Wilshire Blvd, Suite 555, Los Angeles, CA 90025

TOURIST OFFICES OVERSEAS

UK
(☎ 020-7580 8811, fax 7580 8866) 1st floor, Remo House, 310-312 Regent St, London W1R 5AJ

USA
(☎ 312-236 9013/123, fax 236 1125) 33 North Michigan Ave, Suite 224, Chicago, IL 60601
(☎ 212-338 9412, fax 338 9283) 275 Madison Ave, Suite 1711, New York, NY 10016

POST & COMMUNICATIONS

Polish postal and telecommunications services usually share one office, called the *poczta* (post office), where you can buy stamps, send letters, collect poste restante, place long-distance calls and send faxes. Airmail letters take about a week to reach a European destination and up to two weeks if mailed to other continents. Poste restante isn't very reliable – stick to sending mail to the large cities, such as Warsaw, Kraków and Gdansk. Mail is held for 14 working days, then returned to the sender.

Public telephones are few and far between by western standards, and often out of order. Go to a post office: each should have at least one functioning public phone. The new telephones only operate on phonecards, which are available from the post office.

The Internet is becoming popular in Poland and cybercafes are opening in the big cities. Other places providing Internet and email facilities include computer offices, software shops and the like.

MONEY
Costs

Though not the bargain it used to be, Poland is still a cheap country for travellers. Staying at cheap hotels and hostels, eating in medium-priced restaurants, and getting around by bus or train, you should easily be able to get by on around US$30 a day. If you camp or stick only to hostels (where available) and self-cater or eat in cheap bistros, you could cut it to US$20 fairly painlessly.

In restaurants, service is included in the price, so you just pay what is on the bill. Tipping is a matter of choice but in upmarket establishments it's customary to tip 10% of the bill. Bargaining is not common in Poland and is limited to some informal places such as markets, bazaars and a few street vendors.

Changing Money

Travellers cheques are reasonably easy to exchange wherever you go, but you'll get a slightly better rate with cash. Credit cards are becoming more useful – you can use them to pay for upmarket hotels and restaurants, car rentals and long-distance transport. You can also get cash advances with the major cards, and bankomats (ATMs) are widespread in cities and towns.

ONLINE SERVICES

Lonely Planet's Destination Poland page (www.lonelyplanet.com/dest/eur /pol.htm) has a thorough country profile. The Poland National Tourist office has a site (www.polandtour.org); another site (www.explore-poland.pl) covers the country in words and pictures.

For news, travel information, links and other details about Poland, see www.polishworld.com. The online version of *The Warsaw Voice* weekly (www.warsawvoice.com.pl) will help you keep track of Poland's current political, economic and cultural issues.

BOOKS

For a taste of Polish fiction, try Nobel Prize winner Czeslaw Milosz's *The Captive Mind* or Jerzy Kosinski's *The Painted Bird*. Isaac Bashevis Singer, a Polish-born US writer of Yiddish novels and short stories, also won a Nobel Prize, and it's definitely worth dipping into the autobiographical *In My Father's Court*. *Poland* by James A Michener is a well dramatised version of Polish history. Thomas Kenneally's Booker Prize-winning *Schindler's Ark* was the basis of Steven Spielberg's film *Schindler's List*.

Anne Applebaum's *Between East and West* is a highly lauded fusion of travel writing and political history. *God's Playground – A History of Poland* by Norman Davies is one of the best accounts of Polish history. *The Heart of Europe – A Short History of Poland*, also by Davies, is a more condensed account, with a greater emphasis on the 20th century. *Jews in Poland – A Documentary History* by Iwo Cyprian Pogonowski provides a comprehensive record of half a millennium of Polish-Jewish relations in a country which, until WWII, was the major centre of Jewish culture in Europe. Turning to more recent history, *The Polish Revolution – Solidarity 1980-82* by Timothy Garton Ash provides what is perhaps the best insight into the Solidarity era.

FILMS

Speilberg's *Schindler's List* (1993) is required watching. Set in the Jewish ghettos of Kraków and the Plaszów death camp during WWII, it tells the true story of an Austrian businessman,

Oskar Schindler, who saved 1100 Jews who had been workers in his factory.

The early years of Polish cinema were pretty barren, but things picked up after WWII. A dozen remarkable Polish films were made in the period from 1955-63, including Andrzej Wajda's famous trilogy: *A Generation*, *Canal* and *Ashes and Diamonds*. He followed up with *Man of Marble*, its sequel, *Man of Iron*, and *Danton*.

Polish director Roman Polanski made only one feature film in Poland, *Knife in the Water*, before heading to Hollywood and working on a string of hit films.

ENTERING & LEAVING

There are direct flights to Warsaw from major European destinations, as well as from US cities with large Polish communities, such as New York and Chicago. There is no departure tax. Train and bus fares from some European destinations can be as expensive as discounted air fares unless you have some kind of transport pass. Road connections with Poland are good and getting better, but there are still border delays, especially when crossing from other Eastern European countries. Many border crossings to Germany and the Czech Republic have been closed since floods in July 1997 damaged bridges. There are sea connections from the UK and Scandinavia to Gdansk, Gdynia and Swinoujscie. Most services have car-freighting facilities.

PORTUGAL

Portugal is one of the cheapest and most fascinating destinations in Western Europe. It has a rich seafaring past, superb beach resorts, wistful towns and cities, and a landscape wreathed in olive groves, vineyards and wheat fields. Four decades of dictatorship left the country sidelined from Europe's power centres and detached from the progressiveness of modern life for much of the 20th century. Holiday-makers mistook this tardy development for quaintness and Portugal developed a reputation as little more than a cheap charter flight destination for northern Europeans wanting to pep up their summer tans on the Algarve. But this small slice of Europe offers more than beaches and port wine. Away from the crowded resorts of the Algarve is a dusty patina of faded grandeur, outstanding architecture from Moorish to Manueline and a remarkably diverse natural landscape.

WHEN TO GO

Portugal's climate is temperate, and you'll find good weather just about everywhere between April and October, and nearly year-round in the Algarve. The wettest season is from November to March: the soggiest regions are in the extreme north and in the central Serra da Estrela mountain region. The ski season is from January to March (February is best). Peak tourist season is roughly from mid-June to September, except in the Algarve where it really only quietens down in the dead of winter. Carnaval and Easter are two holidays celebrated with gusto all over the country.

At a Glance

Full Country Name: Portugal
Area: 92,389 sq km
Population: 10.5 million
Capital City: Lisbon (pop 650,000)
People: 99% Portuguese, 1% African
Language: Portuguese
Religion: 99% Roman Catholic, 1% other
Government: Parliamentary democracy
Currency: Portuguese escudo = 100 centavos
Time Zone: The same as GMT/UTC; clocks go forward one hour on the last Sunday in March and back on the last Sunday in October
International Telephone Code: 351
Electricity: 220V, 50Hz

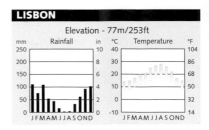

LISBON
Elevation - 77m/253ft

HIGHLIGHTS
Lisbon

The Art Deco facades of Lisbon may be disappearing in a frenzy of re-development, but Portugal's capital is a pleasant city with a diverse range of attractions. Don't miss the Gulbenkian museum and the Oceanarium, the largest in Europe. Wandering through the narrow streets of the city's old quarters is interesting, particularly in the Baixa, Alfama and Bairro Alto districts. A highlight is the Manueline architecture of the Jerónimos Monastery (Mosteiro dos Jerónimos) in Belém.

Historic Towns & Architecture

Rich in architecture and history, Portugal's old walled towns such as Évora and Marvão evoke a timeless atmosphere and are great places in which to linger. Évora, only two hours east of Lisbon, has a Roman temple and more architectural and artistic treasures within its Moorish walls than any place outside Lisbon – the entire centre is listed on the UNESCO World Heritage register. The mountaintop village of Marvão (900m) has a stunning setting and a formidable castle rising from the ruins, with fine views out over the plains below.

Other towns of historic interest worth visiting are Valença do Minho, Bragança, Guimarães and Coimbra.

Architecture buffs should head for the monasteries at Belém (in Lisbon) and Batalha, the palaces of Pena (in Sintra) and Buçaco, and the Bom Jesus do Monte near Braga – a place of pilgrimage for legions of Catholics. Look out for Portugal's most notable decorative art, the painted tiles (usually blue and white) known as *azulejos*. You can see them in the train stations at Porto, São Bento and Aveiro; at Igreja do Carmo in Porto; the National Museum of Azelejos in Lisbon; in Évora; and in Almancil on the Algarve.

National Parks & Beaches

For scenery, you can't beat the mountain landscapes of the Serra da Estrela and the Peneda-Gerês national parks. The former features the highest mountain peaks in mainland Portugal, glacial lakes, Alpine-style meadows and tiny mountain villages. This is also the best place in Portugal for hiking, with a network of well marked and mapped trails that are rarely crowded, even in the height of summer. The Parque Nacional Da Peneda-Gerês, in the far north of the country, is a protected area of granite massifs and rural villages. As well as being a popular hiking destination, the park offers a unique window into a fast-disappearing rural way of life.

At the other end of the spectrum is the Algarve and its famous beaches. While this strip of southern coastline can be overrun with foreign tourists in summer – particularly from Lagos to Faro – there are still a few quiet spots and there's no doubting that the rugged cliffs and sandy bays are alluring. Lagos is easily the most popular resort town, with young package tourists and independent travellers alike – the bars, taverns and nightclubs heave throughout summer. As it also has some of the better Algarve beaches, it's well worth stopping here for some good-time indulgence. If you want something quieter, try heading west of Lagos towards Sagres, where you'll find some wild and relatively peaceful beaches.

Douro Valley

The Rio Douro (Douro River) cuts through the north of the country from Porto to the border with Spain. The mountain-ringed Douro Valley is one of the most beautiful parts of Portugal and is best explored from the city of Porto. Among the highlights is a train ride through the vineyard-terraced slopes of the valley. In Porto itself there are many sights, but how could you leave without spending a day hopping between the famous port wine lodges?

VISA REQUIREMENTS

Nationals of all European Union (EU) countries, as well as those from Canada, Israel, New Zealand and the USA can stay up to three months in any half-year without a visa. As of July 1999, Australian citizens must obtain a visa from their nearest Portuguese consulate before entering the country. South Africans require only a Schengen visa.

Portuguese Embassies & Consulates

Australia
(☎ 02-6290 1733, fax 6290 1957) 23 Culgoa Circuit, O'Malley, Canberra, ACT 2606
Consulate: (☎ 02-9326 1844, fax 9327 1607) 132 Ocean St, Edgecliff, Sydney, NSW 2027

Canada
(☎ 613-729 0883, fax 729 4236) 645 Island Park Drive, Ottawa, Ont K1Y OB8
Consulate: (☎ 514-499 0359, fax 499 0366) 2020 Rue de l'Universite, 17th floor, Montreal, Que H3A 2A5
Consulate: (☎ 416-360 8260, fax 360 0350) 121 Richmond St West, 7th floor, Toronto, Ont M5H 2Kl

Ireland
(☎ 01-289 4416, fax 289 2849) Knock Sinna House, Knock Sinna, Fox Rock, Dublin 18

Itineraries

Two Days
With two days you'll really only have time to visit Lisbon. However, if you're set on a beach and a good time, go to Lagos in the Algarve.

One Week
Spend two or three days exploring Lisbon and the surrounding area, including the monastery at Belém and the atmospheric town of Sintra. From there, go to Évora and Marvão if you like the idea of historic towns; or, if beaches are your preference, head down to Lagos and make your way along the coast to Sagres. Alternatively, travel up the coast, stopping at the fortified hilltop village of Óbidos on the way to Porto, where you can spend a few days exploring the Douro Valley.

Two Weeks
Northern Portugal Start with three or four days in Lisbon, including a day in Sintra, then head up the coast, stopping at Óbidos and the popular fishing village of Nazaré. Continue north, pausing at Batalha for its impressive monastery and a day in the ancient university town of Coimbra. From

here you can head inland to Serra da Estrela National Park (Parque Natural da Serra da Estrela) for some hiking and mountain air. The best bases here are Covilhã and Guarda. Otherwise, continue up to Porto, where you can indulge in port wine and explore the Douro Valley. If you still have time, continue up to the Peneda-Gerês for a unique view of rural village life.

Southern Portugal Start with Lisbon, then travel across to Évora for a couple of days and down to Mourão. From there, travel down to the Algarve, starting with the unspoilt town of Tavira in the east. From Tavira you can make your way along the coast via Faro, Albufeira, Lagos and Sagres, pausing at the many beaches and bays along the way. Finish the trip with a sunset visit to Sagres and Cabo de São Vicente (Cape St Vincent) on the western tip of the Algarve.

One Month
With a month or more you could combine the two-week itineraries or spend more time exploring a particular area.

PORTUGAL HIGHLIGHTS & ITINERARIES

PENEDA-GERÊS
NATIONAL PARK
Hike into a vanishing
way of village life

DOURO VALLEY
Sample port wine
in Portugal's most
picturesque region

LISBON
Marvel at the
Jerónimos Monastery,
emblem of the
enchanting capital

EVORA
Check out the
walled-in wonders of
this World Heritage site

TAVIRA
Ease into the Algarve
from this pretty,
unspoiled town

ATLANTIC
OCEAN

ATLANTIC
OCEAN

SPAIN

SPAIN

To Vigo
To La Coruña
To Ourense
To Madrid
To Málaga

Viana do Castelo
Barcelos
Braga
Guimarães
Vila do Conde
Amarante
Vila Real
Porto
Peso da Régua
Lamego
Espinho
Ovar
Aveiro
Mira
São Pedro do Sul
Viseu
Mangualde
Tondela
Gouveia
Guarda
Figueira da Foz
Coimbra
Luso
Lousã
Covilhã
Pombal
Fundão
Monsanto
Leiria
Castelo Branco
Nazaré
Batalha
Fátima
Alcobaça
Tomar
Caldas da Rainha
Peniche
Óbidos
Abrantes
Castelo de Vide
Ericeira
Santarém
Marvão
Portalegre
Sintra
Vila Franca
Ponte de Sor
Coruche
Mora
Cascais
LISBON
Barreiro
Vendas Novas
Évoramonte
Estremoz
Elvas
Badajoz
Mérida
Setúbal
Montemor-o-Novo
Évora
Alcácer do Sal
Reguengos de Monsaraz
Mourão
Santiago do Cacém
Ferreira
Beja
Moura
Sines
Aljustrel
Serpa
Vila Nova de Milfontes
Mértola
Zambujeira do Mar
Alcoutim
Aljezur
Portimão
Silves
Loulé
Faro
Ayamonte
Huelva
Seville
Lagos
Albufeira
Almancil
Tavira
Vila Real de Santo António
Sagres
Utrera

Chaves
Bragança
Mirandela
Vila Real
Tua
Barca de Alva
Freixo de Espada à Cinta
Miranda do Douro
Zamora
Salamanca
Pinhel
Vilar Formoso
Cáceres

SUGGESTED ITINERARIES

One Week **1** Lisbon • Sintra • Évora • Marvão
2 Lisbon • Sintra • Lagos • Sagres
3 Lisbon • Sintra • Óbidos • Porto • Douro Valley

Two Weeks **1** Lisbon • Sintra • Óbidos • Nazaré • Batalha • Coimbra • Serra da Estrela National Park
2 Lisbon • Sintra • Óbidos • Nazaré • Batalha • Coimbra • Porto • Douro Valley • Peneda-Gerês National Park
3 Lisbon • Évora • Mourão • Sagres • the Algarve

New Zealand

(☎ 09-309 1454, fax 308 9061) 85 Forte St, Remuera, Auckland 5

UK

(☎/fax 020-7235 5331) 11 Belgrave Square, London SW1X 8PP

Consulate: (☎ 020-7581 8722, fax 7581 3085) 62 Brompton Rd, London SW3 1BJ

USA

(☎ 202-328 8610, fax 462 3726) 2125 Kalorama Rd NW, Washington, DC 20008

Consulate: (☎ 212-246 4580, fax 459 0190) 630 Fifth Ave, Suite 310-378, New York, NY 10111

Consulate: (☎ 451-921 1443, fax 346 1440) 3298 Washington St, San Francisco, CA 94115

TOURIST OFFICES OVERSEAS

Canada

(☎ 416-921 7376, fax 921 1353) 60 Bloor St West, Suite 1005, Toronto, Ont M4W 3B8

(☎ 514-282 1264, fax 499 1450) 500 Sherbrooke St West, Suite 940, Montreal, Que H3A 3C6

UK

(☎ 020-7494 1441, fax 7494 1868) 22-25a Sackville St, London W1X 1DE

USA

(☎ 212-719 3985 or toll-free 800 POR-TUGAL, fax 212-764 6137) 590 Fifth Ave, 4th floor, New York, NY 10036-4785

(☎ 202-331 8222, fax 331 8236) 1900 L St NW, Suite 310, Washington, DC 20036

POST & COMMUNICATIONS

Stamps are sold not only at post offices, but also at numerous kiosks and from coin-operated vending machines. For delivery to the USA or Australia, allow eight to 10 days; delivery times for Europe are four to six days.

Most towns have a poste restante service at the central post office. A small charge is levied for each item of mail collected and unclaimed letters are normally returned after a month.

The cheapest and most convenient way to call anywhere is from a card-operated Credifone. Phonecards are widely available from newsagents, tobacconists and telephone offices. For a slightly higher charge you can also make calls from booths in Portugal Telecom offices and post offices, where you pay over the counter after your call is finished.

Post offices operate a domestic and international fax service called Corfax, but it's not cheap. Cybercafes for checking email can be found in Lisbon, Porto and a few other towns. An excellent alternative is the Instituto Português da Juventude (IPJ), a state-funded network of youth centres that usually have a library with free Internet access. Some municipal libraries and a few larger Portugal Telecom offices also have free Internet access.

MONEY
Costs

Although costs are beginning to rise as Portugal falls into fiscal step with the EU, this is still one of the cheapest places to travel in Europe. On a rock-bottom budget – using hostels or camping grounds and mostly self-catering – you could get by on about US$25 a day in the high season. With bottom-end accommodation and the occasional inexpensive restaurant meal, daily costs would hover at around US$30. Outside major tourist areas, prices dip appreciably.

A reasonable restaurant tip is about 10%, and taxi drivers also appreciate a tip of about 10% of the fare. Good-humoured bargaining is acceptable in markets but you'll find the Portuguese tough opponents. Off season, you can sometimes bargain down the price of accommodation.

Changing Money

Though travellers cheques are easily exchanged (at rates about 1% better than for cash) they are very poor value in Portugal because commission fees are so high – sometimes up to 13% for a US$100 cheque. The exception is American Express travellers cheques, which can be exchanged commission-free with Amex agents. Plastic is overall a more sensible alternative and there are *multibancos* (ATMs) in all tourist centres of any size where you can withdraw cash from credit and debit accounts.

ONLINE SERVICES

Lonely Planet has a Web site at www .lonelyplanet.com/dest/eur/por.htm. Portugal Info is to be found at www .portugal-info.net and Portugal for Travellers is located at http://nervo .com/pt.

ICEP, Portugal's state-run tourism organisation, has a site at www.portu gal-insite.pt. Excite City.Net has a site (www.city.net/countries/portugal) that includes links to the homepages of about 20 Portuguese towns. A good site about Lisbon is at www.eunet.pt /Lisboa/i/lisboa.html, but it's not updated very often. It has a listing of museums, bars and clubs, and recom-mendations on restaurants and places to see.

BOOKS

The best general overview of the country is the very readable *The Portuguese – The Land and its People* by Marion Kaplan. Another good read is Rose Macaulay's *They Went to Portugal*, which follows the experiences of a host of travellers from medieval times to the 19th century. The very compelling 'whodunnit' *Ballad of Dog's Beach* by José Cardoso Pires is readable fiction.

Keen walkers should pack the *Landscapes of Portugal* series by Brian & Eileen Andersen, which features both car tours and treks in various regions, and the more detailed *Walking in Portugal* by Bethan Davies & Ben Cole.

FILMS

Wim Wenders' film *A Lisbon Story* had its world premiere in Lisbon in 1994. Originally conceived as a documentary, it acquired a story line as it went along: a movie sound man wanders the streets trying to salvage a film that its director has abandoned, recording the sounds of the city. In the process he falls in love, has a close call with gangsters and is followed by a pack of children.

ENTERING & LEAVING

TAP (Air Portugal), the national air-line, has direct flights to Lisbon from a number of destinations, including Eng-land, France, Spain, the USA and Canada. There are also international flights to Porto and Faro. International departure tax is US$13, but this is included in the price of your ticket. Direct and regular bus services operate from France, Spain and England. Train connections from France and Spain are just as routine, with a number of scenic stops en route. You can also drive, ride, pedal or walk into Portugal, with major border posts open around the clock. Coming from England, you can take the Plymouth-Santander or Portsmouth-Bilbao car-passenger fer-ries to northern Spain and then travel on to Portugal.

ROMANIA

Famed for its Dracula connections, Romania is a country in transition. Horse-drawn carts jostle for space against fast cars whose drivers are talking money on mobile phones, while farm workers watch *Baywatch* courtesy of satellite dishes standing in the rear yard of their medieval farmhouse. Romania is clawing itself forward, slowly and surely sloughing off the remnants of the Ceausescu era. In the middle of the picturesque scenery and the headlong rush to development, parts of the country are being left out. But in 1996 a neocommunist government was voted out and replaced by one talking about genuine reform, so all is not without hope.

Romania brims with gruesome history, majestic castles, medieval towns, great hiking and the cheap skiing

of the 'undiscovered' former Eastern bloc. And the Romanians, despite being among Europe's poorest people, are among the most hospitable in Eastern Europe and will welcome you with open arms. You'll be floored at how different Romania is, but you'll almost certainly see signs that it's chasing the dreams of the rest of the west.

WHEN TO GO

May and June are the best months to visit, followed by September and early October. At these times, you can visit the medieval painted monasteries in southern Bucovina, and enjoy them minus the tourist hordes. Spring and autumn are also the best times for bird-watching in the Danube Delta. Romania has harsh winters, when tourism is centred on the ski resorts like Poiana Brasov, just outside Brasov, and

At a Glance

Full Country Name: Romania
Area: 237,500 sq km
Population: 23 million
Capital City: Bucharest (pop 2 million)
People: 89% Romanians, 6.9% Hungarians, 1.8% Gypsies, plus Germans, Ukrainians
Language: Romanian, Hungarian
Religion: Romanian Orthodox, Roman Catholic, Protestant
Government: Republic
Currency: Romanian leu (plural: lei)
Time Zone: Two hours ahead of GMT/UTC; clocks are turned forward one hour at the end of March and back again at the end of September
International Telephone Code: 40
Electricity: 220V, 50Hz

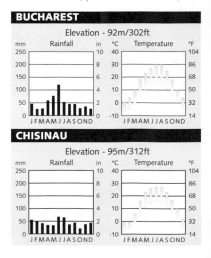

Sinaia. Snow lingers as late as mid-May, and the hiking season doesn't begin in earnest till June. The resorts along the Black Sea coast start filling up in late June and stay packed until mid-August.

HIGHLIGHTS
Museums & Galleries

Not to be missed if you're in Bucharest is the Village Museum, one of Europe's largest and oldest museums, and a microcosm of Romanian rural life. Inside are hundreds of full-scale displays of churches, farm buildings, windmills and traditional houses. Also in Bucharest, the National History Museum tells the story of Romania from prehistoric times to WWI. It's not a museum, but Ceausescu's House of the People is a staggering sight. It's the second largest building in the world after the Pentagon, and while a shocking eyesore on the outside, its interior is a fantastic and opulent showcase of Romanian craftsmanship.

Constanta's archaeological museum has one of the better collections of Greek and Roman artefacts in Eastern Europe. The ethnographical museum in Cluj-Napoca and the Museum of Popular Techniques at Sibiu contain excellent displays of Romanian folk culture. Romania's oldest and finest art gallery is the Brukenthal Museum in Sibiu. Finally, the Danube Museum in Drobeta-Turnu Severin is outstanding for history and natural history, with an aquarium of fish from the Danube.

Castles & Monasteries

Bran Castle, near Brasov in Transylvania, is on everyone's 'must-see' list (even if Count Dracula never slept there), but the ruins of nearby Râsnov Castle are more dramatic and less touristy. Peles Castle at Sinaia is actually a royal palace, but it's an amazingly grandiose castle and easily the finest in Romania. The Gothic Hunedoara Castle, one of Transylvania's architectural gems, is evocative, despite the ugly steel mills surrounding it.

The World Heritage-listed painted churches of Southern Bucovina are among the greatest artistic monuments in Europe. The Voronet and Moldovita monasteries, painted with magnificent frescoes (the Voronet is known as 'the Sistine Chapel of the East') are well worth seeing. In Wallachia, Curtea de Arges Monastery is an impressive piece of 'chocolate box' architecture and hides a host of royal tombs.

Medieval Towns

Romania's best preserved medieval towns are in Transylvania. The fortified city of Brasov has the finest central square in the country and is an excellent base for many points of interest. Sighisoara is a perfectly preserved medieval town that bursts into life for the twice-weekly market but attracts plenty of tourists on other days, while Sibiu is far enough off the beaten track to be spared the tourist trade. Cluj-Napoca is a relaxed little town with cheap accommodation. In Crisana, Oradea is an elegant 19th century Habsburg town just across the border from Hungary.

Hiking & Skiing

Romania has some fabulous hiking areas and most of the mountain ranges have well marked trails. The Bucegi and Fagaras ranges south and west of Brasov provide some of the country's finest hiking. Resorts such as Poiana Brasov, Busteni and Sinaia are some of the best bases from which to start your walks. Sibiu is the best base for hikes into the Fagaras Mountains.

Likewise, there is some very good skiing in Romania and it's much cheaper than in Western Europe. Sinaia has the most challenging downhill runs, while Poiana Brasov has the most reliable snowfalls – it's often possible to ski as late as May.

Itineraries

Two Days
If your time is short, spend a day in the fortified medieval city of Brasov and take a day trip out to the exquisite Peles Castle at Sinaia.

One Week
Spend a couple of days in Brasov, visit the famous Bran Castle and the not-so-famous but equally dramatic Râsnov Castle. Spend a day or two in Sinaia visiting Peles Castle and taking the cable car up to the foot of Mt Furnica. From there, travel up to Sighisoara and (if you're heading west into Hungary) perhaps Cluj-Napoca. If you're heading south to Bulgaria, spend a day in Bucharest. If time permits, journey into the northern part of Romania to visit the monasteries of Southern Bucovina.

Two Weeks
With two weeks you have a chance to spend time in the main towns as well as seeing a slice of Romanian rural life. Spend two days in Bucharest visiting the House of the People, the Village Museum and the final resting places of the Ceausescus. Head up to Brasov for a few days with trips out to Bran and Râsnov castles, then on to Sinaia, which you can use as a base for some hiking. From there travel up to the wonderful medieval town of Sighisoara, then on to Sibiu, Cluj-Napoca and Oradea. From Sibiu you can hike in the Fagaras ranges. Alternatively, skip Cluj-Napoca and Oradea and spend time visiting the frescoed monasteries of Bucovina, particularly Voronet and Moldovita.

VISA REQUIREMENTS

US citizens have the luxury of being able to visit Romania visa-free for 30 days. All other western visitors need a visa, obtainable in advance at a Romanian embassy or upon entry to Romania.

Single-entry transit and single-entry tourist visas valid for 30 days are issued at the border or the airport in Bucharest but, to avoid getting ripped off at some border crossings, it is better to get your visa before leaving home.

Romanian Embassies & Consulates

Australia
(☎ 02-6286 2343 or 6290 2442, fax 6286 2433) 4 Dalman Crescent, O'Malley, Canberra, ACT 2606

Canada
(☎ 613-789 5345, fax 789 4365) 655 Rideau St, Ottawa, Ont K1N 6A3
Consulate: (☎ 416-585 5802/9177, fax 585 4798) 111 Peter St, Suite 530, Toronto, Ont M5V 2H1
Consulate: (☎ 514-876 1792/3, fax 876 1797) 1111 St Urbain, Suite M01, Montreal, Que H2Z 1Y6

Ireland
(☎ 031-668 1336/447, fax 668 15 82) 60 Merrion Rd, Ballsbridge, Dublin 4

UK
(☎ 020-7937 9666, fax 7937 8069, ✉ consul@roemb.demon.cntry) 4 Palace Green, London W8 4Qd

USA
(☎ 202-232 4829/4747, fax 232 4748, ✉ romania@embassy.org, www.embassy.org/romania) 1607 23rd St NW, Washington, DC 20008
Consulate: (☎ 212-682 9120, fax 972 8463) 200 E 38th St, New York, NY 10016
Consulate: (☎ 310-444 0043, fax 445 0043) 11766 Wilshire Blvd, Suite 560, Los Angeles, CA 90025

ROMANIA HIGHLIGHTS & ITINERARIES

VORONET & MOLDOVITA MONASTERIES
See the glory of Romanian art at its finest

SINAIA
For a taste of something different, try Peles Castle, easily Romania's finest

SIBIU
Sink your teeth into the excellent museums or take a hike nearby

BRAN CASTLE
It sucks, but Vlad Tepes (Count Drac in the book) never really lived here

SUGGESTED ITINERARIES

Two Days Brasov • Sinaia

One Week Brasov • Bran • Rasnov • Sinaia • Sighisoara • Cluj-Napoca or Bucharest

Two Weeks Bucharest • Brasov • Bran • Rasnov • Sinaia • Sighisoara • Sibiu • Cluj-Napoca • Oradea

1 Bucharest • Brasov • Bran • Rasnov • Sinaia • Sighisoara • Sibiu • Cluj-Napoca • Oradea

2 Bucharest • Brasov • Bran • Rasnov • Sinaia • Sighisoara • Sibiu • Voronet • Moldovita

TOURIST OFFICES OVERSEAS

UK

(☎/fax 020-7224 3692) 83a Marylebone High St, London W1M 3DE

USA

(☎ 212-545 8484, fax 251 0429) 14 E 38th St, 12th floor, New York, NY 10016

MONEY
Costs

Accommodation will be your biggest expense in Romania. Cheap accommodation is scarce in Bucharest. Expect to pay at least US$25 for a double room with shared bath in any

Moldova

Moldova is a cultural enigma. Once part of the Soviet Union and independent since 1991, this troubled country continues to struggle with national identity and social unity. Squeezed between the north-western corner of Romania and Ukraine, Moldova is ethnically very much part-Romanian, part-Russian. Added to these political tensions are Moldova's money blues brought on by the economy being so closely tied to the sliding fortunes of the Russian rouble. Outside the capital, Chisinau, tremendous poverty prevails. Although the smallest of the former Soviet Republics, Moldova is the most densely populated, with over 4.4 million inhabitants.

Despite these problems, Moldova is a picturesque country – all rolling green hills, white-washed villages, placid lakes and sunflower fields – with an old-world charm that's hard to manufacture. It also has some of the best vineyards in Europe.

Moldova's tourist infrastructure is virtually nonexistent; getting around by public transport can be a pain and Soviet-style bureaucracy will thwart you at every turn. The hardest part, however, is just getting into the country. All western visitors need a visa and (with the exception of US citizens) these are only issued if you have an invitation or prebooked accommodation through a tour company. Contact the following Moldavian consulates:

Romania

(☎ 01-666 5720, fax 312 8631) Str Campina 47, RO-713 26 Bucharest

USA

(☎ 202-667 1130, fax 667 1204) 2101 S St NW, Washington, DC 20008

Changing money can also be a problem. Travellers cheques and credit cards are only accepted at a couple of banks in the capital and there are no ATMs. Carry US dollars cash. The currency is the Moldavian leu, and costs are low compared with Western Europe. However, the old Soviet three tier pricing policy means you'll pay more than locals for hotel rooms, so expect to spend around US$30 a day.

The good news for adventurous types is that travel in Moldova is like nowhere else in Europe. The bustling capital, Chisinau, is a small, green city with an historic heart that only partly survived WWII bombing. Museums, theatres, cafes, colourful markets and reasonably lively bars and discos combine to make a pleasant base. Nearby, Cricova is an underground wine town where you can literally ride through the subterranean cellar streets packed with more than a million bottles of wine. Elsewhere in Moldova there are enough wineries to keep you busy wine tasting for weeks – unfortunately most, including Cricova, can only be visited on officially sanctioned (and very expensive) tours.

The cliff-top Orheul Vechi monastery and the Cave monastery are interesting attractions. The self-declared republic of Trandsdniestr, which sparked a bloody civil war when it declared independence from the rest of Moldova in 1991, offers a unique insight into a communist bastion and a bizarre self-styled state (with its own 'funny money' currency). Travel to this part of Moldova was not recommended at the time of writing.

hotel within walking distance of the centre of most Romanian cities and towns. Accommodation in private homes in the countryside starts at US$10 a night, including a home-cooked breakfast. The cost of dining is rising – Romanians can't afford to eat out, so most restaurants are geared to 'rich foreigners' – but it's still cheap. In Bucharest, however, it's tough to eat for less than US$5 per head, not including alcohol. A bottle of good Romanian wine can be as little as US$1.50. Seeing a film or play costs about US$1, and entrance fees to museums are about 20 cents. Public transport is dirt cheap by western standards.

Tipping is not common in Romania, though you should always round up the bill. Some bartering, but not much, goes on at flea markets. Taxi drivers drive a hard bargain, so always haggle.

Changing Money

It's easy to cash travellers cheques in Romania, but not very easy to replace stolen ones. Only American Express has an office that issues replacements in Bucharest. Cash-dispensing ATMs accepting Visa/MasterCard are becoming increasingly widespread in Romania. Credit cards are widely accepted in hotels, restaurants and shops. They are essential for hiring a car, unless you want to pay cash up front. Marked, torn or very used notes will often be refused at exchange offices. Ensure whatever currency you bring is in good condition.

POST & COMMUNICATIONS

Sending mail is comparatively cheap, and mail in and out of Romania is rapidly approaching western norms. All post offices sell stamps, and there is a poste restante mail service in the central post office in Bucharest and most major cities. Mail is kept for one month.

Direct international calls can be made or received from most private phones and public cardphones. All calls can be made from the bright orange card phones. Magnetic phonecards are sold at telephone offices in every city.

Faxes can be sent or received from any central post office or, in Bucharest, from any Telex-Fax office. Cybercafes are beginning to sprout. So far you can send email and access the Internet in Bucharest, Craiova in Wallachia, Iasi in Moldavia, Mangalia on the Black Sea coast, Sibiu, Sighisoara and Gheorgheni in Transylvania, Timisoara in the Banat, and Sighetu Marmatiei in Maramures.

ONLINE SERVICES

Lonely Planet's Destination Romania (www.lonelyplanet.com/dest/eur/rom .htm) has a detailed country profile and links. The homepage of the Society of Romanian Studies (www .huntcol.edu/pmichels/srs.html) has over 400 hot links to every known Romanian-related Web site. The Romanian Internet Directory has a site (www.bucharest.com) that provides local news, photos of the 1989 revolution and links galore to Romania-related Web sites. Virtual Romania has a site (www.info.polymtl.ca/romania) that has news and dozens of Romanian links.

BOOKS

The Romanians – A History by Vlad Georgescu is a comprehensive contemporary history of the country. *A*

History of Romania, edited by Kurt W Treptow and published by the Romanian Cultural Foundation in Iasi, is a hefty tome tracing the history of Romania from the Stone Age to the 1990s, and is worth its weight in lei. *Kiss the Hand You Cannot Bite – The Rise and Fall of the Ceausescus* by Edward Behr provides fascinating background to the 1989 revolution. Dan Antal's autobiography *Out of Romania* offers startling (and witty) insights into the hardships and cruelties encountered by a youth on the 'wrong side' of the Securitate. The extraordinary cult following that has grown up around Bram Stoker's *Dracula* novel, and its association with Vlad Tepes, is expounded in *In Search of Dracula – History of Dracula and Vampires* by Raymond McNally & Radu Florescu.

FILMS

Romanian cinema has blossomed since the revolution. In 1994 Lucian Pintilie's *O Vara de Neuitat* (Unforgettable Summer) made a small splash at Cannes. Other films to look out for are Mircea Daneliuc's *Senatorul Melcilor* (Senator of the Snails), Radu Gabrea's *Rosenemil, o Tragica Lubire* (The Tragic Love Story of Rosenemil) and Tony Gatlif's *Gadjo dilo* (The Crazy Stranger). In 1996 Fox Studios paid US$1.5 million for film rights to *Almost Adam*, a novel by Petru Popescu, who was born in Romania.

ENTERING & LEAVING

There are plenty of scheduled flights to Romania from a dozen or so western countries and, with a single plane change, from a great many more. Most flights arrive at Bucharest's Otopeni international airport. There are also flights to Timisoara and Constanta.

With an unbeatable train service linking Romania to Western Europe and Russia, there is little reason to travel to or from Romania by bus. Romania's public bus system is virtually nonexistent, and fares offered by the numerous private bus companies operating services to the west rarely compete with the inexpensive comfort of the trains. The exception to this rule is Istanbul, where the bus (12 to 14 hours) is substantially cheaper and faster than the train – and they've banned smoking on it, which is just as well since most Romanians and Turks are chain smokers. There are plenty of trains from Western Europe, Hungary, Yugoslavia, Bulgaria and Turkey, Moldova, Ukraine and beyond. Between May and September, a ferry plies the Black Sea between Constanta and Istanbul. There's no departure tax when leaving Romania, but you have to show your exit card – that's the wee piece of paper they placed in your passport when you entered the country and which you've probably lost by this stage.

SLOVAKIA

Slovakia, the former Czechoslovakia's less glamorous half, emerged dishevelled and sleepy after the 'Velvet Revolution' of 1989, before 'divorcing' the Czech Republic in 1993. Although it's now holding its own in the rebuilding Eastern bloc, there's a refreshing absence of Prague-style glitz and clamour. The capital, Bratislava, is small and cheerful with a surprisingly accomplished cultural life; the High Tatras are as rugged a range as any in Eastern Europe and in winter Slovakia is easily one of the best ski destinations in Europe in terms of value for money.

Slovakia is also rich in architecture, arts and folk culture. In East Slovakia, a string of unspoiled 13th century medieval towns founded by Saxon Germans shelter Gothic artworks, and there are about 180 quaint castles and ruins scattered around the country. The peasant traditions of rural Slovakia are still evident in the villages, and you'll find the Slovaks to be extremely warm, friendly people prepared to go out of their way to help you enjoy their country.

WHEN TO GO

May, June and September are the prime visiting months, with April and October chillier and sometimes cheaper alternatives. Most Slovaks take their holidays in July and August when hotels and tourist sights are more than usually crowded, and hostels are full of students, especially in the Tatra Mountains resort areas. Centres like Bratislava and the mountain resorts cater to visitors year-round. Elsewhere, from

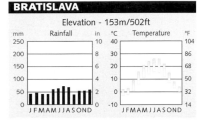

October or November until March or April, most castles, museums and other tourist attractions, and some associated accommodation and transport close down.

HIGHLIGHTS
Bratislava

Many travellers only make it as far as the Slovak capital, just 16km from the Hungarian border. Although cheap

At a Glance

Full Country Name: Slovak Republic
Area: 49,036 sq km
Population: 5.4 million
Capital City: Bratislava (pop 447,000)
People: 86% Slovak, 11% Hungarian, 1.5% Romany, 1% Czech
Language: Slovak, Czech, Hungarian
Religion: 60% Roman Catholic, 30% Protestant
Government: Parliamentary republic
Currency: Slovak crown (Sk)
Time Zone: One hour ahead of GMT/UTC; clocks are turned forward one hour at the end of March and back again at the end of September
International Telephone Code: 421
Electricity: 220V, 50Hz

accommodation is difficult to find, Bratislava is a pleasant, cosmopolitan city with many beautiful monuments, museums and art galleries. Highlights include Bratislava Castle, the Slovak National Museum and the Slovak National Gallery, and taking a ferry to see the Gothic ruins of Devín Castle.

Historic Towns & Museums

Historic towns with well preserved centres include Bardejov in East Slovakia, the fortified Renaissance town of Levoca, and Cicmany village in Central Slovakia, with its unique painted cottages – like a live-in museum of Slovakian artistry. Bardejov also has a curative spa and an excellent *skansen* (open-air museum) that is laid out like a full-scale village. Another excellent outdoor museum is at nearby Svidník. It's a complete village of Rusin culture with traditional architecture, old houses, a school, mill, fire station and more.

The town of Martin is fairly bland but its ethnography museum is worth visiting for its exhaustive collection of Slovak folk items.

Castles & Churches

The fairy-tale castle of Bojnice near Prievidza is Slovakia's best known. It's not the original 12th century Gothic structure but a 20th century reconstruction modelled on a French Romantic castle. The spectacular ruins of Spiš Castle, once the largest in Slovakia, are near Levoca and are best viewed from a distance. Other nearby castles are Lubovna (half in ruins) and the whitewashed Kezmarok Castle, containing an interesting museum.

The traditional wooden churches of East Slovakia are worth seeing. They represent a crossover of Slovak, Polish and Ukrainian cultures and most date from the 18th century. The most accessible are near Bardejov and include Jedlinka, Hervartov and Lukov-Venecia.

Hiking & Skiing

Jasná in the Low Tatras (Nízke Tatry) is Slovakia's best ski resort, and is at its peak from mid-December to April. In the summer months an extensive network of hiking trails makes this a great place for walking. The High Tatras (Vysoké Tatry) are a spectacular range of mountains and Slovakia's biggest

---

Itineraries

Two Days
Have a short visit in Bratislava, taking in the main museums, the castle and a ferry ride to Devín Castle.

One Week
Spend two days in Bratislava, then travel north-east to Bojnice Castle and across to the impressive fortified town of Levoca. From here you can spend the rest of the week visiting, hiking or skiing in the nearby High Tatra Mountains. Alternatively, you could visit the Slovenský raj National Park from Levoca.

Two Weeks
Spend two days in Bratislava and a day at Bojnice Castle. From there it's a short trip north to Cicmany, with its unique painted houses. Travel across to Levoca and the High Tatra Mountains and/or Slovenský raj National Park, then spend a couple of days in Bardejov, with its curative spa and excellent open-air museum. Also visit Svidník and Košice.

One Month
With a month, you can follow the two week itinerary but spend more time skiing or hiking in the mountains, including a trip to Jasná in the Low Tatras and to the Malá Fatra Mountains. Also make side trips to Spiš Castle, the Slovak karst and the wooden churches of East Slovakia.

SLOVAKIA HIGHLIGHTS & ITINERARIES

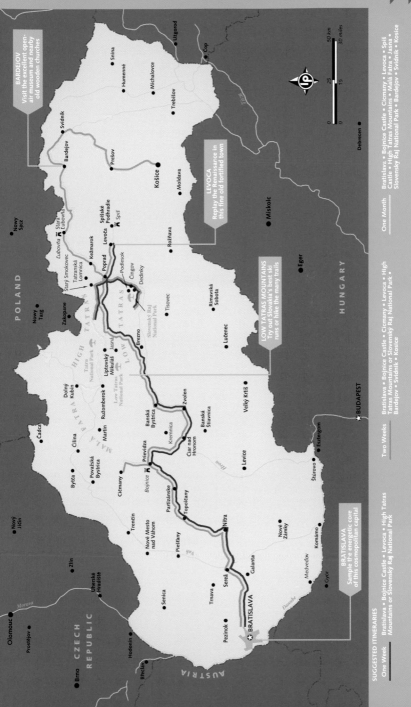

BARDEJOV
Visit the excellent open-air museum and nearby old wooden churches

LEVOCA
Replay the Renaissance in this fine old fortified town

LOW TATRAS MOUNTAINS
Try out Slovakia's best ski runs or hike the many trails

BRATISLAVA
Sample the energetic core of this cosmopolitan capital

SUGGESTED ITINERARIES

One Week — Bratislava • Bojnice Castle • Levoča • High Tatras Mountains or Slovenský Raj National Park

Two Weeks — Bratislava • Bojnice Castle • Čičmany • Levoča • High Tatras Mountains or Slovenský Raj National Park • Bardejov • Svidník • Košice

One Month — Bratislava • Bojnice Castle • Čičmany • Levoča • Spiš Castle • High Tatras Mountains • Malá Fatra • Jasná • Slovenský Raj National Park • Bardejov • Svidník • Košice

outdoor attraction. Again there are extensive hiking trails – although you'll probably have to climb higher than elsewhere to have solitude here – and there are loads of *chaty* (mountain huts) scattered through the area. Good bases are Poprad, the resort centre of Starý Smokovec and Tatranská Lomnica.

Another fine area for walking – with perhaps Slovakia's best mountain scenery – is the rugged ravines of Slovenský raj. Much of this region is covered in dense pine and deciduous forest sheltering rare wildflower species and a range of wildlife including lynx, bears and wolves. Good bases include Cingov, Podlesok and Dedinky.

VISA REQUIREMENTS

Nationals of all European Union (EU) countries, Canada and Switzerland can visit Slovakia visa-free for up to 90 days, and UK and Irish Republic citizens can stay for up to 180 days. US passport holders can stay for 30 days without a visa. Australian, New Zealand and South African travellers must obtain a visa, valid for up to 30 days.

Currently the only border point where Slovak visas can be issued on the spot (for 30 days at the officials' discretion, and only during business hours) is the automobile checkpoint at Petrzalka, near Bratislava in West Slovakia (Berg on the Austrian side). All visitors are expected to register at the district foreigners' police office within three working days, but this is not necessary if you're staying in hotels.

Slovakian Embassies

Australia
(☎ 02-6290 1516) 47 Culgoa Circuit, O'Malley, Canberra, ACT 2606

Canada
(☎ 613-749 4442) 50 Rideau Terrace, Ottawa, Ont K1M 2A1

Czech Republic
(☎ 02-32 05 07) Pod hradbami 1, 160 00 Prague 6

South Africa
(☎ 012-342 2051) 930 Arcadia St, Arcadia, 0083 Pretoria

UK & Ireland
(☎ 020-7243 0803) 25 Kensington Palace Gardens, London W8 4QY

USA
(☎ 202-965 5160) 2201 Wisconsin Ave NW, Suite 250, Washington, DC 20007

POST & COMMUNICATIONS

The postal service is fairly efficient and inexpensive. You can buy stamps in post offices, as well as from street vendors and newsagents. Most larger post offices have a window for poste restante, though the most reliable service is at the main post office in Bratislava.

Coin-operated phones can be used for domestic and international calls, but phonecards are more convenient for international calls. The cards are sold in post and telephone offices and some newsagents. The easiest way to make international calls is from main post offices or telephone centres.

Faxes, telex and telegraph messages can be sent and received at main post offices in the larger cities. Email is possible from Internet cafes in Bratislava and Banská Bystrica.

MONEY
Costs

Slovakia has been relatively slow to privatise, meaning it's likely to remain a bargain for travellers far longer than the neighbouring Czech Republic. Food, admissions and transport are all cheap, and accommodation is manageable except in Bratislava. By staying at cheap hostels and camp sites, sticking to self-catering, pub food and cafeterias, you can get away with US$15 a day in summer. In a private home or better hostel, with meals at cheap restaurants and using public transport, you can get by on US$20 to US$25. To share a clean double room with bath in a mid-range hotel or pension, and enjoy good local or western meals, plan on at least US$30 to US$40. Except for Easter and Christmas/New Year, many bottom and mid-range hotels drop their prices by a third or more outside the summer season.

A tip of 5 to 10% is appreciated in any tourist restaurant with table service.

Changing Money

Travellers cheques can be changed at major banks and post offices. Credit cards can be used in most major hotels, restaurants and shops and most of the larger branches of major banks can give cash advances. ATMs are becoming quite common but shouldn't be relied upon outside of major towns. Be aware that some exchange places might not accept damaged US dollars.

ONLINE SERVICES

Lonely Planet has a Web site, Destination Slovakia, at www.lonelyplanet .com/dest/eur/slk.htm. The EU Net site (www.eunet.sk) provides regional information, travel tips and links to related Web pages at its Slovak site. Central Europe Online is a popular site (www.ceo.cz) with lots of links to Czech and Slovak servers. Bratislava and other major Slovak cities are featured at Slovakia.Com's Web site (www.slovak.com). Slovakia Online (www.savba.sk/logos) provides online reservations at upmarket hotels.

BOOKS

Nineteenth century poet Ivan Krasko's *Verses* is regarded as a masterpiece of Slovak literature. Other outstanding poets of the Slovak National Revival were Janko Kráľ, Pavol O Hviezdoslav and Svetozár H Vajanský. Among post-WWI literary landmarks are Petr Jilcmnický's visionary *Chronicle* and the brilliant village tales of Bozena Slancikova. The Europe-based journalist Timothy Garton Ash's *We the People – The Revolutions of 1989* features gripping first-hand accounts of the revolutions.

ENTERING & LEAVING

There are a handful of flights in and out of Slovakia (US$6 departure tax) but Bratislava is only 64km from Vienna and 215km from Budapest. Several daily buses and trains link Vienna and Bratislava, and there are numerous trains to Budapest. There are no direct trains from West Slovakia (including Bratislava) to Poland; all connections are via the Czech Republic, so if you need a Czech visa, don't get aboard one of these trains without one. From East Slovakia, however, train services to Poland and Hungary bypass the Czech Republic. There are two trains daily to Moscow, both of which pass through Bratislava and Košice.

There are heaps of road borders to and from the Czech Republic, Hungary, Poland and Ukraine. Walking in and out of Slovakia can circumvent the hassle of buying an expensive international ticket. For example, you can easily walk across the bridge over the Danube River between Komárno (Slovakia) and Komárom (Hungary). From mid-April to September, there's a hydrofoil between Bratislava and Vienna, which is a good way to get to Austria.

SLOVENIA

In the eyes of many a Yugoslav despot, Slovenia is the golden goose that got away. Rich in resources, naturally good-looking and persistently peaceful, Slovenia has been doing just fine since breaking away from the Yugoslav Federation in 1991. Travellers in search of an antidote to much of Europe's crowds and high prices can, at least for now, consider it their little secret.

Little Slovenia straddles Eastern and Western Europe. Many of its cities and towns bear the imprint of the Habsburg Empire and the Venetian Republic, while up in the Julian Alps you'd almost think you were in Bavaria. Slovenia may be the gateway to the Balkans from Italy, Austria or Hungary, but it still has the feel of Central Europe.

Except for a brief period in June and July 1991 when Yugoslavia attempted to stop its smallest child from leaving its unravelling nest, there's been no fighting, no war and no terrorism in Slovenia. While Croatia and Bosnia-Hercegovina became embroiled in the bitterest conflict in Europe since WWII, Slovenes got on with making money and keeping out of the limelight.

Slovenia is one of Europe's most delightful surprises for travellers – the amazing variety of settings packed into one small area makes this country a 'Europe in miniature'. An bonus is that Slovenia is a nation of polyglots, and communicating with these friendly, helpful people is never difficult.

WHEN TO GO

September is an excellent month to visit because it's the best time for hiking and climbing, and the summer crowds have vanished. December to March is the high season for skiers, while spring is a good time to be in the lowlands and valleys, as everything's in blossom. Try to avoid July and August, when hotel rates rise and there are lots more tourists, especially on the coast.

At a Glance

Full Country Name: Republic of Slovenia (Republika Slovenija)
Area: 20,251 sq km
Population: 2,051,000
Capital City: Ljubljana (pop 330,000)
People: 91% Slovenian, 7% Serbo-Croatian
Language: Slovenian, Croatian, Serbian, German, English, Italian
Religion: 80% Roman Catholic, 2.4% Eastern Orthodox Christian, 1% Muslim, 1% Protestant
Government: Democratic republic
Currency: Slovenian tolar (SIT)
Time Zone: One hour ahead of GMT/UTC
International Telephone Code: 386
Electricity: 220V, 50Hz

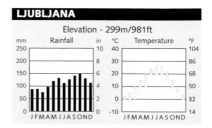

HIGHLIGHTS
Ljubljana

Ljubljana is a relaxed but vibrant capital – only a little over 300,000 people live here, but everything of national importance in Slovenia takes place here. In summer, cafes spill out onto the streets of the Old Town and there's a wide range of cultural entertainment on offer. Don't miss Ljubljana Castle, the National Museum and National Gallery, or an aimless wander around the Old Town and beside the Ljubljanica River.

Historic Towns

Other than Lubljana, the most attractive towns are Ptuj, Škofja Loka, Radovljica, Piran and Kranj. Piran is the classic coastal town and a gem of Gothic Venetian architecture. It gets mobbed in summer but is still a great place to visit. There's a maritime museum and cruises on the harbour. Ptuj is one of Slovenia's oldest and most historically important towns, with a well preserved medieval core and plenty of museums and monasteries. Škofja Loka, with a castle and preserved Old Town, is one of Slovenia's most beautiful towns. Radovljica, an easy day trip from Bled, is another town full of historical buildings.

Castles & Churches

Slovenia was once known as the 'country of castles' and counted more than 1000, but wars and development have taken care of most of them. Of the remaining ones, the most dramatic are the hilltop Bled Castle, Predjama Castle near Postojna, Ljubljana Castle, the 16th century Renaissance Sneznik Castle in Notranjska, Bogenšperk Castle in Dolenjska, Podsreda Castle in the Kozjansko region of Štajerska, Celje Castle and Ptuj Castle.

There are some beautiful churches in Slovenia, too. The Church of St John the Baptist alone is worth the trip to Lake Bohinj. This small medieval church boasts exquisite frescoes. The Church of the Holy Trinity at Hrastovlje (in Primorska) is another evocative, fresco-covered masterpiece. Others worth looking out for are the Church of the Virgin Mary at Ptujska Gora near Ptuj, the Chapter Church of St Nicholas in Novo Mesto, the Church of the Assumption at Nova Štifta near Ribnica and the Church of the Annunciation at Crngrob near Škofja Loka.

Museums

Some of the finest museums in Slovenia include the Dolenjska Museum in Novo Mesto, the Posavje Museum in Brezice, the Blacksmith Museum in Kropa, the Municipal Museum in Idrija, the Saltworks Museum in Secovlje near Piran, the Beekeeping Museum in Radovljica, the Kobarid Museum and, in Ljubljana, the Museum of Modern History and the Slovenian Ethnographic Museum.

Natural Wonders

Triglav National Park is Slovenia's only official national park, and includes most of the Julian Alps lying in Slovenia. Although there are mountains to climb here, there are also easy hikes through forests, meadows and valleys. The Vršic Pass through the Alps is one of the spectacular sights here – follow the paved road from Kranjska Gora to Bovec. This is the beginning of the beautiful Soca Valley, carved by the Soca River. The Škocjan

Caves, at the southern end of the Karst region, are among the foremost underground wonders of the world, while the Vintgar Gorge near Bled and the Upper Savinja Valley in Štajerska are spectacular areas.

VISA REQUIREMENTS

Citizens of Australia, Canada, the European Union (EU), Israel, Japan, New Zealand, Switzerland and the USA do not require visas for stays of up to 90 days. Citizens of other countries can get 90-day visas in advance at any Slovenian embassy or consulate, or 30-day visas on arrival.

Slovenian Embassies

Australia
(☎ 02-6243 4830) Advance Bank Centre, Level 6, 60 Marcus Clark St, Canberra, ACT 2601

Canada
(☎ 613-565 5781) 150 Metcalfe St, Suite 2101, Ottawa, Ont K2P 1P1

UK
(☎ 020-7495 7775) Cavendish Court, Suite One, 11-15 Wigmore St, London W1H 9LA

USA
(☎ 202-667 5363) 1525 New Hampshire Ave NW, Washington, DC 20036

TOURIST OFFICES OVERSEAS

Tourist offices and travel agents specialising in Slovenia include:

Australia
(☎ 07-3831 4400) 323 Boundary St, Spring Hill, 4000 Qld

Canada
(☎ 514-938 4041) 4060 Ste-Catherine St West, Suite 535, Montreal, Que H3Z 2Z3

South Africa
(☎ 011-884 8555) Norwich Towers, 3rd floor, 13 Fredman Drive, Santon

UK
(☎ 020-7287 7133, fax 7287 5476) 49 Conduit St, London W1R 9FB

USA
(☎ 212-358 9686/9025) 345 East 12th St, New York, NY 10003

POST & COMMUNICATIONS

Poste restante mail sent to the main post office in a city or town (such as Ljubljana) is held for 30 days.

The easiest place to make long-distance calls as well as send faxes and

---

Itineraries

Two Days
Spend your time exploring Ljubljana, Slovenia's capital and nerve centre.

One Week
Spend two days in Ljubljana, travel north to Bled and its famous castle, then across to Lake Bohinj, with a visit to the frescoed Church of St John the Baptist. From there you can zip down to spectacular Predjama Castle and the Škocjan Caves, and finish your trip with a day or two in historic Piran on the Adriatic coast.

Two Weeks
With two weeks you'll have time to explore more thoroughly. Spend two days in Ljubljana, then travel up to Bled, with a stop at either Radovljica or Kranj. Visit Lake Bohinj, then (returning via Bled) go to Kranjska Gora and take the mountain road through the Julian Alps (via the Vršic Pass) to Bovec. If hiking is an interest, spend a few days in this area or continue south to Predjama Castle and the Škocjan Caves, then on to Piran. Somewhere into this itinerary you should try to visit the wonderful historic town of Ptuj in the far east of the country.

One Month
Take in the above itinerary, allowing extra time in Ljubljana, Triglav National Park, Soca Valley and Piran. Also visit the Pleterje Monastery, and find some of your own special places.

SLOVENIA HIGHLIGHTS & ITINERARIES

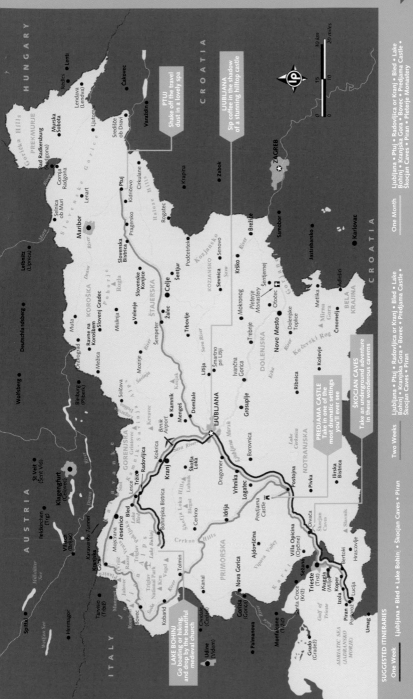

PTUJ
Shake off the travel
dust in a lovely spa

LJUBLJANA
Sip coffee in the shadow
of a stunning hilltop castle

ŠKOCJAN CAVES
Take an underground adventure
in these wonderous caverns

PREDJAMA CASTLE
Take in one of the
most dramatic settings
you'll ever see

LAKE BOHINJ
Go boating, hiking,
and drop by the beautiful
medieval church

SUGGESTED ITINERARIES

One Week Ljubljana • Bled • Lake Bohinj • Škocjan Caves • Piran

Two Weeks Ljubljana • Ptuj • Radovljica or Kranj • Bled • Lake
Bohinj • Kranjska Gora • Bovec • Predjama Castle •
Škocjan Caves • Piran

One Month Ljubljana • Ptuj • Radovljica or Kranj • Bled • Lake
Bohinj • Kranjska Gora • Bovec • Predjama Castle •
Škocjan Caves • Piran • Pleterje Monastery

telegrams is from a post office or telephone centre. Public telephones on the street do not accept coins; they require a phonecard *(telefonska kartica)* or the near-obsolete phone tokens *(zetoni)*. Both are available at all post offices and some newsstands.

Ljubljana has a couple of Internet cafes where you can send and receive email.

MONEY
Costs
Slovenia is still much cheaper than neighbouring Italy or Austria, though prices are increasing. If you stay at hostels and eat in self-serve restaurants, you could easily get by on US$30 a day. Staying in private rooms or guesthouses and eating at medium-priced restaurants will push the daily costs up to US$50 to US$70 a day.

Expect to pay from around US$13 to US$15 for a hostel bed, US$10 to US$30 for a budget hotel and US$5 to US$10 for a cheap meal.

A 'circulation tax' (not unlike value-added tax) is added to the purchase price of most goods and services. Many hotels in Slovenia levy a 'tourist tax' on overnight visitors of about US$2. Tipping is not necessary, since most restaurants add a 10% service charge to the bill.

Changing Money
Nearly all prices are in tolar, but some hotels, guesthouses and camping grounds still quote rates in Deutschmarks, to which the tolar is linked. It's easy to change cash and travellers cheques at banks, post offices, travel agencies and any *menjalnica*, the ubiquitous private exchange offices. There's no black market, but exchange rates can vary. Banks take a commission of 1%, while tourist offices, travel agencies, exchange bureaus and hotels take up to 5%.

Credit cards are accepted at upmarket restaurants, shops and hotels, but elsewhere you must use cash. Only a few of Slovenia's ATMs are accessible to foreign account holders. Credit card holders can get cash advances in tolars from some banks.

ONLINE SERVICES
Lonely Planet's Destination Slovenia site (www.lonelyplanet.com/dest/eur/slo.htm) offers a detailed country profile. The best single source of information on the Internet is the CPTS's SloWWWenia site (www.ijs.si/slo). It has an interactive map where you can click onto more than two dozen cities, towns and ski resorts, as well as information on culture, history, food and wine, getting to and from Slovenia and what's on. Another good site is at http://slovenia.cjb.net. It's heavy on text and pictures, but it's a good introduction to Slovenia.

BOOKS
Independent Slovenia – Origins, Movements, Prospects is a good compilation of essays by Slovenian activists and analysts explaining the hows and whys of Slovenia's independence movement. A superb book with excellent photos and text on Slovenian culture, history and folklore is *Cankarjeva Zalozba* (Mountains of Slovenia) by Matjaz Kmecl.

Slovene for Travellers by Miran Hladnik not only has conversational phrases by topic but also includes excellent cultural information and travel tips. *Deseti Brat* (The Tenth Brother), published in 1866 by Josip Jurcic, was the first full-length novel in Slovenian. It's the tragic and realistic story of an illegitimate son's desire for revenge.

FILMS

Since the 1970s, the most popular films in Slovenia have been those dealing with crime, suspense and comedies, for example Franci Slak's *Hudodelci* ('The Felons; 1987), Jure Pervanje's *Do Konca in Naprej* (To the Limit and Beyond; 1990) and Vinci Vogue Anzlovar's *Babica Gre na Jug* (Grandma Goes South; 1991). More recent successes have been *Ekspres, Ekspres* by Igor Šterk, *Herzog* by Mitja Milavec and Andrej Košak's *Outsider* (1997).

ENTERING & LEAVING

Slovenia's national airline, Adria Airways, has nonstop flights between Ljubljana's Brnik airport, north of Ljubljana, and practically every major city in Europe. There's a departure tax of US$16 for passengers leaving by air, which is usually included in the ticket price.

Buses travel between Slovenia and Italy daily, using Nova Gorica in Slovenia as the easiest exit and entry point. Koper also has good bus connections with Italy. It's also easy to travel by bus to and from neighbouring Hungary. The main train routes into Slovenia come from Salzburg (four to five hours away), Trieste (three hours), Vienna (six hours) and Zagreb (two to three hours). Trains between Amsterdam and Ljubljana take 18 hours. There are dozens of international border crossings if travelling by car, motorcycle, bicycle or even on foot. On weekends between April and mid-October, it's possible to sail between Venice and Portoroz (one of Slovenia's Adriatic coast towns) by catamaran.

SPAN

When you cross the Pyrenees Mountains from France you enter a different Europe. Spain is a treasure-trove of arts and culture, brimming with fabulous flamenco, music, history, painting, literature, food and drink, sport, bullfighting and passionate fiestas. Add to this its complete spectrum of scenery and a unique, well preserved architectural and artistic heritage, and Spain offers a patchwork of fun and fascination that few countries can match.

The exuberance of the Spaniards and the glorious predictability of the summer weather have been attracting refugees from northern Europe's damp and clammy lands for decades, but Spain is much more than a coastal strip of nouveau riche holiday homes and warm English beer. It is drenched in the historical pageantry of empire and conquistadors, the artistic legacy of Goya, Velázquez, Picasso and Dalí, and the romance of Don Quixote, Hemingway and the International Brigades.

More than 60 million foreigners a year visit Spain, yet you can also travel for days and hear no other tongue but Spanish. The more you travel in Spain, the bigger it seems to get. It's surprising just how many Spains there are. Cool, damp, green Galicia is a world away from hot, dry Andalucía, home of flamenco and bullfighting. Fertile Catalunya in the north-east, with its separate language and independent spirit, seems a different nation from the Castilian heartland on the austere *meseta* (tableland) at the centre of the Iberian Peninsula.

WHEN TO GO

The ideal months to visit are May, June and September (plus April and October in the south). At these times you can rely on good weather, yet avoid the sometimes extreme heat – and the main crush of Spanish and foreign tourists. That said, there's decent weather in some part of Spain virtually year-round. Winter along the southern and south-eastern Mediterranean coasts is mild, while in the height of summer you can retreat to the north-west, or to beaches or high mountains anywhere, if you need to get away from excessive heat. If you want to make sure you hit some parties, the best festivals are concentrated between Semana Santa (Easter week) and October.

At a Glance

Full Country Name: Spain
Area: 504,788 sq km
Population: 39.2 million
Capital City: Madrid (pop 2,984,576)
People: Spanish (though Catalans and Basques display a fierce independent spirit)
Language: Castilian Spanish; also Catalan, Galician, Basque
Religion: 99% Roman Catholic
Government: Constitutional monarchy
Currency: Spanish peseta (pta)
Time Zone: One hour ahead of GMT/UTC; clocks go forward one hour on the last Sunday in March and back again on the last Sunday in September
International Telephone Code: 34
Electricity: 220V, 50Hz

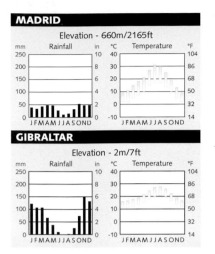

HIGHLIGHTS
Fiestas

Spaniards love to party and no trip to Spain would be complete without factoring a *fiesta* (festival) or *feria* (fair) into the itinerary. Many of these fiestas are based on religious events, but that doesn't mean they are celebrated with any less fervour, drinking and dancing.

The most famous event is Sanfermines (the Running of the Bulls) in Pamplona, a 10 day party in early July that kicks off every morning with a mad scramble of bulls chasing runners through the streets to the bullring. This one attracts a lot of travellers (not to mention Spaniards) and accommodation is very hard to come by. Carnaval is held all over the country in February/March with several days of parades and fancy dress. Seville (Sevilla) is the best place for wild partying during Semana Santa, and it's followed by more celebrating during the Feria de Abril in late April.

Fiestas de San Isidro, in the third week of May, is Madrid's major fiesta, while Festes de la Mercé is a big one in Barcelona in late September. Las Fallas is celebrated in Valencia city in mid-March with fireworks, bonfires and mass partying – this is one of Spain's top fiestas. Unusual festivals include La Tomatina, a wild tomato-throwing festival in Buñol, Valencia, in August; and Feria de Caballo (Horse Fair) in Jerez de la Frontera, Andalucía, in May.

There are many more, so check with tourist offices before planning your trip.

Cities & Towns

Madrid and Barcelona are Spain's most vibrant cities, with the most to see and do. They're a strong contrast, but both are essential experiences if you want a feel for the country.

With its exciting southern atmosphere, Seville isn't far behind the 'big two' for excitement, and introduces you to the distinctive region of Andalucía. Other cities and towns with a particularly strong attraction include Santiago de Compostela and Pontevedra in Galicia; San Sebastián in the País Vasco; Segovia, Ávila, Salamanca, León, Toledo and Cuenca in the old Castilian heartland; Trujillo in Extremadura; Valencia on the Mediterranean coast; and Granada and Ronda in Andalucía.

Museums & Galleries

Spain is home to some of the finest art galleries in the world. The Prado in Madrid has few rivals, and there are outstanding art museums in Bilbao, Seville, Barcelona (including Museu Picasso), Valencia and Córdoba. Fascinating smaller galleries, such as the Dalí museum in Figueres and the abstract art museum in Cuenca, also abound. Tarragona and Teruel have excellent archaeological museums.

SPAIN HIGHLIGHTS & ITINERARIES

SANTIAGO DE COMPOSTELA
Make a pilgrimage to this beautiful medieval town

MADRID
Hit the big fiesta in May, or pack into the renowned Prado any time

SEVILLE
Get a haircut, learn the flamenco, take in a bullfight

BAY OF BISCAY

Cabo Ortegal
Viveiro
Ribadeo
Avilés
Gijón
O Ferrol
La Coruña
Luarca
Ribadesella
Santander
Oviedo
ASTURIAS
Torre Cerredo
(2648m)
Parque Nacional
de los Picos
de Europa
CANTABRIA
Bilt
Cordillera
Cantábrica
Reinosa
Mira
de E
Santiago de
Compostela
Lugo
GALICIA
Ebro
Pontevedra
Ponferrada
Astorga
León
Montes de León
Burgos
Vigo
Tuy
Orense
Puebla de
Sanabria
Benavente
Palencia
Aranda
de Duero
CASTILLA Y LEÓN
Valladolid
Bragança
Chaves
Zamora
Duero
Braga
Guimarães
Tordesillas
Medina
del Campo
Sierra de
Guadarrama
Porto
Salamanca
Segovia
Ciudad
Rodrigo
Ávila
Guarda
Béjar
Cordillera
Central
MADRID
Coimbra
Sierra de Gredos
Almanzor
(2592m)
MADR
Plasencia
Navalmoral
de la Mata
Talavera
de la Reina
Aranjuez
PORTUGAL
Toledo
Cáceres
Trujillo
Sierra de
Guadalupe
Montes de Toledo
Alcázar de
San Juan
Portalegre
Valencia
de Alcántara
CAST
Santarém
Parque Nacional
de las Tablas
de Daimiel
Tajo
Mérida
Guadiana
Ciudad
Real
Manza
LISBON
Badajoz
EXTREMADURA
Valdep
Setúbal
Évora
Puertollano
Zafra
Morena
Beja
Sierra
Bailen
Linares
Córdoba
Úbe
Guadalquivir
Jaén
ANDALUCÍA
Écija
Lagos
Huelva
Seville
Cordil
Faro
Parque
Nacional de
Doñana
Osuna
Granad
Guadiana
Mulhacén
(3478m) S
Antequera
Málaga
Jerez de la
Frontera
Ronda
ATLANTIC
OCEAN
Golfo
de Cádiz
Cádiz
Marbella
Motril
Costa del Sol
To Melilla
Algeciras
Gibraltar (Brit)
Cabo de
Trafalgar
Tarifa
Ceuta (Sp)
Strait of Gibraltar
Isla d
Alboɾ
To Canary Islands
Costa de la Luz

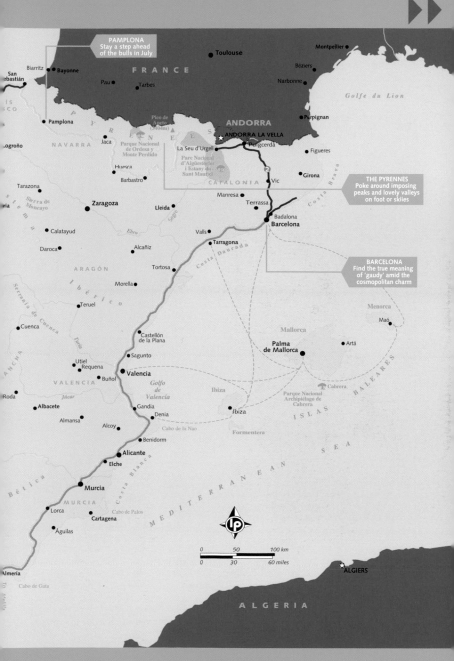

►►

PAMPLONA
Stay a step ahead
of the bulls in July

Montpellier

Toulouse

FRANCE

Biarritz
Bayonne

San
Sebastián

Pau
Tarbes

Béziers

Narbonne

Golfe du Lion

Pamplona

NAVARRA

Jaca

Pico de
Aneto
(3404m)

ANDORRA

ANDORRA LA VELLA

Puigcerdà

Figueres

Logroño

Parque Nacional
de Ordesa y
Monte Perdido

La Seu d'Urgell

Parc Nacional
d'Aigüestortes
i Estany de
Sant Maurici

Girona

Tarazona

Huesca

Barbastro

CATALONIA

Vic

THE PYRENNES
Poke around imposing
peaks and lovely valleys
on foot or skiies

Sierra de
Moncayo

Zaragoza

Lleida

Manresa

Terrassa

Badalona
Barcelona

Calatayud

Ebro

Valls

Daroca

Alcañiz

ARAGÓN

Tortosa

Tarragona

BARCELONA
Find the true meaning
of 'gaudy' amid the
cosmopolitan charm

Ibérico

Morella

Menorca

Teruel

Maó

Cuenca

Mallorca

Serranía de Cuenca

Castellón
de la Plana

**Palma
de Mallorca**

Artà

Sagunto

Utiel
Requena

Valencia

Buñol

VALENCIA

Golfo
de
Valencia

Ibiza

Parque Nacional
Archipiélago de
Cabrera

Cabrera

ISLAS BALEARES

Roda

Júcar

Albacete

Gandia

Denia

Ibiza

Almansa

Alcoy

Cabo de la Nao

Formentera

Benidorm

Alicante

Elche

Murcia

Costa Blanca

MURCIA

Lorca

Cabo de Palos

Cartagena

MEDITERRANEAN SEA

Águilas

Almería

Cabo de Gata

0   50   100 km
0   30   60 miles

★ ALGIERS

ALGERIA

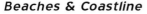

Beaches & Coastline

The Costa Brava in Catalunya is rugged enough not to have been completely overwhelmed by tourist development, and still secretes many pretty coves, villages and beaches. The Baleares

Itineraries

Where you should go depends on what you like doing – every part of Spain has its own compelling reasons to be visited. The basic choice is between a wide-ranging tour that takes you to as many varied parts of the country as you can manage or a narrower focus on a smaller number of places to explore in greater depth. If you want to see a good slice of Spain in short time, consider the following:

Two Days

Head straight to Madrid, Barcelona or Seville depending on how and where you're entering the country. In Madrid, a must-see is the Prado, one of Europe's finest art galleries, although don't overlook Reina Sofía and Thyssen-Bornemisza. But the essence of Madrid, a sprawling and relatively modern city, is in the pulsating streets, bars and nightlife.

Barcelona evokes more history than Madrid and is probably Spain's most stylish city, (and playground of the notorious Gaudi). Highlights include the Picasso Museum, the soaring La Sagrada Familia, rambling along the 1.25km La Rambla boulevard, exploring the Barri Gotic medieval quarter and partaking in the nightlife (again).

Seville, in the deep south, is one of Spain's most exciting cities. Take in the city's enormous Gothic cathedral and La Giralda, and drink the night away with the city's student crowd at Plaza del Salvador. There are also some fine flamenco bars in Seville.

One Week

Spend two days each in Barcelona, Madrid and Seville, allowing one day for travel. Alternatively, if you want to mix cities with beaches or mountains, combine Barcelona with the Costa Brava (Calella de Palafrugell or Cadaqués) or the Pyrenees (the Parc Nacional d'Aigüestortes i Estany de Sant Maurici is the prime hiking and skiing area in Catalunya).

From Madrid you could head up to San Sebastián for a beach or to the Sierra de Gredos for walking. The best beaches near Seville are probably Los Caños de Meca and Bolonia.

Two Weeks

With two weeks you can begin to explore. Start with a few days in Barcelona, then head down the Costa Daurada to Valencia, a vibrant city that is far from overrun with foreign tourists (try to catch the Las Fallas festival in March). Continue down the coastal route past the Costa Blanca (where there are several popular summer resorts) to Granada, backed by the mountains of the Sierra Nevada and boasting the Alhambra fortress. From here you could carry on to the overcrowded 'Britain in Spain' resorts of the Costa de Sol, but it's better to head across to Seville – a highlight of any visit to Spain. You should still have time then to finish the trip in Madrid, perhaps stopping in Cordoba on the way. If you allow a mix of beachside relaxation and city exploration, this trip will easily absorb two weeks.

One Month

Follow the two week itinerary to begin with, perhaps adding a detour to Gibraltar from the Costa del Sol. From Madrid you can begin to explore some of the less-visited northern parts of Spain. Head through Segovia and north-west to Santiago de Compostela – the beautiful medieval city that is the culmination of Spain's most famous pilgrimage (Camino de Santiago). From here it's a pleasant trip along the northern Atlantic coast, passing near Picos de Europa national park (good for walking) and on to the lovely San Sebastian. If it's near the start of July, Pamplona and its famous San Fermines (Running of the Bulls) festival is not far away. Otherwise, continue west to the Pyrenees for some of the best hiking in Spain.

islands have many fine, isolated little beaches, especially on Menorca, while Mallorca's cliff-strewn northern coast is one of the most spectacular in the country. Cabo de Gata in eastern Andalucía is lined with excellent, isolated and (by Spanish standards) underpopulated beaches, backed by some fine, rugged coastal scenery. The Costa de la Luz on Andalucía's Atlantic coast has more good beaches and is relatively underdeveloped; Tarifa at its southern end is one of Europe's top windsurfing centres.

In Galicia, the Rías Bajas and Rías Altas are two series of majestic estuaries not unlike the Norwegian fjords, dotted with good beaches, fishing villages and low-key resorts. Spain's most awesome coastal scenery is here, too. On the Bay of Biscay you'll find the country's best surf beaches and, at San Sebastián, probably its most beautiful city beach.

Mountains & Scenery

The Pyrenees, especially in Catalunya and Aragón, are strung with imposing peaks and lovely valleys. Two of the best areas to head for are the national parks: Aigüestortes i Estany de Sant Maurici in Catalunya and Ordesa y Monte Perdido in Aragón.

In the north-west, the Picos de Europa range, which straddles Cantabria, Asturias and Castilla y León, is justly famous for its wild and beautiful mountain scenery. Galicia is Spain's greenest area – rolling countryside abutting a dramatic coast. In the central west, the Sierra de Gredos and its western offshoots, such as the Sierra de Peña de Francia, contain further impressive ranges and charming, remote valleys, such as those of La

Vera and the Jerte and Ambroz rivers in northern Extremadura. There's yet more impressive mountainous terrain in the Serranía de Cuenca area on the borders of Castilla-La Mancha and Aragón, and in Mallorca's Serra de Tramuntana.

In Andalucía, the mountains around Ronda, the Alpujarras valleys south of the Sierra Nevada and the sierras of Cazorla and Segura east of Baeza stand out for their beauty, while the semidesert scenery east of Almería is weird enough to have been used as the setting for dozens of western movies.

VISA REQUIREMENTS

US, Canadian, Australian, New Zealand and Israeli citizens are among those who may enter Spain as tourists without a visa and stay up to 90 days. European Union (EU) passport holders can come and go as they please. South Africans require a Schengen visa.

Spanish Embassies & Consulates

Australia
(☎ 02-6273 3555) 15 Arkana St, Yarralumla, Canberra, ACT 2600

Canada
(☎ 613-747 2252) 74 Stanley Ave, Ottawa, Ont K1M 1P4

Ireland
(☎ 01-269 1640) 17A Merlyn Park, Balls Bridge, Dublin 4

UK
(☎ 020-7235 5555) 39 Chesham Place, London SW1X 8SB
Consulate: (☎ 0131-226 4568 or ☎ 220 1843) 63 North Castle St, Edinburgh EH2 3LJ

USA
(☎ 202-728 2330) 2375 Pennsylvania Ave NW, Washington, DC 20037

TOURIST OFFICES OVERSEAS

Canada
(☎ 416-961 3131) 2 Bloor St West, 34th floor, Toronto, Ont M4W 3E2

UK
(☎ 020-7486 8077, brochure request ☎ 0891-669920 at 50p a minute) 22-23 Manchester Square, London W1M 5AP

USA
(☎ 212-265 8822) 666 Fifth Ave, 35th floor, New York, NY 10103
(☎ 213-658 7188) 8383 Wilshire Blvd, Suite 960, Beverly Hills, LA, CA 90211
(☎ 312-642 1992) 845 North Michigan Ave, Chicago, IL 60611
(☎ 305-358 1992) 1221 Brickell Ave, Suite 1850, Miami, FL 33131

POST & COMMUNICATIONS

Spanish cities and villages usually have several post offices. Stamps are sold at most *estancos* (tobacconist shops), as well as at all post offices. Mail to other Western European countries normally takes a week; to North America 10 days; and to Australia or New Zealand two weeks. Poste restante mail can be addressed to you at poste restante (or better, *lista de correos*) at any place in Spain that has a post office.

Many pay phones can be used for international and domestic calls. They accept coins and phonecards *(tarjetas telefónicas)*, which are sold at post offices and estancos. Calls from pay phones cost 30 to 35% more than private phones.

Most post offices have a fax service, but you'll often find cheaper rates at shops or offices with 'Fax Público' signs. Spain has plenty of Internet cafes and other public Internet and email services, particularly in cities and tourist areas.

MONEY
Costs

Spain is one of Western Europe's more affordable countries. If you are frugal, it's just about possible to scrape by on US$20 to US$25 a day. This would involve staying in the cheapest possible accommodation, avoiding eating in restaurants or going to museums or bars, and not moving around too much. A more comfortable budget – allowing you to indulge in the Spanish passion for life – would be US$40 a day.

In restaurants the law requires menu prices to include a service charge, and tipping is a matter of personal choice – most people leave some small change if they're satisfied and 5% is usually plenty. Markets and cheap hotels are the only places in Spain where you are likely to bargain.

Changing Money

Travellers cheques can be cashed at banks and exchange offices, and usually attract a slightly higher exchange rate than cash. Credit cards are widely accepted at hotels and restaurants, especially from the middle range up, and also for long-distance train tickets. These days, even small towns have an ATM *(cajero automático)* where you can withdraw from credit and debit accounts. Be careful carrying your money, whether it's cash or plastic, as tourists are a major target of theft.

ONLINE SERVICES

Lonely Planet's Destination Spain page (www.lonelyplanet.com/dest/eur/spa.htm) has loads of information. Discover Spain (www.spaintour.com) is the national tourist office site. It provides all sorts of links to specific sites. Another good site is www.okspain.org, which is handy for tracking tour organisations. The official Spanish Board of Tourism site is at www.tourspain.es/inicioi.htm.

BOOKS

The New Spaniards by John Hooper and *Homage to Barcelona* by Colm Tóibín are readable and fascinating accounts of Spanish society and culture. For a good survey of Spanish history, *The Story of Spain* by Mark Williams is hard to beat. The 17th century novel *Don Quijote de la Mancha* by Miguel de Cervantes is immensely popular, as are Federico García Lorca's plays *Blood Wedding* and *Yerma*.

There's plenty of foreign literature set in Spain – the classic works include Laurie Lee's *As I Walked Out One Midsummer Morning*, Gerald Brenan's *South from Granada*, George Orwell's *Homage to Catalonia*, Ernest Hemingway's romantic civil war novel *For Whom the Bell Tolls*, as well as *The Sun Also Rises* and *Death in the Afternoon*.

FILMS

Two Hemingway novels made into films are *For Whom the Bell Tolls* (1943), starring Gary Cooper and Ingrid Bergman, which was nominated for a best picture Oscar, and *The Sun Also Rises* (1957), starring Tyrone Power, Errol Flynn and Ava Gardner.

ENTERING & LEAVING

Spain has many international airports, including Madrid, Barcelona, Bilbao, Santiago de Compostela, Seville, Granada, Málaga, Almería, Alicante, Valencia, Palma de Mallorca, Ibiza and Maó.

Bus and train travel are other good options, and there are regular bus services to Spain from all major centres in Europe, including Lisbon, London and Paris. Travelling to Spain by train can be more expensive than by bus unless you are under age 26 or have a rail pass. Ferry services connect Spain directly with the UK and Morocco. A departure tax applies when flying out of Spain, but this is included in the price of the ticket at purchase.

Gibraltar

Gibraltar is a curious anomaly – a tiny British colony sticking out of southern Spain. Dominated by the huge 426m-high limestone rock and dozens of English pubs selling plates of fish and chips, Gibraltar (pop 30,000) is a fascinating contrast to the Spanish life just outside its borders.

Considered by ancient Greeks and Romans to be one of the two Pillars of Hercules, Gibraltar was ceded to Britain in 1713 after an Anglo-Dutch fleet had captured it during the War of the Spanish Succession nine years earlier. Since then any moves by Spain to win back sovereignty of the rock have been resisted by Britain and the resident Gibraltarians. It's now a self-governing territory.

For travellers, Gibraltar is easy to enter from Spain. EU citizens, Australians, New Zealanders, Americans, Canadians and South Africans need only a valid passport to cross the border at La Linea. If you need a visa for Spain, make sure it's a multiple entry one so you can return across the border.

Everything about Gibraltar – except the climate – is British. Apart from the pubs and tearooms, the currency is the pound (sterling or the Gibraltar pound, which are interchangeable) and the town is full of high-street stores like Safeway and Marks & Spencer. But the highlight of Gibraltar is the rock itself and the nature reserve that covers its upper reaches. Here, apart from spectacular views across to Morocco, you can see migrating birds such as raptors and storks, and a colony of Barbary macaques, the only wild primates in Europe. A cable car will take you to the top.

Costs in Gibraltar are closer to British than Spanish but you shouldn't need to spend any more than US$30 a day. The territory has its own airport, but the cheapest way to get there is to take a bus to La Linea and walk the 1.5km across the border and into town.

SWEDEN

Sweden has the lot: Danish castles in the south, thousands of lakes and saunas and even a few minor fjords. The north has the Sami people and reindeer, and the midnight sun shines all night long. The only thing missing is the tourists. The nation that gave the world ABBA, the zip, Greta Garbo, Absolut Vodka and IKEA chairs tends to keep a low profile. The last time Swedes fought a war was in 1809, when they lost Finland to Russia. Swedes tend to think of themselves as observers rather than the ones to be observed: they visit other countries, they've accepted a larger percentage of immigrants than almost any other European country, and they enjoy ethnic cuisines with the best French wines.

For the visitor, Sweden has Iron Age graveyards, prehistoric fortresses, open-air rune stones, medieval churches, thousands of protected nature reserves and more than 10,000km of trekking and bicycle paths. The coastal archipelago *(skärgård)* around Stockholm is served by one of the largest fleets of century-old steamers.

There are many free things in Sweden, but when you pay, you pay dearly. Yet the quality is invariably high. Beware: after you've seen one attraction, you may want to see them all!

WHEN TO GO

If you want sunshine, visit between late May and late July, bearing in mind that August can be wet. Many youth hostels, camping grounds and attractions open only in summer, from late June to mid-August. Summer in Sweden can be hot, sunny and beautiful, but travel in winter requires planning and will restrict you to certain areas. Big cities are in full swing year-round.

At a Glance

Full Country Name: The Kingdom of Sweden
Area: 450,000 sq km
Population: 8.9 million
Capital City: Stockholm (pop one million)
People: 90% Swedes, 3% Finns, 0.15% Sami (inhabitants of Lappland); remainder are mainly south-eastern European migrants
Language: Swedish, but English is widely spoken
Religion: Lutheran
Government: Constitutional monarchy
Currency: Swedish krona
Time Zone: One hour ahead of GMT/UTC; clocks go forward one hour at the end of March and back again at the end of September
International Telephone Code: 46
Electricity: 220V 50Hz

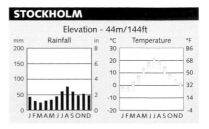

STOCKHOLM
Elevation - 44m/144ft

HIGHLIGHTS
National Parks

There are about 20 national parks in all kinds of landscapes, but the best places to admire the mountains are the giant Sarek and the tiny Abisko in Lappland. Different again is the forest at Tiveden, at the north end of Lake Vättern. Hiking and cross-country skiing opportunities abound in these parks.

Islands

The Baltic islands of Gotland and Öland have a different character to the mainland, and this is reflected in the rare *raukar* (limestone) rock forms and the flora. The islands are also summer centres and cabin holidays are popular. Some 24,000 islands litter the waters off Stockholm and many more are strung along the coastline, providing endless opportunities for exploration.

Historic Towns

When Gothenburg (Göteborg) was founded in the early 1500s, there were already 80 towns established in Sweden. Birka, a Viking town on an island near Stockholm, and the rebuilt Eketorp fortified village on Öland are both special. Lund is the oldest remaining town in Sweden, and Visby is the only walled medieval town left. Other fine examples are Sigtuna, Kalmar, Ystad, Stockholm, Linköping and Eksjö.

Museums

Stockholm's 70-odd museums exhibit world-class treasures. Among the best are the National Museum, and the renowned Skansen, which combines folk-life, wildlife and traditional houses. Similar regional museums and museum villages are popular in Sweden and are often better presented than elsewhere in Europe. Kulturen in Lund, Jamtli in Östersund and Malmöhus Castle in Malmö are among the best.

Castles & Churches

Sweden has hundreds of castles, royal palaces and castle-like manor houses. Skåne has some very fine Danish castles, and the Royal Family still oversees some 10 castles in and around Stockholm. Castles can be palaces with gardens such as Drottningholm near Stockholm, lakeside residences such as Skokloster slott by Lake Mälaren and Vadstena slott, formidable fortresses such as Kalmar and Örebro castles and impressive ruins such as those at Borgholm on Öland. Uppsala slott and Malmöhus also function as museums.

Sweden has 3000 churches, built during the last 900 years. Hundreds of medieval churches can be found in Gotland, Skåne and the Stockholm-Uppsala region. Entry to churches is free, except for the Riddarholmskyrkan burial church in Stockholm. There are many styles of cathedrals; the *domkyrkor* (cathedrals) of Lund (Romanesque), Uppsala (Gothic) and Kalmar (baroque) are fine examples. It's also well worth visiting the wooden Särna *gammelkyrka* (old church) in upper Dalarna.

VISA REQUIREMENTS

Stays of up to 90 days are usually visa free, but citizens of South Africa and Eastern European countries should check requirements with embassies.

Swedish Embassies & Consulates
Australia

(☎ 02-6270 2700) 5 Turrana St, Yarralumla, Canberra, ACT 2600

Itineraries

Two Days
Visit Stockholm, one of Europe's most beautiful national capitals. The Old Town is a particularly fine place to spend time in summer. Don't miss the Royal Palace, the National Museum and Djurgården, the royal park and open-air museum.

One Week
Spend two or three days in and around Stockholm, including North to Uppsala and the ferry or coastal steamer ride through some of the islands of the Stockholm archipelago. From there head west to the port city of Gothenburg.

Two Weeks
Spend three or four days in the Stockholm region and Uppsala, then head west to Gothenburg, and explore the Skåne region including Malmö (which will probably be your entry point if you're coming to Sweden from Denmark), Trelleborg and Lund. This area is easy to tour by bicycle and there are many hostels scattered around.

From there, travel north to the Dalarna region, an area of beautiful scenery, rich folk culture and winter sports. The area is centred on Lake Siljan. Falun is the main town, but places worth a visit include Mora and the village of Särna, gateway to some fine wilderness hiking.

Alternatively, take a ferry from Nynäsham (just south of Stockholm) or Oskarshamn to the historic island of Gotland. A popular summer holiday spot for Swedes, Gotland boasts a fascinating collection of prehistoric sites and medieval churches. It's great to tour from village to village and historic site to forest or beach by bicycle.

One Month
With a month you can cover everything in the two week itinerary more thoroughly, including exploring the Dalarna and Götaland regions. You can also head north through Norrland and past the Arctic Circle to the Sarek and Abisko national parks.

Canada
(☎ 613-241 8553) 377 Dalhousie St, Ottawa, Ont K1N 9N8
UK
(☎ 020-7917 6400) 11 Montague Place, London W1H 2AL
USA
(☎ 202-467 2600, fax 467 2656) 1501 M St NW, Washington, DC 20005
Consulate: (☎ 212-583 2550) Dag Hammarskjold Plaza, 885 Second Ave, New York, NY 10017-2201
Consulate: (☎ 310-445 4008) 10960 Wilshire Blvd, Suite 820, Los Angeles, CA 90024

TOURIST OFFICES OVERSEAS
Australia
Scandinavian Airlines System
(SAS; ☎ 02-9299 9800) 5th floor, 350 Kent St, Sydney, NSW 2000
UK
(☎ 020-7724 5868, @ info@swedish-tourism.org.uk) 11 Montague Place, London W1H 2Al
USA
(☎ 212-885 0700, @ info@gosweden.org) Grand Central Station, New York, NY 10017-5617

POST & COMMUNICATIONS
Letters sent airmail take about a week to reach most parts of North America, a little longer to Australia and New Zealand. Poste restante services are available at the main post offices in large cities such as Gothenburg and Malmö. For smaller places, you will need to specially arrange to have mail held for collection at the local post office, for which you will need the correct postcode.

Almost all public telephones in Sweden now take Telia phonecards. Many Telia booths also accept credit cards. Some post offices have fax services. Larger public libraries have online computers that can be used free of charge, though a limit of one or

SWEDEN HIGHLIGHTS & ITINERARIES

NORWAY

RUSSIA

FINLAND

Arctic Circle

Riksgränsen
Narvik • Björkliden • Karesuando
Abisko National Park
Kiruna

SAREK NATIONAL PARK
Take a walk on Sweden's
real wild side

Malmberget • Pajala
Gällivare • Övertorneå
Sarek National Park
Muddus National Park

Arctic Circle

Mo i Rana
Jokkmokk • Vuollerim

NORWEGIAN SEA

Haparanda
Boden • Luleå
Arvidsjaur
Piteå

Oulu (Uleåborg)

Storuman

Skellefteå

Lycksele

NORRLAND

Umeå

Trondheim
Storlien • Åre • Östersund
Röros
Idre
Sveg
Sårna
Storsjön
Örnsköldsvik
Vaasa

FINLAND

Härnösand
Sundsvall
Hudiksvall
Bollnäs • Söderhamn
Mora
Rättvik • Gävle
Falun
Borlänge
Siljan
Grisslehamn

UPPSALA
Get a liberal education
in this marvellous
little university town

S V E A L A N D

Sala
Uppsala
Turku (Åbo)

HELSINKI ☆

Gulf of Finland

STOCKHOLM
Stroll the maze-like
streets of millennium-
old Gamla Stad

Åland

OSLO ☆
Arvika
Västerås
Kapellskär
Karlstad
Eskilstuna
Örebro
Mälaren
STOCKHOLM ☆

TALLINN ☆

ESTONIA

Strömstad
Hjälmaren
Tiveden National Park
Nyköping • Nyköping
Nyköping
Nynäshamn

GOTLAND
See why Swedes spend
their precious summers here

Kristiansand
Uddevalla
Vänern
Motala
Norrköping
Linköping
Gotland

G Ö T A L A N D

Vadstena
Gothenburg (Göteborg)
Borås
Huskvarna
Jönköping • Eksjö
Västervik
Visby

RIGA ☆

Frederikshavn
Värnamo
Oskarshamn
SMÅLAND
Varberg
Växjö

LATVIA

Grenå
Ljungby
Kalmar
Öland
BALTIC SEA

Halmstad
Helsingborg
SKÅNE
Karlskrona

LITHUANIA

Klaipėda

DENMARK
Landskrona
Lund
Kristianstad
Simrishamn

SKÅNE
Visit imposing Malmöhus
castle or take in the student
atmosphere of Lund

VILNIUS ☆

COPENHAGEN
Öresund Bridge
(completed 2000)
Malmö • Trelleborg
Ystad
Bornholm

RUSS. FED.
Kaliningrad

SUGGESTED ITINERARIES

One Week   Stockholm • Uppsala • Gothenburg

Two Weeks   ① Stockholm • Uppsala • Gothenburg • Lund • Malmö •
Trelleborg • Mora • Särna
② Stockholm • Gotland

One Month   Stockholm • Uppsala • Gotland • Gothenburg • Lund •
Malmö • Trelleborg • Mora • Särna • Sarek National Park •
Abisko National Park

two hours applies. These computers normally have to be booked several hours – sometimes days – in advance. Cybercafes can be found in most cities.

MONEY
Costs

Sweden is very expensive, but it can be bearable if you're careful. If you bring a tent or stay in hostels, buy travel passes, eat at buffets and keep off the booze you might be able to get by on US$40 a day, but you'll be pushing it. Double that budget and you can eat a good meal at least once a day, stay in hotels, visit museums and travel around a bit.

Changing Money

You should encounter few problems if you carry cash in any convertible currency or travellers cheques of international brands. If you've got a credit card or a Cirrus card, bring it – ATMs all over the country will accept it. Forex branches do cheap currency conversions, though they'll charge you a fair bit more for travellers cheques.

ONLINE SERVICES

Lonely Planet's Destination Sweden page (www.lonelyplanet.com/dest/eur/swe.htm) has loads of details. There is another general tourist information site at www.sverigeturism.se. The Global Visitor's Guide to Sweden (www.visit-sweden.com) has a colourful approach and lots of information. The Swedish Institute site (www.si.se/eng/eindex.html) has facts as well as information about studying in Sweden and cultural exchanges. The Stockholm information page (www.stoinfo.se/sverige) has information on the capital.

BOOKS

Check out *Swedish History in Outline* by J Weibull, *A Concise History of Sweden* by A Åberg, or *Swedish Politics During the 20th Century* by S Hadenius.

Nature in Sweden by P Hanneberg is a good introduction to what the wilds have to offer, while *Nordic Folk Art* by M Nodermann and *Manor Houses and Royal Castles in Sweden* by B Söderberg focus on the crafted and created. August Strindberg's troubled life produced dramas both written and enacted. His autobiography *The Son of a Servant* gives remarkable insights into his early life. Revolutionary fiction works include *The Father* and *Miss Julie*.

FILMS

A Ship to India (1947) is a romantic film starring Ingrid Bergman. Sweden's most celebrated director, Ingmar Bergman, has produced a number of masterpieces, including *Fanny & Alexander*.

ENTERING & LEAVING

The main international airport is Arlanda, a half-hour bus ride north of Stockholm. There are daily services to and from most European capitals. Most flights from North American and Asian centres fly through Copenhagen. An airport tax of 14 krona is included in ticket prices.

Buses and trains link up with ferries to provide services to and from Sweden, Denmark, Finland, Norway, Germany, Poland, Estonia and the UK. Swedish ports of entry include Gothenburg, Helsingborg, Malmö and Stockholm, although ferries from north-western Finland head straight for Umeå and Skellefteå in northern Sweden, and services to Germany leave from Trelleborg.

SWITZERLAND

Switzerland conjures up its fair share of cliches: irresistible chocolates, kitsch clocks, yodelling Heidis, humourless bankers, international bureaucracies and an orderly, rather bland national persona. But Harry Lime was wrong on more than one count when, in Orson Welles' film *The Third Man*, he said that 500 years of Swiss democracy and peace had produced nothing more than the cuckoo clock. For a start, the cuckoo clock was invented by the Germans; secondly, the Swiss, who are a brainy lot, have won more Nobel Prizes and registered more patents per capita than any other nation on earth.

Switzerland may be neutral, but it is certainly not flavourless. The fusion of German, French and Italian ingredients has formed a robust national culture, and the country's Alpine landscapes have enough zing to reinvigorate the most jaded traveller. Goethe summed up Switzerland succinctly as a combination of 'the colossal and the well ordered'. The untamed majesty of the Alps and the tidy, just-so precision of Swiss towns prevent Switzerland from ever being one-dimensional or boring.

WHEN TO GO

You can visit Switzerland at any time of year. Summer lasts roughly from June to September, and offers the most pleasant climate for outdoor pursuits. Unfortunately, you won't be the only tourist during this period, so prices can be high, accommodation

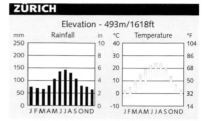

hard to find and the mainstream sights crowded. You'll find much better deals and smaller crowds in the shoulder seasons between April-May or late September-October.

If you're keen on winter sports, resorts in the Alps begin operating in late November, move into full swing around Christmas, and close down when the snow begins to melt in April.

At a Glance

Full Country Name: The Federal Republic of Switzerland
Area: 41,295 sq km
Population: 6.9 million
Capital City: Bern (pop 150,000)
People: 74% Germanic origin, 20% French, 4% Italian, 1% Romansch
Language: German, French, Italian, Romansch
Religion: 49% Roman Catholic, 48% Protestant
Government: Federal republic
Currency: Swiss franc (Sfr)
Time Zone: One hour ahead of GMT/UTC
International Telephone Code: 41
Electricity: 220V, 50Hz

Itineraries

Switzerland is not a big country, but there is a lot of variety and your itinerary will depend on the time of year you visit and your priorities.

Two Days
Visit the international city of Geneva, home of the United Nations and numerous museums, and take a trip on the lake. Don't miss a visit to Château de Chillon, across the lake in Montreux.

If it's mountain vistas you want, spend the time at Interlaken in the Jungfrau region. The scenery is spectacular and you can add a day trip to Bern or a tour of Lake Thun.

One Week
With a week you can spend a couple of days in Geneva and Montreux, with a stop in Lausanne to see the l'Art Brut collection. Then take the Panoramic Express to Interlaken and explore the Jungfrau and Lake Thun region. Continue north to Lucerne and spend some time around the lake, then finish your journey in Zürich, Switzerland's financial and cultural centrepiece.

Two Weeks
Follow the one week itinerary, but spend longer in the Jungfrau region, visiting places like Grindelwald and Schilthorn. During spring and summer this is a superb area for hiking, and in winter skiing is a major activity. Visit the Gruyères cheese dairy after Montreux and include detours to Bern and Basel. If your heart is set on seeing the famous Matterhorn, you can take the train to Zermatt in between Montreux and Interlaken, but this is a private train, so rail passes are not valid.

One Month
With a month up your sleeve you can cover all of the two week route, but continue east from Zürich and explore St Gallen and eastern Switzerland before looping down to take in the Graubünden, Ticino and Valais regions.

HIGHLIGHTS
Alpine Scenery & Resorts
Many people come just to see the mountains, and Switzerland is a country so blessed with impossibly beautiful Alpine vistas that it's difficult to select the best. You can't get much better than the view from Schilthorn, or from its neighbour across the valley, Jungfrau. The three or four-pass tour in the Jungfrau region is unforgettable on a fine day. The mountains and lakes combination seen from one of the summits around Lake Lucerne (Mt Pilatus, Mt Rigi or Mt Stanserhorn) is as seductive as views from higher peaks. The ski resorts invariably provide great panoramas to go with the pistes. They range from traditional chalet villages such as Grindelwald or Klosters, to exclusive, expensive resorts such as St Moritz. Zermatt has excellent skiing and inspiring views of the Matterhorn, while Davos and Verbier offer some of the best skiing in the world.

Historic Town Centres
Rathausplatz in medieval Stein am Rhein is harmonious and perfectly preserved; you'll find the main street in Gruyères is almost as photogenic. Lucerne is worthy of its fame, with a charming medieval centre and a good location right in the scenic heart of Switzerland. Schaffhausen and St Gallen sport historic centres bristling with oriel windows. Bern, with its covered arcades, fountains and clock towers, is unbelievably quaint for a capital city. Murten, and to a lesser extent, Estavayer-le-Lac, proudly display ancient centres ringed by fortifications, virtually unchanged over time.

SWITZERLAND HIGHLIGHTS & ITINERARIES ▶▶

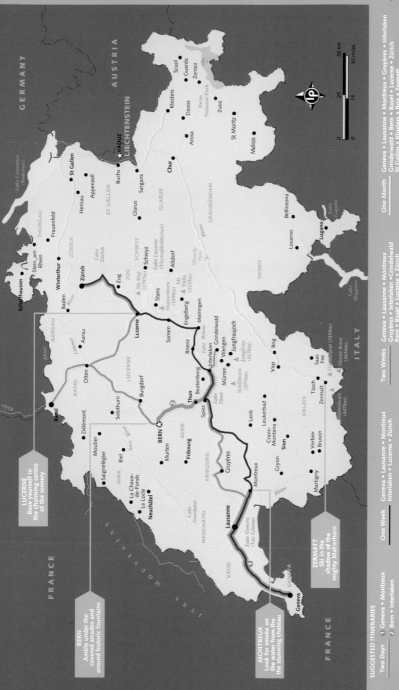

LUCERNE
Base yourself in
the charming centre
of the scenery

BERN
Amble under the
covered arcades and
around historic fountains

MONTREUX
Look for smoke on
the water from the
stunning chateau

ZERMATT
Ski in the
shadow of the
mighty Matterhorn

SUGGESTED ITINERARIES

Two Days
1 Geneva • Montreux
2 Bern • Interlaken

One Week
Geneva • Lausanne • Montreux
Interlaken • Lucerne • Zürich

Two Weeks
Geneva • Lausanne • Montreux
Gruyères • Interlaken • Grindelwald
Bern • Basel • Lucerne • Zürich

One Month
Geneva • Lausanne • Montreux • Gruyères • Interlaken
Grindelwald • Bern • Basel • Lucerne • Zürich
St Gallen • Klosters • Brig • Zermatt

Castles & Churches

There are many interesting castles scattered through the country. The Château de Chillon in Montreux is one of the most famous and occupies a stunning position on the shores of Lake Geneva. Also try to take a day tour (from Interlaken or Thun) to the castles around Lake Thun, such as Schloss Oberhofen.

Basel and Bern both have fine cathedrals. The most impressive abbey churches in the country, quite breathtaking in their scale, are those in Einsiedeln and St Gallen.

Museums & Galleries

Basel and Zürich each have an excellent art museum, the Kunstmuseum and the Kunsthaus. Away from the mainstream, the bizarre l'Art Brut collection in Lausanne is something to see. Zürich's national museum (Schweizerisches Landesmuseum) gives the most complete rundown of Swiss life and times, making all but redundant equivalent regional museums. The sprawling Art and History Museum in Geneva covers a bit of everything. The best clock and watch museum is the Museum of Horology in La Chaux-de-Fonds. For food fans, there are various show cheese dairies (eg at Gruyères and Stein), and the Lindt & Sprüngli chocolate factory in Zürich.

Festivals

Switzerland has plenty of traditional festivals, from village-oriented to national. Carnival *(Fasnacht)*, in February, is celebrated in many towns (Basel, Lucerne and Zürich in particular) with parades and music. Starting in March and continuing through the summer are the unusual cow-fighting festivals in Lower Valais. The famous Montreux Jazz Festival gets swinging in July and the International Festival of Music is held in Lucerne in August.

VISA REQUIREMENTS

Citizens of Australia, Canada, Ireland, New Zealand, South Africa, the UK and the USA do not require visas for visits of up to three months.

Swiss Embassies

Australia
(☎ 02-6273 3977, fax 273 3428) 7 Melbourne Ave, Forrest, Canberra, ACT 2603

Canada
(☎ 613-235 1837, fax 563 1394) 5 Marlborough Ave, Ottawa, Ont KIN 8E6

Ireland
(☎ 01-269 2515, fax 283 0344) 6 Ailesbury Rd, Ballsbridge, Dublin 4

New Zealand
(☎ 04-472 1593, fax 499 6302) 22 Panama St, Wellington

South Africa
(☎ 012-436 707, fax 436 771) 818 George Ave, Arcadia 0083, PO Box 2289, 0001 Pretoria

UK
(☎ 020-7723 0701, fax 7724 7001) 16-18 Montague Place, London W1H 2BQ

USA
(☎ 202-745 7900, fax 387 2564) 2900 Cathedral Ave NW, Washington, DC 20008-3499

TOURIST OFFICES OVERSEAS

Canada
(☎ 416-695 2090, fax 695 2774) 926 The East Mall, Etobicoke, Toronto, Ont M9B 6K1

South Africa
(☎ 011-484 1986, fax 484 1999) c/o Swissair, Swiss Park, 10 Queens Rd, Parktown, POB 3866, Johannesburg 2000

UK
(☎ 020-7734 1921, fax 7437 4577) Swiss Centre, Swiss Court, London W1V 8EE

USA

(☎ 212-757 5944, fax 262 6116) Swiss Center, 608 Fifth Ave, New York, NY 10020

POST & COMMUNICATIONS

Like everything else in Switzerland, the mail and telephone systems are very efficient, and have charges to match.

Mail can be sent poste restante (*Postlagernde Briefe*) to any town with a post office and is held for 30 days.

Public telephone boxes are numerous, and there are invariably some outside post offices. A few telephones take credit cards; many take the Taxcard phonecards, which are available from post offices and other outlets. Some of the larger post offices have special telephone sections, usually open longer hours than the general post office counters. In these booths you pay the total charge at the counter after you've finished making your call. International calls to Europe are cheaper from 9 pm to 8 am on weekdays, and throughout the weekend. The cheap rate to the USA and Canada is from 11 pm to 10 am and on weekends. There's no cheap rate to Australasia.

Telephone offices in post offices also have fax and telex facilities. As you'd expect in such a technologically developed country, email is in common use and cybercafes are opening up in cities and tourist areas.

MONEY
Costs

Costs are higher in Switzerland than anywhere else in Europe. If you camp or stay in hostels, and buy food from supermarkets, you could get by on around US$35 a day after buying a rail pass. If you stay in pensions, enjoy eating out and want to sample the nightlife, count on spending at least twice as much.

Tipping is rarely necessary, as hotels, restaurants and bars are required by law to include a 15% service charge. Even taxis normally have a service charge included.

Changing Money

All major travellers cheques and credit cards are accepted. Commission is not charged for changing cash or cheques, but shop around for the best rates (hotels usually have the worst rates).

ONLINE SERVICES

Lonely Planet's Destination Switzerland site (www.lonelyplanet.com /dest/eur/swi.htm) has a full country profile. Switzerland Tourism's Web site (www.switzerlandtourism.ch) includes SBB and Swissair timetables, and links for useful related organisations (eg the Swiss embassy). The Swiss information page is at www.about.ch.

BOOKS

Why Switzerland? by Jonathan Steinberg is a light and insightful look at Switzerland's social and political life. *George Mikes Introduces Switzerland* is a more sober collection of essays covering all aspects of Swiss life. *Blood Money – The Swiss, the Nazis and the Looted Billions* by Tom Bower is a sobering exposé of one of the sleazier sides of Switzerland's banks.

Max Frisch explores Swiss identity in his novel *I'm Not Stiller*, and examines the idea of detached neutrality in *Homo Faber*. *The Magic Mountain* by Thomas Mann is a weighty, reflective novel set in the Alps. Mary Shelley wrote *Frankenstein* in Switzerland and set much of the action around Lake Geneva. *Heidi*, the famous children's story by Johanna Spyri, is set in the Maienfeld region, just north of Chur.

FILMS

Many films have used the Alps as a backdrop. *After Darkness* (1985), starring John Hurt, is set in Switzerland, and *Five Days One Summer* (1982) has Sean Connery as a doctor who takes a party on a mountaineering trip. Others include *Three Colours Red* (1994), *The Return of the Pink Panther* (1974), the TV film *Hotel du Lac* (1986), *Goldfinger* (1964) and *Golden Eye (1995)*.

ENTERING & LEAVING

The main entry points for international flights are Zürich and Geneva. Basel, Bern and Lugarno airport also have international flights. There is no departure tax when flying out of Switzerland. If you have a rail pass, trains are the best way to travel to Switzerland (train travel within Switzerland is fairly expensive, though). Buses tend to be slower and less comfortable, but are usually cheaper. Getting to Switzerland by road is simple, since there are fast, well maintained motorways through all surrounding countries.

If you have time and money, it's possible to get to Switzerland (Basel) by boat along the Rhine all the way from Amsterdam. Switzerland can also be reached by lake steamer ferries from Germany via Lake Constance, from Italy via Lake Maggiore and from France via Lake Geneva.

Check your Midnight Express stereotypes at the airport and enter this rapidly modernising country with one foot firmly in Europe and one in the Middle East. It's not all Middle Eastern splendour, mystery, intrigue and whirling dervishes, but it is a spicy maelstrom of history, dramatic scenery, a booming tourist trade, warm people and a modern, secular and western-oriented culture.

With over 4000km of Mediterranean and Aegean coast and a fabulous climate, Turkey has understandably become a popular holiday spot, and there are several over-developed resorts and a few unspoilt gems along the convoluted western coast. The best of Turkey is actually out in the countryside and in some of the smaller towns and villages. History plays a big part, too. Many of the most famous sites from classical Hellenic and Hellenistic culture are not in Greece but in Turkey, including such cities as Troy, Pergamum (Bergama), Ephesus, Miletus and Halicarnassus. The Turkish people are generally quite friendly to foreign visitors (especially away from the touristy places, where you are less likely to be dragged into a carpet shop), the cuisine is a savoury surprise and travel in Turkey is cheaper than almost anywhere else in Europe.

WHEN TO GO

Spring (April to June) and autumn (September to November) are best. The climate is perfect on the Aegean

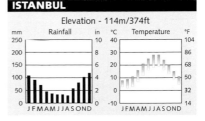

ISTANBUL

Elevation - 114m/374ft

and Mediterranean coasts then, as well as in Istanbul. In high summer the coastal resorts are stinking hot. From late October to early April the beach scene more or less shuts down. There's not much rain between May and October except along the Black Sea coast, but from about mid-June the mosquitoes come out in plague proportions in some areas (don't forget the insect repellent). Eastern Turkey should really be visited from

At a Glance

Full Country Name: Turkey
Area: 779,452 sq km
Population: 64 million
Capital City: Ankara (pop 3.2 million)
People: 85% Turks, 12% Kurds, plus other Islamic peoples, Armenians, Jews
Language: Turkish, Kurdish
Religion: Muslim
Government: Parliamentary democracy
Currency: Turkish lira (TL)
Time Zone: Two hours ahead of GMT/ UTC; clocks are turned forward one hour in late March and back again in late September
International Telephone Code: 90
Electricity: 220V, 50Hz

late June to September, as snow may close roads and mountain passes in colder months.

HIGHLIGHTS
Istanbul
If you only visit one place in Turkey it should be stanbul, former capital of the Ottoman Empire (when it was known as Constantinople). Here you can inhale all the sights, sounds, tea and carpet shops, mosques, bazaars and Byzantine architecture your senses can handle. Don't miss Topkapi Palace, the Aya Sofya (Hagia Sofia), the Blue Mosque and the Kariye Museum. Taking a cruise on the Bosphorus is another highlight, and you just have to tackle the buzzing Grand Bazaar.

Ancient Sites & Architecture
Turkey has so many ancient Greek and Roman sites that you're bound to stumble on a few. Ephesus, the best preserved classical city on the Mediterranean, is easily the most famous and a definite must-see – but go early in the day ahead of the crowds. There's not much left of Troy and many people find it disappointing. The dramatically sited ruins of Termessos, near Antalya, are hard to get to but worth the effort. Aphrodisias, Priene, Miletus and Hierapolis are other well known sites.

Apart from Turkey's famous imperial mosques, Seljuk architecture is worth seeking out. Alanya, Konya, Sivas and Erzurum have good Seljuk buildings.

Beaches
Turkey has some fantastic beaches, although you may find some of the touristy resorts such as Mamaris,

Bodrum and Kusadasi disappointing in high summer. The best beaches are at Pamucak (near Ephesus), Ölüdeniz (near Fethiye), Patara, Antalya, Side and Alanya. The uncrowded, long white-sand beaches of Patara are particularly noteworthy. The Black Sea coast also has a few beaches, notably near Sinop and Unyë. These beaches are more popular with Turkish tourists than foreigners and, compared with the Mediterranean, the waters are *icy*.

Mountains & Valleys
In eastern Turkey, near Malatya, the great mausoleum on Nemrut Dagi (Mt Nemrut) certainly repay an early start to the day. A sunrise trip to the summit of this mountain is a highlight of eastern Turkey. In the extreme east of the country, snowcapped Mt Ararat is pretty much inaccessible, not least because of the Kurdish troubles in the region, but it's spectacular when viewed from afar. It's also famous as the supposed resting place of Noah's Ark.

The incredible 'lunar' landscapes of Cappadocia are perhaps the single most visually impressive feature in all Turkey. Göreme Valley is the place to base yourself for exploring this bizarre spectacle of volcanic pumice, odd rock formations and underground cities. You can stay the night in a hotel carved into the rock. The lush Ilhara Valley, nearby, is a great spot to walk through.

VISA REQUIREMENTS
Citizens of Japan, New Zealand and virtually all the countries of Western Europe need only a valid passport for stays of up to three months. Aus-

tralian, Canadian, UK and US citizens need visas, obtainable in advance from a Turkish consulate, or upon entry to Turkey.

Itineraries

Three Days
Spend at least two days in Istanbul exploring the major sights around the Sultanahmet area, the 'European' area around Beyoglu and a cruise on the Bosphorus, on one of the local ferries. Also take an overnight trip to Iznik and Bursa, or Troy and the Gallipoli peninsula (to see the WWI battlefields). It'll be a bit rushed but it's definitely worth getting out to these places.

One Week
Spend at least two days in Istanbul, then take a ferry and bus to Bursa to see its magnificent monuments, including the Green Mosque. Bursa is also the base for the thermal baths and a good place for a traditional Turkish bath *(hammam)*. From there travel across to the Gallipoli peninsula and Troy (Çanakkale is the best base for both). Australians and New Zealanders in particular will find the WWI battlefields quite moving (the Anzac Day service on 25 April is a good time to be here). Travel down the coast and stay at either Kusadasi or Selçuk for excursions to the ancient cities of Ephesus, Priene, Miletus or Didyma. You may also have time to visit Bergama on the way down the coast. From Kusadasi you can return to Istanbul, continue around the coast, or take a ferry across to Samos and continue through the Greek islands.

Two Weeks
Cover the one week itinerary and add a trip inland from Kusadasi to the spectacular travertine pools at Pamukkale and the ruined city of Hierapolis. Then continue around the coast to Patara, Kas and Side. From there you can head inland via Konya to Cappadocia, where you could easily spend two or three days exploring the Göreme and Ilhara valleys. Alternatively, you can reach Cappadocia with a loop trip from Istanbul via Ankara.

One Month
A month is the minimum amount of time you'll need to explore a reasonable amount of Turkey, and travel is certainly cheap enough to allow you to spend a month here on a budget.

Cover all the areas included in the previous itinerary and add a yacht cruise or coastal highway excursion from Kusadasi, stopping at the many resorts and villages along the way to Antalya. Also visit Termessos from Antalya. After Cappadocia, you can head east to Malatya and take an overnight trip to the summit of Nemrut Dagi.

Another option is taking a tour of the Black Sea coast (rather than the south-west coast). A ferry runs from Istanbul to Trabzon in summer, so you could travel overland one way, visiting the spectacular Sumela Monastery near Trabzon, and take the boat back.

Eastern Tour Any tour of the east will depend on the political situation, and current travel warnings should be heeded. A 14 to 21 day tour for mid-May to early October only would include a circuit beginning in Ankara or Cappadocia and going to Adiyaman and Nemrut Dagi, Diyarbakir, Van, Dogubeyazıt and Mt Ararat, Kars, Erzurum, Artvin, Hopa, Rize, Trabzon, Samsun, Amasya and returning to Ankara via Bogazkale (Hattusas).

Two Months
With two months you could combine some of the previous itineraries. A good loop trip is to travel from Istanbul westward via Çanakkale and around the Aegean and Mediterranean coasts to Antalya, up to Cappadocia, across to Nemrut Dagi, up to Trabzon, then across the Black Sea coast to Istanbul, either by ferry or overland. Amasya is a worthwhile diversion from the Black Sea coast. Of course, you could easily while away your time lazing on the beach or sailing on an extended yacht cruise.

TURKEY HIGHLIGHTS & ITINERARIES

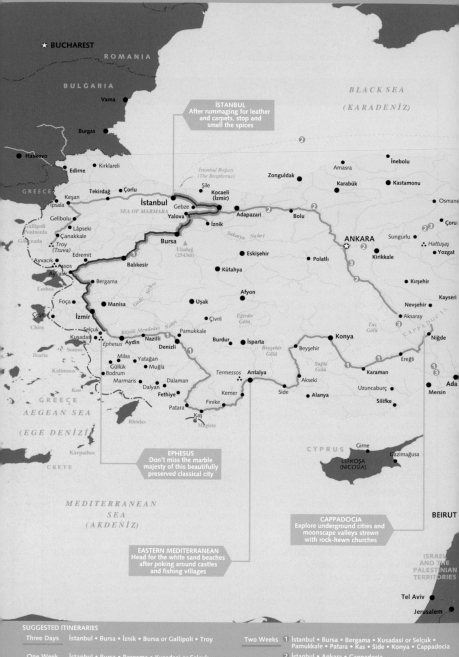

İSTANBUL
After rummaging for leather and carpets, stop and smell the spices

EPHESUS
Don't miss the marble majesty of this beautifully preserved classical city

CAPPADOCIA
Explore underground cities and moonscape valleys strewn with rock-hewn churches

EASTERN MEDITERRANEAN
Head for the white sand beaches after poking around castles and fishing villages

SUGGESTED ITINERARIES

Three Days   İstanbul • Bursa • İznik • Bursa or Gallipoli • Troy

One Week   İstanbul • Bursa • Bergama • Kusadasi or Selçuk

Two Weeks   **1** İstanbul • Bursa • Bergama • Kusadasi or Selçuk • Pamukkale • Patara • Kas • Side • Konya • Cappadocia

2 İstanbul • Ankara • Cappadocia

SUMELA MONASTERY
Hike into the Kaşkar Range to see this stunning cliff-side

NORTH-EASTERN ANATOLIA
Discover the lush mountains and medieval villages of the Georgian Valleys

NEMRUT DAGI
Visit the summit's mighty stone heads and share the spectacular views

RUSSIA

GEORGIA

★ TBILISI

AZERBAIJAN

Vladikavkaz

Sukhumi

Kutaisi

Samsun

Ünye   Ordu   Trabzon   Rize
            Giresun   Hopa   Batumi
Niksar   Sumela Manastırı   Yusufeli   Artvin   Çıldır
                        Gümüşhane   Çoruh Nehri   Göle   Gölü
Tokat   Koyulhisar Şebinkarahisar   Sankamış   Kars   Ani   Kumayri Kirovakan
         Suşehri   Bayburt   YEREVAN ★
                     Refahiye   Kelkit Çayı Tortum   Horasan   Kağızman
Sivas   Zara   Karasu Irmağı   Pasinler   Tuzluca   ARMENIA
         Divriği   Erzincan   Tercan   Erzurum   Arus Nehri   Mt Ararat ▲
                     Fırat Nehri   Ağrı   (5137m)
                                 Tunceli   Doğubeyazıt   AZERBAIJAN
         Karakaya   Kebir   Patnos
         Barajı   Barajı   Bingöl   Muradiye
Elazığ   Özalp
Malatya   Murat Nehri   Muş   Van Gölü Tatvan Van   Darya-ye
Elbistan   Bitlis   Gevaş   Gürpınar   Orümiye
         Gölbaşı   Nemrut Dağı   Kurtalan Siirt   Çatak
Kahramanmaraş Adıyaman   Cilo Dağı   Orümiye
         Atatürk   Siverek Diyarbakır   Şırnak Hakkari (4168m)
Gaziantep Barajı Hilvan   Mardin   Yüksekova
Osmaniye Birecik Şanlıurfa Viranşehir
İskenderun Kırıkhan   Qamishle   IRAN
Aleppo
(Halab)   Mosul   Arbil
         Sabkhat
         el-Gabbul
                                                                  Kirkük
SYRIA   Euphrates Nehri
                     Deir ez-Zur   IRAQ

DAMASCUS   ★ BAGHDAD

LP

0   100   200 km
0   60   120 miles

JORDAN   SAUDI
                ARABIA

Turkish Embassies
Australia
> (☎ 02-6295 0227, fax 6239 6592) 60 Mugga Way, Red Hill, Canberra, ACT 2603

Canada
> (☎ 613-789 4044, fax 781 3442) 197 Wurtemburg St, Ottawa, Ont K1N 8L9

Greece
> (☎ 01-724 5915, fax 722 9597) Vasilissis Georgiou B 8, 10674 Athens

UK
> (☎ 020-7393 0202, fax 7393 0066) 43 Belgrave Square, London SW1X 8PA

USA
> (☎ 202-659 8200, fax 659 0744) 1714 Massachusetts Ave NW, Washington, DC 20036

TOURIST OFFICES OVERSEAS
Australia
> (☎ 02-9223 3055, fax 9223 3204, ✉ turkish@ ozemail.com.au) Room 17, Level 3, 428 George St, Sydney, NSW 2000

Canada
> (☎ 613-230 8654, fax 230 3683) Constitution Square, 360 Albert St, Suite 801, Ottawa, Ont K1R 7X7

UK
> (☎ 020-7629 7771, fax 7491 0773, ✉ tto@ cityscape.co.uk) 1st floor, 170-173 Piccadilly, London W1V 9DD

USA
> (☎ 212-687 2194, fax 599 7568, ✉ tourny@ idt.net) 821 UN Plaza, New York, NY 10017

POST & COMMUNICATIONS
Postal services in Turkey are handled by the Posta Telgraf office, usually known as the PTT, where you can buy stamps, send letters, faxes and telegrams, or make telephone calls. If you are having mail sent poste restante, have it addressed to Merkez Postahane (main or central post office) in whichever town you wish to collect it.

The best way to make telephone calls is with Telekart telephone debit cards, which are sold in shops and kiosks near public phones. Some newer phones also accept credit cards. International calls can be quite expensive: around US$3 per minute to the USA, and even higher to Australia.

Turks are addicted to fax machines. Most businesses including hotels, car rental companies and airlines have them, so they're handy for making reservations. Faxes can be sent from Telekom phone centres, or from your hotel. Major cities and tourist centres have cybercafes. Many small hotels and pensions all around the country have Internet services, which you can access for a fee to send and receive email.

MONEY
Costs
Turkey is a low-slung dollar burner. You can travel on as little as US$15 a day using buses and trains (although there are very few useful train services), staying in pensions and eating one restaurant meal daily. It's possible to travel on less than this if you eat at cheap *lokanta* (restaurants) and snack stalls and don't move around too much. For US$20 to US$45, you can travel on plush buses, kick back in one and two-star hotels and eat most meals in restaurants.

In cheaper restaurants it's not necessary to leave more than a few coins on the change plate. In more expensive restaurants, tipping is customary. Even if a 10 or 15% service charge is added to your bill, you're expected to give around 5% to the waiter directly. Bargaining is pretty common in Turkey – you'd be mad not to bargain for souvenirs. For hotel rooms, bargain if you visit between

November and April or if you plan to stay more than a few nights.

Changing Money

With the value of the Turkish lira always sliding, it's best to change money every few days. Keep an eye on all the zeros on your bills – it's easy to mistake a 500,000 lira note for a 50,000 lira note. Banks and exchange offices are generally only open from Monday to Friday – you may find it hard to convert your travellers cheques on weekends. ATMs are common in Turkish cities, towns and resorts, many of them connected to worldwide cashpoint networks such as Cirrus or Plus and to credit cards (Visa seems to be the most widely accepted). Keep some exchange receipts, as you may need them to change lira back at the end of your stay.

ONLINE SERVICES

Lonely Planet's Destination Turkey (www.lonelyplanet.com/dest/eur/tur.htm) gives a thorough country profile. The *Turkish Daily News* site (www.turkishdailynews.com) has current information, weather and, in the classifieds section, ads for rental apartments, jobs as English teachers and translators etc. *Milliyet*, a prominent national daily newspaper, provides news in slightly rickety but ambitious English at www.milliyet.com/e. As might be expected, the official Turkish government site (www.turkey.org) is rather dry, with full texts of government communiques and speeches, but also visa, passport, consular and economic information, email addresses of Turkish diplomatic missions, and useful links to other sites related to Turkey.

BOOKS

Istanbul – A Traveller's Companion by Laurence Kelly is a delightful collection of choice bits written about Byzantium, Constantinople and Istanbul over two millennia.

Mark Twain's *Innocents Abroad* is a classic account of tourism in Turkey. Many of Twain's observations of Istanbul are still current. *A Fez of the Heart* by Jeremy Seal is a witty inquiry into resurgent Islam and what it means to be a 'modern' Turk. Lord Kinross' *The Ottoman Centuries* is the most readable of the histories of the empire; his *Atatürk, the Rebirth of a Nation* is essential reading for anyone who wants to understand the formation of the republic.

If you want to know your old rocks, grab *Ancient Civilisations and Ruins of Turkey* by Ekrem Akurgal. Turkish fiction available in translation includes the novels of Yasar Kemal (colourful characters and the drama of farming and working-class life) and Orhan Pamuk (a young Turkish novelist with a worldwide following).

FILMS

Perhaps the most famous movie about Turkey is *Midnight Express* (1978), a politically motivated, anti-Turkish diatribe in which a convicted drug smuggler is magically transformed into a suffering hero. Controversial director Oliver Stone created a visually striking and emotionally chilling story in this early work by playing fast and loose with the facts. The classic suspense-comedy *Topkapi* (1964), with Peter Ustinov and Melina Mercouri, is much more fun to watch, as is the James Bond thriller *From Russia With Love* (1963), set in Istanbul.

ENTERING & LEAVING

There are plenty of ways to get into Turkey by air, sea, rail and bus, across the borders of seven countries. There are international airports at Istanbul, Ankara, Izmir and some of the Mediterranean resorts. Turkish Airlines has direct flights from Istanbul to two dozen European cities and New York, as well as the Middle East, North Africa, Bangkok, Karachi, Singapore and Tokyo. Departure tax is around US$12, which is usually included in ticket prices.

By train, the daily *Istanbul Express* links Munich, Slovenia, Yugoslavia, Croatia and Bulgaria to Istanbul. Major European cities such as Frankfurt and Vienna are also well serviced by Turkish bus lines. There are daily train and bus connections between Athens and Istanbul via Thessaloniki. The bus is much faster than the train. You can also travel by bus to Syria, Georgia and Iran, and by train to Armenia. Turkish Maritime Lines runs car ferries from Antalya, Marmaris and Izmir to Venice weekly from May to mid-October. Private ferries run between Turkey's Aegean coast and the Greek islands.

INTERNET ADDRESSES ▶▶

ACCOMMODATION
Bed & Breakfast Channel: www.bbchannel.com
France.com: www.france.com
HomeExchange.com: www.homeexchange.com
Hostelling International: www.iyhf.org
Internet Guide to Hostelling: www.hostels.com
Irish Tourist Board: www.ireland.travel.ie

ACTIVITIES
CameraSurf Homepage: www.uol.com.br/camerasurf
Great Outdoor Recreation Page: www.gorp.com
PADI: www.padi.com
Surfline: www.surfline.com

AIR FARES
eXito: www.exitotravel.com
Expedia: www.expedia.msn.com/daily/home/default.hts
Flight Info.Com: www.flifo.com
Preview Travel: www.previewtravel.com
Travelocity: www.travelocity.com

AIRLINES
AeroContinente: http://200.4.197.130/Acerca-in.htm
Air Courier Association: www.aircourier.org
Air France: www.airfrance.fr
Air New Zealand: www.airnz.com
Alitalia: www.alitalia.com/english/index.html
American Airlines: www.americanair.com
Ansett Australia: www.ansett.com.au
Avensa: www.avensa.com
Avianca: www.avianca.com.co
British Airways: www.british-airways.com
Canadian Airlines: www.cdnair.ca
Continental Airlines: www.flycontinental.com
Iberia: www.iberia.com
International Association of Air Travel Couriers (IAATC): www.courier.org/index.html
Lauda Air: www.laudaair.com
Lufthansa: www.lufthansa.com
Qantas Airways: www.qantas.com
United Airlines: www.ual.com
Virgin Atlantic: www.fly.virgin.com

CAR & MOTORCYCLE
American Automobile Association: www.aaa.com/vacation/idp.html
Australian Automobile Association: www.aaa.asn.au

415

British Automobile Association: www.theaa.co.uk/membership/offers/idp.html
Canadian Automobile Association: www.caa.ca/CAAInternet/travelservices/frames14.htm
New Zealand Automobile Association: www.aa.org.nz

FILM & RADIO
BBC World Service: www.bbc.co.uk/worldservice
Internet Movie Database: www.imdb.com
Radio America: www.voa.gov
Radio Australia: www.abc.net.au/ra

HEALTH
Altitude Sickness: www.princeton.edu/~oa/altitude.html,
    www.gorge.net/hamg/AMS.html
American Society of Tropical Medicine & Hygiene: www.astmh.org
British Airways Travel Clinics: www.britishairways.com/travelqa/fyi/health/health.html
CDC (US Centers for Disease Control & Prevention): www.cdc.gov
Health Canada: www.hc-sc.gc.ca/hpb/lcdc/osh
International Association for Medical Assistance to Travellers: www.sentex.net
International Planned Parenthood Federation: www.ippf.org
International Society of Travel Medicine: www.istm.org
Lariam Action USA: www.suggskelly.com/lariam
MASTA (Medical Advisory Services for Travellers): www.masta.org
Medical College of Wisconsin Travelers Clinic: www.intmed.mcw/travel.html
Mefloquine: www.travelhealth.com/mefloqui.htm,
    www.geocities.com/TheTropics/6913/lariam.htm
Shorelands: www.tripprep.com
Travel Health Information Service: www.travelhealth.com
Travellers Medical and Vaccination Centre: www.tmvc.com.au
WHO (World Health Organization): www.who.ch

INTERNET & TELEPHONE ACCOUNTS
eKno: www.ekno.lonelyplanet.com
Internet Cafe Guide: www.netcafeguide.com
Opening Accounts: www.yahoo.com, www.hotmail.com

MAPS
Hagstrom Map and Travel Center: www.hagstromstore.com
International Travel Maps: www.nas.com/~travelmaps
Rand McNally – The Map & Travel Store: www.randmcnallystore.com
World of Maps & Travel Books: www.worldofmaps.com

MONEY MATTERS
Credit Cards: www.mastercard.com/atm,
    www.visa.com/cgi-bin/vee/pd/atm/main.html
MasterCard ATMs: www.mastercard.com/atm
Oanda Online Currency Converter: www.oanda.com/converter/classic
Visa ATMs: www.visa.com

NEWSPAPERS & MAGAZINES
Bicycling: www.bicyclingmagazine.com
Big World Magazine: www.bigworld.com
Chicago Tribune: www.chicagotribune.com
LA Times: www.latimes.com
Mountain Bike: www.mountainbike.com
National Geographic: www.nationalgeographic.com
New York Times: www.nytimes.com
Outside: http://outside.starwave.com
San Francisco Examiner: www.examiner.com
Southern Cross (UK): www.southerncross.co.uk
Surfer Magazine: www.surfermag.com
Sydney Morning Herald: www.smh.com.au
The Age (Melbourne): www.theage.com.au
The Australian: www.news.com.au
The Globe & Mail (Toronto): www.theglobeandmail.com
The Independent (UK): www.independent.co.uk
The London Telegraph: www.the-planet.co.uk
The Times: www.the-times.co.uk
Time Out: www.timeout.com/london
TNT: www.tntmag.co.uk
Traveller Magazine: www.travelmag.co.uk
Vancouver Sun: www.vancouversun.com

NICHE TRAVELLERS
Access-Able Travel Source: www.access-able.com
Accessible Journeys: www.disabilitytravel.com
American Association of Retired Persons (AARP): www.aarp.org
Elder Treks: www.eldertreks.com
Gay Scape: www.gayscape.com
International Gay & Lesbian Travel Association (IGTLA): www.IGLTA.org
Mobility International USA: www.miusa.org
National Information Communication Awareness Network (NICAN): www.nican.com.au
Royal Association for Disability & Rehabilitation (RADAR): www.radar.org.uk
Society for the Advancement of Travel for the Handicapped (SATH):
    http://sath.org/index.html
Yahoo!: www.yahoo.com/Recreation/Travel/Women

PASSPORTS & VISAS
Embassy Web: www.embpage.org
Governments on the WWW: www.gksoft.com/govt/en/representations.html
Passports Australia, Department of Foreign Affairs & Trade:
    www.dfat.gov.au/passports/passports_faq_contents.html
Passport Office, Department of Foreign Affairs & International Trade (Canada):
    www.dfait-maeci.gc.ca/passport/paspr-2.htm
Passport Office, Department of Internal Affairs (New Zealand):
    http://nform.dia.govt.nz/internal_affairs/businesses/doni_pro/fees.html
Passport Services, The State Department (USA):
    http://travel.state.gov/passport_services.html
UK Passport Agency, The Home Office: www.open.gov.uk/ukpass/ukpass.htm

TEACHING RESOURCES

Dave's ESL Cafe: www.pacificnet.net/~sperling/eslcafe.html
English Expert Page: www.englishexpert.com
International House: www.international-house.org
Job Registry Online Directory: www.edulink.com/JOBS_FILES_LIST/jobopenings.html
Learn Spanish: www.studyspanish.com
New World Teachers: www.goteach.com
Teach English in Mexico: www.teach-english-mexico.com
TEFL Job Centre: www.jobs.edunet.com
World Teach: www.igc.org/worldteach

TRAVEL ADVISORIES

British Foreign & Commonwealth Office: www.fco.gov.uk
Conservation International's Ecotravel Center: www.ecotour.org/ecotour.htm
Council Travel: www.counciltravel.com
Ecotour: www.ecotour.org/ecotour.htm
Ecotourism Association of Australia: www.wttc.org
Encounter Overland: www.encounter.co.uk
Exodus: www.exodustravels.co.uk
Flight Centre: www.flightcentre.com
Global Exchange: www.globalexchange.org
Green Travel Network: www.greentravel.com
Intrepid Travel: www.intrepidtravel.com.au
Journeys International: www.journeys-intl.com
Serious Sports: www.serioussports.com/core.html
Specialty Travel: specialtytravel.com
STA Travel: www.sta-travel.com
Tourism Concern: www.gn.apc.org/tourismconcern
Tourism Offices Worldwide Directory: www.towd.com
Trailfinders: www.trailfinder.com
Travel CUTS: www.travelcuts.com

TRAVEL EQUIPMENT

Karrimor: www.karrimor.com.uk
Lowe Alpine Packs & Apparel: www.lowealpine.com
Macpac: www.macpac.com.nz
Photo.net: www.photo.net/photo
REI: www.rei.com

VOLUNTEER ORGANISATIONS

Australian Volunteers International: www.ozvol.org.au
AmeriSpan: www.amerispan.com/volunteer
Council on International Educational Exchange: www.ciee.org/vol
Earthwatch Institute: www.earthwatch.org/australia/html
Global Volunteers: www.globalvolunteers.org
International Voluntary Service: www.ivsgbn.demon.co.uk
Peace Corps of the USA: www.peacecorps.gov
Tx Serve: www.txserve.org/general/volopp2.html
Australian Volunteers International: www.ozvol.org.au
Volunteer Service Abroad: www.tcol.co.uk/comorg/vsa.htm

OTHER USEFUL SITES

Backpackers.com: backpackers.com
Cybercafe Search: cybercaptive.com
European Rail Travel: www.eurorail.com/railindx.htm
Federation of International Youth Travel Organisations:
   www.fiyto.org/index-old.html
FEMA Tropical Storm Watch: www.fema.gov/fema/trop.htm
Festivals.com: www.festivals.com
Guide to European Festivals: www.festpass.com
Habitat for Humanity: www.habitat.org
International Student Travel Confederation: www.isic.org/index.htm
Lonely Planet: www.lonelyplanet.com
Look Smart Travel: www.looksmart.com
Norwegian Cruise Line: www.ncl.com
Oxfam International: www.oxfaminternational.org
Planeta.com: www2.planeta.com/mader
Rail Europe: www.raileurope.com
Rail Pass Express: www.eurail.com
Rain or Shine: www.rainorshine.com
The Travel Page: www.travelpage.com/dest.htm
Transitions Abroad: www.transabroad.com
Travel Insurance: www.travelinsure.com
Travelocity: www.travelocity.com
UK Railways: www.rail.co.uk/ukrail/home.htm
US State Department Travel Warnings & Consular Information Sheets:
   http://travel.state.gov/travel_warnings.html
Vegetarian Eating: www.cms.dmu.ac.uk/~cph/Veg/veg-uk.html?glasgow
World Events Calendar: www.travel.epicurious.com
World Tourism Organization: www.world-tourism.org/ows-doc/wtich.htm
Yahoo! Travel Directory: www.yahoo.com/Recreation/Travel

WORLD HERITAGE LIST ▶▶

UNESCO's list of 'cultural and natural treasures of the world's heritage' includes the following places in Europe:

Albania
Ancient ruins of Butrint

Austria
Hallstatt-Dachstein (Salzkammergut) cultural landscape
Palaces & gardens of Schönbrunn near Vienna
Salzburg's historic city centre
Semmering Railway

Belgium
Canal du Centre (four lifts)
Flemish Béguinages
Grand-Place, Brussels
La Louvière
Le Roeulx (Hainault)

Britain
Bath
Blenheim Palace
Canterbury Cathedral, St Augustine's Abbey & St Martin's Church
Durham Castle & Cathedral
Edinburgh (old & new towns)
Gough Island Wildlife Reserve
Greenwich
Gwynedd's castles & town walls
Hadrian's Wall
Henderson Island
Ironbridge Gorge
Tower of London
St Kilda
Stonehenge & Avebury
Studley Royal Park & ruins of Fountains Abbey
Westminster Abbey and Palace & St Margaret's Church

Bulgaria
Boyana Church near Sofia
Ivanovo rock-hewn churches near Ruse
Kazanlâk Thracian tomb
Madara horseman relief
Nesebâr's old city
Pirin National Park
Rila Monastery
Srebarna Nature Reserve
Thracian Tomb of Svechtari

Croatia
Dubrovnik's old city
Plitvice Lakes National Park
Porec's Euphrasian Basilica
Split's historic centre with Diocletian's Palace
Trogir's old town

Cyprus
Ancient capital of Paphos
Choirokoitia
Painted churches of Troodos Massif

Czech Republic
Ceský Krumlov's historic centre
Holasovice historic village
Kromeríz Castle
Kutná Hora medieval silver town & Church of St Barbara
Lednice-Valtice
Pilgrimage Church of St John Nepomuk at Zelena Hora
Prague's historic centre
Telc's old city

Denmark
Jelling Kirke
Roskilde Domkirke

Estonia
Tallinn (old town)

Finland
Fortress of Suomenlinna
Petäjävesi Old Church
Vanha Rauma
Verla Board Mill

France
Abbey of St Rémi & Tau Palace at Reims
Amiens Cathedral
Arc-et-Senans' Royal Saltworks
Arles' Roman & Romanesque monuments
Avignon's historic centre
Bourges Cathedral
Canal du Midi
Carcassonne
Chambord's chateau & estate
Chartres Cathedral
Chateau of Versailles & gardens
Church of Saint Savin sur Gartempe
Corsica's Cape Girolata, Cape Porto, Les Calanche & Scandola Natural Reserve
Fontenay's Cistercian abbey
Grande Île section of Strasbourg
Lascaux & other caves in the Vézère Valley
Lyon (historic site)
Mont Saint Michel & its bay

Notre Dame & the banks of the Seine in Paris
Place Stanislas, Place de la Carrière & Place d'Alliance in Nancy
Pont du Gard Roman aqueduct near Nîmes
Roman theatre & triumphal arch at Orange
Santiago de Compostel routes
Vézelay's basilica

Germany
Aachen Cathedral
Abbey & Altenmünster of Lorsch
Augustusburg Castle at Brühl
Bamberg
Bauhaus sites in Weimar & Dessau
Cathedral & St Michael's Church at Hildesheim
Cologne Cathedral
Goslar & mines of Rammelsberg
Lübeck
Luther memorials in Eisleben & Wittenberg
Maulbronn Monastery complex
Messel fossil site
Palaces & parks of Potsdam
Quedlinburg's Collegiate Church, castle & old town
Speyer Cathedral
Trier's Roman monuments, cathedral & Liebfrauen Church
Völkling ironworks
Weimar
Wies' pilgrimage church
Würzburg's Residence & Court Gardens

Greece
Acropolis in Athens
Delos
Delphi archaeological site
Medieval city of Rhodes
Meteora
Monasteries of Daphni, Hossios, Luckas & Nea Moni at Chios
Mount Athos
Mystras
Olympia's archaeological site
Pythagorio & Hereon at Samos
Temple of Apollo Epicurios at Bassae
Thessaloniki's Early Christian & Byzantine monuments
Vergina's archaeological site

Hungary
Banks of the Danube in Budapest & the Castle District
Karst caves at Aggtelek Hollókö traditional village
Pannonhalma Benedictine Abbey

Ireland
Boyne Valley archaeological sites
Skellig Michael

Italy
Agrigento archaeological area
Archaeological area of Basilica of Aquileia
Archaeological areas of Pompeii & Herculaneum
Archaeological sites of Paestum and Velia
Caserta's Royal Palace with the park, aqueduct of Vanvitelli & the San Leucio complex
Castel del Monte
Certosa di Padula
Cilento and Vallo di Diano National Park
Cinque Terre, Portvenere & islands
Costiera Amalfitana
Crespi d'Adda
Historic centre of Florence
Historic centre of Naples
Historic centre of San Gimignano
Milan's Church of Santa Maria delle Grazie & convent including *The Last Supper* by
    Leonardo da Vinci
Modena's cathedral, Torre Civica & Piazza Grande
Padua's botanical garden
Pienza's historic centre
Pisa's Piazza del Duomo
Ravenna's Early Christian monuments & mosaics
Renaissance city of Ferrara
Rome's historic centre
Sassi (traditional stone houses) of Matera
Siena's historic centre
Su Nuraxi fortress at Barumini
Valle Camonica's rock carvings
Vatican City
Venice & its lagoon
Villa Romana del Casale
Vincenza & its Palladian villas
Urbino

Latvia
Riga's (historic centre)

Lithuania
Vilnius' (historic centre)

Luxembourg
Old quarter & fortifications of Luxembourg City

Malta
Hypogeum prehistoric temples at Paola
Megalithic Temples of Malta
Valetta

Netherlands
Amsterdam's Defence Line
DF Wouda Steam Pumping Station
Kinderdijk-Elshout's mill network
Schokland & surrounds
Willemstad, Netherlands Antilles

Norway
Bryggen
Hjemmeluft Petroglyphs
Røros
Urnes stave church

Poland
Auschwitz concentration camp
Castle of the Teutonic Order in Malbork
Kraków's historic centre
Medieval town of Torun
Warsaw's old city
Wieliczka salt mines near Kraków
Zamosc's old city

Portugal
Batalha Monastery
Central zone of Angra do Heroism in the Azores
Côa Valley rock-art sites
Convent of Christ in Tomar
Cultural landscape of Sintra
Évora's historic centre
Lisbon's Monastery of the Hieronymites & Tower of Belém
Monastery of Alcobaça
Oporto's historic centre

Romania
Biertan fortified church
Bucovina painted churches
Danube Delta
Horezu Monastery

Slovakia
Aggtelek Caves and Slovak
Karst Banská Štiavnica medieval mining centre
Vlkolinec folk village near Ruzomberok

Slovenia
Škocjan Caves

Spain
Alcalá de Henares
Altamira Cave
Archaeological ensemble of Mérida
Churches of the kingdom of Asturias
Cuenca's walled city
Burgos cathedral
Doñana National Park
El Escorial near Madrid
Garajonay National Park
Güell park and palace & Casa Mila in Barcelona
Historic centre of Córdoba
La Alhambra, El Generalife summer palace & Albaicín Moorish quarter of Granada
Las Medullas

Mudejar architecture of Teruel
Poblet Monastery
Old town section of Ávila
Old town & aqueduct of Segovia
Old town section of Cáceres
Palau de la Música Catalana and Hospital de Sant Pau, Barcelona
Rock art of Mediterranean basin on Iberian Peninsula
Royal Monastery of Santa María de Guadeloupe
Salamanca's old town
San Millán Yuso and Suso monasteries
Santiago de Compostela's old town & route
Sevilla's cathedral, Alcázar Archivo de Indias
Toledo's historic centre
Valencia's La Lonja de la Seda (silk exchange)

Sweden
Birka
Engelsberg ironworks
Gammelstad, Luleå
Karlskrona
Laponian area
Royal Domain of Drottningholm
Skogskykogården
Tanum rock carvings
Visby

Switzerland
Müstair's Convent of St John
Old city section of Bern
St Gall Convent

Turkey
Archaeological site of Troy
Divrigi's Great Mosque and hospital
Göreme National Park and Cappadocia
Hierapolis-Pamukkale
Istanbul's historic areas
Nemrut Dag
Safranbolu and its traditional timber houses
Walled city of Hattusas
Xanthos-Letoön

Note: For updating this list, see www.unesco.org/whc/heritage.htm.

GLOSSARY

COMMON WORDS

altstadt – old district (Germany)
aperitif – appetiser or drink preceding a meal (France)
au pair – a foreigner who acts as a nanny or undertakes housework, in exchange for board, or payment
autobahn – motorway (Germany)
autoroute – motorway (France)
autostrada – motorway (Italy)

bancomat – ATM (Italy)
bankomat – ATM (Czech Rep)

cajero automático – ATM (Spain)
caves – wine cellars (France)
cerveza – beer (Spain)
chambre d'hôte – private accommodation (France)
chaty – mountain huts (Slovakia)
chianti – Tuscan wine (Italy)

domatia – private accommodation (Greece)
domkyrkor – cathedral (Sweden)

estanco – tobacco shop (Spain)

Fax Público – fax services shop (Spain)
feria – fair (Spain)
fiesta – festival (Spain)
Frascati – wine from the Lazio area (Italy)

gammelkyrka – church (Sweden)
gasthaus – guesthouse (Germany)
gîtes d'étapes – mountain refuges (France)
grappa – spirit distilled from the fermented remains of grapes after pressing (Italy)

heuringen – wine cellar (Austria)

lista de correos – poste restante (Spain)

mehana – tavern (Bulgaria)
menjalnica – private money exchange offices (Slovenia)

Mensa – student cafeteria (Switzerland and Austria)
mezes – appetisers (Greece and Turkey)
multibanco – ATM (Portugal)

ouzeria – bar where ouzo is consumed (Greece)
ouzo – aniseed-flavoured spirit (Greece)

pasts – post office (Latvia)
poczta – post office (Poland)
pommes frites – potato chips (Belgium)
posti – post office (Finland)
pourboire – tip (France)

quarto particular – private accommodation (Portugal)

raki – aniseed-flavoured grape brandy similar to Greek ouzo (Turkey)
raukar – limestone formation (Sweden)
refugis – free shelters for hikers (Andorra)

sangria – a drink including red wine and orange juice (Spain)
schnapps – strong digestive liqueur made from apples, pears, plums or wheat
skansen – open-air museum (Slovakia)

tabac – tobacco shop (France)
tabacchi – tobacco (Italy)
tarjeta telefónica – phonecard (Spain)
tapas – snacks on saucers (Spain)
télécarte – phonecard (France)
telefonska kartica – phonecard (Slovenia)
telekart – phonecard (Czech Rep)
telekarte – phonecard (Latvia)
telekort – phonecard (Scandinavia)

weinstubl – wine cellar (Germany)

zetoni – phone tokens (Slovenia)
zimmer frei – free room or private accommodation (Germany)

AIR TRAVEL GLOSSARY

Baggage Allowance – This will be written on your ticket and usually includes one 20kg item to go in the hold, plus one item of hand luggage.

Bucket Shops – These are unbonded travel agencies specialising in discounted airline tickets.

Bumped – Just because you have a confirmed seat doesn't mean you're going to get on the plane (see Overbooking).

Cancellation Penalties – If you have to cancel or change a discounted ticket, there are often heavy penalties involved; insurance can sometimes be taken out against these penalties. Some airlines impose penalties on regular tickets as well, particularly against 'no-show' passengers.

Check-In – Airlines ask you to check in a certain time ahead of the flight departure (usually one to two hours on international flights). If you fail to check in on time and the flight is overbooked, the airline can cancel your booking and give your seat to somebody else.

Confirmation – Having a ticket written out with the flight and date you want doesn't mean you have a seat until the agent has checked with the airline that your status is 'OK' or confirmed. Meanwhile you could just be 'on request'.

Full Fares – Airlines traditionally offer 1st class (coded F), business class (coded J) and economy class (coded Y) tickets. These days there are so many promotional and discounted fares available that few passengers end up having to pay the full economy air fare.

ITX – An ITX, or 'independent inclusive tour excursion', is often available on tickets to popular holiday destinations. Officially it's a package deal combined with hotel accommodation, but many agents will sell you one of these for the flight only and give you phoney hotel vouchers in the unlikely event that you're challenged at the airport.

Lost Tickets – If you lose your airline ticket an airline will usually treat it like a travellers cheque and, after inquiries, issue you with another one. Legally, however, an airline is entitled to treat it like cash and if you lose it then it's gone forever. Take good care of your tickets.

MCO – An MCO, or 'miscellaneous charge order', is a voucher that looks like an airline ticket but carries no destination or date. It can be exchanged through any International Association of Travel Agents (IATA) airline for a ticket on a specific flight. It's a useful alternative to an onward ticket in those countries that demand one, and is more flexible than an ordinary ticket if you're unsure of your route.

No-Shows – No-shows are passengers who fail to show up for their flight. Full-fare passengers who fail to turn up are sometimes entitled to travel on a later flight. The rest are penalised (see Cancellation Penalties).

On Request – This is an unconfirmed booking for a flight.

Onward Tickets – An entry requirement for many countries is that you have a ticket out of the country. If you're unsure of your next move, the easiest solution is to buy the cheapest onward ticket to a neighbouring country or a ticket from a reliable airline which can later be refunded if you do not use it.

Open-Jaw Tickets – These are return tickets where you fly out to one place but return from another. If available, this can save you backtracking to your arrival point.

Overbooking – Airlines hate to fly empty seats and since every flight has some passengers who fail to show up, airlines often book more passengers than they have seats. Usually excess passengers make up for the no-shows, but occasionally somebody gets 'bumped' onto the next available flight. Guess who it is most likely to be? The passengers who check in late.

Point-to-Point Tickets – These are discount tickets that can be bought on some routes in return for passengers waiving their rights to a stopover.

Promotional Fares – These are officially discounted fares, available from travel agencies or direct from the airline.

Reconfirmation – If you don't re-confirm your flight at least 72 hours prior to departure, the airline may delete your name from the passenger list. Ring to find out if your airline requires reconfirmation.

Restrictions – Discounted tickets often have various restrictions on them – such as needing to be paid for in advance and incurring a penalty to be altered. Others are restrictions on the minimum and maximum period you must be away, such as a minimum of 14 days or a maximum of one year.

Round-the-World Tickets – RTW tickets give you a limited period (usually a year) in which to circumnavigate the globe. You can go anywhere the carrying airlines go, as long as you don't backtrack. The number of stopovers or total number of separate flights is decided before you set off and they usually cost a bit more than a basic return flight.

Stand-By – This is a discounted ticket where you only fly if there is a seat free at the last moment. Stand-by fares are usually available only on domestic routes.

Transferred Tickets – Airline tickets cannot be transferred from one person to another. Travellers sometimes try to sell the return half of their ticket, but officials can ask you to prove that you are the person named on the ticket. This is less likely to happen on domestic flights, but on an international flight tickets are compared with passports.

Travel Agencies – Travel agencies vary widely and you should choose one that suits your needs. Some simply handle tours, while full-service agencies handle everything from tours and tickets to car rental and hotel bookings. If all you want is a ticket at the lowest possible price, then go to an agency specialising in discounted fares.

Travel Periods – Ticket prices vary with the time of year. There is a low (off-peak) season and a high (peak) season, and often a low-shoulder season and a high-shoulder season as well. Usually the fare depends on your outward flight – if you depart in the high season and return in the low season, you pay the high-season fare.

INDEX

Italics indicates maps

notes

LONELY PLANET

ON THE ROAD

Lonely Planet **travel guides** explore cities, regions and countries in depth, with restaurants, accommodations and more for every budget. With reliable, easy-to-use maps, practical advice, great cultural background and sights both on and off the beaten track. There are over 200 titles in this classic series covering nearly every country in the world.

 Lonely Planet Upgrades extend the usefulness of existing travel guides by detailing any changes that may affect travel in each region since the book has been published. Upgrades can be downloaded for free on www.lonelyplanet.com/upgrades

For travellers with more time than money, **Shoestring guides** offer dependable, first-hand information with 100s of detailed maps, plus insider tips for stretching money as far as possible. Covering entire continents in most cases, the six-volume shoestring guides have been known as 'backpackers' bibles' for over 25 years.

For the discerning short-term visitor, **Condensed** guides highlight the best a destination has to offer in a full-colour pocket-sized format designed for quick access. From top sights and walking tours to opinionated reviews of where to eat, stay, shop and have fun.

Lonely Planet **CitySync** lets travellers use their Palm™ or Visor™ handheld computers to quickly search and sort hundreds of reviews of hotels, restaurants, major sights, and shopping and entertainment options, all pinpointed on scrollable street maps. CitySync can be downloaded from www.citysync.com

ESSENTIALS

Read This First books help travellers new to a destination hit the road with confidence. These invaluable pre-departure guides give step-by-step advice on preparing for a trip, from budgeting and arranging a visa to planning an itinerary, staying safe and still getting off the beaten track.

Healthy Travel pocket guides offer practical advice for staying well on the road, with user-friendly design and helpful diagrams and tables.

Pocket-sized, with colour tabs for quick reference, extensive vocabulary lists easy-to-follow pronunciation keys and two-way dictionaries, Lonely Planet **Phrasebooks** cover the essential words and phrases travellers may need.

Lonely Planet's eKno is a communication card developed especially for travellers, with low phone rates, free email and a toll-free voicemail service so that you can keep in touch while on the road. Check it out on www.ekno.lonelyplanet.com

LONELY PLANET

ACTIVITY GUIDES

For those who believe the best way to see the world is on foot, Lonely Planet's **walking guides** detail everything from family strolls to difficult treks, with expert advice on when to go and how to do it, reliable maps and essential travel information.

Cycling guides map out a destination's best bike tours, long and short, in day-by-day detail. With all the information a cyclist needs, including advice on bike maintenance, places to eat and stay, and innovative maps with detailed cues to the rides and elevation charts.

The **Watching Wildlife** series is perfect for travellers who want authoritative information but don't want to tote a field guide. Packed with advice on where, when and how to view a region's wildlife, each title features photos of over 300 species and engaging insights on their lives and environments.

With underwater colour photos throughout, **Pisces Books** explore the world's best diving and snorkelling areas. Each book contains listings of diving services and dive resorts and detailed information on depth, visibility, levels of difficulty and marine life you're likely to see.

MAPS & ATLASES

Lonely Planet's **City Maps** feature downtown and metropolitan maps as well as transit routes, walking tours and a complete index of streets and sights. Plastic-coated for extra durability.

Road Atlases are an essential navigation tool for serious travellers. Cross-referenced with Lonely Planet guidebooks, they also feature distance and climate charts and a complete site index.

LONELY PLANET

FOOD & RESTAURANT GUIDES

Lonely Planet's **Out to Eat** guides recommend the brightest and best places to eat and drink in top international cities. Arranged by neighbourhood and packed with dependable maps, scene-setting photos and quirky features, Out to Eat serves up the lot.

For people who live to eat, drink and travel, **World Food** guides explore the culinary culture of each country. Entertaining and adventurous, each guide is packed with detail on staples & specialities, regional cuisine and local markets, as well as sumptuous recipes, comprehensive culinary dictionaries and lavish photos good enough to eat.

OFF THE ROAD

Journeys is a travel literature series that captures the spirit of a place, illuminates a culture, recounts an adventure or introduces a fascinating way of life. These books are tales to read while on the road or at home in your favourite armchair.

Lonely Planet's new range of lavishly illustrated **Pictorial** books is just the ticket for both travellers and dreamers. Quirky tales and vivid photographs bring the adventure of travel to life, before the journey begins or long after it is over.

Entertaining and adventurous, Lonely Planet **Videos** encourage the same independent approach to travel as the guidebooks. Currently airing throughout the world, this award-winning series features all original footage and music.

TRAVELLERS NETWORK

Lonely Planet online. Lonely Planet's award-winning web site has insider information on hundreds of destinations from Amsterdam to Zimbabwe, complete with interactive maps and colour photographs. The site also offers the latest travel news, recent reports from travellers on the road, guidebook upgrades and a lively traveller's bulletin board www.lonelyplanet.com or AOL keyword: lp

Lonely Planet produces two free newsletters. **Planet Talk** is the quarterly print version, **Comet** comes via email once a month. Each is loaded with travel news, advice, dispatches from authors and letters from readers. Contact your nearest Lonely Planet office to subscribe.

LONELY PLANET

Guides by Region

Lonely Planet is known worldwide for publishing practical, reliable and no-nonsense travel information in our guides and on our web site. The Lonely Planet list covers just about every accessible part of the world. Currently there are fifteen series: travel guides, Shoestrings, Condensed, Phrasebooks, Read This First, Healthy Travel, Walking guides, Cycling guides, Pisces Diving & Snorkeling guides, City Maps, Travel Atlases, Out to Eat, World Food, Journeys travel literature and Pictorials.

AFRICA Africa on a shoestring • Africa – the South • Arabic (Egyptian) phrasebook • Arabic (Moroccan) phrasebook • Cairo • Cape Town • Cape Town city map • Central Africa • East Africa • Egypt • Egypt travel atlas • Ethiopian (Amharic) phrasebook • The Gambia & Senegal • Healthy Travel Africa • Kenya • Kenya travel atlas • Malawi, Mozambique & Zambia • Morocco • North Africa • Read This First Africa • South Africa, Lesotho & Swaziland • South Africa, Lesotho & Swaziland travel atlas • Swahili phrasebook • Tanzania, Zanzibar & Pemba • Trekking in East Africa • Tunisia • West Africa • Zimbabwe, Botswana & Namibia • Zimbabwe, Botswana & Nambia Travel Atlas • World Food Morocco
Travel Literature: The Rainbird: A Central African Journey • Songs to an African Sunset: A Zimbabwean Story • Mali Blues: Traveling to an African Beat

AUSTRALIA & THE PACIFIC Auckland • Australia • Australian phrasebook • Bushwalking in Australia • Bushwalking in Papua New Guinea • Fiji • Fijian phrasebook • Healthy Travel Australia, NZ and the Pacific • Islands of Australia's Great Barrier Reef • Melbourne • Melbourne city map • Micronesia • New Caledonia • New South Wales & the ACT • New Zealand • Northern Territory • Outback Australia • Out To Eat – Melbourne • Out to Eat – Sydney • Papua New Guinea • Pidgin phrasebook • Queensland • Rarotonga & the Cook Islands • Samoa • Solomon Islands • South Australia • South Pacific • South Pacific Languages phrasebook • Sydney • Sydney city map • Sydney Condensed • Tahiti & French Polynesia • Tasmania • Tonga • Tramping in New Zealand • Vanuatu • Victoria • Western Australia
Travel Literature: Islands in the Clouds • Kiwi Tracks: A New Zealand Journey • Sean & David's Long Drive

CENTRAL AMERICA & THE CARIBBEAN Bahamas, Turks & Caicos • Bermuda • Central America on a shoestring • Costa Rica • Cuba • Dominican Republic & Haiti • Eastern Caribbean • Guatemala, Belize & Yucatán: La Ruta Maya • Jamaica • Mexico • Mexico City • Panama • Puerto Rico • Read This First Central & South America • World Food Mexico
Travel Literature: Green Dreams: Travels in Central America

EUROPE Amsterdam • Amsterdam city map • Andalucía • Austria • Baltic States phrasebook • Barcelona • Berlin • Berlin city map • Britain • British phrasebook • Brussels, Bruges & Antwerp • Budapest city map • Canary Islands • Central Europe • Central Europe phrasebook • Corfu & Ionians • Corsica • Crete • Crete Condensed • Croatia • Cyprus • Czech & Slovak Republics • Denmark • Dublin • Eastern Europe • Eastern Europe phrasebook • Edinburgh • Estonia, Latvia & Lithuania • Europe on a shoestring • Finland • Florence • France • French phrasebook • Germany • German phrasebook • Greece • Greek Islands • Greek phrasebook • Hungary • Iceland, Greenland & the Faroe Islands • Istanbul City Map • Ireland • Italian phrasebook • Italy • Krakow •Lisbon • London • London city map • London Condensed • Mediterranean Europe • Mediterranean Europe phrasebook • Munich • Norway • Paris • Paris city map • Paris Condensed • Poland • Portugal • Portugese phrasebook • Portugal travel atlas • Prague • Prague city map • Provence & the Côte d'Azur • Read This First: Europe • Romania & Moldova • Rome • Russia, Ukraine & Belarus • Russian phrasebook • Scandinavian & Baltic Europe • Scandinavian Europe phrasebook • Scotland • Slovenia • Spain • Spanish phrasebook • St Petersburg • Switzerland • Trekking in Spain • Ukrainian phrasebook • Venice • Vienna • Walking in Britain • Walking in Ireland • Walking in Italy • Walking in Spain • Walking in Switzerland • Western Europe • Western Europe phrasebook • World Food Italy • World Food Spain
Travel Literature: The Olive Grove: Travels in Greece

INDIAN SUBCONTINENT Bangladesh • Bengali phrasebook • Bhutan • Delhi • Goa • Hindi & Urdu phrasebook • India • India & Bangladesh travel atlas • Indian Himalaya • Karakoram Highway • Kerala • Mumbai (Bombay) • Nepal • Nepali phrasebook • Pakistan • Rajasthan • Read This First: Asia & India • South India • Sri Lanka • Sri Lanka phrasebook • Trekking in the Indian Himalaya • Trekking in the Karakoram & Hindukush • Trekking in the Nepal Himalaya
Travel Literature: In Rajasthan • Shopping for Buddhas • The Age Of Kali

LONELY PLANET

Mail Order

Lonely Planet products are distributed worldwide. They are also available by mail order from Lonely Planet, so if you have difficulty finding a title please write to us. North and South American residents should write to 150 Linden St, Oakland CA 94607, USA; European and African residents should write to 10a Spring Place, London, NW5 3BH; and residents of other countries to Locked Bag 1, Footscray, Victoria 3011, Australia.

ISLANDS OF THE INDIAN OCEAN Madagascar & Comoros • Maldives • Mauritius, Réunion & Seychelles

MIDDLE EAST & CENTRAL ASIA Bahrain, Kuwait & Qatar • Central Asia • Central Asia phrasebook • Dubai • Hebrew phrasebook • Iran • Israel & the Palestinian Territories • Israel & the Palestinian Territories travel atlas • Istanbul • Istanbul to Cairo on a shoestring • Jerusalem • Jerusalem City Map • Jordan • Jordan, Syria & Lebanon travel atlas • Lebanon • Middle East • Oman & the United Arab Emirates • Syria • Turkey • Turkey travel atlas • Turkish phrasebook • Yemen
Travel Literature: The Gates of Damascus • Kingdom of the Film Stars: Journey into Jordan • Black on Black: Iran Revisited

NORTH AMERICA Alaska • Backpacking in Alaska • Baja California • California & Nevada • California Condensed • Canada • Chicago • Chicago city map • Deep South • Florida • Hawaii • Honolulu • Las Vegas • Los Angeles • Miami • New England • New Orleans • New York City • New York city map • New York Condensed • New York, New Jersey & Pennsylvania • Oahu • Pacific Northwest USA • Puerto Rico • Rocky Mountain • San Francisco • San Francisco city map • Seattle • Southwest USA • Texas • USA • USA phrasebook • Vancouver • Washington, DC & the Capital Region • Washington DC city map
Travel Literature: Drive Thru America

NORTH-EAST ASIA Beijing • Cantonese phrasebook • China • Hong Kong • Hong Kong city map • Hong Kong, Macau & Guangzhou • Japan • Japanese phrasebook • Japanese audio pack • Korea • Korean phrasebook • Kyoto • Mandarin phrasebook • Mongolia • Mongolian phrasebook • North-East Asia on a shoestring • Seoul • South-West China • Taiwan • Tibet • Tibetan phrasebook • Tokyo
Travel Literature: Lost Japan • In Xanadu

SOUTH AMERICA Argentina, Uruguay & Paraguay • Bolivia • Brazil • Brazilian phrasebook • Buenos Aires • Chile & Easter Island • Chile & Easter Island travel atlas • Colombia • Ecuador & the Galapagos Islands • Healthy Travel Central & South America • Latin American Spanish phrasebook • Peru •Quechua phrasebook • Rio de Janeiro • Rio de Janeiro city map • South America on a shoestring • Trekking in the Patagonian Andes • Venezuela
Travel Literature: Full Circle: A South American Journey

SOUTH-EAST ASIA Bali & Lombok • Bangkok • Bangkok city map • Burmese phrasebook • Cambodia • Hanoi • Healthy Travel Asia & India • Hill Tribes phrasebook • Ho Chi Minh City • Indonesia • Indonesia's Eastern Islands • Indonesian phrasebook • Indonesian audio pack • Jakarta • Java • Laos • Lao phrasebook • Laos travel atlas • Malay phrasebook • Malaysia, Singapore & Brunei • Myanmar (Burma) • Philippines • Pilipino (Tagalog) phrasebook • Read This First Asia & India • Singapore • South-East Asia on a shoestring • South-East Asia phrasebook • Thailand • Thailand's Islands & Beaches • Thailand travel atlas • Thai phrasebook • Thai audio pack • Vietnam • Vietnamese phrasebook • Vietnam travel atlas • World Food Thailand • World Food Vietnam

ALSO AVAILABLE: Antarctica • The Arctic • Brief Encounters: Stories of Love, Sex & Travel • Chasing Rickshaws • Lonely Planet Unpacked • Not the Only Planet: Travel Stories from Science Fiction • Sacred India • Travel with Children • Traveller's Tales

Bonus Offer

ekno more than a phone card

Are you sure you've packed everything?

Lonely Planet's ekno is all you need to stay in touch while you're away.

To join simply visit the website or call us on the toll-free access number for the country you are in and press 0 for Customer Service (see list provided).

To qualify for a 10% bonus, just quote this code LPRTF0402 when you join.

Save up to 75% on international calls

from payphones and hotel phones. Call home or ahead from 55 countries. It's simple to use — just keep your account number and PIN handy and dial the toll-free access number for the country you are in. Follow the menu prompts to make a call, check your messages or add more calling time to your account.

Global Messaging

Friends and family can leave you a voice message for free. Each time you use the ekno service you will be notified of new messages. You can listen to your voice messages at the touch of a button. Give your ekno account number to friends and family or swap ekno numbers with new friends you make on the road.

You also get a free email account that works anywhere in the world. Just go to the ekno website to check your messages. Visit:
www.ekno.lonelyplanet.com

Add more calling time while you're on the road

You can purchase additional calling time throughout your trip using your credit card. Simply call our toll-free 24 hour Customer Service team from wherever you are or visit the website. You can even set up auto-recharge so your account will be topped-up automatically when you reach a preset limit.

powered by **ekit**

Lonely Planet's

- Spend less on overseas
- Receive voice messages
- Use your ekno account t

Join ekno before you go!

- Activate your account by calli
  www.ekno.lonelyplanet.c
- Top-up your account and coll
- Set up your voice messaging
- Give your friends and family

You can use ekno from any tou
entering your ekno account nu
your credit card.

Get lost but stay connec

If you're on the move and you
crossing a border at night and
arrange a rendezvous with son
for a friend in London... then y

Using ekno you can..

- Slash your phone costs with c
- Call from over 55 countries t
- Check for new emails on the
- Store important details secur
- Avoid hassles with foreign cu

a great comm

Lonely Planet's **ekno**

Join ekno before you go!

Tear out and keep your ekno cards on you or give them to your travelling partners. Call us toll-free or visit the website to join.

How to join or find out more online

The easiest way to join is online at **www.ekno.lonelyplanet.com**. Quote LPRTF0402 when you join to collect your 10 % bonus.

Your ekno website is also the best place for the most up-to-date information. It is also gives you easy access to all your messages, product updates and account details.

How to join or find out more by phone

Dial the local toll-free access number and press 0 for Customer Service:

USA	1 800 706 1333
Australia	1 800 114 478
UK	0 800 376 2366
France	0 800 900 850
Canada	1 800 808 5773
Italy	800 875 683
Spain	900 931 951
Mexico	001 800 514 0287
New Zealand	0 800 445 108
Germany	0 800 634 8086
Japan	0053 112 0460

Check the website for all other access numbers.

Details correct at April, 2002

Once you've joined use the same access numbers to use all the great ekno phone services.

Where did ekno come from?

ekno – it's Lonely Planet for one number; **ek** means one from Karachi to Kathmandu, from Delhi to Dhaka, and **no** is short for number.

At Lonely Planet we do a lot of travelling, and although we have used heaps of phone cards, we could never find one that offered an integrated communications service across many countries with great rates – one designed especially for travellers. So we decided to build our own.

We joined up with an innovative communications company to bring you a phone card with the lot – competitive costs on international calls from a stack of countries, a powerful voice messaging system that allows you to receive and reply from all over the globe, and a free Lonely Planet email and website service. With ekno you can ring home and home can ring you.

For the traveller who is out of sight but never out of touch.